UNION-MANAGEMENT RELATIONS IN CANADA

UNION-MANAGEMENT RELATIONS IN CANADA

John C. Anderson
Morley Gunderson

Addison-Wesley Publishers
Don Mills, Ontario • Menlo Park, California • Reading, Massachusetts
Amsterdam • London • Manila • Paris • Sydney • Singapore • Tokyo

Printed in Canada

C D E F — THB — 86

ISBN 0-201-18620-9

Canadian Cataloguing in Publication Data

Main entry under title:
  Union-management relations in Canada

Includes bibliographies and index.

ISBN 0-201-18620-9

1. Industrial relations — Canada. I. Gunderson, Morley, 1945- II. Anderson, John C.

HD8106.5.U54   331′.0971   C81-094980-6

To our parents,
Lila and Jack Anderson
and
Ann and Magnus Gunderson

Contents

THE OUTCOMES OF COLLECTIVE BARGAINING

11. Union Impact on Wages, Fringe Benefits, and Productivity
Morley Gunderson   247

APPENDIX 2

Contributors

Roy J. Adams *(Ph.D. — University of Wisconsin)* is an associate professor of industrial relations, Faculty of Business, McMaster University. He has been on faculty since 1973. His research concerns unions and collective bargaining in Canada, the U.S., Britain, Sweden, and Germany.

His major works are as follows: *White Collar Union Growth in Britain and Sweden* (Madison: University of Wisconsin, 1975); "The Recognition of White-Collar Worker Unions," *British Journal of Industrial Relations,* 1973; "Solidarity, Self-Interest and the Unionization Differential Between Europe and North America," *Relations Industrielles/Industrial Relations,* 1974; "Canada-U.S. Labour Link Under Stress," *Industrial Relations,* 1976; "Workers' Participation in Management in West Germany: Impact on the Worker, the Enterprise and the Trade Union," *Industrial Relations Journal,* 1977 (with C.H. Rummel).

His professional activities include: chairman, Commission of Inquiry on Educational Leave and Productivity, Labour Canada, 1978-79; member, Task Force on Literacy and Occupational Health and Safety, Ontario Department of Labour, 1980; president-elect, Canadian Industrial Relations Association, 1980; consultant to Labour Canada, Ontario Department of Labour, and the German Marshall Fund of the U.S.

John C. Anderson *(Ph.D. — Cornell University)* is an associate professor of industrial relations, Graduate School of Business, Columbia University. His major publications appear in *Industrial and Labour Relations Review, Industrial Relations, Relations Industrielles/Industrial Relations, Academy of Management Review,* and *Human Relations.* He is also a member of the editorial board of *Industrial Relations.*

Jean Boivin *(Ph.D. — Cornell University)* has been a professor at the Industrial Relations Department, Laval University since 1972 where he served as chairman from 1976 to 1979. His teaching and research interests cover labour history, collective bargaining, and industrial relations systems. The rapid growth of public-sector labour relations has led him to analyse this phenomenon quite extensively, and most of his publications have dealt with this subject. Jean Boivin was president of the Canadian Industrial Relations Association in 1978, and he is a member of the Industrial Relations Research Association's Executive Board. He was actively involved in the preparation of Quebec's First Economic Summit in 1977, and he acts as an analyst of labour relations for the news media on a regular basis.

Donald D. Carter *(B.A., L.L.B. — Queen's; B.C.L. — Oxford)* is a professor at the Faculty of Law, Queen's University, Kingston and is a faculty associate of the Queen's University Industrial Relations Centre. From 1976 to 1979, he served as chairman of the Ontario Labour Relations Board and from 1972 to 1975 was a member of the Ontario Public Service Labour Relations Tribunal. He has also acted as a labour arbitrator on numerous occasions. Professor Carter is a coauthor of *Collective Bargaining for University Faculty in Canada* and a contributor to *The International Encyclopaedia for Labour Law and Industrial Relations*.

Gary N. Chaison; formerly associate professor, Faculty of Administration, University of New Brunswick, Fredericton, is now in the Department of Management, Worcester University, Worcester, Massachusetts. His principal research interests are in the areas of union government, structure, and growth. His past work has included analyses of union rivalry, certification elections, and officer turnover. He also served as the coordinator of an oral history project dealing with labour and business in the Atlantic Provinces. Presently he is engaged in studies of union mergers and the characteristics of female union officers in Canada. His articles have appeared in such journals as *Industrial Relations*, *Industrial and Labour Relations Review*, *Relations Industrielles/Industrial Relations*, *Labour Law Journal*, and the *Canadian Oral History Association Journal*.

John Crispo is a professor of industrial relations and public policy in both the Faculty of Management Studies and the Department of Political Economy at the University of Toronto. He is also an associate of the University of Toronto's Centre for Industrial Relations. He has served on a number of boards and commissions and as an arbitrator and mediator. He was a member of the Prime Minister's Task Force on Labour Relations. His publications include *The Canadian Industrial Relations System* (Toronto: McGraw-Hill Ryerson, 1978) and *Industrial Democracy in Western Europe: A North American Perspective* (Toronto: McGraw-Hill Ryerson, 1978). He is also a frequent media commentator on a wide range of topics, including industrial relations.

Bryan Downie is a professor of industrial relations and organization behaviour at the School of Business, Queen's University, and a faculty associate of the Queen's University Industrial Relations Centre. He has written a number of books and articles on bargaining and conflict resolution and has done extensive consulting with business, labour, and government in Canada. He has also been appointed by government as a neutral third party in numerous disputes. He is chairman of the Education Relations Commission and the College Relations Commission in Ontario. These two agencies oversee collective bargaining in Ontario education.

Jeffrey Gandz *(Ph.D. — York University)* is associate professor of business administration, School of Business Administration, The University of Western Ontario, in which he teaches courses in organizational behaviour and human-resource management in M.B.A. and executive programs.

H.J. Glasbeek *(B.A., LL.B. (Hons.) — Melbourne, J.D. — Chicago)* is a professor of law at Osgoode Hall Law School. He is the author of *Labour Law in Australia* (with E.I. Sykes) and *Cases and Materials on Industrial Law* (with E.M. Eggleston) and he is a contributor to *The International Encyclopaedia for Labour Law and Industrial Relations*. His current research interests in labour relations and law include the concept of the corporation as criminal, with particular reference to occupational health and safety.

John Godard is an assistant professor in the School of Business at Queen's University. He received an M.B.A. in public policy from the University of Manitoba and is currently completing a Ph.D. in industrial and labour relations from Cornell University. His research interests revolve primarily around the social relations and structure of the firm under collective bargaining, and the structural and behavioural determinants of bargaining and nonbargaining outcomes.

Morley Gunderson is a professor at the University of Toronto where he teaches in industrial relations, management studies, and economics. He obtained his B.A. in economics from Queen's University and his M.A. in industrial relations and Ph.D. in economics from the University of Wisconsin in Madison. His publications have appeared in *Industrial and Labour Relations Review, Industrial Relations, Relations Industrielles/Industrial Relations*, and the *Journal of Human Resources*, as well as the various economic and econometric journals. He is the author of a textbook *Labour Market Economics: Theory, Evidence and Policy in Canada*, McGraw-Hill, 1980, a member of the Executive Committee and the Research Policy Committee of the Canadian Industrial Relations Association, as well as the editorial board of the *Journal of Labor Research* and the *International Journal of Manpower*.

Harish C. Jain *(Ph.D. — University of Wisconsin)* is a professor, personnel/industrial relations area, Faculty of Business, McMaster University.

Professor Jain has published widely in the equal-employment and human-resource-management areas. He is the author of a comparative study entitled *Disadvantaged Groups in the Labour Market and Measures to Assist Them* (Organization for Economic Cooperation and Development, Paris, France, 1979), in addition to being the editor of *Contemporary Issues in Canadian Personnel Administration* (Prentice-Hall, 1974), coeditor of *Race and Sex Equality in the Workplace: A Challenge and an Opportunity* (Labour Canada, 1980), and coeditor of *Behavioral Issues in Management: The Canadian Context* (McGraw-Hill, 1977). His articles have appeared in the *Industrial Relations Journal, Relations Industrielles/Industrial Relations, International Labour Review, Academy of Management Review, Canadian Journal of Behavioural Science*, and *Human Communication Research*, among other professional journals.

He was previously a consultant with the OECD, the Royal Commission on Distribution of Income and Wealth in U.K., the Canadian Employment and Immigration Department, the Canada Department of Labour, the Saskatchewan Public Service Commission, and the Ontario Human Rights Commission.

John B. Kervin *(Ph.D. — Johns Hopkins)* is associate professor of sociology and industrial relations, Centre for Industrial Relations, University of Toronto. His current research interests are in the area of bargaining behaviour and behavioural determinants of strike activity.

Thomas A. Kochan received his Ph.D. in industrial relations from the University of Wisconsin in 1973 and is presently a professor of industrial relations at the Sloan School of Management, Massachusetts Institute of Technology. His major research interests lie in the areas of collective bargaining, conflict and conflict resolution, and organizational change. One of his more recent publications is *Collective Bargaining and Industrial Relations: From Theory to Policy and Practice* (Richard D. Irwin, 1980).

Noah M. Meltz is a professor of economics and director of the Centre for Industrial Relations, University of Toronto. He received his B.Comm. from the University of Toronto and an A.M. and Ph.D. from Princeton University. Professor Meltz was an economist with the Canada Department of Labour before joining the University of Toronto in 1964.

Labour market analysis is Professor Meltz's main area of research interest. He has conducted studies of historical occupational trends in Canada, as well as projections of future manpower requirements. His recent studies have dealt with the role of Canada Employment Centres in the labour market, the relationship between vacancies and unemployment in the postwar period, the occupational structure of earnings in Canada, work sharing and job sharing, and an economic analysis of shortages of tool and die makers.

Professor Meltz is a consultant to the Canada Department of Employment and Immigration, the Economic Council of Canada, the Ontario Ministry of Labour, the Ontario Economic Council, and the Israel Central Bureau of Statistics. He is a past-president of the Canadian Industrial Relations Association.

Desmond Morton *(Ph.D. — University of London)* is a professor of history at the University of Toronto and author of *Working People: An Illustrated History of Canadian Labour.* A past-president of the Canadian Historical Association and chairman of the Canadian Commission of Military History, Professor Morton is the author of ten books and many articles on Canadian labour, military, and political history. His most recent work is *Canada and War: A Military and Political History.* He is currently doing research on Canadian veteran and civil reestablishment after the First World War.

Allen Ponak *(Ph.D. — University of Wisconsin)* is a visiting professor of industrial relations, Faculty of Management, McGill University. Since 1975 he has taught graduate and undergraduate courses in industrial relations, collective bargaining, public policy, and public-sector labour relations at McGill and at the University of British Columbia. His work has been published in major scholarly journals, and he currently is undertaking a nationwide study of faculty unionism. Professor Ponak has served as a consultant to a variety of Canadian and American organizations and is an experienced mediator.

Frank Reid is an associate professor of economics at the Centre for Industrial Relations and the Department of Political Economy, University of Toronto. He obtained his M.Sc. in economics at London School of Economics and his Ph.D. at Queen's University. He is the author of *An Analysis of U.S. Wage Controls and Implications for Canada*; *Wage and Price Behaviour in Canadian Manufacturing* (with T.A. Wilson); and *Sharing the Work* (with N.M. Meltz and G.S. Swartz). In addition to these three books, Professor Reid has published numerous articles in scholarly journals including studies of the economic effects of the Canadian and American controls programs in the *Canadian Journal of Economics* and the *American Economic Review*.

Joseph B. Rose is an associate professor in the personnel/industrial relations area at McMaster University, Hamilton. He has published numerous articles on construction labour relations and public policy.

Kenneth P. Swan *(B. Eng. — R.M.C., LL.B. — Alta.)* is associate professor of law at Queen's University and a research associate of the Queen's Industrial Relations Centre. He is a member of the Labour Law Casebook Group, vice-chairman of the Ontario Crown Employees Grievance Settlement Board, associate editor of *Labour Arbitration Cases*, and an experienced arbitrator of both interest and grievance disputes.

Mark Thompson *(Ph.D. — School of Industrial and Labor Relations, Cornell University)* has taught at McMaster University and is currently an associate professor with the Faculty of Commerce. Formerly he was director of the Institute of Industrial Relations, University of British Columbia, 1974-1977. In addition, he spent two years as a member of the Research and Planning Department, International Labour Office, Geneva, Switzerland. His research interests include: labour relations in mining, strike patterns in Canada, and labour relations in Mexico. His publications appear in *Relations Industrielles/Industrial Relations*, *British Journal of Industrial Relations*, *International Institute of Labour Studies Bulletin*, and *Industrial and Labor Relations Review*.

C. Brian Williams *(Ph.D. — Cornell University)* is a professor of labour relations and labour law, Department of Industrial and Legal Relations, University of Alberta. He is a member of the National Academy Arbitrators, chairman of the Public Service Grievance Appeal Board for the Province of Alberta, and an active mediator.

Preface

Industrial relations in Canada have often been described as diverse, fragmented, and extremely decentralized. As a consequence of eleven legislative jurisdictions, geographic dispersion, and differential economic and industrial development, there has been a tendency for industrial-relations research, policy, and practice in Canada to lack coherence. This has continued to present substantial problems in attempting to provide a comprehensive coverage of industrial-relations problems in the university classroom.

This volume is designed to reduce the substantial void which presently exists in the field of Canadian industrial relations. The book takes an industrial-relations-system perspective and as such has chapters which focus on the environment of labour relations, the parties, the collective-bargaining process, the outcomes of collective bargaining, and the union-management relationship. In addition, given the wide range of Canadian policies and practices, some chapters address current trends or significant policy issues in the Canadian scene.

The book has several important features. First, it is comprehensive in coverage, both in terms of topic areas and the national scope of its coverage. Second, it is designed both to present the basic introductory material and to provide a stepping stone to a more analytic and in-depth treatment of each topic. In this vein, many of the chapters deal with material that is on the frontier of research in industrial relations. Third, the book offers supplementary material which is designed to provide focus and realism to the study of the Canadian industrial-relations system. Each chapter includes a number of questions and a bibliography to direct the student to more specific materials on each subject, and realism is provided through a collective-bargaining simulation and a series of short grievance cases. Lastly, in recognition of the immense problems inevitably encountered by a single author or coauthors in attempting to cover the necessary material in sufficient breadth and depth to reflect the diversity of the Canadian experience, the book is based on contributed chapters from experts on various aspects of the Canadian industrial-relations system. This is designed to ensure that current theoretical, research, and policy issues can be covered in detail.

The book is appropriate for students at various levels. As the chapters will cover basic material as a prelude to more in-depth treatment and analysis of each topic, it is suitable for introductory undergraduate and graduate courses in industrial relations. Also, because more depth is provided, it can be utilized in undergraduate courses on collective bargaining given in third and fourth years, as well as second year MBA classes in most business schools. For the introductory course, it has the distinct advantage of offering more challenging advanced material for the interested student. For more advanced courses it gives a quick refresher before going to the material in more depth. In addition to providing this material for students, the hope is that the book will stimulate academics and practitioners to approach industrial relations from an analytical perspective, along with the traditional institutional, descriptive perspective that tends to dominate the field.

A book of this magnitude and collaborative effort reflects the input of numerous persons beyond the editors and contributors. We are indebted to Deborah Campbell and Joy Glazener for typing and corrections, to David R. Smith for proofreading, and to Margaret MacDonald for copy-editing, proofreading, and coordination. Frank Burns, of Addison-Wesley, provided encouragement and support; his confidence in this project is greatly appreciated. We are particularly indebted to Richard Kalwa, whose contribution went well beyond his tasks of copy-editing, proofreading, and indexing under very stringent deadlines. His substantive suggestions and total involvement in all aspects of the book have been indispensable.

John C. Anderson
Morley Gunderson

THE CANADIAN INDUSTRIAL-RELATIONS SYSTEM

JOHN C. ANDERSON and MORLEY GUNDERSON

1. The Canadian Industrial-Relations System

Industrial relations is an important part of everyday life in Canada. In order to help understand the practice of industrial relations, the industrial-relations system is presented. Dunlop represented this system as composed of three actors — labour, government, and employers — interacting with market, technological, and power contexts, bound together by an ideology to establish a web of rules of the work place. After discussing the critiques of this perspective, a modified version of the industrial-relations system model is presented. The second half of the chapter is devoted to a description of the characteristics of the Canadian industrial-relations system, with particular emphasis on how they relate to the remaining chapters of the book.

Evidence of the functioning (or breakdowns) of the industrial-relations system is available daily to the Canadian public. Newspapers frequently provide the details of "exorbitant" demands of private- and public-sector unions. Strikes are a common occurrence in most Canadian cities, and people become accustomed to avoiding picket lines and to stockpiling goods before strikes start. During the past few years Canadians have watched as industrial-relations problems have influenced national and international policies. Labour-management relations in Canada have impacted the country's position in world markets. Union leaders helped to shape foreign policy as they decided whether or not to load Soviet ships after the invasion of Afghanistan. Recent news reports have highlighted the role of the labour movement in stimulating social and economic change in Poland. Moreover, movies, television, and news reports have tended to reinforce the public's concern that corruption has replaced internal democracy as the primary form of government in many unions.

While industrial relations is an integral part of Canadian society, most people are not now nor ever likely to be union members during their working lives. Unfortunately, for many people the events described above, often dramatized by the media, are their only contact with what they view as the industrial-relations system, and as such, these events play a major role in shaping their opinions about Canadian industrial relations. This is unfortunate because industrial relations, in most cases, does not result in exorbitant settlements, strikes, or changes in public policy. Moreover, industrial relations is not a term restricted to union-management relations nor is it only comprised of the collective-bargaining process. Employees, managers, owners, or self-employed entrepreneurs are all part of the industrial-relations system and are influenced or constrained by that system. Despite the importance of industrial relations to society, most people are not well-informed about it. The objective of this chapter (and the book as a whole) is to provide an overview of the major components of industrial relations in Canada. A conceptual framework for viewing industrial relations is provided in the next section followed by an overview of the characteristics of the Canadian industrial-relations system.

INDUSTRIAL RELATIONS: A CONCEPTUAL VIEW

What Is Industrial Relations?

Broadly speaking the term "industrial relations" refers to the nature of employment relationships in an industrial society (20). Thus, all people who are employed are a part of the industrial-relations system. The Task Force on Labour Relations went further to define the industrial-relations system as "the complex of market and institutional arrangements, private and public, which society permits, encourages or establishes to handle superior-subordinate relationships growing out of employment and related activities" (48, p. 9). This definition stresses the fact that in order to study industrial relations it is important to understand not only the nature of the employment relationship but also the wide range of factors which influence that relationship. Industrial relations, therefore, does not refer solely to the role of unions and collective bargaining in employment (which is referred to here as labour or union-management relations) but also encompasses the role and impact of personnel policies developed by employers; the scope and impact of employment-related legislation enacted by the federal and provincial governments (for example, minimum wages and standards, workers compensation, occupational safety and health, unemployment insurance); and the role of the labour market in establishing the terms and conditions of employment for individuals across occupations, industries, and regions. The above definition also reveals that industrial relations involves choices made by employers and employees not only about the wages and benefits to be paid for a given job or to a given employee, but also about why people accept or leave jobs, how conflicts between employers and employees about working conditions are resolved, as well as choices about which employees are promoted, transferred, or laid off.

Given the wide range of issues related to the study of industrial relations, it is not surprising that labour problems have been studied by economists, political scientists, sociologists, psychologists, lawyers, and historians. Each discipline has selected certain problems to study and has ignored others. Economists have been primarily interested in labour as a commodity, examining the effects of unions and investments in human capital on the wage determination process (30) and the role of labour market variables (supply and demand) and economic conditions in society on the decision-making behaviour of individuals, unions, and firms (36). Political scientists have contributed to our understanding of the internal dynamics of unions and the role of unions in the political process in both the public and private sectors (42). Industrial sociologists have focused on the behaviour of industrial work groups and on the role and determinants of conflict in organizations and society (17). Psychologists, on the other hand, have studied the dynamics of bargaining behaviour (39) and effects of wage-payment systems on individual behaviour (45). Legal scholars and historians have been interested in the development of the labour movement and of the legal, regulatory, and historical framework within which industrial relations has been conducted (9). While these examples are illustrative, rather than exhaustive, they provide an ample overview of the range and diversity of issues studied within the domain of industrial relations.

The large number of different disciplines engaged in studying labour and employment problems has resulted in a long-standing debate and controversy about whether industrial relations is, or should be a discipline in its own right (21, 28, 32). The general tone of these periodic evaluations has been pessimistic (41). In fact, all too often the prognosis has been the return to traditional disciplines and the death of industrial relations as a separate field of study (41).

Milton Derber (12) attributed the divergent tendencies in industrial-relations research to the difficulty of integrating the diverse elements of the field; its identification as an art rather than a science; its tendency to shift emphasis with changes in current problem areas; and the failure of universities to produce Ph.D.s trained in more than one discipline enveloped by industrial relations. In conjunction with these problems has been the inability of industrial-relations theory or research to develop an acceptable unifying conceptual framework.

The solution continually proposed to these dilemmas has been the design and implementation of more interdisciplinary research (41). In fact, Becker (7) has argued that the main strength of institutional industrial relations has been its interdisciplinary focus. That is, few industrial-relations problems are fully understood by adopting the theory and methods of a single discipline. As a consequence, industrial-relations research has often drawn from several disciplines in an attempt to explain any given issue. Another tradition of industrial-relations research has been its orientation toward public policy. In addition, industrial-relations research has been distinguished from its component disciplines by its focus on the underlying processes rather than on just the outcomes of the industrial-relations system. For example, while economists have focused on wage levels and differentials in the market place, industrial-relations researchers have been more interested in the workings of the processes (for example, collective bargaining) that lead to wage differences. Thus, industrial relations as a field has been characterized as unique because of its interdisciplinary focus, its orientation toward public policy, and its interest in the processes which influence the terms and conditions of the employment relationship (7).

Although some writers are more pessimistic than others, there has definitely been a resurgence of research on industrial-relations topics which examines problems by integrating theory and methods from more than one of the core disciplines of industrial relations (2, 4, 40). Unfortunately, however, industrial relations has continued to be plagued by the absence of a unifying theoretical framework. An increase in the volume of interdisciplinary research does not, in itself, guarantee the development of the integrated conceptual framework needed to unify the field of industrial relations.

Dunlop's Industrial-Relations System

The most well-known and controversial attempt to provide a theoretical framework for the field was presented in 1958 in John Dunlop's book entitled, *Industrial Relations Systems* (14). The industrial-relations system was characterized as an "analytical subsystem of an industrial society on the same logical plane as an economic system" (p. 5). The system is comprised of three sets of actors— government, employees and their associations, and employers and their associations — who are bound together by a common ideology. The interactions of these actors produce the main output of the industrial-relations system, a "web of rules" of the work place and the work community. The actors exist within the technical, market, and power contexts of the system which are viewed as the determinants of the web of rules, each context having a selective impact on a subset of the rules (for example, market context impacts mainly on compensation). The characteristics of the industrial-relations system are discussed in more detail below.

The web of rules— The central proposition of Dunlop's theory is that the workings of the industrial-relations system produces a set of rules and regulations which govern the employment relationship. The web of rules define the rights and responsibilities of the actors in the system toward one another. The rules established may be either substantive or procedural. Substantive rules include outcomes of the system such as wages and pay supplements, fringe benefits including health, dental, and insurance programs, sick leave plans, holidays and vacations, and working conditions including rest periods, safety and health protections, and physical conditions. Procedural rules, on the other hand, include those arrangements between the actors which determine the ways in which substantive rules are to be made and applied as well as methods for resolving conflicts about existing rules. Procedures for collective bargaining, grievances, promotion, transfer or layoff would all be considered procedural rules. Thus, substantive and procedural rules combine to define the expected behaviours of each of the actors in the industrial-relations system.

The actors— Dunlop viewed three groups as the major parties to the industrial-relations system; the government, employers and their associations, and employees and their associations. The actors alone, or in combination, determine the web of rules of the system. The government can be viewed as an actor in the system in two different roles: (a) as a regulator, unilaterally establishing both substantive and procedural rules by enacting legislation (for example, collective bargaining and minimum-wage laws); and (b) as a participant, either as an employer in the public sector or as a guardian of the public interest intervening and interacting with employers and employees to determine the outcomes of the system. The definition of actors also reveals that the industrial-relations system may be useful in describing behaviour between an individual employee and employer, a single union and employer, unions and employers or their representatives at the industry or sectoral level, or the interaction of all actors at the society level. Thus, the web of rules can be a result of unilateral decisions of employers or governments or a result of negotiations between individuals and/or unions and employers and/or employer and industry associations.

The contexts of industrial relations— Dunlop argues that the type of substantive and procedural rules as well as the degree to which they are more or less favourable to one set of actors is largely dependent on the nature of the context in which the parties interact. The market, technical, and power contexts of the industrial-relations system may shift the balance of power between the parties, increasing the probability of favourable outcomes to one of the parties. The market context includes the nature of the labour market and product market facing the firm or industry. Dunlop indicates that unions will attempt to expand to control the supply of labour and to expand to cover the total product market of the firm in order to increase their bargaining power with the employer. The market context was also viewed as of particular importance in shaping the compensation package offered to employees.

The technical context of industrial relations refers to the extent to which employees or unions occupy a strategic position in the technical system of the organization or industry. The more control the union has over the technology, the greater the opportunity it has to shape the web of rules in its favour as it can control the operations of the firm. For example, maintenance workers in production technologies are essential to the continuing production of goods and as such have substantially more power to establish favourable rules.

The final context of the industrial-relations system delineated by Dunlop is the power context. This dimension refers to the relative position of the actors in society. In some instances, the government will be the major party shaping the web of rules; in other instances the employers or employees will dominate. The power context, therefore, focuses on the relative power that the various actors have accumulated because of their status in society. The more power residing with employees and their associations by virtue of their relative status, the more likely it is that the web of rules will be weighed in their direction.

The role of ideology— The industrial-relations system is presented as being bound together by a common ideology among the actors. For example, in North America, the values underlying capitalism and business-oriented unionism provide the basis for a collective-bargaining system which accepts the inherent conflict of interests between employers and employees which can be resolved by private contract of the terms and conditions of employment. In an industrial-relations system where a common ideology does not exist, the actors are unlikely to be able to establish procedural rules to govern the relationship, and substantive rules may need to be unilaterally imposed.

Criticisms of the Industrial-Relations-System Model

Much of the debate in industrial relations during the past twenty years has surrounded the applicability or inapplicability of Dunlop's representation of the industrial-relations system (8, 37, 47). Unfortunately, the theory did not provide the unifying framework sought for the field of industrial relations, and hence it did not have as pervasive an impact as was hoped. In fact, the model has been severely criticized on a number of grounds. The most common criticism is that it is only a taxonomy which has resulted in descriptive rather than explanatory research (47). While the industrial-relations system identified a number of components of the system— context, actors, rules, and ideology— the linkages between these components were, in large part, left unspecified. Although Dunlop provided some examples of how the context would be likely to influence the web of rules, the approach has been severely criticized for a failure to provide testable hypotheses which would generate empirical research (8). For example, the characteristics of labour and management organizations, which would increase or decrease their ability to set rules on their own terms, were not identified or discussed. As a result, the various researchers who have relied on the industrial-relations-system model have identified different, and sometimes conflicting, relationships between the same two sets of variables.

Problems of definition and the obscure treatment of rules in the industrial-relations system have been a second source of debate. While the notion of a web of rules of the work place was immediately accepted by the industrial-relations community, many people were confused by the distinction between substantive and procedural rules (47). Although actors in the system could establish both types of rules, some procedural rules were established by unilateral action of the government (for example, collective-bargaining legislation) while others could be determined by the employer (for example, appeals procedures) or jointly between labour and management (for example, grievance procedures, joint employer-employee committees). The theory failed to identify the conditions under which these different types of procedural rules were likely to have a substantial impact on the type and comprehensiveness of substantive rules which govern the work place. Without the availability of a collective-bargaining procedure, research has shown that wages, benefits, and general working conditions are much less favourable to the employees (29). In addition, other procedural rules, like grievance procedures are much less likely to exist. Therefore, the fact that the theory did not clearly distinguish between substantive rules and the mechanisms or procedures which determine them, and that it failed to specify the expected relationship between these two types of rules, have been major contributing factors to the failure of the industrial-relations-systems model to become a unifying theory for the field.

Most industrial-relations theorists adopt the position that an inherent conflict of interest exists between employers and employees in any society (11). Singh (37), as a result, criticizes Dunlop for not developing the importance of the role of conflict in the industrial-relations system. Although the nature of the ideology which binds the actors together within the system may shape the level and type of conflict which is acceptable within the system, its relevance is not discussed. Consequently, some writers have discussed conflict as an output of the industrial-relations system, examining strike activity in particular, while others have focused on the role of conflict as a mediator between the procedural and substantive rules. Thus, once again the lack of specificity in the treatment of conflict and ideology has created confusion in attempts to test the industrial-relations-systems model.

The major criticisms presented above, coupled with many more specific ones, have resulted in a continuing debate concerning the usefulness of the industrial-relations system. Unfortunately, the process of criticism and debate has all too often failed to result in positive changes to the model which would stimulate empirical research designed to test the model. Few studies have yet to use the model as anything more than a framework for descriptive research of industrial-relations practices in different firms, industries, or countries. Modifications have been suggested, however, which make the model more amenable to empirical testing.

A Modified Version of the Industrial-Relations-Systems Model

A number of authors have recommended changes to Dunlop's initial framework. In the Canadian context Craig (10) took the model out of structural terms and represented it in a more conventional systems approach with the use of the input-output framework. With some additional modifications, the resulting framework has several distinct advantages (see Figure 1). First, the framework recognizes that there exists a wide range of inputs to industrial relations beyond the market, technological, and power contexts of the system. Rather than viewing industrial relations as an isolated subsystem, the identification of inputs stresses the direct importance of the economic, legal, political, and sociocultural systems in shaping the actors, their interactions and the outputs of the system.

This framework also recognizes that the determination of the outputs of the

Figure 1

A Modified Version of the Industrial-Relations System

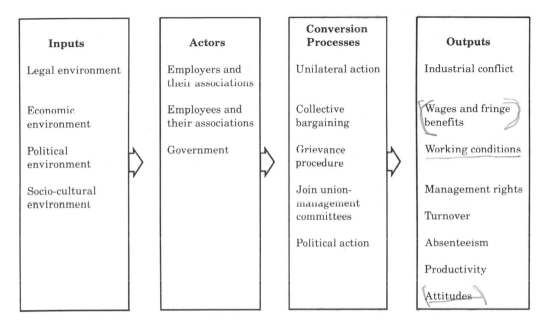

Inputs	Actors	Conversion Processes	Outputs
Legal environment	Employers and their associations	Unilateral action	Industrial conflict
Economic environment	Employees and their associations	Collective bargaining	Wages and fringe benefits
Political environment	Government	Grievance procedure	Working conditions
Socio-cultural environment		Join union-management committees	Management rights
		Political action	Turnover
			Absenteeism
			Productivity
			Attitudes

system, including the web of rules, may result from unilateral action on the part of any of the actors within the system, or through bilateral action as in bargaining, grievance processing, labour-management committees, day-to-day decisions at the work place, or political action by management or the union, or by tripartite involvement on some issue. As a result, it is vital to conceptualize the industrial-relations system as operating on several levels of society with the web of rules being shaped at the firm, industry, sector, or societal level. Moreover, outputs produced at one level inevitably will influence those produced at another.

Third, by distinguishing more clearly between procedural (conversion mechanisms) and substantive rules (outputs), the framework demands a recognition that the web of rules includes not only wages, benefits, and working conditions, but all of the outputs of the conversion mechanisms. These might include such outputs as changes in legislation, productivity, industrial conflict, industrial accidents, turnover, absenteeism, and employee attitudes.

Finally, the framework reveals that it is important to see the system as dynamic rather than static. That is, outputs in one time period or at one level (individual, firm, industry, sector, society) are likely to become inputs for another level or for another time period. For example, political action which succeeds in effecting a change in collective-bargaining legislation (output) will produce a change in the legal environment (an input) from that time forward. Thus, many of the environmental conditions examined as constraints in a static view of the industrial-relations system may, in fact, be under the partial control of the actors when a dynamic perspective is adopted.

While the above conceptual framework addresses some of the criticisms of the industrial-relations-systems model, it does not solve all of them. Most important, it does not provide directly testable hypotheses. Each of the sets of conceptual variables — inputs, actors, conversion mechanisms, outputs — contain a vast number of dimensions which can be identified, measured, and related to variables within the same conceptual set or with variables in other sets. However, as Heneman (20) notes, "every partial system should be anchored in a larger system and an experimenter should provide a bridge from his system over to another system (in terms of variables in common)." Thus, the onus is placed on the researcher to identify the appropriate level of analysis, the perspective to be taken, and the variables considered important in explaining the dependent variable(s) of interest. Then the researcher must show how the work helps us to understand the overall industrial-relations system.

The conceptual framework indicates a series of sequential relationships starting with inputs moving through actors and conversion processes to outputs. In reality, however, theory and empirical research exist to indicate that the characteristics of the inputs and actors may have direct effects on the conversion mechanisms and outputs of the system as well as the indirect ones included in the framework (as indicated by the dotted lines in Figure 1). Therefore, in thinking about the industrial-relations system, it is important to consider the way in which the components of the system interact to shape the industrial-relations outputs.

THE CANADIAN INDUSTRIAL-RELATIONS SYSTEM

As with every industrial-relations system, the Canadian system has many characteristics which make it unique. The purpose of this section of the chapter is to provide an overview of the Canadian scene, using the framework presented above (see Figure 1). This is done to set the stage for the individual chapters in the remainder of the book which focus on specific components of the industrial-relations system. In addition, a preliminary step is taken to describe the linkages between the various components of the system. The state of theory, research, and practice which address these relationships is discussed in the various chapters in the book.

The Inputs of the Industrial-Relations System

The legal environment Public policy has been identified as one of the major factors shaping industrial relations (24). In Canada, there are a number of different types of legislation which influence the characteristics of the actors, the way in which they interact, and the output of the industrial-relations system. In comparison to the United States, legislative control over employment-related matters is quite decentralized. Under the British North America Act, jurisdiction over industrial relations is given to the provinces for all employers not involved in national enterprises. As a result, there are eleven separate jurisdictions, each having at least one statute governing labour relations in the private sector and often having one or more pieces of legislation dealing with the public sector (see Chapter 15). In addition, each jurisdiction has a number of laws which establish minimum standards for the wages and working conditions of employees. Thus, public policies established at provincial and federal levels have a direct impact on the nature of industrial relations in Canada.

Despite the number of separate jurisdictions, and the innumerable specific differences in the content of the laws, the underlying philosophy and approach to the legal regulation of collective bargaining in Canada are substantially similar across the provinces and the federal government (see Chapter 2). Each statute provides for the formation of trade unions through the free choice of a majority of the employees in a unit appropriate for collective bargaining. Individuals' rights to select or not select a bargaining agent are protected from the undue influence of unions and employers by identifying certain behaviours (for example, intimidation, coercion, change in working conditions) as unfair labour practices. If the union wins a majority, it is certified as the exclusive bargaining agent of all employees in the bargaining unit and the employer is required to bargain with the employees' representative in an attempt to establish the terms and conditions of employment for the group. Most collective bargaining laws also provide mechanisms to aid in the resolution of disputes between the parties (for example, conciliation) as well as the conditions under which the strike or lockout may be employed. Moreover, provisions exist to aid in the resolution of disputes over the interpretation and application of a negotiated collective agreement through the establishment of grievance procedures. Thus, collective bargaining legislation is designed to facilitate the establishment and maintenance of a collective bargaining relationship between union and management.

The interactions between labour and management are not the only subjects of regulation, however. More and more provincial and federal legislation has been passed to constrain the unilateral actions of employers by regulating the outputs of the system themselves (see Chapter 4). For example, minimum-wage rates are established by law as are basic working conditions such as hours of work, overtime compensation, and occupational safety and health in the work place. These pieces of legislation are designed to establish a set of minimally acceptable conditions under which employees should work. Employer decisions, which may adversely affect the rights of individuals to jobs, wages, promotions, and due process, are also constrained by human rights legislation (see Chapter 21). Protections, in the form of legislation, are also provided in the case of industrial accidents or unemployment. Thus, it is clear that public policy in Canada has been established and has evolved to set minimums on many of the outputs of the industrial-relations system and, in addition, it establishes procedures by which people may collectively attempt to influence directly the outputs of the system through negotiation with their employers.

Public policy is not always designed to establish minimum industrial-relations conditions. In fact, in response to adverse economic conditions over the past two decades, the federal government has several times attempted to restrict the magnitude of increases in total compensation (wages and fringe benefits) paid to employees, and of prices charged for goods and services. In October of 1975, the Anti-Inflation Board was established to monitor, and, if necessary, to constrain wage and price increases (see Chapter 20). As industrial-relations outcomes are also viewed as changing inputs in the future, in this case inflation rates, the purpose of the program was to attempt to alleviate major sources of inflationary pressures in the economy.

The above examples highlight the fact that the legal environment not only defines the nature of some of the conversion processes (for example, collective bargaining, grievance processing) but that it may be enacted to set upper and lower bounds on the outcomes of the industrial-relations system. Beyond this direct role, public policy also has a substantial role in shaping the expectations and bargaining power of the parties during negotiations. Unions can threaten employers with

Table 1

Characteristics of the Canadian Economic Environment

Year	Inflation Rate	Unemployment Rate	Growth in GNP	Increase in Productivity
1971	2.9	6.4	2.7	3.6
1972	4.8	6.3	6.6	3.8
1973	7.5	5.6	6.9	2.4
1974	10.9	5.4	2.8	−0.6
1975	10.8	7.1	0.2	0.2
1976	7.5	7.1	4.6	2.9
1977	8.0	8.1	2.4	3.0
1978	9.0	8.4	3.4	1.3
1979	9.1	7.5	2.9	0.5

SOURCE: *D. Wood, and P. Kumar (Eds.),* The Current Industrial Relations Scene in Canada, *(Kingston: Industrial Relations Centre, Queen's University, various years).*

action under various statutes should they fail to accept certain demands (for example, occupational health and safety violations) and employers may use other policies such as wage and price guidelines to ignore union demands. Public policy often sets the context in which other environmental influences come into play.

The economic environment — Prevailing economic conditions have played an increasingly important role in determining the nature of employer-employee relations and the outcomes of the industrial-relations system. Economists often suggest that the nature of the macro- and microeconomic context explains very well the nature of the outcomes of the industrial-relations system without reference to the institutional forces (labour, management, collective bargaining) which have been identified above. An understanding of the dynamics of supply and demand in the labour and product markets is seen as providing sufficient information to predict the wages and other terms and conditions of employment offered to employees (see Chapter 4). With this perspective in mind, an examination of the performance of the economy over the past decade reveals that Canada has been faced with increasing levels of inflation and unemployment, an erosion of real wages, a decrease in productivity levels, and a moderate rate of economic growth (see Table 1). All of these conditions are likely to place considerable pressure on the actors in the industrial-relations system in attempting to achieve their goals.

Another important dimension of the Canadian economy is its dependence on exports of raw materials and semi-finished products — forest products, grain, minerals, and oil. The nature of labour relations in these export industries has a large impact on the competitiveness of Canadian goods on the world market. In addition to a dependence on exports, Canada traditionally has been highly dependent on foreign investment to develop these industries.

Kochan (24) identifies several reasons why the economic environment is important in determining the outcomes of the system. First, economic conditions shape the expectations of employees, unions, and management before they enter the bargaining arena. High inflation rates and declining real wage rates increase the expectations of workers for higher wages. Second, economic conditions affect the short-term bargaining power of the parties. Under times of high unemployment, unions are likely to moderate their demands because of decreased job security. Strikes may result in workers being replaced from the available labour pool. Similarly, decreases in economic growth and the productivity of labour may make management much more resistant to labour's demands. Thus, the economic conditions in society will do a great deal to shape the nature of union demands and the militancy with which these demands are pursued.

The political environment — Unlike the nature of political systems in other countries (see Chapter 19), Canada's political context has much less of a direct impact on the functioning of the industrial-relations system than does either the legal or the economic context. At the federal level, Canada is primarily a modified two-party system, dominated by the Conservative and the Liberal parties. However, given the regional disparities in support for these parties, elections often result in minority governments being formed. As a consequence, the New Democratic Party (NDP) has played an important role in recent years as it has often held the swing vote which could result in the dissolution of Parliament after a vote of nonconfidence in the government. Therefore, both parties have been more receptive of the labour-oriented NDP.

At the provincial level, the NDP has been, or presently is, either the party in power or the official opposition in more than half of the Canadian provinces. As the NDP was formed with strong labour support and still maintains a substantial union vote, it is understandable that in most provinces in which they have formed the government that progressive labour and employment-related legislation has been enacted (22). Thus, the orientation and ideology of the political system may also influence the relative bargaining power of labour and management.

The sociocultural environment — As a result of distances and the geographic diversity which characterizes Canada, sociocultural influences on the industrial-relations system are substantial. The demographic characteristics of the workers and the industrial and occupational composition of regions are all likely to have a key influence in determining the attitudes that people have towards unions as well as their preferences for different outcomes related to their employment (24). Research has generally indicated that unionization is less likely to be found among females, more educated individuals, and white-collar and professional employees (24, 33) (see Chapter 16). Changes in the composition of the labour force reveal trends toward increasing labour force participation rates by women, high average levels of education in the population, and a movement toward white-collar and service occupations.

Each of these trends would suggest that the general public's attitude toward organized labour is becoming more negative. Gallup polls over the past decade have in fact, revealed an increasing concern about the role of labour in Canadian society. Only in 1969 (see Table 2) was labour not viewed as the biggest threat to the future of Canada. These conditions suggest that the public is more and more unwilling to support labour's demands for a greater share in the economy.

Changes in the composition of the labour force and of union members have an important impact not only on the general attitudes toward trade unions but also on preferences for certain outcomes of collective bargaining (see Chapter 11). One

Table 2

**"Speaking of our future, which do you think will be the
biggest threat to Canada in years to come —
big business, big labour, big government?"**

Year	Big Business (%)	Big Labour (%)	Big Government (%)
1969	12	26	46
1972	27	36	22
1976	18	43	33
1978	21	38	35

SOURCE: Gallup polls, various years.

group of employees may want higher wages, while another would prefer increased pension benefits and still another health and medical benefits, increased vacations, and daycare facilities (24). Thus, changes in the composition of the labour force is likely to lead to changes in union goals. Furthermore, as the membership of unions becomes more heterogeneous, union leadership will have more difficulty in establishing union goals without conflict, will need to establish more structural mechanisms to ensure democratic representation of members' interests, and will have to be prepared to accept more contract repudiation by the rank-and-file.

In addition to the changing composition of Canadian society, which may impact social attitudes toward industrial relations, Canada also has strong cultural differences which are reflected in the system. Industrial relations in Quebec has developed in parallel with the rest of the country but exhibits many features which are unique to its historical and cultural heritage (see Chapter 18). The belief that the motivations of workers, the goals of labour, management, or the government, or the interactions of the actors are the same across the country would prevent a complete understanding or interpretation of the events in Quebec. Knowledge of differences in philosophy and history (see Chapter 5) are vital to an understanding of the Canadian industrial-relations system.

Conclusion — In the original representation of the environment of industrial relations, Dunlop limited his focus to the market, technological, and power contexts. However, it is clear that a large number of factors influence industrial relations. The legal environment establishes the parameters within which the parties interact and often directly regulates the minimum, maximum, and type of outcomes of the industrial-relations system. The political, economic, and sociocultural environments influence the expectations of employees, unions, and employers with respect to the levels and types of wages and terms and conditions of employment that are preferred, establishing the bargaining goals of the parties. These same factors may also shape the attitudes the parties hold toward one another and toward their preferred forms of interaction. Finally, each of the aspects of the environment of industrial relations affect the bargaining power that each of the parties have at the table. Hence, knowledge of the inputs to the industrial-relations system is necessary to allow interpretation of the role of direct actions of the parties in establishing the outputs of the system.

The Actors in the Industrial-Relations System

The characteristics of union and management organizations as they relate to industrial-relations processes and outcomes is one of the least-researched areas in the field of industrial relations. While descriptions of the internal dynamics and the administration of labour unions are plentiful, the systematic examination of the effects of union organization on conversion processes and outcomes is lacking. Moreover, the situation is even worse vis-à-vis studies of management, which are almost nonexistent. Thus, a description of the actors and their role in the Canadian industrial-relations system is unfortunately more speculative than is desirable.

Management organization — Given the geographic diversity of Canada and the small average size of firms, labour-relations issues in most cases are dealt with at the plant level (see Chapter 6). No national organization or association represents management as a whole within the industrial-relations system. While multiemployer bargaining exists in certain industries (for example, trucking, construction, hospitals), it is still not the most common practice. Thus, the practice of industrial-relations management has tended to be relatively decentralized (see Chapter 8).

For many years the role of U.S. and multinational corporations in Canada raised questions about the degree of freedom that Canadian management had to decide local labour-relations issues. A high proportion of firms in this country are owned or financed by foreign interests. While there has been a decline in recent years, approximately 30 percent of all assets were foreign controlled in 1977, with almost 23 percent of the foreign ownership of assets centred in the United States (38). Moreover, foreign ownership controls over 50 percent of the assets in mining and various manufacturing industries (38): tobacco products (100 percent), rubber products (94 percent), textile mills (58 percent), machinery (64 percent), transport equipment (77 percent), electrical products (69 percent), nonmetallic mineral products (70 percent), petroleum and coal products (92 percent), and chemical and chemical products (68 percent). Thus, foreign ownership tends to control those export industries on which Canada is so dependent and in which labour relations have tended to be the most unstable.

In the early 1970s, it was strongly believed that labour policies in Canadian subsidiary firms were strongly influenced by practices in U.S. parent companies. Complaints were frequently heard about the inability of the management of U.S. firms located in Canada to make decisions on industrial-relations matters without the approval of the foreign corporate headquarters. In a study of five industries, Downie (13) found wide variations in the extent to which the timing of negotiations and wage and fringe benefit changes in the Canadian bargaining unit were influenced by the U.S. corporation. However, over two-thirds of the firms were found to be subject to U.S. influence. While conditions have changed somewhat since 1970, it is still likely that U.S. policies and practices are partially transmitted to their Canadian counterparts.

A recent study of personnel and industrial-relations staff in 250 Canadian organizations suggests that management of industrial relations is increasingly becoming a professionalized function (27). Most of the respondents, who were human resource/labour relations managers (52 percent), reported having a university degree (53 percent) with many having a specialization in personnel, industrial relations, or business administration (43 percent). Moreover, approximately three-quarters of these managers had taken courses in industrial relations before or after employment. Furthermore, 88 percent of the sample believed that young management trainees in the field should have a university degree or formal training in the field. Thus, if these respondents are indicative of the future of industrial relations in Canada, it is clear that it is becoming more professional. This is important given that training, experience, and skill in the management of labour relations have been found to be a significant factor in the ability of management to bargain effectively (2) and to ensure the smooth functioning of the grievance procedure (4).

Specialized departments have also developed in organizations to handle industrial-relations matters. Kumar (27) found that the median size of industrial-relations staff was 16 employees and that the median number of staff per 10,000 employees was 67. While these data do not indicate the relative importance of industrial-relations activities to the organization, it is clear that these firms were devoting substantial resources to the function. How much authority and responsibility are delegated to industrial-relations managers and how effective they are in performing their functions is explored in Chapter 6.

Union organization — Unlike the situation in the United States, membership in Canadian unions has continued to grow during the 1970s from 2.9 million in 1975 to 3.4 million in 1980, representing about 38 percent of the total nonagricultural labour force. However, over 57 percent of employees were covered by collective agreements in 1977; varying from 10 percent of white-collar workers in manufacturing to 89 and 94 percent of white-collar and nonoffice employees, respectively in public administration (46). Thus, unions have made a substantial penetration into the representation of Canadian workers (see Chapter 7).

A total of 208 international and national unions exist in Canada. However, similar to their employer counterparts, most unions are relatively small; only 16 unions have a total membership which exceeds 50,000. On the other hand, a total of 139 unions have memberships under 10,000. As a result, union organization is quite decentralized, with most union activities, including collective bargaining, occurring at the local level.

The growth of unions in Canada has been largely shaped by the environment of the industrial-relations system. Favourable legislation, which has supported union organization by reducing the percentage of employees required to obtain a certification election and, in some provinces, by legislating that individuals must pay dues whether or not they join the union (agency shop), has stimulated union membership growth. A large portion of the growth has occurred in the public sector where the tendency has been for the government to define by statute the composition of bargaining units and automatically to grant existing employee associations exclusive bargaining-agent status (16). The nature of economic and political conditions has also been a stimulant to union growth. Research (15) has revealed that people are much more likely to join unions when inflation and unemployment are on the increase; political support for labour is present; and the labour force is growing. All of these factors have contributed to the growth of Canadian unions.

The nature of union organization has, like management, been influenced greatly by the presence of U.S.-based international unions. The development of the Canadian labour movement has paralleled in many ways the situation in the United States (see Chapter 5). While the struggles for the recognition of trade unions were not as violent in Canada, the organizing process was in large part instigated by the desire of U.S. unions to protect their jobs from lower-paid Canadian craftsmen. Organizing initially focused on craft workers, and it was not until the 1930s that industrial unions, which were interested in organizing all workers without regard to craft, started to appear. Following the United States, craft unions, which were affiliated with the Trades and Labour Congress, and industrial unions, which were affiliated with the Canadian Congress of Labour, merged to form the Canadian Labour Congress in 1956 (23).

Although the Canadian Labour Congress (CLC) was born, a majority of all workers and unions were still affiliated with international unions. In many cases, the constitutions of those organizations required the approval of the international union for collective-bargaining agreements, strikes, and internal government (1). As a result, not just management policy, but union policies and practices were often controlled from south of the border. However, since the late 1960s the proportion of union members affiliated with international unions has dropped from over 70 percent to 46 percent in 1980. Moreover, resolutions passed by the CLC in 1976 required changes in international union constitutions to grant autonomy over local matters to affiliated Canadian bodies. Consequently, the labour movement is presently much less affected by the policies of international unions than in the past.

Like their management counterparts, the leadership and staff of Canadian unions have also become increasingly more professional. Specialized committees, staffs, and departments have been established to provide training to stewards and local leadership, to provide assistance in organizing and grievance processing, to provide research support for collective bargaining, and to provide political action campaigns for dealing with government. While very little research is available which indicates how the rationalization of union structure has impacted their ability to achieve the goals established, it is clear that the trend has been to increased sophistication of both labour and management. This trend may, in part, be responsible for the inroads that unions have made into such realms as classification plans, job evaluation, and pension fund administration.

Government — Both provincial and federal governments are also major actors in the industrial-relations system. Traditionally, government has played a role as a regulator of industrial relations passing legislation to establish the ground rules for interactions between labour and management. This passive approach of government has meant that for the most part the parties have been left to establish privately the terms and conditions of employment for their employees.

However, over the past fifteen years two major changes have occurred in relation to the role of governments in the industrial-relations system. First, governments have become not only regulators of but large employers of unionized work forces (see Chapter 15). This new role as a participant in labour relations has changed the willingness of government to intervene. Actions taken as a regulator are much more likely to influence directly the government's role as an employer, making the government more cautious in legislative change. However, it also appears that the government has an increasing willingness to intervene in disputes, forcing the parties back to work and to the bargaining table, sometimes even imposing settlements on the parties. Thus, this new role as an employer may have increased the government's willingness to intervene directly in the interactions of the other two actors to ensure the smooth functioning of the industrial-relations system.

Conclusion — Over the past decades, control over industrial-relations issues has shifted more and more away from U.S. headquarters of corporations and unions to within Canada. While labour relations has still remained relatively fragmented and decentralized, both sides have increased their skills, expertise, and professionalism, opening the way for more innovative relationships. Unfortunately, at this point research has lagged behind practice so that very little information is available which indicates how these changes in union and management organization have impacted the relationships between the parties in collective bargaining, grievance processing, or in the day-to-day interactions of supervisors and unionized workers. On the other hand, the role of the government in industrial relations has increased, with both provincial and federal governments being willing to intervene in the process. Unfortunately, once again, little research is available which examines the impact of these changes on the outputs of the Canadian industrial-relations system.

The Conversion Processes in the Industrial-Relations System

There are a wide variety of mechanisms through which the inputs reaching the actors in the system may be translated into outputs of the industrial-relations system. In any relationship, often several of these conversion processes will be operating, having an impact on selected sets of outputs. Both parties are likely to select carefully which mechanism is used to deal with any given issue; certain conditions will be changed unilaterally while others will be discussed jointly through bargaining, grievances, political action, or joint committees. Thus, it is important that an examination of the Canadian industrial-relations system not limit itself to only an examination of collective bargaining.

Unilateral action by the actors — Often the terms and conditions of employment and other outputs, like individual behaviour and attitudes, are primarily influenced by the actions of the employer alone. This is most likely to occur: (a) for the 43 percent of the labour force that is not covered by a collective bargaining relationship; and (b) for those issues which are traditionally considered as management's rights.

Given that a large proportion of the labour force, including white-collar, professional, and managerial employees, are not represented by unions, it is the responsibility of management to establish those terms and conditions of employment which will permit the efficient and effective operation of the organization. However, even this situation is not free from constraints. As mentioned previously, legislation exists in all Canadian jurisdictions which establishes minimally acceptable wages and working conditions which must be offered to employees. Moreover, for the employer to be able to recruit quality employees, the wages, benefits, and working conditions offered must be competitive with those available elsewhere in the labour market. Therefore, in reality, at least with certain basic conditions, the employer is further constrained by prevailing conditions. Finally, to continue to avoid unionization employers may have to offer better than average conditions to the organizations' employees. Thus, while the employer in a nonunion context may unilaterally make decisions which determine the outputs of the industrial-relations system, those decisions are often heavily constrained by public policy, the nature of the economic environment, and conditions in the unionized sector.

Whether unionized or not, employers have the right to unilaterally make decisions to ensure the efficient operation and direction of the firm. While unions have made inroads into management rights (see Chapter 12), there are still many aspects of personnel administration and capital allocations which remain within the domain of employers. Thus, organizations establish personnel/human-resource departments in order to establish standards and procedures for selecting employees, systems for analysing, describing and classifying jobs, systems for evaluating the relative worth of different jobs, and systems to analyse training needs, provide training, and evaluate performance. Moreover, decisions concerning the size and allocation of the work force, including promotions and transfers, establishing new jobs, or identifying redundant positions, are traditionally controlled by management, although at times subject to the grievance procedure. Thus, a large number of issues that are vital to the operation of the firm have remained outside union reach. Many of these areas of personnel administration are strongly related to ensuring a motivated, stable, and satisfied work force and, therefore, are important to such outputs of the industrial-relations system as turnover, performance, job satisfaction, absenteeism, and industrial accidents.

Collective bargaining — The most central conversion process to the Canadian industrial-relations system is the collective-bargaining process. As previously mentioned, 57 percent of the labour force are covered by collective agreements. In 1979, most agreements were negotiated for a period of two years (48 percent) with the remainder split between contracts of one year (30 percent) and three or more years (22 percent) in duration. While it is difficult to estimate the total number of collective agreements in force in Canada, statistics indicate that 440 agreements involving 500 workers or more expired in 1980 while another 982 were still in force (46). Given that most negotiations involve less than 500 employees in a bargaining unit, it would be expected that the number of actual collective agreements is much higher.

The collective-bargaining process recognizes the inherent conflict of interests between labour and management (see Chapter 9). Public policy provides that both parties must bargain in good faith in an attempt to reach a collective agreement. Generally, collective bargaining is viewed as a win-lose process; any gains for the union are seen as losses to management. For example, increases in wages, fringe benefits, and job security improve the position of workers at the expense of increased labour costs and reduced discretion for management. As a consequence, the process of collective bargaining takes a substantial amount of time; in 1979 the median time was six months. This distributive process tends to generate a substantial amount of conflict between the parties.

All collective bargaining, however, does not involve the distribution of benefits between labour and management. Walton and McKersie (43) describe the fact that many issues (for example, safety and health) require joint problem solving by the parties to achieve an outcome which is beneficial to both parties. In fact, many authors (35) argue that moving collective bargaining from distributive to integrative will improve labour-management relations in the country substantially, and they have proposed a number of techniques to help the parties make this shift (see Chapter 14). Collective bargaining also involves a substantial amount of negotiation within the union and management teams. This intraorganizational bargaining process is often as difficult as collective bargaining as the parties must establish their priorities in bargaining, resolving internal conflicts along the way. Thus, the collective-bargaining process involves much more than direct interactions between labour and management over wages and working conditions.

The nature of collective bargaining often depends on the prevailing environmental conditions and the characteristics of union and management organizations. As inflation and financial pressures on the firm increase, the resistance of the parties to each other's demands makes settlement difficult and may increase hostility. Similarly, the existence of factions within union and management increase the difficulty of establishing a consistent strategy in negotiations which would facilitate settlement. Without adequate authority delegated to the union and management negotiators, collective bargaining may also become protracted. In general, the expertise, skills, and experience of the parties as well as their interpersonal relationships will determine the extent to which bargaining is likely to be characterized as distributive or integrative. Clearly, these are only a few examples of the ways in which characteristics of the inputs and the actors affect collective bargaining but they do point out that negotiations are not only an interpersonal process.

The grievance process — Once a collective agreement has been negotiated, the vast majority of time allocated by union and management representatives to industrial relations involves the interpretation and application of that agreement (see Chapter 13). Violations of the agreement or differences in the interpretation of the rights and responsibilities of the parties under the agreement may be grieved. All contracts or statutes include a procedure by which these differences may be resolved. Typically, grievance procedures have four steps: (a) the grievant and supervisor informally discuss and attempt to resolve the problem; (b) if unresolved, the grievance is reduced to writing and presented by the employee and union steward to the plant manager or department head; (c) if unresolved, the grievance will be passed up to a higher level of management or the personnel or employee-relations manager; and (d) finally, if the grievance cannot be resolved at this level, it is submitted to an independent arbitrator whose decision is binding upon the parties. At each stage of the grievance process each side normally has seven to fourteen days to respond to the grievance (or managerial response) before placing it before the next step in the procedure.

The grievance process has many functions within the organization other than just resolving disputes. It provides a general communication channel for employee concerns; a pressure-release valve in the employer-employee relationship; a vehicle for training lower level union and management officials; and a mechanism for delegating authority down to the work level (26). Thus, while the grievance process does not provide additional benefits to the worker, it does ensure that the outcomes received through other mechanisms are forthcoming and helps to develop the union-management relationship in a positive way.

The effectiveness of the grievance process is often gauged by the parties in a number of ways (4). First, both sides would like to see grievances settled in the early stages of the procedure so that injustices are not allowed to develop further. This implies that another criterion used is the speed with which grievances are resolved. Members like to have their problems dealt with quickly. However, both of these dimensions of the effectiveness of the grievance process are subordinated to the desire of both parties to receive a just and equitable settlement of the problem (4). The above criteria do not focus at all on the number of grievances as an indicator of the success of the procedure. High rates are not necessarily good or bad as they depend to a large extent on the characteristics of the work force, union and management policies, and the technology of the work (44). The effectiveness of the grievance procedure produces important outputs of the system by helping to maintain worker satisfaction with both work and the union, and therefore, decrease the probability of industrial conflict, turnover, absenteeism, and low performance.

The functioning of the grievance procedure also is in large part dependent on the characteristics of union and management organizations and the relationship between the parties. Research has shown that the training and skill of supervisors and union stewards is the key to making the procedure work (4). Moreover, the more trust and cooperation which exists between the parties, the better the grievance process will function in the organizations. Establishing formal union and management grievance screening committees also appears to contribute to its effectiveness. However, it is important to note that the grievance procedure may also be used strategically by the union leadership to show the union membership that they are being represented or to force management to more seriously consider certain issues at upcoming negotiations.

Joint union-management committees— Frequently, union and management officials discover that there are issues to be dealt with between rounds of negotiations which are of ongoing concern but do not fit within the realm of the grievance procedure (see Chapter 14). Rather than handling these issues on an ad hoc basis, often the parties establish a joint committee. These committees are often established to review and recommend changes to policy on such topics as job-classification systems or job-evaluation plans. They may also be designed to monitor safety and health programs or to administer group incentive procedures or pension plans. Moreover, a committee may be established just to ensure an ongoing dialogue between labour and management during the life of the contract.

Joint committees have several features which distinguish them from other conversion mechanisms (15). First, both union and management have equal representation on the committee, often to the extent of cochairing between the sides or using a rotating chairperson. Second, it is understood that the committee will deal with issues of mutual concern to the parties which when resolved have benefits to both union and management. Issues which are clearly subjects of negotiations are deferred until collective bargaining. Thus, the process is designed to promote integrative bargaining rather than distributive bargaining. The hope is that both union and management will place themselves in a problem-solving mode, generating innovative solutions to joint problems. Thus, these committees are designed to help build cooperation and a responsible relationship between the parties which should help to reduce industrial conflict (25).

The manner in which joint union-management committees function is also related to the nature of the pre-existing relationship between the parties and the characteristics of the actors' organizations. Commitment to these types of committees is essential to making them work (15). As a result committees are often not developed until the union-management relationship has matured, workers are secure, and the union leadership is relatively stable politically. Even once these conditions are present, both sides have to have enough authority to deal with the problems and be prepared and willing to engage in a problem-solving process (25). Given these preconditions, it is not surprising that joint committees are not universally accepted or used in either the private or public sectors in Canada.

Political action— The previous conversion mechanisms have focused on the interactions of labour and management in establishing the terms and conditions of employment. Both parties also have available to them the use of political tactics to attempt to convince government to legislate the outputs of the industrial-relations system. While both management, through such organizations as the Canadian Association of Manufacturers, and unions, through the CLC and provincial federations of labour, lobby for changes in legislation, both the extent and effectiveness of these actions may be questioned.

The Canadian labour movement has for a long time flirted with direct support of a political party, the NDP. While labour still supports the platforms of the NDP, and several local unions in southern Ontario continue to be directly affiliated with the NDP, labour and political parties in Canada have traveled a rocky road (22). The CLC maintains an official policy of being nonpartisan and union members in general vote Liberal in federal elections. Thus, both the role of political action in Canada and its effectiveness in obtaining changes in the outputs of the system must come under close scrutiny.

Conclusion— There are a variety of mechanisms which are available to the actors in the industrial-relations system to transform inputs to outputs. The most prevalent in Canada tend to be those processes which involve bilateral action between unions and employers. The nature of the environment within which the parties function, as well as the characteristics of union and management organizations themselves appear to be the major forces which influence how smoothly these processes work. Thus, again it is important in analysing industrial-relations practices to examine the context in which the interactions occur.

The Outputs of the Industrial-Relations System

The outputs of the industrial-relations system are in large part the result of the unique combination of inputs, characteristics of the actors, and characteristics of the conversion processes used. Therefore, while some general descriptions of the outputs of the Canadian system can be provided, a comprehensive examination of their determinants is left to subsequent chapters which specifically examine industrial conflict (Chapter 10), wages, and fringe benefits (Chapter 11) and management rights (Chapter 12).

Industrial conflict— The practice of industrial relations can result in the manifestation of conflict in a number of ways. Strikes over collective bargaining, wildcat strikes over conditions during the life of collective agreements, general strikes over political issues, mass "sick-outs," and work-to-rule campaigns are all forms of conflict which are frequently used in Canada. Approximately 11 percent of negotiations in 1976, and six percent in 1977 and 1978 resulted in a work stoppage. A total of 1,041 strikes occurred, involving 442,000 employees, with a total of 7,637,000 days lost due to strikes. All strikes taken together only accounted for less than one-third of one percent of total working time available during 1979 (46).

Canada has some of the longest strikes in the world which may substantially impact the country's position in world markets. Moreover, strikes are concentrated in the manufacturing (41 percent) and primary (22 percent) industries which are the specific industries where exports are highest. Therefore, industrial conflict as an output clearly feeds back into other conditions in society which are the inputs to the system at a later time, accentuating the dynamic nature of the industrial-relations system.

Wages and fringe benefits— Collective bargaining has made a substantial impact on the wages and fringe benefits provided to workers in Canada (see Chapter 11). Rather than describing in detail each of the outputs in this realm, the results of a survey (4) of 171 establishments are presented below (see Table 3). The table

Table 3

Incidence of Fringe Benefits
(Percent of Employees with Benefit)

Benefit	Management/ Professional	Office	Nonoffice
Group life insurance and related plans	99.3	98.9	95.5
Provincial health care	100.0	100.0	100.0
Supplementary health insurance plans	98.1	95.3	90.0
Dental care plans	67.6	59.9	60.6
Group legal insurance	.3	1.2	1.7
Group automobile insurance	13.1	9.0	5.4
Group homeowner's insurance	.5	.0	.0
Liability insurance	58.0	43.8	44.6
Formal paid sick leave plans	89.2	82.4	41.5
Sickness indemnity insurance plans	1.0	1.5	40.5
Combined formal paid sick leave and sickness indemnity plans	8.9	14.4	12.8
Long-term disability plans	91.9	77.2	64.5
Retirement savings plans	100.0	99.7	93.5
Paid holidays	94.2	100.0	100.0
Paid vacations	94.2	100.0	100.0
Paid rest periods	67.7	75.6	83.2
Paid jury and witness duty	100.0	99.8	98.7
Time-off for union business	20.9	53.3	86.9
Hours of work	100.0	100.0	100.0
Overtime compensation	46.7	98.6	99.8
Shift-work compensation	25.5	67.0	95.9
Call-back pay	17.3	51.8	89.0
Stand-by pay	15.9	24.5	19.4
Pay for regularly scheduled weekend work	6.1	19.3	3.2
Severance pay plans and retirement allowances	41.6	39.8	26.0
Health and safety plan	63.8	68.8	89.4

SOURCE: Pay Research Bureau, Employee Benefits and Working Conditions, Canada, 1980.

provides information on the percentage of employees who are covered by some provision on each of the different fringe benefits. The diversity of benefits shows how important nonwage issues are to the total compensation of employees. In this sample, benefit payments represented over 40 percent of total payroll expenditures.

Working conditions and management rights — Beyond wages and fringe benefits, the outputs of the industrial-relations system also include a number of noncost items as well as provisions which cover union impact on such areas as personnel administration and general management. Again, rather than discussing each of these areas in detail, selected results of the survey of major collective agreements are provided to illustrate the range of outputs negotiated in this domain (see Table 4).

Table 4

**Provisions in Major Collective Agreements
in Manufacturing — 1977**

Collective Agreement Provision		Number of Contracts	Percentage of Contracts
Seniority in promotion:	no provision	38	11.1
	considered with other factors	.303	88.9
Seniority in layoff:	no provision	17	5.0
	straight seniority	46	13.9
	considered with other factors	277	81.1
Probationary period:	no provision	18	5.3
	one month or less	36	10.6
	one to three months	249	73.1
	four to six months	31	9.1
	other	7	1.9
Posting of job vacancies:	no provision	78	22.9
	provision exists	263	77.1
Notice of layoff:	no provision	121	35.5
	one week or less	180	52.8
	more than one week	9	2.7
	graduated	9	3.5
	other	22	6.5
Recall procedure:	no provision	32	9.4
	inverse order of layoff	45	13.2
	other	264	81.3
Distribution of work during slack periods:	no provision	279	81.8
	provision exists	62	18.2
Distribution of overtime among employees:	no provision	135	39.6
	provision exists	206	60.4
Notice of technological change:	no provision	209	61.3
	less than three months	44	12.9
	three to six months	35	10.3
	other	53	15.5
Training for technological change:	no provision	228	66.9
	provision exists	113	33.1
Employment guarantees in technological change:	no provision	249	73.0
	provision exists	92	27.0
Employment of older or handicapped workers:	no provision	204	59.8
	provision exists	137	40.2

SOURCE: Labour Canada, Provisions in Major Collective Agreements Covering Employees in Canadian Manufacturing Industries *(Ottawa: Labour Canada, 1977).*

Turnover, absenteeism, productivity, and employee attitudes — The industrial-relations practices of employers and unions are also likely to have an impact on the behaviour and attitudes of people within the industrial-relations system. However, within this realm so many other factors also contribute to producing turnover, absenteeism, productivity, and attitudes that researchers must be careful not to conclude that unions and the conversion processes described above do or do not have an impact without controlling these other factors. Recent research has shown that by negotiating various forms of job security that unions do reduce turnover up to 25 percent (6). Moreover, it appears that, at least in manufacturing, unions by providing a voice to workers increase productivity up to 25 percent (18). Finally, unions do seem to increase job satisfaction with pay, promotion, and working conditions (31). While each of these findings are tentative, they do reveal the potential impact that industrial relations may have on individual behaviour and attitudes.

Conclusions — A discussion of the outputs of the industrial-relations system reveals the wide range of conditions which may be impacted. What conditions actually are present to a large extent depends on the other components of the system. Moreover, the particular combination of outputs is likely to reflect the preferences of the actors and their willingness to make trade-offs between outputs. That is, the outputs themselves are probably not independent of one another.

CONCLUDING REMARKS

The Canadian industrial-relations system is an important part of the lives of most Canadians. As employees or employers, Canadians are surrounded by a complex set of legal arrangements, institutional mechanisms, and environmental pressures which in large part determine the terms and conditions under which we work. In order to help understand the complexities of this dynamic system, a framework based on the work of John Dunlop was presented which identifies the major environmental conditions, the characteristics of the actors, and the mechanisms which exist to guide the interactions of the parties in shaping the web of rules or outputs of the system. This framework was then used to describe the characteristics of the Canadian industrial-relations system.

Overall, while descriptive material is available concerning industrial relations in Canada, it is difficult to identify at this point the most important features that determine the outputs of the system. Unfortunately, very little research exists in Canada which examines such issues as the impact of environmental conditions on the expectations and organizational arrangements established by unions and management; the effects of union and management characteristics on the processes of industrial relations; or the relative importance of inputs, actors, and processes on outputs. The purpose of the remaining chapters in this volume is to examine in more detail the characteristics of the industrial-relations system on outputs and the linkages between the components. It is hoped that these discussions will provide the reader with a working understanding of the Canadian industrial-relations system.

REFERENCES AND WORKS CITED

1. Adams, R. "The Canada-U.S. Labor Link Under Stress," *Industrial Relations,* Vol. 15 (October 1976), 295-312.

2. Anderson, J. "Bargaining Outcomes: An IR Systems Approach," *Industrial Relations,* Vol. 19 (May 1979), 127-143.

3. Anderson, J. "Local Union Democracy: In Search of Criteria," *Relations Industrielles/ Industrial Relations,* Vol. 34 (September 1979), 431-451.

4. Anderson, J. "Correlates of the Effectiveness of the Grievance Process." Unpublished paper, Graduate School of Business, Columbia University, 1981.

5. Ashenfelter, O., and J. Pencavel. "American Trade Union Growth: 1900-1960," *Quarterly Journal of Economics,* Vol. 83 (August 1969), 434-448.

6. Becker, B. "Hospital Unionism and Employment Stability," *Industrial Relations,* Vol. 17 (February 1978), 96-101.

7. Becker, B. "The Institutional Method and Industrial Relations Research." Unpublished paper, School of Management, State University of New York at Buffalo, 1980.

8. Blain, A.N.J., and J. Gennard. "Industrial Relations Theory: A Critical Review," *British Journal of Industrial Relations,* Vol. 8 (November 1970), 389-407.

9. Carrothers, A.W.R. *Collective Bargaining Law in Canada* (Toronto: Butterworth, 1965).

10. Craig, A. "A Model for the Analysis of Industrial Relations Systems" (Paper presented to the Annual Meeting of the Canadian Political Science Association, Ottawa, 1967).

11. Dahrendorf, R. *Class and Class Conflict in Industrial Society* (London: Routledge, 1959).

12. Derber, M. "Divergent Tendencies in Industrial Relations Research," *Industrial and Labour Relations Review,* Vol. 17 (July 1964), 598-611.

13. Downie, B. *Relationships Between Canadian-American Wage Settlements* (Kingston: Industrial Relations Centre, Queen's University, 1970).

14. Dunlop, J. *Industrial Relations Systems* (New York: Holt, 1958).

15. Ellis, T. "Cooperation Provisions in Major Agreements," *Monthly Labour Review,* Vol. 89 (March 1966), 283-287.

16. Feuille, P., and J. Anderson. "Public Sector Bargaining: Policy and Practice," *Industrial Relations,* Vol. 19 (October 1980), 309-324.

17. Fox, A. *A Sociology of Work in Industry* (London: Collier Macmillan, 1971).

18. Freeman, R., and J. Medoff. "The Two Faces of Unionism," *The Public Interest* (Fall 1979), 69-93.

19. Goodman, J., E.G.A. Armstrong, A. Wagner, J.E. Davis, and S.J. Wood. "Rules in Industrial Relations Theory: A Discussion," *Industrial Relations Journal,* Vol. 6 (Spring 1975), 14-30.

20. Heneman, H., Jr. "Toward a General Conceptual System of Industrial Relations: How Do We Get There?" in G. Somers (Ed.), *Essays in Industrial Relations Theory* (Ames, Iowa: Iowa State University Press, 1969), pp. 3-24.

21. Hill, S., and K. Thurley. "Sociology and Industrial Relations," *British Journal of Industrial Relations,* Vol. 12 (July 1974), 147-170.

22. Horowitz, G. *Canadian Labour in Politics* (Toronto: University of Toronto Press, 1968).

23. Jamieson, S. *Industrial Relations in Canada* (Toronto: Macmillan, 1973).

24. Kochan, T. *Collective Bargaining and Industrial Relations* (Homewood, Ill.: Irwin, 1980).

25. Kochan, T., D. Lipsky, and L. Dyer. *The Effectiveness of Union-Management Safety and Health Committees* (Kalamazoo, Mich.: W. E. Upjohn, 1977).

26. Kuhn, J.W. *Bargaining and Grievance Settlement* (New York: Columbia University Press, 1961).

27. Kumar, P. *Professionalism in the Canadian P/IR Function: Report of a Survey* (Kingston: Industrial Relations Centre, Queen's University, 1980).

28. Laffer, K. "Is Industrial Relations an Academic Discipline?" *Journal of Industrial Relations,* Vol. 16 (March 1974), 62-73.

29. Lewin, D. "The Impact of Unionism on American Business: Evidence for an Assessment," *Columbia Journal of World Business,* Vol. 13 (Fall 1978), 89-103.

30. Lewis, H.G. *Unionism and Relative Wages in the United States* (Chicago: University of Chicago Press, 1963).

31. Locke, E. "Job Satisfaction," in M.D. Dunnette (Ed.), *Handbook of Industrial and Organizational Psychology* (Chicago: Rand McNally, 1976).

32. Margerison, C.J. "What Do We Mean by Industrial Relations? A Behavioral Science Approach," *British Journal of Industrial Relations,* Vol. 8 (July 1969), 273-286.

33. Moore, W., and R. Newman. "On the Prospects for Trade Union Growth: A Cross Sectional Analysis," *The Review of Economics and Statistics,* Vol. 57 (November 1975), 438-445.

34. Pay Research Bureau, *Employee Benefits and Working Conditions Canada 1980* (Ottawa: Pay Research Bureau, 1980).

35. Peterson, R., and L. Tracy. "Testing a Behavioral Model of Labour Negotiations," *Industrial Relations* Vol. 16 (February 1977), 35-50.

36. Rees, A. *The Economics of Work and Pay* (New York: Harper and Row, 1973).

37. Singh, R. "Systems Theory in the Study of Industrial Relations: Time for Reappraisal?" *Industrial Relations Journal,* Vol. 7 (Autumn 1976), 59-71.

38. Statistics Canada. *Corporations and Labour Unions Returns Act* (Ottawa: Information Canada, 1978).

39. Stephenson, G.M., and C.J. Brotherton. *Industrial Relations: A Social Psychological Approach* (London: Wiley, 1978).

40. Stern, R. "Toward an Empirical Merger: Sociological and Economic Conceptions of Strike Activity," in J. Stern, and B. Dennis (Eds.), *Proceedings of the 28th Annual Meeting of the Industrial Relations Research Association* (Madison: IRRA, 1975), pp. 56-63.

41. Strauss, G., and P. Feuille "Industrial Relations Research: A Critical Analysis," *Industrial Relations,* Vol. 17 (October 1978), 259-277.

42. Truman, D. *The Governmental Process: Political Interests and Public Opinion* (New York: Knopf, 1951).

43. Walton, R., and R. McKersie *A Behavioral Theory of Labour Negotiations* (New York: McGraw-Hill, 1965).

44. Weissinger, W. *The Determinants of Grievance Rates: A Case Study.* Unpublished Master's thesis, Ithaca, N.Y.: Cornell University, 1976.

45. Whyte, W. *Money and Motivation* (New York: McGraw-Hill, 1951).

46. Wood, D., and P. Kumar. *The Current Industrial Relations Scene in Canada* (Kingston: Industrial Relations Centre, Queen's University, 1975-1980).

47. Wood, S.J., A. Wagner, E.G.A. Armstrong, J.F.B. Goodman, and J.E. Davis. "The 'Industrial Relations System' Concept as a Basis for Theory in Industrial Relations," *British Journal of Industrial Relations,* Vol. 3 (November 1975), 241-308.

48. Woods, H.D., A.W.R. Carrothers, J.H.G. Crispo, and G. Dion. *Canadian Industrial Relations* (Ottawa: Information Canada, 1969).

QUESTIONS

1. Outline the main components of an industrial-relations system.

2. What is the "web of rules"? Why is it an important concept to industrial-relations theory?

3. Identify and describe two dimensions of the context of the industrial-relations system and discuss their impact on one output of the system.

4. What role do the actors play in the industrial-relations system?

5. Describe the major processes through which inputs are converted to outputs of the industrial-relations system and specifically which outputs each impacts.

6. Choose an industry with which you are familiar. Using the industrial-relations system concept, describe labour relations in that industry.

THE ENVIRONMENT
OF LABOUR RELATIONS

DONALD D. CARTER

2. Collective-Bargaining Legislation in Canada

Canadian labour legislation has created a tight statutory structure regulating almost every aspect of union-management relations in this country. This structure influences the formation of the collective-bargaining relationship, the conduct and timing of bargaining and, to some extent, even the content of the collective agreement. Collective-bargaining rights are generally acquired by trade unions through processes established by legislation. This same legislation severely curtails the right to strike and in some jurisdictions goes so far as to require the bargaining parties to resort to conciliation procedures. The content of the collective agreement is also influenced by labour legislation as most Canadian jurisdictions require the parties to provide in the agreement a procedure for settlement of disputes arising out of its interpretation or application, and some Canadian jurisdictions now require that union-security provisions be a part of the collective agreement.

The administration of Canadian labour legislation is largely the responsibility of administrative tribunals known as labour-relations boards. However, the resolution of disputes relating to the interpretation and application of collective agreements is left to ad hoc grievance arbitration boards, and Canadian courts still exercise influence over this legal structure when applying and interpreting the general law.

THE INFLUENCE OF LEGISLATION

The course of union-management relations in Canada has been characterized by a high incidence of legal intervention. Statutes enacted by either the federal or provincial parliaments have had a great influence upon the development of collective-bargaining systems in Canada. As will be explained later, Canadian courts have decided that primary jurisdiction over labour relations rests with the provinces. In each province, a system of labour laws confines collective bargaining within a tight statutory framework in which union-management relations are conducted. This framework, although initially modeled upon the American Wagner Act, in many ways now goes further in regulating collective-bargaining conduct than does U.S. legislation.

There has been considerable debate about the virtues of this scale of legislative intervention. It has been argued that such a tight legal framework leaves insufficient room for the natural operation of free collective bargaining. This debate usually focuses on the legislative restrictions limiting recourse to the use of such economic sanctions as strikes, picketing, and lockouts. The concern is that a detailed legislative framework gives the government too prominent a role in what should be a private system of conflict resolution. Neither unions nor management, however, have consistently adopted this position, and there has been a noticeable tendency for both to seek further legislation when it is to their own advantage to do so. This ambivalence on the part of both management and unions toward government intervention has meant that, if anything, the pace of legislative activity has increased in recent years.

This increase in the regulation of union-management relations may also be part of a general trend toward a more regulated society. Collective bargaining is now an established institution within society and its exercise has major social and economic implications. This fact has led many to conclude that union-management relations are too important to be left exclusively in the hands of management and labour and to argue that the public interest must also be considered. The concept of a public interest is usually vaguely defined, but it is often alluded to in those situations where the general public, rather than the parties themselves, appears to be bearing the brunt of economic sanctions, or where it appears that collective bargaining is contributing to an inflationary spiral. In this kind of situation, the industrial-relations system is often perceived as malfunctioning, and a frequent response is to call for more regulation, usually in the form of legislative intervention.

Legislation in Canada has had both a direct and an indirect effect upon union-management relations. Statutes that establish and define the collective-bargaining structure within which unions and management must operate have a very direct effect. Besides this body of collective-bargaining law, however, there also exists a wide array of other legislation that touches upon union-management relations in a more indirect manner. Statutes dealing with minimum standards of employment, worker health and safety, human rights, compensation for work injuries, unemployment insurance, and pensions (many of which are discussed in Chapter 3) all have some influence upon the conduct of union-management relations even though they also apply to those employees (and their employers) who have not embraced collective bargaining. This chapter will deal only with the structure of collective-bargaining law since both employment law and social-security law, although important, have a much less direct impact upon union-management relations than does collective-bargaining legislation.

THE CONSTITUTIONAL DIVISION OF LEGISLATIVE AUTHORITY

The regulation of union-management relations in Canada is divided among eleven different jurisdictions — ten provincial and one federal. The Canadian constitution (the British North America Act) has been interpreted by the courts as giving the greater share of legislative jurisdiction over labour relations to the provinces. The federal government's jurisdiction has been restricted to undertakings falling within its specific legislative authority or, incidentally, to conduct falling within its criminal law powers. Federal legislative power has only been permitted to extend beyond these boundaries in time of national emergency. The Canadian constitutional situation differs markedly from that in the United States where the federal government has a much more extensive jurisdiction than the state governments.

The constitutional division of legislative authority in Canada has meant that most organized employees in Canada fall within provincial labour-relations jurisdiction. Persons employed in manufacturing, mining (except uranium), forest-products industries, construction, service industries, local transportation and provincial and local governments all fall within provincial legislative jurisdiction.

While the provincial systems have much in common (all borrowing heavily from the U.S. Wagner Act), each system also has certain characteristics that distinguish it from the others. The most unique of these provincial systems (discussed in more detail in Chapter 19) can be found in Quebec where the Wagner model appears to have been adapted by the addition of certain elements borrowed from European systems of industrial relations.

The federal government's labour-relations jurisdiction covers a relatively small percentage of all employees, but these include workers in a number of particularly important areas of the economy. All air, rail, shipping, and trucking operations having either an interprovincial or international character fall within the federal jurisdiction as do broadcasting enterprises, banks, uranium mines, and grain elevators. Also under the federal government's labour-relations jurisdiction are federal civil servants (these are covered by a separate collective-bargaining statute, as are public employees in many provinces). Strikes by such federal government employees as air-traffic controllers and postal workers have had a significant impact in Canada. The same can be said of strikes by certain employees in the federal private sector, such as stevedores and airline and railway employees. The impact of labour disputes in the federal jurisdiction means that this jurisdiction is much more important than a simple count of those employees covered by federal labour legislation would indicate.

Difficulties may arise when drawing the line between federal and provincial jurisdiction over labour relations. A business may not fall squarely within a federal undertaking but still may have some functional relationship to it. Since constitutional problems most frequently arise when a trade union is applying to a labour-relations board for bargaining rights, many of these issues are resolved initially by the boards, subject to possible review in the courts. No clear pattern has yet been established in this area. For example, it has been held that a private trucking firm under contract to the post office to collect mail came under the federal jurisdiction even though it was also involved in local operations that would otherwise bring it within provincial jurisdiction. On the other hand, it has been held that persons employed in a parking garage at Toronto International Airport that was operated under contract for the federal government fell within provincial labour-relations jurisdiction.

Other difficulties may arise with the constitutional division of legislative authority. Industries such as trucking, having both local and interprovincial or international components, may bargain as an entire industry, bringing into play both provincial and federal labour laws. As well, large employers operating local undertakings in more than one provincial jurisdiction may agree to national negotiations even though they are still governed by provincial labour legislation. Both the meat-packing industry and the elevator industry have undertaken this kind of national negotiation despite problems caused by the concurrency of provincial laws. Fortunately, many of these problems have been worked out by cooperation among agencies of the governments involved.

One advantage of the Canadian system of divided legislative authority is to allow some diversity and innovation in labour legislation. Although federal collective-bargaining laws enacted after World War II were intended to be used as a model by the provinces, in the years that followed the provinces began to experiment on their own in response to the particular conditions within their respective jurisdictions. Quebec and British Columbia have gone further in this direction, although all of the provinces have to some extent branched out on their own. This diversity has led to some interesting legal innovations, and developments in one jurisdiction have sometimes spread to other Canadian jurisdictions. On the other hand, the presence of eleven different systems of collective-bargaining law in Canada has given rise to a somewhat confusing collection of labour law, and something less than a uniform standard of labour legislation throughout the country. Although the federal jurisdiction has attempted to encourage a more uniform standard, it is quite apparent that legal variety is a "fact of life" of the Canadian labour-relations system.

Some mention should also be made of one other constitutional consideration affecting the distribution of legislative power over labour relations. The British North America Act has been interpreted so as to prevent provincial governments from establishing courts or other agencies with the same kinds of powers as those of the superior courts appointed by the federal government. In other words, the provinces cannot establish their own system of courts to compete with federally appointed courts. This constitutional restriction has given rise to some question as to the legitimacy of provincially appointed labour-relations boards established to administer provincial collective-bargaining laws. These boards have been given a wide remedial mandate, including the reinstatement and compensation of employees discharged in breach of collective-bargaining legislation and the employees discharged in breach of collective-bargaining legislation and the issuing of cease-and-desist orders to restrain strikes and lockouts. It has been held, however, that the exercise of these powers is qualitatively different than the exercise of somewhat similar powers by superior courts because labour-board powers are exercised in a labour-relations context. So long as such powers are exercised in a manner that is necessary to a labour board's labour-relations functions, it appears that provincial labour boards will not be regarded as encroaching upon the traditional powers of a superior court.

THE LOOSENING OF EARLY RESTRICTIONS UPON EMPLOYEE ORGANIZATION

Many Canadian collective-bargaining statutes now contain a preamble expressly stating that it is in the public interest to encourage the practice and procedure of collective bargaining. The Canadian legal structure, however, has not always been so favourably disposed toward collective bargaining. At the time of Confederation there existed in Canada a number of legal restrictions impeding employee organization. The common-law crime of conspiracy (two or more individuals consorting for illegal purposes) could be applied to trade-union organizers, making them liable for criminal prosecution, and separate legislation already existed in some of the new provinces effectively prohibiting collective-bargaining activity. In addition to these restrictions, trade unions (because they were regarded as operating in restraint of trade by interfering with the normal course of business transactions through such actions as strikes) were refused access to the courts and, as a result, were unable to enforce any rights that they might otherwise have.

It was not until the 1870s that some loosening of these restrictions occurred. The strike of Toronto printers in 1872 and the arrests and prosecutions that followed upon it gave rise to public demand for labour-law reform. This demand for reform may also have been encouraged by the fact that a year earlier such reform legislation had been enacted by the English Parliament. The Canadian Trades Union Act of 1872 expressly declared that the purposes of a trade union were not to be considered unlawful merely because they might also be in restraint of trade. At the same time, the Criminal Law Amendment Act legalized peaceful strikes and picketing. A few years later, in 1875 and 1876, the definition of "criminal conspiracy" was amended by legislation to apply only to those trade combinations involving acts expressly punishable by law.

By the end of the nineteenth century, most of the legal restrictions upon trade-union activity had disappeared. At this point, the law relating to conspiracies in restraint of trade clearly excluded from its scope combinations of employees acting for their own reasonable protection— an exclusion still found in present-day federal competition legislation. While trade unions were not completely free of legal fetters at that time, especially in respect of court-imposed restrictions on picketing, it still could be safely said that many of the earlier restrictions had disappeared.

CONCILIATION LEGISLATION

The loosening of legal restrictions did not leave a legal vacuum for long. As trade-union influence gradually increased, it soon became apparent that labour-management disputes were becoming more common in such key areas as railways, mining, and public utilities. Before the end of the nineteenth century some provinces had already legislated to provide mediation or arbitration procedures if the parties mutually chose to avail themselves of such procedures. This requirement of joint consent meant, however, that recourse to such procedures was infrequent as it was usually not in the interest of the stronger party.

Federal legislation providing dispute-resolution machinery, still essentially voluntary in nature, made its first appearance in 1900. The Dominion Conciliation Act allowed the federal minister of labour to appoint a conciliation board either at the request of one of the parties or on the minister's own initiative. This conciliation-board procedure was essentially an exercise in fact-finding, contemplating an investigation of the dispute by a board, the making of specific recommendations by this board, and the publication of the board's recommendations. This procedure was premised on the assumption that, if the public were made aware of labour disputes by means of a public report from a board composed of representatives of the two parties and an independent chairman, resulting public pressure would influence the parties to settle their differences. This fact-finding procedure reappeared in a later federal statute, the Railway Labour Disputes Act of 1903 but, like the 1900 statute, it was not compulsory in the sense that neither party was required to accept the procedure. In 1906 these two conciliation statutes were consolidated into one statute, the Conciliation and Labour Act.

A much more important legislative event occurred in 1907 following a difficult strike of western miners in the previous year. The enactment of the Industrial Disputes Investigation Act of 1907 for the first time made the conciliation-board procedure compulsory and prohibited the parties from resorting to economic sanctions until the conciliation board had completed its investigation and its report was released to the public. Even though the application of the Industrial Disputes Investigation Act was later confined to strictly federal undertakings as the result of a landmark constitutional decision in 1925, *Toronto Electric Commissioners v. Snider,* the conciliation-board procedure was subsequently adopted by most provincial jurisdictions and has become one of the hallmarks of the Canadian labour-law system.

Despite its prominence in the Canadian system, the conciliation board has enjoyed only mixed success. For one thing, the influence of public opinion upon labour disputes is unpredictable, and publicity may serve to harden bargaining positions just as much as it may soften them. The procedure itself usually takes a considerable period of time, and the postponement of the use of economic sanctions until the fact-finding exercise is completed may actually frustrate the collective-bargaining process. These disadvantages to the conciliation-board procedure have caused it to be used infrequently for the resolution of labour disputes in the private sector. The conciliation board still receives some use in both the private and public sectors under federal jurisdiction and in the provincial public sector perhaps because labour disputes in these areas tend to receive more public attention.

Despite this continuing use of the conciliation board, it is safe to say that fact-finding by tripartite conciliation boards has been largely displaced by mediation conducted by a single conciliation officer. This person is usually a full-time government employee whose function it is to act as a channel of communication in labour disputes. The process contemplates that the parties will be brought together through the persuasive efforts of the conciliation officer rather than by the influence of public opinion. Instead of a public inquiry and public report, the conciliation officer relies upon private discussions, usually conducted with each party separately. The conciliation officer does not prepare public reports, and only makes specific recommendations where these would encourage settlement of the dispute. Recourse to the services of a conciliation officer is a precondition to the use of economic sanctions in most Canadian jurisdictions.

THE EVOLUTION OF A LEGISLATIVE FRAMEWORK FOR UNION RECOGNITION

Conciliation legislation was not the complete answer to the problems plaguing Canadian labour relations in the first half of the twentieth century. Canada was becoming an industrialized nation and union membership was on the upswing, making substantial gains during periods of economic prosperity and full employment. During the depression years of the 1930s, however, union membership declined and working conditions deteriorated as the pendulum of economic power swung in favour of employers. Employer economic strength at that time could be asserted in many ways to thwart union organizing efforts. Employees sympathetic to a union could be dismissed at will and new employees could be hired on the condition that they not join a trade union. (The latter condition was referred to as a "yellow dog" contract.) Even where a trade union had organized a majority of employees, employers could still refuse to recognize a trade union by either continuing to deal directly with the employees, or by entering into a "sweetheart" arrangement with a rival company union. Employer opposition at times went even further and violence and intimidation on the part of both employers and unions were not uncommon during this period. The basic problem appeared to be one of union recognition — a matter not dealt with by conciliation legislation.

The Wagner Act Model

This problem of union recognition was addressed first by legislators in the United States when, in 1935, the National Labour Relations Act (usually called the Wagner Act) was enacted by the U.S. Congress. This statute expressly recognized the right of employees to organize and bargain collectively with their employer. Certain types of employer conduct interfering with these rights (often called unfair labour practices) were prohibited. These activities included intimidation or coercion of employees to stop them from joining a union, employer support of a management-dominated company union, and unilateral changes by management in the terms of conditions of employment (for example, promises of increased wages). Employers were also required to recognize unions representing their employees and to negotiate in good faith with these unions. Just as importantly, this legislative scheme was to be administered by a new administrative agency, the National Labour Relations Board, rather than by the courts (which had not enjoyed a reputation of being favourably disposed toward collective bargaining). The legal structure created by the Wagner Act is the basic model for our present system of Canadian labour-relations law.

This American model was not fully introduced into Canada until a few years later. Some limited aspects of the Wagner Act were borrowed by various Canadian jurisdictions during the period from 1937 to 1942, but no jurisdiction, either provincial or federal, provided a complete code governing union recognition or established an administrative agency to apply such a code during that period. With the outbreak of World War II and the consequent shortage of workers, however, union organization became easier and trade-union membership grew significantly despite the lack of legal support.

The Ontario Labour Court

In 1943, Ontario took the next legislative step and introduced a Wagner-style collective-bargaining statute, the only difference being that the administration of the statute was given to a division of the Ontario Supreme Court instead of to an administrative tribunal. The tenure of the Ontario Labour Court (as it was called) lasted only ten months. During that period, the Labour Court performed functions similar to those now carried out by labour boards— assessing the legitimacy of trade unions, describing appropriate bargaining units, and determining whether trade unions enjoyed the support of the employees in the bargaining unit. Despite the fact that it dealt with some large and important applications for bargaining rights, the Labour Court never gained widespread acceptance with organized labour. The trade unions resented the requirement that they be represented by lawyers before the court and disliked the fact that they had no representation on the court itself. The criticisms of labour, and the need to establish a joint federal-provincial structure for the administration of collective-bargaining legislation during wartime, led to the displacement of the Labour Court by an administrative tribunal.

P.C. 1003

In 1944, the federal government through the exercise of its wartime powers established a legal structure containing all of the elements of the Wagner Act model, including an administrative tribunal to apply this new law. The Wartime Labour Relations Regulations (P.C. 1003) made under the War Measures Act embraced a long list of industries considered to be essential for the war effort and extended federal collective-bargaining law over most areas of economic activity within Canada. The regulations established a Wartime Labour Relations Board as the permanent tribunal for the administration and application of these laws. Provision was made for the establishment of local (provincial) boards, although matters of policy were still to remain the responsibility of the federal board. Most provinces suspended their own legislation totally making the federal order applicable to all economic activity within the province (the exceptions being Quebec and Saskatchewan). The impact of the federal labour-relations regulation cannot be overstated as, at one stroke, it brought most of the economic activity in Canada within a single, comprehensive system of collective-bargaining law.

Postwar Legislation

The end of the war brought a return to a divided responsibility for labour relations as the provinces began to reclaim their jurisdiction. By this time, however, the pattern had been set and the Wagner model had become firmly established throughout Canada. In anticipation of the repeal of the wartime regulations, the federal government enacted a collective-bargaining statute in 1948 containing the same basic elements as the wartime scheme. This statute was intended to be a model code to be followed by the provinces in order to provide some uniformity of labour legislation throughout Canada. Most provinces enacted substantially similar legislation at about the same time, reinforcing the pattern that had been established by the federal government. Despite their common beginning, some interesting mutations began to develop in the different Canadian labour systems in the years that followed. Not only do these systems now show considerable diversity, but there also exist significant differences between these systems and their American progenitor.

THE GROWTH OF PUBLIC-SECTOR LEGISLATION

Collective-bargaining legislation in Canada was initially directed toward employees in the private sector. Although most of this legislation simply did not refer to public servants, legislative silence alone was sufficient to exclude from its coverage any employee of the Crown. By the rules of statute interpretation, the Crown is not bound by legislation unless there is an express provision in the statute to this effect. Moreover, collective-bargaining legislation in some jurisdictions expressly excluded such groups of public employees as teachers, police, and fire fighters. Municipal employees (other than fire fighters and police), however, were generally covered by collective-bargaining legislation as were employees of Crown corporations.

Until the 1960s, there appeared to be little movement in the direction of extending collective-bargaining rights to public employees. Up to that time, public servants themselves did not appear to be inclined to embrace collective bargaining, perhaps because of its blue-collar connotations or perhaps because the general public at that time still regarded collective bargaining by public servants as unthinkable. The aggressive assertion of economic demands, and the possibility of a withdrawal of public services was seen by many as a challenge to the very sovereignty of the state. And there were also many who considered that public servants had no need to organize because of what appeared to be a much greater measure of job security enjoyed by employees in the public sector.

Attitudes began to change by the 1960s. Governments had increased in size, a factor that may have contributed to a growing feeling of frustration and alienation on the part of public servants. Trade unionism began to look increasingly attractive to public servants as unionized blue-collar trade employees in the private sector obtained substantial gains in wages and fringe benefits. As well, many white-collar workers in the private sector were becoming organized, removing some of the perceived social stigma of collective bargaining for public servants.

The watershed came in 1967 with the enactment of the Public Service Staff Relations Act — a statute creating a new and distinct collective-bargaining structure for federal public servants. While this scheme borrowed some aspects of the Wagner model, it also contained a number of innovations that put Canada in the vanguard of legislative reform. The coverage of this statute in one respect was wider than private-sector legislation, bringing within its scope professional employees and low-level managers (both groups that had been traditionally excluded from private-sector collective-bargaining legislation). The new statute gave public servants the option of either compulsory arbitration or strike action as the ultimate means of resolving any bargaining impasse. The right to strike, however, was qualified by a restriction preventing employees designated as providing services necessary for the safety and security of the public from withdrawing their services. The range of bargainable issues was made somewhat wider where the strike option, rather than arbitration, was chosen as the procedure for impasse resolution.

Shortly after the passage of the federal statute, a number of provincial jurisdictions followed suit. Some provinces borrowed the model of the Public Service Staff Relations Act, while other provinces took a different route, usually by refusing to extend the right to strike to public employees and instead providing for compulsory arbitration of bargaining disputes. By the middle of the 1970s, however, a general pattern of distinct collective-bargaining structures for public employees had been established throughout Canada. While there is considerable variance among these structures, their existence acknowledges the fact that collective bargaining by public servants is now firmly established throughout Canada.

The growth of collective-bargaining structures for public employees occurred at a much faster rate in Canada than in the United States. While public employees in Canada still face some restrictions on their rights to strike and bargain, Canadian legislators in general have been more favourably disposed to extend collective-bargaining rights to public employees than their American counterparts. It should be noted that in recent years trade-union growth has occurred primarily in the public sector, and unions representing public employees now rank among the largest labour organizations in Canada.

SOME DISTINCTIVE FEATURES OF CANADIAN LABOUR LEGISLATION

Canadian collective-bargaining legislation, although owing a substantial debt to the Wagner Act, possesses some indigenous characteristics that distinguish it from the American legal structure. Not only do collective-bargaining structures for public employees appear to be better developed in Canada than in the United States, but in the private sector as well there exist some important differences between Canadian and American approaches.

The Certification Process

A distinguishing feature of virtually all Canadian collective-bargaining legislation is that it provides a relatively simple procedure by which trade unions can acquire collective-bargaining rights. Under this procedure a trade union may apply to a labour board and, where it establishes that it represents a majority of a particular group of employees, it receives a certificate giving it exclusive bargaining rights for all employees in the bargaining unit (as elaborated in Chapter 8). This procedure, called certification, is the principal method by which trade unions acquire bargaining rights, although bargaining rights may also be acquired by an employer voluntarily recognizing the union.

Unlike the United States where the employee vote is used, the usual method by which trade unions establish their representative character is through simple evidence of membership (the lone exception is Nova Scotia where the employee vote is mandatory). As a general rule, the employee vote in Canada is a secondary procedure for establishing representativeness, to be used only by the labour boards where there is some doubt about the reliability of the membership evidence submitted by the union. For example, in Ontario the board need not direct a vote if over 55 percent of the employees in the bargaining unit are union members.

Extensive Restrictions on Strike Action

Canadian collective-bargaining legislation in all jurisdictions except one (Saskatchewan) severely curtails the use of economic sanctions. Strikes for the purpose of gaining recognition are expressly prohibited, as are strikes occurring during the life of a collective agreement. Even where the parties are bargaining for collective agreement, the right to strike is postponed in most Canadian jurisdictions until the parties have exhausted certain dispute-settlement procedures, usually conciliation but sometimes a strike vote as well. Because these procedures have been made a precondition to the use of economic sanctions, they have often been regarded as being merely indirect restrictions upon the right to strike and lockout. Indeed, there are some who argue that the restrictive aspect of these procedures tends to impair their usefulness in resolving conflict.

Compulsory Grievance Arbitration

The complete restriction upon strikes and lockouts during the life of the collective agreement has meant that some alternative mechanism must be used to resolve disputes relating to the interpretation and administration of the collective agreement. As a result, Canadian collective-bargaining legislation generally requires that there be included in collective agreements a procedure for final and binding resolution of any unresolved disputes arising under that agreement. Unlike the United States where such procedures are completely a matter of negotiation between the parties, grievance resolution in Canada has a public element and, while the parties may fashion their own grievance procedure, they are not free to dispense with such machinery. This public aspect to grievance arbitration means that in Canada there has generally been greater public regulation of the grievance-arbitration process than in the United States.

Recognition of the Right to Union Security

Canadian labour legislation expressly recognizes the legitimacy of those arrangements that a union may negotiate for its own financial security. Unions are permitted by the legislation to bargain for such arrangements as the "closed shop" (the requirement that a person be a member of the union before being hired), the "union shop" (the requirement that a person join the union upon being employed) and the "dues shop" or "Rand formula" (a requirement that a person at least pay union dues as a condition of employment). In addition, some Canadian jurisdictions go even further by making the "Rand formula" mandatory, while others only go so far as to require the employer to collect dues on behalf of the union where authorized by the employee. This approach contrasts sharply with that taken in some American jurisdictions where "right-to-work" laws have restricted union-security arrangements.

ADMINISTRATION OF LABOUR LEGISLATION IN CANADA

An account of Canadian Labour legislation would not be complete without mention of the institutions responsible for administering these laws. From a labour-relations perspective, the primary legal institution is an administrative tribunal commonly known as the labour-relations board. An administrative tribunal is a public agency, created by statute but having some independence from the executive branch of government. Two other institutions, ad hoc arbitration boards and the courts, also have important roles to play in the administration of the legal structure although their roles are less prominent than that of the labour boards.

Labour-Relations Boards

Labour-relations boards, as administrative tribunals, derive their authority from the very collective-bargaining legislation that they administer since these statutes not only impose rights and obligations on trade unions and employers but also provide the structure and procedure for the assertion of these rights. Each of the eleven Canadian jurisdictions has established its own structure to administer its collective-bargaining laws. The usual structure has been the labour-relations board, although a variation of this pattern can be found in Quebec where the responsibility for administering its collective-bargaining statute is divided between public officials called investigative commissioners and a provincial labour court.

Labour-relations boards, while generally reporting to the government through the ministry of labour, are still regarded as having some autonomy from ministries or departments of labour. The functions performed by labour boards are both administrative and adjudicative in nature. The boards, as a rule, are tripartite in composition, being composed of independent chairmen, representatives of trade unions, and representatives of employers. The chairmen and board members are appointed for either a fixed term (sometimes set out in the statute) or at the pleasure of the government. In the larger more industrialized jurisdictions, the apointments are usually full-time, while in the smaller jurisdictions part-time appointments are more prevalent. In addition, labour boards employ support staffs of civil servants to carry out their administrative function.

In the manner that they carry out their adjudicative function, labour boards bear some resemblance to the courts. The chairmen presiding over labour-board hearings make evidential and procedural rules, and reasons are usually provided for any decision of significance. Board procedures, however, are marked by greater informality and are generally more expeditious than those of the courts. There is no requirement that the parties be represented at the hearing by a lawyer.

The presence of board members representing the two sides in the collective-bargaining process is another characteristic of labour boards that distinguishes them from the courts (one exception is the federal board where the members do not have a representative role). The appointment of board members occurs only after consultation with either the major employer associations or the major trade-union associations, as the case may be. These representative board members are experienced labour-relations practitioners who bring to the boards an expertise that is applied in the decision-making process. Regular contact is maintained between the board members and labour and management groups to ensure that board members do not get out of touch with their respective constituencies.

The presence of these representative board members serves to make board decisions more acceptable in the labour-relations community, but it also means that labour boards are far less removed from particular disputes than any court would be. This is generally regarded as being acceptable, partly because the presence of both union and employer members on boards means that biases can be offset. The representative role of the board members, however, can cause problems where a party before the board has no association with the major interest groups represented by the board members. This situation could occur where a labour board is faced with a dispute between rival trade unions, one a member of a major trade-union association and the other outside the association, or where a dissident employee complains about the conduct of both the union and the employer.

Labour boards were established initially for the purpose of administering the statutory procedures for the acquisition, transfer, and termination of bargaining rights. Applications for bargaining rights and complaints relating to employer and union conduct during the organization of employees constituted the bulk of the case load at that time. Once collective-bargaining relationships were established by labour boards, any further matters arising from that relationship were left to be resolved in other forms. Such matters as strikes and picketing, and to a lesser extent, the conduct of the parties at the bargaining table were dealt with by the courts while disputes relating to the interpretation of collective agreements were referred to ad hoc boards of arbitration.

Even though matters relating to the organizational stage of collective bargaining still form the core of the labour boards' jurisdiction, the 1970s have seen an expansion of board jurisdiction to cover other aspects of the bargaining process. Most boards now have the power to issue directions restraining illegal strikes and lockouts and to determine whether bargaining conduct is inconsistent with the statutory duty to bargain in good faith. The labour-relations board in British Columbia now has wide authority to regulate and control picketing. In two provinces, Ontario and British Columbia, labour boards also have a limited jurisdiction to arbitrate collective-agreement disputes. Going even further, British Columbia and the federal government have now provided their boards with authority to arbitrate first-agreement bargaining disputes. This expansion of labour-board jurisdiction in the 1970s has quite clearly increased both the visibility and the importance of labour boards.

The primary function of labour boards, however, is still to grant or withdraw bargaining rights, applying criteria either found in the legislation itself or developed through the boards' own decision-making process. To this end the board must deal with such issues as the eligibility of employees to bargain collectively, the eligibility of unions to represent employees, the appropriateness of the collective-bargaining constituency, and the validity of union membership evidence. On all of these issues there now exists a comprehensive body of labour-board decisions interpreting the standards established in the legislation.

The labour boards also possess a wide statutory power to remedy violations of collective-bargaining legislation. The discretionary aspect of this remedial power offers the boards a wide scope to apply their special expertise in fashioning a remedy appropriate to the industrial-relations situation with which they are faced. At times, labour boards may refuse to grant any remedy at all if this response appears to be justified by the particular situation.

Not only are labour-board remedies discretionary, but they also possess a significant accommodative aspect. Many of these remedial sections expressly provide for an accommodative approach to be taken initially through the intervention of a board official, often called a labour-relations officer. Before the hearing of a disputed matter, a labour-relations officer usually will be appointed to endeavour to obtain a settlement. If accommodation is reached, as it is in a high percentage of cases, the matter is never heard by the board. This active accommodative role of the labour boards is another significant feature that distinguishes labour boards from courts.

A corollary of this accommodative approach is that boards sometimes refuse to issue any order where the conduct in question has been discontinued by the time of the hearing of the matter. The Ontario board, for example, has clearly articulated that it will not issue a direction or declaration in respect of illegal strike or lockout action when such conduct ceases before the hearing, unless there has been a past pattern of such conduct, or a likelihood of further occurrences, or where the particular matter has more general implications.

As the accommodative aspect of the labour boards' remedial powers has assumed greater importance, there has been a decline in the use of criminal prosecutions to deal with labour-relations problems. Although many collective-bargaining statutes still make any contravention of their provisions a criminal offence, such prosecutions are now quite rare. Usually such prosecutions cannot be undertaken without the consent of the labour-relations board, a two-step procedure that makes the prosecution route slow and costly. Moreover, consent to prosecute may not always be forthcoming as the labour boards have come to regard prosecution as a secondary remedial route. Studies have indicated that very few prosecutions are pursued even where consent to prosecute is granted.

Damages are another remedy within the discretion of the labour boards. A damage award, although intended primarily to compensate the party injured by a violation of the collective-bargaining statute, does have a certain punitive aspect as the award must be paid by the party contravening the legislation. The amount of damages, however, reflects the extent of the loss incurred and not the seriousness of the conduct causing such loss, giving rise to the possibility that damages awarded to an injured party might exceed the amount that might be levied by way of a fine if the matter had been made the subject of a prosecution. Most damage awards imposed by labour boards are in respect to loss of income suffered by employees who have been discriminated against in their employment because of trade-union activity. Recently, however, labour boards have, on occasion awarded damages to trade unions where serious contraventions of the legislation have interfered with their right to represent employees. In these cases, labour boards have ordered that a trade union be "made whole" for its lawyer's fees, litigation expenses, and organizational expenses flowing from the breach of the collective-bargaining statute. Despite the broad remedial mandate of the labour boards, damages flowing from illegal strikes are not usually claimed before labour boards but are left to arbitration.

Arbitration Boards

Arbitration boards, although not directly involved in the application and administration of labour legislation, still play an important part in the overall legal structure established for collective bargaining in Canada. Arbitration boards are usually ad hoc in the sense that they are established to deal with only one particular dispute, and their composition is tripartite in nature (being made up of an independent chairman, a nominee of the employer, and a nominee of the union). On occasion the arbitration function may be performed by a single independent arbitrator rather than a tripartite board.

A distinction must be drawn between grievance (or rights) arbitration and interest arbitration even though the two types of boards are similar in appearance. Grievance arbitration involves the resolution of disputes arising out of the interpretation and application of the collective agreement, requiring an arbitration board to perform the function of contract interpreter. Interest arbitration, on the other hand, requires an arbitration board to resolve bargaining disputes, in essence determining wages and other terms and conditions of employment encompassed by the collective agreement for the parties.

Interest arbitration is not a common feature of the Canadian industrial-relations structure, although it does receive some use in the public sector when strikes are prohibited. In the private sector, however, there is little enthusiasm for this method of dispute resolution since there are a number of problems associated with its use. The procedure of interest arbitration requires an ad hoc arbitration board to hear representations from the employer and the union and then to make a collective agreement for them. This procedure gives the appearance of being adjudicative but the issues before the board are usually economic in nature, requiring a particular decision about the allocation of economic resources. The guidelines provided to the board to resolve such disputes are often vague, and even contradictory. Not surprisingly, arbitration awards often give the appearance of being more a compromise between the opposing positions of the parties than the result of the application of established principles.

The presence of arbitration, moreover, may discourage the parties from making concessions prior to arbitration, placing the burden of establishing the appropriate compromise upon the arbitrator. Recognizing this problem, some parties have adopted a variation of interest arbitration called "final-offer selection," restricting the arbitration board to choosing the final offer of one of the two parties. This puts pressure on each party to provide a reasonable final offer in the hope it will be accepted. The procedure, however, may not be workable where a dispute is complicated by a number of unresolved bargaining issues, since the "all-or-nothing" approach may simply be too blunt an instrument in this kind of situation.

A final criticism of interest arbitration is its incompatibility with the operation of a free-enterprise economy. It has been argued that there is no justification for treating the price of labour differently than any other price, and that both should be freely negotiated. Not suprisingly, neither Canadian employers nor Canadian unions appear to have much appetite for interest arbitration, and even its usefulness in the public sector is being questioned.

Grievance arbitration, on the other hand, plays an important part in the Canadian labour-relations structure. A procedure for the final and binding resolution of disputes arising from collective agreements is made mandatory in all but one Canadian jurisdiction (Saskatchewan). Despite these statutory roots, grievance arbitration is a hybrid process, containing both public and private elements. Collective-bargaining legislation mandates only the basic procedure, leaving the parties free to improve upon this model in order to meet their own needs. In fact, there now exist in the rail, longshoring, trucking, mining, and garment industries some interesting variations from the standard model of arbitration. Grievance arbitration (and interest arbitration), moreover, is a procedure distinct from commercial arbitration — a fact that has been legislatively recognized in most Canadian jurisdictions by the exclusion of this process from the statutory structure established for the arbitration of commercial disputes.

Grievance-arbitration boards are generally ad hoc in nature, although in the case of certain large bargaining units more permanent arbitration structures have been established. Once it is decided to take a grievance to arbitration, the general practice is for the parties to establish a board of arbitration by each of them first nominating a representative and then selecting a chairman by mutual agreement. A variation of this procedure is for the parties to simply select a sole arbitrator by mutual agreement. In the event that the parties are unable to agree upon a chairman or sole arbitrator, the government may exercise its statutory power and make the appointment. In one jurisdiction (Ontario) either party has the option of applying immediately for the appointment of a single arbitrator by the government.

The arbitration board, once constituted, convenes a hearing of the grievance at a time and place agreed upon by the parties. Hearings are usually held in a location close to the place of work, and the procedures followed by the board are normally quite informal. The parties are often able to agree upon a statement of facts avoiding the need for more formal evidential procedures, and in many arbitrations the parties (more often trade unions) do not employ lawyers to present their cases. Nevertheless the courts still regard arbitration procedures as being adjudicative and have required arbitration boards to follow certain fundamental judicial procedures. These procedural requirements, often referred to as the rules of natural justice, have introduced a legal element into the arbitration process and may be one reason why many Canadian arbitrators have legal backgrounds.

Grievance arbitration is essentially an adjudicative process requiring an arbitration board to make findings of fact and then to assess these facts in the light of certain arbitral standards. The primary source of these standards is the collective agreement itself, and initially arbitration boards look to the language of the agreement to determine whether the parties have formulated a rule that can resolve the grievance. Where collective-agreement language is vague and ambiguous, however, arbitration boards may have to look outside the collective agreement for assistance. In this situation, considerations such as the past practice of the parties, previous arbitration decisions dealing with similar issues, relevant legislation, and even general doctrines of equity may be taken into account.

It has often been said that the grievance-arbitration process is the creation of the parties themselves. To a large extent, the parties do control the process by formulating procedures, selecting the adjudicator, and ultimately bearing the costs of the process (each party paying its own costs and the costs of its nominee, and paying half the costs of the arbitrator). Nevertheless, grievance arbitration in Canada is mandated, and this aspect of the process has also given rise to a certain amount of legislative regulation of both its structure and procedures.

Courts

The role of the judiciary in the Canadian collective-bargaining structure should not be overlooked. Except for the brief Ontario experiment with a labour court, the federally appointed judges of the superior courts have never directly administered Canadian collective-bargaining legislation. Nevertheless, superior courts still play a prominent role in labour-relations law because of their general jurisdiction to administer civil and criminal law, their power to review the decisions of labour boards and arbitration boards, and their role as the ultimate interpreter of the Canadian constitution. Provincially appointed courts (provincial criminal courts) also have a role in dealing with breaches of collective-bargaining legislation, although such prosecutions usually require labour-board consent. One jurisdiction (Quebec) has gone so far as to constitute a provincially appointed court to administer certain parts of its collective-bargaining legislation.

Generally speaking, the role played by the courts, especially the superior courts, has not found much favour with trade unions. Until quite recently, the criminal and civil law was applied by the courts in such a way as to curtail picketing and strike activity, and judicial review of labour-board and arbitration decisions tended to restrict the application of collective-bargaining principles. The earlier application of the restraint-of-trade doctrine by the courts also meant that trade unions for a long time could not avail themselves of the courts to assist their own claims, forcing them to rely on other institutions. The formalism and expense of judicial proceedings, moreover, were additional irritants that did nothing to mitigate trade-union distrust of the courts.

Recently, the judiciary has been playing both a less prominent and a less controversial role in the Canadian industrial-relations system. The expansion of labour-board jurisdiction has meant that labour boards have assumed some of the jurisdiction once exercised by the courts, especially in respect of strikes and picketing. Legislatures have enacted more specific provisions confining the role of the courts, and the courts themselves now appear to exercise more restraint when reviewing decisions of labour tribunals. Recent judicial decisions, moreover, appear to reflect a more balanced approach to labour-relations problems, perhaps because a number of recent appointments to the bench have come with first-hand knowledge of the Canadian industrial-relations system.

SUMMARY

Canadian labour legislation has created a tight statutory structure regulating almost every aspect of union-management relations. While the Canadian legal structure owes much to the American model of the Wagner Act, some significant differences distinguish the Canadian system of collective-bargaining law. Compulsory conciliation procedures have found much greater favour in Canada, and the right to strike in Canada is more closely confined by statute than in the United States. On the other hand, Canadian legislation provides a much less cumbersome certification procedure and goes further in recognizing the legitimacy of union-security provisions. Canadian legislators, moreover, have gone further in extending collective-bargaining rights to public-sector employees than their American counterparts.

The primary responsibility for the administration of Canadian collective-bargaining legislation lies with the labour-relations boards. These administrative tribunals now have a jurisdiction over most aspects of the collective-bargaining relationship. The resolution of grievances arising from collective agreements, however, is still largely the responsibility of boards of arbitration constituted by the parties on an ad hoc basis. The judiciary, although having a less prominent role in the Canadian labour-relations structure, still has a significant impact because of its responsibility to apply and interpret the general law.

ADDITIONAL REFERENCES

1. Arthurs, H.W. *Collective Bargaining by Public Employees in Canada: Five Models* (Ann Arbor, Mich.: Institute of Labor and Industrial Relations, 1971).

2. Arthurs, H.W., D.D. Carter, and H.J. Glasbeek. *Labour Law and Industrial Relations in Canada* (Toronto: Butterworth, 1981).

3. Brown, D.J.M., and D.M. Beatty. *Canadian Labour Arbitration* (Agincourt, Ont.: Canada Law Book, 1977).

4. Brown, D.J.M. *Interest Arbitration*, Task Force Study No. 18 (Ottawa: Queen's Printer, 1968).

5. Carrothers, A.W.R. *Collective Bargaining Law in Canada* (Toronto: Butterworth, 1965).

6. Carter, D.D. *The Expansion of Labour Board Remedies* (Kingston: Queen's University Industrial Relations Centre, 1976).

7. Labour Relations Law Casebook Group. *Labour Relations Law: Cases Materials and Commentary*, 2nd ed. (Kingston: Queen's University Industrial Relations Centre, 1976).

8. Report of the Task Force on Labour Relations. *Canadian Industrial Relations* (Ottawa: Queen's Printer, 1968).

9. Weiler, P.C. *Reconcilable Differences: New Directions in Canadian Labour Law Reform* (Agincourt, Ont.: Carswell, 1980).

10. Weiler, P.C. "The Administrative Tribunal: A View From the Inside," *University of Toronto Law Journal*, Vol. 26 (1976), 193.

11. Willes, J.A. *The Ontario Labour Court 1943-1944* (Kingston: Queen's University Industrial Relations Centre, 1979).

QUESTIONS

1. Discuss the problems associated with the increasing regulation of the Canadian industrial-relations system.

2. Explain the constitutional division of legislative authority over labour relations in Canada.

3. Describe the evolution of Canadian collective-bargaining law since Confederation.

4. Compare the private-sector collective-bargaining structure in Canada with that found in the public sector.

5. What are the significant differences between the Canadian collective-bargaining structure and its U.S. counterpart? Explain.

6. Distinguish the functions performed by arbitration boards from those performed by labour-relations boards.

7. How do labour boards differ from courts? Explain.

8. Explain the difference between grievance arbitration and interest arbitration.

HARRY. J. GLASBEEK

3. The Contract of Employment at Common Law

This chapter describes the basic legal rules governing contract of employments con-cluded outside the collective-bargaining regime. It takes into account some essential legislative provisions which will affect the contents of such contracts. The chapter compares the essence of the employment relationship when governed by common law on the one hand and collective-bargaining legislation on the other. The analysis suggests that differences between the regimes may be less important than similarities.

This chapter has two interrelated purposes. The first is to demonstrate that the attributes of the institution known as the common-law contract of employment form the central part of all employment relationships in Canada today, whether or not such relationships are said to be governed by common law or by another legal regime such as collective bargaining. If this can be shown, it will have important implications for students of union-management relations. In particular, it will raise questions about the validity of the commonly shared assumption that the condition of workers has greatly improved as a result of individual contracting being, to a large extent, replaced by controlled collective bargaining. The second objective of the chapter is to detail, in a relatively nontechnical way, the legal rights and duties created by the common-law rules governing the contract of employment.

IDEOLOGY OF THE CONTRACT OF EMPLOYMENT

Working for wages under a negotiated contract is not, historically speaking, a long-established phenomenon. Even though, at the end of the thirteenth century, some wage labour could be said to have arisen in England as manorial systems and customary services fell into disuse and serfs purchased their liberty, coming to work on leased land, it was not until the advent of the Black Plague in the mid-fourteenth century that the scarcity of labour spotlighted the fact that some reliance on this mode of production had developed. The result was the enactment of a statute, which in effect took away the right to bargain for wages and, most importantly, took away the unhindered mobility of labourers. Workers of certain classes had to work for whosoever commanded them, they could not leave their employ without permission, and were remunerated at a rate based on conditions which existed before the Black

Plague made labour a scarce commodity. This approach to wage labour remained dominant over the centuries. In the reign of Henry VIII, large numbers of unemployed persons wandered around the countryside, partly as a result of the Crown's attack on the monasteries. To counter the increasing lawlessness and social unrest, the famous *Statute of Apprentices* was enacted. It, like the Black Plague statute, tied workers to particular employers for specified periods, to work under conditions established by justices of the peace. Thus, even at this late stage, free contracting for wage labour was not the norm. But the economic pressures generated by the coming of the Industrial Revolution began to create pressures for change. During the sixteenth century, cloth manufacturing became a real alternative to craft production. Craft gilds were finding it increasingly difficult to control production, and people came flooding into towns as work in agriculture became progressively less available. Despite the continuation of the regulatory scheme set up by the *Statute of Apprentices*, contracting between increasing numbers of mill and factory owners, on the one hand, and the great number of people seeking work in the towns on the other hand, became more and more common. Indeed, workers occasionally sought to have the restrictive statute apply to them as the new free contracting arrangements did not suit them well. But this was a losing battle, and Adam Smith wrote that, by 1776, the fixation of wages by justices of the peace had fallen entirely into disuse. Individual contract making had taken its place.

These changes did not take place in a vacuum. At the same time as the needs of the new kinds of entrepreneurs were being identified by lawmakers in the labour-relations area, they were also being given recognition in other spheres. Contract had, as we know it today, evolved. Novel kinds of commercial relationships developed as the production of new goods and services led to new rationalizations in manufacturing and merchandizing methods. This put pressure on a legal system that was fashioned to handle many fewer dealings of a less variegated kind. In particular, a rather expansive but nonetheless fixed writ system, developed during feudal times, was recognized, from a technical point of view, to be no longer effective. The notion of this writ system had been that there were only a specific number of kinds of claims which could be made and that, unless a claimant could bring his action in a way that met the procedural requirements of an established form of action, he would fail. This rigidity was so unsuited to the facts of commerce of the Industrial Revolution that it began to be replaced by a general law of contract. The development from the writ system to modern contract law suited the new forms of enterprise in very tangible ways. Entrepreneurs were not aided simply because the legal process became more streamlined. The rules and principle of liability also were changed substantially, to the undoubted advantage of entrepreneurship.

Under the pre-Industrial Revolution system, there was no pressing legal need to differentiate between serious promises of different kinds. For instance, the relationships between demanders and suppliers did not warrant the courts to treat statements made during serious negotiations, on the one hand, and statements found in final agreements, on the other hand, very differently. In a similar vein, courts were not terribly perturbed if prices for goods or services had not been agreed on by the disputants by the time a dispute arose. Just as they were willing, given the right form of action, to treat a serious anteagreement promise as binding, they were prepared to imply a reasonable price for the supply of goods and services. In the market economy which subsequently developed, however, entrepreneurs had a real interest in having options kept open as long as possible in order that the optimum market price could be obtained. Further, the logic of the market dictated that, once one party had convinced another of the appropriateness of a particular price, that party should be able to take advantage of the bargain. There was thus a need for rules which differentiated between promises which could be enforced because they represented an agreement between bargainers as to a particular price and those which were merely stages in bargaining about what the price ought to be. Modern texts on contract law now encapsulate this development by defining an enforceable contract as an agreement which both parties intended should be binding, where one party made an offer of specific terms which were accepted by the other, and where the promises sought to be enforced were given in exchange for consideration. Consideration means that a promise is enforceable if something is given in return for it by the person seeking to enforce the promise.

What becomes apparent from this sketch is that it was seen by the legal system that competitive ideals could best be advanced by letting people use their resources to get the best possible deal and then enforcing that deal without inquiring into its fairness or reasonableness. The market mechanism would, if people were free to inform themselves and to shop around, produce results which were acceptable because of the logic of the economic variables prevalent in the market. The old writ system with its enforcement of promises as such and its unabashed imposition of reasonable prices, even in the face of parties' solemn agreements, was not capable of giving the free-market precepts a free field of play. Changes were necessary.

Courts, of course, cannot simply say that there is a dawning of a new age and that, therefore, lovingly established principles have to be overturned. Courts seek to make changes as smoothly as possible and, if feasible, justify new approaches by claims that they are abiding by deeply held social convictions and mores. In support of the new contract doctrines courts developed, they were able to argue that the new rules reflected ancient beliefs which, as a result of changing social and economic circumstances, now could be given more life and meaning. These basic beliefs held that common law had an all-abiding respect for individuals and individualism which had to be protected from suppression by the state and, now that feudalism and group control mechanisms (such as merchant and craft gilds) had broken down, they also had to be safeguarded from collective pressures created by concerted activities. Thus, on the one hand, courts should keep legislative interference with individual action to a minimum and, on the other hand, should promote self-assertion by individuals.

The institution of the new contract doctrines was thus central: by permitting voluntary agreement making between sovereign individuals, it echoed both philosophical and prevailing market tenets. Unsurprisingly, this turn of events was hailed as a great jurisprudential leap forward. Sir Henry Maine acclaimed, as have most lawyers since, the evolution of modern contract as a marvelously progressive development. Maine welcomed it because it represented the end of a status society. By this he meant that no longer would people's rights, duties, privileges, and obligations be determined on bases such as where they were born, to whom they were born, or their sex or age. From then on, the legal rights, duties, privileges and obligations of any person were to arise from that person's ability to freely win rights his willingness to take on responsibilities. Ability, and perhaps luck, were to be the determinants. This was seen as a liberating movement.

Whatever the philosophical merit of the development described, it had an immediate and depressing impact on workers. Their lot was not improved by the law's reflection of the ideals of the age. Individual contract making on the basis of *legal* equality between persons who were grossly unequal *economically* led to very poor employment conditions for workers. This was aggravated by the fact that courts refused to examine the reasonableness of wage bargains. In addition, where there was a dispute in a situation in which no specific agreement had been entered into by the employer and the employee, the courts came to find that such matters were ruled, as a matter of law, by certain premises justified by practices of a pre-individual-contract-making era. That is, a sense of continuity was provided. But the pre-Industrial Revolution relationships assumed that a servant was something like a piece of property of his master. Notions derived from status principles — the essence of relationships of that kind — ought logically to have had no place in the new age of laissez faire. But their incorporation, as well as meeting the judiciary's need for legitimating its modification of legal principles, also happened to coincide with entrepreneurs' needs. It had the effect of supporting the proposition that investors of capital should not in any way be inhibited in the use they made of their capital unless they expressly bargained away their right to do so.

The upshot of this revolution in law was that rules developed which made workers the disadvantaged party in employment relationships. The rules and concepts which emerged were the basic rules and concepts applied to Canadian employment relationships from their inception. They still constitute the ruling framework, despite the fact that statutory collective bargaining has become the focus of public attention. This is so because collective bargaining is not universal. It is also true because, even when collective bargaining takes place, the new legal conceptual framework has not displaced the old one. This is what one would expect if it is correct, as argued above, that individual-contract-of-employment law was peculiarly well-suited to satisfy the ruling ideology and if adherence to that ideology and all that it entails has not been publicly abandoned. Any new legal scheme developed in this ideological context would naturally rely on proven mechanisms to achieve its aims, even if particular social or political circumstances led to the acceptance of dramatically different organizational relationships. In particular, trade unions are, in principle, antithetical to the judicial premises developed in respect of individual contract making. Inevitably, the common-law courts sought to repress them. When this could not be done, law had to accommodate them. But the legal system is resilient. Accommodation is not the same as capitulation. Given society's continued support for free-market enterprise precepts, the law could be expected to rely on the tried and true means of supporting that economic and philosophical system. The remainder of this chapter thus divides into two parts: (a) a discussion of the legal attributes of the individual contract of employment; and (b) an assessment of the persistence of these common-law concepts in collective-bargaining law.

ENTERING INTO A CONTRACT OF EMPLOYMENT

Types of Contracts of Employment

Like contracts generally, a contract of employment is a voluntarily entered into agreement between two legally capable persons who had an intention to create legal relations. There must have been an offer of certain terms, an acceptance thereof, and consideration given for promises before the agreement can be enforced at law. The parties may enter into their agreement by writing down the terms of their agreement and signing such a document. However, it is only necessary to do so when contracts are entered into for a term longer than one year. This is a remnant of seventeenth-century legislation, the *Statute of Frauds*. Its purpose was to avoid having to rely on fading memories when a dispute between parties to a long-term contract arose and when the danger of perjury was, therefore, great. The time span chosen was arbitrary and created logical difficulties for the courts. The courts have, therefore, developed many means to avoid the hardships caused by requiring a written memorandum of agreement in all cases to which the *Statute of Frauds* apparently should apply. Overall then, there are very few cases where writing is a prerequisite to enforcement of a contract of employment. Some contracts are always so, for example, apprenticeship agreements and schoolteachers' contracts in certain jurisdictions such as Ontario, Manitoba, and Alberta.

A contract of employment can thus often be entered into by the parties expressing their agreement orally. Typically, however, the existence of the contract will be implied from the conduct of the parties. An employee will just commence work, obey the employer's commands, and receive certain benefits.

There may be a specific agreement as to how long the contract of employment is to last. Such contracts will terminate on the specified date or, as is occasionally stipulated, when particular tasks have been performed. These are known as fixed term contracts. Much more common, however, are agreements in which there is no explicit nor implicit understanding about duration. At one stage, English common law presumed that such contracts were to last for one year and, should the parties continue as they were, for another year, and so forth. This presumption of yearly hiring had its origin in the predominance of certain peculiar employment situations, in particular, domestic service and agricultural labour. As the special needs of these forms of employment decreased in significance, the common-law courts jettisoned the presumption. Today, a contract which does not include a termination date will not be interpreted as a yearly contract unless there is a custom which indicates it ought to be treated in that way.

Where the contract was open-ended as to termination, the courts sometimes regarded it as a periodic hiring agreement, the length of the period being ascertained by reference to various features of the contract, especially the method of payment of wages. For example, if wages were paid monthly, the contract would be read as being a contract for the hire of labour for one month, which would be renewed to last for another month at the end of the first month if the parties just continued their relationship. But, generally, this approach has been abandoned. It simply is not consonant with the way that employers and employees view their relationship. They think of it as an agreement which is to continue until it is ended by agreement or nonperformance. That is, where parties have not put in a termination date, the contract of employment is best seen as one of indefinite duration, terminable by reasonable notice. The courts have adopted this notion.

Capacity to Contract

As in all other contractual relations, the parties to a contract of employment must be sane and be acting of their own free will in order to enter into an enforceable agreement. This general rule is subject to some qualifications and refinements.

Traditionally, minors, that is, people under a specific age — now usually eighteen — can only enter into certain kinds of enforceable contracts. These are agreements for the supply of necessities such as food, clothing, and shelter. Contracts which clearly inure to the benefit of minors are also enforceable. Early on, it was held that contracts of employment and apprenticeship should be regarded as beneficial to minors unless they contained such adverse terms that this presumption was rebutted. This judicial attitude permitted the exploitation of infants. Today, legislation has been enacted to prevent such possible abuses. The statutes in various Canadian jurisdictions typically forbid the employment of minors in certain industries altogether, and in other occupational areas they permit employment only on certain terms so that schooling will not be unduly interrupted. Often, permission of the parents has to be obtained before minors may be hired. Another common provision requires the appropriate minister to declare the work not to be dangerous to the physical well-being of the minors. The moral health of minors is also to be protected. Typically, these statutes provide that minors cannot work after midnight without parental permission and that minors should not be employed in such enterprises as hotel work, entertainment lounges, and the like. The paternalistic spirit of these statutes is underscored by the common provisions that none of the restrictions on child employment exist when the minor is employed in a family undertaking.

Migrants constitute another group of persons who cannot freely enter into contracts of employment. In order to protect work opportunities for Canadian citizens and permanent residents, the *Immigration Act* provides that to obtain a visa to enter Canada, a person must have an employment authorization. Such an authorization will be given after a Canadian employer has identified a need for a particular worker which cannot be satisfied by hiring a Canadian citizen or permanent resident. Further, the employer must satisfy the investigating immigration officer that the job being offered provides conditions which would be acceptable to a Canadian citizen or permanent resident. When the job ends, the employment authorization terminates. Should the job description change, the employer has to satisfy the immigration office again that the initial criteria are still met in order to be able to retain the migrant in his employ. No employment authorization will be given where the hiring of migrant workers might affect the power balance of an ongoing labour dispute.

Once a collective agreement has been concluded between an employer and a trade union, the employer cannot negotiate any variations in terms with any of the individuals in the bargaining unit. The notion is that the collective-bargaining regime is not to be undermined by private dealings and that, therefore, all bargaining is to be between the employer and the bargaining agent for all members in the bargaining unit.

Purpose of the Contract

Like all other contracts, a contract of employment will be unenforceable if it is entered into for an unacceptable purpose. For instance, where the objective is to contravene criminal law, such as a conspiracy to restrain trade or to breach a statute which prescribes certain minimum working conditions, the contract may be unenforceable, at least in respect of those parts which are illegal. Similarly, contracts which offend public morality may be unenforceable.

Requirements of Fairness in the Formation of Contracts of Employment

Every legislature in Canada has enacted human-rights statutes, which prohibit amongst other things, discrimination in hiring practices on the basis of such criteria as race, national origin, colour, religion or creed, sex, and marital status. While these are the most common grounds, there are other prohibited grounds, varying from jurisdiction to jurisdiction. For example, discrimination on the basis of physical handicap is prohibited in Manitoba, New Brunswick, Nova Scotia, Prince Edward Island, and the federal sphere; discrimination on the basis of political belief is prohibited in British Columbia, Newfoundland, Prince Edward Island, and Quebec.

The implementation of these human-rights schemes is usually left to an administrative agency, most often known as a human-rights commission. Typically, the commission requires that complaints be lodged with it, alleging a breach of the governing statute. A field officer will be sent out to investigate whether or not there has been a violation. If the investigating officer fails to mediate the dispute and believes there is a breach of the statute, it will be reported to the pertinent minister. This may lead to the establishment of a board or tribunal hearing. In some jurisdictions, the commission itself may present the case, in others the original complainant may do so. The boards and tribunals have been given remedial powers which include ordering an end to an established discriminatory practice and awarding compensation. Such orders may be enforced in ordinary courts.

The advertising and posting of job vacancies must also comply with human-rights legislation. Similarly, in all jurisdictions except Alberta, employment agencies have been made subject to human-rights statutes. In some provinces, the power of employment agencies to exploit persons in the labour market has been limited by a licensing and regulatory system. These schemes usually provide that only licensed employment agencies may operate and that licensees can only charge employers a fee for services provided.

The need to protect individuals from discrimination in hiring is recognized even when the employment relationship is covered by collective bargaining. Unions are permitted to bargain for security clauses, that is, terms in a collective agreement which bolster union security by requiring every member in the bargaining unit to pay dues to the union, or by requiring union membership as a prerequisite to becoming or remaining an employee. This is an endorsement of the collective regime as opposed to the individual-contracting system governed by common law. But, manifestly, individuals could, as a result of security provisions, be just as seriously discriminated against as they could be under common law. Consequently, trade unions may not be recognized or certified, if their constitutions make it impossible for certain persons to belong to the trade union because of such factors as race, nationality, sex, or creed. This prevents discrimination in hiring in much the same way as it is prevented in the individual-contracting situation. In addition, bargains will not be recognized as collective agreements where their terms discriminate on enumerated proscribed grounds, which usually correspond to the human rights proscribed grounds of discrimination.

RIGHTS AND DUTIES OF EMPLOYERS UNDER A CONTRACT OF EMPLOYMENT

The parties are free to provide for whatever conditions they like. The conditions will be expressly provided for in the contract, or implied from the conduct of the parties or the custom in the industry. In addition, whether or not contracts provide for certain terms, courts will imply them, unless it is clear that the parties intend them not to be part of their contractual relationship. As was indicated in the first section, the terms which courts were willing to insert as a matter of law from the inception of the modern contract doctrine were based on their view of what must have been the intentions of the parties. Their understanding of the essential nature of the contract of employment was, therefore, the determining factor in the creation of these implied terms. This, in turn, was coloured by their need to show historical continuity with the precept of a dominantly feudal society.

As a result, courts thought that the essence of the contract of employment was that a worker offered services in return for wages. That is, the contract of employment was seen as being distinct from other freely negotiated contracts in that it was a contract of service. For a long time, this was reflected in the language used by lawyers who referred to the relationship as being a master-servant one. This language has now been replaced by the terms employer and employee. This suggests that the relationship is now qualitatively different and, in particular, that the element of service is no longer the essence of the employment relationship. Let us, therefore, first turn to the rights and obligations implied by common-law courts in contracts of employment to determine how integral the concept of service is to such relationships.

Employer's Duty to Pay Remuneration

It is perhaps of some interest that courts were not always sanguine that, if the parties had not expressly agreed that there should be remuneration for work done, there should be such payment. The argument raised was that it would depend on the circumstances. For example, if the services were rendered by relations or by close friends, an inference might be drawn that there should be no remuneration payable. This trend is only of historical interest as, today, it is customary to assume that services are not gratuitously rendered in the absence of an express agreement to this effect.

Rates are usually spelled out by the parties or are payable according to the custom in the industry. Where the latter situation arises, the court has to guess at the reasonable price for labour. A similar exercise is undertaken by the courts in the rather infrequent situations where services have been rendered without a contract having been negotiated or, more commonly, where a contract is unenforceable for some reason. An example of this is where there is no memorandum in writing which satisfies the requirements of the *Statute of Frauds*. In such cases, the courts are able to fashion a noncontractual remedy. The notion is that a person should be rewarded for the value bestowed on the recipient of services. Although not necessarily coincident with the amount recoverable on the basis of the customary rate of pay in the trade or industry, it will seldom yield vastly different results.

One of the few problems which arises out of the old notions of the contract of employment relating to remuneration for services is that it is still the law that payment is deemed to be due in arrears. That is, a worker has to have given service for a stated period before becoming entitled to receive pay for that service. What it means in practice is that, if a worker is hired on the basis of having to complete a discrete task which will only be done if services are rendered for a particular period — for instance, the harvesting of a crop — the worker will not be entitled to any pay until the task is performed in its entirety. A worker who leaves during the period set aside for the performance of the contract may not be able to recover pay for the services already rendered, subject to the restitutionary principles referred to above. Today, however, courts are reluctant to read contractual arrangements as contracts of entirety.

All Canadian jurisdictions have legislation which regulates the form of payment. Statutes prescribe that payment shall be by cheque or in cash. The reason underlying these provisions reveals a great deal about the nature of the employment relationship. It was common practice for employers to pay their workers by giving them goods instead of money. It was easy to overvalue the goods and thus to underpay the workers, in the sense that they were paid less than the contractually arranged rates. There were many variants of this technique which was known as "truck." Thus, some employers instead of money would issue vouchers which were only redeemable by purchasing goods at a specified store, usually a company store. The requirement that payment of wages be in cash or by cheque obviates most of these problems. When it is necessary to make an assessment of whether or not the worker has received the minimum wage as prescribed by statute, the employer is allowed to compute, as part of remuneration paid, food and lodging provided to the worker, up to a specified amount. In addition, the employer is permitted, by statute, to subtract from the amount of wages owed, sums for payments to charities, insurance schemes, union dues, or plans which benefit the worker, provided the worker agrees to such deductions.

All jurisdictions in Canada also provide for wage floors. This is a direct interference with the precepts of contract principles. Typically, a board or a commission is empowered to make a specific order for a minimum-wage rate aimed at a particular industry or a general order governing minimum-wage rates in respect of all employees covered by the minimum-standards statute. The kinds of employees covered vary from jurisdiction to jurisdiction but nearly always excluded are domestic servants and various categories of agricultural workers. Members of the family of the employer, some professional employees, and employees who, in particular geographic regions of the country, require special treatment, for example, in the fishing or timber industry, are often excluded from statutory coverage. Part-time student workers and employees in recreational facilities may also be excluded or treated differently.

A large number of persons in the work force have their basic conditions of employment governed by minimum-standards legislation. Thus, the Ontario Ministry of Labour's *Annual Report 1978-1979* indicated that 250,000 workers, about 10 percent of the Ontario work force, received the minimum wage. There are thus a great number of workers whose weak market position is so apparent that the legislature has seen fit to protect them from the rigorous implementation of sacrosanct contract principles.

In this context, it is appropriate to note that many people who are protected by minimum-standards statutes are met with the argument that they are not truly employees. That is, they are characterized as entrepreneurs who have entered into contracts, knowing that there were risks and as such should be rugged enough to bear the cost of these materialized risks. This argument is the essence of contract law: freely entered into agreements by sovereign individuals are enforceable without regard to the terms of the agreement. This doctrine has some exceptions, such as where one party has been mistaken or misled, or coerced in some way. In addition, if the contract is one of employment, certain terms are guaranteed for the employee. This makes it clear that the employment contract is viewed differently to other kinds of contracts. Thus, when persons making a minimum-standards application are faced with the argument that they are independent contractors rather than employees, the essential nature of employment as opposed to other contractual relationships is put in issue.

Initially, a contract of employment was differentiated from other contracts by the fact that one party could exercise control over the other. This highlighted the real economic gap between the parties as well as the fact that the employer had physical control over both the contents of the task to be performed and its mode of performance. While the exercise of physical control still leads to a finding of an employment relationship when one party renders services to another in return for remuneration, other tests have had to be devised where such a finding cannot be made, as it is no longer clear that lack of physical control can be equated with the independence which denies an employment relationship. For instance, it is common to infer an employment relationship where the hirer supplies all the equipment and tools to the service renderer. However, courts do not automatically deny the relationship where the service renderer supplies equipment or tools. Courts have sought to provide themselves with rather mechanical tests to determine whether or not the contract before them is one of employment. Thus they have differentiated between a contract of service and a contract for services, the idea being that the former indicates that the contract is one for whatever service the hirer asks to be performed in the manner the hirer demands, the latter referring to contracts for delivery of specified goods and/or services, the performance of the tasks being left to the enterprise of the hired person. But, of course, in order to differentiate between the contracts in this way the courts require criteria; the mere formulation of the difference does not provide these criteria.

In the same way, another popular semantic formula was one which declared that if a hired person is part and parcel of the hirer's organization, then that person is an employee. This formulation permits the inclusion of many people who cannot be physically controlled by their hirers because of their high level of individualized skills — doctors in hospitals, and engineers in public works departments, etc. But this test does not (just as the contract of service/contract for services test does not) provide criteria to determine whether a person is part and parcel of an organization or not. A formula which does provide such criteria is found in *Montreal v. Montreal Locomotive Works Ltd.* (1947) 1 D.L.R. 161, 169 (P.C.).

> It has been suggested that a fourfold test would in some cases be more appropriate, a complex involving (1) control; (2) ownership of the tools; (3) a chance to profit; (4) risk of loss.

This test requires the courts to examine the reality of the economic position of the parties. Thus, even though remuneration may be left uncalculated, the actual relationship may be one in which the hirer is in a dominant position, dictating terms to a person who does not, in fact, operate as an entrepreneur in a market. To take an extreme example, the service renderer who, on paper, appears to be an entrepreneur may only have one customer, the hirer, being therefore completely dependent on the willingness of the hirer to use the entrepreneur's services. In such cases, the offeror of services may be classified as an employee for the purpose of benefiting from minimum-standards legislation. Even the collective-bargaining schemes have recognized that reality may give the lie to the appearance of independence, and, often, to the parties' perceptions. Thus, legislation has been enacted permitting such self-styled "entrepreneurs" to form and join unions of employees as a category described in a telling phrase: "dependent contractors."

The tribunals, boards, and courts find it difficult to develop consistency in decision making when faced with the question of whether there is an employment relationship. However, it is implicit in the foregoing that an employment contract is differentiated from other contractual relationships because one of the parties is seen as being in a subservient position. We will return to this shortly.

In addition to legislative minimum-wage provisions, a guaranteed floor is also provided by legislation requiring employers who obtain government contracts to provide specified wages and conditions of employment as minima.

Another major inroad on the principle that the parties are free to contract for any remuneration they choose is legislation which provides that there shall be no discrimination in pay on the basis of sex. This legislation is far from uniform. The most common form prescribes equal pay for equal work, regardless of the sex of the employee. But the difficulty of interpretation is great. When is work equal? Much depends on the criteria specified in the statute. It may say the work must be identical, in which case it may be read as meaning that the work done must be the same in all respects. It may provide that the work must be substantially the same, requiring the same or similar exercises of skill, effort, and responsibility, which will lead to comparisons of a different sort. Although there had been a tendency to be more liberal in applications of this kind, the overall effect has not been as positive as many people would like, in part because comparisons are usually restricted to certain jobs.

To broaden the comparisons that are possible, a relatively new form of equal-pay legislation is being promoted, requiring equal pay for work of equal value. This kind of statute, currently in existence at the federal level, presents serious problems for implementation, for example, it requires the development of job-content evaluations. This creates difficulties since the creation of job classification, content, and evaluation criteria must be done within the framework of the employer's production needs, and this will lead to fundamental questions about who runs the enterprise. These questions may not be so revolutionary if they are raised as part of the bargaining process, but if they have to be resolved by an external tribunal or board (as will be the case under the legislation), they will raise very sensitive issues. This can be gleaned from the existing federal legislation which provides that a genuine seniority, merit, or bona fide occupational differentiation may justify differences in rates. The last two justifications create hurdles for large-scale equalization: arguments in respect of merit or bona fide occupational classifications are very hard to counter when made by the person who is the risk taker in an enterprise. A great deal of controversy and confrontation around this aspect of interfering with rates of pay in freely entered into contracts can be anticipated.

Two more legislative instances of interference with free contracting for remuneration must be mentioned. Under federal unemployment insurance, apart from some few excepted employment situations, all employees must contribute a set proportion of their earnings, up to a particular amount, to an unemployment insurance fund. The employers contribute an amount which is calculated by reference to the employee's contributions, at present 1.4 times the employee's premium rate. The government also contributes to the fund from general revenue. When an insured person (that is, a contributing employee) becomes unemployed, that employee becomes entitled to initial benefits, if continuous employment for a set period can be established. Claimants are entitled to a week's payment from the fund for every week of insured employment up to a specific number of weeks. After that period has elapsed, extended benefits (paid for out of the government's contributions to the fund) become payable. These permit one week of benefits to be paid for every two weeks of insured employment, again for a specified period. On top of all that, extra benefits are available in regions of the country where the incidence of unemployment exceeds that of other regions. The amount of unemployment benefits paid is, at the moment, about 60 percent of the average weekly earnings of the insured person, up to a fixed amount.

There are some barriers to entitlement. The most significant one is that the claimant must prove to be ready, willing, and able to take suitable employment. Time is given to find a job but, as time elapses, the claimant may be asked to reduce expectations in respect of both suitability and pay. Another disqualifying situation is being on strike, unless the claimant shows no intent to return to work for the struck employer. Leaving employment without good reason or by dismissal because of misconduct may also operate as partial barriers to benefit entitlement. These kinds of problems call for the exercise of discretionary judgments, made by the Employment and Immigration Commission. Disputed decisions are taken to the minister for determination, after which, there is an appeal to an Umpire, who is a federal or provincial superior or county court judge. Where the dispute is one relating to whether or not a claimant worked as an employee, there is a further appellate level, the Pension Appeal Board.

Federal legislation also requires that all employees and employers (except for migratory work, foreign government workers, and the like) pay remuneration-based contributions to provide for retirement incomes. The retirement income scheme is known as the Canada Pension Plan. Persons who earn over a certain minimum amount (at present, $1300) must pay a set proportion of their wages into a government fund. The employer matches this contribution. The rates are set on the basis of a formula which will yield a specified benefit upon retirement. This will be a portion of the year's maximum pensionable earnings, that is, those earnings subject to contributions. Contributions and retirement income are adjusted to inflation. The plan also provides for disability and servicing spouses' pensions. A contributor's pension rights are fully portable from employer to employer and a formula has been devised to allow benefits (at a lower rate) to persons who are irregularly in the work force.

Federal legislation also provides an Old Age Security Pension. Everyone who has resided in Canada for forty years after the age of eighteen is entitled to the full benefit of this pension upon reaching sixty-five. The scheme is not financed by direct employer-employee contributions and is only mentioned for the sake of completeness. On top of the Old Age Security scheme, there is a federal Guaranteed Income Supplement, based on a means test. In addition, there are a variety of provincial schemes and, of course, privately bargained for pension schemes. The latter are most commonly found in that part of the private sector where collective bargaining occurs.

Employer's Duty to Provide Work

Employers, by definition, have control over the enterprise, and therefore can decide what work is to be done and when. There may be periods in which they do not want any work done, yet may not wish to dismiss the employees concerned. The question which has arisen from time to time is whether, in such circumstances, employers must provide their employees with work to do.

Where the work is of a special kind, the courts have implied that the employer is under a duty to provide work. As may be imagined, these situations are very uncommon. One such case is where the employee's remuneration depends on the number of things made or sold. Courts have ruled that such employees should be provided with that amount of work (things to make or sell) which will enable them to earn the average amount earned when the contract was running its more ordinary course. Where the contract provides that a guaranteed minimum remuneration be paid, the employer's duty is limited to providing only such amount of work as would yield the minimum rate as opposed to an average of earnings.

A second situation in which the common-law courts have decreed that the employer is charged (by implication) with a duty to provide work is where the employee has a great stake in performing the contract, in receiving public recognition, almost as much (or more so in some cases) as in being paid for the services rendered. Typical of successful claimants are actors and singers, or managerial employees in certain industries. Note here that, as a corollary to this doctrine, courts have on a very few occasions treated a failure to provide an employee with work of the calibre rightfully expected as an insult and a breach of contract, entitling the employee to obtain appropriate relief.

Apart from these exceptional circumstances, common law has not required employers to provide work in the absence of an agreement by the parties to the contrary. But the courts recognize that not to require the employer to provide work but to simultaneously permit the employer to insist that the employee should remain available and willing to perform contractual duties upon request, would not fit in easily with the notion that a contract is truly a bargain between equals. To use the jargon of contract law, the contract would lack mutuality. This phrase reflects the sense which courts have that they should be loath to uphold one-sided agreements, unless the parties' intentions deny any other interpretation. Yet, the courts have generally been quick to assume that an employee's contract is one of service and, therefore, that onerous incidents will not necessarily let them treat a contract of employment as one which lacks mutuality. Here, in the context of the duty to provide work, however, the courts have stayed closer to general contract principles than to the position that there is something special about a contract of employment. They have held that, if employers want their employees to remain available and willing to perform, they need not provide work, but they must pay the employees their ordinary remuneration. This is subject to the proviso that employers may be able to discharge their burden of having to pay remuneration if they can show that it could never have been the intention of the parties that employers alone bear the burden of lack of productive activity by their employees. An example of this is provided by a case where gradual deterioration of the plant led to its closure because of the danger it presented to the safety of employees.

The problem, then, is that the common-law courts do not permit an employer (in the absence of a trade custom) to suspend an employee. In addition, it means that, in effect, an employer cannot lay off employees during a slack period; he must dismiss his employees or pay them. But dismissal has been made relatively costly by the fact that notice or pay in lieu of notice must be given. In the particular circumstance of a retrenchment in times of economic slackness, an employer will, in all probability, want to dispense with the services of a number of employees. In such cases, legislative provisions in respect of notice or pay in lieu of notice come into play. Typically, provincial statutes provide that where mass terminations occur, periods of notice, which increase in length with the number of workers dismissed, must be given. This heightens the cost of termination considerably and, in a negative sense, may help to protect employee's jobs or, at least, lessen the pain of dismissal.

Under collective bargaining, however, the participants commonly assume that an employer has a right to suspend, as opposed to terminate, employment. In the context being discussed at present, this means that employers, by abiding with certain prearranged conditions included in the collective agreement based on seniority principles, can lay off employees for various periods. The statutory provisions requiring group termination notice will not come into play as long as the retrenchment is a temporary layoff. This is defined as a suspension for a relatively lengthy period (typically thirteen weeks) during which the employer still makes some contributions by way of supplementary unemployment benefits, pension contributions, and the like. This helps both the employer and the employees, the latter because they have a claim on a job. But that job opportunity may never materialize and, when it does not, the chances of getting group termination pay may have been lost because the employee, in dire circumstances during the layoff, was unavailable when recalled because of accepting another job or being forced into one as a claimant for unemployment insurance benefits. Such unavailability relieves the employer from the statutory obligation of group termination notice. There is no way of assessing whether employees are better off by accepting terms in a collective agreement regulating the employer's right to lay off, rather than relying on their rights under the law of individual contract of employment.

A similar conundrum is presented by the issue of reduction of hours. At common law, in the absence of an established custom, a unilateral reduction by the employer in the number of hours to be worked would be a failure to provide work as agreed and, therefore, require continuation of payment of remuneration for the nonworked hours. Under collective bargaining the received wisdom is that, in the absence of a contrary provision in the agreement, the employer may unilaterally reduce hours and pay only for the hours worked. This view must be based on the notion that contract of employment law plays no part when a collective agreement prevails and/or that, in reality, employees are hired by the hour and no breach of contract is involved in reducing a work week by hourly lots.

Clearly, these admittedly abstruse difficulties stem from our legal system's failure to identify the separateness of the individual-contract-of-employment and collective-bargaining regimes, a failure which, it is the thesis of the article, is attributable to the fact that it is not understood that the underlying precepts of the two systems are not discrete.

Employer's Responsibility for the Employee's Conduct

Where an employee's behaviour causes injury to another, a question may arise about the legal liability of the employer to that injured person. The common-law courts produced two doctrinal means by which to make employers so responsible. Note here that this development runs counter to a basic common-law premise that no person should be liable to compensate another for injury suffered unless it can be shown that the injury was the result of wrongdoing by the defendant. In legal language, fault must be proved. As a consequence, the fault of the employee being personal, it is difficult to equate it with fault on the part of employer.

One tack the common-law courts initially took was to hold that the employer owed a duty of care to the injured person, one which could not be delegated to his employees. Thus, the employee's act was really the act of the employer. The notion that the employer could not delegate his duties in any way corresponded much more closely to existing conditions in an era during which employers had more physical control over their enterprises than they do now. Unsurprisingly, this mechanism for making employers responsible for their employees' actions is seldom relied upon today. It is not startling to learn that this doctrine is known as the master's-tort theory of responsibility. Note that it is advantageous where, for some reason, the employee who actually inflicted the injury cannot be sued by the victim, as the master remains personally responsible for breach of his nondelegable duty.

Current employers have vicarious liability for the actions of employees. That is, employers are held liable for injuries inflicted by their employees when acting in the scope of their employment. Two things must be proved by the victim to recover from the employer. First, the employee's conduct must have been such that it amounts to fault. Second, the employee's harmful act must have taken place while engaged in the scope of employment. Several difficult decisions have to be made by the courts: Does it matter that the employer had prohibited the particular conduct which caused the harm? Is a particular variation from the routine of doing a task so much a frolic of the employee's that the employer cannot be made responsible for it? If the harm done by the employee was intentional, as opposed to accidental, should the employer be held responsible? No answers can be provided to questions such as these in the abstract. Decisions vary with the courts' appraisal of the extent of deviation from the scope of employment and their belief about the reason for holding an employer vicariously liable.

There are various theories for the imposition of vicarious liability. One is the notion that the employer should be responsible because he has control over his employees. This is just another version of the master's-tort theory if it means that the acts of the employees are those of the master's. But employers may be held liable even if they exercised all diligent care in choosing their employees and in supervising them; that is, when they meet their apparent personal duty of care. If so, they are held liable not because they have a nondelegable duty but because those who benefit from the creation of risks should bear the costs of those risks. Another rationale is based on a simple economic-efficiency argument, namely, the loss incurred by the injured person as a consequence of the enterprise of the employer should be allocated to the employer because he is in a much better position than the victim or the employee to spread the loss throughout society. Depending on which of these rationales is perceived to be the most significant, differing answers will be given to questions concerned with how much variation beyond the normal scope of employment the employer should be made responsible for.

Even though vicarious liability does not depend on the peculiar nature of the contract of employment, the pervasive nature of the distinction drawn between contracts of service and contracts for services had led the courts to hold that vicarious liability for the acts of independent contractors should be restricted to those cases where the enterprise is inherently ultradangerous. Some softening in this position can be seen in modern times, perhaps because, inasmuch as cost spreading is a major aim of the vicarious-liability doctrine, some independent contractors are in no better position than most employees to spread loss throughout society.

Employer's Duty to Provide a Safe Work Environment

Initially, the common-law courts set their face against the proposition that workers should be entitled to compensation for injuries suffered at work. Conceptually, this resistance was based on pure contract principles. It was assumed that the worker, when entering into the contract of employment, had voluntarily agreed to accept the risks of the work environment. That is, in the freely negotiated terms about allocation of costs, workers were assumed, in the absence of a term to the contrary, to have agreed to bear the cost of injury to themselves. As it became clear that this was not compatible with the reality of the relationships, fall-back positions were evolved by the courts. One was the application of a principle which had developed independently of contract-of-employment law. This was the doctrine that, to recover compensation for injuries inflicted by anyone else's negligence, the injured person had to have been blameless. Any contributory negligence on the employee's behalf would lead to a total denial of liability. Injured workers often had a difficult time proving that their negligence in no way contributed to the accident. The second rule which made it very difficult for workers to be compensated was one which became known as the doctrine of common employment. It prevented workers from recovering compensation from their employers where their injuries were the result of fellow employee's acts. The notion was that the workers assumed the risk of their fellow employees' carelessness. Manifestly, such a doctrine made it very awkward in many of the traumatic injury cases in respect of which workers sought compensation.

Both these common-law doctrines have been abrogated by legislation: the common-employment doctrine no longer exists and the contributory negligence of an injured person merely affects the amount of damages awarded. While the law was evolving in this legislative way, courts also sought ways round the harsh doctrines they had developed. Consequently, they began implying into every contract of employment a duty to be discharged by the employer in respect of safety of employees. This was said to be a nondelegable duty and consisted of an obligation: (a) to provide competent fellow workers; (b) to provide safe tools, machinery, and equipment; (c) to provide a safe place of work and safe access to that place of work; and (d) to provide a safe system of working. Being a nondelegable duty, the employer cannot discharge it merely by delegating it to competent managers or hiring independent contractors (to supply tools or machinery), although, in some cases, showing that reasonable reliance was placed on competent suppliers was found to be a good defence for employers.

As a result, an injured worker could sue the employer for breach of contract or in tort for damages suffered. It was also established that no employee could be forced to obey instructions by the employer which would jeopardize physical safety. Naturally, employees were not well-placed to disobey an instruction on this ground, for if they could not eventually establish that they had been reasonable in such refusal, the courts would hold the employer entitled to dismiss such employees without notice. The only way an employee's exercise of this right would give rise to a judicial trial would be where the employer had treated the refusal to obey as a reason for abrupt termination of the contract of employment, and the employee had brought an action for wrongful dismissal. Manifestly, employers may, by the very existence of the rule, have been more restrained in their demands; further, many times they may have conceded employees' right to refuse to work in certain conditions. But, on balance, the right to refuse existed more in theory than in fact.

Similarly, the right to bring an action in damages was hedged in by difficulties; employees had to prove appropriate causal connections (most difficult in disease cases) and an absence of care by the employer; there were problems about proving the quantity of damages; and there were costs associated with bringing proceedings. On the other side, employers were far from satisfied with the uncertainties associated with common-law actions. Canada abandoned recourse to these remedies very early in its history. All provinces now have a workers' compensation statute which is the sole source of compensation for workers injured at work. The only exception to this are injuries suffered by workers in a few, specially scheduled industries where common-law doctrines are continued.

The amounts paid to workers under these workers' compensation schemes are 75 percent of the workers' earnings, not to exceed a specified amount. Where the worker has been permanently disabled, there may be an award of up to 75 percent of the worker's previous earnings, depending on the extent of the disablement. Where the disablement is slight, the award may be made by paying a lump sum. Otherwise, a monthly pension is awarded. Where the worker has died as a result of a work-related accident, a lump sum is payable to the dependants for funeral expenses and the like. A monthly pension will also be paid to the dependants. One of the obvious advantages of schemes of this nature is that it is possible to review the conditions of the worker frequently. The injured worker is to be provided with all medical and therapeutic aid, hospitalization expenses, and rehabilitative care.

Diseases arising out of working conditions are also compensable, but on a much less universal scale. Schedules in the statutes list a number of diseases and indicate that there is a presumption that the suffering of such a disease is compensable if the worker was employed in a scheduled industry. In some provinces, the worker must have been employed at any time in the twelve months previous to the manifestation of the disabling disease, in others there is no time limit. Where the disease complained of is not listed, the burden is on the worker-applicant to show that the disease is work-related.

These schemes are funded on a collective basis. Industries covered by the statutes are grouped by types, the relevant employers paying into a collective fund for their industry group. The sum levied from each employer is calculated on the basis of the estimated payroll for the coming year. The Workers' Compensation Board (as the administrative agency running the scheme is usually called) calculates the contribution rate on the basis of the known hazard in a particular group of industries. At the end of the year, the rate is adjusted based on actual payroll and actual accident rates. An advantage that the schemes bestow is that the board can adjust for particularly hazardous enterprises in a group. There is also power to provide for preventive regulation. But it is fair to assert that the preventive efforts of the schemes have seldom been pushed very far. In the main, they have consisted of setting up advisory bodies, mainly comprised by appropriate employers, which publicize obvious safety problems.

By generally removing fault notions, the compensation schemes have reduced a source of controversy, but areas of dispute remain. The questions of whether the injury arose out of or in the course of employment, whether the disease is a compensable one, and the extent of disability are all potentially contentious issues.

The above section deals with duties owed to employees with respect to safety and enforcement by the award of compensation to injured employees. Recently, in line with a growing awareness of the dangers posed to workers by the use of toxic substances in manufacturing processes, omnibus-type legislation has been enacted, aimed directly at prevention rather than compensation. The most far-reaching legislation is to be found in the federal jurisdiction, Ontario, Saskatchewan, and Manitoba. These statutes provide for the imposition of a set of obligations on both employers and employees in order to attain certain standards of safety in the work environment. Usually, there is provision for regulations to be passed after appropriate recommendations by an agency created for this purpose. The agency will be given the task of evaluating the feasibility of imposing safety standards in the work place. It is given research facilities. The amount of money given in this respect is of the utmost importance in view of the difficulties inherent in setting appropriate exposure levels to the thousands of chemical substances in use in manufacturing. The agency is aided by an inspectorate which not only has the task to enforce the existing standards, but also has to report on the need for more regulation or deregulation. The enforcement process involves consulting with the employers and employees, making recommendations, imposing fines and, where there is immediate danger, ordering the cessation of work until the premises comply with essential safety standards. As well, these statutory schemes seek to improve the safety of the work environment by providing for joint employer-employee safety committees. In some jurisdictions, the appropriate minister is given the power to appoint committees comprised of an equal number of employer and employee representatives. In others it is mandated that, where the work force exceeds a certain number, a joint committee of this kind be appointed. Committees must make inspections regularly, may make joint recommendations, call inspectors where needed, or where no agreement as to appropriate action can be reached. Employers are under an obligation to make available information about levels of exposures of particular workers, new substances introduced to the plant, medical advice respecting employees, and so on.

In addition, where workers have a reasonable apprehension of danger, they are entitled to refuse to work until the situation is remedied. Where a supervisor feels that the worker's fear is misplaced, the joint committee (or a safety representative who may be appointed in lieu of such a committee in some cases) may be asked to adjudicate. Workers are not to be disciplined where their belief is judged to be reasonable. Employees who refuse to accept the work may be asked to do other equivalent work. It is an open question as yet as to whether or not the employee will be considered disciplined if the remuneration rate is less for this other task than the one in respect of which the employee is normally employed. As was seen, at common law, it was always open for an employee to refuse to work in unsafe conditions. But such a worker, not supported by a legislative scheme of the kind described, ran a great risk: if the refusal was thought unreasonable by a court, there was no question but that the employer could dismiss such an employee. Further, even if it was a reasonable refusal, it was considerably easier for an employer to rid himself of such a troublesome worker. This note about the practical improvement of the worker's lot draws attention to the fact that the parties are free to bargain about safety in the work environment and all the schemes permit such agreement making, provided the terms are at least equal in their provision for safety to the legislative schemes. For instance, they must provide for joint committees with, at least, the same powers of inspection, access to information, and right to make recommendations as the legislatively mandated committees have.

The efficacy of these elaborate schemes is still not established. Much will depend on the political will supporting the work of the agencies which are to set standards. Much also depends on economic circumstances. These will dictate whether a standard can be imposed in view of the effect on the competitive position of an industry or people within it.

RIGHTS AND DUTIES OF EMPLOYEES UNDER A CONTRACT OF EMPLOYMENT

This chapter has emphasized that the essence of a contract of employment is that it is a contract of service. This is amply illustrated by an examination of employee duties which common-law courts have implied as a matter of law into every contract of employment, unless there is a specific term to the contrary in the contract. Broadly, these duties fall into two categories. One is comprised of the duties to obey and to use appropriate skill and care. Then there are those duties which may be described as the duties of good faith and fidelity. The first set of duties clearly can only be operative during the life of the contract of employment; the latter may extend beyond this period. The existence of both is only explicable on the basis that courts do not see the contract of employment as one of cooperation or mutuality, but rather as one between a superior and an inferior or, if you will, a master and servant. Where an employee is in breach of these implied duties, the employer may successfully bring an action for damages or exercise a right to terminate the contract of employment without giving notice.

Duty to Obey

While an employee is entitled to refuse to obey an employer's order which is unlawful or dangerous, the employee must obey all other reasonable orders. An employer may dismiss an employee without notice if the employee's disobedience is willful. What seems to be connoted by "willful disobedience" is some deliberate design or purpose by the employee to derogate from his duty under the contract. From case law, it appears that disobedience is likely to be characterized as willful if it is accompanied by insolence. Thus, swearing at a manager or employer, or any other open flouting of authority accompanying a refusal to obey an order is likely to amount to willful disobedience. What can an employer reasonably require employees to do? There is no short answer to this query. Manifestly, inasmuch as the contract expressly provides for a circumscribed area of performance by employees, orders requiring an employee to carry out a non-agreed-upon task will not automatically be characterized as willful disobedience. Such a limitation on employer power may be implied from custom or usage. The duties of an employee are much more likely to be specifically spelled out where a collective agreement governs the relationship than where one does not. But, even there, there will be plenty of room for controversy. Examples of the difficulty are cases in which managers ask employees to make coffee, to pick up dry cleaning or the car; or, situations in which the employer, despite the existence of a well-established modus operandi, determines that shifts should be changed, or that different days or hours ought to be worked.

When the parties work on the basis of an individual contract of employment, the likelihood is that, unless there is something clearly to the contrary, the employer will be entitled to treat refusal to obey by employees in all the examples listed above as disobedience of the kind which entitles dismissal without notice. This is so because common-law courts see the right of an employer to manage operations as he deems fit as being of paramount importance. In the absence of an explicit term or a well-established custom to the contrary, the employer is entitled to demand that employees shall work overtime; refusal by employees will amount to actionable disobedience. The only excuse which employees may offer is that they are unable — because of illness, or transport breakdown, or the like — to comply with the order. This truly awesome power of employers to command has been blunted greatly by legislation. Minimum-standards legislation now provides that employees cannot be asked to work more than a certain number of hours per day and per week. Permits may be given to exceed such limits in specific circumstances. The point being made here, though, is that left to themselves, the courts view the right of the employer to demand and the duty of the employee to obey to be the essence of the relationship. Nothing could underscore more heavily what the law perceives the true nature of the contract of employment to be: it sees it as a contract of service.

Duty to Exercise Skill and Care

It was once thought that an employer could dismiss an employee for failure to use appropriate skill and care. This rule has been qualified, not because the underlying philosophy has changed but rather because employers' operations have changed greatly. The basis for the rule was that, by offering to serve, the employee was contractually bound to a certain quality of service. The reasonableness of service was, therefore, to be determined by criteria based on the basis of the employer's needs. Now that the enterprise has become so complex it is seen as unfair to attribute such holding out to an employee: the skill requirements for the job are best understood by the employer, as the employee is not usually in a position to assess the operative needs of the enterprise. The rule has, therefore, become that only if an employee lays claim to special expertise will the employer be entitled to treat lack of reasonable skill and care as a reason for dismissal without notice. It appears that lack of skill will not be a ground for instant dismissal unless it amounts to willful misconduct. This does not, of course, mean that an employer is forced to retain an inefficient employee if willful misconduct cannot be established. An employer can always terminate such a contract by giving appropriate notice.

As a corollary, it is pertinent to point out that, even if the duty of the employee to exercise skill and care is much less onerous than it used to be, it still has legal significance. One aspect is that it has been judicially determined that if an employee makes the employer vicariously liable for the employee's neglect, the employer will be entitled to indemnification from the negligent employee. The doctrine is based on the theory that the employee has breached the duty to exercise reasonable skill and care. In practice, employers seldom seek such indemnity because, as a rule, the employees will be judgment-proof. Further, the industrial relations which would ensue would be far from ideal. But the power is there and it reveals, once again, the true nature of the contractual relationship.

Duty of Good Faith and Fidelity

This duty is imposed on employees on the basis of the interrelationship of two constructs. The first is that the employer is, by assumed definition, in competition with existing and potential like enterprisers. The second is that the employer has reposed a trust in employees which they must respect as part of their contractual obligation. The result is that an employee may not breach that trust in any way which harms the employer's competitive position. The impact this chain of reasoning has on the nature of the contract of employment is quite dramatic. It means that employees cannot argue that what they do in their nonworking time is their own business. The greater the ambit given to phrases like "protection of the employer's competitive position," or "trust," the greater the fetter on freedom of activity of employees.

Employees of employer A who help a rival to set up business while still employed by A and who use their knowledge acquired while working for A to do so will be restrained from such conduct. To complete the remedy, the rival may be restrained from using the knowledge so acquired. Similarly, where employees take away such information as customers' lists and use these to set up a rival business themselves, they may be restrained. In this category of case, the employer will be able to exercise his right arising out of an employee's implied obligation even though the contract is no longer on foot.

To be able to restrict employees (and potential competitors) in this way, the employer has to show that the information, product, or process taken away for use was a trade secret. A trade secret differs from a copyrighted or a patented idea in that anyone who comes by the confidential information other than by revelations by persons forsworn from disclosure is entitled to use it for his own purposes. The essence of a trade secret in this context, then, is that the employer must have made it clear that he did not want information about his products or processes or technology or customer lists to be revealed to anyone. It does not matter that the information is available elsewhere: disclosure by the employee will be a breach of the duty of good faith and fidelity. It may lead to instant dismissal and/or a restraining order plus an accounting for lost profits.

To determine whether or not the disclosure concerned a trade secret worthy of this kind of protection, the court will not only look to see whether the employer clearly (expressly or impliedly) made it known that there should be no disclosure, but also whether the information disclosed was of a kind which gave an advantage to a competitor which otherwise would not have been obtained. Note here that sometimes employers will directly seek to achieve the same result by expressly inserting into the contract of employment a restraint of trade clause. Typically this will prevent an employee from using knowledge acquired during employment for outside use within a given time and space. Such terms will be enforced by the courts if they are deemed reasonable. On the whole, the question of reasonableness is tackled in much the same way as is the issue of the protection of trade secrets when giving life to the employee's duty of good faith and fidelity. That is, the right of the employer to be protected in his competitive position is to be balanced against the right of the employee to become a competitor and the public's right in fostering competition generally.

This focuses attention on two remaining consequences of the employee's implied duty of good faith and fidelity. First, an employee cannot help but learn during the employment period. A blanket prohibition on the right of such an employee to use such acquired knowledge and skill in the pursuit of self-interest on the basis that it would breach the duty of good faith and fidelity to the former employer would be antithetic to free-enterprise notions. Thus, where the knowledge to be used is not a trade secret, the courts will not restrain the use of that knowledge at the behest of the former employer. Drawing a line between naturally acquired knowledge and trade secrets is extremely difficult.

Second, it has been implicit in this discussion of the employee's duty of good faith and fidelity that the product of an employee's efforts is to be seen as the rightful property of the employer. A vexing question arises when the employee invents something of use to the employer: to whom does the invention belong? Once again, a balance has to be struck between encouraging the enterprising efforts involved in inventing and the protection of the competitive position of the employer. The latter's interest must be weighed, because either he has inserted a specific clause in the contract of employment which guarantees him the benefit of any inventions made by employees, or it is perceived that the duty of good faith and fidelity permits him to claim that employees must yield the product of their labour to him. In the former case, the employer will be given the benefit for which he has contracted. In the latter, facts such as when and where the invention was made, whose materials were used, the level of employment of the particular employee in relation to the invention are all pertinent to the adjudication. The starting position seems to be that the employee holds the benefit of an invention on trust for the employer unless the surrounding facts indicate that a contrary finding should be made. Again, the servile nature of the contract-of-employment relationship as perceived by the law is revealed.

Termination of Employment

A contract of employment, like any other contract, can be terminated because performance under it is complete or because the specified time of duration has expired. The former situation hardly ever exists in the employment area and the latter, although more common, is also exceptional. Other than that, the contract itself may stipulate how it is to be ended and, where it does not, the parties may end it by giving each other appropriate notice or by the rightful treatment by one party of the other's breach as a fundamental one. These two bases for termination require further consideration, but first some other less important modes of termination need to be mentioned.

Like all contracts, contracts of employment will terminate if they are frustrated. This merely means that performance of the contract becomes impossible because of a supervening event outside the control of the party seeking to rely on the frustration argument to avoid obligations under the contract. Examples of such uncontrollable events would be the accidental burning down of a plant, the long illness of an employee whose personal contribution was essential to the enterprise (for instance, an actor's), and so on. When a contract is frustrated it ends at the time of the frustrating event, leaving the parties in whatever position they are, without further recourse.

Contracts of employment, being contracts of personal service, will be terminated by the death of either of the parties (where they are human beings). Rights which had vested at the time of death, for example, the wages of a deceased employee, are not extinguished by the death. Similarly, employees in a partnership can claim that the employment has terminated when one of the partners leaves the partnership if it can be shown that the personal relationship between that partner and the employees was an important ingredient of the contract. Where the partnership is altered by a replacement of one person for another, employees might be in a position to treat the contract as terminated. Normally, employees just continue to work in such circumstances, and the employment contract will be deemed to continue as if it had been renewed with the new partnership on the same terms as had originally been agreed upon. Minimum-standards legislation prescribes that where there is a sale (which usually includes a lease, a transfer, or any other manner of disposition) of a business (which usually includes an activity, trade, undertaking, or any part thereof), the employment shall not be deemed to be terminated and the duties that the vendor owed to his former employees shall now be owed to them by the purchaser.

The most common means of termination of a contract of employment is by the giving of notice. Where there is no provision in the contract, and it is characterized as one of indefinite duration — the most common circumstance — the courts will imply a period, labeled "reasonable notice," which must be given by either party to terminate the contract. The parties have the right to pay a sum of money, calculated on the basis of the wage rate multiplied by the notice period, rather than continue to work together for that specified time. As a matter of practice, the question of whether or not reasonable notice has been given usually arises when an employee complains of dismissal without just cause and with inadequate notice.

As one would expect, the assessment of what a reasonable notice period is, is fraught with difficulty. No rule can be enunciated. The custom in the industry in the relevant geographic area may determine the amount of notice. In the absence of a clearly established custom, courts may look to the periodicity of payment. It is not unusual for courts to hold that where an employee gets paid on a weekly, biweekly or monthly basis, one week, two weeks or a month's notice is to be given. But this is no more than a crude rule of thumb. The courts will also take into account "the capacity in which the employee is engaged, the general standing in the community of the class of persons, having regard to their profession to which the employee belongs, the probable facility or difficulty the employee would have in procuring other employment in case of dismissal, having regard to the demand for persons of that profession, and the general character of the services which the engagement contemplate." [*Speakman v. City of Calgary* (1908) 1 A.L.R. 454]. This kind of test makes it very difficult to forecast how much notice should be given in all cases where the employee is not seen as menial or low-skilled, the assumption in these cases being that little notice is required, usually no more than the periodicity of payment indicates or minimum-standard legislation prescribes.

There is legislation in all jurisdictions which provides that a minimum period of notice must be given to employees. In the majority of cases, the protection is only provided to employees who have been continuously employed for at least three months. The periods of notice to be given vary. Thus, in some jurisdictions (Alberta, Nova Scotia, Ontario), it is tied to length of service, in others one flat period is provided for regardless of length of service (Canada, Prince Edward Island, Saskatchewan). In Nova Scotia, no one who has been continuously employed for ten years can be terminated by giving notice. Where an express term, a custom, or an implied term give a right greater than the statute, the longer period of notice may be claimed.

The statutory minimum notice does not usually have to be given where there has been a temporary layoff. This is not treated as a termination of the contract of employment under these statutes. They provide definitions of temporary layoffs by reference to time of layoff and the continued assumption by the employer of some of the obligations of the contract such as, for example, pension plan contributions, supplementary unemployment benefit payments, and so on. Where the layoff is to be permanent, however, that is, a termination of the contract, notice which at least complies with the statutory minimum must be given. Further, if the layoff is a group termination, the minimum period of notice which must be given is increased. For instance, if an employer intends to lay off more than 50 persons in a four-week period, the employer is to notify the appropriate ministry so that manpower decisions can be made and coordinated. The employees must be given at least four weeks' notice or pay in lieu of notice. The periods of notice increase with the number of persons to be laid off; for instance, under the federal statute, if more than 300 people are to be laid off as a group, they must receive sixteen weeks' notice or pay in lieu thereof.

The final means of terminating a contract of employment is dismissal of employees for cause. The discussion of the legally implied duties imposed on employees revolved around this issue: the cases arose because an employer, seeking to justify his peremptory dismissal of an employee, would claim that the employee had breached an implied duty. The legal reasoning is that such a breach by the employee undermines the essence of the contract of employment, entitling the employer to terminate it without giving notice or pay in lieu thereof.

Failure by an employee to obey a reasonable order by the employer will, if it is willful as defined earlier, permit dismissal without notice. In general, if the employee's conduct can be said to be a willful repudiation of obligations to abide by the essential elements of the contract, it will be treated as willful misconduct giving occasion for termination for cause. Thus, as well as willful disobedience, repeated insolence, drunkenness (at the work place), or morally improper behaviour (for example, sexually harassing fellow employees), may amount to willful misconduct. Criminal activity may also be so characterized. If the criminal offence occurs at the place of work, it will nearly always justify dismissal for cause, that is, without notice. Where the criminal activity occurs elsewhere and outside the hours of work, the crucial question will be how the employee's conduct relates to work duties and to the business position of the employer. (For instance: Is the employer's good will likely to be adversely affected? Is the productivity of other employees likely to be diminished?) Much will thus depend on the peculiar facts of a case. The employer loses the right to treat the conduct of an employee as just cause if he knowingly accepts or condones that breach. On the other hand, the employer may, when defending a termination for cause, rely on a breach of an employee's duty of which he was not aware at the time of dismissal.

REMEDIES FOR BREACH OF CONTRACT

Employer Remedies

The foremost remedy of an employer in respect of a breach of contract by his employee is summary dismissal. The employer cannot, in the absence of an express or implied term to the contrary, suspend an employee for a willful repudiation of the contract by the employee. This is the corollary of the judicially evolved rule that, while there is no duty on the employer to provide work, he must either terminate the contract or continue to pay the employee; he cannot fail to provide work and refuse to pay, that is, suspend the contract for a while. This sharply differentiates the remedial tools available to an employer governed by individual-contract-of-employment law from those provided for by the collective-bargaining regimes. Under the federal labour statute, the technique developed under collective-bargaining regimes to review an employer's exercise of his purported right to dismiss summarily has been made applicable to the individual-contract-of-employment situations which fall under federal jurisdiction. Employees so governed who have been employed by one employer for twelve months, may complain of summary dismissal to an inspector appointed under the act to investigate and to mediate. If the problem is not resolved, the employee may ask an adjudicator to make a determination in the same way as a grievance arbitrator appointed pursuant to a collective agreement would.

As with breaches in all contractual relationships, the injured party may seek financial compensation for losses. An employer can sue an employee for breach, in addition to or instead of exercising his right to dismiss summarily. Typically this may be done where the employee has damaged the employer's property as a result of the breach. However, an employer cannot deduct such a loss from the wages owing to the employee; a separate claim must be made. An employer may also sue for failure to give appropriate notice where this amounts to a sizeable period and, therefore, a sizeable amount. In some cases, the difficulty of replacing a particular employee (who left in breach) because of his special skill or knowledge may give rise to an action for damages. This will be rare and, even where the situation arises, seldom worth the employer's effort. This is so because, like all other claimants in contract damage cases, the employer's right to compensation will be diminished in amount by the obligation to mitigate his losses. That is, the employer will have had to take all reasonable steps to replace his lost employee to minimize the losses due to the termination of the contract. Finally, sometimes an employer seeks to insert into the contract a term to the effect that, in case of breach by employees, a certain sum shall be payable to the employer. Where the amount specified is subsequently seen as merely an agreed-upon estimate of the loss that would be occasioned by a breach, the courts may enforce such a term. They will not do so, however, where they see the term as one which was intended to deter a breach; they will see this as a penalty clause and refuse to uphold it as a basis for the employer's claim for contractual damages.

Whereas the contract of employment is ruled by universal contract rules in respect of damage claims arising out of breach, it is treated differently in relation to another standard contractual remedy: specific performance. Because a contract of employment is one of personal service, its very nature demands that the parties should not be forced to work with one another. Thus, an employer cannot force an employee to comply with even his reasonable wishes: he may dismiss or sue the employee, but if the employee refuses to cooperate the law will not compel abiding by the contractually agreed-upon terms. By way of symmetry, the employer who summarily dismisses an employee will not, if it is subsequently shown that he did not have cause to terminate the contract, be forced to rehire the employee; the obligation can be satisfied by the payment of damages. This provides a sharp contrast with the collective-bargaining situation in which both labour-relations boards and grievance-arbitration boards have the power to reinstate employees they adjudge to have been wrongfully dismissed. That is, there will be specific performance of the employment relationship.

There are situations which arise under the common law controlling individual contracts of employment which seem to lead to something like specific performance. Where a contract explicitly provides that an employee undertakes to render services exclusively for the employer, this clause will not be upheld by the grant of an injunction sought by the employer to prevent an employee from leaving his service. But where a similar result is sought by seeking an injunction to prevent breach of a contractual stipulation to the effect that the employee will not, during the term of the contract, render any of the services to be rendered for the employer for any other person, the courts may grant the order restraining an employee from accepting other employment. The distinction made in the cases is between enforcing a positive covenant, that is, one requiring performance of the existing contract, and enforcing a negative covenant, that is, requiring the employee not to work in a particular way. The latter is acceptable because it may well leave the employee free not to perform the contract he wants to abandon. This assumes that the enforcement of the negative covenant will not, in fact, amount to the enforcement of the existing contract. To require the courts to make distinctions of this kind is to present them with un-enviable tasks. To illustrate: The famous actress, Bette Davis, had entered into a contract which both required her to render her acting services exclusively to Warner Bros. and forbade her to accept acting work with any other person during the term of the contract. An injunction to force her to render services for the employer was refused; an injunction forbidding her to accept work as an actress with any other person for the remainder of the contract was granted. This was justified on the basis that the actress was a person of intelligence, capacity, and means and that there was no evidence that, were she to refuse to fulfil her contract with Warner Bros., she would not be able to employ herself both usefully and remuneratively in other spheres of activity. That is, she was not effectively being forced to carry out the contract of employment.

Employee Remedies

Where an employee has been dismissed and such termination was wrongful because there was no justifying cause for summary dismissal, or because appropriate notice was not given, the employee may recover, by way of damages, the amount of pay in lieu of notice that should have been received, less any amount that the employee could have earned by accepting reasonably available alternate employment. An employee may seek to recover by bringing a complaint under the minimum-standards legislation where the notice to be given will not exceed the minimum. This is cost free. In some jurisdictions, it is also possible to bring an action for damages in courts of very low jurisdiction and, therefore, with a low cost structure, where the amounts claimed will not exceed small, specified sums. In those jurisdictions, there are modern replicas of the truly ancient (1349) English *Master and Servant Act* which not only made it a crime for servants to leave their service but also imposed criminal sanctions on masters if they did not provide guaranteed conditions. The modern equivalents have translated this into an employer obligation to pay wages due. This permits actions for damages or arrears of wages up to a certain amount.

Although punitive damages will not be awarded to employees who can show that not only were they wrongfully dismissed but that they also suffered a loss of dignity, there is some recent case law which permits the damage assessment to take into account the fact that the employee had become so depressed by the employer's treatment as to become ill. So far this development has been restricted to employees of an executive, professional nature, suggesting that the aggravated-damages award is a recognition that such employees are not employed just on the basis that they will be remunerated, but that it is also a condition of their employment that prestige and pleasure are tangible benefits which they have a right to expect.

Bankruptcy and the winding up of a company may also amount to a breach of contract. An employee may sue for damages in the usual way. Often there will be an arrears in payment of wages in the case of a bankruptcy. The employee may then seek to recover as a creditor. This does not place the employee in a sound position. Under the *Bankruptcy Act,* the employees are not secured creditors, and thus they collect after secured creditors have exercised their rights. Amongst nonsecured creditors, they rank fourth in order of priority of creditors. In addition, the statute does not protect employees in as many words, but rather clerks, servants, traveling salesmen, labourers or workmen, giving rise to interpretative difficulties. Similarly, employees are creditors in respect of wages, salaries, commission or compensation, and questions, such as whether severance pay due under a minimum-standards statute falls under this rubric, may arise. Such questions are complicated by the fact that the minimum-standards legislation is provincial, and the bankruptcy legislation is federal: issues as to whether the definition of wages in the former are applicable in the latter may arise.

Protection is sometimes afforded to employees by making directors of corporations personally responsible for wages and vacation pay accrued. This has required legislative interference with the notion that the corporate entity is a person separate from its members.

COLLECTIVE BARGAINING — A COMPARISON

This chapter is primarily concerned with setting out basic rules relating to the law of the individual contract of employment. Collective-bargaining legislation and practices are examined elsewhere in this anthology. The attempt to compare the two legal regimes which follows is necessarily flawed by its brevity. But, it is hoped that it may serve a purpose. The development of the construct now referred to as the contract of employment was a direct response by the common law to the recognition of the establishment of new economic relationships, namely, modern capitalism. Inasmuch as these economic relationships have not altered fundamentally, it ought to follow that legal regimes concerned with employment relationships have not changed basically; adaptation should merely reflect modifications of the economic relationships. This would prevail even more so because the legal system does not like abrupt deviations from past practices and norms.

The essence of the individual contract of employment as developed by the law has been seen to be a relationship of service. This accords with the notion that an entrepreneur in a competitive society should be free to invest and to dispose of his capital as he sees fit and be subjected to as little external noneconomic restraint as is consonant with social needs. The upshot of legal acquiescence with this approach is the imposition of onerous duties on the employee as compared with those which burden the employer. The only real exception is that an employer has a nondelegable duty to provide a safe work environment and even this duty, as was seen, has had to be complemented by positive enactments to better protect the rather hapless employees.

Redress of the imbalance of bargaining power was sought by the workers, over the opposition of the courts. Gradually, the pressure for concerted activity by employees came to be recognized as being irresistible; it was legitimized, resulting in the sophisticated legislative collective-bargaining schemes in existence today. It is natural, therefore, for these schemes to be hailed as evidence of true progress, in the sense that a countervailing force to overly strong enterprisers has been positively fostered by the legal system. But this has led to too great a claim being made for collective bargaining: it is frequently assumed that the bad old days of master-and-servant law have gone; that the law which permitted, even promoted, the exercise of dominance by an employer over an employee, to an extent which robbed the latter of dignity, has been left behind. The individual-contract-of-employment regime is perceived as belonging to an inferior stage, as being conceptually totally different. This is even reflected in judicial pronouncements which are normally very careful to avoid overt references to political claims. Thus, a majority of the Supreme Court of Canada has asserted that once parties are governed by a collective agreement entered into under the appropriate labour statute, the contractual relationship of employment and its common-law incidents have no legal significance whatsoever, except for the purposes of hiring and termination [*McGavin Toastmaster Ltd. v. Ainscough* (1975), 54 D.L.R. 3rd]. What follows are several briefly elaborated arguments to show that this line of reasoning may really obscure our view of the state of labour relations.

First, it is to be noted that even under collective-bargaining regimes all the initial decisions remain an employer's to make. Thus, how much to invest, where to do so, what products shall be made, what amount, what quality, what processes are to be used, what substances are to be employed, and so on, are all decisions left to the employer. This was, of course, the true source of the power of the employer vis-à-vis the employee when the contract of employment was the basic legal construct cementing the relationship: the initial imbalance in economic power coloured the nature of the agreement struck. That is why individual-contract-of-employment law is seen as a reflection of an unacceptable state of affairs. While trade unions are in a better position to overcome these barriers to equality of economic power because of their new collective-bargaining rights, it is notable that they very seldom directly limit the scope of employers in their investment and deployment of capital decision-making power. That is, the unions' right to bargain about such matters is, as it was for individuals under common-law contract, largely theoretical. To underscore this by a topical illustration, note that employers seem to be all too free to close down their enterprises and take their capital elsewhere; unions could, like individuals under the common law, put terms into the agreement preventing such closures or, at least, make them very costly for employers. Typically they do not do so and are seemingly, like individuals under common-law contract law, incapable of doing so: they are seeking legislative assistance. Their impotence stems from the continuance of the imbalance in power arising out of the reality of economic relationships. The mere existence of collective-bargaining legislation has not altered this. The enhancement of the individual worker's power is not immediately apparent. The claim that there has been such enhancement may well be an overstatement.

Second, inasmuch as the argument is that the contract-of-employment doctrines display an assumption that a superior-inferior relationship is to be accepted, and that collective-bargaining regimes do not share this assumption, it also is of dubious merit. This characterization of the common-law contract is justified on the basis that employers could (and can) treat their employees as servants, as commodities, as a matter of law. This is how the right of an employer to summarily dismiss employees for breach of one of the legally imposed duties is rightly perceived. But note that, as a matter of fact, each of the grounds for which an employee could be discharged at common law, has been held to have been just cause for discipline by an employer of an employee under the collective-bargaining regimes. Thus, willful disobedience is such a ground; so are repeated instances of insolence, drunkenness (at the work place or away from it), immoral behaviour, or criminal activity (at the work place or away from it). As well, the employer can discipline an employee for not exercising good faith and fidelity.

There is, of course, a great difference in result. Arbitration boards, unlike common-law courts, have been given an arsenal of remedies. Not all breaches of these employee obligations will lead to dismissal; such actions as suspensions, reprimands, loss of seniority, warnings, and compelled apologies, may all be substituted for the employer's attempt at discharge. This suggests a serious limitation on the right of the employer to exercise his economic power at will with the support of legal rules. Certainly, it is often asserted that these developments have really contributed to employee dignity and security. Yet, the argument is not all that persuasive. One of the advantages the employer gets out of this system is that an arsenal of calibrated punishments has been made available to facilitate whipping the work force into shape. At common law, the employer's main weapon was the ease with which recalcitrant and unproductive workers could be replaced. This tool was not always freely available and, in a period of union militancy and economic conditions favourable to employees, self-assertion by employees was hard to resist. Under collective-bargaining regimes, it is assumed that an employer has a right to a productive, conforming work force, whatever the economic realities. Arbitration boards will help rehabilitate delinquent employees, and aid in correcting aberrant behaviour.

Yet, the creation of the possibility of reinstatement which did not exist at common law can be seen as an advance for the workers' cause, even if offset somewhat by the arguments just made and by the fact that workers have given up a large proportion of their right to strike. Be that as it may, what is important for the purposes of the assessment being made here is that the presumptions underlying the arbitral jurisprudence about the extent of the employer's managerial power are unchanged from those developed by common-law judges. If the legitimation of concerted action by employees had in fact been due to an abandonment of common-law contract notions with its acceptance of unequal distribution of powers, one might have expected that collective-agreement law would have developed on the basis that the share of power was to be redefined by the new countervailing powers, that nothing was to be assumed to be a given. Indeed, as has been seen, the Supreme Court of Canada has indicated that this ought to be the basis of collective-bargaining jurisprudence. Yet, where the parties have failed to include express terms to the contrary, the assumptions about the contents of employer power or, in the language of collective agreements, prerogative of management, turn out to be the same as they were at common law. This is surely not coincidental; the claim that the employee is no longer a servant vis-à-vis a master, but a true contracting party with control over his own destiny, seems somewhat overblown.

To underscore this point with two further illustrations, note that, just as at common law, under collective bargaining the employer's right to demand that a worker spend all his time working for the employer is only limited by express terms, a custom or statutory law. Arbitrators under collective agreements have consistently held that overtime is compulsory. Clauses which set out the ordinary hours of work are not seen as setting out maximum hours, but merely as the basis for the calculation of overtime rates. Similarly, arbitrators, in the absence of anything to the contrary in the collective agreement, always assume that the prerogative of management gives the employer the right to unilaterally reduce the hours of work to be made available to employees, even though there is a clause setting out the ordinary hours of work. This is all the more remarkable for, as has been seen, at common law the employer cannot reduce the hours of work and not pay employees their normal remuneration unless there is an express term or custom to the contrary. The list of similarities in treatment of the reserved power of employers by the two supposedly totally differently oriented regimes is endless.

Third, an argument is made that employees governed by collective bargaining obtain much better conditions than do employees outside that industrial-relations sector. Lack of space and expertise prevent a serious critique of this claim. It suffices, however, to point out that economic studies are far from sanguine that the conditions which prevail in much of the collective-bargaining sector are due to the fact of concerted activity as opposed to other economic factors, such as the concentration of the industry, its geographical location, or dispersion. Certainly, it is manifest that collective bargaining primarily takes place in those sectors of the economy which seem more concentrated than others or in the public sector. In any event, it would seem imprudent to claim that the quantitative improvements in working conditions due to collective bargaining have been such that they have made a qualitative difference to the relationship, that is, that servants-employees have become employees-contractual partners.

SUMMATION

Legal rules governing the employment relationship do not, in themselves, tell much about the contents or daily practices of the relationship. But legal rules are expressions (albeit sometimes attenuated) of political will. As such they provide a means to evaluate how society perceives what relationships ought to be. In this light, an appreciation of the rules relating to what many now consider the dated common-law rules relating to employment may shed some light on the true nature of the widely hailed phenomenon of collective bargaining. It may be a way to get at the essence of the whole of our industrial-relations system; it may be a prism through which a valuable perspective, which otherwise might remain obscured, can be gained.

QUESTIONS

1. (a) A painter is hired to paint a chain of stores owned by a franchisor. The painter supplies his own transport, does his tasks without supervision of any kind, choosing his own working hours. He injures a customer of one of the stores by his negligence. The franchisor is sought to be made liable for the painter's negligence on the basis that the painter was its employee. Discuss the issues likely to arise.
    (b) The above franchisor's franchisees have found that, after working seven days a week, twelve hours a day, they have been making less than the minimum wage. Their earnings are tied to profits; they have a good deal of discretion in

the day-to-day running of the store. But they are selected by the franchisor who has a right to terminate their engagement by giving notice; the franchisor can insist that certain kinds and amount of inventory shall be taken by the franchisees. Do our franchisees have a right of action under the minimum-wage statute?

2. What is the difference between an independent contractor and an employee? When is the difference important?

3. "The common law's rejection of specific performance as a remedy means that employees not covered by a collective agreement are at the mercy of the whim of their employers: they can be dismissed at will." Discuss.

4. "The concept of equal pay for work of equal value imposes impossible difficulties on the market place. Who is to determine when work is of equal value? It ought to be left to the market. This legislative concept must be defeated. Fairness has no place in our economic system." Discuss.

5. "There is no such thing as an absolutely safe environment. The parties should be left to themselves. The recent development of the mandated joint committee system is, therefore, to be welcomed; the governmental standard setting is not." Discuss.

6. "Chinese restaurant owners should be able to hire only Chinese waiters and waitresses, and women's hairdressing establishments should be able to hire female employees only, without bearing the burden of being termed discriminators." Discuss this in light of the human-rights legislation in your jurisdiction.

7. Do individuals participate more in regulating their working conditions when they contract by themselves or when they are covered by a collective agreement?

8. (a) "Unemployment insurance benefits are calculated to make people work shy." Discuss.

   (b) If unemployment insurance benefits are not payable to workers on strike, should depreciation allowances be given to employers who are struck?

9. If an employee sets up a business in his own time which is similar to that of his employer and which operates in a nearby geographic area, does the employer have potential remedies against his employee? What are they?

NOAH M. MELTZ

4. The Canadian Labour Market

The labour market provides a context and can set limits within which union-management relations operate. The age structure of the labour force, the occupations and industries in which the demand for labour is changing, the levels of unemployment, overall and within particular sectors, all influence the attitudes and strategies of the parties to collective bargaining.

In addition, society's willingness to invest in education and training as well as to institute legislation governing labour market relations, such as minimum wages, maximum hours, occupational licensing and unemployment insurance, all affect the eventual outcome of employment, earnings, and unemployment.

INTRODUCTION

The labour market is a crucial element in union-management relations. In the industrial-relations system, it is an important input that sets limits within which the various actors — labour, management, and the government — operate. In some circumstances, the labour market influence may be so pervasive that in fact it dictates the final outcomes, leaving the actors with little, if any, room to manoeuvre.

Union-management relations are affected by various aspects of the labour market including the age and sex structure of the labour force; its occupational and industrial composition and the extent to which it is trained and educated; the extent of unemployment; and barriers to entry or movement among labour markets. Government legislation also affects the functioning of markets both in terms of entry requirements (and possible barriers) and the setting of standards for such things as minimum wages and maximum hours.

This chapter explores the various aspects of the labour market which affect union-management relations (22). First, the concept of the labour market is examined in terms of its various dimensions and how it functions. Second, the outcomes of the labour market are examined with particular emphasis on its malfunctioning and its implications for industrial relations. Third, key aspects of labour market developments are discussed, including such topics as labour force structure, earnings, unemployment, and government legislation. Finally, reference is made to some peculiarities of the Canadian labour market. The chapter concludes with the implications for policy and research needs.

78

THE CONCEPT OF THE LABOUR MARKET

The labour market is the mechanism by which the demand for and the supply of labour are brought together to determine employment, wage and salary rates and, as a residual, unemployment. Each of these factors, in turn, has a variety of components or dimensions. The determinants of the various components of labour supply and demand are discussed more extensively in both Gunderson (19) and Ostry and Zaidi (30). The discussion in this section provides an overview of that material, emphasizing its relationship to union-management relations.

Labour Supply

Labour supply has both quality and quantity dimensions. The quality dimensions refer to such factors as motivation and alienation (subjects within the purview of personnel and organization behaviour) as well as education and training (subjects which have been analysed in the context of manpower economics and human-capital theory).

The quantity dimensions of labour supply are numerous, basically involving the size of our population (births less deaths plus net immigration), the extent to which it participates in labour market activities, and the hours the population worked, for those who participate in the labour market. The economic determinants of these various components— births, net immigration, labour force participation, and hours of work — have been the subject matter of considerable research on the supply side of labour markets.

Economic analysis has focused, for example, on the importance of the high opportunity cost of having children for women whose potential labour market earnings are high and hence who would forgo substantial earnings and perhaps a career in raising a family. Other things equal, such women tend to have fewer children, and they tend to have them closer together in time so as to minimize the disruption to their labour market activities. These changing birth patterns can have obvious future implications for the size and age structure of the labour force, which in turn can affect such industrial-relations phenomena as union growth, skill shortages, youth employment, and internal union trade-offs between pensions and wages.

The decision to participate in labour force activities, as opposed to household work, schooling, or retirement, has also been the subject of considerable research. The underlying theoretical framework is the "work-leisure model" which treats the purchase of "leisure" (a catchall for nonlabour market activities) the same as the purchase of any other commodity. Therefore, as nonlabour income or wealth increases, we buy more of everything including leisure; and as the price of leisure (the wage rate or opportunity cost of leisure) increases, we buy less leisure and engage in more labour market activities. Thus the increased labour force participation of married women is attributed, in part, to their increased expected wage and hence high (opportunity) cost of not working in the labour market. More recently, the effect of inflation eroding the real wealth of families may also compel more married women to work out of economic necessity. The trend towards the early retirement of males is also attributed in part to the increase in family wealth over time.

The same work-leisure choice model is used by economists to predict changes in hours of work for those who participate in labour market activities. The long-run decline in hours of work is attributed by economists to our increased demand for leisure time associated with rising income: this demand is manifest through trade unions and legislature pressures for reduced hours of work. Increasingly, this reduction is taken in the form of longer vacations and a shorter work-week rather than reduced hours-per-day, in part because fixed costs of commuting make the reductions in hours-per-day less economical than a reduced work-week or a longer vacation.

The work incentive or labour supply effects of various income maintenance programs has also been analysed through the work-leisure model. In most circumstances, income maintenance programs have the direct effect of reducing the incentive to work both because they provide income and hence reduce the need to work, and also because they often tax labour market earnings, usually implicitly by requiring the recipient to forgo all or some of the transfer payment upon working. This is the case, for example, with respect to welfare and unemployment insurance, the latter of which will be analysed in more detail in a subsequent section.

Labour Demand

While many of the quantity dimensions of labour supply are analysed through the work-leisure choice model, labour demand on the part of firms is analysed as a derived demand, derived from the demand for the firm's output. Faced with a wage increase, other things equal, firms will reduce their labour demand mainly because, in the long run, they substitute other factors of production for the more expensive labour. This reduction in employment associated with the wage increase (perhaps caused by unions or minimum-wage increases) will be large if the firm can easily substitute other factors of production for labour; if it cannot pass the cost increase on to consumers without reducing demand for the product and hence the derived demand for labour; or if labour costs are a substantial portion of total costs so that the firm cannot absorb the wage-cost increase.

Interaction of Supply and Demand in Various Market Structures

The interaction of the supply of and demand for labour occurs in a variety of market structures, each of which can have an important impact on the wage and employment outcomes. Because the demand for labour is a derived demand, derived from the demand for the firm's output, then the product market structure faced by the firm can influence its labour market decisions. Firms that are monopolists in the product market, for example, will restrict their output to maintain an artificially high price for their product: this in turn causes them to reduce their derived demand for labour. As long as they are competitive buyers of labour they would have to pay the going wage rate; nevertheless, they would employ less labour as monopolists as opposed to if they behaved competitively. Similarly, oligopolistic firms (small number in the product market) may be very sensitive to the pricing decision of their fellow oligopolistic firms. In such circumstances, they may try to absorb a considerable range of wage increases without changing product prices, because of uncertainty as to how their fellow oligopolistic firms will respond to price changes.

Not only does the way the firm behaves in the product market have implications for its derived demand for labour and hence its wage and employment decision, but so does the way it behaves in the labour market itself. Firms that are competitive buyers of labour (no matter what their product market situation) would have to pay the going wage rate; however, some firms (termed monopsonists) may dominate the local labour market for particular skills, in which case they are wage setters not wage takers.

Clearly the structure of the product market and the labour market in which the firm operates can influence its wage and employment decisions and provide various ranges within which the industrial-relations actors must operate. The issue is compounded when one considers the large public sector (for example, government, health, education) where the economic constraints are replaced by, or at least supplemented with, political constraints.

The possible existence of dual or segmented labour markets also complicates the wage and employment determination process. According to dual labour market analysis (discussed in more detail in chapter 21) the labour market is segmented into noncompeting groups. The primary or core labour market generally consists of high-paying jobs with good working conditions, reasonable job security, and opportunities for training and advancement. The secondary or peripheral labour market consists of jobs with the opposite characteristics. In part because of these poor working conditions, workers in the secondary labour market exhibit high absenteeism and turnover and lack the motivation for self improvement: this, in turn, reduces these workers' chances of leaving the secondary labour market. For this reason, and because of discrimination, custom and tradition, the secondary and primary labour markets remain segmented from each other, with little chance for workers to advance from the secondary to the primary labour market.

Matching of Supply and Demand

The actual bringing together of labour demand and labour supply occurs through a variety of mechanisms which often differ by occupation. With respect to the job-search procedure of workers, the single most important means of finding a job is by checking with employers in the area, followed by checking with friends or relatives. Other methods, in order of importance, are checking with trade unions; placing or answering advertisements in local papers; contacting Canada Employment Centres, checking with employers outside the area, and contacting private employment agencies (21, p. 53). The role of union hiring halls, primarily found in construction, has been subject to some question as they can be a means of discriminating among workers as well as penalizing employers who have not cooperated with the union (3).

Employers can also affect the job-matching process through their recruiting, promotion, and training procedures as well as through changes in their wage structure or the redesigning of the job. For example, a firm may try to reduce a persistent shortage of a particular skill by any combination of recruiting, promotion, training, raising the wage premium for that job or redesigning the job so that its component parts could be done by others or by capital equipment.

IMPLICATIONS OF THE FUNCTIONING AND MALFUNCTIONING OF LABOUR MARKETS

The numerous dimensions of labour supply and demand interact in alternative market structures to determine wage and employment outcomes. They also influence other outcomes, such as unemployment and artificially low wages, that are regarded as signs of malfunctioning of markets.

According to economic theory, wage rates, along with other considerations which are combined in the phrase "net advantages," play a central role in allocating labour among different potential employers. It is assumed that workers are rational and in attempting to maximize their own satisfaction they move to the highest paying employer, all other things being equal. If all other things are not equal then adjustments will take place through wages or non-wage considerations which, together with wages, make up the net advantages: benefits, opportunities for career advancement, quality of the work environment, location, congeniality of work associates, and so on (35).

In addition, however, there are costs of moving and a variety of considerations involved in the decision to change one's employer or to search for a job. In spite of these factors, research has shown that the tendency is for individuals to respond to differences in net advantages, including wages, as theory would predict (35, 25). According to microeconomic theory, in the absence of collective bargaining, an increase in wage rates is a signal that there is insufficient supply. The introduction of collective bargaining or other "interferences" such as minimum wages can complicate the signals which emanate from the market.

A smoothly functioning market would be one in which there are no actual barriers to entry or exit and both job seekers and employers know the current and likely future situation. Even in such a smoothly functioning market, however, there could still be some unemployment but it would only arise from changes in the demand for labour (cyclical unemployment) or from the movement of workers into and out of the labour market (frictional unemployment). The latter would arise from the entry of young workers, the reentry of persons who had been absent from the market, retirement, death, or disability of persons previously in the market.

A malfunctioning market can result from a number of factors. Artificial barriers to entry, created by such factors as occupational licensing, discrimination, or unnecessary age, education, training or residence requirements, tend to reduce the supply of labour and increase the wage rate. Individuals who obtain employment after the introduction of such barriers are clearly the beneficiaries of higher wages and perhaps more secure employment. Persons excluded from the protected market may end up being penalized by being forced to engage in even greater competition for a job in nonprotected markets (32).

As discussed in more detail in Chapter 11, there are differences in views among researchers about the impact of unions. One study estimated that unions have raised wages in Ontario by between 10 and 17 percent (39). There is less agreement, however, on the employment impact of unions. Some suggest that the impact has been detrimental to employment (42), while others argue that unions have shocked management into improving efficiency thereby having a positive net effect on balance (15).

The likely impact of unions or any type of professional association depends ultimately on the nature of the labour market under consideration. If there are few alternative ways to enter an occupation, then the union or association can have a major impact, in the short run, on wage rates and employment levels. On the other hand, if there are a number of ways of entering the occupation, in terms of acquiring the requisite skills or gaining access to employment, then the union's impact will be much smaller.

KEY LABOUR MARKET DIMENSIONS AFFECTING UNION-MANAGEMENT RELATIONS

Labour market developments have important implications for union-management relations. The more important of these dimensions include: the age and sex structure of the labour force; the occupational, industrial, and geographic structure of the labour force; earnings differentials; unemployment rates; education, training and immigration; and legislation. Each of these will be examined in turn.

The Age and Sex Structure of the Labour Force

The age and sex structure of the labour force can affect union-management relations in a number of ways. Prime-age workers (those for example, twenty-five to fifty-four years of age) tend to be most stable in their attachment to the labour force. This is particularly true for males and increasingly so for females. In the past, women tended to remain in the labour force only until they were married. Increasingly, women are returning to the labour force after childbearing, and their attachment is moving upward toward that of men while male labour force participation has actually declined somewhat in the past several decades. For example, female labour force participation rates (proportion of females actually working or seeking employment) increased from 16 to 40 percent between 1901 and 1971 while the male participation rate declined from 88 to 76 percent during the same period.

Youth (persons under twenty-five) tend to change jobs much more frequently than persons in other age groups. As a result they are less likely to be interested in unions or collective bargaining than other persons who feel they have a longer-run interest in the results of collective bargaining. Several decades ago, this lack of interest in union affairs also tended to characterize women, but this attitude has changed significantly as a result of their more permanent attachment to the labour force.

As individuals near retirement, their preferences within collective bargaining shift towards pension and related benefits, and away from a concentration on the size of the wage package. There clearly can be sharp differences within a bargaining unit between younger workers with families to support, who are interested in the amount of take-home pay, and older workers who are prepared to accept a reduced take-home pay in favour of putting more money into a pension plan. Workers of different ages and family responsibilities may also place different emphasis on such factors as health and safety, medical benefits, and seniority.

While the age structure of the labour force has been getting younger as a result of the post-World War II baby boom, this will tend to change as a gradual aging occurs in the 1980s (30, p. 14). This, in turn, will affect the mix of workers' demands at the bargaining table.

Changes in the Occupational, Industrial, and Regional Structure of the Labour Force

Occupations and industries experience differences in the cyclical and seasonal nature of employment and hours of work as well as differences in long-run patterns of growth (or decline). An occupation is a type of work (such as medical doctor, teacher, welder, salesperson, machine operator) while an industry represents a type of product or service being produced (such as agriculture, forestry, manufacturing, retail trade, government).

Occupations are also differentiated by the types of education and training which are required, as well as the level of responsibility and experience. Professional and technical occupations require the most education while skilled trades require the greatest amount of training. One usual way of classifying occupations is to distinguish between blue-collar (that is production and related work), and white-collar (clerical, sales, and professional employment).

Blue-collar workers traditionally have been the most highly organized and white-collar the least. Some white-collar workers, such as medical doctors, dentists, and lawyers, belong to professional associations which perform many functions similar to those of craft unions. Since 1965, many groups of white-collar workers have become unionized, including nurses, teachers, and government employees. In fact, the government sector is now the most highly unionized industry sector in Canada (4, p. 60).

An occupation or industry which is growing will tend to be in a better position to increase wages and improve working conditions than one which is experiencing little growth or may even be declining. Also, all things being equal, an industry that is more prone to cyclical swings in employment could be expected to pay higher compensating wages relative to sectors which are more stable.

Geographical regions have their own particular mix of industries and occupations. This is evident in the case of Canada's different regions. Manufacturing occupies a larger proportion of the labour force in Ontario and Quebec while primary industries are relatively more important in the Prairies and the Atlantic Provinces. Growth rates in the labour force differ by region, with the largest gains being in the West (British Columbia and Alberta) and Ontario, while relative declines have occurred in the Atlantic region and Quebec (30, p. 63). The existence of multiplant operations or federal government standardization may, on the other hand, overcome the effects of geographic isolation. Regional differences in labour supply can lead to different patterns in employment, wages, and working conditions.

Earnings Differentials

Earnings by occupation and industry are both a result of the operation of labour markets and a determinant of market operations. Market forces of supply and demand set the general boundaries for the employment-wage rate dimensions (19). The determination of earnings is affected both by collective bargaining between unions and management and by government regulations such as minimum wages, training, and education requirements. In addition, the wage rates negotiated by one union may become the goal of another union in its collective bargaining.

Empirical studies, such as that of Meltz and Stager (25) on the pattern of occupational earnings differentials, indicate that there are changes in the relative earnings of occupations over time and that some occupations tend to follow patterns similar to other occupations, such as policemen and firemen, and plasterers and masons. There are also above-average and below-average occupations which appear to retain their rankings over time. That is, the high-wage occupations of forty years ago are still the high-wage occupations of today. Some changes have occurred, however, which are usually associated either with the decline of an industry (for example the deterioration in the relative position of the railroads) or a major change in technology (such as the huge increase in air traffic and in the earnings of airline pilots). The dispersion of earnings among occupations seems to have followed cycles of narrowing (1911-21 and 1941-51) and widening (1921-31, 1951-61, and 1961-71), with a long-run narrowing between occupations with high and low earnings.

Earnings by industry have also shown considerable stability over short and moderately short periods of time (30, p. 54). In contrast to occupations, there seems to have been few long-run changes in the interindustry dispersion over time although there are noticeable cyclical patterns.

Regional differentials in earnings are affected by the mix of industries and occupations as well as by differences in earnings due to purely regional factors. Over time, the regional dispersion of wage rates has narrowed, although there have been cycles similar to those for occupations.

Unemployment Rates

The unemployment rate is a rough measure of available but unused labour services. It also tends to be used as a measure of the demand for labour, although, for reasons discussed below, the vacancy rate is probably a better measure (34). The general level of demand for labour is relevant to union-management relations since it provides an indication of the likely ability of employers to recruit other workers if their work force goes on strike. Demand for labour can also affect the willingness of workers to go on strike since when demand for labour is high there will be alternative jobs open to strikers on a part-time or full-time basis. Low unemployment rates (and high vacancy rates) tend to strengthen the bargaining position of the union and weaken the bargaining hand of employers. The reverse is true for high unemployment rates and low vacancy rates.

All other things being equal, one would expect major differences in the rate of unemployment to have some impact on the rate of change in wages. The relation between the two rates has been the subject of much research following the pathbreaking work of A. W. Phillips (31), who determined that, for the United Kingdom, there was an inverse relation between the level of unemployment and the rate of change in wages during the period 1861 to 1957. (For a detailed discussion see 19, pp. 259 281, and 30, pp. 240 256).

Recent research has questioned whether the unemployment rate is a satisfactory measure of labour market demand, since after the mid-1960s the unemployment rate no longer was a statistically significant predictor of wage changes (20, 36). The weakening of the explanatory power of the unemployment rate appears to be due to changes in the composition of the labour force toward more youth and women as well as changes in government regulations such as the 1971 revisions in the Unemployment Insurance Act which provided more liberal benefits to a wider segment of the labour force (34). For these reasons the vacancy rate, which is not as affected by these factors, has been found to be a better measure of the demand for labour and hence a better predictor of wage changes (33).

Education and Training

Education and training programs as well as immigration are important sources of the supply of labour, and these have a sizable impact on wage and employment determination. In the economic literature, education and training are examined in terms of human-capital theory. In order for an individual to undertake education and training, there has to be some return for the investment of time and money which is being used. The money investment is direct, in the form of such expenses as tuition, fees, and books, and the investment is indirect, in terms of the earnings which are forgone while the person is in school.

In the case of both education and training, the government is heavily involved in subsidizing or completely covering the costs. Education is one of the largest single items of expenditure by provincial governments, while the Department of Employment and Immigration, which provides funds for training, is one of the larger federal government departments.

Over the long term, there has been a substantial increase in the level of education of persons in the labour force. This long-run trend accelerated in the 1960s, particularly with the increased importance placed on the contribution of education and training to the productivity of the country (12).

The increase in levels of education has been credited with having a direct impact on union-management relations in Canada. Crispo and Arthurs (5), for example, suggest that rising education levels, with concomitant increases in expectations, are a factor in the growing militancy of the trade-union movement in Canada.

The increase in education is also related to the change in the occupational structure of the labour force which, as was observed above, has shifted significantly toward professional and other white-collar workers. The increase in unionization among these groups may also be related to the increasing expectations associated with the higher levels of education.

Education and training requirements can also be used as barriers to entry into particular occupations. The setting of artificially high standards can be used to reduce the supply of labour and thereby foster increases in wages and security of employment. Persons excluded by the barriers to entry may end up with lower wages and possibly less secure jobs (19, pp. 313-314). The effect of such occupational licensing has been discussed with respect to a small number of occupations and trades, such as doctors, dentists, lawyers, and skilled tradesmen. In order to estimate the precise impact, however, it is necessary to determine how much of training is excessive in terms of the minimum levels of competency, and how many persons have been excluded from taking education or training who have the requisite abilities and are prepared to pay the full costs of undertaking training. While some research has been conducted on these subjects (7, and other references cited in 19, p. 323), there are many complicating factors which prevent a precise conclusion as to their overall impact.

Over the long term, immigration has only made a small net contribution to Canada's population growth because the large number of persons entering the country has almost been offset by large numbers emigrating to the United States. It has been estimated that only between 10 and 15 percent of the net increase in the labour force between 1861 and 1971 resulted from immigration even though 10 million persons entered the country during this period (30, p. 16).

In the post-World War II period, there was a significant net gain through immigration. A larger proportion of immigrants than non-immigrants entered the labour force and were concentrated in professional and technical occupations as well as more skilled crafts and production jobs in manufacturing and construction. This pattern was partly the result of Canadian immigration policies which attempted to fit immigration into the needs of the economy for more skilled and educated manpower (30, pp. 15-20).

Immigration has been an important source of educated and skilled manpower for Canada. Moreover, it has been a subject of concern for trade unionists. In the early years of the century, immigration was viewed by trade unions as a means by which employers could undercut wages by recruiting nonunion newcomers who might also be more docile. In fact, at the turn of this century, the high increase in the labour force, largely through massive immigration of unskilled workers, was followed by a lowering of real wages (30, pp. 234-235). However, during the post-World War II expansion, unions did not object to immigration, perhaps because the economy was so buoyant and because the government reduced immigration during periods of recession (27). At the turn of this century, immigrants were generally unskilled; however, in the post-World War II period, emphasis was placed on recruiting skilled workers. The fact that there had been a shortage of skilled workers in Canada may have contributed to the labour movement's acceptance of large-scale immigration.

Attention has recently focused on skill shortages in Canada which have been compounded by the decrease in immigration. This decrease is partly associated with the rise in living standards in Europe which has made Canada a relatively less desirable place in which to relocate. In addition, the federal government has been consciously reducing immigration in order to encourage greater training in Canada to fill skill shortages from the ranks of the unemployed. This issue is being examined by two federal government task forces: the Parliamentary Task Force on Employment Opportunities in the 80s; and Employment and Immigration's Task Force on Labour Market Development. Government policy on education and training as well as on immigration will have a major impact on the supply of particular kinds of labour, which in turn will ultimately affect union-management relations in particular occupations and industries.

Legislative Developments Which Impinge on the Labour Market

Government legislation, both federal and provincial, sets direct limits on the operation of the labour market and its outcomes. With the exception of Unemployment Insurance, which is run by the federal government, most workers are subject to provincial laws in the fields of employment standards and labour relations. Federal jurisdiction in these matters, being confined mainly to the transportation and communication industries, covers less than 10 percent of the labour force.

Employment standards, discussed in Chapter 3 in detail, include minimum wages, maximum hours, rates of pay for overtime, equal-pay provisions and various benefit provisions along with notice of layoffs, dismissal, and vacation pay. Economic theory predicts that in the long run, minimum-wage laws will have an adverse effect as employment will be reduced relative to what it would have been in the absence of the minimum wage. Although it is difficult to determine the precise impact of minimum-wage laws, largely because so many other factors are also changing over time, empirical evidence supports the predictions of economic theory that minimum-wage laws lead to adverse employment effects, particularly for teen-agers (19, pp. 135-136; 30, pp. 248-249, 304-307).

In the past century, there has been a major reduction in the hours worked per day, per week and per year in Canada. In 1870, the standard hours of work in manufacturing industries were 64 hours per week. A century later, in 1976, the average was

39.4 hours per week. The daily hours dropped over the same period from more than 10 to less than 8. The number of work-days was also reduced, and on an annual basis hours have declined, especially in the last several decades, due to the increase in the number of statutory holidays and vacations (30, pp. 78-91).

This long-term decline in hours worked reflects our increased wealth and hence ability to afford working less. These preferences are manifested through collective bargaining as well as government legislation. As Ostry and Zaidi (30, pp. 83-84) indicated: " . . . the chief rallying-point for early trade unions was the movement for shorter hours . . . the first attempt to form a national federation of unions in Canada stemmed from the famous Toronto Printers' Strike in 1872 — a strike fought over the nine-hour (day) issue." The labour market impact of the reduction in hours is difficult to ascertain. However, it is generally accepted that the initial reduction in hours from the long work-days resulted in increases in productivity from less fatigued workers. Whether or not there are further productivity gains to be made by lowering the work-day from the present figure of slightly under eight hours per day is subject to debate.

Premium rates for overtime are both provided for in legislation and the subject of collective bargaining between unions and management. The premium rate has the effect of discouraging the use of labour for additional hours because the overtime cost may be between 50 and 100 percent more than the regular wage rate. Unions have argued that reducing the formal work-week beyond which premium rates are necessary will "spread the work." With the exception of some industries where overtime premiums are customary, overtime tends to be a cyclical phenomenon with increased use for short periods when demand for labour is high.

The impact of unemployment insurance on the labour market has also been the subject of recent controversy in Canada. Grubel, Maki, and Sax (17), and Reid and Meltz (34) suggest that changes in the Unemployment Insurance (UI) Act in 1971 contributed to raising the measured rate of unemployment in Canada by between 0.8 and 1.9 percentage points. This result presumes that the more generous UI provisions induced some persons to spend more time searching for a job while unemployed, and that other persons may have been induced to enter the labour force with the intention of becoming eligible for unemployment benefits. In addition, a more generous UI program increases the incentive for firms to lay off workers in response to temporary reductions in demand. The implication that changes in the UI provisions raised the unemployment rate has been bitterly contested by the labour movement. Trade-union representatives refused to endorse a 1976 Economic Council of Canada report which suggested such a result (14, Preface).

SOME UNIQUE ASPECTS OF THE CANADIAN LABOUR MARKET

There are several unique aspects of the Canadian labour market which have an impact on the nature of union-management relations in Canada. These aspects include: the division of jurisdiction between the federal and provincial governments; the vast distances, relatively thin population and separate regions which characterize the country; the importance of resource industries especially in certain regions; the open nature of the economy; and the importance of foreign-based multinational corporations. Each of these aspects is discussed in turn.

Federal-Provincial Jurisdictional Issues

The scope of the labour market is divided jurisdictionally between the federal and provincial governments, with less than 10 percent of the labour force subject to federal labour relations legislation. While education is under provincial jurisdiction, training has been viewed as shared, or at times, solely under federal jurisdiction because of the federal government's overall responsibility for economic matters. These divisions have led to conflicts over the administration of programs relating to the labour market (9). While the federal government operates a national system of employment offices (Canada Employment Centres), the Province of Quebec has established its own employment service (Quebec Manpower Centres).

In the early 1960s, when manpower policy was being developed beyond simply encouraging immigration, programs tended to be on the basis of shared costs between the federal and provincial government. In Ontario, for example, this funding provided the basis for the development of the community college system, known as the Colleges of Applied Arts and Technology (CAATs). The Canada Department of Employment and Immigration's Canada Manpower Training Program is still a major source of funds for the CAATs (23).

The heavy reliance on institutional as opposed to on-the-job training has been the subject of much criticism (13, 14) and is currently under review. Any change in the composition of training would have to take into consideration the implications for provincial institutions.

In terms of union-management relations, the division of jurisdiction has led to some differences in training programs for various skills and also to some fragmentation in labour markets through barriers to mobility, especially in certain trades such as those in the construction industry in Quebec. The implication is that the Canadian labour market is less responsive to labour market demands than it would be if there were a more unified approach to education, training, and mobility.

Distances

The Canadian population being spread over a distance of 3000 miles and having major language and cultural differences, has helped create a more isolated and a less integrated labour market. One result is the persistence of significant regional differences in unemployment rates, as exemplified by the fact that the unemployment rate in the Atlantic Provinces has tended to be almost three times that of the Prairie Provinces (30, p. 16).

Differences in unemployment rates, along with differences in the composition of labour supply, can affect labour relations. In Nova Scotia, for example, the threat of Michelin closing down its operations if unionized, effectively led to legislation that prevented the unionization of multiplant operations in this area of high unemployment.

Importance of Resource Industries

Resource industries (forestry and mining, including coal and oil) along with agriculture and hydroelectric power generation, are significant export industries in the Canadian economy. While these industries are now largely capital intensive, employing only a fraction of the labour force (7.5 percent in total, excluding hydroelectric power), there is some impact on union-management relations in certain regions of the country.

In British Columbia and in the Atlantic Provinces, forestry operations are unionized. In British Columbia, wages set in this sector tend to have an important impact on other wage settlements. In Ontario and Quebec, unionized workers in mining and hydroelectric generation are also important pace setters. Oil and gas workers clearly have benefited from the enormous price increases in these sectors.

The Open Economy

International trade is particularly important to Canada's economy. In 1979, exports of goods and services represented 29.3 percent of Canada's Gross National Expenditure while imports were equivalent to 31.5 percent. Aside from the trade in automotive products under the Canada-U.S. auto pact, the bulk of Canada's exports are made up of primary products. Since imports tend to be manufactured products, the manufacturing sector is perhaps smaller than it might be under a closed economy. However, the standard of living may be higher due to the concentration on primary products, where Canada has a comparative advantage. The subject of international trade, tariff barriers, and the impact on the country is one of continuing debate in Canada.

Foreign-Based Multinationals

Another topic of debate is the role of multinational corporations in Canada. Not only are investment policies subject to scrutiny by the Foreign Investment Review Agency (FIRA), but recently their policies concerning plant closings have been under scrutiny (8, 40). One concern is that multinationals, responding to political pressure in the parent country, may close down a Canadian branch rather than one in the parent country, even though economic criteria alone would dictate closing the branch in the parent country before the one in Canada.

Any consideration of the role of multinational corporations also has to consider the role of international unions, many of which organize the same companies in the two countries. From the standpoint of the labour market, the issue is the degree to which multinationals have affected the level of employment, as well as the composition of employment, in Canada. There is no unanimous view on this subject, although the amount and composition of investment would suggest that the *level* of employment is higher than it might otherwise have been in the absence of such investment. With respect to the composition of employment, the debate is whether the proportion of research and development personnel as well as senior management would be higher if the corporation were based in Canada (6, 37).

SUMMARY AND POLICY IMPLICATIONS

The labour market provides a context and can set limits within which union-management relations operate. The age structure of the labour force, the occupations and industries in which demand for labour is changing, the levels of unemployment overall and within particular sectors, all influence the attitudes and strategies of the parties to collective bargaining.

In addition, the willingness of society to invest in education and training as well as to encourage immigration and legislate labour market relations through such factors as minimum wages, maximum hours, occupational licensing, and unemployment insurance, all affect the eventual outcome of employment, earnings, and unemployment.

By the same token, the labour market itself is affected by the results of union-management relations. A wage rate negotiated by a union operates similar to a minimum wage in that the firm will not hire anyone for less. In addition, the collective agreement usually sets out conditions for layoffs (usually involving the least senior employees) and provisions for such factors as training, promotion, vacations, holidays, and benefits. As a result, an understanding of the operation of markets must also include the impact of the range of issues settled between management and unions.

A final set of considerations affecting the labour market are those special characteristics which make up the Canadian economy and society. Geographic distance, divided federal-provincial jurisdiction, an important resource-based sector as well as a heavy participation of foreign-based companies, all have their impacts on the Canadian labour market and in turn on union-management relations.

Some Policy Implications

From the government perspective there are several aspects of the labour market which warrant consideration in a union-management context. The present concern over skill shortages requires consideration of, and union involvement in, long-run policy formation relating to apprenticeship. On the other hand, the question of occupational and skill licensing has to be carefully considered to ensure that artificially high requirements are not introduced (11). With respect to union hiring halls, the Task Force on Industrial Relations in 1968 proposed that these functions be taken over by Canada Employment (then called Manpower) Centres. The validity of this proposal might be again reviewed.

For unions, an understanding of present and prospective labour market developments is essential in considering their particular long-run position. Whether an industry sector will grow or decline will have a major impact, not only on collective bargaining, but also on the strength and status of a union. Technological changes can alter the demand for labour and in turn can affect jurisdictions between unions. An ongoing examination of these changes might mitigate some of the conflict which could arise from them.

Employers must also be concerned with the union-management aspects of the labour market. Two particular considerations can be cited. First, in attempting to meet skill shortages, cooperation with unions may be necessary. Second, in estimating their future manpower requirements, firms will have to consider the possible impact of changes in wage rates rather than estimating "needs" in isolation from the market. Increases in wage rates could result in smaller numbers of employees being required than might have been thought. This in turn could alter government estimates of training and immigration requirements.

Clearly an understanding of how labour markets function — and malfunction — is crucial to an understanding of union-management relations. Equally important, however, is an understanding of how union-management relations affect the operation of labour markets. It is essential not only to know the impact that specific industrial relations institutions will have on the labour market, but also to understand why these peculiar institutions and characteristics of the labour market arise and evolve. It is hoped that a balanced understanding of the interaction of labour market analysis and union-management relations will help in devising sensible public policies in both these important areas.

REFERENCES AND WORKS CITED

1. Canada. Parliament. Standing Committee on National Finance. *Report on Canada Manpower* (Ottawa: 1976).

2. Canada. *Task Force on Employment Opportunities in the 80's* (Ottawa: House of Commons, 1980).

3. Canada. Task Force on Labour Relations. *Canadian Industrial Relations* (Ottawa: Queen's Printer, 1968).

4. *Corporations and Labour Unions Returns Act.* Report for 1978, Part II — Labour Unions. Statistics Canada, Cat. 71-202 Annual (Ottawa: Supply and Services Canada, 1980).

5. Crispo, John, and H.W. Arthurs. "Industrial Unrest in Canada: A Diagnosis of Recent Experience," *Relations Industrielles/Industrial Relations,* Vol. 23, No. 2 (1968), 237-264.

6. Daly, Donald J. "Weak Links in 'The Weakest Link,'" *Canadian Public Policy,* Vol. 3 (Summer 1979), 307-317.

7. Dodge, David. "Occupational Wage Differentials, Occupational Licensing and Returns to Investment in Education," in S. Ostry (Ed.), *Canadian Higher Education in the Seventies,* Economic Council of Canada (Ottawa: Information Canada, 1972), pp. 133-175.

8. Donner, Arthur. "Plant Closings Are Becoming a Social Issue," *The Globe and Mail,* September 8, 1980.

9. Dupré, J. Stefan, David M. Cameron, Graeme H. McKechnie, and Theodore B. Rotenberg. *Federalism and Policy Development: The Case of Adult Occupational Training* (Toronto: University of Toronto Press, 1973).

10. Dymond, W.R. (Chairman). "Canadian Manpower Policy: A Policy in Search of a Problem." Proceedings of the Industrial Relations Research Association (December 1972), 69-78.

11. Dymond, W.R. (Chairman). *Training for Ontario's Future: Report of the Task Force on Industrial Training* (Toronto: Ontario Ministry of Colleges and Universities, 1973).

12. Economic Council of Canada. *Second Annual Review, Towards Sustained and Balanced Economic Growth* (Ottawa: Queen's Printer, 1965).

13. Economic Council of Canada. *Eighth Annual Review, Design for Decision-Making: An Application to Human Resource Policies* (Ottawa: Information Canada, 1971).

14. Economic Council of Canada. *People and Jobs, A Study of the Canadian Labour Market* (Ottawa: Information Canada, 1976).

15. Freeman, Richard B., and James L. Medoff. "Two Faces of Unionism," *The Public Interest* (Fall 1979), 69-93.

16. Goldman, Barbara. *New Directions for Manpower Policy* (Montreal: C.D. Howe Research Institute, 1976).

17. Grubel, Herbert, D. Maki, and S. Sax. "Real and Insurance-Induced Unemployment in Canada," *The Canadian Journal of Economics,* Vol. 8 (May 1975), 174-191.

18. Gunderson, Morley. "The Case for Government Supported Training," *Relations Industrielles/Industrial Relations,* Vol. 29 (December 1974), 709-726.

19. Gunderson, Morley. *Labour Market Economics, Theory, Evidence and Policy in Canada* (Toronto: McGraw-Hill Ryerson, 1980).

20. Kaliski, S.F. *The Trade-Off Between Inflation and Unemployment: Some Explorations of the Recent Evidence for Canada,* Economic Council of Canada, Special Study No. 22 (Ottawa: Information Canada, 1972).

21. Maki, Dennis R. *Search Behaviour in Canadian Job Markets,* Economic Council of Canada (Ottawa: Information Canada, 1972).

22. Meltz, Noah M. "Manpower Research: Its Economic Aspects and its Application to Industrial Relations," International Conference on Trends in Industrial and Labour Relations, 1972 (Jerusalem, Israel: Jerusalem Academic Press, 1974), 304-315.

23. Meltz, Noah M. "Implications of Manpower and Immigration Policy," in Lawrence H. Officer and Lawrence B. Smith (Eds.), *Issues in Canadian Economics* (Toronto: McGraw-Hill Ryerson, 1974).

24. Meltz, Noah M. "Identifying Sources of Imbalances in Individual Labour Markets," *Relations Industrielles/Industrial Relations,* Vol. 31, No. 2 (1976), 224-246.

25. Meltz, Noah M., and David A.A. Stager. *The Occupational Structure of Earnings in Canada 1931-1975,* Anti-Inflation Board of Canada (Hull, Quebec: Supply and Services Canada, 1979).

26. Moore, Larry F., and Larry Charach. *Manpower Planning for Canadians: An Anthology* 2nd ed. (Vancouver: Institute of Industrial Relations, University of British Columbia, 1979).

27. Morton, Desmond, with Terry Copp. *Working People, an Illustrated History of Canadian Labour* (Ottawa: Deneau and Greenberg, 1980).

28. Newton, Keith. "The Rationale for Government Involvement in Manpower Training in Canada: Theory and Evidence," *Relations Industrielles/Industrial Relations,* Vol. 32, No. 3 (1977), 399-414.

29. Organization for Economic Co-operation and Development. *Manpower Policy and Programmes in Canada* (Paris: 1966).

30. Ostry, Sylvia, and Mahmood A. Zaidi. *Labour Economics in Canada,* 3rd ed. (Toronto: Macmillan of Canada, 1979).

31. Phillips, A.W. "The Relation Between Unemployment and the Rate of Change of Money Wage Rates in the United Kingdom, 1861-1957," *Economica,* Vol. 25 (November 1958), 283-299.

32. Rees, Albert. *The Economics of Work and Pay,* 2nd ed. (New York: Harper and Row, 1979).

33. Reid, Frank. "Unemployment and Inflation: An Assessment of Canadian Macroeconomic Policy," *Canadian Public Policy,* Vol. VI: 2 (Spring 1980), 283-299.

34. Reid, Frank, and Noah M. Meltz. "Causes of Shifts in the Unemployment-Vacancy Relationship: An Empirical Analysis for Canada," *Review of Economics and Statistics,* Vol. 61 (August 1979), 470-475.

35. Rottenberg, Simon. "On Choice in Labor Markets," *Industrial and Labor Relations Review,* Vol. 9 (1956), 183-199.

36. Rowley, J., and D. Wilton. "Empirical Foundations for the Canadian Phillips Curve," *Canadian Journal of Economics,* Vol. 7 (May 1974), 240-259.

37. Safarian, A.E. "Foreign Ownership and Industrial Behaviour: A Comment on 'The Weakest Link,'" *Canadian Public Policy,* Vol. V:3 (Summer 1979), 318-335.

38. Stager, David, and Noah M. Meltz. "Manpower Planning and the Professions," *Canadian Journal of Higher Education,* Vol. VII, No. 3 (1977), 78-83.

39. Starr, Gerald. *Union-Nonunion Wage Differentials.* (Toronto: Ontario Ministry of Labour, 1973).

40. United Automobile Workers. *Auto in Crisis.* Brief submitted to the Ontario Government by the Canadian UAW Council (Ottawa: September 15, 1980).

41. Wilkinson, Bruce. *Studies in the Economics of Education,* Department of Labour (Ottawa: Queen's Printer, 1965).

42. Wright, David McCord (Ed.). *The Impact of the Union* (New York: Harcourt Brace, 1951).

QUESTIONS

1. Discuss, with reasons, the effect that the level of unemployment has on the relative positions of management and unions in the bargaining process.

2. "The age composition of a bargaining unit should not have any impact on the priority of issues raised at the bargaining table." Discuss whether you agree or disagree.

3. The level of education of persons in the Canadian labour force has increased significantly in the post-World War II period. Discuss how this has affected the attitude of workers toward trade unions.

4. Discuss how the labour market sets limits which affect the outcome of union-management relations.

5. Explain, with reasons, the opposition of trade unions to mass immigration into Canada in the early part of the century.

6. Discuss how changes in the industrial structure of the labour force can affect the potential for trade unionism.

DESMOND MORTON

5. The History of Canadian Labour

Canadian labour history has usually focused on the complex family tree of central organizations or on the movement's political activities. Important as these are, the growth of Canadian labour organizations from a few thousand members in the 1860s to 40 percent of the present nonagricultural work force is primarily due to legislated extension of collective-bargaining rights. Political and economic activities for the main body of Canadian unions have not been contradictory but mutually supportive.

INDIVIDUALISM OR SOLIDARITY

History forever interferes with those who want to forget past practices or start with a clean slate. The current climate of labour-management relations may be affected for generations by bitter memories of past struggles. Cape Breton miners and steelworkers still recall the jibe from J.E. McClurg, general manager of BESCO in 1925, that they could not "stand the gaff" (42). Miners in the Sudbury basin approach negotiations with International Nickel having long memories of struggle against powerful absentee owners. Like the battle honours of a distinguished regiment, past struggles are important reminders to union members of the courage and solidarity that built past gains and that may well be necessary again. Labour history, with its theme of the struggle for painful progress, becomes a weapon in the union arsenal. For both labour and management it can be a means of gaining experience and understanding.

Industrial relations primarily boils down to a conflict between individual and group interests. In North America, the pioneering, individualistic spirit was strong. The new world held out a promise of cheap land, freedom, and the myth that anyone could make a fortune had just enough truth to make it convincing. Pioneer labour in the forests or in canal and railway building was almost always linked to the prospect of eventual ownership of a farm or business. Those who accepted the permanent status of a hired person had failed to meet the challenge of the new country.

Early Unions
At the same time, North American circumstances cried out for organization and cooperation. Pioneer life was unendurable without neighbourly support. Immigrants

turned to communal associations like the St. Andrew's Society or the Orange Order for help in finding work or for support in illness and bereavement. Early workers' organizations developed from the common interest their members shared in an occupation or trade. Such organizations collected funds to meet the threats of unemployment or invalidity, dispelled the terror of a pauper's burial by accompanying members on their last journey, and organized occasional banquets, picnics, and processions to heighten members' conviviality and self-esteem. "United to Support, not Combined to Injure," proclaimed the banner of the Toronto Typographical Union, Canada's oldest continuing union local. "We Bury Our Dead," boasted Quebec's Ship-Labourers' Benevolent Society.

Such organizations were limited to workers who, by special skills or local labour market conditions, could command more than a subsistence wage and who could afford the cost of mutual insurance, to say nothing of regalia and entertainment. "People of the same trade," Adam Smith had noted, "seldom meet together, even for merriment or diversion, but the conversation ends in some conspiracy against the public or in some contrivance to raise prices." Early labour organizations fulfilled Smith's sour prophecy. When they could, unions in early nineteenth-century Canada set their rates and notified their employers, often in politely worded newspaper advertisements. Saint John ship labourers, according to Eugene Forsey, "ruled the port with a rod of iron," quitting work in a body to attend any member's funeral. Printers in Toronto established a firm union rate of thirty-three cents per thousand ems of hand-setting. Coopers, moulders, and glass blowers set their own pace and rates and often recognized a "Blue Monday" to recover from a weekend's dissipation, with the promise to "Give her Hell" on Tuesday and the rest of the week (11, 17, 22, 32).

The law agreed with Adam Smith: union efforts to set rates were conspiracies in restraint of trade. In the common law, strike action was considered an interference with the employer's trade. Even planning or threatening a strike constituted conspiracy since two or more people were inevitably involved. Unions in theory and sometimes in practice were subjected to legal sanctions merely for performing their natural functions. Individual workers were subject to statutes such as the Masters and Servants Act which provided a prison term for anyone who left employment without a master's permission.

BROADER CONNECTIONS

Early labour organizations in Canada were tiny, local, and evanescent. Since records have vanished or were never kept, we shall never learn about all of them. Only in the mid-nineteenth century was there a noticeable move for broader connections. There were many reasons for this. The new railways made movement easier. Knowledge about wage rates and working conditions in New York or Boston offered arguments for local improvements. Mutual insurance schemes became more efficient and generous if the risks were widely shared. Above all, bargaining power based on scarcity of skilled workers could be effective only if unions included an entire trade or craft.

International Unions

These advantages seemed possible with the "New Model" unionism represented by the Amalgamated Society of Engineers (ASE) in Great Britain and by such imitations as the Moulders' Union in the United States. Both were among the first unions to establish branches or locals in Canada. ASE members brought their union connection to Canada as skilled tradesmen for the Grand Trunk Railway. William Sylvis began rallying local Canadian associates to his Moulders' Union during an 1863 organizing tour. Typographers, carpenters, painters, coopers, the shoemakers of the Knights of St. Crispin, and other craft organizations followed suit.

Craft-based unionism emphasized distinctions between trades and even between skills within a single trade. Helpers, apprentices, and the unskilled represented a threat of dilution to the craft or of replacement during a strike. The issue of "bucks" or helpers lay at the heart of thirty years of conflict between the Moulders' Union and employers (19, 36, 40).

Workers also looked to their own communities for links. Organizing all the trades and labour organizations of a city or town into a single assembly or union over-looked jurisdictional differences. Such an association might be a vehicle for financial backing or, by the 1880s, for boycotts in support of a strike. The common focus was often political action, but it extended easily to the busy social and educational programs of ambitious union leaders.

The Nine-Hour Movement

The era of Canadian Confederation combined high hopes and unusual economic prosperity. Such circumstances persuaded union leaders in Toronto, Hamilton, Montreal, and smaller centres to organize ambitious central labour organizations and, in 1872, to launch a coordinated bid for a nine-hour day. The drive was too ambitious. Hamilton employers, where the movement began, fought back. Toronto printers jumped the gun in a dispute with an old enemy, George Brown, publisher of the *Globe*. However, Canadian labour organizations drew widespread attention. The prime minister, Sir John A. Macdonald, embarrassed his old Liberal antagonist, Brown, by passing a Trade Unions Act, legalizing (within severe limits) union activity.

In 1873, Toronto labour leaders summoned delegates to form a Canadian Labour Union (CLU). Cost of travel limited representation to Ontario but the CLU's debates were an impressive foretaste of Canadian union concerns for a century to come. Resolutions included the need to organize, the inadequacy of apprenticeship training, opposition to mass immigration, and the novel idea that workers should have their own representatives in Parliament (6, 50, 51).

The early 1870s proved a false dawn for Canadian unionism. Macdonald's labour legislation included a statute that declared most effective strike tactics to be criminal offences. By the time that the law and the Masters and Servants Act had been amended to make them more tolerable to unionists, Canada was deep in a depression. Most of the optimistic labour organizations, including the CLU, collapsed for lack of support. Labour leaders turned to politics, campaigning for or against the Conservatives' panacea for prosperity: a National Policy of high tariffs to protect Canadian manufacturing.

The Knights of Labor

Canadian unionism revived slowly during the 1880s, but its progress was hurried by the dramatic influx of a totally new kind of organization, the Holy and Noble Order of the Knights of Labor. Founded as a secret society in Philadelphia in 1868, the Knights grew slowly until 1879 when their principles were diluted, and the tight rules of secrecy were relaxed.

For American and then Canadian workers, the Order's mixture of radical idealism and practical caution proved infectious. Preaching the fundamental worth of working people, the evils of monopoly, and the ultimate cooperative commonwealth, the Knights opened their assemblies, without distinction of race or sex, excluding only lawyers, bankers, and the liquor industry. They also advocated moderation, education, and opposition to strikes except as a desperate last resort.

The Knights entered Canada in 1881. Their "mixed assemblies" which ignored craft barriers were ideal for Canadian towns or cities too small to support a single local of carpenters or metalworkers. They arrived at a time when the industrialization promoted by Macdonald's National Policy was creating factories and jobs but also shocking critics because of foul working conditions, frequent accidents, and exploitation of women and children workers.

The Knights of Labor created assemblies in every part of Canada except Prince Edward Island and the Northwest Territories. They overcame opposition from the Catholic hierarchy to become a force in Montreal and Quebec. At their height, they numbered perhaps fifteen thousand members in Canada but many thousands more passed through its ranks. They revived the labour leaders of the 1870s and launched a new generation.

The Knights' enthusiasm for education produced labour newspapers, and the radicalism of their ideals created Canada's first serious social criticism. Both Liberals and Conservatives came to terms with labour's apparent strength, debating factory safety legislation, extending the voting franchise, choosing prominent Knights as candidates in a few seats, appointing a federal royal commission to investigate the relations of capital and labour and launching the idea of Labour Day. In 1894, Parliament established the first Monday in September, to recognize the Knights' most basic proposition: the dignity of labour.

However, the Order sank as it had risen, though more slowly in Canada than in the United States. In part, it was a victim of success. Floods of new members could never be indoctrinated in the Knights' philosophy and tactics. They struck or were locked out and their prompt defeat gave credence to the craft union suspicion that ill-paid unskilled workers could never be organized.

In both Canada and the United States, political involvement provoked bitter personal and ideological rivalries. Hamilton, a major centre for the Order, saw the organization shattered by such disputes. Toronto and Ottawa shared the experience. Employers used the differences between the Knights and older craft unions, now organized in the American Federation of Labor (AFL), to provoke conflict. The AFL's president, Sam Gompers, concluded from the experience that both partisan politics and dual unionism (two unions organizing the same industry) were fatal to a sound labour movement. By the 1890s, the Knights were defunct in the United States and a fading remnant in Canada (25, 33, 34, 51).

The Trades and Labour Congress

Gompers' uncompromising principles would be adopted in Canada only in 1902. Until then, the Knights and craft unionists struggled to work together. In 1883, and again in 1886, a revived Toronto Trades and Labour Council summoned delegates to a "national" congress. Thereafter, the Trades and Labour Congress (TLC) of Canada would meet annually until 1956 when it became a major partner in creating the Canadian Labour Congress (CLC).

Calling itself the "Parliament of Canadian Labour," the TLC attempted to develop a political program and to promote it as best it could in Ottawa and the provincial capitals. Delegates regularly demanded shorter hours of work, inspectors to enforce factory acts, control of European immigration, and an absolute ban on Orientals. They demanded free education for children and the exclusion of women from dangerous factory and mining occupations — acts that would restrict the labour market as well as serve humanitarian purposes. The TLC also wanted the Senate abolished and supported democratic innovations such as proportional representation and the referendum.

Frustrated in their lobbying efforts for these and other concerns in Ottawa, TLC leaders next argued the case for direct labour representation. A tiny handful of unionists won election as Liberals or Conservatives between 1887 and 1900; their ineffectiveness led labour radicals to appeal again and again for unionists to forget their "foxy or proxy" supporters in the old parties and to develop a distinctive labour party and program.

Hinterland Unions

Despite its boast of national representation, the TLC spoke essentially for central Canada. Craft unionism extended from Halifax (and even St. John's in a then-independent Newfoundland) across to Victoria, but it had little impact on the resource industries which the National Policy expected to support central Canadian industries. Coal mining, an important development of the 1870s in both Nova Scotia and British Columbia, was both highly skilled and dangerous but miners were isolated and at the mercy of owners and operators. James Dunsmuir, developer of Vancouver Island's coal fields, used the Royal Navy and then the militia to prevent unions in his mines. When San Francisco failed as a source of strike-breakers, Dunsmuir turned to China. Racial prejudice against Chinese immigrants was fanned by their role as strikebreakers.

In Nova Scotia, there was no Dunsmuir, and the Orient was too far off. The Provincial Workmen's Association (PWA), founded in 1879, survived bitter strikes and the use of the militia because the province's mine owners were too numerous and divided. However, the PWA's power in the mines and the legislature faded fast with the advent of the Dominion Coal Company. By buying up small mines and defeating the PWA when it attempted to organize a new steel mill in Sydney, the company soon reduced the union to a subservient status, dependent on dues collected by the employer (42, 52, 56).

GROWTH AND DIVISION

From 1873 to 1896, Canada had combined substantial growth and economic expansion with a mood of hard times. Without much warning, the mood began to change in 1896. A new Liberal government under Wilfrid Laurier found itself afloat on a wave of prosperity. Factories expanded. The West opened for settlement and boasted of being the breadbasket of the world. A single transcontinental railway was not enough: Canada needed three.

Canadian workers shared the expansive mood but not the benefits. Their weapon would be Sam Gompers' AFL, already in the full flood of an organizing boom in the United States. Fearful that American corporations would switch their factories northward if Canadian workers were cheap and unorganized, Gompers commissioned a Hamilton carpenter and former socialist, John Flett, as a full-time organizer.

The Berlin Convention, 1902

Flett's whirlwind organizing campaign, backed by other part-time AFL organizers, transformed Canadian unionism. Communities from Charlottetown to Windsor felt his impact. In many, the history of unionism dates from Flett's visit.

Employers, politicians, and other unionists objected to the AFL invasion. The TLC's president, Ralph Smith, a Liberal-Labour M.P. and the first British Columbian in the post, called for a Canadian Federation of Labour independent from and equal to the AFL. The issue was addressed at the TLC's 1902 convention at Berlin (now Kitchener). Both sides were organized. Flett urged his new locals to affiliate. Labour radicals came in force, suspicious that Smith was merely planning to tie the Congress to the Liberals. Other unionists were angry that delegates who had long dominated the TLC came from nonexistent assemblies of the Knights of Labor. In the showdown, Smith was defeated. Even his own Nanaimo union refused his credentials.

The Berlin meeting affected only a few thousand Canadian unionists, but it confirmed the dominance of international craft unionism. The Knights and "dual" Canadian unions were forced out of the TLC and set up their own rival "national" organization. It was and remained a feeble alternative, whose persistent survival gave Canadian labour all of the ill effects of "dual unionism" that Gompers could have feared. Though Canadian unionists had made the Berlin decision, their choice was immediately condemned by employers, and it would be denounced by academic nationalists. The former feared that Gompers' AFL unionism was too powerful; the latter condemned it as too moderate. Canadian workers wanted the strength and experience of the powerful craft unions because they wanted to share in a North American standard of living. In time, employers would find that the business philosophy of Gompers' brand of unionism could ensure stability and moderation in contract negotiation. That did not make unionism congenial, and it remained convenient for employers and governments to exploit anti-American sentiment for anti-union purposes (5, 12, 28, 54).

Radical International Unions

The AFL was not the only international labour movement to cross the Canadian border. Gompers' bitter rivals in the Western Federation of Miners broke into British Columbia's new hardrock mining industry. The United Brotherhood of Railroad Employees tried to organize Canadian Pacific Railway employees. Later, the Industrial Workers of the World (IWW), the "Wobblies," waged free-speech fights in Edmonton, Victoria, and other western cities, and found support in the lumber camps and construction crews. The AFL's independent-minded affiliate, the United Mineworkers, invaded the Alberta coal fields, but it was checkmated in a year-long struggle to oust the Provincial Workmen's Association on Cape Breton Island in 1909-10 and in an even harsher struggle to bring any kind of unionism to Vancouver Island in 1913-14.

The years before 1914 were far from the era of rustic tranquility evoked in Stephen Leacock's *Sunshine Sketches*. In the midst of unprecedented immigration and industrialization, Canadians were shocked by some of the most violent and extensive strikes in their history. Thousands of soldiers and militia guarded mines, railway bridges, and streetcars or escorted strikers to jail. When Alberta miners went on strike, prairie residents found their winter coal supplies in jeopardy. For their part, employers adopted labour-saving devices, "scientific management," and an array of union-breaking techniques devised by the Citizens' Industrial Association in the United States. Within a few years, unions in Toronto, Hamilton, and other Canadian cities had been dealt serious setbacks (4, 10, 44, 55).

Mackenzie King and the IDI Act

Such turbulence demanded a government response. In 1900, Laurier's government opened a small Department of Labour. Its best-known official was a youthful William Lyon Mackenzie King at the outset of a career dedicated, by his own account, to the joint service of the underprivileged and the Liberal Party. King may have been a fussy bachelor and a dedicated careerist; he was also an able negotiator, convinced that reasonable people could settle any dispute. In addition, he had learned that publicity could be a negotiator's most useful weapon. In the 1900s, King became the government's all-purpose industrial negotiator. In the process, he discovered that some employers and most radical unionists were distinctly unreasonable. He also refused to see why union recognition should ever become an issue worthy of a strike.

King's industrial-relations philosophy was embodied in what he considered a supreme achievement in a very long career: the Industrial Disputes Investigation (IDI) Act of 1907. The IDI Act met a demand many Canadian unionists had urged until then: compulsory, government-sponsored investigation of industrial disputes. During the investigation, there could be no strike and no lockout. For Canada's weak unions, the act meant a chance to face employers and state their case. However, as American unions had discovered, any arrangement which allowed employers to continue operations, stockpile, train strikebreakers, and victimize selected unionists could make an eventual strike much longer and probably hopeless. But for the time being, such objections to King's legislation were buried in a chorus of praise.

On the strength of the IDI Act, King entered Parliament in 1908 to become Canada's first fullfledged minister of labour. Whatever labour critics might say, King's career as both a politician and an industrial-relations specialist had been launched. When he was defeated in 1911, he found a new career helping the Rockefeller family with its numerous labour problems. King's ingenuity led to the idea of "Employee Representation Plans" as a substitute for "unreasonable" unions. Ironically, a Canadian invention became better known in the 1920s as the "American Plan" (15, 18, 21, 66).

The First World War

When war came in 1914, the Laurier boom had burst. Canada had overexpanded. Two of the three transcontinental railways skidded toward bankruptcy, threatening to take the rest of the economy with them. The unemployed far outnumbered Canada's 170,000 unionists. The TLC, in radical hands since 1911, condemned war as a capitalist plot, but unionists raced to enlist or joined employers in a clamour for war contracts. By 1916, a labour surplus had become such a shortage that the new Imperial Munitions Board was dreaming up ingenious ways to entice women to work in the new munitions factories. Equal wages with men were promised if not delivered. As the war drained almost half a million men into uniform and hundreds of thousands into industry, wages rose but not enough to match unprecedented inflation. When the government tried to finance the war by borrowing and increasing the money supply, prices soared.

Unions had always been active in the metal-manufacturing industries. As these became munitions plants, union membership grew. Unionism entered new areas like the civil service and even police forces. In wartime, strikes were obviously unpatriotic and many industries were subjected to the IDI Act, which was extended to cover all war industries.

By 1917, workers were angry enough to walk out in defiance of the IDI Act. Their leaders, angry that the wartime Conservative government never consulted them and had imposed conscription over their objections, tried to contest the 1917 election. The result was a humiliating setback, but union militants were not deterred. Many of them had come to think of the "general strike" as labour's ultimate political weapon. In Winnipeg in the summer of 1918, municipal employees gave the idea a modest try. Backed by some of the city's unions and aided by a conciliatory group of citizens, the civic workers won their demands (55, 58, 63).

By the end of the war, workers in the Canadian West were full of fight. They had always been more radical than their eastern counterparts. As early as 1902, British Columbia unionists had sent a couple of socialists to the provincial legislature. By 1918, labour victories were common in the cities and mining districts of British Columbia, Alberta, and Manitoba. However, when the TLC met at Quebec in 1918, eastern moderates dominated. Wartime leaders were rejected. Tom Moore, a Niagara Falls carpenter, began a presidency that lasted until 1943. Indignant western delegates agreed to meet in Calgary in March, 1919. Some of them had more ambitious plans. Far from planning strategy, the Calgary meeting became the starting point for a wholesale western secession from the TLC to form a completely new "One Big Union" (OBU), free from craft barriers and "business union" values.

The Winnipeg General Strike and the OBU

Plans for the "One Big Union" were still taking shape when Winnipeg's metalworkers decided to try the general strike again, this time to force recognition from their employers. Response was enthusiastic. On May 15, 1919, at 11 A.M., between 25,000 and 30,000 Winnipeggers walked out — twice as many as held union cards.

This time, neither governments nor citizens were tolerant. The war was over, Europe was in turmoil and both politicians and property owners were terrified by talk of the revolution. When the strike committee tried to authorize essential services, it was accused of usurping government authority. Returned soldiers defied union appeals and government orders and demonstrated in the streets — for and against the strike. Penniless workers began trickling back to work. The government fired striking postal workers; the city dismissed unionized policemen. Railway brotherhoods ordered members back to work on pain of losing their pension. On June 17, strike leaders, real and presumed, were seized in predawn arrests. When strikers demonstrated in protest, Royal North-West Mounted Police and special constables drove them from Main Street. By June 26, the Winnipeg General Strike was over (2, 8, 43, 46).

The One Big Union idea died too, after a brief, heady start in the wake of the general strike. The general strike itself was hopelessly discredited as a bargaining tactic. Instead, labour in postwar Canada turned to politics. North End Winnipeg sent J.S. Woodsworth, a clergyman jailed for supporting the strike, to Parliament in 1921. In Nova Scotia, Ontario, Manitoba, Alberta, and British Columbia, postwar provincial elections saw more labour victories than ever before. In Ontario and Alberta, labour and farmer members were joined to form governments, ousting the traditional parties (9).

Labour in the Twenties

In general, though, the postwar years were full of disappointment and division for Canadian unionists. Political partnership with farmers broke down because of conflicting rural-urban interests. The TLC's more conservative leadership preferred to lobby for influence instead of uselessly threatening Liberal or Conservative power. The Congress also took a leading role in crushing the One Big Union schism in the West. By 1921, its western affiliates were weak but reunited.

Some divisions were caused by the TLC itself. In 1921, its biggest national affiliate, the Canadian Brotherhood of Railway Employees (CBRE), was forced out as a "dual union" by the Brotherhood of Railroad and Steamship Clerks. The CBRE's leader, Aaron Mosher, swept up the fragments left over from the 1902 break to form an aggressively nationalist All-Canadian Congress of Labour in 1926.

Since 1900, Quebec's Catholic hierarchy had tried to match "materialistic" unionism with its own confessional syndicates. French Canada's bitter resentment of conscription and a resulting mood of nationalism gave the Catholic syndicates a new impetus. By 1921, they too could form a central organization and add a new accent to the discordant voice of Canadian labour.

On the opposite flank, a Canadian Communist party was also formed in 1921. Its members eagerly sought influence in their own unions, provided a noisy opposition at TLC conventions and were expelled by exasperated fellow unionists. In 1927, orders from Moscow ended "boring from within" and began "parallel unionism." An abortive attempt to take over Mosher's organization failed. Instead, the Communists founded their own central body, the Workers' Unity League, and then proceeded to create its affiliates.

A labour movement fragmented among craft, Catholic, nationalist, and revolutionary organizations had little influence on government and none at all on employers. The United Mineworkers, who had finally beaten the PWA in 1917, fell victim to internal divisions and persistent wage cutting by absentee employers. The same combination of internal and external problems afflicted miners in the West as well. As if fragmentation were not enough for unions, judicial appeals decided in 1926 that labour relations were in the constitutional domain of the provinces, not Ottawa. Even old-age pension, the one social benefit that labour's parliamentary representatives could extract from the postwar Liberal government, depended on provincial consent (37, 55, 57, 61).

The Great Depression

Neither Canadian labour nor the provinces were in any condition to face the crisis of the 1930s. In fact, considering the extent of the economic disaster, union membership was surprisingly robust, declining only by about one-eighth from 319,000 in 1929 to a low of 281,000 in 1935. In the first four years of the decade, wage rates fell far more slowly than prices.

The Depression left few Canadians unaffected but its real impact was on the young, the unskilled, and on Westerners. Union leaders pressed governments for unemployment insurance and public works, but only the Workers' Unity League tried hard to organize. The League's efforts ended sometimes in bloodshed and often in defeat — in Estevan, Stratford, Flin Flon, Noranda, Blubber Bay — but even setbacks added something to Canada's sparse tradition of class struggle. Communists also led in organizing the unemployed and the wretchedly paid workers in government relief camps (20, 24, 26, 39).

The Depression sent some Canadians desperately hunting for political remedies. Voters turned to charismatic leaders like Duff Pattullo of British Columbia or Mitchell Hepburn of Ontario, who professed a comforting mixture of sympathy for change and for old-fashioned values. Desperate Albertans scrapped a farmer government in favour of Social Credit and the Biblical oratory of William Aberhart. A scattering of western radicals, socialists, and labour reformers met in Calgary in 1932 and Regina in 1933 to create the Cooperative Commonwealth Federation (Farmer Labour Socialist). Its leader was Winnipeg's labour M.P., J.S. Woodsworth but, apart from Aaron Mosher, few Canadian trade unionists wanted anything to do with the CCF.

In 1935, Communists sent unemployed workers on an "On-to-Ottawa" trek. It ended in bloodshed at Regina on July 1. The beneficiaries were not the Communists but the Liberals. With this further evidence of their slogan, "King or Chaos," they swept back to power in the autumn (3, 7, 67).

INDUSTRIAL UNIONISM

The CIO in the U.S. and Canada

The year 1935 had other events that affected Canadian labour from afar. Moscow commanded the Workers' Unity League to dissolve. Communists must join other labour organizations to fight fascism. In Washington, the Wagner Act became law. American unions could now win recognition from obdurate employers in supervised certification votes. A National Labour Relations Board could punish unfair practices by management (after 1947, by unions). The Wagner Act, plus courage and ingenuity, allowed Depression-hardened organizers to crack open the huge plants that had defied unionization for sixty years. New industrial unions, ignoring barriers of craft or trade, organized anyone who worked, claiming that President Franklin Delano Roosevelt wanted them to sign a card. Splitting from an entrenched, craft-dominated AFL in 1937, the initials of the new Congress of Industrial Organizations (CIO) became as magic a symbol as the Knights of Labor had been in the 1880s.

In Canada, the CIO sounded like magic too, as news came of victories in Akron and Flint and Pittsburgh. In Oshawa in the spring of 1937, workers at the big General Motors plant signed up in the CIO's United Auto Workers and demanded a contract. Opposition came less from the company than from Premier Hepburn, who was convinced that the CIO was a Communist conspiracy bent on seizing Ontario's gold mines. A penniless CIO could help its Canadian affiliate only with brave words and bluff— barely enough to win a compromise settlement. CIO unions were stalled in their organizing drive in Canada. The organizers, sharply divided between CCF and Communist sympathies, fought each other (1, 45).

The Second World War

In 1939, Canada again found herself in a world war though its impact only hit home with the Nazi blitzkrieg in the spring of 1940. Once again, wartime lifted Canadians out of a deep economic depression. By 1941, the manpower shortage was so acute that the government introduced national selective service for men and women. Avoiding earlier errors, Mackenzie King's wartime government determined to finance the war on a pay-as-you-go basis, with high taxes. A burst of inflation was stopped with sweeping price controls. A National War Labour Board ordered wages held at 1925-29 levels. A flood of wartime directives froze workers in essential occupations, removed able-bodied men from nonessential occupations and severely controlled employers' rights to hire and fire and employees' rights to quit or switch jobs.

A fragmented labour movement met the war in fragmented ways. TLC leaders stayed in close touch with King and his labour minister, Humphrey Mitchell. Communist unionists, on Moscow's orders, initially disrupted the war effort and then, when Hitler invaded Russia in 1941, supported it fanatically. The CCF generally supported the war effort but used it as a chance to make both union and political gains. In 1939, two years after the AFL expelled its new industrial unions, the TLC followed suit. Promptly, they linked up with Mosher's organization in a new Canadian Congress of Labour (CCL).

As in 1914-18, war brought an organizing scramble. This time, Canada turned out ships, aircraft, vehicles, artillery, radios, and radar sets as well as shells and fuses. Every kind of raw material, from steel and aluminum to synthetic rubber and uranium oxide, was needed. Every war industry could be unionized. For the new industrial unions, it was a golden opportunity but craft unions forgot their principles and joined the rush, bringing stronger finances and more experience. By 1944, Canada had 724,000 union members, twice the 1939 total (1, 20).

The National War Labour Order

The road was not always smooth for the unions. C.D. Howe, King's minister of munitions, had no sympathy with them. Neither did most of the "dollar-a-year" men who helped him manage the economy, nor key employers like H.G. Hilton of the Steel Company of Canada. A bitter midwinter strike in 1941-2 showed Kirkland Lake's gold miners how easily the IDI Act could defeat a union recognition bid. Even when organized, unions were bound by wartime wage controls.

By 1943, with the war's outcome no longer in doubt, some unions were ready to rebel. In January, the United Steelworkers struck for a fifty-five-cent-an-hour wage. Howe fumed but the government gave in. Other strikes followed until 1943 came close to rivalling 1919 as a year of labour conflict. Something had to be done. King turned to the War Labour Board. Its chairman, Judge C.P. McTague, had been a reluctant participant in the Kirkland Lake fiasco. His report was clear. Too many strikes were not about money or hours but the simple, basic right to organize. Canada must have an equivalent of the U.S. Wagner Act.

For King, convinced of his own expertise, that advice was painful. It questioned the perfection of his IDI Act. However, it was also clear to him that workers were deserting his Liberal Party in droves for a growing CCF. In 1943, the Canadian Congress of Labour had actually endorsed the CCF shortly after the party had come close to victory in Ontario. Desperately, King took his party leftward. In 1944, the

Liberals approved family allowances and promised universal health and hospital insurance and a postwar guarantee of full employment. In February, 1944, King's cabinet approved P.C. 1003, the National War Labour Order, combining both McTague's recommendations and the principles of the IDI Act. For the first time in Canada, clear rules provided for the definition of bargaining units, certification and recognition of unions and enforcement of fair labour practices. Combined with the IDI Act's conception of investigation and cooling-off periods, P.C. 1003 established the basis of Canadian labour legislation. Translated into a federal statute in 1948 and eventually adapted and modified by ten provincial labour-relations systems, the 1944 regulation remains Canadian labour's basic guarantee (41, 52).

The Rand Formula

The extent of that guarantee was tested when peace returned in 1945. A union might be certified but its effectiveness depended on financial support. In the fall of 1945, the United Auto Workers struck the Ford Motor Company in Windsor, demanding a guaranteed checkoff of dues from every employee. A long, tense strike, marked by a car blockade of the plant, ended in arbitration. Mr. Justice Ivan Rand scolded the union for its tactics but conceded that every worker in the plant benefited from representation and every worker must pay dues even without choosing to join the union. The Rand Formula became a basis for union security (49).

Postwar Strikes

Opinion polls showed that most Canadians expected their country to return to a depression after the war. Employers were confident that hard times would tame the brash new unions. Instead, the Liberal government now knew how to produce full employment. Canadians had fifteen years of unsatisfied appetites for homes, cars, refrigerators, and even kitchen tables. Compulsory wartime savings and generous veterans' benefits gave them purchasing power. Manufacturers could sell anything they could hire workers to produce.

When industrial unions coordinated their 1946 bargaining strategy, Canada was in a boom, not a bust. Although employers fought union demands and King's government, nervous about postwar inflation, also tried to curb wage demands, the only result was longer strikes. Employers with orders to fill simply had to give in. British Columbia woodworkers, lake seamen, workers for the powerful textile trust at Valleyfield and Hamilton, and steelworkers at Sydney and Sault Ste. Marie helped to make 1946 one of Canada's three most costly years for strikes (the others were 1919 and 1976). The rubber industry lost 800,000 man-days of production and wages. More strikes followed in 1947. The Packinghouse Workers dealt with three powerful companies working under nine provincial labour laws. A settlement was possible only after Saskatchewan's new CCF government broke a common provincial front. Not all strikes were victories, however. Nova Scotia fishermen and Cape Breton miners lost bitter battles.

Yet there was little of the violence and desperation of past labour struggles. Even at Hamilton, where Stelco's mill was blockaded for weeks, a veteran labour mayor, Sam Lawrence, and a well-managed police force cooled tensions. Strikes were long but settlements were realistic compromises. There were no obvious differences among Communist, CCF, or nonpartisan unions in their bargaining tactics. There was, however, an increasingly bitter underlying rivalry. By 1947, it could not be contained (1, 13, 31).

Labour's Cold War

CCF suspicion of the Communists began with J.S. Woodsworth; it was amply reciprocated. In the war years, Communists effectively nullified the CCL endorsement of their political rivals. In 1945, the CCF blamed stunning setbacks in federal and Ontario elections on local alliances between Liberals and hard-working Communist organizers. CCF unionists vowed revenge long before the Cold War made anti-Communism fashionable. Aided by the Communists' own errors, the CCF had driven Communist influence from the CCL by the end of 1949. In the less political TLC (which also endorsed the Liberals in 1945) the Communist issue focused on the Canadian Seamen's Union (CSU). At first, TLC leaders defended the Communist-run CSU even after its president (and the TLC's secretary-treasurer) Pat Sullivan claimed that the Communist party had ordered violent and costly strikes in 1946 and 1947 for Soviet policy reasons. AFL pressure and his own exasperation at CSU tactics caused Percy Bengough, the Congress president, to switch his stand. In a sordid episode, the Canadian union was wiped out by the invading Seafarers' International Union (SIU) and by a federal policy of disposing of a deep-sea merchant fleet (14, 29, 59, 62, 67).

In 1950, serious Communist influence was removed from both the CCL and the TLC. What had begun as a struggle between Communists and democratic socialists was caught up in the Cold War. Some Communist unions, notably the United Electrical Workers and the United Fishermen and Allied Workers, survived to rejoin the Canadian Labour Congress in 1972. Others dissolved into non-Communist unions.

By 1950, most of the distinctions between the TLC and the CCL had faded. Wartime organization drives had blurred old distinctions between craft and industrial unionism. Both congresses were dominated by internationally based unions. Both had eliminated Communist influence; both endorsed Canada's Cold War foreign policy and free collective bargaining. Both repeatedly pledged themselves to a reunion of what American pressure had split asunder in 1939. Only the CCL's link to the CCF and the personal rivalry of two old men, Bengough and Mosher, kept them apart.

The Asbestos Strike

Indeed, reunion might even extend to the Catholic unions. The once quiescent syndicates no longer espoused Catholic social corporatism and adherence to the chaplains. In 1949, a long violent strike at Asbestos pitted the Catholic syndicates against provincial police sent by the conservative, nationalist government of Maurice Duplessis. In the ultimate settlement, neither side could claim much of a victory but a key segment of Quebec labour and intellectual opinion had split with the old clerical nationalism. The split was confirmed when a Catholic union struck Dupuis Frères, French Canada's answer to the English-owned department stores and a national institution. If Canadian labour could unite, the Canadian and Catholic Confederation of Labour might be part of the merger. A million and a quarter Canadian unionists would stand in one body (64, 65).

The Canadian Labour Congress

As any business could testify, competition can have its costs. Rival unions wasted money on raiding, not organizing. With only 350,000 members in 1952, the CCL was unlikely to narrow the gap to the TLC's 522,000. Its drive to organize the T.

Eaton Company as a breakthrough to white-collar workers had proved a costly failure. Newfoundland's entry into Confederation in 1949 had added only a few thousand members to each congress. When Percy Bengough retired, his successor, Claude Jodoin, was acceptable to the CCL and perhaps also to the Catholic confederation. But a Canadian merger had to wait for the Americans. Not until the AFL and CIO signed a no-raiding pact in 1953 could negotiations begin. Mosher's retirement after an embarrassing quarrel in his own union finally cleared the decks. In 1956, not long after the American organizations had come together as the AFL-CIO, the Canadian Labour Congress (CLC) was born (23, 29).

The biggest potential stumbling block, political action, was discreetly deferred to the new CLC's 1958 convention. By then, the CCF seemed to have been flattened beyond recognition in the Diefenbaker landslide. With the consent of CCF leaders and much grumbling from its rank and file, the Canadian Labour Congress committed itself to building a new party for labour, the CCF, and "the liberally minded." Three years of persuasion, education, and organizing culminated in Ottawa in the summer of 1961 with the formation of the New Democratic Party (NDP). Then, as it had promised, the CLC slipped discreetly away to allow the NDP to find friends among old CCFers, new labour backers, and sceptical voters (29, 48, 67).

UNIONS AND GOVERNMENTS

Union Setbacks

The high hopes of the merger movement were not realized. By 1957, Canada's postwar prosperity was fading fast as European and Japanese industries returned to world competition. Unemployment and recession pushed Canadians into a conservative, antiunion mood as the Diefenbaker years began. The prestige of the new Canadian Labour Congress meant nothing when the Duplessis government crushed an illegal strike at Murdochville in 1957 or when Joey Smallwood abruptly decertified the International Woodworkers of America in the midst of a bitter 1959 strike. The congress could not even prevent a powerful affiliate, the Carpenters' Brotherhood, from invading the IWA jurisdiction at the Newfoundland premier's invitation. By 1960, the Catholic unions made it clear that they would not join. Instead, under Jean Marchand, they abandoned the last traces of confessionalism and emerged in 1960 as a nationalist and militant Confederation of National Trade Unions (CNTU). It was a portent of Quebec's quiet revolution (27, 30).

The congress faced other setbacks. Canadian unions had prided themselves on their freedom from gangsterism. The painful exception was the Seafarers' International Union, whose brutal tactics against the Canadian Seamen's Union continued through the 1950s under its ex-convict president, Hal C. Banks. Not until 1960 did the congress expel the SIU, and then it had to plead for government help to end Banks' reign of terror. A Royal Commission found seventy-five documented instances of violence and wondered pointedly why union leaders had not complained before (35).

Political Frustrations

Even political action was a disappointment. Under the former Saskatchewan premier, Tommy Douglas, the NDP won nineteen seats in 1962, eighteen in 1963 and even after its electoral support climbed to its plateau of 18 percent in 1965, parliamentary strength hovered at twenty seats. Old CCFers had protested the trade-union link; many CLC affiliates, particularly among the craft unions, conspicuously ignored the new party. In British Columbia, where the NDP made its greatest gains, Premier W.A.C. Bennett passed legislation banning union financial contributions. Other politicians muttered similar threats. In Ottawa, the NDP link was an excuse for the Diefenbaker government to ignore CLC nominees for government appointments.

The most important single goal of the merger was to organize the unorganized. In an antiunion climate, governments made certification harder. "In the field of Labour-Management Relations," claimed a 1958 Ontario legislature committee, "the dominant public interest lies in the preservation of public peace and the protection of the individual worker against oppression" (48, p. 247). Oppression meant unions. Employers learned new techniques to drag out certification procedures. The Murdochville strike was the outcome of five years of delay. Union strength grew slowly, but the share of potential membership fell from 33.3 percent in 1956 to only 29.4 percent in 1964.

Meanwhile, technological change wiped out entire occupations. Two desperate strikes could not save the Brotherhood of Locomotive Firemen from the advent of diesel engines. In 1964, Toronto printers, members of Canada's oldest continuing union, launched a futile strike against drastic technological changes in the city's three newspapers. A year later, even the cautious locomotive engineers risked their jobs to protest run-throughs made possible by the Canadian National Railway's new equipment. After investigation, Mr. Justice Samuel Freedman criticized the men but he also urged a radical modification of an old doctrine, the inviolability of a labour contract. Unions, he argued, should be able to negotiate the impact of technological change even during the life of a contract.

Freedman's suggestions became only one of a host of union demands during the 1960s. Organizers wanted to change certification rules so that abstainers were not automatically "no" voters. Younger workers were fed up with the outworn Mackenzie King theory that "cooling-off" periods and protracted mediation eased tensions. The truth was likely the opposite, as more and more wildcat strikes demonstrated. The CNTU wanted to break up national bargaining units which favoured its CLC rivals. In Ontario and British Columbia, unionists went to jail to protest the easy granting of ex parte injunctions to employers. High on the list of problems facing a reelected but minority Liberal government in 1963 was the challenge of civil-service unionism.

Public-Sector Unionism

Public-sector unions had existed in the post office since 1891. Saskatchewan's CCF government gave its employees the right to bargain and strike in 1944. Those were exceptions. Civil servants traditionally traded low pay for job security, pensions, and — in the public mind — easy workloads. By the 1960s, those advantages were gone. Unionized workers had won similar security and fringe benefits in the private sector. Promised wage gains for civil servants had been repeatedly postponed in the Diefenbaker years in a failing effort to balance the budget. By 1963, Liberals, Tories, and New Democrats all promised federal employees to bring in collective bargaining. Quebec's example in 1964, granting the right to strike, set the pace.

In 1967, Parliament adopted the Public Service Staff Relations Act (PSSRA). Modeled closely on familiar labour-relations legislation, the PSSRA was as important a statutory landmark as the IDI Act or P.C. 1003. It challenged the theory that only Parliament could control public spending although governments in practice would continue to try to use public-service salaries to curb general wage demands. Under the PSSRA, bargaining units could opt for compulsory arbitration or the right to strike. Weak and divided civil-service federations forgot old grievances and merged as the Public Service Alliance of Canada.

Across Canada, provincial governments followed Ottawa's example although Alberta and Ontario denied public-sector workers the right to strike. The merger of the TLC and CCL rival unions in a more powerful Canadian Union of Public Employees (CUPE) coincided with a dramatic increase in public spending on education, health, and social services. Like civil servants, public-service employees were ready to be organized. By the early 1970s, CUPE strength had soared to make it the largest union in Canada. Public-sector organizing extended to professionals as nurses and teachers abandoned historic prejudices against unionism and strike action.

The Woods Task Force

The tide of change seemed to reach a peak in 1966, with a wave of wildcat strikes, the rejection of negotiated settlements by union members, the first railway strike since 1950, and the first of a painful succession of national postal strikes. At Montreal, where the rush to complete Expo 67 had allowed construction workers to extract record wages, the normally passive longshoremen closed the port until their demands were met. When St. Lawrence Seaway workers threatened to follow suit, a government negotiator brought peace with an unprecedented 30 percent wage increase. Amidst a storm of criticism, the federal government bundled up its labour-relations problems and handed them to a "task force" headed by Professor H.D. Woods of McGill University.

By the time Woods reported, Canada had a majority government and a new prime minister. Pierre Elliott Trudeau had backed the Asbestos strikers in 1949, voted NDP in 1963, and joined the Liberal government with the CNTU's Jean Marchand in 1965. Unionists, like other Canadians, found him enigmatic and unpredictable, strangely cold to the pragmatic and material concerns of ordinary workers. They were bewildered by astonishing switches from promising "no more free stuff" in his 1968 election to transforming unemployment insurance into a huge income-maintenance plan by 1972; from denouncing wage controls in 1974 to imposing them in 1975.

Unions and Nationalism

One Trudeau position was clear: his disdain for emotional nationalism, in Canada or in his native Quebec. Canadians felt differently. Quebec nationalism, punctuated by the October crisis of 1970 and a near-general strike in 1972, elected a provincial government in 1976 pledged to Quebec independence. Canadians as a whole, resentful of their failing branch-plant economy and United States policy in Vietnam, experienced a wave of anti-American feeling. Canadian unions, with their international connections and their continuing divisions in Quebec, were acutely vulnerable. Within the CLC, the growth of Canadian-based public-service unions ended the old dominance of the internationals. The 1972 CLC convention avoided disruption only by surrendering to demands from the Quebec Federation of Labour for greater autonomy and financial resources and to CUPE's insistence on autonomy guidelines for international-union affiliates.

Pressure on international unions was heightened by the annual publication of statistics collected under a new Corporations and Labour Unions Returns Act which cheerfully exaggerated the amount of money Canadian unionists sent to American-based union headquarters. Since many Canadian districts in fact represented a serious financial drain on parent unions, the trend of the 1970s was for friendly separation and greater autonomy. The Communication Workers of Canada and the Canadian Paperworkers Union emerged from international affiliation into full independence. Other unions, threatened by splits and raids from a flock of small, fervently nationalist independent unions, either followed suit or improved services to Canadian members (16).

More dramatic was the impact of radicalism and nationalism on Quebec unions. Sometimes, it seemed that Marxism had replaced Catholicism as an ideological pillar. In fact, unions became vehicles of revolutionary protest for young people and intellectuals angry at English dominance of the Quebec economy and at a Liberal provincial government that stood squarely in the path of independence. A 1972 "Common Front" of the CNTU, the Quebec Federation of Labour, and the teachers' union set out ostensibly to bargain for the province's public employees; months of fiery speeches and strikes gave the image, if not the substance, of a civil war against the government of Robert Bourassa. The tactics failed. Bourassa was triumphantly reelected in 1973, the labour alliance was shattered in the struggle for union jurisdiction over the huge James Bay hydroelectricity development, and Quebec nationalists learned to work more quietly and systematically, for the Parti Québécois victory to come in 1976.

The Anti-Inflation Board

For most Canadians, inflation, unemployment and the local symptoms of deindustrialization rivaled nationalism as preoccupations. The blame might be spread among the Trudeau government, the Arab-dominated world oil cartel, and multinational corporations; however, unions were also handy scapegoats. Canada's collective-bargaining system generally had been praised by the Woods Task Force, and it was altered only in details by the new federal labour code of 1971 and by legislation in the three western provinces that fell to the NDP between 1969 and 1972. Certification became easier; technological change might be negotiated more frequently; and union members gained more control over safety and occupational health. However, to fight inflation, unions still had to lead their members out on strike. A public, attuned to judge causes by the amount of noise they made, could easily believe that wage demands fueled inflation, not vice versa (60). On Thanksgiving Day, 1975, the Trudeau government unveiled a sweeping program of controls designed to curb inflation. The most obvious target of the new Anti-Inflation Board was union bargaining power.

Protest and Recession

Unions fought back. The CLC coordinated court challenges, protest rallies, and a national "Day of Protest" on the anniversary of controls. A few union insiders, anticipating a long period of government-administered controls, developed an ingenious case for a tripartite government-management-labour operation of the economy with an all-powerful CLC playing all the cards for its affiliates. Such schemes dissolved by 1978 when controls, with all their anomalies and distortions, abruptly ended. As it had feared, Canadian labour emerged to fight for catch-up gains in an economic setting of plant shutdowns, mass layoffs, and the highest unemployment since the 1930s. As it had before in hard times, the labour movement tightened its belt and remembered that it was a political as well as an economic force. Belatedly, the CLC, under a younger and more aggressive president, Dennis McDermott, set out to see what it could do for its neglected political partner, the New Democratic Party.

In what is termed its "parallel campaign," the CLC and its more politicised affiliates set out to win union members for the NDP through direct contacts in the work place and through telephone canvassing of their homes. For the first time, union political action had moved past the traditional resolutions and modest financial contributions. Results showed how little heed most union members gave to their leaders' urging.

Political militancy and nationalism strained the unity of the Canadian Labour Congress. New Quebec legislation, designed to end costly union rivalry on construction sites and to support national unionism, led to charges of raiding by the Quebec Federation of Labour against the building trades. An even older grievance was the CLC practice of representation at conventions by rank-and-file unionists, in contrast to the AFL-CIO practice of representation by union officials. The upshot was a major break in March 1981 between the congress and some of its venerable and conservative affiliates.

It was a worrying development in a decade which promised Canadian labour more than a fair share of frustrations and anxieties. As usual, Canadian unionism could assemble a confusing balance sheet of setbacks and achievements. By the 1980s, the myths that women and professionals would never join unions had been exploded — though experience had proved that they would do so only on their own terms. In a century, unionism had transformed the poor in Canada from a majority to a minority.

The changes had come only because of laws and politics. Further changes would come only when law and politics allowed.

REFERENCES AND WORKS CITED

1. Abella, I. *Nationalism, Communism and Canadian Labor* (Toronto: University of Toronto Press, 1973).

2. Allen, R. *The Social Passion: Religion and Social Reform in Canada* (Toronto: University of Toronto Press, 1971).

3. Avakumovic, I. *The Communist Party in Canada: A History* (Toronto: McClelland and Stewart, 1975).

4. Avery, D. *Dangerous Foreigners: European Immigrant Workers and Labor Radicalism in Canada, 1896-1932* (Toronto: McClelland and Stewart, 1979).

5. Babcock, R. *Gompers in Canada: A Study in American Continentalism Before the First World War* (Toronto: University of Toronto Press, 1975).

6. Battye, J. "The Nine-Hour Pioneers: The Genesis of the Canadian Labor Movement," *Labour/Le Travailleur,* Vol. 4 (1979), 25-26.

7. Beeching, W., and P. Clarke. *Yours in the Struggle: Reminiscences of Tim Buck* (Toronto: N.C. Press, 1977).

8. Bercuson, D. *Confrontation in Winnipeg. Labour, Industrial Relations and the General Strike* (Montreal: McGill-Queen's University Press, 1974).

9. Bercuson, D. *Fools and Wise Men: The Rise and Fall of One Big Union* (Toronto: McGraw Hill-Ryerson, 1978).

10. Bradwin, E. *The Bunkhouse Man* (Toronto: University of Toronto Press, 1972).

11. Cooper, J.I. "The Quebec Ship-Labourers' Benevolent Society," *Canadian Historical Review,* Vol. 30 (1949), 336-343.

12. Copp, J.T. *The Anatomy of Poverty: The Condition of the Working Class in Montreal, 1897-1929* (Toronto: McClelland and Stewart, 1974).

13. Copp, J.T. *Industrial Unionism in Kitchener* (Elora: Cumnock Press, 1976).

14. Copp, J.T. *The IUE in Canada* (Elora: Cumnock Press, 1980).

15. Craven, Paul. *"An Impartial Umpire": Industrial Relations and the Canadian State* (Toronto: University of Toronto Press, 1981).

16. Crispo, J. *International Unionism: A Study of Canadian-American Relations* (Toronto: McGraw Hill-Ryerson, 1967).

17. Cross, M.S. (Ed.). *The Workingman in the Nineteenth Century* (Toronto: Oxford University Press, 1974).

18. Dawson, R.M. *William Lyon Mackenzie King: A Political Biography, Vol 1* (Toronto: University of Toronto Press, 1958).

19. Desrosiers, P., and D. Heroux. *Le Travailleur Québécois et le Syndicalisme* (Montreal: Les Presses de l'Université du Québec, 1973).

20. Dumas, E. *The Bitter Thirties in Quebec* (Montreal: Black Rose, 1975).

21. Ferns, H.S., and B. Ostry. *The Age of Mackenzie King* (Toronto: James Lorimer, 1975).

22. Fingard, J. "The Winter's Tale: Contours of Pre-Industrial Poverty in British America, 1815-1860," *Historical Papers* (1974), 65-94.

23. Forsey, E. "The Movement Toward Labour Unity in Canada: History and Implications," *Canadian Journal of Economics and Political Science,* Vol. 24 (1958), 78-83.

24. Gray, J. *The Winter Years* (Toronto: McClelland and Stewart, 1966).

25. Hann, R. "Brainworkers and the Knights of Labor," in G. Kealey and P. Warrian (Eds.), *Essays in Canadian Working Class History* (Toronto: McClelland and Stewart, 1976), pp. 35-57.

26. Hanson, S.D. "Estevan 1931," in I. Abella (Ed.), *On Strike: Six Key Labor Struggles in Canada, 1919-1949* (Toronto: James, Lewis and Samuel, 1974), pp. 33-77.

27. Hattenhauer, R.J. *A Brief Labor History of Newfoundland* (St. John's: Queen's Printer, n.d.).

28. Heron, C., and B. Palmer. "Through the Prism of the Strike," *Canadian Historical Review,* Vol. 58 (1977), 423-457.

29. Horowitz, G. *Canadian Labour in Politics* (Toronto: University of Toronto Press, 1968).

30. Isbester, F. "Quebec Labour in Perspective," in R. Miller and F. Isbester (Eds.), *Canadian Labour in Transition* (Scarborough, Ont.: Prentice-Hall, 1971), pp. 240-266.

31. Jantzi, D. "The Ford and Stelco Strikes," in R. Laxer (Ed.), *Union Organization and Strikes* (Toronto: OISE Publications, 1978), pp. 40-78.

32. Kealey, G.S. (Ed.). *Canada Investigates Industrialism* (Toronto: University of Toronto Press, 1973).

33. Kealey, G.S. *Toronto Workers Respond to Industrial Capitalism* (Toronto: University of Toronto Press, 1980).

34. Kennedy, D. *The Knights of Labour in Canada* (London: University of Western Ontario Press, 1950).

35. Kwavnick, D. *Organized Labour and Pressure Group Politics: The Canadian Labour Congress, 1956-1968* (Montreal: McGill-Queen's University Press, 1971).

36. Langdon, S. "The Emergence of the Canadian Working Class Movement, 1845-1875," *Journal of Canadian Studies,* Vol. 8 (1973), 3-13 (May), 8-26 (August).

37. Latham, A.B. *The Catholic and National Labor Unions of Canada* (Toronto: University of Toronto Press, 1930).

38. Laxer, J. *Canada's Unions* (Toronto: McClelland and Stewart, 1976).

39. Liversedge, R. *Recollections of the On-to-Ottawa Trek* (Toronto: McClelland and Stewart, 1973).

40. Logan, H.A. *Trade Unions in Canada* (Toronto: Macmillan, 1948).

41. MacDowell, L. "The Formation of the Canadian Industrial Relations System During World War II," *Labour/Le Travailleur,* Vol. 3 (1978), 175-196.

42. MacEwen, P. *Miners and Steelworkers of Cape Breton* (Toronto: Samuel Stevens and Hakkert, 1976).

43. Masters, D.C. *The Winnipeg General Strike* (Toronto: University of Toronto Press, 1950).

44. McCormack, R. *Reformers, Rebels, and Revolutionaries: The Western Canadian Radical Movement, 1899-1919* (Toronto: University of Toronto Press, 1978).

45. McKenty, N. *Mitch Hepburn* (Toronto: McClelland and Stewart, 1967).

46. McNaught, K., and D. Bercuson. *The Winnipeg Strike, 1919* (Toronto: Longman, 1974).

47. Morton, D. *NDP: Social Democracy in Canada* (Toronto: Samuel, Stevens and Hakkert, 1977).

48. Morton, D., and J.T. Copp. *Working People: An Illustrated History of Canadian Labour* (Ottawa: Deneau and Greenberg, 1980).

49. Moulton, D. "Windsor, 1945," in I. Abella (Ed.), *On Strike: Six Key Labour Struggles in Canada, 1919-1949* (Toronto: James, Lewis and Samuel, 1974), pp. 129-162.

50. Ostry, B. "Conservatives, Liberals and Labour in the 1870's" *Canadian Historical Review,* Vol. 41 (1960), 93-127.

51. Palmer, B. *A Culture in Conflict: Skilled Workers and Industrial Capitalism in Hamilton, Ontario, 1860-1914* (Montreal: McGill-Queen's University Press, 1979).

52. Phillips, P. *No Power Greater: A Century of Labour in B.C.* (Vancouver: B.C. Federation of Labour, 1967).

53. Pickersgill, J. *The Mackenzie King Record, Vol. 1* (Toronto: University of Toronto Press, 1960).

54. Piva, M.J. *The Condition of the Working Class in Toronto, 1900-1921* (Ottawa: University of Ottawa Press, 1979).

55. Robin, M. *Radical Politics and Canadian Labour, 1880-1930* (Kingston: Queen's University Industrial Relations Centre, 1968).

56. Robin, M. *The Company Province, Vol. 1* (Toronto: McClelland and Stewart, 1972).

57. Rodney, W. *Soldiers of the International: A History of the Communist Party of Canada, 1919-1929* (Toronto: University of Toronto Press, 1968).

58. Siemiatckyi, M. "Munitions and Labour Militancy: The 1916 Hamilton Machinists' Strike," *Labour/Le Travailleur,* Vol. 3 (1978), 131-152.

59. Stanton, J. *Life and Death of the Canadian Seamen's Union* (Toronto: Steel Rail, 1979).

60. Stewart, W. *Strike* (Toronto: McClelland and Stewart, 1976).

61. Struthers, J. "Prelude to Depression: The Federal Government and Unemployment, 1918-1929," *Canadian Historical Review,* Vol. 58 (1977), 277-293.

62. Sullivan, J.A. *Red Sails on the Great Lakes* (Toronto: Macmillan, 1955).

63. Thompson, J.H. *The Harvests of War: The Prairie West, 1914-1918* (Toronto: McClelland and Stewart, 1978).

64. Trudeau, P.E. (Ed.). *The Asbestos Strike* (Toronto: James Lorimer, 1974).

65. Vadeboncoeur, P. *En Grève: L'Histoire de la C.S.N. et des Luttes Mênées Par Ses Militants de 1937 à 1963* (Montreal: Editions du Jour, 1973).

66. Whittaker, R. "The Liberal Corporatist Ideas of Mackenzie King," *Labour/Le Travailleur,* Vol. 2 (1977), 127-169.

67. Young, W. *The Anatomy of a Party: The National CCF* (Toronto: University of Toronto Press, 1969).

QUESTIONS

1. "Boundaries were made by the bosses." Assess the impact of international influences on the development of a trade-union movement in Canada.

2. What was the contribution of William Lyon Mackenzie King to the practice of industrial relations in Canada?

3. What were the goals in establishing central labour organizations in Canada, and what obstacles did they have to overcome?

4. Time lost through strikes reached record levels in 1919, 1946, and 1976. Is there a pattern in the rise and decline of labour militancy in Canada?

5. Assess the legal and political developments which led to the emergence in Canada of (a) craft unions, (b) industrial unions, *or* (c) public-service unions.

6. Unions in Canada have differed from American unions by helping to establish a sympathetic political party. What are the arguments for or against this course of action?

7. In 1976, the Canadian Labour Congress briefly endorsed the concept of "social corporatism." Assess the influence of corporatist thinking in the philosophy of industrial relations in Canada.

8. American labour history is dominated by "great men" like Samuel Gompers or John L. Lewis. Comment on the contributions of similar influential figures in Canadian labour history or explain their absence.

9. "Une province qui n'est pas comme les autres." How far does Quebec's sense of being different extend to the labour movement? What elements are comparable?

THE PARTIES
IN LABOUR RELATIONS

JOHN H. GODARD and THOMAS A. KOCHAN

6. Canadian Management Under Collective Bargaining: Policies, Processes, Structure, and Effectiveness

This chapter first provides a general overview of the debate over management under collective bargaining and proposes an "interest group" approach to analysing managerial policies and practices. Based upon the findings from a recent study of Canadian firms, a descriptive analysis of managerial policies, processes, structure, and effectiveness under collective bargaining is then presented. The analysis draws extensively from the field of organization theory. Some of the findings are: pattern bargaining is widespread as a managerial policy; labour-relations decisions are highly centralized in Canadian firms; and managers seem less concerned with their ability to bargain effectively than they are with the morale and productivity of workers.

Management is a central participant in labour relations. An understanding of management is therefore essential to a balanced view of any labour-relations system. Yet, to date, the analysis of management under collective bargaining has not progressed much beyond that of theoretical debate. In general, related research has focused upon narrow and specific issues or has been anecdotal and impressionistic in nature. While a few more comprehensive analyses have been attempted, these have involved studies of major corporations in the United States and may have only limited applicability to the Canadian context (19, 32).

In this chapter, existing theory and research are built upon and extended to the Canadian context, based primarily upon the preliminary findings of a recent study of labour relations in Canadian firms.[1] The purpose is to provide a descriptive analysis of the organizational characteristics and effectiveness of management under collective bargaining in Canada. Various theoretical issues are examined, but it is beyond the scope of this analysis to engage in a comprehensive discussion of the theoretical debate over management or of the sources of variation in managerial

1. We would like to thank the Conference Board in Canada, Labour Canada, and the New York State School of Industrial and Labour Relations (Cornell University) for their assistance at various stages in this research. However, we take full responsibility for the findings presented in this chapter.

characteristics and effectiveness from one firm to the next. Instead, a general orientation to management under collective bargaining is provided, and readers are alerted to the need to be aware of the diversity which exists across different firms.

The analysis is divided into five sections. The first section is intended to briefly familiarize readers with the debate over management and to establish a general foundation for understanding managerial policies and practices in labour relations. Sections two through four examine, respectively, the labour-relations policies and priorities of management; the labour-relations processes of management, and the structural arrangements through which these processes are performed and coordinated; and the evaluations of Canadian managers of their effectiveness in labour relations under collective bargaining. Section five consists of a qualitative analysis of three unionized Canadian firms.

MANAGEMENT UNDER COLLECTIVE BARGAINING: GENERAL FOUNDATIONS

Despite the historical pattern of managerial resistance to unionization, the actual impact of unionism upon management has been the subject of an intensive debate which predates the institution of collective bargaining as it is known today. In this section, a brief overview of this debate is provided, along with relevant research findings. The field of organizational theory is then drawn upon to place this debate into perspective and establish a general foundation for the remainder of the analysis.

The Debate Over Management Under Collective Bargaining

According to conventional neoclassical economists, the primary, if not the sole, objective of management is to maintain and enhance the firm's competitive position and profitability by maximizing cost effectiveness and productivity. Unionism only serves to frustrate this objective by artificially inflating labour costs and interfering with managerial decision-making flexibility (11, 31). Hence, unionism is believed to have an entirely negative impact (at least from the managerial perspective).

The assumptions made by neoclassical economists have been criticized by a wide variety of authors. One major criticism, most closely associated with the arguments of institutional economists, is that neoclassicists fail to consider the functional consequences which unionism can have for efficiency and productivity (11, 31). Grievance and seniority provisions established under collective bargaining may ensure that workers are treated equitably and consistently, thereby resulting in higher morale and lower turnover, and hence higher productivity and lower hiring and training costs. Unionism also pressures management to search continually for more effective methods of production and induces increased efficiency and productivity by "shocking" management into rationalizing the production process.

A second major criticism, most closely associated with the writings of J.K. Galbraith (13) and, to some extent, with the Marxist school of thought (5, 15, 16), is that the neoclassical approach is predicated upon overly simplistic assumptions about the objectives of management. It is contended that, while managers undoubtedly view costs and productivity as important, they also place a high premium upon acquiring power and control and reducing uncertainty in their environment, even to the point where this is incompatible with economically "rational" behaviour. Accordingly, unionism is potentially instrumental to these objectives. First, the collective agreement fixes wage levels and thereby shelters management from the cost uncertainties otherwise caused by unpredictable wage fluctuations in the labour market. Second, unions help to establish and enforce rules and procedures for regulating and controlling the day-to-day behaviour of workers. Third, they are instrumental in communicating worker concerns and problems to management. It is also maintained that, where unionism has a significant impact upon wages, this is as much because management has been willing to absorb or pass on higher labour costs to consumers as it is because of union power per se.

Finally, a third argument, best illustrated by Alan Flanders' "responsibility theory of management" (10), is that managers are committed to an ethos of social responsibility which they consider to go hand in hand with their position of power and status in society. Consistent with this ethos is a fundamental belief in the right of workers to organize if they so choose, and a recognition of the legitimacy of collective bargaining, provided that unions do not interfere with the firm's productivity or force management to compromise its responsibilities to other interests in society.

Existing research provides only limited and somewhat ambiguous findings as to which of these views can be considered most accurate. On the one hand, indications are that unionism does lead to higher labour costs and slightly lower profitability, particularly under oligopolistic product-market conditions (11, 19, 20). On the other hand, there are indications to suggest that, on the average, unionism can be associated with lower turnover and higher productivity (11, 19). But the direction and magnitude of these effects seems to vary considerably from one firm to the next. Although this variation seems to depend upon the context specific to the firm, and more important, the policies and practices of management itself, researchers have lacked an adequate conceptual framework for analysing the policies and practices of management as an interest group involved in a bargaining relationship. They have also been unable to convincingly explain why, if unions do indeed have positive effects upon management, managers still generally resist union organizing efforts. In short, research has lacked an adequate foundation for understanding managerial behaviour and for placing the debate over management into perspective.

Understanding Management: A General Foundation

In recent years, organizational theorists have increasingly come to view organizations as composed of coalitions of multiple interest groups with competing and often conflicting goals (1, 14, 18, 22). Management constitutes one of the key interest groups — employees, suppliers, creditors, government regulatory agencies, and so forth, constitute others. Each group seeks to achieve its goals, either by forming coalitions with or bargaining with other groups. Regardless of what its ultimate motives are, management must amass and maintain sufficient power and autonomy to assert itself vis-à-vis other groups. Thus, in addition to pursuing the economic objectives of maximizing cost effectiveness and productivity, management seeks to maintain and enhance its power relative to other organizational interest groups, gain control over the behaviour of other groups, and reduce the amount of uncertainty which other groups can introduce into the organization.

Although, in the long run, the economic objectives of management may take priority over the objectives of obtaining power, control, and certainty, there is little a priori reason to expect this to be the case. There may even be conflicts between these objectives. For example, a managerial decision to avoid the uncertainty of a strike in the short run may require granting a higher wage concession than is in management's long-term economic interests. Indeed, the more powerful competing interest groups become (for example, the more powerful the union), the more management must adapt its behaviour and pay attention to its noneconomic objectives. Thus, the nature of managerial behaviour and the importance management places on alternative objectives is likely to be contingent upon the power of the competing interest groups with which it deals. Since the power of these groups varies across settings and over time, an understanding of managerial behaviour requires an understanding of the political, historical, and economic contexts in which the firm exists, and the implications for managerial power, control, and certainty as well as for cost effectiveness and productivity.

THE LABOUR-RELATIONS POLICIES AND PRIORITIES OF MANAGEMENT

In nonunion firms, managerial policies have in general been — and continue to be — to avoid unionization. The practices which serve these policies can include: coercive tactics involving physical and psychological intimidation; union "substitution" practices involving company-established grievance systems (usually without binding arbitration) and wage levels at or above union scale; paternalistic practices involving company-sponsored social events, profit sharing, and even free turkeys at Christmas; and, finally, more advanced "human-relations" practices involving worker-management consultation, information sharing, and job redesign and enrichment (4, 15, 19). Although the nature and sophistication of the practices employed tend to vary according to the size and resources of the firm, managerial resistance to unionization can be explained by more than the economic objectives of management. For example, Reinhard Bendix, in his classic *Work and Authority in Industry* (4), has shown that managers have historically propagated antiunion ideologies in order to maintain and enhance their power and authority in the work place, and that unionization represents a threat to management's self-image. Freeman and Medoff (11) have commented that unionization is resisted in part because it entails a substantial risk for management; although it can have positive effects upon the firm, whether or not these will outweigh its potentially negative effects is uncertain until after a union has actually become established. Furthermore, Goldman and Van Houten (15) have made the case that unionization is resisted primarily because the right of workers to strike is a source of uncertainty to management, even though the strike weapon may not be used frequently and may not entail substantial long-term costs for management when it is used.

Where a union organizing drive has been successful, management can continue to resist collective bargaining by taking a "hard line" in negotiations, encouraging lengthy strikes designed to "break" the union, bypassing union officials by making direct appeals to the workers, and even relocating operations. Most often, however, managers eventually come to accept unionism as a fact of life. A U.S. Conference Board study found that once approximately 40 percent of a firm's employees are unionized, the top labour-relations priority tends to shift from avoiding further unionization to achieving the best possible bargain (19). The same study found that only 3 percent of 600 unionized firms surveyed failed to give some priority to establishing and maintaining cooperative relations with union officials, and that over 40 percent assigned this objective a high priority relative to other labour-relations objectives. This of course does not mean that cooperative relationships are attained or that managers do not often take steps to weaken union power. Yet it does suggest that once unionism has become sufficiently established, management's response tends to change from one of resistance to one of adaptation. This entails the development of specific policy positions on specific issues pertaining to the collective agreement.

Compensation Policies

It is conventionally assumed that managers attempt to set wages and benefits at the minimum level necessary to attract and retain workers of sufficient skills and abilities given the technological requirements of the firm. This normally entails the payment of wages and benefits that are in line with local labour market conditions. Unions not only attempt to push wages and benefits above this level, but also attempt to establish and maintain a "pattern" of comparable settlements across unionized firms with similar characteristics. Hence, where bargaining patterns are prevalent, this is typically viewed as contrary to the objectives of management (9, 19, 24, 25, 27).

There is reason to believe, however, that management may not always be as resistant to pattern bargaining as is conventionally assumed. The U.S. Conference Board study (21) found that industry settlements ranked among the top three criteria taken into account when managers set their wage and benefit targets in 68 percent of firms surveyed, while local labour market conditions received a similar ranking in 51 percent of these firms. Firms assigning greater weights to industry settlements tended to have multiplant agreements, to be larger in size, to be more highly unionized, and to have lower labour-to-total-cost ratios. Sixteen percent of the firms surveyed assigned a high priority to national trends, 19 percent to major union settlements in other industries, and 26 percent to maintaining equitable patterns across all of their operations. Although the findings of this study should be considered tentative, they seem to indicate that managerial accommodation to (or perhaps even support of) pattern bargaining is widespread in the U.S., varying to some degree with the context in which bargaining occurs.

In order to gain some insight into the wage and benefit policies of Canadian managers, a question to this effect was included in a recent survey of Canadian firms. This study involved a mail survey of 300 unionized firms from the manufacturing, retail, and public-utility sectors. (While the response rate was approximately 50 percent, only the first 93 responses were available at the time of writing.) Firms were asked to indicate on a seven-point scale the extent to which they attempt to follow other company, industry, or union settlements when negotiating wages and pension and insurance benefits in the major agreement for their firm. Canadian managers should be especially prone to pattern bargaining, primarily because the Canadian economy is much more highly concentrated than its American counterpart (that is, on the average there are fewer firms competing in each industry), and the existing evidence is that anticompetitive practices are considerably more prevalent (28). The responses of 90 firms participating in the study are reported in Table 1. A response of "one" indicates that management does not attempt to follow other settlements at all, while a response of "seven" indicates that they attempt to follow other settlements very closely. From this table, it is clear that pattern bargaining, in one form or another, is highly pervasive in Canada, at least in the firms surveyed. Fifty-eight percent of the participants answered with a response of six or seven with respect to wages. While attempts to follow other settlements are

Table 1

**Pattern Bargaining: Extent to Which
Other Settlements Are Followed**

Bargaining Item	Not at All 1	2	3	4	5	6	Very Closely 7
				(Percent)			
Wages	-	2	1	14	24	32	26
Pension and insurance benefits	-	3	6	28	19	21	23

SOURCE: *Preliminary results of mail survey to Canadian firms based on 90 usable responses (n = 90).*

significantly lower with respect to pensions and insurance benefits, perhaps because of administrative complexities or difficulties of comparison (24, 25), they are still highly pervasive, with 44 percent of respondents answering with a response of six or seven. Furthermore, fewer than ten percent answered with a response of less than four on both wages and pension and insurance benefits.

Of course, these findings may only reflect managerial adaptations to union power and not managerial preferences per se. They also do not indicate the type of settlements followed. Yet they do indicate that attempting to follow the settlements reached in other firms is strongly entrenched within the compensation policies of Canadian managers.

The Relative Importance of Selected Bargaining Issues

Collective bargaining involves a series of trade-offs between the preferences of management and those of the union. As a result, management must approach the bargaining process with an understanding of the relative importance it gives to each of the issues negotiated. This is likely to vary in accordance with both managerial interests and the extent to which the union raises that issue in negotiations.

In order to determine the relative importance which management assigns to various issues, participants in the survey were presented with a list of bargaining (and behavioural) issues and asked to rate these issues on a scale ranging from "one" (least important) to "four" (most important). They were also instructed to assign at least one issue a value of one and at least one issue a value of four. For analytical purposes, the bargaining issues included can be divided into four categories: (a) compensation issues; (b) job-security and management-rights issues; (c) procedural issues; and (d) union-security and rights issues. The results are reported in Table 2. For each issue, the most frequent response is circled, provided that the frequency of this response is roughly one-and-one-half times or more of the next most frequent response for that issue. Also included is a column indicating the percentage of respondents assigning a value of either three or four on each issue.

Not surprisingly, compensation issues tend to be the most important bargaining issues. Wage levels are clearly of greatest importance, followed by paid time off, wage-administration issues, pensions, and insurance plans. This is understandable.

Table 2

The Relative Importance of Selected Bargaining and Behavioural Issues

Issues	Least Important 1	2	3	Most Important 4	Percentage of Firms Responding with "3" or "4"
	(Percent)				
Bargaining issues					
Compensation					
Average wage level	3	2	30	(65)	95
Wage administration (skill differentials, incentive pay, etc.)	14	13	(55)	18	73
Pension plans	13	18	(43)	26	69
Insurance plans (health, life, etc.)	9	23	(56)	12	68
Paid time off (vacations, etc.)	1	24	(54)	21	75
Cost-of-living adjustments	34	7	22	37	59
Management rights					
Severance and layoff issues	22	(42)	20	16	36
Subcontracting issues	27	21	23	29	52
Technological change issues	21	29	32	18	50
Procedural					
Seniority provisions	9	22	(48)	22	70
Grievance system	8	34	42	16	58
Work-place rules and discipline	5	30	(49)	15	64
Union security and rights					
Union security and rights (e.g. membership requirements, dues checkoff, release time)	35	34	20	12	32
Behavioural issues					
Worker attitudes and morale	1	17	(50)	32	82
Productivity of workers	1	7	28	(64)	92
Voluntary quit rate	35	30	26	9	35
Absenteeism rate	3	22	(45)	30	75
Health and safety	1	7	40	52	92

SOURCE: As for Table 1 (n = 90).

In recent years the Canadian economy has, on the one hand, been in a state of recession, thereby making managers more sensitive to wage costs. On the other hand, the real earnings of workers have been steadily declining (34), thereby placing greater pressure on union officials to be more militant with respect to wages. Indeed, when these factors are taken into account, it is interesting that 35 percent of the respondents indicated that wage levels are in fact *not* the most important issue in their firms.

The bimodal response pattern with respect to cost-of-living adjustments is also interesting. Approximately one-third of the respondents rated this issue as most important and another one-third labeled it as least important. COLA clauses, as they are commonly referred to, have historically been resisted by management, because they provide for automatic wage increases based on inflation during the life of the contract and, therefore, introduce uncertainty into the wage bargain. In times of high inflation, as have been experienced in recent years, they become an increasingly important bargaining issue as unions attempt to introduce or strengthen them in order to protect the incomes of their members.

Two explanations may account for this finding. First, it may simply be that many firms have come to accept the uncertainties caused by inflation as a fact of life and have adapted accordingly. Second, roughly 30 percent of major agreements in Canada are of only one year duration (34), thereby making the introduction of a COLA clause unnecessary and perhaps even a "nonissue" in negotiations.

The response patterns for job-security and management-rights issues showed great variability but, on average, were ranked lower in importance than compensation issues and procedural issues. These issues are potentially quite important since they can strike at the heart of managerial prerogatives and can negatively affect managerial flexibility, power, and control, as well as productivity per se. Thus, these relatively low rankings are surprising given that unions view these issues as important for the job and income security of their members, and as these same issues have received increased emphasis due to the economic conditions of recent years. The most plausible explanation is that there are many firms where job and income security has not been a problem. As a result, these issues are either not raised in negotiations, or, where they are raised, the specific provisions sought do not involve a strong threat to managerial prerogatives.

The relative importance of procedural issues is somewhat easier to explain. While there are a number of arguments suggesting that provisions pertaining to these issues can have positive effects upon worker morale and productivity through standardized rules and procedures that result in consistent and equitable treatment for workers, procedural issues can also have negative effects upon management's flexibility in assigning, promoting, and disciplining workers. Thus, management's concern with these issues is typically not whether standard rules and procedures should be incorporated into the contract — in fact many nonunion firms voluntarily establish similar rules and procedures (11) — but rather what the nature and comprehensiveness of these provisions should be. This concern is likely to be strongest in firms where the work flow or technology is relatively unstandardized and requires frequent changes in workloads and in the nature of the tasks performed (8, 29). It is also important, particularly with respect to seniority provisions, in firms where a number of jobs require specialized skills and experience, in other words, where the technology is complex (8, 29). Conversely, in firms with relatively simple and highly standardized technologies, as is the case in assembly-line operations, the establishment of highly standardized rules and procedures may have an entirely positive impact.

In short, the importance of procedural issues is expected to vary considerably, and the survey results indicate that this is generally the case. Of the three issues included in this category, seniority seems to be the most important and to vary the most, perhaps indicating that it can have the greatest effect upon managerial flexibility and that this effect is highly sensitive to technological considerations.

Finally, there is little doubt that union security and rights are, in general, of lowest importance from the managerial perspective. It appears that the majority of Canadian managers have put the ideological arguments over union security behind them and appear to accept the conventional wisdom espoused by many industrial-relations professionals, namely that secure union leaders are under less pressure to prove their worth to workers. The payoff to management is presumably in less militancy and greater certainty in bargaining.

In summary, there does seem to be a general pattern in the relative importance of the bargaining issues examined. Compensation issues are rated as most important, followed in order by procedural personnel issues, job-security and technological-change issues, and union-security issues. However, this pattern is far from a uniform one. A great deal of variability exists, particularly with respect to job-security issues and, to a lesser extent, with respect to procedural issues. While some suggestions have been provided concerning those factors which might explain this variability, these suggestions should be viewed as tentative in nature.

Importance of Behavioural Issues

For comparative purposes, participants in the Canadian survey were asked to rate the importance of: (a) worker attitudes and morale; (b) worker productivity; (c) voluntary quits; (d) absenteeism; and (e) health and safety. Although these issues do not conventionally fall within the domain of bargaining, they were included because they tend to reflect many of the concerns which underlie the policies and practices of management under collective bargaining. Moreover, a number of authors have argued that the terms of the collective agreement can have important impacts upon them. Furthermore, the results of the U.S. Conference Board study indicated that managers rated concerns over the productivity and morale of their workers very high relative to more traditional bargaining issues.

Returning to Table 2, it is clear that behavioural issues are considered extremely important by Canadian managers. Worker attitudes and morale, worker productivity, and health and safety are second only to wages as the greatest concerns of these managers, while absenteeism is comparable in importance to procedural issues. The voluntary quit rate, on the other hand, does not rate as very important, perhaps reflecting the labour-market conditions of recent years. But overall, the findings show that the concerns of these managers go beyond the specific provisions negotiated in the collective-bargaining agreement to include more general concerns over the attitudes and behaviour of their work force.

MANAGERIAL STRUCTURE AND PROCESS UNDER COLLECTIVE BARGAINING

Just as managerial policies must be adapted to meet the realities of collective bargaining, so must managerial processes. As indicated in Figure 1, these processes revolve around the three tasks of preparing for negotiations, participating in negotiations (see Chapter 9), and administering the provisions of the collective agreement (see Chapter 13). This section discusses the first of these tasks and then examines the structural arrangements through which all three are performed and coordinated, including the size and degree of specialization of labour-relations staff, the scope of labour-relations staff responsibilities, and the extent to which authority over labour relations is centralized within management.

Managerial Preparations for Bargaining

In order to learn how management prepares for bargaining, semistructured interviews were conducted with senior labour-relations executives in nine major Canadian corporations. The nature and sophistication of managerial preparations for bargaining range considerably. For example, one firm with extensive operations in the retail sector undertakes virtually no preparation whatsoever. Management simply waits until the union presents its demands, at which point the general manager for the the division or divisions involved meets and discusses these demands with the corporate president and is given an informal mandate, which can be changed subject to a telephone conversation if the division manager feels this is warranted. In other firms, however, a more complex sequence is involved. This sequence typically includes: monitoring worker attitudes and concerns; monitoring union developments; monitoring industry and/or local wages and benefits; conducting general background research; and developing initial bargaining proposals.

Monitoring worker attitudes and concerns — This process essentially serves two functions. First, it enables management to identify those problems which may be affecting worker attitudes and morale. Second, it provides management with some indication of the types of issues which the union will bring to the bargaining table and the extent to which workers are prepared to strike over them. While this process can be highly sophisticated, involving comprehensive discussions with and surveys of workers, such a high level of sophistication can be both time consuming and expensive. As a result, most of the firms studied follow a less ambitious, informal approach, whereby line managers convey their impressions about worker attitudes and morale to labour-relations executives, either in writing or in an informal meeting.

Monitoring union developments — Monitoring union developments serves to keep management abreast of internal union political processes and, hence, provides management with an understanding of the types of pressures that union negotiators will be subject to in negotiations, particularly those pressures stemming from the national or international level of the union. This process can involve "under-the-table" discussions with union leaders, monitoring other sets of negotiations conducted by the union, and even subscribing to union publications.

Monitoring industry and/or local wages and benefits — As earlier discussed, most Canadian firms attempt to follow wage and benefit patterns established by other company, industry, or union settlements. The extent to which management has concrete information as to the nature and composition of these settlements can be of critical importance for its success in following this policy. Thus, it is not surprising that this process tends to be highly sophisticated, at least in the firms studied. Most of these firms conduct a formal survey of the firms whose settlements they attempt to follow. In one large public utility, over 100 firms are included in the survey. In addition, many of these firms employ secondary sources of information, such as private wage and benefit surveys and government data.

Figure 1

**Managerial Labour-Relations Processes
Under Collective Bargaining**

Preparing for Bargaining

Monitoring operative attitudes and concerns

Monitoring union developments

Monitoring local and/or industry wage developments

Conducting background research for bargaining

Developing wage proposals

Developing benefit proposals

Conducting Negotiations

Costing union demands

Negotiating major contracts

Advising the chief negotiator

Deciding re strikes/lockouts

Deciding upon "final package"

Developing contract language

Contract Administration

Advising line managers about the contract

Handling grievances at the final stage prior to arbitration

Handling arbitrations

Determining suspensions

Conveying suspensions to the union

Conducting general background research for bargaining — General background research typically involves identifying those nonwage provisions which have been problematic for line managers and developing a preliminary agenda of prospective bargaining issues. In some of the firms examined, this involves an informal process of simply discussing the existing contract with line managers. However, in others, it is much more sophisticated. For example, one firm obtains formal submissions from line managers as much as eight months in advance of the start of negotiations and carefully develops an initial agenda which can consist of as many as 200 items. This firm also carefully reviews all arbitrations that have occurred during the life of the preceding contract in order to determine what modifications in contract language may be called for. Another firm establishes subcommittees consisting of both line and staff personnel, each of which focuses upon specific areas of negotiations.

Developing bargaining proposals — Clearly, the development of specific bargaining proposals represents the pinnacle of bargaining preparations. In general, the process by which these proposals are developed is related to the level at which negotiations take place. For example, in one firm, where bargaining is conducted on a plant-by-plant basis, plant-level personnel are responsible for developing proposals but must obtain the approval of division-level management, which must in turn consult with managers at the corporate level. In another firm, which bargains on a multiplant basis, senior labour-relations officials prepare a comprehensive report with recommendations; this report is then presented to the firm's designated bargaining committee, which in turn discusses it with senior management before proposals are developed. In many of the firms we examined, the union itself has an indirect input. That is, many of these firms do not develop any specific proposals until after they have a preliminary, often informal, meeting with union officials in order to determine what the union's demands are likely to be. Also notable is that in one of the firms investigated, wage and benefit proposals tend to be developed in accordance with budget estimates provided by the senior labour-relations executive far in advance of the conduct of any actual research.

The Size and Degree of Specialization of Labour-Relations Staff

In many respects, labour relations is unique as a functional area within management. On the one hand, the success with which labour-relations processes are performed and coordinated can have a major impact not only upon managerial costs, but also upon such factors as worker attitudes and morale, managerial flexibility, and the degree of uncertainty facing the firm. As in most functional areas of this importance, there are a number of technical advantages to allocating this function to highly trained and specialized staff experts. Labour-relations processes can be highly complex in nature, and the greater the information and expertise brought to bear upon these processes, the greater management's effectiveness is likely to be, other things being equal. Where economies of scale permit, it is in the interests of management to divide and subdivide responsibilities for these processes to as great an extent as possible, for the more the processes are specialized, the greater the information and expertise which are brought to bear upon them (21).

On the other hand, a high degree of specialization can have a number of disadvantages, depending upon the task requirements of the functional area involved (21). These disadvantages can be especially problematic with respect to labour relations. First, the functional demands of collective bargaining can be highly variable, tending to peak immediately prior to and during negotiations and slacken in interim periods. Often, it is not viable to have as many staff specialists as would otherwise be desirable, as the workload simply does not justify it in slack periods. Second, adherence to and administration of contract provisions is almost by definition the day-to-day responsibility of line managers. While staff specialists can assist line managers by providing them with advice about the contract and by handling grievances and arbitrations, the day-to-day conduct of labour relations still remains largely a line responsibility. Third, labour relations, perhaps more than any other functional area within management, is highly interdependent or "tightly coupled" with other functional areas. The conduct of labour relations can have a direct

Table 3

Full-Time Equivalent Labour-Relations Staff

Full-Time Equivalent	Percent of Firms
Less than 1	15
From 1 to 4	46
From 4½ to 10	20
From 10½ to 30	14
Over 30	6

SOURCE: As for Table 1 (n = 92).

impact not only upon line managers, but also upon managers in personnel, finance, accounting, and so forth. Labour relations must therefore be highly integrated and coordinated with these functions. One approach to ensuring that this is the case is to have individuals whose responsibilities cut across various functional areas, thereby resulting in a lower degree of specialization than would otherwise be the case. In sum, there are a number of considerations which tend to offset the technical advantages of a high degree of specialization.

In order to determine how specialized labour relations is in Canadian firms, information was obtained on each of the following: (a) the full-time equivalent of the total number of individuals devoting one-third or more of their time to labour-relations activities (excluding line supervisors), which is referred to as the "size" of labour-relations staff; (b) the number of individuals devoting their full time to labour relations, as a percent of the total number of individuals involved, which is referred to as "functional specialization"; and (c) whether or not firms with at least one full-time specialist have individuals who further specialize by devoting their full time to contract administration, research, or contract negotiations, which is referred to as "task specialization."

Size— As indicated in Table 3, close to one-half of the firms in our sample have the full-time equivalent of between one and four individuals with labour-relations responsibilities; however, this figure varies considerably, with 15 percent of the firms reporting a full-time equivalent of less than one, and 6 percent reporting a full-time equivalent of over thirty. As expected, this is largely explained by differences in the number of unionized workers; this variable accounts for 50 percent of the variability in the size of the labour-relations staff (correlation = .74). Yet, from Table 4 it is evident that this relationship is not a linear one. That is, the number of unionized workers per full-time equivalent tends to be significantly higher in firms where the number of unionized workers is higher — a finding which is similar to a finding of the U.S. Conference Board study. Thus, there appear to be economies of scale in labour relations. While the staff requirements in labour relations increase as the number of unionized workers increase, this relationship is not a proportionate one, as there are diminishing returns to increasing the size of the labour-relations staff.

Table 4

**Ratio of Unionized Workers to Full-Time
Equivalent Labour-Relations Staff**

Ratio	Percent	Frequency	Average Number of Unionized Workers
Under 200 to 1	27	19	350
Between 200 and 400 to 1	41	29	2815
Over 400 to 1	32	22	6154

SOURCE: As for Table 1 (n = 70).

NOTE: One firm was an extreme outlier and therefore dropped from this calculation.

Functional specialization— Functional specialization is generally quite low in the participating firms. While over 80 percent of these firms have at least one full-time specialist, and the number of full-time specialists is highly correlated with the number of unionized workers (correlation = .80), Table 5 indicates that only 40 percent of these firms reported that two thirds or more of the total number of labour-relations staff are assigned to labour relations on a full-time basis. While this is as expected, somewhat unexpected are the findings which emerge when the sample is broken up in accordance with differences in the total number of labour-relations staff. As a general rule, functional specialization should increase as the total number of labour-relations staff increases. Yet, our results indicate that functional

Table 5

**Functional Specialization: Number of Full-Time Specialists
by Total Number of Full and Part-Time Specialists Combined**

Total Number of Full- and Part-Time Specialists	Percent of Total IR Specialists That Are Full-Time			
	11% or more	33% or more	66% or more	90% or more
1 to 4 (n = 33)	88	85	45	27
5 to 10 (n = 22)	95	68	27	9
11 or more (n = 23)	97	75	44	22
Total weighted percent	92	77	40	21

SOURCE: As for Table 1 (n = 78).

NOTE: Firms were excluded if they did not have at least one full-time equivalent labour-relations specialist.

specialization tends to be lower in firms which have from five to ten labour-relations staff members (full- or part-time) than in firms with less than five or greater than ten labour-relations staff members. These results are strengthened by our additional finding that the degree of functional specialization is only weakly correlated with the number of unionized workers (correlation = .31).

While these results may simply reflect an anomaly in our data, an alternative explanation is that there are certain "core" functional requirements which collective bargaining imposes upon management. These cause management to increase the number of full-time specialists as the number of unionized workers increases, even though these specialists might be underutilized in slack periods. Beyond a certain point, these core requirements are met and, therefore, management increases the number of part-time staff members. These part-time staff members are less likely to be underutilized in slack periods and are often located at the plant level, where administrative requirements become sufficient to warrant some degree of specialization but are insufficient to warrant full specialization. At a further point, however, slack periods are likely to be less pronounced, as more contracts are involved, and the administrative requirements at the plant level are greater. It is then necessary to increase the percentage of full-time specialists. Thus, certain threshold effects appear to exist. The points at which these threshold effects occur are undoubtedly a function of more than the number of unionized workers and the number of contracts (for example, contract duration, grievance rate, number and average size of plants, and so forth). But the likelihood that they do exist provides some insight into the complex trade-offs surrounding the degree of specialization in labour relations.

Task specialization — In view of our findings for functional specialization, it is not surprising that, as shown in Table 6, task specialization is also relatively low. Of those firms with at least one full-time labour-relations staff member, only 28 percent reported at least one full-time contract-administration specialist, only 18 percent

Table 6

**Role Specialization: Percent of Firms
Specialized in IR Subareas**

Subarea	Number Specializing	Percent Specializing	Average Full-Time Equivalent
Contract administration and/or grievance handling	19	28	20
Research or similar preparations for dealing with unions	12	18	26
Contract negotiations	10	15	27

SOURCE: As for Table 4 (n = 67).

NOTE: Firms with no full-time specialists were excluded.

reported at least one full-time research specialist, and only 15 percent reported at least one full-time negotiating specialist. The results also show that the number of areas of task specialization in firms with at least one full-time labour-relations specialist is significantly correlated with the number of unionized operatives (correlation = .67). Also of note is that 70 percent of the firms reporting at least one area of task specialization have a total labour-relations staff number in excess of ten (compared to 30 percent with a total of from five to ten). This finding is consistent with the threshold effect discussed above. In other words, even though there is a significant correlation between task specialization and the number of unionized workers, this relationship does not seem to take effect until after a threshold point has been reached.

What, then, can be concluded about the size and degree of specialization of labour-relations staff in these Canadian firms? An overwhelming majority of firms employ at least one full-time labour-relations specialist, but beyond this, functional and task specialization are quite low. This is probably due to the unique characteristics of labour relations as a functional area within management. Size and specialization are also closely related to the number of unionized workers in the firm, but these relationships are by no means perfectly linear, tending to be characterized by economies of scale and threshold effects.

Labour-Relations Staff Responsibilities

Now that the size and degree of specialization of labour-relations staff has been examined, the next question is: What is the scope of labour-relations staff responsibilities? In order to answer this question, it is useful to begin by drawing upon the distinction made by organizational theorists between boundary-spanning roles and major decision-making or executive roles (2, 33). In general, boundary-spanning roles entail two sets of responsibilities: gathering and processing information about other interest groups with which management deals; and, representing management in its interactions with these groups (2). Accordingly, these responsibilities serve two functions: to supply those in executive positions with the information they require to make effective decisions; and to establish and maintain stable and predictable relationship patterns with these groups, thereby reducing the degree of uncertainty with which management must cope.

It is clear that the majority of labour-relations activities involve boundary-spanning responsibilities. All of the processes identified with respect to preparing for bargaining consist primarily of information gathering and processing, as do processes which serve to support the conduct of negotiations and the adminstration of the agreement, such as costing union demands, and advising line managers about the contract. Other processes, such as negotiating the major agreement, developing contract language, and handling grievances and arbitrations, involve external representation. On the other hand, decisions over strikes and lockouts, the "final package," and the determination of suspensions can be viewed as of major importance, and do not fall within our definition of boundary-spanning responsibilities.

With this in mind, it is useful to rephrase the question: To what extent are the responsibilities of labour-relations staff limited to a boundary-spanning role rather than inclusive of a decision-making or executive role? The answer to this question is an important one. Because of their role in the organization, individuals involved primarily in boundary-spanning activities tend to value long-run stability and predictability, and emphasize the importance of maintaining cooperative relation-

Table 7

Location of Primary Labour-Relations Staff Responsibilities

Staff Responsibility	IR Staff	Line Mgmt.	Percent Shared Between IR and Line	No Location of Responsibility or Use of Outside Consultants
Preparing for bargaining				
Monitoring operative attitudes and concerns	66	21	7	5
Monitoring union developments	84	10	—	6
Monitoring local and/or industry wage developments	79	15	7	1
Conducting background research for bargaining	78	10	8	3
Developing wage proposals	78	9	10	2
Developing benefit proposals	75	16	8	1
Negotiations				
Costing union demands	76	20	2	2
Negotiating major contracts	78	14	5	3
Advising the chief negotiator	52	19	13	16
Deciding re strikes/lockouts	37	14	15	2
Deciding upon "final package"	44	34	20	2
Developing contract language	79	8	9	3
Contract administration				
Advising line managers about the contract	77	10	9	3
Handling grievances at the final stage prior to arbitration	74	19	5	2
Handling arbitrations	69	20	7	5
Determining suspensions	49	35	12	5

SOURCE: As for Table 1 (n = 86).

NOTE: Responses for "developing wage proposals" (n = 75) and advising chief negotiator (n = 85).

ships with members of other interest groups. In contrast, line managers tend to emphasize the importance of short-term cost effectiveness and productivity. This conflict over objectives is one which has often been documented by labour-relations researchers (20, 32), and is of considerable significance because it underscores the implications that the answer to our question can have for the complexion of managerial policies and outcomes.

The answer to our question is presented in Table 7. From this table, it is clear that processes which involve boundary-spanning activities are primarily the responsibility of labour-relations staff far more often than are those which involve major decisions. Labour-relations staff members have primary responsibility over decisions about strikes and lockouts, the "final package," and suspensions in less than 50 percent of the firms in the study, while they have primary responsibility over most boundary-spanning activities in three-quarters or more of these firms. But even though there is a relatively strong pattern in these results, the tendency for labour-relations staff to have primary responsibility over major decisions in almost half of these firms should not be overlooked. As a result, it can be concluded that there is almost an even split between the number of firms where labour-relations staff play a decision-making role and the number of firms where they are restricted solely to a boundary-spanning role.

Centralization of Authority

Perhaps the clearest indication of how labour-relations processes are coordinated is the degree to which the effective authority for making or approving major decisions or procedural changes resides with managers at top levels within the firm, or, in other words, is centralized. According to organizational theorists (17, 23, 30, 33), there are essentially two broad considerations that are linked to the degree of centralization. First, the more dependent management is upon a particular critical resource (for example, labour), and the greater the ability of suppliers of that resource to withdraw or withhold that resource (for example, the ability of workers to strike), the more centralized management authority is likely to be. On the other hand, the greater the frequency and variability of the activities specific to particular processes, the more decentralized authority over these processes is likely to be.

With respect to labour relations, it is clear that management is highly dependent upon labour, and that the right of workers to strike can provide them with a considerable amount of ability to withhold their supply of this resource. Thus, authority over labour relations should in general be highly centralized. (Indeed, the U.S. Conference Board study found this to be the case in the firms it examined.) Beyond this general degree of centralization, it can be expected that the degree to which certain processes are centralized will vary according to differences in the importance and nature of the processes themselves.

Results obtained from our survey of Canadian firms are reported in Table 8. This table presents the percentage of firms where authority resides at the plant or operating level, at the divisional level *or* higher, at the corporate level *or* higher, and at the parent-firm level. Because only 61 percent of the firms in the sample reported that they have a divisional level, and only 60 percent reported that they have a parent-firm level, perhaps the most reliable indication of centralization is obtained by examining the percentage of firms where authority resides at the corporate level (see column 3) and by comparing this to the percentage of firms where authority resides at the plant or operating level (see column 1). These data indicate that, in general, labour relations is indeed quite highly centralized, at least in the firms surveyed. As might be expected, deciding about strikes and lockouts, deciding upon the "final package," and developing wage and fringe proposals are among the most centralized processes, as they are both highly important and least frequent. Advising line managers and handling grievances at the final stage prior to arbitration are relatively less centralized, which can be explained by the tendency for these processes to be relatively frequent and variable, and to involve matters of procedure.

Table 8

Centralization of Authority in Labour Relations

	Operating/ Plant Level	Divisional Level or Higher	Corporate Level or Higher	Parent Firm Level	No Location of Authority Identified
Preparing for bargaining		(Percent)			
Monitoring operative attitudes and concerns	24	67	48	5	9
Monitoring union developments	18	75	65	6	7
Monitoring local and/or industry wage developments	17	81	64	7	2
Conducting background research for bargaining	15	84	71	8	2
Developing wage proposals	9	87	76	11	3
Developing benefit proposals	11	87	77	13	3
Negotiations					
Costing union demands	12	83	65	8	5
Negotiating major contracts	16	81	66	11	3
Advising the chief negotiator	11	66	57	8	22
Deciding re strikes/lockouts	8	90	84	19	2
Deciding upon "final package"	8	90	79	15	2
Developing contract language	15	81	68	8	5
Contract administration					
Advising line managers about the contract	27	65	51	6	8
Handling grievances at the final stage prior to arbitration	27	70	54	7	3
Handling arbitrations	19	77	62	6	5
Determining suspensions	47	48	33	3	5

SOURCE: *As for Table 1 (n = 88).*

NOTE: *Responses for "developing benefit proposals" (n = 77).*

Somewhat surprising, however, is the tendency for determining suspensions to be quite decentralized. One reason for this may be that the information required to make this decision exists only at the operating level, and that the impact of this decision is restricted to the operating level. Also of note is the relatively low level of centralization for monitoring worker attitudes and concerns. This, no doubt, is explained by the tendency for this process to be highly informal and to involve information which is typically gathered by operating or plant level personnel.

MANAGERIAL EFFECTIVENESS UNDER COLLECTIVE BARGAINING

Managerial interests cannot be viewed as necessarily consistent with those of other interest groups participating in the organization. They tend to revolve around the noneconomic objectives of power, control, and certainty as much as they do around the economic objectives of cost effectiveness and productivity per se. Accordingly, to learn about managerial effectiveness in labour relations, it is necessary to obtain the perceptions of managers themselves rather than to rely solely on "objective" measures such as turnover, absenteeism, labour costs, productivity, strike rates, and so forth (12, 14, 18). While more objective measures are no doubt valuable (especially from a public-policy perspective), they do not reflect the subjective concerns of managers themselves or the extent to which these concerns are shaped by non-economic as well as economic considerations. In fact, in discussions with labour-relations executives in Canadian firms, it was found that these executives typically lack objective measures of their firm's performance in labour relations, especially with respect to behavioural outcomes such as turnover, absenteeism, and worker productivity. This finding is consistent with that of the U.S. Conference Board study, which found that only 20 percent of the 600 firms surveyed had a formal procedure for evaluating their labour-relations effectiveness, and that most firms relied upon subjective rather than objective criteria (19).

This section examines managerial effectiveness in labour relations from the perspectives of senior labour-relations executives in Canadian firms, basing the analysis, first, upon the extent to which these executives view various bargaining and behavioural outcomes as favourable to their firm, and second, upon the evaluations of these executives of their firm's relationship with the major union with which they bargain. In examining these data, it is important to keep in mind that the perceptions of senior labour-relations executives may differ from those of managers in other functional areas within their respective firms.

Managerial Evaluations of Bargaining and Behavioural Outcomes

As indicated in Table 9, there tends to be a great deal of variability in the evaluations which senior labour-relations executives have of particular bargaining and behavioural outcomes. However, a common pattern can be identified. First, these executives tend to evaluate bargaining outcomes as quite favourable to their firms. These issues received a score of five or more (on a seven-point scale) in at least two-thirds of the firms in the study, and a score of six or seven in at least 40 percent of these firms. Those outcomes which tend to be the most favourably evaluated are wage levels, paid time off, cost-of-living adjustments, union security and rights, grievance systems, and insurance benefits. Those which tend to be least favourably evaluated are wage administration, pension plans, work-place rules and provisions for discipline, severance and layoff provisions, subcontracting provisions, and seniority rights and provisions. In general, however, these differences are relatively minor and cannot be viewed as highly significant.

On the other hand, the results with respect to behavioural outcomes do appear to be highly significant. Most striking is the tendency for worker attitudes, absenteeism rates, and productivity to receive the least favourable evaluations. While it would be wrong to conclude that these evaluations would necessarily be any higher in the absence of a union, these results do indicate that the behaviour of workers clearly presents the greatest problem for the firms in our study, perhaps explaining our

Table 9

**Managerial Evaluations of Bargaining and
Nonbargaining Outcomes**

Outcomes	Very Poor 1	2	3	4	5	6	Very Good 7	Rated 6 or 7
	(Percent)							
Average wage level	1	1	4	13	23	37	20	57
Wage administration (skill differentials, incentive pay, etc.)	2	1	9	19	26	30	13	43
Pension plans	3	2	4	21	21	20	27	47
Insurance plans (health, life, etc.)	-	-	7	13	29	33	18	51
Paid time off (vacations, etc.)	1	1	6	9	28	30	25	55
Cost-of-living adjustments	5	1	2	14	21	17	35	52
Severance and layoff issues	2	-	8	25	15	34	16	50
Subcontracting issues	6	1	4	22	19	28	19	47
Technological-change issues	1	1	-	28	21	29	20	49
Seniority rights and provisions	2	2	7	18	27	23	21	44
Grievance system	1	1	3	16	27	34	18	52
Work-place rules and provisions for discipline	1	1	7	16	35	29	11	40
Union security and rights (e.g. membership requirements, dues checkoff, release time)	2	-	6	21	17	28	27	55
Worker attitudes and morale	1	6	9	38	31	9	4	13
Voluntary quit rate	2	1	7	28	20	25	16	41
Absenteeism rate	1	11	17	32	22	11	6	17
Productivity of workers	2	3	9	34	38	13	1	14
Ability to avoid strikes	4	2	6	18	9	30	30	60
Health and safety	-	-	9	24	33	18	15	33

SOURCE: As for Table 1.

earlier finding that these matters tend to be considered of highest importance in these firms.

Also noteworthy is the tendency for managers to view their firm's ability to avoid a strike quite favourably, with 60 percent of respondents assigning this item a value of "six" or "seven." This is interesting, as the "strike weapon" is commonly considered to be the primary source of union power.

In sum, it would appear that, although there is a considerable amount of variance from one firm to the next, managers in unionized Canadian firms tend to view those outcomes pertaining to worker behaviour as relatively least favourable to their firms, and those outcomes pertaining to collective bargaining as relatively most favourable. While it cannot be concluded from these findings that behavioural

Table 10

Managerial Evaluations of Union-Management Relations

Positive Statements	1 or 2	Strongly Agree 1	2	3	4	5	6	Strongly Disagree 7
When the company and union negotiators reach agreement, it sticks.	73	39	34	15	4	2	5	-
Union leaders and management officials try to cooperate as much as possible.	33	9	24	32	18	8	9	1
The union is effective in bringing up genuine employee concerns.	19	2	17	27	19	19	14	1

Negative Statements	1 or 2	Strongly Disagree 1	2	3	4	5	6	Strongly Agree 7
Union leaders and management officials distrust each other.	51	13	38	18	12	10	7	2
Union leaders and management officials try to weaken each others' power.	43	15	28	20	21	9	8	-
The relations between union leaders and management officials are hostile.	64	32	32	14	13	7	3	-
The negotiating behaviour of union officials is erratic and inconsistent.	41	11	30	21	12	12	5	9

SOURCE: As for Table 1.

outcomes are either positively or negatively affected by unionism, it can be concluded that obtaining favourable results in collective bargaining is generally not as problematic for management as is commonly supposed.

Managerial Evaluations of Union-Management Relations

In order to obtain managerial evaluations of various aspects of their relationship to the major union with which they bargain, participants in the Canadian survey were asked to indicate the extent to which they agreed or disagreed with a number of positive and negative statements about their relationship. The results are reported in Table 10. A low rating indicates a favourable evaluation, while a high rating indicates an unfavourable one.

Our findings are somewhat ambiguous. For example, while almost two thirds of our respondents tended to disagree (that is, assigned a value of "one" or "two") with the statement that union-management relations are hostile, only one-third tended to agree with the statement that union and management officials try to cooperate as much as possible. There is also a high degree of variability for most of the statements included, indicating that union-management relations vary considerably from one firm to the next. Of note, however, is that these respondents tended to give the statement "the union is effective in bringing up genuine employee concerns" the most negative rating. A number of authors have argued that unionism can serve as an effective mechanism of communication between workers and management. In general, our findings indicate that these managers do not believe this to be the case. Although 19 percent tended to agree with this statement, 15 percent tended to disagree, and 65 percent were ambivalent, assigning this statement a value of three, four, or five. This finding, coupled with our earlier finding that worker behaviour represents the greatest problem for management, may indicate that — at least from the managerial perspective — unionism often does not have the positive behavioural effects which some authors maintain that it can have. In short, proponents of this viewpoint may be overstating their case.

THREE CASE STUDIES

In presenting the survey data in the preceding sections, we constantly emphasized the variability in labour-relations structures, policies, and practices that exist across Canadian firms. In this final section, we present three brief case profiles in order to illustrate this diversity more vividly and in order to point out how these variations reflect differences in the economic and technological environments of the firms and the strategic choices made by management. The firms discussed here are selected because they illustrate differences in environment and organizational characteristics and, therefore, are not necessarily representative of all unionized firms in Canada.

Firm A

Firm A is a large retail chain which is highly unionized and bargains at the divisional level of the company. The major division is a retail store that operates in a highly competitive product market. Its major competitors include other major chains as well as smaller independent retailers who have, in recent years, banded together to achieve economies of scale associated with bulk purchases. While the major chains are unionized, the smaller ones are not. Consumers in this industry discriminate primarily on the basis of price, so that any general price increase that is not industry-wide can result in a serious loss of volume. Therefore, any increases in wages that are not industry-wide can have severe consequences for this firm's competitive position. On the other hand, a strike of anything more than a few days in length may cause consumers to patronize competitors and these losses are expected to continue after the strike is ended.

The senior labour-relations executive of this firm clearly sees the union as having a highly deleterious effect. From his perspective, the firm has historically been in a weak bargaining position vis-à-vis the union. This has led the firm to concede to a number of union demands in the past which now put the firm at a competitive disadvantage. He believes, however, that unionism is an inescapable fact of life for this firm. The union is well established and the firm cannot relocate operations to avoid unionization.

Firm B

Firm B is a large manufacturer of a diversity of durable industrial products. It has a large number of unionized plants dispersed across Canada with an average size of between 150-200 employees. Bargaining is done on a plant-by-plant basis. This firm is subject to only a limited amount of competitive pressure, since its output tends to be differentiated and produced to customer order. Finally, this company is horizontally integrated, that is, in the event of a strike at one plant other plants are able to compensate for lost production.

Senior labour-relations executives in this firm indicated that, with the exception of one or two plants in Quebec, they consider their experiences with unions to be highly positive. In fact, they expressed the view that unions in some respects are indispensable as a means of communicating with their workers. In particular, they suggested that unions act as mechanisms for guarding against arbitrary treatment by line supervisors since any such treatment would be conveyed to senior managers through grievance and formal bargaining processes. In addition, these executives have found union leaders to be instrumental in conveying company decisions to workers and thereby preventing the spread of inaccurate information through the "grapevine."

This firm follows a policy of wage parity across company operations and does not consider local labour-market wage rates when negotiating for a particular plant. This is a policy which the union has historically advocated with considerable vigour. Moreover, both union officials and management tend to share similar criteria and judgments over what constitutes a reasonable wage increase so that the range over which wages become a serious issue in bargaining is extremely limited.

Nonwage issues are also seldom a source of dispute in negotiations, and most recent bargaining over these issues involves clearing up previous contract-language ambiguities rather than dealing with new substantive considerations. Issues such as contracting out and technological change are, by mutual agreement, not considered within the formal scope of bargaining but are dealt with on a day-to-day basis as they arise in particular plants.

This firm would, therefore, seem to be the archetype for what traditional industrial-relations professionals define as a "mature" bargaining relationship. Management has adjusted to the union, scrutinized its labour-relations functions, altered its decision criteria to conform to the needs of the union and the requirements for peaceful negotiations, and developed a cooperative informal working relationship with union leaders at the local levels. Note that these patterns have developed within a less competitive market context than the one present in Firm A in the retail industry.

Firm C

Firm C is a large capital-intensive industrial chemical company with a large number of plants dispersed across Canada (ranging in size from 50-600 employees) and negotiating approximately twenty-five contracts with a dozen different unions. The firm is owned by a multinational chemical company with subsidiaries world-wide. Historically, the industry has been dominated by this parent firm and one other large multinational company, and competition has been low, particularly in Canada. Competition has been increasing in recent years, however.

When unionism was increasing in the post-World War II years, this firm followed a policy of active acceptance and, in fact, invited unions into the organization. As a result, the company became 100 percent unionized. In recent years, however, this company has begun to gradually close down unionized plants and to follow a policy of indirect union avoidance in newly established plants. It has done so by establishing comprehensive personnel management systems in each of its new operations. As a result, the company is currently only two-thirds unionized.

The chief labour-relations executive in this firm indicated that he believed unionism can be a very valuable asset for management, particularly as it acts to counteract the behaviour of overly ambitious plant managers who might otherwise sacrifice human considerations for short-term production and profit objectives. This executive also indicated that the company has always had very favourable relations with union officials. They have tended to communicate well with one another and to develop a mutual appreciation and respect for each others' problems. In recent years, however, union officials have been under increased pressure to enter into tougher bargaining, particularly with respect to establishing wage parity across company operations. When product markets were growing and profits were high, the company was somewhat prepared to give in to these considerations. However, in recent years, this has not been the case, and an increasing number of strikes have resulted. Given the company's high level of capital intensity, strikes are extremely costly.

Thus, this firm appears to be moving away from a policy of active acceptance of unions to one of indirect union avoidance as it experiences both increasingly competitive pressures and increasingly aggressive union behaviour and bargaining. The company has not, however, attempted to alter the status quo in those plants that are still unionized. Rather, the firm appears to be following what has been referred to as a "double-breasted" strategy whereby it cooperates with unions to the extent possible in existing plants and takes whatever steps necessary to insure that new plants will remain nonunion.

Implications from the Case Studies

While one must always be cautious about generalizing from case studies, these three cases are presented to illustrate two key points that are masked by the overall quantitative data presented in the earlier sections. The first point they illustrate is how management policies, structures, and evaluations of labour relations differ in response to different market and organizational contexts. The retail firm that operates in a highly competitive and partially nonunion industry is in a weak bargaining position relative to its union and, therefore, has not yet developed sophisticated policies and structures for "managing" its labour relations. Instead, it historically accepted the union presence and the competitive disadvantages that resulted from union-induced higher labour costs, seeking to recoup these costs by economies of scale, more aggressive marketing, and other managerial strategies. Alternatively, the union could help this firm by organizing all of its competitors, however it appears to have been unsuccessful at doing so. In contrast, firms B and C have greater discretion to manage their labour relations because of their larger size and more protected market positions. They, therefore, have professionalized, specialized, and centralized their labour-relations functions and developed what we might term actual "strategies" for influencing their union-management relationships.

The discretion enjoyed by firms B and C illustrates our second key point, namely, that given some market protection employers can choose different strategies for responding to trade unions. Note that one of these firms recently began to exercise its discretion and to utilize its specialized expertise by moving from the traditional pattern of "mature" labour relations wherein the union is accepted as a permanent and legitimate party within the firm to a policy of transferring its operations into a nonunion environment. In short, union avoidance, rather than organizational adaptation to the requirements of collective bargaining, seems to be this firm's strategy for minimizing uncertainty and maximizing control over its labour relations.

Thus, these three cases illustrate both the diversity of organizational responses to unions that are present across different contexts at any single point in time as well as the changing patterns of response that appear to be emerging in some North American firms. If the strategy of union avoidance grows in Canada as it has in the United States in recent years, the picture of labour relations will change dramatically in the next decade. The changes will be in a direction that will test the very foundations under which labour laws in both Canada and the United States have been based for almost a half-century, namely that collective bargaining is a valued institution in industrial society that is to be encouraged, accepted, and protected. Whether this will be a significant and growing trend in the years to come cannot be predicted at this point in time. Clearly, however, it is a potential trend worth watching.

Concluding Remarks

In the opening paragraph to this chapter, we stated that management is a central participant in labour relations, and that an understanding of management is essential to gaining a balanced view of any labour-relations system. Yet it must be emphasized that, although management is a central participant, it is not the only one. While managerial policies and practices obviously have important consequences for managerial effectiveness, they have equally important consequences for workers and other interest groups affected by the behaviour of the firm. Furthermore, it is clear that there are certain inherent conflicts of interest between managers and employees. Managerial policies and practices must, therefore, be viewed accordingly.

REFERENCES AND WORKS CITED

1. Aiken, M., and S.B. Bacharach. "The Urban System, Politics, and Bureaucratic Structure," in Lucien Karnik (Ed.), *Organization and Environment* (London: Sage Publications, 1978), pp. 199-250.

2. Aldrich, H.E. *Organizations and Environments* (Englewood Cliffs, N.J.: Prentice-Hall, 1979).

3. Alexander, K.O. "Conglomerate Mergers and Collective Bargaining," *Industrial and Labor Relations Review,* Vol. 24 (1971), 335-353.

4. Bendix, R. *Work and Authority in Industry* (New York: Harper and Row, 1956).

5. Braverman, H. *Labor and Monopoly Capital* (New York: Monthly Review Press, 1974).

6. Clegg, S., and D. Dunkerly. *Organization, Class and Control* (London: Routledge and Kegan Paul, 1980).

7. Craypo, C. "Collective Bargaining in the Conglomerate, Multinational Firm: Litton's Shutdown of Royal Typewriter," *Industrial and Labor Relations Review,* Vol. 29 (1975), 3-25.

8. Doeringer, P.B., and M.J. Piore, *Internal Labor Markets and Manpower Analysis* (Lexington, Mass.: D.C. Heath, 1971).

9. Flanagan, R.J. "Wage Interdependence in Unionized Labor Markets," *Brookings Papers on Economic Activity,* Vol. 3 (1976), 635-681.

10. Flanders, Alan. "Collective Bargaining: A Theoretical Analysis," *British Journal of Industrial Relations,* Vol. 6 (1968), 2-19.

11. Freeman, R.B., and J.L. Medoff. "The Two Faces of Unionism," *The Public Interest,* Vol. 57 (1979), 69-93.

12. Friedlander, F., and H. Pickle. "Components of Effectiveness in Small Organizations," *Administrative Science Quarterly,* Vol. 13 (1968), 289-304.

13. Galbraith, J.K. *Economics and the Public Purpose* (Boston: Houghton Mifflin, 1973).

14. Georgiou, P. "The Goal Paradigm and Notes Toward A Counter Paradigm," *Administrative Science Quarterly,* Vol. 18 (1973), 291-310.

15. Goldman, P., and D.R. Van Houten. "Uncertainty, Conflict, and Labor Relations in the Modern Firm 1: Productivity and Capitalism's 'Human Face,'" *Economic and Industrial Democracy,* Vol. 1 (1980), 63-98.

16. Hyman, R. *Industrial Relations: A Marxist Introduction* (London: Macmillan, 1975).

17. Jacobs, D. "Dependency and Vulnerability: An Exchange Approach to the Control of Organizations," *Administrative Science Quarterly,* Vol. 19 (1974), 45-49.

18. Keeley, M. "A Social-Justice Approach to Organizational Evaluation," *Administrative Science Quarterly,* Vol. 23 (1978), 272-291.

19. Kochan, T.A. *Collective Bargaining and Industrial Relations* (Homewood, Ill.: Irwin, 1980).

20. Kochan, T.A., and R.N. Block. "An Interindustry Analysis of Bargaining Outcomes: Preliminary Evidence From Two-Digit Industries," *Quarterly Journal of Economics,* Vol. 19 (1977), 431-452.

21. Pfeffer, J. *Organizational Design* (Arlington Heights, Ill.: AHM, 1978).

22. Pfeffer, J., and G.R. Salancik. *The External Control of Organizations: A Resource Dependence Perspective* (New York: Harper and Row, 1978).

23. Pugh, D.S., D.J. Hickson, C.R. Hinings, and C. Turner. "The Context of Organization Structure," *Administrative Science Quarterly,* Vol. 14 (1969), 92-114.

24. Reder, M. "The Theory of Union Wage Policy," *Review of Economics and Statistics,* Vol. 34 (1952), 34-45.

25. Rees, A. "Union Wage Policies" in Industrial Relations Research Association, *Interpreting the Labour Movement* (Madison: IRRA, 1952).

26. Robbins, S.P. *Organizational Behaviour, Concepts and Controversies* (Englewood Cliffs, N.J.: Prentice-Hall, 1979).

27. Ross, A.M. *Trade Union Wage Policy* (Berkeley: University of California Press, 1953).

28. *Report of the Royal Commission on Corporate Concentration* (Ottawa: Supply and Services Canada, 1978).

29. Selznick, P. *Law, Society, and Industrial Justice* (Russell Sage Foundation, 1969).

30. Shortell, S.M. "The Role of Environment in a Configural Theory of Organizations," *Human Relations,* Vol. 30 (1977), 275-302.

31. Simons, H.C. *Economic Policy for a Free Society* (Chicago: University of Chicago Press, 1948).

32. Slitchter, S.J., J. Healy, and E. Livernash. *The Impact of Collective Bargaining on Management* (Washington: The Brookings Institution, 1960).

33. Thompson, J.D. *Organizations in Action* (New York: McGraw-Hill, 1967).

34. Wood, W.D., and P. Kumar. *The Current Industrial Relations Scene in Canada, 1980* (Kingston, Ont.: Queen's University, Industrial Relations Centre, 1980).

QUESTIONS

1. What are some of the arguments that, from the managerial perspective, unionism can have positive as well as negative consequences for management?

2. How do the authors view the nature of organizations and the motives of management? What are the implications for managerial behaviour in labour relations?

3. What are some of the reasons for managerial resistance to unionization and some of the resistance tactics employed?

4. What are some of the advantages and disadvantages to having a high degree of specialization in labour relations?

5. What are boundary-spanning roles and what responsibilities do they entail? To what extent are labour-relations staff responsibilities limited to a boundary-spanning role, and what might the implications of this be?

6. What are the reasons which may explain the high degree of centralization of authority over labour relations in Canadian firms?

7. Why is it necessary to obtain the perceptions of managers themselves in order to gauge managerial effectiveness in labour relations?

8. How do managers view the behavioural effects of unionism? How might this be reconciled with research findings that unions do, in general, have positive effects upon turnover and productivity?

GARY N. CHAISON

7. Unions: Growth, Structure, and Internal Dynamics

This chapter presents an introduction to the institutional character of the union movement in Canada. Trends in union growth are examined, with particular attention to union organization by region and by industry, female union membership, and the emergence of the Canadian national unions. Various forms of intra- and interunion structures are reviewed and the concept of union jurisdiction is described along with basic union types. International unionism, union fragmentation, and union mergers are discussed along with the internal dynamics of unions as reflected in their governing systems and the characteristics and turnover of officers. The concept of union democracy is explored through a consideration of its principal components: membership participation, officer selection, and due process. The chapter attempts to develop an appreciation of the diversity in union structures and the dynamics of interunion relationships and union governance.

The term "the labour movement" is often used in a way as to suggest that it is a single homogeneous entity, a group of organizations lacking in any unique or distinguishing characteristics. This misconception, though certainly shared by many, ignores the diversity of union types and structures and prevents one from fully appreciating the complexity of our industrial-relations system. In 1980, the Canadian labour movement consisted of 734 unions, 3.25 million union members, thousands of union officers and staff employees, and numerous intra- and interunion structures for organizing, bargaining, and governance (22). This chapter will present an introduction to the institutional character of this movement through an overview of union growth, structure, and internal dynamics.

UNION GROWTH

Trends in Union Growth

Canadian workers organized and negotiated with employers prior to Confederation. In the late eighteenth century, the first recorded strikes occurred among voyageurs and St. Lawrence River pilots. There are accounts of unions of skilled workers in the Maritime Provinces prior to the War of 1812, and by the 1830s ongoing unions had

147

been formed among printers in Quebec and Ontario (23). In the 1840s and 1850s, unions represented such skilled tradesmen as printers, carpenters, shoemakers, tailors and shipwrights. In the following decade, the U.S.-based international unions gained a foothold in Canada among workers in the construction, railroad, and printing industries. The remainder of the nineteenth century saw repeated efforts to centralize the labour movement by consolidating city-wide unions into national unions and by forming federations of national unions. At the turn of the century, unions tended to be small and represented mostly skilled craftsmen. These workers were more readily organized, primarily because they were more secure than unskilled workers in their employment relationships and, therefore, less easily replaced by employers in time of conflict (20). The tendency to recruit members from among the most skilled had served to severely reduce the potential for union growth. However, in the past half century, the size and composition of trade unions changed dramatically as collective bargaining spread to new groups of workers, first to semiskilled and unskilled workers in mass-production industries (for example, autos, steel, and textiles) and later to white-collar, professional and public-sector workers.

Table 1 presents the number of union members since 1911 (the first year of fairly reliable figures), and it shows union membership as a percentage of the nonagricultural work force. This latter proportion, often called "union density," offers an estimate of the number of potentially organizable workers who have joined unions. It excludes those who are extremely difficult to organize, namely farm workers and the self-employed. In the period during and immediately following World War I, union membership expanded rapidly, from 166,000 in 1914 to 378,000 in 1919, reflecting favourable legislation. The period 1920 to 1935 saw a decline in membership as employers renewed their antiunion efforts and as unions found it difficult to make the structural adaptations necessary for organizing mass-production workers. However, the latter half of the 1930s was marked by the resurgence of industrial unionism, (that is, unions which organized workers by industry rather than craft). There were numerous militant and successful organizing campaigns carried out primarily by U.S.-based unions. Although employment declined in the 1930s, union membership grew, largely because of the efforts to expand union membership into new sectors of the work force. During World War II, union membership rose rapidly from around 360,000 to over 700,000 members, and density increased by almost eight percentage points. This rapid union growth occurred mainly in the mass-production industries, and it was assisted by the introduction of labour legislation which protected workers' rights to join unions. While this growth continued in the immediate postwar period, it slackened in the 1950s, and membership and density declined in the early 1960s. This period from 1950 to 1965 was a time when unions had saturated both their traditional strongholds in the skilled trades and their newer jurisdictions in the mass-production industries and they were having difficulty devising methods and finding resources to recruit new groups of workers (20). There had also been a rapid increase in the proportion of the labour force in white-collar and service occupations — groups which unions were less prepared or inclined to organize than industrial workers. Moreover, by this time, there had been a deterioration of the image of unions; they no longer enjoyed the sympathy and support that was given to them earlier when they were considered "underdogs" in their relations with employers (14, 20).

Table 1

Union Membership in Canada
1911-1980

Year	Union Membership (Thousands)	Union Membership as a Percent of Nonagricultural Paid Workers	Year	Union Membership (Thousands)	Union Membership as a Percent of Nonagricultural Paid Workers
1911	133	—	1946	832	27.9
1912	160	—	1947	912	29.1
1913	176	—	1948	978	30.3
1914	166	—	1949	1,006	29.5
1915	143	—	1950a	—	—
1916	160	—	1951	1,029	28.4
1917	205	—	1952	1,146	30.2
1918	249	—	1953	1,220	33.0
1919	378	—	1954	1,268	33.8
1920	374	—	1955	1,268	33.7
1921	313	16.0	1956	1,352	33.3
1922	277	13.6	1957	1,386	32.4
1923	278	13.2	1958	1,454	34.2
1924	261	12.2	1959	1,459	33.3
1925	271	12.3	1960	1,459	32.3
1926	275	12.0	1961	1,447	31.6
1927	290	12.1	1962	1,423	30.2
1928	301	12.1	1963	1,449	29.8
1929	319	12.6	1964	1,493	29.4
1930	322	13.1	1965	1,589	29.7
1931	311	15.3	1966	1,736	30.7
1932	283	15.3	1967	1,921	32.3
1933	286	16.7	1968	2,010	33.1
1934	281	14.6	1969	2,075	32.5
1935	281	14.5	1970	2,173	33.6
1936	323	16.2	1971	2,231	33.6
1937	383	18.2	1972	2,371	34.4
1938	382	18.4	1973	2,591	36.1
1939	359	17.3	1974	2,732	35.8
1940	362	16.3	1975	2,884	36.9
1941	462	18.0	1976	3,042	37.3
1942	578	20.6	1977	3,149	38.2
1943	665	22.7	1978	3,278	39.0
1944	724	24.3	1979	—	—
1945	711	24.2	1980	3,397	37.6

SOURCE: J. K. Eaton, "The Growth of the Canadian Labour Movement," Labour Gazette, Vol. 75 (1975), 648-649, for the years 1911-1973: Labour Canada, Labour Organizations in Canada, 1980 (Ottawa: Labour Canada, 1980), p. 18, for the years 1974-1980.

NOTE: a. Data on union membership for all years up to and including 1949 are as of December 31. In 1950 the reference date was moved ahead one day to January 1, 1951. The data for subsequent years are as of January 1. Data was not collected for 1979.

The latter 1960s and the 1970s were marked by renewed growth in union membership and higher union density, as service, white-collar, and professional workers were organized in large numbers by unions, particularly in the public sector. A major contributing factor was the introduction of provincial and federal legislation protecting the right of public-sector workers to join unions. These recent increases in union membership have tended to offset declining or stable membership in the more traditional areas of union organizing (14, 15).

Since 1911, total union membership has increased more than twenty-five times from around 133,000 to almost 3.4 million members. A half century ago, approximately 13 percent of nonagricultural paid workers belonged to unions. In 1980, this proportion stood at almost 38 percent. The expansion of the labour movement to its present size has also involved important trends in its structure and membership.

Union Organization by Region and Industry

Union membership is most concentrated in Ontario and Quebec. In 1977, 65.1 percent of the total Canadian union membership was in these provinces. British Columbia accounted for 13.8 percent while the proportion for Alberta was 6.4 percent. Less than 15 percent of total membership was found in the remaining six provinces (25). This concentration of union membership is a result of the size of their labour forces rather than any greater propensity to unionize in one area than another. For example, in 1975, the proportion of nonagricultural paid workers in unions was 32.2 percent in the Atlantic Provinces, 33.8 percent in Quebec, 31.8 percent in Ontario, 30.1 percent in the Prairie Provinces and 36.5 percent in British Columbia (3).

As indicated in Table 2, both the number of union members and the extent of unionization vary widely by industry. More than half of the union members in Canada are in manufacturing and in the community, business, and personal-service sector. Almost 15 percent of the total are in public adminstration (that is, municipal, provincial, and federal government employees), and almost 10 percent are in construction. While these figures indicate where the union members are, they do little to suggest the degree of unionization by industry.

One way to solve this problem is to examine the proportion of an industry's work force who are union members. However, there is an important difference in the number of union members and the number of employees covered by collective agreements. Under many collective agreements, workers are not required to join the union that negotiates for them. Thus, the full extent of unionization is more accurately suggested by the proportions of workers in the various industries who were represented by a bargaining agent (rather than only those that *joined* a union). In 1977, 57 percent of all employees were covered by collective agreements. The highest degree of representation was in the public sector with 91 percent of employees covered by collective agreements. The remaining industries varied widely and included 77 percent in logging, 72 percent in transportation, communication, and other utilities, 64 percent in mining, 61 percent in manufacturing, 50 percent in services, 21 percent in trade, and 2 percent in finance. Apparently, there are substantial areas in which unions can continue to grow, notably the service and trade sectors, although the strongholds of collective bargaining, whether such earlier ones as in transportation or later ones as in the public sector, may be nearing a saturation point (30).

Table 2

Union Membership by Industry and Sex, 1977

Industry	Union Members	As Percent of Total Members	Female Union Members	As Percent of Total Female Members	Female Members As Percent of Total Members in Industry
Agriculture	2,980	0.1	476	0.1	16.0
Forestry	32,666	1.0	857	0.1	2.6
Fishing and trapping	3,188	0.1	34	0.0	1.1
Mines, quarries, oil wells	63,635	2.1	1,479	0.2	2.3
Manufacturing	868,870	28.1	164,539	18.6	18.9
Construction	302,954	9.8	3,092	0.4	1.0
Transport, communication, utility	439,416	14.2	76,133	8.6	17.3
Trade	132,050	4.2	45,773	5.2	34.7
Finance, insurance, real estate	7,884	0.2	5,028	0.6	63.8
Service	781,470	25.2	436,245	49.3	55.8
Public administration	460,126	14.9	151,848	17.1	33.0
Industry unspecified	132	—	—	—	—
Total	3,095,371	99.9[a]	885,504	100.2[a]	28.6

SOURCE: *Labour Canada*, Industrial and Geographic Distribution of Union Membership in Canada, 1977 (Ottawa: Labour Canada, 1979), pp. 3-4.

NOTE: a. Does not equal 100.0 percent because of rounding.

Female Union Members

Table 2 indicates that most union members are men. In 1977, women comprised only 27.7 percent of all union members. Female union membership tends to be concentrated in the trade, public-sector, community, business, and personal-service industries (the latter including many female teachers) (25). Large numbers of women, though fairly small proportions of total union membership, are found in manufacturing and transportation, communication, and utilities (21).

While the proportion of union members who are women currently is low, there has been a considerable increase over time. In 1966, only 17 percent of union members were women, and in the years 1966-1976, the number of women in unions increased by 160 percent while the number of male members increased by only 40 percent. Furthermore, women now comprise a majority of the membership in forty-three percent of the unions, and these include such large ones as Centrale de l'enseignement du Québec, Fédération des affaires sociales, the Service Employees International Union, the International Ladies Garment Workers Union, and the Amalgamated Clothing and Textile Workers Union. Women also constitute large percentages of the membership of the major public-sector unions, notably the Canadian Union of Public Employees (40.8 percent in 1976) and the Public Service Alliance of Canada (35.7 percent) (29).

Growth of National Unions

The recent surge in union growth in the public and service sectors has largely been accomplished through the efforts of Canadian national unions, as opposed to unions which are international or which are highly localized in scope. As Table 3 indicates, the membership of national unions about doubled every decade from 1911 to 1960, increased at a slower rate in the 1960s, but more than doubled in the past decade.

Table 3

National Canadian Unions
(Selected Years)

Year[a]	Number of National Unions	Membership (Thousands)	As Percent of Total Membership
1911	10	14	10.5
1920	18	24	6.4
1930	30	48	14.9
1940	38	97	26.8
1951	52	206	20.0
1960	50	433	29.7
1970	65	753	34.7
1980	128	1,703	50.1

SOURCE: Labour Canada, Labour Organizations in Canada *(Ottawa, Labour Canada, various years).*

NOTE: a. The data for 1911-1949 is for the last day of the year, while that for 1951-1980 is for the first day of the year.

Table 4

Unions with 50,000 or More Members, 1980

Union	Membership	As % of Total
1. Canadian Union of Public Employees	257,180	7.6
2. United Steelworkers of America	203,000	6.0
3. National Union of Provincial Government Employees	195,754	5.8
4. Public Service Alliance of Canada	155,731	4.6
5. United Automobile, Aerospace, and Agricultural Implement Workers International Union of America	130,000	3.8
6. United Food and Commercial Workers of Canada	120,000	3.5
7. International Brotherhood of Teamsters, Chauffeurs, Warehousemen, and Helpers of America	91,000	2.7
8. United Brotherhood of Carpenters and Joiners of America	89,010	2.6
9. Centrale de l'enseignement du Québec	81,033	2.4
10. Fédération des affaires sociales	70,000	2.1
11. International Brotherhood of Electrical Workers	68,637	2.0
12. Service Employees International Union of Canada	65,000	1.9
13. International Association of Machinists and Aerospace Workers	61,500	1.8
14. Canadian Paperworkers Union	61,500	1.8
15. International Woodworkers of America	61,300	1.8
16. Laborers International Union of North America	51,176	1.5
Others Less than 50,000	1,634,900	48.1
Total	3,396,721	100.0

SOURCE: Labour Canada, Labour Organizations in Canada, 1980 *(Ottawa: Labour Canada, 1980), pp. 16-17.*

The number of national unions rose at a considerably slower rate, leveled off in the 1950s, increased again in the 1960s, and almost doubled in the 1970s. Most of the newly created unions in the 1970s represented professional or public-sector workers on a regional or provincial basis (8, 9). Often these associations became bargaining agents without changing the scope of their operations or without consolidating with other associations. This tended to increase the number of very small unions and brought about a high degree of union fragmentation.

National unions also have found their place among the largest unions in Canada. Table 4 lists the sixteen unions with 50,000 or more members in 1980. Six of these are national unions (numbers 1, 3, 4, 9, 10, and 14) and, with the exception of the Canadian Paperworkers Union, they all are in the public sector. Most of these unions have shown themselves to be major political powers within their labour federations and are among the fastest growing and most militant unions in Canada.

The implications of union fragmentation and the declining relative size of the internationals are discussed later in this chapter, and the evolution of many national unions from professional and public-sector associations is examined in other chapters. The rapid expansion in the national unions was brought about primarily through the new inroads of unionism in the past fifteen years, and this has gone far to alter the profile of the Canadian labour movement.

UNION STRUCTURE

While contemporary unions may engage in a variety of economic, social, and political activities, the principal role of the union in North America is that of an employee representative in the negotiation, administration, and enforcement of collective-bargaining agreements. These functions are described in detail in later chapters.

The union movement consists of a variety of union types and inter- and intraunion structures. The union itself is the employee association which is governed by a constitution, enters into bargaining relationships with employers, and collects dues and assessments from its members. There are three major types of unions in the Canadian context. An *international union* charters subordinate bodies and represents employees in both Canada and the United States but has its headquarters and usually the vast majority of its members in the United States. The *national union* is national or regional in scope, organizing employees at more than a single location or from more than a single employer. Both international and national unions are usually comprised of various locals, at the single-plant or single-firm level. Such locals are often termed "affiliates" to denote their ties to a national or international body. If such an affiliation is not present, the union is generally termed a *local independent union*. The distinction between local and national unions has become rather hazy over time as a large proportion of those organizations categorized as national unions are actually single-province or even single-employer in scope, particularly in the public sector (9). Many have only one subordinate body, a characteristic one would expect to see only in the local independent unions. Nevertheless, it is important to differentiate between those unions which are international in scope and those which are not.

Examples of the eighty international unions include the United Steelworkers of America, the International Brotherhood of Teamsters, the United Automobile Workers, the International Association of Machinists, and the United Food and Commercial Workers. Among the 128 unions classified as national are the Canadian Union of Public Employees, the Canadian Union of Postal Workers, the Canadian Paperworkers Union, the National Union of Provincial Government Employees, and the Canadian Brotherhood of Railway, Transport, and General Workers. In 1980, there were 242 local independent unions, including the Halifax Police Association, the Professional Association of Residents and Interns of British Columbia, the Eaton Employee Association of Victoria, and numerous faculty associations at universities (22).

As indicated previously, the basic organizational unit of the national or international union is the *local union*. The local constitutes the smallest subordinate body of the union and has its own system of governance with elected officers, meetings, and a constitution. Members pay their dues to the local and a portion of this, a per capita fee, is remitted to the parent union.

In some cases, locals of a union will join together in a particular area in order to coordinate their bargaining, organizing, and political activities. These *intra*union structures or intermediate bodies are called *district councils, joint boards* or *conferences*. At times, unions or locals of unions in a particular industry may combine on an areawide basis and form an *allied trade federation*, also known as a *union council*, *union federation*, or *joint council*. Allied trade federations frequently deal with questions of union jurisdiction to prevent interunion rivalries over the right to represent particular groups of workers. Allied trade federations have governing bodies and conventions, and they receive dues from member unions. They are generally found where workers are organized into unions by their craft, as in the construction, maritime, and printing industries. Allied trade federations are *inter*union structures, as opposed to district councils which are *intra*union bodies (22).

Union Jurisdiction and Union Types

A union's jurisdiction is its claim to organize and represent a specific portion of the work force. The defining of a jurisdiction has the effect of drawing the boundaries of the union's organizing territory relative to those of other unions. This claim is legitimized by entering into bargaining relationships for "units" or groups of workers within the jurisdiction, either through employer recognition or labour-relations board certification of the union's representational status. The jurisdiction is actually more of a statement of organizing intent or a demarcation of an area of possible long-term future growth than any declaration of immediate organizing objectives. In many cases, unions claim jurisdictions far beyond their ability to organize so as not to have these job territories claimed by other unions in the future. The union's jurisdiction is stated in its constitution as a description of jobs, work processes, industries, geographical areas, or a combination of these. For example, the jurisdiction of the International Association of Machinists is a detailed listing of work processes and is covered in eight pages of its constitution (19). In contrast, the jurisdiction of the United Paperworkers International Union is defined as "all workers employed in and around establishments in the pulp and paper industry and related industries and such other establishments as decided by the International Executive Board" (27, Article III).

The manner in which union jurisdictions are or should be specified and organized has been a source of serious and continuing conflict within the labour movement. Most of the earliest unions limited their membership to workers in a particular craft or skill. These organizations, called *craft* or *horizontal unions*, were found primarily in the construction, railroad, and printing industries. The unionization of employees in the mass-production industries in the 1930s brought about the rapid growth of *industrial* or *vertical* unions, which organized all workers in a particular industry regardless of their craft or skill. There are two recent variations of this union type: the *semi-industrial union* representing all workers at a given work site, and the *multi-industrial union* for all workers in several industries (4).

There are few if any pure industrial or pure craft unions. Reflecting the emergence of new work processes and even new industries, most craft unions have come to organize some units on an industrial basis. For example, aside from organizing workers performing specific crafts, the Carpenters have been active in organizing noncarpenters in the Canadian sawmill and logging industry, and the International Brotherhood of Electrical Workers represents nonelectrical workers in the power-generating and communications industries. Furthermore, industrial unions such as the Auto Workers have not been reluctant to organize locals on a craft basis when this was most effective or required for certification by a labour-relations board.

In addition, new forms of unions have appeared which span all or several industrial and craft jurisdictions. A *general union* reserves the right to organize all workers in all industries. Although they appear mostly in European industrial-relations systems, there have been some North American general unions, notably the powerful International Brotherhood of Teamsters, with its over two million members, and the less successful District 50, Allied and Technical Workers which merged into the Steelworkers in 1972. *Conglomerate unions*, while not as indiscriminate in organizing as the general unions, are former industrial or craft unions which selectively expand into a new jurisdiction, much as a corporation would diversify and expand into new markets. For example, through both mergers and organizing campaigns, the Steelworkers has ventured into the mining, chemical, and stone products industries. Other unions which might be considered conglomerate in nature would include the Laborers, the Machinists, and the Brotherhood of Railway and Airline Clerks. The terms *multi-industrial union* and *conglomerate union* are often used interchangeably.

In reality, there are no concrete rules or permanent patterns of union jurisdiction. A jurisdiction is far more than the technical definition contained in the constitution; it is a statement of past traditions, a warning to potential trespassers, and a hope for future growth (4). The special problems of jurisdiction arising in the construction industry will be discussed in a later chapter.

Development and Structure of International Unions

The most unique and controversial characteristic of the Canadian labour movement is the presence of international unions. As defined earlier, these unions have headquarters in the United States, and they organize workers in both Canada and the United States. With rare exceptions, their Canadian membership is a small minority, often less than 15 or 20 percent of their total membership. The internationals range in size from the United Steelworkers of America (203,000 Canadian members in 1980) and the United Auto Workers (130,000), to the Flint Glass Workers (115) and the Plate Printers (118). The combined Canadian membership of the internationals was over 1.5 million in 1980 (22).

Table 5, an updated version of a table initially compiled by Adams (1), illustrates the changing importance of the internationals. The organization of Canadian workers by unions based in the U.S. began in the 1860s and 1870s as craftsmen moved across the border while being represented by the same union. Often small and isolated local unions in Canada were strengthened by establishing ties with the developing national unions in the United States (13). American craft unions generally considered the organization of Canadians as a natural extension of their right to organize within their jurisdiction. Around the turn of this century about 95 percent of the union members in Canada belonged to internationals. While this proportion declined with the development of new Canadian national unions in such areas as manufacturing and transportation, the trend was reversed in the late 1930s with the rapid organization of the mass-production industries by international unions. However, starting around the mid-1960s, there have been substantial gains by Canadian national unions among public-sector and professional workers, with the effect of dramatically reducing the proportion of Canadian union members in inter-

Table 5

Proportion of Canadian Union Members in International Unions, 1902-1980
(Selected Years)[a]

Year	Percent	Year	Percent
1902	95.0	1949	70.9
1911	89.7	1954	71.4
1921	72.8	1959	72.4
1929	72.1	1964	71.4
1934	57.4	1969	65.0
1939	60.4	1977	49.0
1944	64.6	1980	46.3

SOURCES: *1902 — C. B. Williams, "The Development of Canadian-American Trade Union Relations:*
   Some Conclusions," Relations Industrielles/Industrial Relations, *Vol. 21 (1966), 342, Footnote 14.*
   1911 — I. Breckner, and S. S. Reisman, Canada-United States Economic Relations *(Ottawa: Queen's*
   Printer, 1957), p. 205.
   1921-1964 — Labour Canada, Union Growth in Canada, 1921-1967 *(Ottawa: Information Canada, 1970),*
   p. 106.
   1969-1980 — Labour Canada, Labour Organization in Canada *(Ottawa: Labour Canada or Supply*
   and Services Canada, various years).

NOTE: *a. The membership data for 1921-1949 is for the last day of the year, while that for 1951-1980 is for the first*
   day of the year.

nationals. Since 1976, international unions could no longer claim to have a majority of the union members in Canada.

The relationships between the headquarters of international unions and their Canadian members have varied widely. Locals and intermediate bodies are creations of, and subordinate to, union headquarters in the United States. Some international unions have decided to grant substantial autonomy to their Canadian members and locals in bargaining and governance. In such cases, intermediate bodies may be established exclusively for Canada, and these are administered by Canadian leadership under a separate constitution with little if any interference from international headquarters. At the other extreme, the highly centralized decision-making processes and structures in some international unions have meant that U.S. officers or staff, or conventions dominated by U.S. membership, have had controlling power in questions of officer selection, dues increases, bargaining priorities, and even the right of the Canadian membership to strike.

The role played by the international unions has been at the centre of a continuing debate. Among the major points of contention are whether: (a) international unions can or even want to satisfy the special employment and bargaining needs of Canadians; (b) international unions have created a fragmented labour movement marked by a large number of small unions incapable of best serving the membership; (c) the approach to politics taken by internationals is inappropriate to Canada; (d) the international unions spend more or less to service their Canadian membership than they receive in dues and fees from them (1). The arguments for and against international unionism have been reviewed in various studies (1, 3, 28). Although generally not conclusive, the arguments may be relevant to the case against specific internationals at one time or another.

Recently, international unions have found that their Canadian members are asking for greater degrees of autonomy, and that the members may go so far as to disaffiliate if their demands are not met. In 1970, the convention of the Canadian Labour Congress, reacting to the demands for greater autonomy, passed a resolution for minimum standards of self-governance for locals and intermediate bodies of international unions. These were expanded at the 1974 convention and include: (a) the election of Canadian officers by Canadians; (b) the right of Canadian officers and members to determine policies that deal with national affairs; (c) the authority for Canadian officers to speak for their union in Canada; (d) separate affiliation for Canadian sections in international trade secretariats; and (e) assurance from international unions that their Canadian members will not be prevented "by constitutional requirements or policy decisions from participating in the social, cultural, economic, and political life of the Canadian community" (5, pp. 48-49). While it is difficult to measure the overall degree to which these standards are being followed, there does appear to be a trend toward greater self-governance on the part of Canadian sections of international unions. In many instances, Canadian divisions or conferences have been created and, led by Canadian officers, the members are playing a greater role in decisions about organizing, bargaining, and political activities. Some unions, for example, the Oil, Chemical, and Atomic Workers, have granted such a high degree of autonomy that the Canadian membership has established a new national union.

There have also been disaffiliations from international unions when the Canadian membership believed that their parent union failed to recognize their special needs in bargaining or their reasons for resisting or supporting a particular union merger (9). These factors prompted the formation of such unions as the Canadian Paperworkers Union, the Brewery Workers Union of Canada, and the Canadian Chemical Workers Union. With the continuing drive for autonomy more disaffiliations will probably arise, either peacefully, through grants of increased governing autonomy, or as hostile reactions to failures in providing autonomy. While international unions may represent a declining proportion of workers in Canada, their presence continues to provide a unique element in the dynamics of union-relationships.

Function and Structure of Labour Federations

More than three-quarters of the union members in Canada are in unions that have joined one of the labour federations. Table 6 indicates the size of the various federations. The Canadian Labour Congress, by far the largest federation, was formed by the 1956 merger of the Trades and Labour Congress and the Canadian Congress of Labour. The former was organized primarily among craft-type unions in 1896 while the latter was a creation of the industrial unions in 1940. At the present time, the CLC is composed of 69 international unions, 22 national unions and 107 locals which are directly chartered by the labour federation. The second largest federation is the Confederation of National Trade Unions (CNTU), or Confédération des syndicates nationaux (CSN), formerly known as the Canadian and Catholic Confederation of Labour. Established in 1921, this organization is based primarily in Quebec and has only ten affiliates. In 1972, some unions seceded from the CNTU because of disagreements over political action, and they started a new federation

Table 6

Union Membership by Congress Affiliation, 1980

Congress Affiliation	Members	As Percent of Total
CLC	2,329,067	68.5
CNTU	187,186	5.5
CSD	43,824	1.3
CCU	27,350	.8
AFL-CIO only	3,441	.1
Unaffiliated international unions	100,506	3.0
Unaffiliated national unions	613,813	18.1
Independent local organizations	91,534	2.7
Total	3,396,721	100.0

SOURCE: Labour Canada, Labour Organizations in Canada, 1980 *(Ottawa: Labour Canada, 1980), p. 19.*

called the Congress of Democratic Unions (La Centrale des syndicats démocratiques-CSD). It was formed to further a policy of independence from political parties and presently has 3 affiliates and 174 directly chartered locals. The fourth federation, the Confederation of Canadian Unions with 13 affiliates, was organized in 1969 as an association of exclusively national unions (22).

A labour federation is not a bargaining agent or representative of employees. Workers do not belong to a labour federation but rather join a union which is affiliated with the federation (or directly chartered by it). As a voluntary association of unions the labour federation coordinates the relations between affiliates, acts as a voice for affiliates in representation to governments, and provides services which some affiliates might not be able to afford. With respect to coordination between affiliates, most federations require that affiliates refrain from raiding each other (that is organizing each other's members). Disagreements over such disputes are resolved by impartial umpires, and violations of no-raid agreements can result in the suspension or expulsion of the affiliate from the federation. Federations also serve as a coordinating centre for the joint organizing campaigns of their affiliates, particularly when such campaigns can be a source of conflict between unions because of overlapping jurisdictions.

The labour federations also act as a voice for their affiliates in attempting to influence legislation in such areas as labour relations, economic development, adjustment to automation, pension reform, unemployment insurance, workmen's compensation, and wage and price guidelines. This is done by the submission of briefs to legislative hearings and lobbying at the federal and provincial capitals (6).

In addition, federation activity encompasses services which affiliates might not be able to afford individually or for which they might lack the required expertise. These include extensive labour-education programs for union members and staff, research and publication programs, assistance in organizing, and research for collective bargaining.

The diverse functions of the federations are carried out through an organizational and governing structure aimed at coordinating affiliate activities and providing services on a national and regional basis. National and international unions are affiliated directly to the CLC while on the provincial level their locals are members of one of the ten CLC *provincial federations of labour*. On the community or district level, the locals of affiliates are members of associations called *local labour councils*. Provincial federations and local labour councils may be viewed as the intermediate bodies of the labour centre, formed to carry out such functions as legislative lobbying, research, and labour education on a provincial and community basis.

Although the CNTU represents workers mostly in the province of Quebec, it has the organizational structure of *federations* and *central councils*. The federations are composed of affiliated unions which organize in the same or related fields while central councils join together unions or union locals in a city or region. In most instances, affiliated unions are required to join and remain in CNTU federations and councils (12).

The differences in the philosophies and policies of the two major federations, the CLC and the CNTU, are discussed in chapters on labour history and on the labour movement in Quebec.

Union Mergers

A union merger is the combining of two or more unions to form a single union, in the process of which one or more of the merging unions loses its separate identity. Mergers occur as an amalgamation or an absorption. An amalgamation involves two or more unions of roughly equal size which form a new organization. An absorption is the merging of one union into a considerably larger one. Some absorptions may entail the complete submergence of one union into another while others may be types of affiliations which provide varying degrees of autonomy for the absorbed union (8).

The reasons for union mergers have been well documented. Frequently, a merger is an attempt to reverse membership decline or stagnation. The underlying causes for this inability to expand may include declining employment in the union's jurisdiction, unsuccessful defences against the organizing campaigns of other unions, and the inability to organize new groups of workers. Some merging unions are growing but, nevertheless, they join together to better their financial position and raise the quality of their services in organizing, lobbying, and grievance handling. Mergers also result from a desire to increase bargaining power relative to that of an employer which may have been involved in a merger itself or which may negotiate on a multi-industry or multiunion basis. Finally, some unions, such as those in the printing and railroad industries, have merged to offset organizing problems caused by the effects of technological change on traditional craft lines (7).

The terms of a merger are shaped by the compromises reached in negotiations. In many cases, merger negotiations have failed because of the reluctance of union leaders to vacate their positions, differences in union structure, such as the degree of local autonomy, and differences in union governing practices, such as the methods for electing officers or the frequency of conventions. Other barriers to mergers have included the extreme hostility created by intense rivalry between the unions, membership pride and loyalty to their union, and fears about inadequate representation in the new union for specialized crafts (7).

In Canada, there are additional barriers to mergers because of the presence of international unions and the desire for greater autonomy expressed by their Canadian members. Mergers between international unions are negotiated at U.S. headquarters. In some cases, the Canadian membership may resist these mergers because of a fear of a loss of autonomy within the new union. For example, some Canadian locals of the Mine, Mill, and Smelter Workers fought unsuccessfully against their union's absorption into the United Steelworkers of America. In other instances, Canadian sections of internationals have disaffiliated rather than have their status changed through a merger. This factor prompted the Canadian locals of the Brewery Workers to disaffiliate from their parent organization when the latter was absorbed by the Teamsters in 1973. At times, Canadian sections of internationals have tried to merge but were prevented from doing so by one or both parent unions. This occurred in the unsuccessful merger negotiations between the Canadian sections of the International Rubber Workers Union and the International Chemical Workers Union. Finally, there have been cases where a Canadian national union attempted to merge with an international but the membership of the former expressed fears that they would be neglected within the larger union. In such instances, a merger may not be consummated unless there is an agreement to establish an autonomous or semiautonomous Canadian section (8).

Union mergers often require that parties be sufficiently motivated to overcome substantial barriers and negotiate an agreement which integrates union governing structures and practices. In Canada, additional merger barriers are created because of recent Canadian reactions to international unionism. As a result, the union merger pace in Canada has been slow, with only thirty-five mergers from 1956 to 1977. These mergers have been primarily between international unions (nineteen mergers) and between national unions (thirteen mergers). Only three mergers have been between national and international unions (8).

Fragmentation of the Labour Movement

The labour movement in Canada is said to be characterized by a high degree of union fragmentation, reflecting the presence of numerous small unions. In 1980, more than two-thirds of the national and international unions had less than 10,000 members, and forty unions had less than 1,000 members (22). It has been claimed "that the rising costs of union administration cannot be met by the smaller organizations and that there is a resulting deterioration in the quality of such functions as organizing, bargaining, research, administration, and education" (9, p. 2). A number of observers of union structure have suggested that mergers could be the most effective means to build fewer and larger unions in Canada (9). However, as emphasized in the preceding section, the frequency of mergers is affected not only by the political and structural barriers faced by unions operating entirely in Canada, but also by recent Canadian reactions to international unionism.

A recent study by Chaison (9) questioned the assumptions about the harmful effects of union fragmentation. It was shown that the rapid increase in the number of unions was largely a result of the emergence of public-sector and professional-employee bargaining agents. Many of these new unions are not really national in scope but represent employees in a single province, have few locals, and may negotiate only a few contracts, or deal with a single employer. Because of the very limited scope of bargaining activity and the distribution of their membership, their size would not necessarily make them ineffective. But it was also recognized that fewer and larger unions could still provide some advantages, notably "enhanced lobbying activity on the national level, increased organizing and strike funds, and the ability to maintain large, full-time professional staffs for research, bargaining, and organizing" (9, p. 5).

While there may be some doubt as to whether small size is necessarily a factor that reduces union effectiveness, it is generally agreed that a key characteristic of the Canadian labour movement is the extent of its fragmentation. The preponderance of small unions is a direct result of the highly decentralized bargaining structures in Canada as well as the evolution of public-sector and professional unionism. These topics will be covered in detail in subsequent chapters.

INTERNAL DYNAMICS OF UNIONS

Union Government and Administration

Although there exist wide variations in the details of union governing practices, there are certain elements shared by most unions regardless of size, type, or geographical distribution of membership. Unions are political institutions in which: (a) governing and administrative relationships are established through a written constitution; (b) the day-to-day administration of the organization is accomplished by elected officers and their appointed staff; and (c) policy decisions are proposed to, then scrutinized, and either approved or rejected by union membership at local meetings or by their representatives at national conventions.

The union constitution specifies the rules which govern relationships between the member and his union, the various union structures (for example, locals, intermediate bodies, bargaining committees), and the union and other unions (for example, procedures for handling jurisdictional disputes and authorizing mergers). It also lists the duties and powers of officers at all levels and provides the means for their selection. Finally, the constitution describes aspects of the general administration of the union, such as the collection of dues, the holding of meetings, and the calling of conventions.

The constitution provides only the basic framework for union governance. The actual exercise of political power within the union and the relationships between union bodies may be shaped by such factors as union traditions, the level at which bargaining and organizing decisions are made, the extent of organized opposition in the union, and the personal leadership style of the union officers. Most union constitutions carefully specify procedures, such as those for selection of convention delegates or officers and the remission of per capita dues, but they are quite broad in designating the power and authority of union officers and the causes for discipline of union members.

The chief executive officer of the union is often called the president, national president, general president, or executive or national director. He or she generally has broad powers to interpret the constitution, appoint staff and committee members, preside over meetings of the union's councils, boards and conventions, and direct and supervise the overall functioning of the union. There is also a secretary and treasurer or secretary-treasurer who direct financial transactions (receive income, issue cheques, make investments), keep records and minutes of council and convention meetings and prepare official correspondence. Also, unions have vice-presidents, variously called vice-president, senior vice-president, executive vice-president, regional vice-president, and international vice-president, among other titles, depending upon the practice or tradition of the union and the rank of the officer. Generally, one or more of the higher ranking vice-presidents assist the president and are elected at large, while others may be elected on a district or regional basis and administer intermediate bodies. The number of vice-presidents in a union may vary from as few as three or four to as many as thirty.

The union officers administer the affairs of the union with the aid of appointed staff. Larger unions usually have directors and staff assistants in several departments, including those for education, public relations, organizing, economic and legislative research, political education, and finance.

Most unions have a governing body, called an executive board or council, which has the power to direct the affairs of the union, issue or revoke charters of locals and intermediate bodies, and authorize the expenditure of funds. If necessary, it usually can take possession of the property of a local union and administer its affairs for the purpose of correcting corruption or financial malpractice, or assuring the performance of obligations under the collective-bargaining agreement. This is called placing a local in trusteeship. The executive board or council often consists of the chief executive officer, the vice-presidents, and at times staff directors and regional representatives. It can meet as frequently as monthly or may convene only once or twice a year.

The day-to-day running of the union is carried out by the principal officers, generally the president, secretary-treasurer and some senior vice-presidents. Decisions regarding administrative matters and policy are usually made by the executive board or council. The supreme governing body of the union is the convention which can meet as often as annually or as infrequently as once every five years. Delegates from locals and intermediate bodies are selected or elected to represent their constituencies. Union officers are often nominated and elected at the convention. Major policy decisions are made through the passage of motions or approval of committee reports.

Characteristics of Union Leaders

It is extremely difficult to generalize about the nature of union leadership in Canada. In some unions, particularly those known for militant organizing and bargaining, the union officer may play the role of the charismatic leader, uniting and directing the organization in time of great struggle and challenge. On the other hand, larger, older, and more conservative unions might have a centralized and bureaucratic control structure and here the officers might serve more as union managers than as leaders. Furthermore, the motivation for obtaining and staying in office varies according to union structure and size. In most smaller unions and locals, the executive officers may be part-time and unpaid and serve their organizations because of their sense of dedication to trade unionism. At the other extreme, positions in the larger unions can offer such attractions as high salaries, prestige and status in the community, and the power to appoint a large number of union staff as well as control the disposition of huge pension funds.

Union leaders are not specifically trained for their positions. Rather, they work their way up through the union, at one time having performed the work of the membership that they represent. The path for leadership advancement is from local to intermediate to national positions. As Estey notes, however, the mobility of the leader is limited to within the union:

> Unlike corporate executives, whose managerial talents are readily transferrable and who can move with relative ease from one industry to another, union leaders rarely, if ever, shift from one union to another, less because their managerial talents are too specialized than because rank-and-file attitudes still discourage it. (17, p. 56)

Contemporary Canadian union leaders often find themselves under considerable pressure to satisfy a membership which judges them primarily on the basis of immediate bargaining gains rather than long-term achievements. This situation was summarized by Finn:

> The immersion in the day-to-day routine of protecting their members' interests keeps the union leaders fully occupied. They have little time to devote to long-term planning or to the broader social issues affecting workers. They stagger from one internal crisis to another, reacting rather than initiating, giving priority to those developments that most immediately threaten their own security and well-being. (18, p. 92)

Certainly the principal tasks of union leaders vary considerably. Leaders in larger unions or locals may have to reduce internal dissent among a geographically dispersed or occupationally diverse membership. Depending on the level at which negotiations take place, national and local leaders might also find themselves continuously reacting to membership expectations for increasingly greater gains in collective bargaining (18). The leader must also devote considerable time to directing nonelected staff, including organizers, negotiaters, lawyers, and research personnel.

Most union officers in Canada are men. In 1977, only one out of every six union executive board members was a woman, although women accounted for more than one-quarter of the total union membership. Women also tended to be underrepresented on the executive boards of the CLC, the CNTU, and even those unions with the largest number of women members. In general, the involvement of women in union government is highest at the local and intermediary levels and lowest in positions of greater authority and responsibility. To a certain degree, this reflects female responsibilities in the family. Union activities usually are conducted outside of working hours and women with families might find it particularly difficult to find the time to hold positions of higher responsibility. Furthermore, women with small children may leave the labour force for several years and consequently they cannot establish the long record of union activity needed to reach higher office, particularly in the larger unions. When women do hold officer positions, they tend to be in the smaller organizations and those with a high proportion of female union members (29).

Election and Tenure in Office

Union officers at national, intermediate, and local levels are elected to their positions. Variations in the frequency and format of elections are found between unions as well as between the different levels of the union's governing structure. Elections at the local and intermediate level tend to be more frequent than those at the national level. Relative to large unions, the smaller unions have shorter intervals between conventions and elections. Locals, particularly smaller ones, may have the membership vote directly through secret ballot. This method is also used for some intermediate and national bodies, through the use of a mail ballot or voting at the local union hall. An alternative and more popular procedure for larger unions or for the selection of high-level union officers is through the vote of delegates attending the union convention.

Observers of union government frequently have noted that national union leaders usually are quite secure in their position. Active political opposition is rare, and when it does appear it tends to be ineffective. The officer is often capable of controlling the union's channels of communications and has the opportunity to develop national prestige — an important advantage denied to potential opponents. Incumbent leaders can also maintain a near monopoly over political skills within the union, and they are in a position to build an effective political machine, complete with patronage appointments to union staff. In sum, the national union officers are able to perpetuate their term in office through a combination of power, prestige, and skill (11). On the other hand, the tenure of the local union leader is said to be considerably less secure, particularly in the smaller locals, where officer compensation is low. Here, both the desire and ability to stay in office are less than at higher levels or in larger union bodies (10).

The causes and frequency of turnover among the presidents of Canadian national unions has been examined in a number of empirical studies. Chaison and Rose (11) found that leaders left office for nonpolitical reasons more often than for political reasons. Almost one-third of the surveyed cases left for nonpolitical reasons, such as voluntary retirement because of age and health, union rules against successive years in office, or the incumbent's death in office. Few changes in leadership were for political reasons such as a defeat in an election or the failure of governing bodies to nominate the incumbent for further office. However, in many situations it was difficult to judge whether there were political reasons for leaving office, as would be the case for example when the leader refused to run or assumed another position within the union.

Another study by Chaison and Rose (10) indicated that union growth increased the ability and/or desire of presidents to remain in office, probably because of enhanced status, compensation, and political skills. In addition, presidents of older and larger unions tended to serve for longer terms than presidents of younger and smaller unions. This finding suggests that there may be a relationship between presidental turnover and stages of union growth. The early formative years for unions would be marked by relatively unstable leadership, but as unions mature (and grow) there is a more centralized organizational structure and reduced membership control of the governing process. Turnover rates decline, and there is an increase in the tenure of presidents (24).

It appears that there are both political and nonpolitical reasons for officer turnover, and turnover rates are related to a variety of union characteristics. In general, the leadership of organized labour is constantly changing. For example, nearly eighty percent of Canadian national unions experienced at least one case of presidential turnover from 1963 to 1972. Similarly high turnover rates were found for international unions. In both types of organization, election defeat was seldom the cause for the incumbent leaving office (11).

The Concept of Union Democracy

Over the years an expectation has developed that unions should function as democratic organizations with membership participation in the selection of officers as well as in decision making related to union administration and collective bargaining. As Barbash observed: "The union is judged not only by whether it performs its functions effectively, but whether it performs them democratically" (4, p. 142). Legislation in the United States and Canada has attempted to protect the rights of union members to participate in the political activities of their union. These rights have also been encompassed in the democratic obligations of affiliates spelled out in the Codes of Ethical Conduct of the CLC and the AFL-CIO. Despite efforts to promote union democracy through legislation and regulation, there still remains some disagreement over its meaning. While several definitions of union democracy have been offered, one of the most comprehensive was suggested by Edelstein and Warner:

> Democracy ... is a decision-making system in which the membership actively participates, directly or indirectly through its representatives, in the making and implementation of policy and in the selection of officials, for all levels, on the basis of political equality and majority rule. Furthermore, the system operates on the basis of the accountability of officials, the legitimacy of opposition, and due process for the protection of the rights of individuals and minorities. (16, p. 30)

Edelstein and Warner expanded on this definition by pointing out that each dimension of democracy can be reached to a different degree and that attempts to characterize an overall level of democracy can only be accomplished in a crude manner. Furthermore, the different aspects of democracy can be examined at the national, local, and intermediary levels.

It would appear that three major facets of union democracy are membership participation, officer selection, and due process. A brief discussion of these should indicate some of the difficulties encountered in measuring union democracy. While many of the conclusions presented below were reached with regard to unions in the United States, there is no evidence to suggest that they would not also apply to Canadian unions.

Membership participation — It is frequently observed that most union members refrain from participating in their organizations. As Estey (17) notes, only about 10 to 15 percent of the members go to the ordinary union meetings, and it is often difficult to get a majority for meetings dealing with such important issues as the election of officers or the ratification of a proposed collective agreement. It should not be assumed that this low level of participation is necessarily a result of the efforts of union officers to control information and decision making:

> Whatever the reasons for this apathy — whether the issues are becoming so complex that they cannot be properly evaluated by the ordinary member; whether the traditional union emphasis on economic objectives leaves the membership with the attitude that the union is simply providing an insurance function, which it is up to the administration to perform as best they can; whether the sheer size of the typical union today leaves the member feeling that his or her vote cannot change things anyhow; or whether the union meeting cannot compete for the members' spare time with the many recreational activities available — whatever the reasons, it is an observed fact that attendance at union meetings is usually confined to a small fraction of total membership. (17, p. 54)

The degree and quality of membership participation may vary from union to union. Greater levels of participation would be found in smaller locals which are relatively autonomous from their parent national or international union and which perform particularly important functions, such as operating hiring halls. Participation can be be enhanced by having more convenient meeting places, skilled leaders, well-run meetings, and democratic procedures. Membership participation is also dependent upon past experiences. Workers, such as minority skill groups in the union, who found that participation paid off in the past, are more likely to participate in the future (26). However, even increased participation need not be a sign of democracy. Anderson has emphasized:

> Attendance figures can tell more about how many friends the union leader has rather than indicating the extent to which the meeting acts as a forum for debate and democratic decision making. Despite the fact that attendance at meetings rises and falls depending on issue or climate — this tells us little about how tightly controlled the agendas are, or how the floor is manipulated by the chair. (2, p. 488)

Of course, there are measures of participation other than attendance at meetings, such as the informal contacts with leadership, or membership in union caucuses. But whatever measures are adopted, the point remains that participation can be a meaningful indicator of union democracy only if it has the effect of influencing decisions within the union.

Selection of officers — Majority rule is often viewed as the cornerstone of the union's claim to democracy. Union officers who wish to remain in office would certainly be responsive to the desires of the voting members. The election process provides the means to hold incumbent leadership accountable for its decisions as well as allowing members to participate in the organization by voting, supporting candidates, or even running for office.

While union members in North America do elect their officers, the mere fact that there are elections does not necessarily indicate the presence of union democracy. First, it should be recognized that, with the exception of the International Typographical Union, there are no opposition parties that function continuously in unions at the national level. When active opposition does occur, it is usually against a particular leader in an election rather than as a continuing and formalized aspect of the union's political processes.

The desire for union leaders to remain in office often results from the higher salary and prestige attached to their positions. At the local level, or for smaller unions, leaders give up less when they leave office. In such cases, there would be less resistance to opposition and greater turnover of officers. However, while local turnover has been found to be negatively related to the size of locals and to levels of compensation, this may not necessarily indicate a high degree of union democracy but may be more of a sharing of leadership tasks and privileges by a local elite (10).

It was indicated earlier that the union leader on the national level is rarely defeated, does not even face meaningful opposition in elections, and that turnover of officers is more often caused by such factors as retirement because of age or health, or death in office. The infrequency of election defeat is not necessarily the sign of undemocratic structures or practices but reflects the power, prestige, and political skills of the leader.

In sum, the means for the selection of officers may appear democratic on the surface because of provisions for secret ballot elections, the use of majority rule, and the apparent open procedures for entering and supporting opposition candidates. But the actual functioning of the election process and the turnover of officers may tell us more of the desires of officers to retain their positions than the ability of the opposition to defeat them. Again, the key factor indicative of democracy is the one most difficult to measure: the extent to which the incumbent leader is responsive to the influence of the membership in his quest to remain in office.

Due process — Unions frequently have clauses in their constitutions stating in part that a member may be disciplined for engaging in conduct "unbecoming a union member" or "detrimental to the welfare of the union or the labour movement in general." Such disciplinary action could be directed against critics of union leaders and could consequently hinder internal democracy. One measure of union democracy is the degree to which a member may receive due process in the application of union discipline, for example, the right to receive a notice of the charges, to be present at a hearing, to present evidence, to receive a judgment based on evidence, and to appeal the procedure to a higher body. The ability to appeal disciplinary actions on procedural and substantive grounds protects supporters of the opposition in the union by limiting the powers of incumbent officers (16).

Most union constitutions contain broadly worded disciplinary clauses coupled with detailed procedures for hearing and appeals. Frequently, the union's executive council is the initial court of appeal, and the national convention is the stage for final appeals. Very few unions have appeal procedures which are controlled by the membership or which are external to the union. An example of the external appeal procedure would be the Public Review Board of the United Auto Workers, which acts on the final appeals of discipline cases and is staffed by public members who have no connection with the union (16).

The union member's right to due process is enunciated in legislation and federation Codes of Ethical Conduct. While external appeal procedures are rare, there is no evidence that there is *widespread* use of union discipline procedures to stifle opposition to incumbent leadership or to discourage membership participation (4).

We have come to expect and even demand democratic governance of unions because of their role as employee representatives and their position as the largest voluntary associations in our society. Initially, our major concern was to devise structures to enhance union democracy. More recently, attention has turned to the informal and the dynamic aspects of democracy. This emerging viewpoint was expressed by Anderson:

> . . . the ultimate test of the extent of union democracy is whether individual members within the union are able to influence decisions that they perceive to affect their vital interests, goals or welfare. Are members able to mobilize enough influence or power to participate in and affect the decisions that are of greatest concern to them, or is power so concentrated within the hands of the leadership or some minority faction so as to preclude effective participation and conflict resolution through the "democratic process"? (2, p. 448)

The questions surrounding union democracy are becoming increasingly sophisticated and tend to reflect the functioning of the actual rather than the ideal labour union. The internal structures and governing procedures of unions are more often being seen as arrangements which may facilitate democracy rather than as any measure or guarantee of it (26). The emerging concept of union democracy, while not providing for convenient and simple answers, is a recognition of the dynamic and complex institutional character of the North American trade union.

REFERENCES AND WORKS CITED

1. Adams, R.J. "Canada-U.S. Labour Link Under Stress," *Industrial Relations,* Vol. 15 (1976), 295-312.

2. Anderson, J.C. "Local Union Democracy: In Search of Criteria," *Relations Industrielles/ Industrial Relations*, Vol. 34 (1979), 431-449.

3. Bain, G.S. *Union Growth and Public Policy in Canada* (Ottawa: Labour Canada, 1978).

4. Barbash, J. *American Unions: Structure, Government and Politics* (New York: Random House, 1976).

5. Canadian Labour Congress. *Constitution of the Canadian Labour Congress* (Ottawa, CLC, 1978).

6. Canadian Labour Congress. *Notes on Unions: The Structure of Labour in Canada* (Ottawa: CLC, 1979).

7. Chaison, G.N. "Comment: Union Mergers and Industrial Environment," *Industrial Relations,* Vol. 17 (1978), 119-123.

8. Chaison, G.N. "Union Mergers and International Unionism in Canada," *Relations Industrielles/Industrial Relations,* Vol. 34 (1979), 768-777.

9. Chaison, G.N. "Union Mergers, Union Fragmentation and International Unions in Canada." Paper presented at the Seventeenth Annual Conference of the Canadian Industrial Relations Association, Montreal, June 1980.

10. Chaison, G.N., and J.B. Rose. "An Analysis of Annual Turnover Rates for Canadian Union Presidents," *Relations Industrielles/Industrial Relations,* Vol. 32 (1977), 547-564.

11. Chaison, G.N., and J.B. Rose. "Turnover Among the Presidents of Canadian National Unions," *Industrial Relations,* Vol. 16 (1977), 199-204.

12. Confederation of National Trade Unions. *Statutes and By-Laws* (Montreal: CNTU, n.d.).

13. Crispo, J. *International Unionism* (Toronto: McGraw-Hill, 1967).

14. Eaton, J.K. "The Growth of the Canadian Labour Movement," *Labour Gazette,* Vol. 75 (1975), 643-649.

15. Eaton, J.K. *Union Growth in Canada in the Sixties* (Ottawa: Labour Canada, 1975).

16. Edelstein, J.D., and M. Warner. *Comparative Union Democracy* (New York: Wiley, 1976).

17. Estey, M. *The Unions: Structure, Development and Management,* 2nd ed. (New York: Harcourt Brace Jovanovich, 1976).

18. Finn, E. "State of the Unions: Labour's Love Lost," *Maclean's,* May 1974, pp. 22, 90, 92.

19. International Association of Machinists and Aerospace Workers. *Constitution of the IAMAW* (Washington: IAMAW, 1977).

20. Kruger, A.M. "The Direction of Unionism in Canada," in R.U. Miller and F. Isbester (Eds.), *Canadian Labour in Transition* (Scarborough, Ont.: Prentice-Hall, 1971), pp. 85-119.

21. Labour Canada. *Industrial and Geographic Distribution of Union Membership in Canada, 1977* (Ottawa: Labour Canada, 1979).

22. Labour Canada. *Labour Organizations in Canada, 1980* (Ottawa: Labour Canada, 1980).

23. McKendy, F.J. "History and Structure of the Labour Movement in Canada: History," *Labour Gazette,* Vol. 73 (1973), 146-153.

24. Rose, J.B., and G.N. Chaison. "Presidential Tenure in Canadian National Unions," *Labor Law Journal,* Vol. 28 (1977), 355-360.

25. Statistics Canada. *Corporations and Labour Unions Returns Act: Report for 1977, Part II, Labour Unions* (Ottawa: Statistics Canada, 1979).

26. Strauss, G. "Union Government in the U.S.: Research Past and Future," *Industrial Relations,* Vol. 16 (1977), 215-242.

27. United Paperworkers International Union. *Constitution of the UPIU* (New York: UPIU, 1972).

28. Waisglass, H.J. "Continental Unionism: Gain or Drain," *Labour Gazette,* Vol. 72 (1972), 528-531.

29. White, J. *Women in Unions* (Ottawa: Canada Government Publishing Centre, 1980).

30. Wood, W.D., and P. Kumar (Eds.). *The Current Industrial Relations Scene in Canada, 1979* (Kingston: Queen's University Industrial Relations Centre, 1979).

QUESTIONS

1. Describe the differences in the degree of unionization by industry. Are these differences related in any way to the relatively small proportion of female workers who are in unions?

2. What are the principal differences between national, international, and local independent unions? Provide one or two examples of each. What factors caused the recent growth in the number and size of the national unions?

3. Describe the intermediate bodies of labour unions and of labour federations. What roles do these bodies play?

4. What is meant by a union's jurisdiction? Describe the differences in the jurisdictions of craft, industrial, and general unions. Provide examples of each union type. What is meant by a conglomerate union?

5. Briefly describe the development of international unionism in Canada. Discuss the controversy surrounding the operation of these unions and the recent attempts of the Canadian membership to achieve greater degrees of autonomy.

6. Describe in detail the functions and structure of the Canadian Labour Congress. Discuss the recent CLC policy regarding the self-governance of locals and intermediate bodies of international union affiliates.

7. What are the principal forms of union mergers? Why do unions merge, and what factors may hinder merger attempts? Describe the barriers to mergers created by the presence of international unions and the desire for greater autonomy on the part of the Canadian membership.

8. Define union democracy. To what extent can levels of union democracy be measured by membership participation, the selection and turnover of officers, and due process?

COLLECTIVE BARGAINING
IN CANADA

JOHN C. ANDERSON

8. The Structure of Collective Bargaining

The structure of collective bargaining in Canada has frequently been described as decentralized and fragmented. This decentralization has been identified as the cause of increased industrial conflict (strikes) and of inappropriate wage and fringe benefit settlements as a result of leapfrogging and whipsawing tactics used by unions. This chapter desribes the types and evolution of bargaining structures operating in the public and private sectors in Canada. The major forces shaping the structure of collective bargaining are outlined. Finally, the implications of increased centralization of collective bargaining are discussed.

Critics of the Canadian industrial relations system have often argued that collective bargaining is much too fragmented and decentralized to function effectively (10, 17). That is, rather than negotiations occurring at the industry, provincial, or national level, most bargaining is between a single union and a single employer in a single location. Furthermore, even where more than one union represents different groups of employees in a plant, the unions often still negotiate separately with the employer over the terms and conditions of employment. This decentralized collective-bargaining structure has been identified as the cause of increased industrial conflict. For example, management representatives of construction companies often complain that a decentralized bargaining structure inevitably results in the industry being shut down every summer as one trade (for example, carpenters, plumbers, electricians) after another goes on strike to support demands for increased wages and benefits. Moreover, decentralized bargaining often allows unions to "leapfrog" over settlements reached by other unions in the industry or geographic region or to "whipsaw" an employer as different unions negotiate different benefits and then demand parity after the settlements have been reached. Thus, the structure of collective bargaining is viewed by the parties as a key factor shaping the process and outcomes of collective bargaining.

The structure of collective bargaining is viewed as so crucial that change, in particular increased centralization of bargaining, is frequently cited as almost a panacea to current problems in collective bargaining. Legislative changes in several provinces have attempted to resolve the unique problems of the construction industry by legislating province-wide bargaining (27). The introduction of collective bargaining by provincial employees has frequently included the statutory definition of a few province-wide bargaining units (2, 14, 31). The Province of Quebec has gone even further to establish province-wide bargaining for other public employee groups including teachers (8). A commission in Ontario recommended more centralization of collective bargaining among hospital employees (1). Furthermore, in March 1978 a special Industrial Inquiry Commission was established by the then federal minister of labour, John Munro, to examine the advantages and disadvantages of wider-based collective bargaining in federal industries, including transportation, grain handling, and communications — three industries which have had a relatively high incidence of strike activity (7). Across industries and jurisdictions, there has been definite pressure toward the increased centralization of the structure of collective bargaining.

Unfortunately, while policy makers have legislated changes in collective-bargaining structure, and labour-relations practitioners are painfully aware of the implications of different bargaining structures, very little is actually known about the forces which influence the choice of alternative structures or about their consequences for the relative bargaining power of the parties, levels of industrial conflict, or the functioning of the bargaining process. The purpose of this chapter is to outline the concept of bargaining structure, to describe the evolution of collective bargaining structures in Canada, and to discuss the major causes and consequences of the centralization or decentralization of the structure of collective bargaining.

THE CONCEPT OF BARGAINING STRUCTURE

Definition

As bargaining structure may take on many different forms in different industries, providing a precise definition of the concept is difficult. Kochan (18, p. 84) defines bargaining structure as "the scope of employees and employers covered or affected by the bargaining agreement. The *formal* structure is defined as the negotiation unit, that is, the employees and employers that are legally bound by the terms of an agreement. The *informal* structure is defined as the employees or employers that are affected by the results of a negotiated settlement through pattern bargaining or some other nonbinding process." However, as Weber (30) notes, even this definition encompasses a potential multiplicity of different units: the election unit, the negotiation unit, and the unit of direct impact.

The election unit— The basic building block of bargaining structure is the group of employees who, through common interests or circumstances, decide that they wish to be represented by a union. These employees and their selected union then either ask the employer for voluntary recognition or apply to one of the provincial labour-relations boards or Canada Labour Relations Board for an election to prove that the bargaining agent (union selected by the employees) represents the interests of the majority of the employees in the election unit. If a majority of the employees in the election unit who vote select the union as their representative, the labour-relations board will certify the union as the exclusive bargaining agent of all employees in the election unit.

Prior to the election, the labour-relations board may be asked to make a determination as to whether or not the election unit defined in the union's application for certification constitutes a unit appropriate for collective bargaining. Often the employer will contest the inclusion of certain employees (for example, managerial and confidential employees) and the exclusion of the others. The union may only be applying to represent the crafts (electricians, machinists, and so on) performing maintenance duties in a single plant of a large manufacturing company. On the other hand, the employer may argue that the unit appropriate for collective bargaining includes both production and maintenance employees in all plants in the city operated by the firm. Furthermore, the employer may want certain supervisory employees excluded from the unit. It would then be up to the labour-relations board to decide whether a craft-based unit or an industrial unit (composed of all production employees regardless of occupation) is appropriate, whether the unit should include a single plant or several, and whether or not supervisory employees should be included in the unit. The board's decision would be the legal definition of the election unit.

In arriving at a determination, the labour-relations board typically takes into consideration several of the following factors (18). First, a degree of community of interests exists among employees. Under this criterion, it is unusual for clerical and production employees, professional and nonprofessional employees, full-time and part-time employees or supervisory and nonsupervisory employees to be included within the same unit unless it is their express interest. Second, the prior history of bargaining within the firm or industry will be considered as well as the decision-making structure of the employer on personnel issues related to the groups under consideration. If an informal bargaining relationship has existed in the past, it is likely that the de facto unit suggested by this relationship will be upheld by the board. Third, the impact of the alternative units on the stability or conflict potential of the union-management relationship will be examined. Labour-relations boards are generally reluctant to define election units which will increase the likelihood of industrial conflict. Finally, the interests of the employees for union representation are usually considered when other factors do not provide a clear answer to the definitional question. (A more detailed discussion of the role of public policy in shaping bargaining structure is provided in the next section.)

The negotiation unit While the labour-relations board may certify a union as the exclusive bargaining representative of an election unit, which is deemed appropriate for collective bargaining, actual negotiations may not necessarily occur between the election unit and the employer. That is, the negotiation unit may actually, by agreement of the parties, be some combination of election units. Therefore, the negotiation unit is "the unit within which formal collective bargaining takes place" (30, p. 14).

The combination of election units into a negotiation unit may be at the instigation of either the union or management, although both must agree for a binding collective agreement to be signed. Unions representing employees in different election units but employed by the same employer may decide to negotiate together. Alternately, the employer may wish to have a negotiation unit composed of similar groups of employees in several plants or to combine with other employers in the same industry. Thus, while the election unit is typically decentralized to a level of a single union and single employer, the negotiation unit may be broader, ranging from a few election units and a single employer to several election units and several employers.

The unit of direct impact— Often negotiations between one union and employer have an impact on other union-management relationships which are not directly involved in the negotiations. The spill over reveals that the unit of direct impact of any set of negotiations is often much broader than the negotiation unit. This may occur for several reasons. First, employers often have informal arrangements which result in the wage and benefits increases negotiated by unions being passed on to nonunion employees within the organization. Therefore, clerical, professional, and managerial employees may directly benefit from the outcomes of collective bargaining. Second, collective bargaining with one negotiation unit may establish the pattern for the other negotiation units within the same industry or geographic region. Moreover, the pattern setting relationship may be either formal or informal.

Two examples of informal pattern bargaining are the automobile industry (20) and municipal collective bargaining. In the auto industry, the United Automobile Workers usually select one of the Big Three automobile manufacturers based on the prospects for a good settlement and stall negotiations with the other companies until the settlement is reached with the target firm. The pattern having been established is then negotiated and ratified, usually with much less difficulty with the other manufacturers.

In Canadian municipal negotiations, both intercity and intracity pattern bargaining occurs. Intercity pattern bargaining often occurs in the following way. The Canadian Union of Public Employees (CUPE) establishes national bargaining goals in each round of negotiations and attempts to negotiate them in key municipalities within a region to establish a pattern which can be used to get other other city governments to accept those union demands. For example, in 1981 one CUPE bargaining goal was to obtain an equalization of the base hourly wage rate of the outside units and the clerical units consistent with the concept of equal pay for jobs of comparable worth. In British Columbia, while this was an item on the table in most municipal negotiations, it was not a major issue in the Greater Vancouver or Greater Victoria districts until the municipalities of Surrey and Nanaimo agreed to the union demands. While neither Vancouver nor Victoria ultimately agreed to this particular demand, it is sure to be raised in subsequent negotiations now that the pattern is partially established. However, this example also emphasizes that this type of pattern bargaining is essentially an informal process with no guarantee that the unit of direct impact will differ to any great extent from the negotiation unit.

Intercity pattern bargaining may also be a formal process, however. Another example from the public sector in British Columbia reveals how rigid the adoption of the formal pattern may actually be. Fire fighters' negotiations in British Columbia are dominated by the outcomes of collective bargaining in Vancouver. Over 80 percent of the municipalities in the province with collective agreements have included a provision agreeing to either settle for the same salary as the Vancouver fire fighters or to give some fixed proportion (for example, 90 percent) of the base Vancouver salary to their fire fighters.

Intracity pattern bargaining is also common in Canadian municipal negotiations (3). Although less often than in the past, fire fighters are granted the same percentage wage increase as police officers if not exact parity of minimum and maximum salaries. Frequently, unions representing city employees will formally meet to plan bargaining strategy, agreeing to allow negotiations with one union (often the CUPE local representing outside workers) to establish the wage pattern for other unions. As a result, the other unions will stall their negotiations until the chosen union has settled with the city. Thus, no matter what form pattern bargaining takes, the consequence is often to substantially expand the scope of the employees impacted by the settlement beyond the formal negotiation unit.

Figure 1

Types of Collective Bargaining Structures

Bargaining Structure	Examples
Single-Employer Forms	
Single plant — single union	Forestry, mining, manufacturing
Single plant — multiunion	Communications
Multiplant — single union	Transportation
Multiplant — multiunion	Manufacturing
Multiple-Employer Forms	
Multiple employer — single union	Over-the-road trucking, fishing
Multiple employer — multiunion	Construction industry

Types of Bargaining Structure

Figure 1 presents a list of the various types of bargaining structures which are common in the Canadian industrial-relations system. The categories presented refer to the negotiation unit rather than the election unit or the unit of direct impact. Moreover, it can be seen that the bargaining structures all involve combinations of basic employer and employee structures. As the election unit is most frequently a single-employer single-union form of bargaining structure, most of these structures involve increased centralization of bargaining which has been mutually agreed to by the parties.

Employer combinations — Employers may combine into a multiemployer labour-relations association by applying to the provincial labour-relations board for certification as an employers' association. This is frequently done in the construction industry. Once certified, employers may not withdraw from the employers' association and bargain separately with their employees without changing their certification status through the labour-relations board. Any agreement negotiated by the association is binding upon all certified employers. However, in many provinces no provision exists within the labour-relations legislation for the certification of an employers' association. Under these circumstances, employers may agree to form a voluntary association and become signatory to any collective agreement negotiated by the employers' association. Each employer signs a contract agreeing to be bound by the decisions of the association with respect to collective bargaining. However, before each subsequent round of bargaining each employer may decide to revoke the authority given to the association and bargain separately with their employees. Finally, a group of employers may decide to bargain together but to sign separate collective agreements with the local unions representing their own employees. In this case, the employers' association has no formal power over its members but rather may provide both research and bargaining expertise as well as information which helps coordinated bargaining occur.

Union combinations — Combinations of unions or election units are often a response to employer actions especially in the case of multiemployer bargaining. It is rare that unions will attempt to become recertified when faced with a more centralized bargaining structure. Rather, unions respond through either *coalition* bargaining or *coordinated* bargaining. Under coalition bargaining, the unions representing employees in the different election units agree to form a coalition and to negotiate a single collective agreement which would be binding on all of the unions involved in the coalition (21, 22). This arrangement is similar to a signatory employers' association. However, given the degree of differences in the philosophies and priorities of unions, coordinated bargaining is more frequent. The unions involved arrange common expiration dates to their collective agreements, agree to prepare for negotiations together, share information, and actually sit down together at the bargaining table, exhibiting a common front to the employer. However, each union signs a separate collective agreement with the employer(s) and may even negotiate some special provisions individually.

Thus, changes in the basic structure of collective bargaining often require agreements among representatives of a number of local unions, different national unions, and several employers in order to increase the centralization of bargaining. Often agreements between these groups on their priorities and strategy and tactics may create internal conflicts. The trade-offs between the needs for democracy and representation and increases in bargaining power in selecting an appropriate bargaining structure are discussed in a later section of this chapter.

BARGAINING STRUCTURE IN CANADA

In order to examine the extent to which the structure of collective bargaining in Canadian industry has remained fragmented and decentralized over the past decade, the level at which negotiations actually occurred for bargaining units involving 500 or more employees was determined from data provided in the *Collective Bargaining Review* for the period 1969 through 1977. Before describing these data, however, it is important to note that because they only include relatively large bargaining units, the degree of centralization of collective bargaining is likely to be overstated. That is, it is highly likely that smaller bargaining units will be engaged in collective bargaining at the level of a single plant and single union. Furthermore, the results also exclude the construction industry which has been evolving toward a more centralized form of collective bargaining, and therefore, in this respect, centralization may be underrepresented. However, this information does provide a good overview of collective-bargaining structure in Canada.

Collective-Bargaining Structures: 1969 to 1977

The number and percentage of bargaining units engaged in negotiations under six alternate collective-bargaining structures for each year between 1969 and 1977 are presented in Table 1. Several conclusions are readily apparent from this table. First, the most common bargaining structure in any year involved negotiations between employees represented by a single union working in a single plant for an employer. Between 42 and 51 percent of all negotiations occurred under this structural form. Moreover, the second most frequently adopted bargaining structure only involves combining employees represented by the same union but working in more than one plant of the employer into a single negotiations unit. This practice is common in industries like automobile manufacturing where a single employer (for example, GM) has several plants in which the production workers are members of the same

Table 1

Frequency of Alternate Bargaining Structures: 1969-1977

Bargaining Structure	1969 # [a]	1969 % [b]	1970 #	1970 %	1971 #	1971 %	1972 #	1972 %	1973 #	1973 %	1974 #	1974 %	1975 #	1975 %	1976 #	1976 %	1977 #	1977 %
Single-Employer Structures																		
Single plant—Single union	154	49.2	149	49.4	165	48.8	179	51.4	160	47.6	179	43.0	202	47.8	198	42.3	272	44.7
Single plant—Multiunion	2	0.6	11	3.6	4	1.2	2	0.6	9	2.7	6	1.4	10	2.4	30	6.4	37	6.1
Multiplant—Single union	101	32.3	75	24.8	109	32.2	84	24.1	103	30.7	147	35.3	136	32.1	139	29.7	185	30.4
Multiplant—Multiunion	1	0.3	5	1.7	2	0.6	3	0.9	6	1.8	6	1.4	6	1.4	8	1.7	5	0.9
Multiemployer Structures																		
Single union	49	15.6	58	19.2	54	16.0	78	22.4	53	15.8	71	17.1	63	14.9	77	16.5	102	16.8
Multiunion	6	2.0	4	1.3	4	1.2	2	0.6	5	1.4	7	1.8	6	1.4	16	3.4	7	1.1
Total all structures	313		302		338		348		336		416		423		468		608	

SOURCE: *Labour Canada*, Collective Bargaining Review, 1969-1977.
NOTES: a. *Number of negotiations, involving 500 or more employees, with that particular bargaining structure.*
b. *Percent of employees with that particular bargaining structure.*
c. *Bargaining structure categories were developed by the author for the purposes of coding the data from the* Collective Bargaining Review. *The resulting categories are more detailed than those used by Labour Canada.*

union (for example, UAW). Another 24 to 35 percent of negotiations during the nine years occurred under this structure of multiplant-single union. Overall, between 72 and 81 percent of negotiations, depending on the year, involved a single-employer single-union bargaining structure. Single-employer multiunion structures were rare. Thus, the results presented in Table 1 reveal that collective bargaining is still substantially a decentralized process in Canada today. Moreover, given these figures only refer to large bargaining units (that is, more than 500 employees), it is likely that collective bargaining is even more decentralized than indicated here.

Multiemployer forms of collective bargaining also appear to be adopted in a relatively small proportion of the union-management relationships in Canada. Approximately 20 percent of the negotiations involved more than one employer bargaining with one or more unions. It most cases (about 83-98 percent), multiemployer bargaining takes place with representatives of only a single union on the other side of the bargaining table. Therefore, an examination of Table 1 reveals that even when collective bargaining moves toward a more centralized form, whether it involves a combination of several plants of a single employer or several employers, it is most likely to occur in negotiations with the same union. It is rare that formal negotiation units are composed of more than one union. Thus, employers may be more willing or able to resolve intraorganizational conflicts of interests than are unions.

The final conclusion that can be drawn from Table 1 is that, at least over the last decade, the structure of collective bargaining has remained remarkably stable. While the percentage of units involved in negotiations under a single-employer single-union bargaining structure has declined somewhat, the percentage of units in each structural alternative has not changed by even 10 percent. Two changes are evident, however. The average size of bargaining units has steadily increased over the nine-year period. This can be seen by the increase in the number of bargaining units which have more than 500 employees in them. Secondly, during 1976 and 1977 the number of units involved in single-employer multiunion bargaining tripled. This may indicate that coalition bargaining is becoming more acceptable to unions. However, it may also only reveal the willingness of unions to combine when faced with adverse economic and legislative conditions (21). In this case, the introduction of the Anti-Inflation program may have stimulated union cooperation.

Collective-Bargaining Structures by Industry

The degree of centralization or decentralization of collective-bargaining structure is shaped by such a complex range of factors (see next section of the chapter) that it is unlikely that the same structural form would be adopted in every industry. Table 2 presents the number and percentage of bargaining units negotiating under each of the six bargaining structures by industry grouping. These figures represent the combination of data for all years under investigation (1969-1977). Even a cursory glance at the figures reveals that there is substantial variation in the bargaining structures adopted both across and within industries. For example, only in one industry (mining) does a single bargaining structure encompass more than 70 percent of the bargaining units. In fact, in half of the industries, less than 60 percent of the bargaining units negotiate under one structure. At the same time, however, clear trends do appear in the choice of bargaining structure by industry.

In Table 2, the circled percentages indicate the most predominant form of bargaining structure in that industry. Using these figures as indicators, it seems that the

Table 2

Alternate Bargaining Structures By Industry: 1969-1977 Combined

Industry	Total, All Structures[a]	Single-Employer Structures								Multiemployer Structures			
		Single plant—single union		Single plant—multiunion		Multiplant—single union		Multiplant—multiunion		Single union		Multiunion	
	#[b]	#[b]	%[c]	#	%	#	%	#	%	#	%	#	%
Fishing	20	2	10.0	0	0	2	10.0	0	0	13	65.0	3	15.0
Forestry	69	48	69.6	0	0	10	14.5	0	0	11	15.9	0	0
Mining	119	90	75.6	8	6.7	10	8.4	0	0	11	9.2	0	0
Manufacturing	1163	705	60.6	28	2.4	198	17.0	21	1.8	192	16.5	19	1.6
Communications	779	403	51.7	67	8.6	92	11.8	11	1.4	190	24.4	16	2.1
Transportation	475	103	21.7	1	0.2	272	57.3	4	0.8	79	16.6	16	3.4
Trade and finance	197	49	24.9	4	2.0	65	33.0	1	0.5	74	37.6	4	2.0
Public administration	729	259	35.5	3	0.4	431	59.1	4	0.5	31	4.3	1	0.1
Total all industries	3551	1659	46.7	111	3.1	1080	30.4	41	1.2	601	16.9	59	1.7

SOURCE: Labour Canada, Collective Bargaining Review, 1969-1977.

NOTES: a. *Total of negotiations involving 500 or more employees.*
b. *Number of negotiations with that particular bargaining structure.*
c. *Percent of negotiations with that particular bargaining structure. Percentages may not sum to 100 because of rounding.*

single-plant single-union bargaining structure is the most common form in mining (75.6 percent), forestry (69.6 percent), manufacturing (60.6 percent), and communications (51.7 percent) industries. Moreover, if we include multiplant negotiations with the same employer, the comparative figures increase to 84.0, 85.1, 77.6, and 63.5 percent, respectively. Thus, all of these industries involve very decentralized collective bargaining.

Two other industries have predominantly single-employer bargaining structures: transportation and public administration. However, in both of these industries, collective bargaining is more likely to involve more than one plant or location. Bargaining structures in public administration are, as expected, almost entirely single employer (94.6 percent), split between single-plant and multiplant forms. These figures reflect that public-sector bargaining outside of the municipal sector often involves a number of different government departments, schools or school districts, airports, or hospitals which are operated by the same employer. Moreover, the bargaining units are primarily defined occupationally, rather than geographically or functionally, which increases the likelihood of multiplant (multilocation) bargaining structures.

The transportation industry, similarly, is single-employer dominated (80 percent). However, certain types of transportation involve primarily within-city movement of people, goods, or services (for example, municipal transport, local delivery — 21.7 percent) while other parts of the industry involve point-to-point delivery, often between storage facilities of the same company (57.3 percent), or between facilities of several employers as in over-the-road trucking (16.6 percent); as a result, the structure of collective bargaining in this industry is less concentrated than in others. The bargaining structure adopted appears to reflect the scope and type of services offered by the employer. Moreover, this choice is simplified by the domination of one union, the Teamsters.

Consistent with the discussion of bargaining structure in general, the data presented in Table 2 reveal that multiemployer alternatives do not dominate many industries. Two exceptions do exist. Eighty percent of collective bargaining in the fishing industry involves more than one employer. Maritime associations representing fishermen are most often composed of owner-operators of a single boat who gain power and coordination by negotiating as a group with union representatives. The construction industry (data not presented here — see Rose (27)) also involves a similar formation of associations of construction companies for the purposes of collective bargaining in order to establish standard wage rates across the industry within a particular city or region. The communications and transportation industries also have a significant proportion of their negotiations (that is, over 20 percent) under multiemployer bargaining structures. Both of these industries are under federal jurisdiction and regulated, which may contribute to this centralization; again this stems from the need to maintain standard wage rates across the industry.

Finally, the trade and finance industries, although consistently involving single-union structures have a substantial proportion of the bargaining units negotiating under single-plant (24.9 percent), multiplant (33 percent), and multiemployer (37.6 percent) structures. This dispersion across the various bargaining structures may reflect the tremendous variety in types of business, employees, and jurisdictions represented within this industry. Moreover, the description of bargaining structure in this industry reemphasizes the fact that although the overall proportions of bargaining units adopting various bargaining structures have remained surprisingly stable over the past decade, there is still a great range of complex factors which may influence union and management's choice of an appropriate structure. The next section of this chapter examines some of the main determinants of bargaining structure.

THE DETERMINANTS OF COLLECTIVE-BARGAINING STRUCTURE

The previous description of the wide variation in the type of bargaining structures adopted in Canadian industries reveals that the structure of collective bargaining does not simply evolve out of the bargaining relationship but rather that it often is a deliberate choice made by the parties. Either union or management may attempt to adopt a particular bargaining structure in order to impose real or perceived costs on the other party during bargaining. As Deaton and Beaumont (11) point out this is usually done by increasing the ability of either party to obtain gains in collective bargaining through the use of whipsawing tactics. However, the choice may also be made because of the potential benefits of increased administrative efficiency or of maintaining market-wide uniformity. However, the benefits of decentralization or centralization of bargaining structure are likely to be different for union representatives than for management officials. As a consequence, the initial choice and evolution of the structure of collective bargaining is inevitably a result of negotiation between the parties and as such is also a product of the relative bargaining power of union and management.

While labour and management are central to the choice of an appropriate bargaining structure, the government may also play an important, and often determining role in the degree of centralization of bargaining structure. For the benefit of society (or the political strength of the party in power) the government may decide to establish legislative criteria which favour the increased centralization of collective bargaining. For example, a lessening of industrial conflict is often cited as a benefit of centralization (28), a benefit which government officials are likely to view as a positive influence on productivity, the economy generally, and the labour-relations climate of the jurisdiction. However, whether the choice is made unilaterally or in combination by unions, management, and/or government, the selection of a bargaining structure occurs within a complex environment of economic, legal, political, and power factors which must be examined as part of any discussion of the determinants of bargaining structure. Given the key role played by government, the role of government policies is discussed first, followed by a review of the influence of economic factors, organizational and representational factors, the nature of the issues, and tactical and power considerations. Finally, the few empirical studies of the determinants of bargaining power which have been undertaken are discussed.

Government Policies

In Canada, the nature of government policies and the distribution of governmental authority over labour-relations matters have a profound impact on the structure of collective bargaining. These policies both have a direct impact through legislation designed to determine the actual composition of the election unit as well as an indirect impact through legislation which may place pressure on the parties to expand or contract the scope of the negotiation unit or the unit of direct impact, thereby influencing the informal as well as the formal bargaining structure.

Direct influence— The greatest limitation placed on the degree of centralization of the structure of collective bargaining is a result of the distribution of authority over labour-relations matters between the federal and provincial governments. In 1925, the *Snider* case interpreted the British North-America Act as granting sole authority in labour-relations matters to the provinces except for firms which are involved in certain national markets (for example, transportation, communications) or under conditions of a national emergency. Consequently, the provinces have the right to establish any criteria they wish for the certification of bargaining units and, in implementing these criteria, to make any administrative rules concerning the scope and composition of the bargaining units. Given that only approximately 15 percent of the labour force are in industries under federal jurisdiction, by definition only a small proportion of collective bargaining is likely to be conducted in a national bargaining structure. Therefore, the distribution of jurisdiction over labour relations itself has an important impact on the degree of centralization of collective bargaining possible in Canada.

Each jurisdiction within Canada influences the formal bargaining structure with two types of decision rules. First, the relevant labour-relations board often has to decide whether it favours broad industrial (multioccupation) bargaining units or narrow occupationally or craft-based units. In general, most Canadian jurisdictions have favoured including maintenance and craft workers within units of production workers when all work together. The scope of the bargaining unit is also affected by decisions concerning the inclusion of professional and part-time employees in bargaining units composed of nonprofessional and full-time employees, respectively. The labour-relations boards have generally been reluctant to include either of these groups in bargaining units with other employees (9). Professionals may be included in nonprofessional units when a majority of the professional employees vote to be so certified. Thus, whether the bargaining unit is narrow or broad is greatly influenced by the decisions of labour-relations boards.

Another way in which labour-relations boards shape bargaining structure is through the positions which they adopt on multiplant and multiemployer bargaining units. Rarely will any labour board require that certification elections be held at the multiplant or multiemployer level. A notable exception in Canadian labour relations occurred in Nova Scotia in 1980 with the passage of the Michelin Bill. This piece of legislation required that if an employer had more than one plant within the jurisdiction that any petition for certification must be made by a bargaining agent representing employees in an appropriate bargaining unit across all plants. Critics argued that this piece of legislation was equivalent to the Nova Scotia government entering the field of union busting. Allegedly, Michelin had threatened to close its two existing plants and not to continue plans to build a third if one of its plants was successfully organized by a union. As employees in the other plant would not support a unionization attempt, requiring a multiplant bargaining structure resulted in the failure of the union to obtain certification as a bargaining agent.

Labour-relations boards also influence bargaining structure based on their role in the establishment of employers' associations. If the provincial labour legislation provides a procedure whereby employers may petition for certification (often termed accreditation) as an employers' association, it helps to overcome many of the problems associated with signatory or voluntary associations as the certification process results in the formal delegation of employer authority to the association. This places increased pressure on the union or unions involved to adjust their bargaining structure to the same level of centralization. Legislation in British Columbia does permit certification of employer associations. As a result, in comparison with other jurisdictions, there is a much greater degree of multiemployer bargaining. For example, not only have construction and forest-products firms developed employers' associations but British Columbia is unique in the establishment of several multiemployer structures (both certified and signatory) in the municipal sector. Municipalities in greater Victoria, greater Vancouver, mid-Vancouver Island, and the Okanagan region have all at one time bargained under a multiemployer bargaining structure. Although the success with these structures has been mixed, their existence in part has been due to favourable legislation.

The domain in which government policies have had the greatest impact on the form of bargaining structure adopted is the public sector. In this sector, the government has had the unique position of being both the employer and the regulator. As Feuille and Anderson (12) note, at most levels in the public sector, bargaining units have been statutorily defined and certification automatically granted to existing unions or associations. Moreover, in the provincial public sector recent legislation has defined broad bargaining units. For example, both British Columbia (2) and Saskatchewan (31) established two-tier bargaining structures with a master agreement negotiated at the service-wide level covering conditions of service-wide application with supplementary agreements negotiated by a relatively small number (10 to 12) of occupationally based units. Similarly, the Province of Quebec passed legislation to adopt province-wide bargaining for several public employee groups including teachers. Furthermore, in the health sector legislative support has been provided for the movement toward province-wide bargaining in British Columbia and Ontario (1).

Government policies may also influence the informal bargaining structures by identifying or structuring the unit of direct impact. For example, in the federal public service while negotiations occur between Treasury Board and narrowly defined occupational groups, these occupational bargaining units are classified into five broad occupational categories which in most cases are represented by a single union. As a result, natural pattern setting and following arrangements are established by the certification process. A few unions negotiate with a single employer for a large number of bargaining units. The collective agreements which are settled as a result of pattern bargaining are almost identical (at least at the level of the five broad occupational categories) so that de facto centralized bargaining occurs (4, 6).

Pattern bargaining is also often directly influenced through the establishment of criteria for arbitration awards in the public sectors. Frequently, compulsory arbitration statutes directly or indirectly identify the comparison bargaining units to be used or the internal relativities to be maintained. Moreover, the use of a small number of arbitrators, as in the Canadian federal public service tends to increase the probability that awards will be uniform and patterns adhered to (5). Finally, legislation in Quebec provides under certain circumstances for the extension of negotiated wages and benefits in an industry to newly organized or nonunion firms. Thus, government policies are also likely to directly influence the extent and scope of pattern bargaining, that is, the informal bargaining structure.

Indirect influence — Other government policies often have a role in shaping the informal and ultimately the formal structure of collective bargaining. For example, the implementation of wage-and-price guidelines under the jurisdiction of the Anti-

Inflation Board (AIB) stimulated substantial coordination between unions, resulting in an increase in coordinated or coalition-bargaining structures. Moreover, as the nature of historical relationships in total compensation between occupations was one of the exceptions to the guidelines, the AIB forced unions and employers to become substantially more aware of the extent and nature of pattern bargaining which occurred within their industry. Thus, the AIB may have had a centralizing effect on collective-bargaining structure by forcing changes in both the formal and informal structures.

Government regulatory policies also have an influence on the structure of collective bargaining. In regulated industries, wage competition is often removed as not only profits but wages end up being standardized across firms and both unions and employers would prefer collective bargaining to occur at the industry level.

The examples provided reveal that government policies exert a tremendous influence on the shape of bargaining structures. This happens both directly through the criteria established for determining the scope and composition of appropriate bargaining units on both the employer and employee sides as well as through the identification of relevant comparisons in pattern bargaining. Indirectly, other government policies may shape the expectations of the parties and the patterns which they follow.

Economic Factors

Weber (30) stresses the fact that unions will attempt to change the structure of collective bargaining to match the nature of the labour and product markets facing the firm. This is done in order to take wages out of competition in the market and thus, give unions a greater chance of getting substantial wage increases. For example, an appropriate bargaining structure for the construction industry would be a multi-employer structure within a particular geographic location. This is due to the fact that construction companies typically sell their products and services within a local area and the product market includes a large number of sellers. Moreover, labour is obtained within the local labour market. On the other hand, the trucking industry involves a national product market and a national labour market so that it would be expected that a union would attempt to establish a national multiemployer structure either through a single unit or pattern setting in order to maximize both bargaining power and administrative efficiency.

The nature of labour and product markets would have a similar impact on employer decision making. In particular, an appropriate bargaining structure based on labour market forces helps to ensure stability in the organizational work force. If the union has organized all workers in the industry, there is likely to be less mobility between firms due to differences in wages and working conditions. Moreover, on the product market side, most employers would prefer that the whole market or industry was unionized or nonunion. This is because the partial organization of the product market would provide a competitive advantage to the nonunion employers with lower labour costs. Thus, both unions and employers will push towards the centralization of bargaining structure only to the point that the structure matches the market structure in which the firm operates.

Organizational and Representational Factors

Several authors (18, 30) have also identified a number of organizational and representational factors which may place pressure on both unions and employers to centralize or decentralize the bargaining structure. Kochan (18) points out that the growth of large corporations has led to a centralization of decision making on industrial-relations matters. In response, unions are forced to attempt to expand the bargaining structure until the critical corporate decision maker is involved in the bargaining. For many years this was a major problem for Canadian bargaining structures as the critical decision makers on both the union and management sides were in the United States. Therefore, it was impossible for the formal bargaining structure to expand to the level demanded by union or management organizational structures. Frequently, attempts were made by union representatives to negotiate wage and benefit parity provisions with U.S. unions in order to legitimize the pattern-bargaining arrangements established informally. However, changes in economic conditions during the 1970s (for example, differences in economic growth, a floating exchange rate) made parity provisions unworkable.

An even greater difficulty created by attempts to expand bargaining beyond the borders or even to centralize bargaining within a jurisdiction was the need to ensure the continuing representation of the interests of lower-level union and management participants. Politics within unions, the demands for internal democracy, and leadership fears of loss of influence, status, or position all tend to exert a decentralizing pressure on collective bargaining. Differences in interests within a union or rivalry between unions greatly reduce the chances for coordinated bargaining at a more centralized level. For example, Adams, Beatty, and Gunderson (1) indicate that rivalry and competition between the Service Employees International Union (SEIU) and the Canadian Union of Public Employees (CUPE) has been a major obstacle to province-wide bargaining in the hospital industry in Ontario.

Public-sector unions and employers in Saskatchewan (14, 31) have partially resolved this problem in two ways. First, elaborate procedures were established to guarantee that lower-level participants on both sides have opportunities to provide input into the formulation of demands and bargaining strategy. For example, in province-wide teacher bargaining, the union bargaining strategy is circulated to local officials. Subsequently, regional meetings are held with local officials to discuss the strategies and priorities. Finally, a vote of local representatives is conducted. Second, a two-tier bargaining structure was adopted in 1973 with such issues as salary, longevity pay, group insurance, sick leave, and retirement negotiated into a master province-wide collective agreement. Other local issues are then negotiated by the local representatives into a supplemental agreement. Thus, both structural and internal process changes are required to ensure that the bargaining structure meets both the representational pressures toward decentralization and economic and organizational pressures toward centralization.

The Nature of Bargaining Issues

Weber (30) also argued that the collective-bargaining structures could vary depending on the nature of the issue being considered. Clearly the two-tier bargaining structures in Saskatchewan described above and their predecessors in B.C. are examples of one form of change in bargaining structure due to the commonality or specificity of the issue under consideration. Similarly, it is not uncommon in the public and private sectors for bargaining units to combine when discussing certain fringe benefits with the employer that have uniform application to all employees no matter which bargaining unit. For example, city unions in the majority of large Canadian municipalities negotiate wages separately but join together when changes in pensions or major fringe benefits such as hospitalization, dental plans, or group insurance are proposed (3). Similarly, in the federal public service issues of service-wide concern by mutual agreement may be removed from the individual occupational bargaining structure and considered by the National Joint Council, which is comprised of representatives of the employer and the major federal unions (6). However, when the vast majority of all bargaining occurs at the single-plant single-union level, there is not much room for easy expansion of bargaining on particular issues.

Tactical and Power Factors

Alterations in bargaining structures may also be due to the desire of one or both parties to increase their bargaining power. Most of the literature suggests that both union and management operate in such a manner as to increase their ability to whipsaw the other party. However, in most cases this would support the maintenance of decentralized bargaining structures. Centralization often increases the power of the union by both increasing the size of the bargaining unit and therefore, the potential impact of any job action by the workers and by increasing the professionalization of the representatives at the table. Moreover, centralization limits management's ability to shift production from one facility to another in the case of a strike and hence, increases union bargaining power. Thus, centralization is often depicted as a factor which is likely to substantially increase union power. On the other hand, as it also limits the unions' ability to whipsaw and provides management with the same benefits of economies of scale, the choice of a bargaining structure for tactical or power reasons is likely to result in the assessment of several of the factors discussed above as well as the historical features of the particular union-management relationships involved.

Empirical Studies of the Determinants of Bargaining Structure

Although a number of determinants of collective-bargaining structure were identified, evidence for their relative importance in determining the joint choice by union and management of a bargaining structure is severely limited. While a number of case studies provide insight into the causes of a bargaining structure in a particular industry, few studies have investigated the determinants of bargaining structure across firms or industries. Moreover, none of those which do exist have examined collective-bargaining structures in Canada. Therefore, two studies (11, 16) are examined below only to provide some suggestive evidence on the importance of the factors discussed.

Deaton and Beaumont— This study (11) examines those factors which differentiate between single and multiemployer bargaining structures in 970 establishments in manufacturing in Britain. Based on the belief that the parties change bargaining structure to impose costs on the other party, to increase administrative efficiency, or to maintain market uniformity, the authors argue that both technical and market factors and institutional factors shape bargaining structure. Multiemployer bargaining structures were hypothesized to be present when: (a) a wage payment by results system did not exist; (b) there was a competitive product market; (c) firms were spatially concentrated in the same area; (d) the establishment size was lower; (e) the firm was not foreign-owned; (f) firms did not have a personnel function developed; (g) union rivalry existed; (h) the skills of employees in any given firm were replaceable; and (i) no hypothesis was offered for union density. In general, the results supported the hypotheses; all variables except the nature of the wage system and the skill replaceability variables were significant and had the expected relationship. Union density (percent unionized) was found to increase the probability of a multiemployer bargaining structure. Using these market and institutional characteristics, 64 percent of the firms could be correctly classified as bargaining in a single- or multiemployer structure. Adding a series of industry dummy variables resulted in 80 percent of the firms being correctly classified.

These results support strongly the role of the market and the desire for administrative efficiency in shaping multiemployer bargaining. Deaton and Beaumont (11) point out that in Britain the choice of a bargaining structure is solely an employer's decision. This difference from the Canadian experience helps to explain why union density and union rivalry, which would be expected to lead to decentralization due to the potential to whipsaw the employer and the need to represent employee interests, respectively, have the opposite relationship in this British sample.

Hendricks and Kahn — This study (16) examines the determinants of single-employer versus multiemployer and firm-wide vs. single-plant bargaining structures under which 3,056 manufacturing industry collective agreements were negotiated in 1975. The authors argue that the choice of a bargaining structure involves both union and management's choice function, the congruence between them, and the ability of both parties to enforce their choice. Management's choice is viewed as being a function of the potential gains to flexibility of management decision making, economies of scale, the alteration of bargaining power through pooled resources or whipsawing, and the labour to total cost ratio for the firm. The union decision, on the other hand, is based on the potential for interunion or intraunion rivalry, economies of scale, and increases in bargaining power through the use of whipsawing tactics. Variables assessing union strength, the fragmentation of unions, the spatial concentration of the product market, the concentration of the product market, employer power, and labour cost to total cost ratio were included in the study.

The results of the study revealed that multiemployer bargaining was less likely when: (a) unions were moderately strong; (b) fragmentation and rivalry among unions were high; (c) employer power was high due to a high concentration ratio and large average plant size; and (d) firms within the industry were spatially dispersed. Examining only those firms with single-employer bargaining, the results indicated that the probability that collective bargaining would be decentralized to the plant level was greater when: (a) union strength was moderate; (b) there was high fragmentation and rivalry among unions; (c) employer power was low due to a low concentration of firms in the market and small average plant size; (d) the firm was operating in a local market; and (e) there were relatively low labour costs to total costs. Overall, the results are surprisingly constant whether the decision involves centralization of bargaining structure within a single employer or across multiple employers. Moreover, the results support the importance of employer and union power, economies of scale, and representational factors identified in the theoretical literature as determinants of the structure of collective bargaining.

CONSEQUENCES OF ALTERNATE COLLECTIVE-BARGAINING STRUCTURES

The decision to adopt a particular bargaining structure involves expectations by union and management of the potential consequences of their choice. Employers are typically interested in reducing the use of whipsawing by unions, which may result in out-of-line settlements and higher labour costs. Unions, on the other hand, typically expect to increase their bargaining power either by expanding the potential cost to the employer of a strike or through the use of whipsawing. In addition, unions, more than employers, as political institutions are interested in ensuring the representation of their members' interests at the same time as maximizing bargaining power. Beyond union and management, the government often has an interest in the form of bargaining structure adopted because of its potential impact on the economy and often because of a desire to control the level of strike activity (7). Often these three sets of expectations of the major actors in the Canadian industrial-relations system are in conflict and as such the direction of evolution of bargaining structure and its consequences are unclear. Unfortunately, the consequences of alternate collective-bargaining structures have not been a topic of much empirical research. As a result, the discussion of the impact of bargaining structure on the bargaining process, the outcomes of collective bargaining, the level of industrial conflict, and the representation of participants' interests will be to a large extent speculative.

Consequences for the Bargaining Process

Very little has been written about the changes which occur as a result of increased centralization of collective bargaining. Muir (24) has suggested that centralization will be beneficial in that it tends to be accompanied by the increased professionalization of the negotiating process. Both labour and management are more likely to use skilled and experienced negotiators when only a single set of negotiations occurs. Moreover, centralization is likely to ensure that the individuals with the authority to settle agreements are actually involved in the bargaining process. Centralization also has its costs, however, as a greater number of individuals on both sides of the table need to be informed, consulted, and involved in the final decision-making process, increasing the problems associated with intraorganizational bargaining. Thus, it is likely that the actual process of collective bargaining will take more time.

The complete evaluation of the consequences of centralization of collective bargaining in a Canadian jurisdiction was conducted by Wetzel and Gallagher (31, 32) on the public-service sector in Saskatchewan. Based on interviews (32) with union and management officials, their research reveals that centralization did slow negotiations. This occurred both as a result of the number of people involved but also because the visibility of settlements across groups increased and, consequently, bargaining representatives were often reluctant to settle before other public-sector groups had reached agreement. There was also a dramatic change in the composition and orientation of management's industrial-relations representatives. Increased skill and expertise of the negotiators made bargaining smoother although these individuals also had less of an understanding of day-to-day operating problems which increased the time taken to settle. Finally, intraorganizational problems in unions and increased informal bargaining within groups also contributed to an extension of the time required to reach an agreement. Thus, each of the anticipated consequences for centralization of collective bargaining was present in the Saskatchewan experience.

Interestingly, Wetzel and Gallagher (31) also discovered that there were two impacts on the issues dealt with in bargaining. First, the range of issues was limited more than when bargaining was decentralized. Feuille, Hendricks, and Kahn (16) found a similar result in U.S. manufacturing and suggest that employers may be willing to trade off higher wages for reductions in fringe benefit and working conditions provisions which may be inappropriate for some of the employers involved in a multiemployer-bargaining structure. Second, Wetzel and Gallagher discovered that as centralization occurred, internal comparisons between occupations became less relevant and the importance of outside comparisons increased. Thus, centralization may also change the way certain issues are dealt with in collective bargaining.

A study (25) of transit bargaining units in the western United States is somewhat supportive of the Saskatchewan experience. While increases in unit size and scope, and reductions in fragmentation did not increase the frequency of renegotiation of contracts, they were positively related to the length of negotiations (although not significantly). Moreover, units that were broader in scope were less likely to have interference in the bargaining process by management, community or elected officials not directly involved in bargaining.

Consequences for Bargaining Outcomes

The expected consequences of centralization or decentralization of collective-bargaining structures on the outcomes of bargaining are quite clear. Through centralization, employers expect to decrease union whipsawing and as a result to lower labour costs and standardize wages and benefits across the bargaining units affected. Unions, on the other hand, should prefer decentralization if it increases their ability to whipsaw the employer and gain additional outcomes favourable to their membership. Several studies have examined this consequence.

Metcalf (23), in a sample of British firms, found that decentralization of bargaining structure was associated with higher wages for unionists. Thompson, Mulvey, and Farbman (29) also found that the relative earnings in decentralized industries in Great Britain were greater than in industries characterized as having centralized bargaining structures. In a U.S. study, Hendricks (15) also found that single-firm contracts led to higher union wages than industry-wide contracts. Going beyond wages to examine the comprehensivenss of collective agreements in two-digit industries, Kochan and Block (19) discovered that the percentage of single-firm contracts was positively related to more favourable outcomes for the union. Moreover, the percentage of multifirm contracts in an industry was negatively related to the level of outcomes. Thus, the evidence which is available strongly supports the contention that centralization will decrease the positive benefit to unions of the use of whipsawing tactics.

Consequences for Industrial Conflict

Public policy makers have often been interested in the potential of centralization of collective bargaining for reducing the level of strike activity. As the actual number of negotiations in an industry or the economy are reduced, the potential number of strikes is also reduced. While this has rarely been directly tested, some evidence is available. Perry and Angle (25) discovered that the more fragmented the bargaining structure in the transit department in a municipality, the greater the number of strikes. Similarly, Roomkin (26) found that as unions centralized control over the decision to strike (which often accompanies centralization of bargaining) the number of strikes decreased. However, as Weber (30) suggests, centralization may also decrease the satisfaction of the membership and increase the probability of wildcat strikes. As Stern and Anderson (28) revealed in their analysis of the 1975 postal strike, centralization of both union and bargaining structure created a large number of internal conflicts which resulted in some locals going back to work before the strike officially ended while others remained on strike after a settlement had been reached. While there is still not enough research to be conclusive, it may be that centralization may create a trade-off between national-level strikes being reduced and local wildcat strikes being increased.

Consequences for Representational Issues

Centralization of collective-bargaining structure is likely to increase the feeling of remoteness that local union officials and union membership have toward the collective-bargaining process and the union leadership. As a result, Weber (30) argues that not only wildcat strikes but also failures to ratify collective agreements and voting union leadership out of office are likely to increase substantially as centralization increases. Intraorganizational bargaining, obtaining input, and providing information back to the constituents become more time consuming as centralized bargaining structures are implemented. Thus, a move toward centralization must be able to provide tangible benefits in bargaining outcomes or administrative efficiency which will offset any political costs associated with the lessened ability of union or management to ensure representation of the interests of a diverse group of constituents.

Perry and Angle (25) examined the consequences on internal union affairs of increasing the size and scope of the bargaining unit and reducing fragmentation of bargaining units in the transit industry. Bargaining structure was not found to be significantly related to member satisfaction with union efforts or satisfaction with the union leadership. However, as unit size and scope increased, both the member evaluation of the union's internal processes and members' perceived influence in decision making decreased substantially. Therefore, centralization reduces the feeling of representation by members.

Centralization of bargaining structure also may create problems for the local administration of the collective agreements. Wetzel and Gallagher (31) found that centralization of teacher collective bargaining in Saskatchewan decreased the flexibility of management in dealing with grievances, creating problems for local union-management relations. Moreover, it was also discovered that management officials at lower levels developed the attitude that bargaining was someone else's responsibility, and they were unwilling to devote time to labour-relations matters, the long-term consequence being that skills needed to ensure good labour relations at the local and ultimately national level will not be developed.

CONCLUDING COMMENTS

Labour-relations practitioners are quick to point out that the structure of collective bargaining is one of the most important factors shaping the process and outcomes of collective bargaining. Unfortunately, very little attention has been directed towards understanding those factors that influence the decision of union and management officials to adopt a particular bargaining structure. The choice is presented by most writers as based on a calculation of the increase in bargaining power (usually through the use or elimination of whipsawing tactics) and the increase in administrative efficiency through economies of scale, or the benefits of maintaining market-wide uniformity. Theory and research suggest that the major factors which influence the actual bargaining structure include: (a) government policies; (b) economic or market factors; (c) organizational or representational issues; (d) tactical or power factors; and (e) the nature of the issues being negotiated. In this chapter, the role that each of these factors plays in shaping bargaining has been discussed.

Centralization of collective-bargaining structures has often been viewed as a panacea for many of the ills of the industrial-relations system. It is expected to reduce industrial conflict, increase professionalization, eliminate out-of-line settlements, and as a result benefit the overall economy. The only cost associated with centralization is related to the losses in the ability of union and management representatives to deal with local issues, to resolve internal conflicts, to provide opportunities for input, and to get consensus on priorities, bargaining strategy, and the final settlement. Thus, the parties making a choice of a centralized bargaining structure need to consider the balance between the positive aspects of increased bargaining power and the potential negative consequences to representation of constituent interests. Moreover, these decisions must be made with a full understanding of the legal, political, economic, and institutional context in which bargaining occurs.

REFERENCES AND WORKS CITED

1. Adams, G., D. Beatty, and M. Gunderson. "Structural Issue of Centralized Bargaining in Health Services: Canada, U.S. and Britain" in A. S. Sethi (Ed.), *Industrial Relations and Health Services* (London: Croom Helm, forthcoming).

2. Anderson, J. C. *An Empirical Analysis of the Union Democracy Construct.* Unpublished Master's thesis, Cornell University, 1976.

3. Anderson, J. C. *Union Effectiveness: An Industrial Relations Systems Approach.* Unpublished Doctoral thesis, Cornell University, 1977.

4. Anderson, J. C. "Determinants of Bargaining Outcomes in the Federal Government of Canada," *Industrial and Labor Relations Review,* Vol. 32 (January 1979), 224-241.

5. Anderson, J. C. "Arbitration in the Federal Public Service," in J. Weiler (Ed.), *Interest Arbitration* (Toronto: Carswell, forthcoming).

6. Anderson, J. C., and T. Kochan. "Collective Bargaining in the Public Service of Canada," *Relations Industrielles/Industrial Relations,* Vol. 32 (1977), 234-249.

7. Bairstow, F., M. Dubinsky, and R. Smith. *Report of the Inquiry Commission on Wider-Based Collective Bargaining* (Ottawa: Labour Canada, 1978).

8. Boivin, J. "Labour Relations in Quebec," in J. Anderson and M. Gunderson (Eds), *Union-Management Relations in Canada* (Toronto: Addison-Wesley, 1981).

9. Carter, D., and J. Woon. *Union Recognition in Ontario* (Ottawa: Labour Canada, 1981).

10. Crispo, J. *The Canadian Industrial Relations System* (Toronto: McGraw-Hill Ryerson, 1979).

11. Deaton, D. R., and P. B. Beaumont. "The Determinants of Bargaining Structure: Some Large Scale Survey Evidence for Britain," *British Journal of Industrial Relations,* Vol. 18 (July 1980), 199-216.

12. Feuille, P., and J. C. Anderson. "Public Sector Bargaining: Policy and Practice," *Industrial Relations,* Vol. 19 (Fall 1980), 309-324.

13. Feuille, P., W. Hendricks, and L. Kahn. "Wage and Nonwage Outcomes in Collective Bargaining: Determinants and Tradeoffs," *Journal of Labor Research,* Vol. 2 (Spring 1981), 39-54.

14. Gallagher, D., and K. Wetzel, "Centralized Multi-Employer Negotiations in Public Education: An Examination of the Saskatchewan Experience," *Journal of Collective Negotiations in the Public Sector,* Vol. 9 (Fall 1980), 281-295.

15. Hendricks, W. "Labor Market Structure and Union Wage Levels," *Economic Inquiry,* Vol. 13 (September 1975), 401-416.

16. Hendricks, W., and L. Kahn, "The Determinants of Bargaining Structure in U.S. Manufacturing Industries," *Industrial and Labor Relations Review,* forthcoming.

17. Jamieson, S. *Industrial Relations in Canada* (Toronto: Macmillan, 1973).

18. Kochan, T. *Collective Bargaining and Industrial Relations* (Homewood: Irwin, 1980).

19. Kochan, T., and R. Block. "An Interindustry Analysis of Bargaining Outcomes: Preliminary Evidence From Two-Digit Industries," *Quarterly Journal of Economics,* Vol. 91 (August 1977), 431-452.

20. Levinson, H. "Pattern Bargaining: A Case Study of the Automobile Industry," *Quarterly Journal of Economics,* Vol. 74 (May 1964), 296-317.

21. Lewin, D., and M. McCormick. "Coalition Bargaining in Municipal Government: The New York City Experience," *Industrial and Labor Relations Review,* Vol. 34 (January 1981), 175-190.

22. McLean, R. "Coalition Bargaining and Strike Activity in the Electrical Equipment Industry, 1950-1974," *Industrial and Labor Relations Review,* Vol. 30 (April 1977), 356-363.

23. Metcalf, D. "Unions, Incomes Policy and Relative Wages in Britain," *British Journal of Industrial Relations,* Vol. 15 (July 1977), 157-175.

24. Muir, J. D. "Decentralized Bargaining: Its Problems and Direction in the Public Education Systems of Ontario and the Western Provinces," *Relations Industrielles/ Industrial Relations,* Vol. 26 (1971), 124-145.

25. Perry, J., and H. Angle. "Bargaining Unit Structure and Organizational Outcomes," *Industrial Relations,* Vol. 20 (Winter 1981), 47-59.

26. Roomkin, M. "Union Structure, Internal Control and Strike Activity," *Industrial and Labor Relations Review,* Vol. 29 (January 1976), 198-217.

27. Rose, J. *Public Policy, Bargaining Structure, and the Construction Industry* (Toronto: Butterworth, 1980).

28. Stern, R., and J. Anderson. "Canadian Strike Activity: Union Centralization and National Diversity," in J. Stern (Ed.), *Proceedings of the Thirtieth Annual Winter Meeting of the Industrial Relations Research Association* (Madison: IRRA, 1978), 132-140.

29. Thompson, A., C. Mulvey, and M. Farbman. "Bargaining Structure and Relative Earnings in Great Britain," *British Journal of Industrial Relations,* Vol. 15 (July 1977), 176-191.

30. Weber, A. "Stability and Change in the Structure of Collective Bargaining" in L. Ulman (Ed.), *Challenges to Collective Bargaining* (Englewood Cliffs: Prentice-Hall, 1967), pp. 13-36.

31. Wetzel, K., and D. Gallagher. "Centralization of Bargaining in Saskatchewan's

Provincial Public Sector: Objectives and Experience." Unpublished paper, University of Saskatchewan, February 1980.

32. Wetzel, K., and D. Gallagher. "Local Negotiator Perceptions of Bargaining Under a Two Tier Structure." Paper presented at the Eighteenth Annual Conference of the Canadian Industrial Relations Association, Halifax, May 1981.

QUESTIONS

1. Define collective-bargaining structure and describe the difference between formal and informal bargaining structures.

2. Describe the differences between election unit, negotiation unit, and unit of direct impact.

3. Describe the types of bargaining structures that are predominant in Canadian industries.

4. How does labour legislation impact the structure of collective bargaining?

5. What impact does the economic environment have on the choice of a bargaining structure?

6. What are the advantages and disadvantages of a centralized collective-bargaining structure for a union?

7. What are the advantages and disadvantages of a centralized collective-bargaining structure for the employer?

8. How does collective-bargaining structure influence industrial conflict?

C. BRIAN WILLIAMS

9. Negotiating the Union-Management Agreement

The collective-bargaining process is a major determinant of the outcomes of the Canadian industrial-relations systems. Since the early 1940s, most employees have enjoyed the right to join trade unions for the purpose of negotiating with the employer over the terms and conditions of employment. This chapter presents a conceptual model which describes the process of compromise by union and management in negotiations. The relative bargaining power of the parties is identified as the major factor which shapes the timing of settlement and the content of the collective agreement. Characteristics of the environment, organizational arrangement of union and management, interpersonal, personal, and bargaining history factors may act as sources of bargaining power to the parties. The stages of preparation for and execution of the collective-bargaining process are outlined including several tactics useful to the parties in achieving settlement.

The industrialization of society inevitably leads to the development of a conflict of interests between employees and employers. In a competitive environment, a major goal of the employer is to maximize profits and in doing so, to minimize the costs associated with maintaining an effective work force. In addition, management wants to maintain sole authority over the operations of the enterprise. On the other hand, employees want to protect their economic position by improving their wages and benefits as much as possible, as well as having some say over important work-related decisions. In different countries, the conflict between these economic goals of employees and employers is dealt with through a variety of means such as government intervention and regulation, political action by the parties, or unilateral action by employers. However, in Canada the major way in which the conflict of interests between workers and management is resolved is through the collective-bargaining process. That is, a union or association representing the interests of employees *collectively* on a periodic basis attempts to establish the terms and conditions of employment with management through a process of mutual accomodation, compromise, and bargaining. This process has become an integral part of the Canadian economic system.

Despite the prevalence of collective bargaining as an institution, it is not without its critics. Collective bargaining has often been attacked because of its adversarial nature. The Federal Task Force on Labour Relations described this problem in the following manner:

> There is a basic characteristic of the collective bargaining system that is seemingly contradictory. Paradoxical as it may appear, collective bargaining is designed to resolve conflict through conflict, or at least through the threat of conflict. It is an adversary system in which two basic issues must be resolved: how available revenue is to be divided, and how the clash between management's drive for productive efficiency and the workers' quest for job, income and psychic security are to be reconciled. Other major differences, including personality conflicts, may appear from time to time but normally they prove subsidiary to these two overriding issues. (3, p. 119).

Downie goes even further, describing collective bargaining as being characterized by a win-lose approach which promotes a cleavage between the parties because each side wants to win. Issues which are placed on the bargaining table are viewed competitively with an improvement in favour of the union being viewed as a loss by management. This adversarial situation is likely to result in low trust and secrecy between the parties; mental inflexibility on the part of the negotiators, which creates an unwillingness to view the other party's proposals as reasonable; bilateral threats; and settlements which are only likely to occur under crisis conditions, for example, an impending strike or lockout. Consequently, a search continues for alternatives to adversarial bargaining (see chapter 14).

The dissatisfaction with the collective-bargaining process, in large part, may be misplaced as this conflict-resolution mechanism has successfully resulted in settlements in the vast majority of negotiations between labour and management for over four decades. The focus of this chapter is on the actual process of negotiating the collective agreement between union and management. The evolution and scope of collective bargaining is presented first as a backdrop to a discussion of how negotiations work; the role of bargaining power in achieving a settlement, and finally, the planning and execution of the effective negotiator's role and function are examined.

EVOLUTION AND SCOPE OF COLLECTIVE BARGAINING

Evolution of Collective Bargaining

The first clearly identifiable origin of what is today termed the negotiation of union-management agreements dates back to the early 1900s. The government of Canada, a visible partner in the emerging industrial nation of Canada, found itself dealing with one of the inevitable consequences flowing from the movement to an industrial state — union-management conflict. Conflict in the form of a work stoppage often exists with the precipitating issue being the terms and conditions under which people work.

However, the labour disputes of those days were quite different in character from the labour disputes of today in that the recognition of a union was inextricably bound to the dispute over terms and conditions of employment. At that time, no legislation existed which guaranteed workers the right to join unions and then to bargain collectively with the employer. Our present-day system for deciding the recognition issue (certification) was not set in place until the late 1930s and early 1940s. In reality, the disputes were frequently over recognition of the union, and the resolution of the recognition issue was a necessary prerequisite to the resolution of the dispute over terms and conditions of employment. In a very real sense, the resolution of terms and conditions of employment was frustrated by the unresolved issue of recognition.

In the Conciliation Act of 1900 the government of Canada moved to resolve the dilemma by expressing confidence in a system which it termed "conciliation." The term "conciliation" as used in that act is what today is called "negotiations." Conciliation encouraged the parties to come together in a discussion, dialogue, or a "long jaw" to discuss issues relating to terms and conditions of work and to do so prior to the exercise of a work stoppage. It placed complete confidence in the ability of unions and management to resolve conflicts over the terms and conditions of employment if they would only meet with one another, identify the specific issues, and, through a discussion or a dialogue, move to resolve them, and come to an agreement. In the context of the day, which was not committed to the idea of a dialogue or discussions, this step represented a novel and, indeed, a revolutionary idea. Of course, in endorsing the conciliation system, the act was implicitly encouraging recognition of the union by the employer. It was equally true that the success of this system was limited to the acceptability of the implied assumption of recognition of the union by the employer. However, acceptability was very difficult to obtain (11, 25).

Although the "conciliation" concept found some acceptance in some relationships, its use and acceptance was very limited compared to the rapidly growing number of union-management relationships in Canadian industry. The implicit assumption or requirement of recognition simply proved to be too great an obstacle.

It was not until the late 1930s and early 1940s that provisions were set in place, through public policy, that not only dealt with limiting the application of conciliation in industry, but also put into place the foundations of the union-management negotiating system of today. First, the process of certification was introduced. Second, the introduction of the contemporary system of "compulsory collective bargaining" occurred. The long-standing dilemma dating from the early 1900s had finally been resolved.

Under certification, the issue of recognition was removed from the realm of resolution solely by the parties and placed in the hands of the Labour Board. Compulsory collective bargaining provided not only a reaffirmation of the earlier idea that disputes over terms and conditions of employment could best be settled through the process of dialogue and discussion, but it also established a virtually complete commitment to it as "the system" for the collective determination of terms and conditions of employment. Under these two principles the system of union-management agreement negotiations grew very quickly throughout Canadian industry.

The current labour legislation provides for a majority of employees in a unit appropriate for collective bargaining to select a union to act as their exclusive representative with management in establishing the terms and conditions of employment. Prior to the expiry of an existing collective agreement, either party may notify the other of their desire to negotiate changes in the contract. Both parties are required by statute to bargain in good faith with the intention of concluding a mutually agreeable set of terms and conditions of employment. Should the parties have difficulty in reaching a settlement, most jurisdictions provide for the assistance of a mediator in resolving the issues in dispute. Finally, the parties may exercise their right to use the ultimate sanction, a strike or lockout to induce the other party to settle.

The Scope of Collective Bargaining

One of the most remarkable characteristics of our collective-bargaining system has been its ability to function in very different structures, industrial settings, and employee occupations. Today, it is asked to perform in yet still different situations. Although developed in the private sector and initially employed by unions representing employees in the traditional industrial occupations, today's applications are highly diverse (9, 26).

In its early days, and even today, the vast majority of Canadian union-management negotiations take place at the local-plant level. The primary participants are members of the union's local-plant negotiating committee and members of local management. Traditionally, it is a local or "grass roots" activity. However, against this traditional setting examples abound of the activity structured in settings involving several plants and several employee groups of the same employer. Examples also exist of multiemployer and employee negotiations involving different employers and their employees. The former is often described as "company-wide bargaining" and the latter as "multiemployer bargaining." Although the structure of bargaining is more complex, the objective is still to negotiate an agreement covering all plants, employers, and employee groups within the given structure (6).

In addition to different structures, collective bargaining can also be observed in many differing industrial settings. The size of employer and employee groups range from the very small to the very large. The fields of activity include resource development, manufacturing, transportation, construction, agribusiness, and service. There is hardly a field of industrial activity that has not experienced union-management negotiating activity. The greatest growth has occurred in its extension into new and quite varied employment occupations. From the traditional occupations of trades, manufacturing, and transport, sometimes referred to as the "blue-collar" occupations, collective bargaining now covers a large variety of "white-collar" workers such as school teachers, virtually all occupations in the health-service field, employees of government and its agencies, commercial airline crews, university professors, and even physicians and surgeons. Today, the union-management negotiating process pervades virtually all aspects of Canadian industrial employment activity. Thus, the employment of the system in such diverse settings is certainly a testimony to its acceptance, if not confidence in the union-management negotiating process.

In addition to an overall expansion in the industries and occupations covered, the scope of collective bargaining has also enlarged in terms of the range of issues which find their way to the bargaining table. Originally, collective bargaining focused quite narrowly on issues of wages and working conditions. However, over time not only have the number of pay-related and fringe-benefit provisions increased, but unions have made substantial inroads into areas traditionally considered to be the sole right of management in attempting to ensure the efficient operation of the organizations. Therefore, provisions in such areas as technological change, work methods, promotion and layoff procedures, and productivity improvement are frequently found in collective agreements. Thus, the number and range of issues have also increased and become more complex since collective bargaining became an institutionalized conflict-resolution mechanism in Canadian society.

NEGOTIATING THE AGREEMENT — A CONCEPTUAL VIEW

The negotiation of the union-management agreement is an essential part of the Canadian collective-bargaining system. Despite its periodic nature, and the fact that the negotiation activity does not occupy the most time and effort given to transactions in the collective-bargaining system as a whole, it is often viewed as the most glamorous and important activity within the Canadian collective-bargaining system. This is especially true given that the future of the parties can be greatly affected by the outcomes of negotiations and that the failure of the collective-bargaining system to produce an agreement will inevitably lead to a work stoppage.

Despite its high profile and visibility, some participants and nearly all observers of union-management negotiations know little of how and why the negotiation process works. Unfortunately, there are no credentials needed by either side to sit at the union-management negotiations table. Possibly, this is why sometimes the negotiating process does not work too well.

Similarly, given the complexity of the collective-bargaining process, it has been the subject of study and scrutiny by a large number of scholars from a variety of perspectives. Labour-management negotiations have often been described as only ritual and ceremony. That is, the parties often know from the outset what an acceptable settlement is likely to be but engage in ritualistic tactics and the ceremony of threats and compromise in order to meet the expectations of union members and top management or shareholders. The process has also been depicted as solely based on the exercise of power. Both parties engage in a series of strategies and tactics designed to increase their power vis-à-vis their opponents. Both union and management attempt to use threats and strength to impose costs on the other party. Collective bargaining has also been studied as if it were a game involving two players with a fixed amount of resources to allocate, using various strategies and tactics to shift the allocation in their favour. Moreover, psychologists have been very interested in attempting to understand the underlying psychological processes involved in attempting to influence the perceptions of the other party. Finally, industrial-relations researchers have been interested in analysing the institutional and historical forces which act as major determinants or constraints on the collective-bargaining process. Thus, collective bargaining is a very complex process which involves aspects of ritual and ceremony, power, psychological dynamics, and a history in the relationship. No single approach will adequately describe the negotiating process.

Union-Management Negotiations — Uncertainty and Certainty

As the negotiation of the union-management agreement is complex, it often means that both parties will be making decisions in the face of uncertainty. Uncertainty arises because in negotiations neither party has full and complete information with respect to the position of the other side until the process is over. This is because the parties to the negotiating process do not provide it; nor do they want to provide it. Information has to be sought out, and the process of negotiations — dialogue and discussion — is the source from which this more complete information comes. As a result, it is useful to view the negotiating process as a process of moving from uncertainty and limited information to certainty and more complete information. Therefore, in union-management negotiations uncertainty exists about: (a) how long negotiations will last; (b) whether there will be a settlement; (c) what will be the terms of a settlement; (d) whether there will be a work stoppage; and (e) whether the parties will be able to achieve their objectives in negotiations.

However, when the union-management agreement is negotiated, it is not in a condition of total uncertainty and without any information at all. To be sure, some certainty exists and some information has been obtained, but it is only a small portion of what will be gathered by the time the process has been concluded. For example, each side knows with whom they will be negotiating, what the initial proposals of the parties are, approximately when the process will start, and, full certainty and information on their own position, strategy, and approach. The trouble is that neither party has such certainty and information about the preferences of the other side. It is only through the actual negotiating process that union and management will begin to learn the same kinds of information from the point of view of the other side.

Union-Management Negotiations — A Model

With some appreciation of the role of uncertainty and information flow in negotiations, a model is constructed which: (a) presents what is known about the negotiating process; and (b) tries to relate what is known to the functioning of the negotiating process itself. To start, let us assume that negotiation of a union-management agreement is about to begin and that the only issue to be negotiated is a wage increase. First, it is important to specify what is known for certain about the process. Some of the certainties are listed below:

1. The negotiations will have a starting point, time "t." Often this is specified with respect to the precise time, date, and place.

2. The negotiations will have an end. It is extremely rare that negotiations once started do not come to an end at some point in time. The end of the negotiating process will be called "t + n" with "n" representing the length of time it takes to get from the start to the end.

3. Negotiations will be assumed to end with either an agreement on the issue or a work stoppage. This condition is virtually built into the statutory framework within which union-management negotiations take place. Even in those cases where negotiations lead to a work stoppage it can still be said with a high degree of probability that at some point of time an agreement will be reached.

4. Unlike other forms of negotiations, the parties to union-management negotiations are not free to transact with other parties. This further adds to our certainty that once negotiations start, there is only one real end solution, and that is in fact a collective agreement.

5. Each side knows the proposals they have for negotiation as well as those of the other side. Let us assume for purposes of illustration that our initial position is a 5-percent wage increase while the other side is requesting a 15-percent wage increase.

6. From the foregoing information it can be said that the degree of difference between the parties at the point of their initial positions is 10 percent.

7. Each side knows its own objectives, strategy, and negotiating techniques as well as their true position as it relates to the wage increase. The true position represents what the party would be prepared to settle for and is likely to be considerably different than the 5-percent initial position.

Figure 1

Labour-Management Negotiating Model

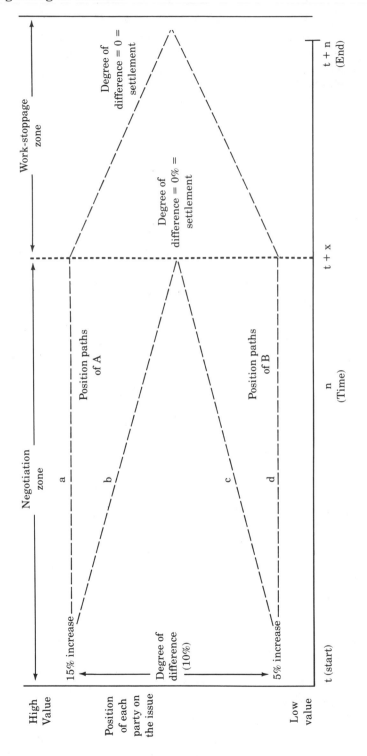

8. In most jurisdictions, the nature and form of involvement of other parties in our negotiating process such as conciliation are known. That is, it is known from public policy whether intervention will likely take place or not and that if it takes place it will take place some time after time "t" and probably towards the conclusion of the negotiating process itself.

9. From a study of the initial positions of the parties at 5 and 15 percent and a 10-percent degree of difference, it can be stated that if the parties hold to their initial positions throughout the negotiating process they will not reach an agreement, and a strike will most certainly occur.

10. If there is going to be a settlement in negotiations, the degree of difference of 10 percent must be reduced to zero. In fact, a useful way of thinking of an agreement or a settlement on an issue such as wages is not to focus so much on what the monetary amount of the settlement is but on the fact that a settlement or agreement is reached when the degree of difference between the parties has been reduced to zero.

These additional certainties have been portrayed in Figure 1. Figure 1 also reveals the following:

1. The position of parties A and B through time is shown by the broken line and is labeled (a), (b), (c), and (d) and represents each party's position path or concession line through time. Position paths (a) and (d) represent position paths where no reduction in the degree of difference takes place through time and the degree of difference remains at 10 percent. If these position paths occur, (a) negotiations will not lead to a settlement; and (b) a work stoppage will take place.

2. Position paths (b) and (c) represent position paths where there is a reduction in the degee of difference through time. In this case, the model portrays the situation where the degree of difference is reduced to zero during the course of negotiations. In this situation, the settlement position is represented by a wage increase of 10 percent. This means that party A moved from its initial position of 15 to 10 percent while party B improved its position from 5 to 10 percent.

Clearly, Figure 1 tells us quite a bit about the true objective of the negotiating process: to reduce the degree of difference on the issues during the period of time falling within the negotiating zone. If this degree of difference reduction occurs then the negotiating process is working. If this degree of difference is not reduced then the negotiating process is a failure, and it will leave the reduction of differences to a work stoppage.

This model is clearly a simplified representation of the collective-bargaining process. However, it is a useful heuristic device to illustrate the basic nature of negotiations. It also reveals that negotiations between union and management often go through a series of stages. In the first stage, typically the union presents its proposals for changes to the collective agreement, including a wide variety of monetary and nonmonetary issues. In the initial set of meetings both sides attempt to assess their opponents' preferences for settlement on the issues in negotiations and to predict the point at which the other side would resist any further change in their position on the issue (resistance point). During these periods, neither party is likely to make many concessions from their initial demands or offers. In fact, it is in these initial meetings that collective bargaining is best described as ritualistic and ceremonial in nature.

Once the parties have evaluated their opponents' resistance points on the major issues under consideration, collective bargaining often moves into a second stage where the parties attempt to obtain tactical commitments from the opponents in order to reduce the difference between them on the issues. At this stage, "horse trading" occurs where each party begins to drop its less preferred issues from discussion in exchange for concessions on the more important issues. Tactically, each side is working to get the other side to make a commitment to important issues without divulging its true preferences. This process is likely to both reduce the number of issues being negotiated as well as decrease the difference between the parties on the remaining issues.

The final stage in the bargaining process comes as the parties converge on a settlement. As indicated by Figure 1, the threat of an impending work stoppage often provides the motivation for the parties to settle. The convergence occurs as both parties feel pressure both from their constituents as well as from the tactics used by the other party to induce an agreement. Union pressure tactics such as slowdowns, sickouts, or work to rule are often used during this final stage to convince management of the seriousness of the union's strike threat.

To this point, the discussion of the collective-bargaining process has assumed that it is, in fact, a win-lose situation, or in Walton and McKersie's (24) terms, distributive bargaining. However, not all of the bargaining process involves the distribution of fixed resources between union and management. Three other major components of the bargaining process have also been identified by Walton and McKersie (24). First, they note that not all issues are distributive in nature; some are integrative. That is, resolving some issues may be of mutual interest to both union and management, for example, safety and health of employees. Under these circumstances, it would be advantageous for both parties to adopt a problem-solving rather than adversarial approach to bargaining. Unfortunately for most union-management relationships, the adversarial, low trust situation which characterizes most negotiations makes problem solving extremely difficult.

The collective-bargaining process not only involves negotiations between representatives of union and management but also involves substantial negotiations within the union and management sides. Walton and McKersie (24) refer to this process as intraorganizational bargaining. It is often as difficult as the collective-bargaining process itself as it requires that differences in preferences between different groups of union members or management officials are resolved prior to bargaining or as concessions are made so that most people affected will accept the results of negotiations. The failure of the intraorganizational-bargaining process is likely to result in internal conflict among individuals on either side and may well weaken its position vis-à-vis the other party or may potentially result in a failure of the relevant constituency (that is, union members or management officials) to ratify any agreement negotiated by their representatives.

Beyond the integrative, distributive, and intraorganizational-bargaining process, Walton and McKersie (24) also describe a fourth component of collective bargaining, attitudinal structuring. The bargaining process also involves both parties' attempts to set the climate for negotiations. This is often done by influencing the other side's perceptions of the level of trust, friendliness, cooperation, or hostility in the relationship. Thus, when examining the collective-bargaining process in any particular context, it is important to examine not only the concessionary behaviour of the parties over time but also the nature of the issues in dispute, the dynamics of the internal relationships within each side's organization, and the nature of the overall relationship between the parties.

Bargaining Power

While the above discussion provides a description of the collective-bargaining process, it does not reveal what causes A and B to move from their initial positions or what the likely outcomes of the bargaining process are going to be. To answer these questions it is important to examine the role, determinants, and function of bargaining power in union-management negotiations. There is no shortage of definitions of bargaining power nor of explanations of its role in the negotiating process. In general, bargaining power may be defined as one's ability to resist the proposal of another in favour of a proposal more favourable to one's self. In the extreme, either A or B (in Figure 1) could force the other to settle on its terms. Seldom in union-management negotiations is this the case. More often, each side has to compromise, moving from the initial position to something respectively greater or less than the initial position.

Chamberlain (5) provides a more analytical definition of bargaining power by focusing on the costs of agreement and disagreement associated with any particular settlement. When the costs of disagreeing with the position of the other party exceed the costs of agreeing with the other party, a settlement is highly likely. The assessment of costs can be economic as in evaluating the dollar costs of a wage increase (agreement) versus the losses associated with reduced business during a strike (disagreement). On the other hand, the analysis of costs of agreement and disagreement can also include political, organizational, or personality characteristics such as employee morale, problems with employer policies, or public sentiment. Thus, the bargaining power of either party may be manipulated by changing the actual or perceived costs of agreement and disagreement associated with the terms and conditions of the settlement.

One of the major problems a negotiator has in assessing the bargaining-power relationship is that once again, a formulation has to be conducted in the context of uncertainty. From each party's point of view, it has very good knowledge of what the consequences of failing to come to a settlement will be and what the "costs" will be if it does not settle. Likewise, each party knows the extent to which it is prepared to "go" to avoid these costs and consequences. However, the ability to assess the bargaining-power position with respect to the other party is quite limited since only the latter truly knows for sure. Again, that is where negotiating skills, experience, and abilities come into play. Obviously a miscalculation or imperfect assessment can have serious consequences such as causing a work stoppage when in fact, had full information been present, a settlement would have been available at the bargaining table in direct negotiations. Often the true position is hidden within the labyrinth of bluff, overstatement, and, in some cases, positions and statements that in no way reflect the true position of either party in negotiations. There is much use of theatrics and outright misrepresentation in the field of union-management negotiations. This is to be expected because one is working in a field where full disclosure of one's position is extremely rare. One can never be sure where the truth lies and in order to arrive at the truth one has to play the process out to its very end.

Determinants of Bargaining Power

A detailed and exhaustive review of the determinants of bargaining power is beyond the scope of this paper. It is a subject that has received extensive examination in negotiations literature. However, the discussion presented below is useful in understanding the role of bargaining power in determining how and why the negotiating process functions. It draws upon and also draws together the thoughts and observations of a number of bargaining-power analysts.

Bargaining-power determinants are both economic and noneconomic. Often, regrettably, analysts frequently stress the economic over the noneconomic factors. Such stress or emphasis has prompted Professor Harold W. Davy to comment:

> Perhaps most important of all, the men and women directly involved in collective bargaining as a process know that what we glibly refer to as "bargaining power" is in fact a many-faceted entity embracing much more than economic strength or, as the economists often put it, the capacity or power to reach an agreement *on one's own terms*. The latter conception overemphasizes the economic strength component of bargaining power.
>
> Preoccupation with the word "power" causes a tendency to forget or minimize the word "bargaining." There is also an implication that in any negotiation one party necessarily "wins" something and the other party "loses" something. This kind of reasoning rejects the view that the ultimate goal of management and union is the development of a *mutually satisfactory* contractual relationship.
>
> The preceding discussion is not merely playing with words. In sophisticated collective bargaining relationships there is a joint understanding that bargaining power is a composite of economic and noneconomic factors. (8, p. 98)

Indeed, determinants of bargaining power are both economic and noneconomic in nature. To Professor Davy the major determinants are: (a) the knowledge, skill, and experience of the principal negotiators and their back-up men; (b) the historical pattern of the particular union-management relationships; (c) the impact on the bargaining table of *external forces and conditions*, economic *and* political, which at one time may strengthen the management hand and at another the union's; and (d) *internal* pressures operating on both negotiating parties, such as friction or conflict within the union or within the management hierarchy which may have an eroding impact on their position at the bargaining table (8, p. 98).

Professor Jonathan S. Monat in his analysis of Dunlop's determinants of bargaining power defines each of the dimensions in the following terms:

> Strategic technological position creates bargaining by virtue of location and position in the production process. This is not identical with skill, but the withdrawal of a strategic work group's skills will lead to restriction or shutdown of the production process. The greater the strategic technological position of the work group, the greater will be its bargaining power.
>
> . . . on the other hand, management will have greater bargaining power if it is able to continue operations by shifting production to other plants which have not been struck. In the longer run, management might weaken work group or union bargaining power by job rotation practices, re-arrange job skills to require a greater proportion of skills outside the bargaining unit, or automation . . . .
>
> A work group is strategic in the labour market if the skills it encompasses are in short supply and there are few substitutes for these skills . . . . Management can protect or increase its labour supply through training and retraining programs, subcontracting, or reorganization of the work.
>
> A work group is strategic in the product market if the demand for the employer's product is inelastic. If the demand for a product is inelastic, the employer can pass increased labour costs on to the consumer without product demand decreasing . . . .

If a work group is strategic in the labour or product markets, it can more readily exact a price for its services. The greater a work group's strategic position in either or both markets, the greater will be its bargaining power. Thus, strategic position in the market structure is sufficient to give a work group bargaining power . . . .

Dunlop includes as community institutions favorable to the development of labour organizations such things as a legal system, free public education, the labour press, and political parties and organizations. The union itself becomes a dominant political influence favoring labour organizations. It changes its attitudes concerning the union's role in society and the use of such tactics as strikes. Hence, as the union gains political power, it is likely to make greater use of its bargaining power. To maintain balance, management must seek to influence those same institutions or create new institutions for this purpose . . . .

Bargaining power also depends on ideals and beliefs held by workers and managers. Do they adhere to the Protestant Ethic or is there a strong push for increased leisure? Are the goals of management compatible with collective bargaining? The more workers and managers adhere to a leisure ethic, desire more spendable income, and demand property rights, the greater will be the expectations that bargaining power will be used against the employer. (16, pp. 131-140)

In summary, the degree of bargaining power held by the parties is a function of many variables, some of which are virtually unique to the time and context of a particular set of negotiations. Bargaining power is also dynamic, leading to constantly changing bargaining-power relationships between the parties as time and context change.

Recent research on collective bargaining in the public sector has attempted to be more systematic in identifying the sources of bargaining power which may shift the balance of costs of agreement or disagreement in favour of one party or the other. First, characteristics of the environment may change the costs associated with a settlement. As suggested by Dunlop, the labour market (particularly the level of unemployment) and the nature of the product market (profit levels and general inflation) can be favourable either to labour or management. Similarly, public policy, political conditions, and public attitudes may also be more or less supportive of labour or management's position at the bargaining table. Second, organizational arrangements such as internal conflicts within the negotiating teams, the amount of authority delegated to the negotiators, or the pressure tactics used by the parties may also impact their bargaining power. Internal conflict and a lack of authority are likely to reduce the negotiating effectiveness of either party by creating difficulties in maintaining a unified front. Third, the interpersonal and personal characteristics of the parties may also have an impact on bargaining power. Such factors as the training, skill, and experience of the parties as well as the level of trust or hostility in the interpersonal relations may also act as sources of bargaining power by increasing the probability that the negotiators will be able to alter the perceptions of their counterparts about either the likelihood of a strike if a *favourable* settlement is not reached or about the impact of other sources of bargaining power on the costs of agreement and disagreement. Finally, the bargaining history of the particular union-management relationship is also likely to impact strongly the balance of bargaining power in the negotiations.

Both management and union negotiators are keenly aware of the importance of bargaining power. They understand fully that its presence or absence can be an aid or limitation to their effectiveness in negotiations. They approach the matter quite pragmatically, planning to make use of bargaining power when they have it and trying to minimize its relevance when they do not have it.

Practical union-management negotiators do not experience a burning need to measure or weigh their own or opponent's bargaining power in a precise fashion before they shape and structure their strategies and approaches to negotiations. Their operational knowledge and judgments are regarded as sufficient for all practical purposes. Negotiators do not need to have bargaining power defined in precise quantitative terms to know where they stand.

Negotiators usually know a great deal about each other's bargaining strengths or weaknesses without refining such knowledge into precise mathematical calculations. On the other hand, there are occasions where such estimates of the other party's capacity to resist or to concede have proved wrong or have been far off the mark when put to the ultimate test of a work stoppage. The best-informed negotiators can, on occasion, overestimate or underestimate the other party's staying power in a particular situation. However, more often than not, experienced negotiators have a firm understanding of the many ingredients that blend to comprise each party's bargaining power in specific short-run situations.

NEGOTIATING THE AGREEMENT — PLANNING AND EXECUTION

As John P. Sanderson has so aptly put it: "negotiation is more of an art than a science" (21, p. 15). As such, there is no "one way" or "best way" to negotiate. Like any creative activity, approaches may vary but as always the objective of an acceptable agreement remains as the main guide to conduct and behaviour. However, while there are no cut-and-dried ground rules it is possible to identify conventions or protocols of general application relating to the planning and execution of the union-management negotiating process. One excellent statement was set out in the work of G.G.M. Atkinson. According to Atkinson:

> Any discussion of conventions is complicated by the fact that in some countries . . . there is no source which gives universally accepted legitimacy to any conventions . . . . If they are present it is because they have evolved as a relationship between the parties has matured and because the parties, probably for reasons of long-term self-interest, prefer them to operate.
>
> . . .as the relationship between the two sides matures, an understanding begins to develop about what is "fair" in bargaining and what is not. Each side begins to accept that "ground rules" or "conventions" are necessary if there is to be any confidence or predictability in what is otherwise a very uncertain and insecure situation. Because conventions evolve it is impossible to give any which are universally observed. (2, p. 38)

Atkinson identifies some seven conventions. Some of the more relevant are set out below together with brief observations on each.

Past bargaining determines the issues for future bargaining — How do the parties know what is negotiable and what is not? This convention encourages the negotiator to consider the past and ask the question: "Has this issue come up in our relationship before?" But what if the issue is new and precedent does not help, or the particular interpretation of precedent is not accepted by one of the parties? What if there is disagreement on whether there is or is not a precedent for this particular issue? In the final analysis, if there is conflict over the legitimacy of the issue, the final outcome will be decided within the bargaining-power relationship between the parties. As Atkinson (2) has so cogently noted: "the message is inescapable — with power goes precedent and with precedent goes negotiation."

Existing agreements should be upheld — It is an axiom in union-management negotiations that what has been achieved through negotiations should only be changed through negotiation. This is possibly the most important convention of all, for if there is no certainty with respect to implementation, then why bother to negotiate in the first instance? However, there is nothing immutable with respect to existing agreements. If in the course of the review of an existing agreement or through its administration it is apparent it is not operating as intended, there is nothing to prevent its renegotiation. Such a process is quite right and proper. However, what does constitute a breach of this convention is for one side to unilaterally impose an agreement in its full form after it has been allowed to "slip" or "not be applied" for some period of time.

A time scale relating to settlement should be known before or established early in negotiations and then honoured by the parties — There is nothing more frustrating for a party to negotiations than to recognize the prospective date of settlement stretching indefinitely into the future. Of course, it is very difficult to give the date on which an issue or an agreement will be settled. However, there is considerable value in giving indications of the time at which negotiation sessions will be convened and to keep the passage of time between these negotiating sessions to a minimum. Stevens (23) points out that with cyclical negotiations, the expiry date of the last agreement may serve as a real aid to the negotiators as it allows the two sides to plan the negotiating strategy accordingly. Moreover, in general, it serves to give an added touch of urgency and meaning to the negotiations. In addition, the sense of a "deadline" gives the parties a known period in which they are free to negotiate outside of the fear of a rupture in the basic relationship between the parties.

Each side should normally be prepared to move from its original position — As noted earlier, a willingness to move from the original position is one of the main ingredients of bargaining, and any attempt by either side to interfere with this convention will not only produce misunderstanding of an extreme and costly kind, but also cause considerable resentment and with it a soured relationship for the future. Certain terms are used by negotiators which identify the various positions on an issue taken in negotiations. First, there is the "ideal settlement" which may be defined as the most favourable settlement which could realistically be achieved in negotiations. It is at this level or thereabouts that each opens negotiations for its own side. Second, there is the "realistic settlement" which is that point of settlement fully justified by bargaining power and which should be reached with reasonable skill in negotiations and in the absence of any adverse circumstances. Third, there is the "fall-back position" which may be defined as the point beyond which confrontation will be preferred. Fourth, there are the "parameters of bargaining" which represent the area of overlap between the two sides. Atkinson (2) has incorporated this terminology into a model, and it is given in Figure 2. An examination of Figure 2 shows that there is an area where the positions of the parties overlap, and this "positive contract zone" indicates that there is an opportunity for settlement.

Sanctions may be used as part of bargaining but not instead of it — This is a convention which is easier to write and talk about than to implement. Clearly, a

Figure 2

Parameters of Bargaining

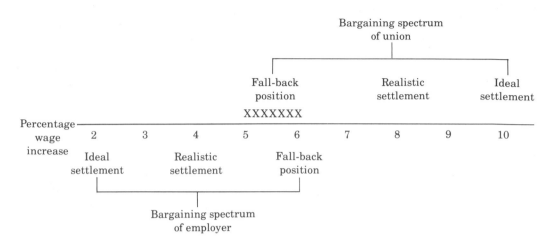

SOURCE: *Adapted from G.G.M. Atkinson,* The Effective Negotiator: A Practical Guide to the Strategies and Tactics of Conflict Bargaining *(London: Quest Research, 1977), p. 51.*

NOTE: XXXXXXX: *Area of settlement*

sanction will be preferred to negotiation either if its user has no faith in the bargaining process or if it is seen as being a strategic manoeuvre to the party's advantage. While the first approach may be countered by more effective negotiating machinery and greater bargaining expertise, the latter use of sanctions is part of the power game and can only be countered by equal or greater power being brought to bear against it. However, it should be fairly clear to both sides over the long term that to substitute sanctions in place of negotiation is just as foolhardy as to replace negotiation by autocratic control. This is not to say that in the last analysis the opportunity to incorporate a sanction into the bargaining situation is not a necessary part of free negotiation. However, when it assumes more importance than negotiation itself, it is not only a breach of a very necessary convention but also a blow to the voluntary bargaining process itself.

Bargaining should be fair — It is very difficult indeed to define precisely what is meant by "bargaining fairly." In Canada, there is no clearly defined concept of what is meant by "bargaining in good faith" or "bargaining fairly." However, Atkinson (2) has identified a number of elements that in his opinion go to make up the concept of "fair bargaining." These elements are: (a) an offer once made should not be withdrawn unless it was clearly conditional at the time of making it or the circumstances surrounding it have changed significantly; (b) there should be no denial of what has previously been unambiguously accepted; (c) no attempt should be made to achieve a settlement on a negotiable issue outside of negotiations itself until direct negotiations have failed; (d) there should be a demonstrated willingness to bargain on any issue which has been accepted as negotiable; (e) information given in confidence or as an informal statement should not be used as a means of achieving formal commitment; (f) opponents should be allowed to retain some semblance of credibility with their own side even in defeat; (g) there should be no trickery in the final agreement; and (h) a bargain once made should be implemented in that form (2, pp. 46-47).

Planning the Collective-Bargaining Process

Effective planning by both parties is the key to successful negotiations. As Randle and Wortman have put it:

> In collective bargaining, only the negotiation process is more important than the preparations that must be made for it. Moreover, the success of collective bargaining is directly proportional to the thoroughness of the preparations. Industry has begun to realize that labour negotiations make or break the company, but industry has been much slower in realizing that the months of preparation may be equally critical. By constant reference to the labour contract, the employer is continually reminded of its importance; however, he often loses sight of the fact that the quality of the contract is more often than not the direct result of the preparation made. Too often he fails to realize that the signing of the contract merely signals the beginning of preparations for the next one. Collective bargaining is a continuous process which is just as permanent and integral an aspect of business as purchasing, production, or sales; and as such should be given the same serious consideration and careful advance planning. (19, p. 145)

The greatest singular benefit from effective planning and preparation is maximizing the probability of reaching an acceptable agreement. Other benefits include the following: (a) greater confidence of both sides in the negotiating process comes from seeing people in negotiations well prepared; (b) bargainers are not caught by surprise and are prepared and equipped to deal with almost any eventuality within negotiations; (c) effective preparation and planning speeds up the negotiating process, and speed in negotiations creates negotiation's momentum and a feeling that "we are getting somewhere"; and (d) it is possible to think more constructively in the planning phase of activities than during the stress and turmoil of the negotiating process itself (19, pp. 145-146).

In order to maximize the benefits to be gained from effective planning, planning must be long-term, continuous, and a day-to-day affair. Although there is no exact formula or guideline for effective planning, we can clearly discern the major steps or activities. Randle and Wortman identify three major stages or phases (19, pp. 146-147). They are: (a) determination of general policies; (b) determination of the negotiators, support staff, the issues to be negotiated, and the gathering up of relevant data and information; and (c) prenegotiation sessions to set the scene for the execution of the actual negotiations that will follow. An overview of each stage or phase is set out below.

General policies — Each party sets out its general policies to ensure that it approaches negotiations with a sense of unity and a common front. Management may try to protect its acceptable level of profits. At the same time, it seeks equally to maintain and develop an effective and efficient labour force. It is also obliged to consider its competitive position and the probable impact of the upcoming negotiations on this position. It will also give consideration to its basic attitudes towards negotiations, be it a "hard-nosed" approach to fight the union at every step or a more "accommodative" approach to use the union and the negotiations as instruments to a more effective and efficient work force. Lastly, it has to reconcile internal management views towards the negotiations which will necessarily arise due to the "political" nature of the management cadre. Out of all of this will emerge its general policies towards the labour-management negotiating process.

In a similar vein, the trade union will likewise establish its general policies. Internally, the union is essentially a political institution and political considerations have much to do with the way in which it approaches and conducts its negotiations. A politically dependent union official seeks to maintain membership support. But often the membership is not of one mind with respect to its expectations in negotiations. Different occupational groups seek to be treated differently. Skilled work groups generally jealously guard their position in the occupational wage structure. On the other hand, less-skilled occupations often have a more strategic importance in the production process and in any work stoppage. The age of the membership is another factor. Younger workers often look for different improvements (for example, wages) than older workers (for example, pensions and other fringe benefits). The union also seeks to maintain or advance its position in the trade-union community, particularly in comparing its gains to the gains made by related trade-union organizations and particularly locals of the same union. The union leadership is well aware of the consequences of not getting for its members the gains obtained by other unions. Lastly, the local union invariably is part of a national or international trade-union structure, and as such the local may be obliged to negotiate within constraints placed upon it by the parent body, for example, conditions under which the parent will support local strike activity, economically or otherwise, and dictates with respect to what the collective agreement should or should not contain. Again, like management, the union is obliged to formulate a number of general policies towards the forthcoming negotiations.

Negotiators, issues, and data — Invariably, both union and management establish committees or "negotiating teams" to represent their respective interests in negotiations. Composition of these teams will vary depending upon the structure within which negotiations are to take place, that is, single employer, multiplant, or multiemployer. The size of the team will vary with the size of the employer and the employee groups. The larger the enterprise, the greater the complexity of labour-management relations. In addition, less reliance is likely to be placed on operating personnel and greater reliance is placed on a professional labour-management-relations staff. Invariably, members of the management team have a demonstrated skill in interpersonal relations, often a skill learned from experience at the negotiating table, as well as acceptability and compatibility with members of the union negotiating team. Consultants are frequently employed by management, often as a reflection of the absence of managerial talent to do the union-management negotiating job. The use of these consultants (especially lawyers) remains a controversial issue, as they are often unfamiliar with the history of the union-management relationship and likely to desire a settlement at any cost. The union team will probably bring together two levels of union representation — the local and the national or international body. Most union negotiating teams are comprised of local union officials, with the national or international personnel supplying support, advisory, and back-up functions. Usually the union team is also from among the "grass-roots" membership. Normally the composition of the union team will have been agreed upon by the members and the persons on it elected by the local membership itself. The issues placed on the bargaining table arise from both the union and the employer. However, in terms of the total number of issues introduced, the number presented by the employer remains relatively small.

Table 1

Sources and Issues in Negotiations

1. Company policies
   a. Variations in policy and practice
   b. Difficulties in administrating existing policies
   c. Need for new policy directions

2. Administration of current agreement
   a. Troublesome provisions
   b. Ambiguous wording in agreement

3. Suggestions from supervisors, foremen, and employees

4. Analysis of current agreement grievances

5. Arbitration decisions

6. Agreement violations (job action)

7. Agreement terms in other agreements

8. Attitude or morale surveys

9. Suggestion systems

10. Law, administrative decisions, and court decisions

11. Exit interviews

SOURCE: Adapted from C. Wilson Randle, and Max S. Wortman, Jr., Collective Bargaining: Principles and Practice
(Boston: Houghton Mifflin, 1966), pp. 159-169.

There are four general types of issues which are often negotiated: (a) changes in the agreement designed to give management more operating flexibility; (b) improvements in economic and job-security provisions; (c) changes in the agreement to correct problems in the administration of the current agreement; and (d) issues available for "trading-off" purposes against an issue raised by the other side. The sources from which issues emerge in the first instance are numerous. Table 1 brings together the major sources as identified by Randle and Wortman (19) and includes both union and management inputs into the formulation of issues.

The negotiators from both sides must be fully informed with respect to current events, issues, trends, and developments affecting the labour-management relationship. This information is often obtained by reading a wide variety of reports, studies, surveys, analyses, journals, newsletters, and government documents, all of which are usually available and deal with current developments in any given industry or activity (12).

The issues placed on the bargaining table by the trade union are frequently based on prevailing practices in the industry or within the geographical region. This

Table 2

Representative Types of Data and Information Used in Negotiating the Union-Management Agreement

Wage Data Necessary

1. Internal (company) wage structure by occupations and rates
2. External (outside the company) wage structure by occupations and rates — by industry, geographical area, union and national
3. Description of plan for employee progression
4. Detailed description of incentive plan, if one exists
5. Detailed description of job evaluation plan, if one exists
6. Beginning rates for male and female employees
7. Plan for employee upgrading, if any
8. Average hourly earnings
9. Average straight-time hourly earnings
10. Average weekly earnings
11. Average straight-time weekly earnings
12. Description of any recent wage increases — for example, cost of living

Hours Data Necessary

1. Number of hours in normal work-day
2. Number of hours in average work-day
3. Number of hours in normal work-week
4. Number of hours in average work-week
5. Starting and quitting time for each shift

Employee Data Necessary

1. Number of employees by sex and by shift
2. Number of employees by sex and seniority
3. Age distribution of employees
4. Employee services available:
    a. Medical services
    b. Credit union
    c. Recreational facilities
    d. Cafeteria
    e. Plant newspaper or magazine
    f. Any others (list)
5. Chronological history of wage and fringe benefit increases

Productivity Data Necessary

1. Production per man-hour
2. Labour costs per unit of production
3. Technological equipment added during contract period
4. Percentage of labour cost to total cost

Fringe Data Necessary

1. Description of shift differentials
2. Description of overtime payment plan
3. Description of pension plan
4. Description of group insurance plan
5. Description of employee compensation plan if separate
6. Description of safety program

7. Description of all policies on such items as call-in pay, call-back pay, sick leave, severance pay, holiday pay, rest periods, and so on

Documents to Be Secured

1. Employee handbooks
2. Statements to employees
3. Copy of last contract
4. Copy of grievance procedure
5. Copy of wage progression plan
6. Copy of pension plan
7. Copy of group insurance policy
8. Copy of employee accident compensation policy if separate from (7)
9. Copy of incentive plan
10. Copy of job evaluation plan
11. Copies of all other policies and plans related to negotiations

SOURCE: C. Wilson Randle, and Max S. Wortman, Jr., Collective Bargaining: Principles and Practice *(Boston: Houghton Mifflin, 1966), pp. 171-172.*

practice of comparing the terms of the collective agreement in question with others within the industry or geographical area results in the generation of a large volume of statistical data ranging from comparisons based upon specific agreement provisions to comparisons based upon more broad industry-wide statistics and data. While the process of negotiations often generates a large volume of data and statistics, there is frequently little agreement on what it all means. Frequently, the parties to the negotiations introduce only those data or statistics that support their position to the exclusion of the presentation of the complete picture. An illustration of the representative types of data used in negotiations is set forth in Table 2.

Prenegotiating sessions — After both parties have completed their preparation and planning, they normally move towards a prenegotiating session. Particularly from the employer's point of view, this is a period of concern and nervousness while awaiting the commencement of the first negotiating session. The usual practice is for the parties to meet together to get acquainted, to establish the ground rules for the negotiating session, to set the agenda, and above all, to formally present their proposals to one another. The objective of course is to get jointly organized for the upcoming sessions and to ensure smooth and successful negotiating sessions. The actual exchange of proposals at this time gives each of the parties an opportunity not only to study them and formulate an initial reaction, but also to obtain clarification to ensure that both sides interpret them in the same way. In addition, as a result of the prenegotiating sessions both sides will have an opportunity to analyse the proposals presented by the other side and to determine their expectations about the settlement of each issue, in both economic as well as noneconomic terms. As a result, after the first negotiating session the parties will not only be familiar with all issues in negotiations but also be able to prepare responses, counterproposals, arguments, and supporting factual data, and information. In addition, the prenegotiating session will permit the parties to get to know one another better and hopefully, through the cooperative act of getting themselves organized, lead to mature, effective, and constructive negotiating sessions.

Execution of the Collective-Bargaining Process

The execution of the actual union-management negotiating process is the epitome of the creative character of union-management negotiations. While one can write and talk about this activity in a limited way, skill and ability in negotiating can only be truly learned and understood through the experience gained in actual participation in negotiating. Unfortunately, this experience may be very difficult to obtain. However, there are a number of excellent simulations available that can be used as surrogates for the actual negotiating process (13).

One of the best descriptions of executing the negotiating process has been set out by Atkinson (2). The process of execution is contained within four consecutive stages or phases. Further, within each stage there are a number of tactics or approaches that can be used to attain its particular objective. The number of possible tactics available in each stage are virtually endless. Atkinson discusses a total of seventy specific tactics. Of course, their effectiveness turns on the experience, judgment and skill of the negotiator using them. While a detailed study of these tactics is beyond the scope of this chapter, the objective and central thrust of activities in each of the four stages presented by Atkinson (2) are presented below.

Stage I: Exploring the realistic settlement — The objective of Stage I is to gain information on the other side's "realistic settlement" without revealing information on one's own. The tactics employed are designed to do just that. Once a position has been put forward one is in a position to: (a) attack the proposition and its supporting arguments, leaving the proponent to defend them; and (b) determine the degree of importance attached to each issue as well as any willingness to move on the issue. The effect is to "open the other side up" to the extent that one can make informed judgments on the firmness of the position advanced and, as a corollary, the likelihood of the "realistic settlement" being other than that advanced. As Atkinson concludes:

> The strategy for Stage I now emerges. It operates at two levels. First, immediately prior to bargaining, you will have used some "pre-negotiation devices" to find out all you can about the position he is likely to adopt, the arguments he is likely to use and your counters to them. Second, in the negotiation itself you will be trying both to encourage him to do the talking (but on lines which you control), and also to avoid indicating your own position until you consider it appropriate. (2, p. 96)

Stage II: Thrust and counterthrust — The objective of Stage II is to demonstrate the weaknesses of the other side's position to the point of forcing a change in expectations. At the same time, one does so while reinforcing the strength of one's own position to the point of convincing the other side of the fairness of one's own expectations. This is a most critical phase of the negotiations for if the other side is not convinced of the need to move they may decide to stand and fight. It is the stage that presents a real test of the negotiator's skills and, above all, calls for the utmost of patience and tenacity. The tactics employed are designed to: (a) undermine the arguments of the other side; (b) undermine the credibility of the other side; (c) support and give credibility to one's own arguments and position; and (d) prevent the other side from making a premature commitment. Atkinson summarizes Stage II activities as follows:

> The objective of Stage II is not difficult to identify. You attempt to structure, in your favour, the expectation of what your opponent really thinks he will get out of the bargaining situation. This will only be possible if he is made to realize that his

position is weaker and/or that yours is stronger than he had first appreciated. So your strategy will be on the one hand to undermine his confidence in his position and in his own personal ability to hold it. And on the other to support your own position and credibility. Since Stage III is to do with movement by both sides towards a settlement, you will wish to ensure that this process does not start until you have structured the expectations of your opponent to your own greatest advantage. (2, p. 112)

Stage III: The move to accommodation — The objective of Stage III is to encourage movement by the other side from its original position while hinting of a possible movement from one's own position. However, to obtain movement, tactics must be selected which are designed to encourage it and to permit it to take place with the least loss of credibility. To encourage movement it is important to create in the other side a belief that there are elements in the negotiating scene that not only require it but also allow it. Such a belief can be created by making it clear and convincing that: (a) the other side cannot hold to its original position; (b) the desire to settle can only be fulfilled if movement occurs; (c) there is a possibility of a similar movement on your part; and (d) movement can be made with a minimum loss of credibility. The absence of any of these qualities may lead to a deep reluctance for either party to move from the original position. It follows that the tactics selected are designed to encourage movement and to facilitate the abandonment of previous commitments.

Stage IV: Accommodation — The objective of Stage IV is to reach an accommodation and to have the accommodation set out in the memorandum of agreement. There are three types of difficulties that can occur. First, the other side may be most reluctant to give up without some way of accommodating their loss of credibility. Second, a "sweetener" in the form of a concession may be needed to close the deal. Third, there may arise problems in the incorporation of the terms of settlement into a memorandum of agreement. The tactics used in Stage IV include: (a) tactics designed to make the commitment to your position credible; (b) tactics designed to encourage the other side to come to a final agreement; and (c) tactics designed to ensure a smooth movement to implementation of terms of agreement and the execution of the memorandum of agreement.

SUMMARY AND CONCLUSIONS

The collective-bargaining process is one of the central activities in the Canadian industrial-relations system. Despite the fact that it only occurs at one-, two-, or three-year intervals, it is this process which determines, in large part, the nature of the terms and conditions of employment for a majority of the Canadian labour force. The purpose of this chapter was to provide an introduction to the nature of the union-management negotiation process as well as a view of the way in which the parties prepare for it.

Collective bargaining is an extremely complex activity which involves decision making on a wide variety of economic and noneconomic issues. Preferences must first be established through intraorganizational bargaining within the union and management teams. Negotiations then occur over both distributive and integrative issues between union and management representatives within a context of uncertainty. Given the uncertainty in the process, the relative bargaining power of each party becomes the primary determinant of the timing and content of the union-management agreement. Bargaining power may be derived from a variety of environmental, organizational, interpersonal, personal, and bargaining-history factors.

The chapter concludes with a discussion of the preparation for and execution of the collective-bargaining process. In conjunction with a simulated collective-bargaining experience, this should provide a good basic understanding of the collective-bargaining process.

REFERENCES AND WORKS CITED

1. Ashenfelter, Orley, and George E. Johnson. "Bargaining Theory, Trade Unions, and Industrial Strike Activity," *American Economic Review,* Vol. 59 (1969), 35-48.

2. Atkinson, G.G.M. *The Effective Negotiator: A Practical Guide to the Strategies and Tactics of Conflict Bargaining* (London: Quest Research, 1977).

3. Canadian Industrial Relations, *Report of the Task Force on Labour Relations* (Ottawa: Minister of Supply and Services Canada, 1969).

4. Centre for Industrial Relations, University of Toronto. *The Collective Bargaining Process.* Videotape, 1976.

5. Chamberlain, Neil W. *Collective Bargaining* (New York: McGraw-Hill, 1951).

6. Christy, Robert J. "The Structure of Collective Bargaining," in S.M.A. Hameed (Ed.), *Canadian Industrial Relations* (Toronto: Butterworth, 1975), 187-204.

7. Cullen, Donald E. *Negotiating Labour-management Contracts* (Ithaca, N.Y.: New York State School of Industrial and Labor Relations, 1965).

8. Davy, Harold W. *Contemporary Collective Bargaining* (Englewood Cliffs, N.J.: Prentice-Hall, 1972).

9. Hameed, S.M.A. (Ed.), *Canadian Industrial Relations* (Toronto: Butterworth, 1975).

10. Healey, James J. (Ed.) *Creative Collective Bargaining* (Englewood Cliffs, N.J.: Prentice-Hall, 1965).

11. Jensen, Vernon H. "Notes on the Beginning of Collective Bargaining," *Industrial and Labor Relations Review,* Vol. 9 (1956), 225-234.

12. Kelly, Laurence A. *Collective Bargaining Information Sources* (Ottawa: Labour Canada, 1975).

13. Lewiski, J., and G. Swimmer. "A Collective Bargaining Simulation," in S.M.A. Hameed (Ed.), *Canadian Industrial Relations* (Toronto: Butterworth, 1975), pp. 267-282.

14. Levinson, Harold M. *Determining Forces in Collective Wage Bargaining* (New York: Wiley, 1966).

15. Mabry, Bevars D. "The Pure Theory of Bargaining," *Industrial and Labor Relations Review,* Vol. 18 (1975), 479-502.

16. Monat, Jonathan S. "Determination of Bargaining Power: Three Models," in H.C. Jain (Ed.), *Canadian Labour and Industrial Relations* (Toronto: McGraw-Hill Ryerson, 1975).

17. Pen, J.A. "A General Theory of Bargaining," *American Economic Review,* Vol. 42 (1952), 24-42.

18. Peters, Edward. *Strategy and Tactics in Labour Negotiations* (New London: National Foremen's Institute, 1955).

19. Randle, C. Wilson, and Max S. Wortman, Jr. *Collective Bargaining: Principles and Practice* (Boston: Houghton Mifflin, 1966).

20. Ryder, Meyer S., Charles M. Rehmus, and Sanford Cohen. *Management Preparation for Collective Bargaining* (Homewood, Ill.: Dow-Jones-Irwin, 1966).

21. Sanderson, John P. *The Art of Collective Bargaining* (Toronto: Richard De Boo, 1979).

22. Slichter, Sumner H., James J. Healy, and E. Robert Livernash. *The Impact of Collective Bargaining on Management* (Washington: The Brookings Institute, 1960).

23. Stevens, Carl M. *Strategy and Collective Bargaining Negotiations* (New York: McGraw-Hill, 1963).

24. Walton, R.E., and R.B. McKersie. *A Behavioural Theory of Labour Negotiations: An Analysis of a Social Interaction System* (London: McGraw-Hill, 1965).

25. Williams, C. Brian. "Notes on the Evolution of Compulsory Conciliation in Canada," *Relations Industrielles/Industrial Relations,* Vol. 19 (1964), 298-324.

26. Williams, C. Brian. "Collective Bargaining in the Public Sector: A Reexamination," *Relations Industrielles/Industrial Relations,* Vol. 28 (1973), 17-33.

QUESTIONS

1. Describe the evolution and scope of collective bargaining in Canada.

2. Describe the major sources of certainty and uncertainty involved in negotiating a union-management agreement. Why are these important to the process of coming to an agreement in collective bargaining?

3. What is bargaining power? Identify three sources of bargaining power and outline their impacts on the process of negotiations.

4. Outline and discuss Walton and McKersie's four dimensions of the collective-bargaining process.

5. Why is it important that the parties prepare for collective bargaining? What types of information should they gather and why?

6. Describe Atkinson's four stages of the bargaining process and identify two tactics associated with each.

JOHN C. ANDERSON and MORLEY GUNDERSON

10. Strikes and Dispute Resolution

This chapter describes the frequency, size, and duration of strikes in Canada since the turn of the century. The functions of strikes are outlined. Most of the research on the causes of strikes has focused on the correspondence between increased strike activity and the peak of the business cycle as well as on the impacts of prevailing economic conditions on strikes. In addition, however, the nature of the community in which the strike occurs, the internal characteristics of the union and management negotiators, the trust or hostility between the parties, and the history of the bargaining relationship may contribute to the probability of a strike. In addition to examining the range of causes of strikes, this chapter discusses the role of dispute-resolution procedures and the potential consequences of strikes.

The Canadian system of collective bargaining establishes a mechanism whereby union and management representatives may voluntarily (with a minimum of government intervention) reach an agreement on the terms and conditions of employment in the work place. In doing so, the system also recognizes that there is an inherent conflict of interests between the employer's desire for control of an efficient and profitable enterprise and the employees' desire for increased wages, fringe benefits, and control over their day-to-day working methods. A natural and relatively frequent consequence of this conflict of interest is the inability of labour and management to resolve their disputes at the bargaining table. Thus, the system also institutionalizes the right of the parties to use a number of methods to attempt to induce their opponents to settle on their own terms. The unions' ultimate economic weapon is the total withdrawal of the employees' services by striking. Correspondingly, management may decide to stop production and lock out the employees until such time as the union is willing to accept the employer's offer. The strike or lockout or, more realistically the threat of a strike or lockout provides a major inducement for the parties to make concessions and compromises in collective bargaining rather than bearing the potentially high economic losses (sales, profits, and customer good will for employers; wages and benefits for employees) and psychological costs (loss of morale and increase in hostility) which may result from job action.

While the costs of a work stoppage may be high to both employees and management, one of the most visible outcomes of union-management relations in Canada is strike activity. Strikes play a variety of functions both in the union-management relationship and in society: supporting bargaining demands, providing a release of pent-up frustrations, providing management with an opportunity to clean and overhaul plant and equipment, supporting or protesting government policy, showing solidarity with workers' causes elsewhere in the world (as was the case in August 1981 when the air-traffic controllers refused to handle U.S. flights in support of the strike of controllers in that country). Just as strikes have different purposes, it is clear that there is a complex and wide-ranging set of conditions which are likely to combine to cause a strike. In any given union-management relationship, the prevailing economic conditions, community characteristics, internal dynamics of union and management organizations, the nature of the relationship, and the history of collective-bargaining experiences may contribute to producing a settlement or a strike. Moreover, the effectiveness of dispute-resolution procedures established through public policy may influence the probability of a strike. Thus, if policy makers are interested in influencing strike activity in Canada, it is important that they have a complete understanding of the causes of strikes. Finally, a strike or lockout may have a variety of consequences, ranging from achieving a settlement in that particular dispute to impacting public policy, foreign trade, and citizens in the community in which the work stoppage has occurred.

The purpose of this chapter is to provide an overview of the causes and consequences of strike activity in Canada. First, a description of the frequency, size, and duration of strikes and the distribution of strikes by industry and province is presented. The functions and causes of strikes are then discussed, focusing on both the economic and noneconomic causes. In addition, the role of dispute-resolution procedures in reducing strike activity is outlined. Finally, the chapter concludes with a brief discussion of the potential consequences of strikes.

BASIC DESCRIPTION OF STRIKE ACTIVITY

Some Measurement Problems

As with most seemingly simple statistics, the measures of strike activities are replete with problems — problems that are accentuated when comparisons are made over long periods of time or across diverse countries (for a discussion of measurement problems see 9, 22, 32, 54, 58, 59, 60, 66). Measurement problems include what to count as a strike (in Canada strikes involving a total loss of less than ten working days are excluded), how to treat political strikes or days of protest, how to treat those who may not officially be on strike but are not working because of the strike, and how to determine when some protracted strikes have ended. Quantitative studies of strike activity are also difficult to compare because of differences in the measures of strike activity that are utilized (66).

Most developed economies, Canada included, publish strike statistics (actually work stoppages which include strikes plus lockouts) in three series: (a) *frequency* or number of strikes per year; (b) total *number of workers* involved in strikes; and (c) *volume* or total days lost through strikes, often expressed as a percent of estimated working time. These raw measures, however, do not directly indicate the average *size* of each strike (that is, the average number of workers involved) or the average *duration* (that is, the average length of time each worker remains on strike). Hence, the raw measures by themselves would not indicate if a high volume of strike activity, as measured by days lost, was due to a large number of strikes (frequency),

Table 1

Various Measures of Strike Activity, Canada 1901-1979

Year	Frequency[a]	Size[b]	Duration[c]	Volume Person-Days Lost[d]	As Percent of Working Time
1901	99	243	30.6	737,808	—
1902	125	102	16.0	203,301	—
1903	175	219	22.4	858,959	—
1904	103	111	16.9	192,890	—
1905	96	130	19.7	246,138	—
1906	150	156	16.2	378,276	—
1907	188	181	15.3	520,142	—
1908	76	343	27.0	703,571	—
1909	90	201	48.6	880,663	—
1910	101	220	32.9	731,324	—
1911	100	292	62.4	1,821,084	—
1912	181	237	26.5	1,135,787	—
1913	152	267	25.6	1,036,254	—
1914	63	154	50.5	490,850	—
1915	63	181	8.3	95,042	—
1916	120	221	8.9	236,814	—
1917	160	314	22.4	1,123,515	—
1918	230	347	8.1	647,942	—
1919	336	443	22.8	3,400,942	0.60
1920	322	187	13.3	799,524	0.14
1921	168	168	37.1	1,048,914	0.22
1922	104	421	34.9	1,528,661	0.32
1923	86	398	19.6	671,750	0.13
1924	70	490	37.7	1,295,054	0.26
1925	87	333	41.2	1,193,281	0.23
1926	77	310	11.2	266,601	0.05
1927	74	301	6.8	152,570	0.03
1928	98	179	12.8	224,212	0.04
1929	90	144	11.7	152,080	0.02
1930	67.	205	6.7	91,797	0.01
1931	88	122	19.0	204,238	0.04
1932	116	202	10.9	255,000	0.05
1933	125	212	12.0	317,547	0.07
1934	191	240	12.5	574,519	0.11
1935	120	277	8.7	288,703	0.05
1936	156	223	8.0	276,997	0.05
1937	278	259	12.3	886,393	0.15
1938	147	139	7.3	148,678	0.02
1939	122	336	5.5	224,588	0.04
1940	168	361	4.4	266,318	0.04
1941	231	377	5.0	433,914	0.06
1942	354	322	4.0	450,202	0.05
1943	402	543	4.8	1,041,198	0.12
1944	199	378	6.5	490,139	0.06
1945	197	488	15.2	1,457,420	0.19

Table 1

Various Measures of Strike Activity, Canada 1901-1979

Year	Frequency[a]	Size[b]	Duration[c]	Volume Person-Days Lost[d]	Volume As Percent of Working Time
1946	226	615	32.5	4,515,030	0.54
1947	234	442	22.9	2,366,340	0.27
1948	154	278	20.7	885,790	0.10
1949	135	347	22.1	1,036,820	0.11
1950	160	1,203	7.2	1,387,500	0.15
1951	258	398	8.8	901,620	0.09
1952	219	513	24.6	2,765,510	0.29
1953	173	315	24.1	1,312,720	0.14
1954	173	327	25.3	1,430,300	0.15
1955	159	378	31.2	1,875,400	0.19
1956	229	387	14.1	1,246,000	0.11
1957	245	329	18.3	1,477,100	0.13
1958	259	430	25.3	2,816,850	0.25
1959	216	440	23.4	2,226,890	0.19
1960	274	180	15.0	738,700	0.06
1961	287	341	13.6	1,335,080	0.11
1962	311	239	19.1	1,417,900	0.11
1963	332	251	11.0	917,140	0.07
1964	343	293	15.7	1,580,550	0.11
1965	501	343	13.7	2,349,870	0.17
1966	617	667	12.6	5,178,170	0.34
1967	522	483	15.8	3,974,760	0.25
1968	582	384	22.7	5,082,732	0.32
1969	595	516	25.3	7,751,880	0.46
1970	542	483	25.0	6,539,560	0.39
1971	569	421	12.0	2,866,590	0.16
1972	598	1,181	11.0	7,753,530	0.43
1973	724	481	16.6	5,776,080	0.30
1974	1,218	477	15.9	9,221,890	0.46
1975	1,171	432	21.5	10,908,810	0.53
1976	1,039	1,512	7.4	11,609,890	0.55
1977	803	271	15.2	3,307,880	0.15
1978	1,058	380	18.4	7,392,820	0.34
1979	1,050	440	16.9	7,834,230	0.34

SOURCE: Strikes and Lockouts in Canada *(Ottawa: Labour Canada, 1977, 1978, 1979).*

NOTES: a. *Number of strikes in existence during the year, whether they began in that year or earlier.*
   b. *Average number of workers involved per strike, calculated as the number of workers involved divided by the number of strikes.*
   c. *Average days lost per worker on strike, calculated as total person-days lost divided by the number of strikers involved. This is a measure of the average length of time that each worker who is on strike remains on strike. An alternative measure of duration is the average length of each strike which would be calculated as the days lost divided by the number of strikes.*
   d. *Product of frequency (strikes) times size (strikers/strikes) and duration (days lost/striker). Numbers approximate because of rounding.*

a large number of workers involved in each strike (size), a series of long strikes (duration), or some combination of the three components.

As illustrated in Table 1, however, some basic manipulations of the raw numbers enable the calculation of the three components of the total volume of strike activity — frequency, size, and duration. As first illustrated by Forchheimer (23), these three components, when multiplied together, give the overall volume of strike activity, total days lost. Expressed as a percent of time worked this is a measure of the severity of overall strike activity in the economy.

Canadian Strike Activity

As the last column of Table 1 indicates, the severity of overall strike activity in Canada increased quite dramatically after the mid-1960s. The average days lost, approximately .36 percent of estimated working time, was seldom exceeded in *any* of the years prior to the 1960s. This high level of strike activity corresponds to what Jamieson (28) has labeled Canada's third wave of industrial conflict. (The first wave began in 1900 and peaked in 1919; the second wave began in the late 1930s and peaked in 1946.) A distinguishing characteristic of this third wave, however, is that it has been sustained at such a high level for a long period of time, suggesting a fundamental, structural change to sustained levels of strike activity that previously would have been thought of as reaching crisis proportions. On an international basis (see Chapter 20) during the 1970s Canada ranked second only to Italy in terms of days lost per worker due to strikes. This high volume of strike activity, however, occurs in part because strikes in North America tend to be of long duration (36, 40).

Components of Strike Activity

The first three columns of Table 1 indicate the contribution of each of the components of strike activity — frequency, size, and duration — to the overall volume of strike activity. The separate components indicate that Canada has always had strikes of fairly long duration. In fact, the average of seventeen days between 1966 and 1979 was down somewhat from the average of nineteen days for the 1901 to 1965 and 1947 to 1965 periods. Since the mid-1960s the components that have increased the most are the average frequency and size of strikes: in the period 1966 to 1979 the average frequency and size respectively were 750 strikes involving 581 workers per strike, compared to 261 strikes involving 402 workers per strike in the 1946-to-1965 period. The large-sized strikes in 1972 and 1976 respectively reflect the "Common Front" strike of civil servants in Quebec and the "Day of Protest" throughout Canada to protest the wage controls instituted in October 1975.

Much of the increase in the frequency of strikes, especially after 1974, occurred because the average length of the contract shortened during the inflationary period of the 1970s. This meant that more contracts were being negotiated each year and the larger number of strikes reflects in part this heavier bargaining calendar. As Table 4 of Chapter 20 illustrates, since the mid-1960s the proportion of contracts ending in a strike did not change much since the mid-1960s (except for a dramatic drop in 1977 and 1978 after the wage-controls program). What increased was the number of shorter (for example, one-year) agreements. Thus if the frequency series were broken down into its components parts (strikes per contract times contracts per year) one would see that the frequency increase since the mid-1970s occurred mainly because of an increase in the number of contracts being negotiated, not because of an increase in the probability that each contract would end in a strike.

This does not mean that Canada's worsening strike record since the mid-1960s was purely a statistical artifact due to the increased number of contracts up for renewal. One would expect that when the contract length shortens, then we would have fewer strikes per contract renewal because discontent has not had as long to build up: in the extreme, if a new contract were renegotiated daily it is unlikely that any one contract would end in a strike. In addition, we would expect strikes to be of shorter duration because pent-up frustration would not have built up for an extended period. The fact that the percent of settlements ending in a work stoppage (Table 4 of Chapter 20) and the average duration of strikes did not decrease dramatically when the length of the contract shortened substantially attests to the fact that our strike activity did increase since the mid-1960s. In essence, our volume of strike activity has increased since the mid-1960s because the increase in the number of contract renewals (due mainly to a shortening of the length of the contract) was not offset by a corresponding reduction in the proportion of contracts ending in a strike or the average duration of a strike. Clearly, in describing our strike picture it is important to distinguish the separate components of strike activity.

Separating the components of the overall volume of strike activity may be useful because the causes of strikes can differ from each component. Stern (66), for example, suggests that strike frequency, which represents the decision to call a strike, may be most responsive to economic conditions. The size of strikes, which represents the mobilization of workers, may be more reflective of the size and structure of the bargaining units, the nature of the workers, and the existence of interunion alliances. The duration of strikes may also reflect conditions specific to that particular strike, including interpersonal relations or basic philosophical differences between the parties.

For the purpose of designing public policies to reduce strike activity, it is useful to know the causal factors associated with each component of strike activity. This is so because if the overall volume of strike activity of a country is high because of a large contribution from one component, then public policies can focus on the factors that influence that particular component.

Contract Status at Time of Strike

It may also be important to distinguish strikes by the status of the contract at the time of the strike. First-contract or recognition strikes occur over the establishment of a first collective agreement; contract-renewal strikes occur over the renegotiation of an existing collective agreement; and "wildcat" strikes occur during the term of an existing collective agreement. (Wildcat strikes in Canada have been described and analysed in 8, 20, 21.)

Table 2 gives the various measures of strike activity according to the status of the contract at the time of the strike. During the 1970s, for all measures of strike activity, the largest proportion occurred during the renegotiation of an existing collective agreement. Recognition or first-agreement strikes accounted for 11.4 percent of strikes and lockouts but because they tended to occur mainly in small establishments they only involved 1.7 percent of workers on strike. In spite of their illegality in all jurisdictions except Saskatchewan (21), wildcat strikes during the term of an existing collective agreement accounted for 23.2 percent of all strikes and lockouts and 31.0 percent of workers involved in strikes. Their short duration, however, explains why they only accounted for 8.0 percent of person-days lost due to strikes.

Table 2

**Strikes and Lockouts by Contract Status for
Various Measures of Strike Activity, Canada 1970-1979
(Percent)**

Contract Status	Strikes and Lockouts	Workers Involved	Person-days Lost
First agreement	11.4	1.7	3.4
Renegotiation of agreement	63.9	67.0	88.3
During term of agreement	23.2	31.0	8.0
Other[a]	1.5	0.3	0.3
Total	100.0	100.0	100.0

SOURCE: *Calculated as the average over the period 1970-1979 from data given in* Strikes and Lockouts in Canada *(Ottawa: Labour Canada, 1970-1979).*

NOTE: a. *Includes instances where there was no collective agreement prior to the work stoppage and the conclusion of a final agreement was not a basic issue.*

Clearly, the underlying causes of these different types of strikes may be different. Recognition strikes may reflect the inexperience of the parties, an especially important factor because the inexperience is likely to lead to misperceptions and a lack of knowledge about each other's position. Wildcat strikes, on the other hand, occur in response to a particular work situation or working condition; however, they may reflect pent-up frustration and be an alternative to what workers regard as an ineffective grievance procedure. They may also reflect rank-and-file discontent over the contract negotiated by their leadership. All too often, the discussion and analysis of strikes assumes that strikes are a relatively homogeneous phenomenon and they are analysed as regular end-of-contract disputes. Clearly the determinants of strikes may differ depending on the type of strike.

Industry and Regional Variation

As indicated in Table 3, there is also considerable industrial and regional variation in strikes in Canada, and there is considerable variation within an industry or province over brief periods of time. Relative to the 1975 to 1979 average of approximately one day (more precisely, .94 days) lost per worker per year due to strikes, the sectors that were *not* strike-prone were trade, finance, services, and public administration. The strike-prone industries were fishing and mining, followed by manufacturing and construction. In fact, based on more disaggregated industry figures, Jamieson (29) indicates that construction, mining and smelting, transportation equipment (mainly automobiles), iron and steel, lumber, and pulp and paper accounted for over one-half of all person-days lost in strikes during 1966 to 1975, even though they employed less than 15 percent of Canada's labour force. Common characteristics of these sectors include their sensitivity to business-cycle conditions or their relatively high degree of isolation — the latter being a factor emphasized by Kerr and Siegel (35) in their discussion of the interindustry propensity to strike.

Table 3

**Person-Days Lost per Paid Worker by Industry
and Province, Canada 1975-1979**

Industry/Province	1975	1976[a]	1977	1978	1979	1975-79 Average
Industry						
Agriculture	.00	.00	.00	.00	.00	.00
Forestry	.81	.56	.35	.97	1.31	.80
Fishing	24.63	.05	2.14	.12	.00	5.39
Mines	8.55	4.02	.60	10.82	9.12	6.62
Manufacturing	2.89	2.37	.89	1.31	1.42	1.78
Construction	1.90	5.35	.76	2.33	.14	2.10
Transport/Utilities	1.80	.79	.67	1.16	1.31	1.15
Trade	.23	.13	.09	.16	.14	.15
Financial	.36	.03	.02	.01	.07	.10
Services	.33	.56	.14	.16	.27	.29
Public Administration	.61	.09	.16	.37	.86	.42
Province						
Newfoundland	2.70	.93	.66	2.21	.34	.97
Prince Edward Island	.05	.23	.00	.37	.09	.15
Nova Scotia	1.03	.74	.09	.24	.14	.45
New Brunswick	.84	1.18	.18	.51	.44	.63
Quebec	1.44	2.85	.56	.78	1.38	1.40
Ontario	.97	.50	.33	.85	.70	.67
Manitoba	.45	.27	.05	.77	.08	.32
Saskatchewan	.68	.50	.11	.56	1.07	.58
Alberta	.56	.15	.09	.56	.07	.29
British Columbia	1.96	1.60	.15	.45	.62	.96
Total	1.30	1.36	.38	.83	.84	.94

SOURCE: Calculated as person-days lost due to strikes and lockouts divided by the number of paid workers in each industry and jurisdiction. The strike and lockout figures are from Strikes and Lockouts *(Ottawa: Labour Canada, 1975-1979). The number of paid workers are from Statistics Canada,* Labour Force Annual Averages 1975-1978, *No. 71-529, and* The Labour Force, *December 1979, No. 71-001.*

NOTE: a. 1976 figures do not include the October 14 Day of Protest.

The provincial figures do not exhibit such extreme variation; nevertheless, Quebec and British Columbia appear to have the highest volume of strike activity. To a large degree this reflects the concentration of strike-prone industries in those provinces. This is borne out in econometric studies (11, 15) which indicate strike probabilities in the private sector in Canada to be fairly similar across regions when other factors, including industrial distribution, are held constant.

Summary of Basic Picture

Since the mid-1960s Canada's strike record has been fairly dismal both by international standards and in comparison to our historical record. We appear to be sustaining a wave of strike activity that is unprecedented in its severity and length. Much of this reflects a continuation of the long-duration strikes that have characterized our strike history; however, both the frequency and, to a lesser extent, the size of strikes have increased substantially since the mid-1960s.

While most strikes occur during the renegotiation of a collective agreement, a substantial number of illegal wildcat strikes occur during the term of the collective agreement. Recognition or first-agreement strikes occur quite often; however, they do not involve many workers and hence do not contribute much to the total person-days lost due to strikes.

There is substantial industry and regional variation, with Quebec and British Columbia having the highest volume of strike activity in part because they have a concentration of strike-prone industries including fishing, mining, construction, lumber, and pulp and paper. These strike-prone sectors tend to be particularly sensitive to business-cycle conditions, or they involve a relatively high degree of isolation.

FUNCTION AND CAUSES OF STRIKES

Functions of Strikes

Since strikes can serve a variety of purposes and occur for a variety of reasons, it is not really feasible to talk about unique causes of strike activity. Strikes may occur to win recognition of a particular union or to win concessions from management. They may reflect pent-up unresolved grievances over working conditions, or spontaneous acts in response to a particular working condition. (The latter would often result in a wildcat strike during the term of an existing collective agreement.) Strikes may be a cathartic event providing a safety valve for pent-up frustration, or they may be a political act of worker solidarity or a way of getting a vacation. They may also be used by union leaders to solidify the rank and file, to find out what the rank and file really wants and is prepared to give up, or to lower the expectations of the rank and file as the strike runs its course.

Causes of Strikes

The multiple purposes of strikes highlight an important distinction that must be made in the analysis of the causes of strikes. Strikes usually are the result of a breakdown in negotiation between *two* parties; they do not result if one party gives in. Thus, factors that change the bargaining power or ability of one party to withstand a strike should not necessarily affect the level of strike activity. If this is perceived by the other party then that other party should be more willing to give in rather than incur a strike. In the extreme, in a world of perfect information, strikes would serve no useful function: both parties would realize each other's position and settle accordingly, dividing up the cost saving from having avoided a costly strike. Hence, the often-cited statement by Hicks (27, pp. 146-147): "The majority of actual strikes are doubtless the result of faulty negotiation . . . . Any means which enables either side to appreciate better the position of the other will always make a settlement easier; adequate knowledge will always make a settlement possible."

Obviously, the real world is not one where information is perfect. In fact, strikes serve the important function of extracting information and conveying that information to the parties. Even strikes that appear futile at a given point in time may serve the purpose of making the threat of one party credible at some future date. To make threats credible, the parties may have to engage in otherwise costly activities, such as strikes. Also, as Hicks (27, p. 146) points out: "Weapons grow rusty if unused, and a Union which never strikes may lose the ability to organize a formidable strike, so that its threats become less effective."

This suggests that in examining the determinants of strikes, we should look at factors that influence the information content of strikes, especially those factors that create misperceptions or a divergence of expectations between the parties. In addition, we should examine factors that affect the joint costs and benefits, to both parties, of strikes as mechanisms to achieve whatever purpose they serve. Whatever their purpose (that is, whatever benefits strikes provide in conveying information, modifying expectations, releasing pent-up frustration, achieving political ends, solidifying the rank and file or providing a vacation) they should be less prevalent when their costs to both parties are high. It is the total cost to *both* parties that is crucial since if strikes are costly only to one party then that party will have to "bribe" the other party by agreeing to an unfavourable agreement. It is only when all mutually beneficial bribes are exhausted that strikes should occur, and only then if they are a cheaper means of attaining their purpose than are alternative procedures. For this reason some recent studies have focused on variables affecting the total costs of strikes to both parties as key determinants of strikes (33, 34, 50).

In summary, strikes can serve a variety of purposes, including the crucial functions of extracting and conveying of information, and the making of future threats credible. Whatever the purpose of strikes, however, the joint decision to incur a strike or lockout can be affected by a variety of factors including those that affect the cost to both parties of the strike as a dispute-settlement procedure. It is in this sense that we discuss these factors as determinants of strikes.

Categorizing Strike Determinants

There are almost as many ways of categorizing the causes of strikes as there are ways of classifying strikes themselves. To a certain degree, the categorization reflects the perspectives of the different disciplines that have contributed to our understanding of strike activity. Economists have focused on the economic environment (notably the business cycle, market characteristics, and inflationary expectations); sociologists have focused at the macrolevel on class conflict and dramatic changes in the social system and in the relations of production, and at the microlevel on the process of bargaining and on interpersonal relations; political scientists and historians have emphasized the political environment and the importance of the strike in achieving political ends; and industrial-relations analysts have emphasized dispute-resolution procedures and characteristics of the bargaining structure and relationship.

For our purposes, we have categorized the determinants of strikes under the rubrics of economic and noneconomic factors, the latter includes legal and procedural factors, political and historical factors, characteristics of the various actors and of the bargaining structure, and personal and interpersonal relationships. Many of these categories are obviously interdependent and overlapping: they are utilized simply as a convenient way of summarizing the current theoretical and empirical literature, and to illustrate its interrelatedness — and at times the isolation of particular disciplinary perspectives.

ECONOMIC DETERMINANTS OF STRIKES

The economic determinants of strikes can be categorized according to the ways in which strikes have been analysed empirically: the early studies of strikes and the business cycle; the more recent studies of the time pattern of aggregate strike activity; and recent cross-section studies that seek to explain variation in strikes across industries, unions, regions, cities, or collective agreements as the unit of observation.

Business Cycles and Strike Cycles

The earliest economic studies of the time pattern of aggregate strike activity focused on the relationship of strikes to the business cycle. The expectation was for a positive procyclical relationship with strikes being highest at the peak of a business cycle. The reasoning for this (usually derived in an ad hoc fashion) was that at the peak of a business cycle (when unemployment is low and profits are high) workers would be willing to incur the cost of a strike, largely because they were more likely to be able to find jobs elsewhere and because they felt employers could pay more since profits were high and inventories low. This line of reasoning, however, begs the question of why the parties should not settle for large wage increases in such circumstances. More bargaining power in the hands of labour should lead to larger wage settlements, not necessarily more strikes.

In spite of their inadequate theoretical explanation, the earliest studies of aggregate strike activity tended, with some notable exceptions, to find a positive relationship between strikes and the business cycle (25, 26, 30, 45, 48, 51, 75, 76). Some of the studies also found that the peak of the strike cycle tended to come slightly before the peak of the business cycle. Griffen (25) suggested that this may mean that strikes may influence the business cycle rather than vice versa; that is, a high level of strike activity may cause a subsequent economic decline. More realistically, this phenomenon occurs because there was a maximum divergence between the views of union and management at the peak of the cycle. And this happens because unions base their demands on current or lagging indicators like employment, wage changes in other firms, and the cost of living. On the other hand, management bases its concessions on indicators that lead the cycle like business failures, security prices, and contracts and orders (51). Consequently, a maximum divergence between the expectations of unions and management takes place just before the peak of the business cycle resulting in the strike peak leading the business-cycle peak.

Recent Studies of Time Pattern of Aggregate Strike Activity

The more recent studies of the time pattern of aggregate strike activity differ from the earlier studies both because they endeavour to establish a more rigorous theoretical relationship between strikes and various measures of business-cycle activity, and also because they use more sophisticated statistical techniques to try to disentangle the complex relationship between strikes and various measures of economic activity.

Most of the recent studies take as their departure the model developed by Ashenfelter and Johnson (3). Theirs was the first attempt to develop a formal model whereby strikes resulted from optimizing behaviour. The essence of their model is that firms decide on the "optimal" profit-maximizing duration of the strike by trading off strike costs with expected future wage costs in their profit-maximizing decision. Subsequent theoretical work has analysed the analogous decision with respect to unions (16), and for both parties in the same model (19, 31, 49). In addition, some recent studies have formalized models emphasizing how strikes may result when union leaders and management have objectives that are different not only from each other, but also with respect to their constituents (44, 69).

While they differ considerably in the precise specification of the variables, most of the recent studies relate various measures of aggregate strike activity to a variety of explanatory variables reflecting measures of aggregate business conditions. While most of the studies use annual or quarterly observations, some (11, 15) pool both time series and cross-section data by using the individual contract as the unit of observation. Explanatory variables used to reflect aggregate business conditions include the unemployment rate (or proxies such as job vacancies or the deviation of output from its trend), profits, and real wages (in some cases money wages and inflation entered as separate explanatory variables). In addition, some studies try to measure the long-run time trend as well as discrete changes in strike activity that may occur in response to such phenomena as wage-price controls or legislative changes that may affect strike activity. While there are always some exceptions found in particular studies, the empirical results generally find economic factors to be important determinants of the time pattern of aggregate strike activity.

Unemployment— A negative relationship between strikes and unemployment (or its proxies) has been documented in the United States (3, 31, 44, 55, 63), the United Kingdom (14, 47, 53, 57), and in Canada (11, 15, 61, 62, 71). Some Canadian studies, however, find the *number* of strikes to be positively related to unemployment or its proxy (12, 72) although the duration or total time lost due to strikes is negatively related to proxies for unemployment (12), or the relationship is statistically insignificant (72). In general, it appears that the relationship found in the earlier business-cycle studies — that strikes are less likely in depressed periods of high unemployment and more likely in periods of prosperity — is also found in the more recent econometric studies, although this relationship does not appear to be as strong or as pronounced in Canada (63, 71).

Money wages — Increases in money wages tend to be associated with reduced strike activity in the United States (3, 31) and in the United Kingdom (47, 57). In Canada, the relationship has been found to be statistically insignificant (71), of the opposite sign (12) and negative for the number of strikes but statistically insignificant for the size, duration, or volume of strike activity (72).

Inflation — Inflation, especially if unanticipated (4, 21, 31) has generally been associated with increased strike activity in the United States (3, 31, 44, 55), in the United Kingdom (14, 47, 53, 57), and in Canada (12, 18, 21, 62, 71, 72). Kaufman (31), in fact, attributes the resurgence of strikes in the United States in the 1970s to the fact that unanticipated inflation created marked divergences in the expectations of the parties.

Real wages— Real wages are affected by both money wages and inflation. If money wages increase faster than prices so that real wages rise, then strike activity tends to dissipate in the United States (17, 31, 55, 63, 69), in the United Kingdom (14, 47), and in Canada (11, 63). McLean (41, 42), however, provides some evidence to suggest that a large increase in real wages can raise workers' expectations relative to the employers' ability to pay, and this can lead to subsequent increases in strike activity.

Profits— There does not appear to be a consensus in the empirical literature on the impact of profits on strike activity. In the United States, both negative (55) and positive but statistically insignificant relationships have been found (3, 31, 60), and in the United Kingdom both positive (47, 57) and statistically insignificant negative relationships (14) have been found. In Canada, negative relationships have been found (61, 72), although positive and statistically insignificant relationships were found for the size and total-time-lost measures of strike activity (72). While there is no consensus on the impact of profits on strikes, there is some evidence that prolonged "strike waves" occur when profits have been steadily eroded by an extended period of rising labour costs (55).

Time trend — A positive time trend indicating an increasing level of strike activity over time, when other factors are held constant, has been documented in the United Kingdom (47, 53, 57) and in Canada in the post-World War II period (62, 71, 72), although a negative trend has been found in the United States (3, 31, 60).

Conclusion — In summary, the more recent econometric analysis of aggregate strike activity over time tends to confirm the importance of economic determinants of strikes. In particular, strike activity diminishes in periods of high unemployment and increases in periods of inflation or when real wages are eroded. In addition, in Canada economic factors were more successful in explaining the frequency of strikes than their size or duration (18, 20, 21, 72), and they were more successful in explaining recent strikes as opposed to strikes prior to World War II when union-organizing strikes were prominent (63). The ability of economic factors to explain strikes was highest for contract-renewal strikes, second highest for first-agreement strikes and lowest for wildcat strikes during the term of the contract (18, 72). In addition, the relationship between economic factors and strike activity seemed weaker in Canada than either the United Kingdom or especially the United States.

Canada-United States — This weaker relationship between strikes and economic factors in Canada could occur for a variety of reasons, although at this stage only speculation is possible. First, because Canada is smaller than the United Kingdom and the United States, its strike activity may be more dominated by "unusual events": in essence, a few particular strikes may dominate the picture, especially for strike measures that involve size, duration, or person-days lost. Second, to the extent that long-duration strikes are more prominent in Canada, and to the extent that strike duration is not as explicable by economic factors as is strike incidence, then Canadian strike activity (at least measures involving duration) will be less dependent on economic activity. Third, strikes during the life of the contract are more often illegal in Canada than in the United States where the right to strike during the contract is often negotiable. Since there is more pressure in Canada to wait until the contract expires before striking, it is less likely that strike activity will reflect economic conditions at the time of the strike. In essence, in Canada there is less flexibility to strike in response to current economic conditions, although illegal wildcat strikes occur frequently, and they appear to be responsive to economic factors (20). Fourth, as suggested by Vanderkamp (71), there may simply be differences in the political and sociological environment between Canada and the United States, and these differences may make Canadian strike activity less dependent on economic activity.

Cross-Section Studies and Economic Variables

The importance of economic factors in explaining strike activity has also been tested in cross-section studies (sometimes pooling time-series data also) which try to explain differences in strike activity across unions (52), cities (64), regions (7), industries (13, 39, 42, 43, 47, 50, 56), or collective agreements (11, 15). Empirical studies at the microlevel using the collective agreement as the unit of observation are particularly informative since they involve the level of analysis of the bargaining unit where bargaining actually occurs, and they often enable the incorporation of numerous explanatory variables describing the negotiators and the negotiation process (68).

Unfortunately the cross-section studies of strike activity are exceedingly difficult to compare because of the different units of observations (industry, union, region, collective agreement) and because of the different explanatory variables used to explain strike variation or control for the other relevant factors. In general, however, it appears that characteristics of the economic environment are not as consistently or quantitatively important in explaining strike activity in the cross-section studies as they are in the aggregate time-series studies. Presumably their effect is dominated by noneconomic factors that do not change much over time (and hence that do not "explain" much of the variation in the time pattern of aggregate strike activity). It is to these noneconomic factors that we now turn.

NONECONOMIC DETERMINANTS OF STRIKES

The vast majority of the research on strike activity has focused on the role of economic variables in explaining aggregate indicators of strike activity. In contrast, current research (1, 2, 5, 10, 37, 38) which may be classified as noneconomic [1] has moved beyond economic factors because of their inability to predict the probability of strikes at the level of the bargaining relationship (7). Drawing from previous theory and research in sociology, psychology, and industrial relations, an attempt has been made to recognize that pressure on the parties in the collective-bargaining process is also shaped by political, legal, organizational, interpersonal, personal, and historical forces. Any of these forces may produce a divergence in the expectations of the parties during negotiations resulting in a strike. Unfortunately, the limited number of studies undertaken from this perspective and the substantial differences in samples and measures used make comparisons difficult. However, in general, the results do tentatively suggest that noneconomic factors do play a key role in explaining the probability of a strike (1, 2, 38) and even its duration (10). With these caveats in mind, we will discuss the main noneconomic determinants of strikes under the following categories: population and community characteristics, union and management organizational characteristics, negotiator and bargaining-process characteristics, and bargaining history.

Population and Community Characteristics

Sociological investigations of the determinants of strike activity have viewed strikes as an example of collective behaviour. The mobilization of workers, while sometimes economic, is also organizational and political in nature. As Stern (65, p. 57) notes: "strikes retain some basic elements of social movement collective behavior. There is a need for rapid mobilization of a relatively large number of participants, a well-developed system of communication, a favourable political climate, and the ability

---

1. It is somewhat of a misnomer to categorize the determinants of strikes as economic or noneconomic since many of the noneconomic factors (such as legislative change) may have their effect on strikes by altering the economic costs and benefits of strikes to the parties. Conversely, many of the economic or market variables may operate through intervening variables which are categorized as noneconomic.

to sustain activity over some length of time. These elements may be analyzed as products of organizational characteristics as well as economic conditions." As a result, sociologists have attempted to identify characteristics of the community and the union which may increase the mobilization and threat potential of the bargaining unit. Moreover, conditions which increase the unions' ability to mobilize their membership are likely to raise the expectations of the workers, but they will not necessarily impact managements' expectations about a settlement and, therefore, this divergence of expectations between union and management may raise the likelihood of a strike.

In a study of U.S. metropolitan areas, Stern (64) found that substantial differences did exist between high- and low-conflict cities. For example, cities with a high incidence of strikes were found to be significantly larger. Moreover, high-conflict cities were found to have more of the labour force employed in manufacturing, fewer females in the labour force and more employees in unions. Each of these conditions has been identified as increasing the mobilization potential as these groups are more likely to be dissatisfied and have pent-up frustrations which may be released through strike action.

Interestingly, in a study of Canadian public-sector employees Anderson (1) did not find any of these variables to be significant in explaining the decision to strike. However, a variable measuring the level of strike activity in the private sector during the previous three years within the community was consistently important in explaining the incidence of public-sector strikes. Together, the results of these two studies suggest that certain population and community characteristics are associated with a high or low level of conflict in the community as a whole, and that the level of militancy in the community as a whole is likely to be very predictive of the probability of a strike in a given union-management relationship. Thus, militancy of labour in the geographic area may be a major factor in the mobilization of workers in any bargaining unit within the region.

While Stern's (64) analysis of the intermetropolitan frequency of strikes examined the most complete set of community characteristics, Britt and Galle (6) and Shorter and Tilly (58) chose degree of unionization, average plant size, and average union size as indicators of mobilization and threat potential, respectively. Degree of unionization and average plant size, an indicator of the degree of worker alienation, were found to be positively associated with the incidence of strikes. However, when Stern (65) reanalyzes Britt and Galle's (6) data including measures of bargaining structure, the relationship appears to become unstable.

As with the economic research discussed previously, most of the sociological studies which focus on strike activity have been at the industry or community level of analysis. When the theory is applied at the level of the bargaining relationship, population and community characteristics do not generally play an important role in explaining impasses or strikes (1, 38, 74). However, the results do suggest that there may be a combination of population and industry characteristics which produce a higher level of militancy in the community which may carry over into individual union-management relationships increasing the likelihood of a strike.

Union and Management Organizational Characteristics

Intraorganizational conflict — Walton and McKersie (73) point out that a major component of the bargaining process is the negotiations which occur within the union and management sides. Often there is a great diversity of interests which results in potentially conflicting goals and priorities for the collective-bargaining process. Factions often exist within the union on the basis of age, sex, occupation, seniority, or political affiliation. Unless mechanisms exist within the union to resolve these conflicts, the potential for a strike may increase because of the inability of union members to agree on management's offers. Stern and Anderson (67) reveal how during the 1975 strike, internal differences within the Canadian Union of Postal Workers over the importance of technological change had a great impact on the duration of the strike as well as its initial occurrence. Management officials often use these types of internal conflicts to get an early settlement to the strike by appealing to the faction most favourable to its position.

Internal conflict is not limited to the union organization. Management officials often have major disagreements over priorities and the stand to be adopted on various issues at the bargaining table. While this type of conflict is most pronounced in the public sector where differences between management and elected officials are frequent, it is not uncommon for line and staff managers in the private sector to have disputes during collective bargaining. Research on municipal employees in both Canada (1) and the United States (38) indicates that internal conflict tends to increase the probability of negotiations breaking down and a strike being called. It is difficult for an agreement to be reached between union and management representatives when major differences in expectations for a settlement exist within the membership of each side.

Inadequate decision-making authority — In the 1960s and early 1970s, a major problem cited in collective bargaining was that the final decision on management's position resided in the U.S. headquarters of parent companies of Canadian subsidiaries. Union negotiators often believed that they were dealing with little more than a messenger boy who ran back and forth between the table and top management. Inadequate decision-making authority in the hands of the management negotiator increases the probability of a strike for two reasons. First, union leaders may feel that the only way to bring the real decision makers to the bargaining table is to put pressure on through a job action. Second, as the real decision makers are not involved in the day-to-day negotiating process, it increases the likelihood that they have unrealistic expectations about the point of settlement or inaccurate perceptions of the expectations of the union. Both of these perceptual distortions are likely to produce a divergence in union and management expectations which will increase the probability of a strike. Research suggests, however, that inadequate authority is more likely to be an important cause of breakdowns in negotiations when arbitration rather than the right to strike is the final action to be taken by the parties (1, 38).

Management and union policies — Specific management and union policies may also contribute to strikes. Unfortunately, research on this area is almost non-existent. Kochan (37) suggests that employer policies of hard bargaining and union resistance may increase the probability of strikes. However, no empirical evidence is available to support this contention. On the union side, Roomkin (52) examined the role of union policies requiring national approval of subordinate contracts and national approval of all strikes in determining strike frequency. Weak support was found for the hypothesis that more decentralized unions had a greater propensity to strike. However, the relationship was only significant for those unions which functioned in local product markets. Thus, the impact of union and management policies in determining strikes is basically an unexplored area.

Negotiator and Bargaining Process Characteristics

Union and management trust or hostility — Walton and McKersie (73) also note that collective bargaining involves the attempts of both parties to structure their opponents' attitudes. Interpersonal sources of conflict may make it extremely difficult for union and management representatives to accept the other side's position, to back down from an extreme position taken early in bargaining, or to compromise. As a result, hostility and a lack of trust may increase the probability of a strike. Research by Anderson (1) and by Kochan and Baderschneider (38) found a measure of attitudinal hostility to be strongly related to the probability of an initial impasse in the public sector. The Canadian study (1), however, reveals that this variable may be very important in the final decision to strike when other environmental and organizational sources of conflict are more significant.

Negotiator skills and experience — As previously noted, Hicks (27) stated that most strikes were the result of faulty negotiations. Inexperienced negotiators are more likely to provide incorrect cues to their opponents, generating unrealistic expectations about the terms of settlement. Moreover, inexperience may lead a negotiator to become overcommitted to a position which may be unacceptable. Movement from that position may then be impossible without a loss of face with both the other side and the negotiator's own constituency. Thus, a lack of skill and experience on the part of either or both negotiators is likely to increase the probability of a strike.

Anderson's (1) study of municipal unions in Canada found that while measures assessing the skill and experience of union and management negotiators were not significant in predicting the occurrence of the strike, strikes were significantly less likely to occur where the management negotiator had received formal training in labour relations. In contrast, Kochan and Baderschneider (38) and Anderson (1) discovered a lack of negotiator skill and experience to be very significant in predicting impasse experiences of public-sector unions under systems without the right to strike. Thus, it is possible that the determinants of a strike are different than the determinants of the use of arbitration or fact finding.

Bargaining History

Whether or not a strike is going to occur in a given round of negotiations may be affected as much by the historical context of the relationship as by current economic and noneconomic conditions. Past struggles and hostilities are likely to carry over to current negotiations (24, 69). Kochan (37) presents data from both the private and public sectors which indicates that the probability of an impasse almost doubles if negotiations had broken down and an impasse had been declared in the previous round of negotiations. Moreover, the probability of impasse continues to increase if two previous rounds of negotiations are considered. While no information is available on how the strike history of a union-management relationship impacts the current probability of a strike, it is probable that a history of militancy will be indicative of future behaviour.

Conclusion

A review of the research on the noneconomic determinants of strike activity reveals that unfortunately while many of the variables identified intuitively seem important in explaining the decision to strike, empirical tests of these propositions are limited, both in terms of number and the range of union-management relationships examined. Moreover, the vast majority of studies which investigate the importance of noneconomic factors are cross-sectional, and thus do not provide a good indication of their importance relative to economic factors which are likely to be stable at any one point in time. Thus, before public policy may be shaped to impact the determinants of strikes, we need to examine more carefully the interaction of economic and noneconomic factors.

DISPUTE-RESOLUTION PROCEDURES

A fundamental premise of Canadian collective bargaining is voluntarism. That is, union and management representatives should have the right to come to an agreement on the terms and conditions of employment without government intervention. However, given that breakdowns in the ability of the parties to resolve their differences without assistance occur frequently, all Canadian jurisdictions have established a number of procedures to assist the parties in resolving their disputes. In this section, the major purposes and types of dispute-resolution procedures are discussed, including conciliation or mediation, conciliation boards or fact finding, arbitration, and other governmental responses to industrial conflict.

Purposes of Dispute-Resolution Procedures

As strikes may play different functions for the parties, dispute-resolution procedures may also have different purposes. Canada was one of the few countries to adopt a system of compulsory conciliation during the early 1900s. In the current context, compulsory conciliation required that the parties prior to any job action avail themselves of the services of a conciliator appointed by the provincial labour-relations board. The conciliator typically met with the parties and reported the possibilities of a settlement to the minister of labour. After the report had been filed and a specified period of time had elapsed (usually seven or fourteen days), then the union obtained the right to strike, and management the right to lock out. In some jurisdictions, if conciliation was unsuccessful, the dispute would be forwarded to a conciliation board charged with investigating the dispute and reporting to the minister. Again, this step was compulsory, and a strike or lockout could not occur until it was completed. Thus, a major purpose of the compulsory-conciliation process was not necessarily to induce a settlement but at the least to provide a *cooling-off period* to allow hostilities to decrease, emotions to ebb, and it was hoped, give the parties a renewed opportunity to examine the matters in dispute.

The above example, however, also illustrates several of the other major purposes of dispute-resolution procedures. The intervention of a neutral third party to the collective-bargaining process often helps to inject new alternatives, perspectives, and compromises which may have been overlooked by the parties. Thus, the intervention may also help to provide *additional information* or *ways of viewing the problem*.

Often at the point of impasse the parties may be overcommitted to positions from which they cannot retreat without losing face with their respective constituencies. Conciliators, mediators, fact finders, and arbitrators often provide the opportunity for negotiators to save face by attributing changes in their positions to the suggestions or insistence of the third party. Therefore, dispute resolution may help to resolve *interpersonal* and *political problems*.

Dispute resolution often has an additional purpose of informing the public of the nature of the issues under contention as well as the positions of the parties. It is the objective of disclosure to induce both *public awareness* and *public pressure* on the parties toward settlement. Unfavourable press should induce both union and management to compromise rather than be the object of public scorn.

Each of the above purposes have assumed that the underlying reason is to help the parties to voluntarily resolve their differences prior to a work stoppage. For certain occupations, usually police, fire fighters, and hospital employees, several jurisdictions prohibit strikes and provide dispute-resolution procedures to act as *strike substitutes*. Thus, in several jurisdictions, the parties must take any issues unresolved in collective bargaining to some form of arbitration.

Dispute-resolution procedures, therefore, may have a number of purposes. Impasse procedures may be designed only to force the parties to rethink their positions and cool off before making the decision to strike. Furthermore, they may help the parties to achieve a settlement by providing information, new ways of viewing the problem, resolving interpersonal or political problems, or by bringing public pressure to bear on the parties. Alternately, the procedures may be designed to impose a settlement on the parties, as is the case with arbitration, while at the same time prohibiting strikes or lockouts.

Types of Dispute-Resolution Methods

Mediation — Mediation is the most common form of third-party intervention. The mediator acts as a facilitator for interaction between union and management and has no power or authority to impose a settlement. The objective of the mediator is to help the parties voluntarily reach a settlement. Often the mediator, while not successfully inducing a settlement, helps to reduce the number of issues in dispute by getting the parties not to hold back concessions.

To be successful the mediator needs to be acceptable to the parties. Acceptability and trust are necessary for the mediator to obtain confidential information about the parties' resistance points and bargaining strategies. For without this data, it is virtually impossible for the mediator to help shape a settlement.

Kochan (37) indicates that early in the mediation process, obtaining trust, learning the issues and obstacles to settlement, assessing the climate of negotiations, and identifying the roles of the various members of the negotiating team are the main tasks for the mediator. During this time the mediator is likely to be challenged by the parties and must appear to be trustworthy and listening in order to gain credibility. During the next stage the mediator begins to get involved in exchanging proposals and looking for areas of compromise. This requires constant probing and questioning of the resistance points of the parties and, therefore, a more active and aggressive approach by the mediator. Finally, in the later stages of the process as settlement is closer the mediator becomes even more aggressive negotiating with both parties, suggesting proposals and pushing both sides towards a settlement. During all of these stages, the mediator may have to aid the parties in resolving intraorganizational conflicts, help the negotiators save face, and suggest compromise solutions.

Fact finding — Fact finding, a role often performed by conciliation boards, is a more formal process than mediation. The fact finder or fact-finding board is charged with the responsibility of investigating the issues in dispute and making formal recommendations to the labour-relations board and possibly the public. Similar to mediation, however, the recommendations of the fact finder do not have to be adopted by the parties but are just another piece of information for consideration in the negotiations. Typically, the fact-finding process will include formal briefs from both union and management as well as a formal hearing where both parties will be allowed to present their views.

The objective of fact finding is also to obtain a settlement voluntarily between the parties. However, typically this procedure adds the inducement of bringing public pressure to bear on the parties as a consequence of the public release of the outcomes of the process. In practice, however, very little public outcry is heard as a result of a public fact-finding report, and whether or not a settlement is achieved depends on the nature of the recommendations of the fact finder and the motivation of the parties to settle.

Arbitration — There are a large number of forms of arbitration which need to be distinguished before describing the procedure itself. First, arbitration involves the parties submitting the issues in dispute to an arbitrator or arbitration panel whose decision is *binding* on both union and management. Second, arbitration may be either *voluntary*, where the parties voluntarily agree to submit their differences to arbitration, or *compulsory*, where the law requires that if the parties cannot come to an agreement then all unresolved issues must be submitted to arbitration. Finally, arbitration may either be conventional or final-offer. Under *conventional arbitration*, the arbitrator is allowed to make any award which he or she thinks is appropriate, selecting some positions of either party or modifying them as necessary. In contrast, under *final-offer arbitration* the arbitrator must select either the exact position of the union or management on a *total-package* basis or an *issue-by-issue* basis. These distinctions apply to the notion of interest arbitration (referring to the establishment of the terms of a new collective agreement) as opposed to grievance arbitration (referring to the *interpretation* of the terms of an existing agreement), the latter type of arbitration being discussed in Chapter 13.

Arbitration, especially in its compulsory form, has been criticized as an unacceptable strike substitute (2) as it does not provide the same inducements to the parties to settle as a strike would. Specifically, arbitration has often been found to chill genuine collective bargaining. This occurs because the parties, knowing that the arbitrator is likely to split the difference between their final positions, hold back concessions during bargaining in fear of losing at arbitration. Arbitration has also been criticized because over time, once the parties have used arbitration in each subsequent round of negotiations the parties will continue to rely on the arbitrator to determine their terms and conditions of employment. Both of these criticisms were found to be strongly supported when examining the arbitration system in the Canadian federal public service (2).

Other forms of dispute resolution — In the Canadian public sector, the government has often taken an alternative approach to resolving disputes, especially strikes by public employees. More and more frequently, both the federal and provincial governments have been willing to pass special legislation requiring the termination of a strike and forcing the parties back to the bargaining table. Thus, strikes may be prevented through mediation and fact finding, prohibited and replaced by arbitration, or ended through special legislation.

THE CONSEQUENCES OF STRIKE ACTIVITY

What differences do strikes make on the outcomes of collective bargaining? Do strikes have any impact on the performance of the Canadian economy? Do strikes have a lasting effect on the union-management relationship? Do strikes have any impact on the profitability of the firm, given that strikes are not only the result of a divergence of expectations between union and management but also involve strategic decisions by union and management with the intention of maximizing the return of the strike to their constituents.

Conventional wisdom would indicate that strikes have a generally negative impact on the economy. Critics often argue that Canada's position in the world market has declined substantially because of importers' fears that unstable labour relations will create difficulties for meeting delivery deadlines. Strikes by grain handlers and forest-product workers are cited as cases in point. Moreover, the long duration of Canadian strikes is frequently identified as a contributor to the decline in productivity per man-hour. The poor labour-relations climate is charged with hindering foreign investment in Canada because of its negative impact on profitability. Furthermore, anecdotal evidence suggests that no one wins in a long strike since even workers do not recapture their lost wages during the strike through the negotiated wage increases.

Each of these criticisms suggests that strikes have generally negative consequences for workers, employers, and society alike. Unfortunately, at this point each of the above statements remains an unsupported supposition. Very little empirical research has investigated the impact of strikes. Policy makers and researchers have been so concerned with the causes of strike activity based on an assumption that they are undesirable events, that few have questioned whether or not strikes have positive or negative consequences. On the other hand, research quite clearly indicates that the existence of the right to strike (in comparison with arbitration) ensures that the collective-bargaining process involves true negotiation and compromise between labour and management.

CONCLUDING COMMENTS

The purpose of this chapter was to introduce the reader to the nature, causes, and consequences of strike activity in Canada. Since the mid-1960s, the incidence and duration of strikes have been on the rise. A wide range of economic and noneconomic factors are found to be related to strike activity. Public policy has generally adopted an approach to reduce strike activity through the establishment of dispute-resolution procedures which focus on the noneconomic causes of strikes. Unfortunately, while there is a well-developed body of literature on the important economic conditions which increase the probability of a strike, both theory and research on the role of noneconomic factors are virtually nonexistent. Moreover, almost no attention has been paid to the consequences of strikes for employees, employers, or society. Thus, in general, before we can decide whether or not strikes in Canada are excessive, or whether or not we are able to effectively intervene to resolve strikes, substantially more attention needs to be directed to this important industrial-relations issue.

REFERENCES AND WORKS CITED

1. Anderson, J.C. "Determinants of Collective Bargaining Impasses: Effects of Dispute Resolution Procedures," in R. Petersen and G. Bomers (Eds.), *Industrial Relations and Conflict Management* (New York: Martinus Nijhoff, 1981).

2. Anderson, J.C., and T.A. Kochan. "Impasse Procedures in the Canadian Federal Service:

Effects of the Bargaining Process," *Industrial and Labor Relations Review*, Vol. 30 (1977), 3, 282-301.

3. Ashenfelter, O., and G. Johnson. "Bargaining Theory, Trade Unions, and Industrial Activity," *American Economic Review*, Vol. 59 (1969), 35-49.

4. Blejer, M. "Strike Activity and Wage Determination under Rapid Inflation: The Chilean Case," *Industrial and Labor Relations Review*, Vol. 34 (1981), 356-364.

5. Brett, J., and S. Goldberg. "Wildcat Strikes in Bituminous Coal Mining," *Industrial and Labor Relations Review*, Vol. 32 (1979), 465-483.

6. Britt, D., and O. Galle. "Structural Antecedents of the Shape of Strikes: A Comparative Analysis," *American Sociological Review*, Vol. 35 (1974), 642-651.

7. Burton, J.F., and C.E. Krider. "The Incidence of Strikes in Public Employment," in D.S. Hamermesh (Ed.), *Labour in the Public and Non-profit Sectors* (Princeton University Press, 1975), pp. 135-182.

8. Clack, G. "Strikes during the Term of Collective Agreements." Statistics Research Committee of the Canadian Association of Administrators of Labour Legislation, 1975.

9. Clack, G. "A Brief Primer on the Use and Misuse of Strike and Lockout Statistics." Statistics Research Committee of the Canadian Association of Administrators of Labour Legislation, 1977.

10. Cooper, W.H., and J.C. Anderson. "Canadian Strike Duration: An Exploratory Analysis." Unpublished working paper, School of Business, Queen's University, 1980.

11. Cousineau, J.M. "The Effect of Economic Activity on Strikes: A Search for a Determinate Solution," *Cahier No. 8009* (Montréal: Departement de Science Économique et Centre de Recherche en Développement Économique, Université de Montréal, 1980).

12. Cousineau, J., and R. Lacroix. "Activité Économique, Inflation et Activité de Grève," *Relations Industrielles/Industrial Relations,* Vol. 31 (1976), 341-358.

13. Creigh, S., and P. Makeham. "Variations in Strike Activity within UK Manufacturing Industry," *Industrial Relations Journal*, Vol. 11, 5 (Nov.-Dec. 1980), 32-37.

14. Davies, R.J. "Economic Activity, Incomes Policy and Strikes — a Quantitative Analysis," *British Journal of Industrial Relations*, Vol. 17 (1979), 205-223.

15. Dussault, F., and R. Lacroix. "Activité de Grève: un Test des Hypothèses Explicatives Traditionnelles," *Canadian Journal of Economics*, Vol. 13 (1980), 632-644.

16. Eaton, B.C. "The Worker and the Profitability of the Strike," *Industrial and Labor Relations Review*, Vol. 26 (1973), 670-679.

17. Edwards, P.K. "Time Series Regression Models of Strike Activity: A Reconsideration with American Data," *British Journal of Industrial Relations*, Vol. 16 (1978), 320-334.

18. Fisher, E.G. "The Effects of Changes in Labour Legislation on Strike Activity in British Columbia: 1945-75," *Working Paper No. 79-1* (Edmonton: Faculty of Business Administration and Commerce, University of Alberta, 1979).

19. Fisher, E.G. "A Strike-as-an-Investment Theory of Bargaining Under Uncertainty," *Working Paper No. 79-2* (Edmonton: Faculty of Business Administration and Commerce, University of Alberta, 1979).

20. Fisher, E.G. "The Pattern and Selected Features of Strike Activity, Particularly Wildcat Strikes, in British Columbia: 1945-75," *Working Paper No. 80-2* (Edmonton: Faculty of Business Administration and Commerce, University of Alberta, 1980).

21. Fisher, E.G., and M.B. Percy. "Unanticipated Output and Consumer Price Movements and Their Influence on the Occurrence and Duration of Wildcat Strikes," *Working*

Paper No. 80-3 (Edmonton: Faculty of Business Administration and Commerce, University of Alberta, 1980).

22. Fisher, M.R. *Measurement of Labour Disputes and their Economic Effects* (Paris: OECD, 1973).

23. Forchheimer, K. "Some International Aspects of the Strike Movement," *Bulletin of the Oxford University Institute of Statistics*, Vol. 10 (1948), 9-24.

24. Gouldner, A. *Wildcat Strike: A Study in Worker Management Relationships* (New York: Harper and Row, 1965).

25. Griffen, J. *Strikes: A Study in Quantitative Economics* (New York: Columbia University Press, 1939).

26. Hansen, A. "Cycles of Strikes," *American Economic Review* (1921), 616-621.

27. Hicks, John R. *The Theory of Wages*, 2nd ed. (New York: St. Martin's Press, 1963).

28. Jamieson, S. "The Third Wave Reconsidered — Labour Unrest and Industrial Conflict in Canada, 1960-1975." Paper presented to the 14th Annual Meeting of the Canadian Industrial Relations Research Association, Fredericton, N.B., June 1977.

29. Jamieson, S.M. "Industrial Conflict in Canada 1966-75," *Economic Council of Canada Discussion Paper 142* (Economic Council of Canada, 1979).

30. Jurkat, E., and D. Jurkat. "Economic Function of Strikes," *Industrial and Labor Relations Review*, Vol. 2 (1949), 527-545.

31. Kaufman, B. "Bargaining Theory, Inflation, and Cyclical Strike Activity in Manufacturing," *Industrial and Labor Relations Review*, Vol. 34 (1981), 333-355.

32. Kelly, L.A. "Measuring Strike Activity," *Research and Current Issues Series No. 33* (Kingston: Queen's University, Industrial Relations Centre, 1976).

33. Kennan, J. "Collective Rationality and the Economic Theory of Strikes," *Working Paper 77-18* (Hamilton: McMaster University, 1977).

34. Kennan, J. "Pareto Optimality and the Economics of Strike Duration," *Journal of Labor Research*, Vol. 1 (1980), 77-94.

35. Kerr, C. and A. Siegel. "The Interindustry Propensity to Strike — An International Comparison," in A. Kornhauser, R. Dubin, and A.M. Ross (Eds.), *Industrial Conflict* (New York: McGraw-Hill, 1954), pp. 189-204.

36. Kinsley, B.L. "Trends in Canadian Strikes 1917-1972," *The Labour Gazette*, Vol. 76 (1976), 28-33.

37. Kochan, T. *Industrial Relations and Collective Bargaining* (Homewood, Ill: Irwin, 1980).

38. Kochan, T. and J. Baderschneider. "Dependence on Impasse Procedures: Police and Fire Fighters in New York State," *Industrial and Labor Relations Review*, Vol. 31 (1978), 431-449.

39. Maki, D.R., and K. Strand. "The Determinants of Strike Activity: An Inter-industry Analysis," *Proceedings of the 17th Annual Meeting of the Canadian Industrial Relations Association* (Montréal: Université du Québec, 1980), pp. 103-138.

40. Malles, P. *Canadian Industrial Conflict in International Perspective* (Ottawa: Informetrica, 1977).

41. McLean, R. "Coalition Bargaining and Strike Activity in the Electrical Equipment Industry, 1950-1974," *Industrial and Labor Relations Review*, Vol. 30 (1977), 356-363.

42. McLean, R. "Interindustry Differences in Strike Activity," *Industrial Relations*, Vol. 18 (1979), 103-109.

43. Mitchell, D.J.B. "A Note on Strike Propensities and Wage Developments," *Industrial Relations*, Vol. 20 (1981), 123-127.

44. Nelson, W., G.W. Stone Jr., and J.M. Swint. "An Economic Analysis of Public Sector Collective Bargaining and Strike Activity," *Journal of Labor Research*, Vol. 2 (1981), 77-98.

45. O'Brien, F. "Industrial Conflict and Business Fluctuations: A Comment," *Journal of Political Economy*, Vol. 73 (1965), 650-654.

46. O'Reilly, C., N. Parlette, and J. Bloom. "Professional Workers and Strike Activity," *Industrial Relations*, forthcoming (1981).

47. Pencavel, J. "An Investigation into Industrial Strike Activity in Britain," *Economica*, Vol. 37 (1970), 239-256.

48. Peterson, F. "Strikes in the United States 1880-1936," *Bulletin No. 561* (U.S. Department of Labor, Bureau of Labor Statistics, 1938).

49. Rabinovitch, R., and I. Swary. "On the Theory of Bargaining, Strikes and Wage Determination Under Uncertainty," *Canadian Journal of Economics*, Vol. 9 (1976), 668-684.

50. Reder, M. and G. Neumann. "Conflict and Contract: The Case of Strikes," *Journal of Political Economy*, Vol. 88 (1980), 867-886.

51. Rees, A. "Industrial Conflict and Business Fluctuations," *Journal of Political Economy*, Vol. 60 (1952), 371-382.

52. Roomkin, M. "Union Structure, Internal Control and Strike Activity," *Industrial and Labor Relations Review*, Vol. 29 (1976), 198-217.

53. Sapsford, D. "A Time Series Analysis of U.K. Industrial Disputes," *Industrial Relations*, Vol. 14 (1975), 242-249.

54. Shalev, M. "Problems of Strike Measurement," in C. Crouch and A. Pizzorno (Eds.), *The Resurgence of Class Conflict in Western Europe Since 1968* (London: Macmillan, 1978), pp. 321-334.

55. Shalev, M. "Trade Unionism and Economic Analysis — the Case of Industrial Conflict," *Journal of Labor Research*, Vol. 1 (1980), 133-174.

56. Shorey, J. "An Inter-Industry Analysis of Strike Frequency," *Economica,* Vol. 43 (1976), 349-365.

57. Shorey, J. "Time Series Analysis of Strike Frequency," *British Journal of Industrial Relations*, Vol. 15 (1977), 63-75.

58. Shorter, E., and C. Tilly. *Strikes in France, 1830-1968* (London: Cambridge University Press, 1974).

59. Silver, M. "Recent British Strike Trends: A Factual Analysis," *British Journal of Industrial Relations*, Vol. 11 (1973), 66-104.

60. Skeels, J. "Measures of U.S. Strike Activity," *Industrial and Labor Relations Review*, Vol. 27 (1971), 515-525.

61. Smith, D.A. "The Determinants of Strike Activity in Canada," *Relations Industrielles/ Industrial Relations*, Vol. 27 (1972), 663-678.

62. Smith, D.A. "The Impact of Inflation on Strike Activity in Canada," *Relations Industrielles/Industrial Relations*, Vol. 31 (1976), 139-145.

63. Snyder, D. "Early North American Strikes: A Reinterpretation," *Industrial and Labor Relations Review*, Vol. 30 (1977), 325-341.

64. Stern, R. "Intermetropolitan Pattern of Strike Frequency," *Industrial and Labor Relations Review*, Vol. 25 (1976), 218-235.

65. Stern, R.N. "Economic and Sociological Explanations of Strikes: Toward an Empirical Merger," in G. Somers (Ed.), *Proceedings of the 28th Annual Winter Meeting of the Industrial Relations Research Association* (Madison: IRRA, 1975).

66. Stern, R.N. "Methodological Issues in Quantitative Strike Analysis," *Industrial Relations*, Vol. 12 (1978), 32-42.

67. Stern, R.N., and J.C. Anderson. "Canadian Strike Activity: Union Centralization and National Diversity" in G. Somers (Ed.), *Proceedings of the 30th Annual Winter Meeting of the Industrial Relations Research Association* (Madison: IRRA, 1978), pp. 132-140.

68. Swidinsky, R., and J. Vandercamp. "A Microeconomic Analysis of Strike Activity." Mimeo. Department of Economics, University of Guelph, 1981.

69. Swint, J.M., and W.B. Nelson. "The Influence of Negotiators' Self Interest on the Duration of Strikes," *Industrial and Labor Relations Review*, Vol. 32 (1978), 56-66.

70. Turner, H., G. Roberts, and D. Roberts. *Managerial Characteristics and Industrial Conflict* (Cambridge: Cambridge University Press, 1977).

71. Vandercamp, J. "Economic Activity and Strikes in Canada," *Industrial Relations*, Vol. 9 (1970), 215-320.

72. Walsh, W. "Economic Conditions and Strike Activity in Canada," *Industrial Relations*, Vol. 14 (1975), 45-54.

73. Walton, R., and R. McKersie. *A Behavioral Theory of Labor Negotiations* (New York: McGraw-Hill, 1965).

74. Watkins, T. "The Effects of Community Environment on Negotiations," *Journal of Collective Negotiations in the Public Sector*, Vol. 1 (1972), 317-327.

75. Weintraub, A. "Prosperity vs. Strike: An Empirical Approach," *Industrial and Labor Relations Review*, Vol. 19 (1966), 231-238.

76. Yoder, D. "Economic Changes and Industrial Unrest in the United States," *Journal of Political Economy*, Vol. 48 (1940), 222-237.

QUESTIONS

1. What measures of strike activity are typical? What information does each provide about strikes?

2. Describe the main functions that strikes play.

3. How are the business cycle and strikes related?

4. Identify and describe three of the economic determinants of strike activity.

5. Identify and describe three noneconomic determinants of strike activity.

6. Describe the four main dispute-resolution methods.

7. How does mediation work to reduce the likelihood of a strike?

8. In your opinion, what impact do strikes have on the Canadian economy?

9. "Unequal bargaining power on the part of one of the parties in the negotiation process has implications for wage determination, not for strikes." Discuss.

10. Why may one expect the relationship of strike cycles to business cycles to be different in Canada and the U.S.?

THE OUTCOMES OF
COLLECTIVE BARGAINING

MORLEY GUNDERSON

11. Union Impact on Wages, Fringe Benefits, and Productivity

The impact of unions on compensation provides an excellent example of an area where our understanding can be furthered by a judicious blend of industrial relations with knowledge from another discipline— in this case, economics. This theme is portrayed throughout the chapter as it moves from a discussion of union goals and power, to the methods used by unions to attain their objectives, to the actual impact of unions on wages, wage structures, fringe benefits, and productivity.

Few topics in labour market analysis have received as much attention as the measurement of the union impact on wages. From the variety of studies there has emerged a consensus on some questions, limited agreement on many, and fundamental disagreement on others. The purpose of this chapter is to outline the extent of our knowledge in this area, highlighting the points of agreement and disagreement. Particular attention is paid to placing the issue of the union impact on compensation (which has traditionally been analysed by economists and econometricians) into a broader industrial-relations perspective. This is particularly appropriate to having a better understanding of the avenues (such as the bargaining structure) through which unions affect wages, the variety of nonwage outcomes that can result, and the feedbacks that are important.

Goals of unions are first discussed, followed by an analysis of the determinants of union power and the methods whereby unions achieve their goals. Problems in measuring the union impact are discussed, followed by an examination of the empirical evidence emphasizing not only wages and wage structures but also fringe benefits, working conditions, and productivity.

UNION GOALS

Although the focus of most of the economic analysis of unions is on their impact on compensation, it is important to put this in a broader perspective. In fact, the rationale for unions may have more to do with ensuring a modicum of job security and due process at the work place rather than the economic objective of higher

247

compensation. Hence, the grievance procedure and contract provisions on such matters as seniority and dismissal are as important as, if not more important than, compensation objectives. In addition, as a first step to attaining these job security and compensation objectives, unions must achieve their objective of being recognized as the sole bargaining agent.

Even when the focus is only on the compensation goal, unions have no clear single objective. Maximizing the wages of union members does not take into consideration the adverse employment effect that could emanate from such a policy, and obviously unions are concerned about the employment prospects of their members, although they may not attach much weight to the employment prospects of nonunion workers. Maximizing the wage bill (wages times employment) of union members would recognize both the wage and employment objectives of unions, as well as the possible trade-off between the two. However, this objective could imply, under certain conditions, that unions would lower their wage below the nonunion wage so as to increase employment and to increase the wage bill of union members. In addition, maximizing the wage bill suggests that equal weight is given to the wage and employment component of the wage bill objective.

It appears more reasonable to assume that unions care about both the wages and employability of their members, but that these components may be given different weights. The weights obviously may depend upon the voting power of persons affected. For example, union wage gains may go to voting union members, whereas employment reductions associated with a high union wage increase may occur in the form of fewer new people being hired. To the extent that such potential new recruits do not have a vote in the current union policies, then unions may favour wage gains at least up to the point where such gains would affect the employability of existing union members. Similarly, to the extent that union policies may reflect the preferences of the median union voter, new recruits may have little say in union decisions. In such circumstances, reductions in the demand for union labour may result in the layoff of younger workers rather than reductions in hours or wages of the average union members.

The relative weights that unions attach to the various components of their overall goals may also depend upon overall economic conditions. For example, in periods of recession unions are unlikely to take money wage cuts even if such cuts could preserve employment opportunities. This may reflect the fact that the reduction in employment opportunities may be concentrated in nonunion employees such as probationary workers, part-timers or those on outside contracts, or on younger members who represent a minority of union votes.

The objectives of unions are further complicated by the various internal union trade-offs that are involved between union members and between union leaders and the rank and file. Different groups within the union may have different preferences as well as the political power to affect these preferences. Older workers may prefer generous pensions — younger workers may prefer wages; females may prefer job flexibility — males may prefer job security; married workers may prefer dental and medical plans — single workers may prefer longer vacations. The weights associated with these different preferences will depend, in part, upon the intensity with which these groups hold their preferences as well as on their political power within the unions. To the extent that unions will reflect the wishes of the median union voter, there may be some concern that the preferences of younger workers or minorities may not be adequately reflected.

Differences between union leaders and the rank-and-file membership may also affect union goals. In fact, there is some empirical evidence to suggest that union leaders tend to place greater emphasis on wages relative to other issues than do rank-and-file members (30). At times, union leadership also is accused of being too much like management; at other times they are accused of being too radical and politically active. Clearly, union leadership may have goals that differ somewhat from those of the rank and file; nevertheless, their political survival depends on their reflecting the wishes of their members and consequently they will always be trying to gauge the intensity of preferences (and political power) of their constituent group. Strikes may be a means to this end, and they may also be utilized by union leaders to scale down the expectations of some of the membership that otherwise may accuse the leadership of "selling out" too early.

UNION POWER

Internal Power

The power of a union to fulfil its demands depends, in part, on a common consensus within the union with respect to its goals. This agreement must come from the various groups within the union, from the leadership and the rank and file, and from other unions as well as affiliated bodies. Jurisdictional disputes, rank-and-file discontent with union leadership, and rivalry within the rank and file may all dissipate the energies of the union and prevent it from providing a united front.

External Power and Elasticity of Demand for Labour

In addition to this internal source of power, union power to affect its wage demands depends on the particular objective circumstances it faces. Most of these factors can be summarized under the rubric of the "elasticity of demand" for union labour. In general, the demand for union labour will be inelastic, and hence wage increases will not be dampened by a large adverse employment effect, if: (a) labour cost is a small proportion of the total cost of production; (b) there are few good substitute products for those produced by union labour; and (c) there are a few good substitute inputs for unionized labour or such substitutes are expensive.

Labour cost portion — If the costs of unionized labour are a small proportion of the total cost in a firm, then the firm will more easily be able to absorb union wage increases: the resultant cost increases simply will not matter much relative to the total cost picture of the firm. This may be the case, for example, with respect to certain skilled crafts or small professional groups or in capital-intensive industries. It may, in part, explain reluctance of these groups to merge with larger groups where their own wage demands would be subsumed in the demands of the larger group.

Substitute products — If there are few good substitutes for the products or services produced by unionized labour then union wage-cost increases may be passed on to the consumer in the form of price increases without there being a substantial reduction in the demand for those products and therefore in the derived demand for union labour. This may be the case, for example, if the product is protected from foreign competition by a tariff or import quota, or if the product is advertised through the union label, or if the whole industry is organized so as to prevent the substitution of nonunion-made products for union-made products.

Substitute inputs — If there are few good substitute inputs for union labour, or if such substitutes are expensive, then unions can obtain wage increases without having to worry about such substitute inputs being used for unionized labour. Hence, unions will be very concerned about technological change and other processes that represent a substitution of capital for union labour. This is evidenced by their concern over the new microtechnology and their desire to have collective agreements reopened if major technological change occurs. Restrictive work practices ("featherbedding" rules) are also designed in part to prevent the substitution of other inputs for union labour. Professional associations also try to control the substitution of nonprofessional workers and paraprofessionals for professional workers.

Nonunion labour can also be a substitute for union labour and firms may try to use nonunion labour by contracting out, and by the use of probationary workers, supervisory personnel who are not in the bargaining unit, or "scab" labour during a strike. Unions obviously will try to control the use of such nonunion labour, and in some instances will seek direct control through the hiring hall or the use of the union shop whereby all persons in the bargaining unit are required to join the union as a condition of employment. If they cannot directly control the use of scab labour, unions will at least seek to have them pay union dues as is required under the agency shop.

To the extent that a reserve of low-wage labour in the economy is also a threat to union labour, then unions may support full-employment policies, income-maintenance programs, and restrictive-immigration policies so as to reduce that reserve of low-wage labour. If the size of the pool of low-wage labour itself cannot be controlled, unions will at least want to make that pool of labour more expensive, and hence they may support wage-fixing policies (minimum wages, equal pay, fair wages on government contracts, and wage-extension decrees) as well as labour-standards programs that make the use of such nonunion labour more expensive. This is not the only reason for union support of these policies, but it may be one of the reasons.

Noncompetitive Markets

The degree of competition that prevails can also affect the power of unions and hence their ability to win gains for their members. Noncompetitive situations can prevail in both the product market (the service market in the case of the public sector) and in the labour market, with both situations affecting the power of unions.

Monopoly in the product market — Conventional wisdom suggests that firms that are monopolistic in the product market have a greater ability to pay out of monopoly profits, and hence unions can garner high wage increases in such circumstances. In addition, if they are regulated monopolists, they may be concerned about their public image and hence may try to "buy" good labour relations by paying high wages, and they may feel that they can pass wage increases on to the public in the form of regulated rate increases.

While these arguments are plausible, they do not necessarily imply that unions can get larger wage increases when product markets are noncompetitive, or monopolistic in the extreme. Monopolies may have a greater ability to pay, but this also means that they may have a greater ability to resist union wage demands. In essence, they may use their monopoly profits to resist unionization, to set up structures (for example, extensive nonunion supervisory labour or capital equipment) that weaken the power of unions, or that allow them to withstand a lengthy and costly strike — after all, the monopolist, by definition, will not lose market share during a strike. In addition, monopolists that are regulated may try to keep union wage costs to a minimum to appear cost-conscious to the regulatory agency, and if rate increases are based on the capital base, then monopolists may have an added incentive to expand their capital base at the expense of labour costs. In essence, the impact of monopoly on the ability of the union to win wage increases is theoretically ambiguous: the net effect of these opposing forces must be ascertained empirically.

Public-sector employees — As discussed in Chapter 15, there is the presumption that unions in the public sector may be quite powerful because their employers are not subject to a competitive profit constraint. In essence, the political constraint in the public sector is not as binding as the profit constraint of the private sector. Union wage increases can be passed on to taxpayers who must have the essential services and cannot buy them elsewhere, who are often ill-informed about the "tax-price" of public services, and who exercise their prerogatives only occasionally by voting on a package of issues of which the wage costs of services may be only a small part. Of real concern is the possibility that public-sector employers may try to save on current wage costs by granting liberal deferred wages, to be paid by future generations of taxpayers and possibly when another political party is in power. Such deferred wages can come in the form of liberal retirement pensions or job security.

While these arguments do suggest that public-sector unions should be quite powerful, there are also forces — usually more subtle — working in the opposite direction. Taxpayer scrutiny is increasingly severe, and taxpayers' sympathies may reside with employers, forgetting that it takes two sides to create a dispute. Politicians may seek to curb inflation by moderating public-sector wage settlements, and they may even prolong or foster strikes to gain the media exposure that is crucial to their prominence. Employers in the public sector, unlike in the private sector, do not usually lose their (tax) revenues during a strike. Public-sector unions themselves may find it difficult to exert pressure if their right to strike is circumscribed or if their membership is reluctant to withhold essential services.

In essence, the power of unions in the public sector relative to the private sector is theoretically ambiguous. Hence, the differential impact of unions in the private and public sector is ultimately an empirical proposition.

Monopsony — Noncompetitive conditions may also prevail in labour markets that are dominated by a single employer — termed a monopsonist to designate that the firm is a monopolistic buyer of labour. Such firms are so large relative to the size of the local labour market that they have to raise wages to attract additional workers; conversely, they do not lose all of their work force if they lower wages. They will be extremely sensitive to raising wages to attract additional workers because they will have to pay these higher wages to their existing work force in order to maintain internal equity in their wage structure. This will serve to depress wages paid by monopsonists relative to what they would pay if they were competitive buyers of labour.

Monopsonists are ripe for union organizing because in such circumstances union wage increases, at least for a certain range, can actually lead to the monopsonist hiring more labour (18). This paradoxical result occurs because when faced with a fixed union wage that they must pay to all their workers, monopsonists are no longer constrained in their hiring decisions by the fact that they have to raise wages to attract additional workers; all workers are paid the union rate for each job. Monopsonists are worse off because they have to pay the higher union wage, but they are more willing to hire additional workers at that wage because they do not have to raise wages (including those of their existing workers) to hire more workers.

In such circumstances, the wage demands of unions, at least for a range of wage increases, are not constrained by the possibility of reduced employment opportunities. Clearly there is room for considerable bargaining in these circumstances in that there is a range of wage increases that the monopsonist can absorb. With so much to gain and lose one would expect a high degree of conflict in organizing and in bargaining — an observation that seems borne out in the isolated one-industry towns that characterize monopsony.

METHODS OF ACHIEVING COMPENSATION GOALS

Given their various objectives and sources of power, unions use a variety of methods — some direct, others indirect — to achieve their compensation goals. The direct methods usually have to do with the setting of union wage rates; the indirect methods usually involve changing the conditions and power relationships under which collective bargaining take place. Different methods may be followed by different unions, and the same union may change its methods over time as objective circumstances (the economy, legislation) change. The main methods through which unions achieve their compensation goals are collective bargaining and interest arbitration, restricting labour supply, altering the demand for union labour, wage fixing in the nonunion sector, and altering the bargaining environment, process, and structure.

Collective Bargaining and Interest Arbitration

Collective bargaining is the most direct and the most common way for unions to influence the compensation of their members. Because the collective agreement, by law, has to cover all members of the bargaining unit, then the collective agreement rate will also apply to nonunion members of the bargaining unit. The ultimate sanction of the union, where it is allowed, is the strike; however, other sanctions such as work to rule (following exactly the requirements of the contract, company policy, or law, to the detriment of productivity), abuse of the grievance procedure, and even sabotage are possible.

The direct determination of compensation through the collective-bargaining process tends to be followed by industrial unions. They are constrained, in competitive markets, by the factors discussed in the previous section that influence the elasticity of demand for their labour, and hence the extent to which union wage increases would be countered by reductions in the overall work force of the organization.

Where the right to strike is not allowed, as in many elements of the public sector, then interest arbitration is usually used to determine the terms of a new collective agreement. Various criteria used by arbitrators include private sector comparability, prevailing community rates, ability to pay, productivity, cost-of-living changes, minimum required living standards, and the need to recruit and retain a viable work force. Unions will obviously try to convince the arbitrator to use criteria that are favourable to their position, and they will abandon these criteria when they become unfavourable.

Restricting Labour Supply

Craft unions and professional associations will try to affect their compensation indirectly through control of labour supply. Devices used by craft unions include such factors as the hiring hall, apprenticeship ratios, and high union dues, as well as more extreme devices like discrimination. By restricting labour supply to the trade, wages will be higher than they would be in the absence of the restriction.

Professional associations behave much like craft unions in their ability to control the supply of labour to their profession. This ability may be quite powerful as in the case of self-licensing professions, such as medicine or law, whereby only those with the *licence* may practice; or it may be less powerful as in the case of certified professions, whereby others can practice, but only those who are *certified* can use the requisite title. In the latter case, substitutes are possible, but they may be imperfect substitutes in the sense that they cannot use the professionally designated title.

This power of occupational self-licensing was usually granted by law to the profession, ostensibly to protect the public interest when the public was required to purchase certain professional services that were often complicated to evaluate, infrequently purchased, and involved severe adverse consequences if the services were improperly provided. Because the provision of the services was so complicated, only members of the profession itself were deemed capable of deciding how they should best be provided. Hence, the profession was given the power to regulate itself. Thus, self-regulating professions were put in the unique position of determining not only the demand for their services (only they could tell their clients how much of their services to purchase), but also the supply of their services through self-licensing.

Under such circumstances, there is the possibility that professional groups may try to artificially raise their salary by increasing the demand for and reducing the supply of their services. Even if this is not a conscious intent, it may be a by-product of their desire to provide only the highest-quality service to the consuming public. This potential is even greater under circumstances where third parties or public revenues are used to pay for the service.

Devices that can be used by professional groups to control the supply of labour to their occupation include the entry and exit rates for professional schools, training requirements for new entrants, requirements with respect to residence or citizenship, and control over the extent to which paraprofessionals can perform the service. Policies that pass the cost of these restrictions on to new entrants into the profession are particulary attractive to incumbent professionals (who are the ones who decide on the requirements) because the latter group would appropriate the benefits of the higher compensation, while the new professionals would bear many of the costs. Hence, increasingly stringent training requirements, with "grandfather" clauses stating that incumbent experienced professionals do not have to meet these requirements, could be expected. Once the new professionals become incumbent professionals, they may have a tendency to require even further stringent requirements: the potential for costly overqualification is obvious.

Altering Demand for Union Labour

Unions could also increase the wages of their members by increasing the demand for union labour and by making that demand more inelastic so that union wage increases would not be dampened by the threat of employment cuts. From our previous discussion of the determinants of the elasticity of demand for labour we saw that unions may do this through supportive advertising (for example, the union label) and contract provisions on technological change, contracting out, or restrictive work practices. At the political level, unions may also support protective tariffs, import quotas, and controlled immigration. They would also support income-maintenance programs and aggregate-demand policies that would reduce the pool of low-wage or unemployed labour.

Wage Fixing in the Nonunion Sector

As an indirect way of altering the demand for union labour, unions may also support wage-fixing policies that would raise the wages of nonunion labour, thereby reducing the substitution of such labour for union labour. The main elements of wage-fixing legislation are minimum wages, equal pay for equal work, fair wages on government contracts, and wage extension by decree.

Unions have to walk a fine line in supporting such legislation, however, because it could clearly be used as a substitute for unionization: if legislation can take care of workers, then clearly there would be less need for unions. It is ironic, in fact, that much wage-fixing legislation originated with the (hidden) objective of reducing the need for unions. Over time, however, unions have been able to utilize such legislation for their own ends to reduce nonunion competition.

Altering the Bargaining Environment, Process, and Structure

In an even more indirect fashion, unions may try to affect their compensation gains by altering the environment, process, and structure in which collective bargaining takes place. Quantifying the importance of these various factors and examining a broad array of collective-bargaining outcomes has been the focus of an emerging new industrial-relations literature on union effectiveness and bargaining outcomes (1, 7, 29).

Especially in times of wage controls, unions could be expected to bargain for changes in their bargaining environment or structure that would enhance their *future* wage gains; with current wage increases being restricted, they may well trade off current for future wages. In fact, as a quid pro quo for their acceptance of wage restraints, governments may give the labour movement a political concession that would enhance their future bargaining position.

Environment — There are various aspects of the environment in which collective bargaining takes place that unions may try to alter in their favour, especially through their central organization and through political action. Changes in labour-relations legislation can obviously alter relative bargaining strengths as, for example, if legislation requires the closed shop whereby nonunion workers in the bargaining unit are required to pay union dues. Having aspects of health and safety and minimum-labour standards covered by legislation also enables unions to concentrate their bargaining on other factors.

The overall economic environment can also affect union bargaining power; hence, unions support full-employment policies, in part, so that employers do not always have a pool of low-wage labour as a potential substitute for union labour. As discussed in Chapter 10, it is also the case that the union strike threat is more effective in times of prosperity and full employment when inventories are low, personal savings are replenished, and alternative jobs are available.

Unions may also try to alter the distribution of power relationships in society as a whole. This will be regarded as especially important by those who feel that the wages of workers are determined not only by the human-capital characteristics of workers (as emphasized by neoclassical economists) and by the characteristics of jobs (as emphasized by dual- and segmented-labour-market perspectives), but also by the distribution of power relationships in society which determine relative shares of income for the various groups. Attempts by unions to obtain a social contract or tripartitism can be regarded as attempts to alter the overall power relationship within which collective bargaining takes place.

Process — Unions may also try to alter the process of collective bargaining in a manner that is conducive to their objectives. In general, most aspects of the process are ones for which both parties feel that there is potential for mutual gain; this is the case, for example, with respect to continuous bargaining, joint committees, or productivity bargaining. Other elements of the process, however, will benefit one party more than the other, and in such circumstances one would expect the losing party to trade off such elements only in return for other concessions. This could be the case, for example, with respect to contract expiration dates or the use of third parties.

Structure — The structure of bargaining — in particular the degree of centralization of the bargaining and negotiating units — can have an obvious effect on bargaining outcomes. To a large degree, the structure is imposed by labour-relations boards in their determination of the appropriate bargaining unit. In Canada, this has traditionally led to decentralized units in part because a requirement for more centralized units would have effectively precluded some organizing drives. The structure is essentially malleable, however, and can be affected by such factors as union mergers, the merging or breaking away of bargaining units, and accreditation of employers' associations. The structure is also affected by collective bargaining; the setting of common expiration dates on contracts, for example, effectively dictates a form of centralized bargaining. A degree of centralization also results under pattern bargaining when a specific contract sets the pattern for related sectors and under interest arbitration when certain wage awards set a precedent. The decree system also, whereby mutually agreed-upon rates are extended throughout the industry, is effectively a form of centralized bargaining.

While the structure, and in particular the degree of centralization, can have an obvious impact on bargaining outcomes, there is not a consensus on the expected direction of that impact. Centralized structures may give unions monopoly power and a greater threat because they can shut down a whole sector. These unions are also not as subject to "whipsawing" whereby multiplant employers can shift production to other firms in the event of a strike. Employers are also more willing to concede in centralized systems whereby a uniform wage increase for all employers in a given product market does not give a competitive advantage to any one employer. On the other hand, with greater union power comes greater responsibility, with unions that bargain centrally being under public and government pressure to exercise restraint in the national interest; this may be especially prevalent in times of wage-price restraint. In addition, centralized bargaining can prevent a single union from disrupting a whole sector by shutting down the weakest link. Centralized employer structures may also enable employers to behave as monopsonists, paying a lower wage because they dominate the labour market.

In theory then, the degree of centralization can have an indeterminate impact on bargaining outcomes. Unfortunately, little empirical evidence exists on the actual effect of centralized versus decentralized bargaining structures—a serious omission because the degree of centralization is a variable over which policy makers have an element of control. Swidinsky (50, p. 16) provides empirical evidence from Canadian data to suggest that "negotiated wage settlements tend to be higher under a centralized bargaining structure (multiemployer and employers' association negotiation units) than under a decentralized structure (employer-wide and single-plant negotiation units)." However, the differences were not very great, being approximately one percentage point (p. 19).

Swidinsky cites evidence from the United States (19) and from Britain (51) indicating that centralized bargaining actually leads to slightly lower wage settlements, although there are exceptions and the relationship can be complex depending upon the degree of centralization of employers and employees as well as the structure of product markets. In essence, the limited number of empirical studies do not find uniform results; however, they do suggest that whatever the impact of centralization on bargaining outcomes, it is likely to be very small and may not be uniform across jurisdictions. This result should not be surprising, however, since it is unlikely that either labour or management would bargain away a structure that would seriously affect its long-run bargaining position, nor is it likely that such a structure would be imposed upon the parties by a legal arrangement.

It is also the case that it would be extremely difficult to detect empirically the impact of different bargaining structures, since those that are bargained for and that can be expected to increase wages are likely to require unions to accept lower current wages as a concession to obtain the more favourable bargaining structure. In addition, for those elements of structure that are determined legislatively, causality may work in both directions. That is, in order to achieve a balance of power, labour boards may provide low-wage sectors with a structure that would enhance their future power. Thus, it should not be surprising to find sectors with low-wage settlements having a bargaining structure that is conducive to high settlements if low wages were accepted as a trade-off for future bargaining power, or if boards try to enhance the power of low-wage sectors with a bargaining structure that would increase their future power. Clearly, the estimation of the effect of bargaining structure on collective-bargaining outcomes requires a careful specification of the expected relationship that recognizes the dynamic nature of the timing of the relationship as well as the two-way causality.

This is in fact true of any attempts to measure the effectiveness of unions in obtaining various collective-bargaining outcomes. What is a beneficial outcome to the union (for example, a union security clause) that is obtained as a trade-off for lower wages in one round of bargaining, may be a measure of union power and effectiveness in a subsequent round, leading to higher wage settlements. What is a trade-off for wages in one period may lead to higher wages in subsequent periods. It is therefore crucial to recognize these trade-offs and feedbacks in an attempt to measure the effects of various union characteristics on collective-bargaining outcomes.

SOME PROBLEMS IN ASCERTAINING THE UNION IMPACT

Attempts to quantify the impact of unions have met with numerous estimation problems, the most important being that of separating cause and effect and that of controlling for quality differences.

Separating Cause and Effect

Conventional wisdom suggests that causality runs in the direction of unions causing higher wages in the union sector. However, there are reasons to suggest that causality may also operate in the other direction; that is, that unions are more likely to arise in situations where high wages already persist. In such circumstances, estimation procedures that do not account for this reverse causality may erroneously give credit to unions for creating a union-nonunion wage differential. Simultaneous-equation estimation procedures are required to account for this reverse causality.[1]

There are numerous possible rationales for causality running in the direction of high wages "causing" unionization, as well as vice versa. Ashenfelter and Johnson (3) — who were the first to formally deal with the simultaneity problem — argued that unionization may be more likely to arise in high-wage sectors because they are easier to organize, and because the high wages may enable workers in such sectors to afford to buy more of everything including union services.

The "exit-voice" theory advanced by Hirschman (20) can also be used to explain the causality from high wages to unionization. Hirschman argued that the traditional mechanism of economists — competition or the threat of "exit" — was not always a preferred or available device in all markets. There are situations where exit is precluded or where it is preferable to try to improve the situation not by leaving or threatening to leave (that is, exit), but rather by utilizing various forms of "voice." In fact, where exit is precluded or difficult, then voice becomes a more important device for improving the situation.

Some firms may pay high wages to reduce turnover, to have a large queue of applicants, or to be known as a model employer. Workers in these firms would be reluctant to leave because of the high wages — that is, exit is reduced. When exit is reduced they will turn to voice as the mechanism to improve their situation. Unions can be recognized as the institutional embodiment of voice whereby workers attempt to have a say in their work environment (12, 13, 16). The causality runs from high wages and hence reduced exit to unionization as the form of voice.

An appealing element of this perspective is that it reconciles the view of industrial-relations analysts, who emphasized the importance of the union in achieving due process and job security at the work place, with a view of economists who emphasized the wage impact of unions. Unions are associated with *both* higher wages for their members and job security and due process at the work place.

Quality Differences

Another problem in measuring the pure wage impact of unions occurs because there are likely to be quality differences between union and nonunion workers if union workers have a wage advantage over nonunion workers. Firms that pay the higher union wage rate are likely to have a longer queue of applicants relative to firms that pay the lower nonunion rate, and this will occur whether unions cause the higher wage or are a result of it. In such circumstances, union firms can be more selective in their hiring and recruiting procedures, thereby obtaining higher-quality workers

---

1. In econometric terminology, the simultaneous-equation estimation techniques are required to account for the fact that unionism is endogenous (itself a function of wages) rather than simply an exogenous determinant of wages. To the extent that one is estimating the impact of unions that have been in existence for a considerable period of time, however, it may be reasonable to assume such unionization to be exogenous and hence to use single-equation estimates (30, pp. 336-338; 40, pp. 104-111).

with more of such factors as education, training, and experience. Such firms may also try to increase the job assignment, for example, by increasing the pace of work; however, such adjustments will be resisted by the union lest they offset the union wage impact itself.

In these circumstances, it is extremely important to control for differences in the characteristics of workers and job assignments in measuring the pure impact of unions on wages. Otherwise these "omitted variables" may lead to an upward bias in the union impact, because the union-nonunion wage differential would reflect better quality workers and perhaps more onerous job assignments in the union sector as well as the pure impact of unions on wages.

Measurement Techniques and Data

The vast majority of studies of the union impact have focused on measuring the union-nonunion wage differential since only union and nonunion wages can be observed. This does not necessarily reflect the impact of unions on the wages of their members since unions can affect the wages of nonunion workers (in a manner to be discussed subsequently). In essence, because the nonunion wage can be affected by unions it need not reflect the wages that would be paid in the absence of unions. Although some studies (for example, 2) have tried to estimate the nonunion wage itself and thereby control for the effect of unions on nonunion wages, most have simply estimated the union-nonunion wage differential, recognizing that this may reflect the impact of unions on both union and nonunion wages.

To be able to attribute the union-nonunion wage differential purely to the impact of unions it is necessary to control for other wage-determining factors that may influence the wage differential. These factors usually include the characteristics of the workers (for example, education, experience, sex) and the characteristics of the jobs (for example, occupation, industry, region). As indicated previously, it is extremely important to control for these factors since, faced with a union wage increase, employers will try to be more selective in their hiring decisions, and they may try to change the nature of job assignments.

The impact of these factors is usually controlled for through the use of multiple-regression analysis which indicates the effect on wages of each explanatory variable, including a measure of unionization, while holding the other wage-determining factors constant. The regression equation is usually estimated from aggregate industry data relating the wages in an industry to the proportion of the industry that is unionized, or on disaggregated data of individual establishments or workers that are both unionized and nonunionized. Simultaneous-equation estimation techniques have increasingly been used to account for the possibility that unionization and labour quality may be affected by wages.

IMPACT OF UNIONS

In varying degrees, the numerous empirical studies of the impact of unions have attempted to account for the measurement problems just discussed. Unions can have an impact on various aspects of compensation including wages and wage structures, nonunion wages, fringe benefits, and productivity. The important impact of unions on job security and due process as well as their possible impact on inflation and unemployment are beyond the scope of this chapter.

Impact on Wages and Wage Structures

Lewis and earlier studies — The classic work of H. Gregg Lewis (37) both reviews and reanalyses the existing literature in the United States and provides new estimates up until the year 1963. While there was considerable variation in the estimated impact in the studies reviewed by Lewis, he attributed much of the variation to methodological differences. Lewis' estimate of the union-nonunion wage differential, based on his own work and a reanalysis of the earlier studies, was approximately 10-15 percent, being larger in recessions and smaller in periods of inflation, reflecting the fact that unions induce wage rigidity over the business cycle, insulating wages from cyclical fluctuations.

Post-Lewis studies — Since Lewis' work there have been numerous additional studies estimating various aspects of the union impact and usually utilizing new data sets where the unit of observation is the individual establishment or worker. These studies, many of which have been reviewed elsewhere (42, 49), provide some tentative generalizations, although for almost every generalization, there are exceptions in some particular studies.

The more recent estimates tend to be higher than the 10-15 percent recorded by Lewis; estimates in the 20-30 percent range are typical. The impact tends to be greater in large establishments and for females and when a large part of the relevant jurisdiction is organized. The impact is higher for blue-collar workers than for white-collar workers, and it can be exceptionally high in certain specific sectors like construction. Unions appear to have reduced overall wage differentials (14) and possibly income inequality (21). Union wages appear to be less subject to cyclical fluctuations, although there are notable exceptions (41), and they are less responsive to differences in the individual characteristics of workers (4, 9, 43).

Perhaps somewhat surprisingly, the union impact tends to be smaller in the public than the private sector. After reviewing some nineteen studies of union wage impacts in the public sector, Lewin, Horton, and Kuhn (36, p. 54) conclude that "the average wage effect of unionism in a public sector is roughly in the order of 5 percent. This is a considerably smaller impact than is popularly asserted and is perhaps between one-half and three-quarters less than the estimated impact of private sector unions."

Simultaneous-equation estimates — Studies that have tried to account for the fact that high wages may "cause" unionism as well as vice versa show mixed results. Some (3, 16, 17) find the union impact to be statistically insignificant or quantitatively unimportant, and other more recent studies find it to remain both statistically significant and large (6, 7, 9, 24, 26, 33, 35, 39). While disconcerting in the sense that these studies do not provide a consensus of evidence on this important question, nor a reconciliation of their results, this should not be surprising since it is a well-known econometric phenomenon that simultaneous-equation estimates can be extremely sensitive to the specification of the relationship.[2]

Canadian Studies

Since there are so few Canadian studies of the union impact, they can be summa-

2. The simultaneous specification requires the use of an instrumental variable that affects unionization but does not affect earnings. Such variables are not readily apparent, and the results may be sensitive to the instrumental variable that is used. It may simply be the case that the available data does not enable identifying the underlying structure of the complex relationship between unions and wages.

rized on a study-by-study basis. In general, they tend to confirm the patterns found in the United States studies, although there are some differences.

Starr — Utilizing establishment data[3] from the Canada Department of Labour 1969 Occupational Wage Rate Survey, Starr (49) estimates the union-nonunion wage differential for production workers in Ontario to lie within the range of 10 to 17 percent. The union impact tends to be greater in heavily organized industries, in situations where labour costs are a small portion of total costs, and in large plants and monopolistic product markets, and it is also more significant for unskilled than skilled workers and for blue-collar as opposed to white-collar workers.

Kumar — Although it was not designed specifically to measure the impact of unions, Kumar's study (31) related interindustry variation in unskilled wages to a variety of wage-determining characteristics, including the proportion of employees covered by a collective agreement. He finds a statistically significant and positive relationship between the extent of unionization and the wages of unskilled workers. Calculations (11) indicate that the implied union-nonunion wage differential is 17 to 23 percent.

Christensen and Maki — Aggregate industry wage data is also used by Christensen and Maki (7, 39). They estimate that an increase of 10 percentage points in the proportion of workers covered by a collective agreement is associated with a 4.2 percent increase in wages for the average production worker. Their results were not affected when simultaneous-equation estimation techniques were utilized to take account of the possibility that unionization may be a function of wages or that labour quality may be higher in the union sector (39). In their subsequent study, (7) they also concluded that the union wage effect was not much larger under a union shop (32.6 percent) whereby all employees in the bargaining unit are required to join the union, as opposed to the open shop (30.7 percent) whereby members of the bargaining unit need not be union members nor pay union dues. Hence they conclude that union power is not increased by the union shop. (Based on more disaggregated United States data, however, they do find that the union shop increases the union wage gains (6); hence, their conclusion based on the more aggregate Canadian data should be regarded as tentative.) They also find that the union wage effect was substantially larger for internationally based unions (31 percent) as opposed to nationally based unions (15 percent).

MacDonald and Evans — MacDonald and Evans (38) also relate aggregate industry wage data for production workers to the proportion of employees covered by a collective agreement and calculate the union-nonunion wage differential as 24.0, 11.3, and 13.6 for skilled, semiskilled and unskilled workers respectively, over the period 1971-1976.[4] The differential is smaller the greater the proportion of the industry that is organized, suggesting that as the industry becomes more organized

---

3. The study by Starr is the only one in Canada to use microeconomic data at the level of the individual establishment. In his study, wages in a particular occupation are related to whether or not the occupation is covered by a collective agreement. The other Canadian studies use aggregate industry data, relating wages in the industry to the proportion of workers unionized or covered by a collective agreement. There is no Canadian data that provides union status of individual workers; hence, it is difficult to make comparisons with most of the recent U.S. studies which are based on such data.

4. Their utilization of data, for the period 1971-1976 enables more accurate estimates than those from their earlier study (11) based only on 1971 data because the pooled time-series cross-section data enables more precise controls for differences in possible omitted variables (such as worker quality) since it is reasonable to assume that these factors will not change much in the same industry over time. In econometric terms, this enables the estimation of a "fixed-effect" error-component model.

nonunion wages rise more rapidly from the "threat" effect than do union wages from the "coverage" effect, the latter reflecting the difficulty of substituting towards nonunion output as coverage increases. The differential tends to be slightly larger in periods of inflation, suggesting that union wages are not as "sticky" as conventional wisdom suggests, perhaps because inflation is increasingly anticipated.

Impact on Nonunion Wages

There are a variety of mechanisms whereby unions can affect the wages of nonunion workers. To the extent that unionized wage increases reduce employment opportunities in the unionized sector the excess supply of labour from the unionized sector should serve to depress wages in the nonunion sector. This may be mitigated if unions are able to featherbed, requiring the use of excess supplies of labour in the union sector. On the demand side, the demand for nonunion labour, and hence the nonunion wage, will be affected in an indeterminate manner by an increase in the wages of union workers. The demand for nonunion labour may increase to the extent that it can be substituted for the now more expensive union labour. Unions will clearly resist such a substitution but it may occur in a subtle fashion, for example through contracting out, by using nonunion supervisors, or even by relocating to a nonunion sector. In addition, there may be a shift in output demand from the products produced by the more expensive union sector to those produced in the cheaper nonunion sector. (This may be minimized if the whole sector can be organized). On the other hand, the demand for *some* nonunion labour may decrease to the extent that it is complementary to union labour or to the extent that firms reduce their scale of output (in the extreme, perhaps even closing down) in response to the higher union labour cost; in such circumstances the firms may employ less of both union and nonunion labour.

Institutionally, there are other forces at work whereby nonunion wages are affected by unionization. As discussed previously, unions can affect nonunion wages through their support of wage-fixing legislation, which applies mainly to the nonunion sector. In addition, nonunion firms may raise their wages to avoid the *threat* of becoming unionized. In the extreme, they may pay wages in excess of the going union wage rate to avoid what they regard as other costs (notably interference with managerial prerogatives) associated with becoming unionized. Nonunion firms may also be compelled to raise their wages so as to compete with unionized firms for a given work force, or to restore traditional wage relativities that may have existed prior to unionization. This argument, however, ignores the fact that nonunion firms should not have to worry about recruiting problems or restoring traditional wage patterns because they will have a supply influx of workers who cannot get jobs in the high-wage union sector; in essence, market forces suggest that their recruiting problems will be lessened and that there will be less pressure to maintain a traditional wage pattern.

Clearly, there are a variety of institutional, market, and legislative forces at work whereby unions affect the wages of nonunion workers. Since these forces do not all work in the same direction, it is not possible to state theoretically the expected impact of unions on the wages of nonunion workers; one must appeal to the empirical evidence.

In his earlier work, Lewis (37, p. 194) concludes that unionism has probably lowered the wages of nonunion workers but by a small amount, by less than 3 or 4 percent. Kahn finds that nonunion wages are decreased by unionism (25, 27);

however, the overall average effect masks considerable variability, with some groups such as nonunion white males receiving a large wage increase from unionism. Rosen (45) indicates that the threat effect (the extent to which nonunion wages are raised to avoid the threat of unionization) is negatively related to the extent of organization of the industry; this somewhat surprising result may reflect the fact that once the industry is highly organized those persons who remain unorganized are unlikely ever to become organized and, hence, pose no potential union threat.

Impact on Fringe Benefits

As indicated in the introductory chapter, unions bargain for a wide range of factors in addition to wages. In fact, some recent empirical evidence (13, 23) indicates that unions increase the fringe benefits of their members even more than they increase their wages. There are numerous reasons why all parties — labour, management, and the government — in the industrial-relations scene may prefer fringe benefits over wages as a form of compensation (18, p. 204). Workers may prefer the tax advantage, economies of scale and administrative simplicity of group purchases, and the chance to avoid wage controls. Employers may also benefit from the specific fringe-benefit purchases of their employees to the extent that they facilitate the planning and operation of the production process and reduce turnover. Governments may prefer fringe benefits (and hence grant favourable tax treatment) because expenditures on items like pensions and workers' compensation and unemployment insurance may reduce pressure for government expenditures in these areas.

While there are these reasons for the existence and growth of fringe benefits, the question remains as to why this growth should have been greater in the union than nonunion sector. That this has occurred is not surprising to industrial-relations analysts who have long regarded unions as a main vehicle for winning fringe benefits; but the question remains as to why fringe benefits have been a preferred form of compensation for union workers even more than nonunion workers. There are theoretical reasons to suggest why this is so.

To the extent that union workers are made better off as a result of unionization, they can afford to buy more of everything including fringe benefits; this will be especially important to the extent that they enter higher tax brackets and fringe benefits are not taxed. In addition, being a political institution of "voice" (12, 16), unions can be expected to represent the wishes of the average worker (more specifically, the median voting member) as opposed to the marginal worker whose interest is most likely to be represented by the mechanism of "exit" or mobility. Since the average worker is more likely than the marginal worker to be older, with seniority and with a family, then these collective preferences are more likely to favour fringe benefits, especially pensions and life, accident, and health insurance. In addition, the collective preferences of senior employees are more- likely to prefer layoffs (which would fall on younger workers) as opposed to wage or hour reductions as devices to cope with reductions in demand. This portrayal of the collective preferences of workers is regarded as one of the important communication functions that unions are able to perform.

Fringe benefits in the form of deferred compensation may also be more prevalent in unionized establishments. Deferred wages may be a preferred form of compensation for employers because they would provide employers with a threat to ensure effort from their work force (32). In addition, they would reduce turnover since employees who quit would lose some or all of their deferred wages (for example, pension and vacation rights). Employees may willingly accept deferred wages if they are given a sufficiently high wage to compensate for some of it being deferred (and hence its receipt being uncertain), and/or if they are provided with sufficient guarantees that employers will ultimately pay the deferred wages. Such guarantees are more likely when they are provided in a collective agreement which, for example, prevents arbitrary dismissal. In essence, unionization makes the payment of fringe benefits in the form of deferred wages a feasible compensation scheme. Hence we would expect such fringe benefits to be associated with unionization.[5]

Impact on Productivity

Although recognized for a long time by industrial-relations analysts (48) the potential positive impact of unions on various aspects of productivity has only recently been analysed and quantified by labour economists (5, 8, 16). As indicated by Freeman and Medoff (16), there are two dominant views of trade unions. The monopoly view regards unions as creating economic inefficiency by raising wages above the competitive norm, by inducing strikes, or by requiring featherbedding work rules which compel the employer to use inefficient amounts of union labour. An alternative view regards unions as having some positive effects on productivity by reducing turnover, "shocking" management into more efficient practices, improving morale and cooperation among workers, providing information about the collective preferences of workers, and by improving communications between labour and management.

As indicated throughout this chapter, the preponderance of empirical literature on the impact of unions has focused on the extent to which unions raise wages above the competitive wage that otherwise would prevail. That unions do this would not be denied by trade unionists since one of the avowed purposes of the trade union movement is "to take labour out of the market." To the extent that there is this wage impact, however, it will lead to inefficiencies in that management will utilize excessive amounts of capital and nonunion labour relative to the higher-priced union labour, and it will utilize excessively high-quality union labour. Rees (44) has estimated that these inefficiencies have led to an output loss of approximately 0.14 percent of gross national product in the United States in 1957.

While the preponderance of studies have focused on this wage impact of unions, there is a growing econometric literature on the more positive impacts of unions on various aspects of productivity. Specifically, unions have been found to lower quit rates (15, 34) and raise output per worker (5, 8, 16). Based on the estimated magnitude of these productivity increases, Freeman and Medoff (16, p. 80) suggest: "In manufacturing, productivity in the organized sector appears to be substantially higher than in the unorganized sector, by an amount that could roughly offset the increase in total costs attributable to higher union wages."

There is also evidence that unionized environments have more strenuous work

5.   This also highlights another problem associated with measuring the impact of unions on wages. The average union-nonunion wage differential may not reflect the deferred wages that union members are likely to have. The problem is compounded by the fact that the current wages of union workers are likely to be lower because some of their wages are being deferred; on the other hand, they are raised somewhat to compensate for the uncertainty of these deferred wages. A complete measurement of the union wage impact would require a comparison of the lifetime wage profile of union and nonunion workers. Reverse causality is also at work here. That is, the causality is running from a higher union wage profile to unionization (which is necessary to ensure payment of the deferred wage portion) rather than vice versa.

conditions, for example a structured work setting, inflexible hours, and a faster work pace. This may reflect the fact that unionism is more likely to occur in response to such working conditions or that employers are able to respond to the union wage advantage by changing the conditions of work. Without being able to disentangle the true cause and effect, Duncan and Stafford (10) estimate that about two-fifths of the union-nonunion wage differential reflects a compensating wage for these more onerous working conditions. Kalachek and Raines (28) find that employers are able to offset some of the union wage-cost increase by more stringent hiring standards, notably with respect to the education qualifications of their workers.

While these productivity-inducing effects are likely to offset some of the wage-cost increases due to unionism, it is unlikely that they offset all of them. If they did, then one would expect to see managers, or at least stockholders, welcoming the encroachment of unions — a phenomenon that is not usually observed except for "company unions" that management controls. In essence, at least some of the wage gains of unions represent real gains to union workers and real costs to employers, otherwise one would not expect to see workers organizing or employers resisting unionization.

CONCLUDING OBSERVATIONS

There is probably no single statement concerning the impact of unions that can be made with absolute certainty. This even applies to the question of whether unions have *any* impact on the compensation of their members. For every generalization, there are at least some studies that are in disagreement.

Perhaps this should not be surprising, given the large number of studies based on different methodologies and data sets and given the subtle complexities of what, on the surface, appears to be a relatively simple measurement problem. In spite of this seemingly negative conclusion, the variety of studies have provided us with some generalizations that seem to be more robust than others.

It appears that unions have had a positive impact on the compensation of their members, and this impact is larger for females, blue-collar workers, and workers in the private as opposed to the public sector. Overall, unions have probably reduced wage disparities and have had a larger impact on fringe benefits than wages.

Some of the more recent avenues of research have highlighted the complexities that are involved in this relationship; however, more work is needed before firm generalizations can be made from these statistics. Unionism may be a result of, as well as a cause of, high wages. Also, unionized establishments may adjust to costly union wage increases by raising their hiring standards and altering their work conditions. Unions may also have a beneficial impact on productivity, and this may offset some of the wage-cost increase associated with unionism.

These new research issues in the area of union impact relate to various phenomena that have been discussed extensively in the literature on descriptive, institutional industrial relations. Understanding this literature can therefore contribute to our knowledge of the feedbacks that are involved and the mechanisms that enhance union effectiveness in attaining a broad array of outcomes. In that sense, further understanding in the area of union impact will probably come from utilizing the institutional industrial-relations literature to indicate the feedback adjustments and interrelated processes that are important, combined with the newer econometric techniques that can account for these complex relationships in estimating the impact of unions. Progress in understanding this area, as in so many in industrial relations, will come from a judicious blend of theory, institutional knowledge, and statistical analysis.

REFERENCES AND WORKS CITED

1. Anderson, J. "Determinants of Bargaining Outcomes in the Federal Government of Canada," *Industrial and Labor Relations Review,* Vol. 32, (1979), 224-241.

2. Ashenfelter, O. "The Effect of Unionization on Wages in the Public Sector: The Case of Fire Fighters," *Industrial and Labor Relations Review,* Vol. 24 (1971), 191-202.

3. Ashenfelter, O., and G. Johnson. "Unionism, Relative Wages and Labor Quality in U.S. Manufacturing Industries," *International Economic Review,* Vol. 13 (1972), 488-507.

4. Block, F., and M. Kuskin. "Wage Determination in the Union and Non-Union Sectors," *Industrial and Labor Relations Review,* Vol. 31 (1978), 183-192.

5. Brown, C., and J. Medoff. "Trade Unions in the Production Process," *Journal of Political Economy,* Vol. 86 (1978), 355-378.

6. Christensen, S., and D. Maki. "Labour Union Effects on Wage Gains." Mimeo, Simon Fraser University, 1980.

7. Christensen, S., and D. Maki. "The Union Wage Effect in Canadian Manufacturing Industries," *Journal of Labor Research* (forthcoming).

8. Clark, K. "The Impact of Unionization on Productivity: A Case Study," *Industrial and Labor Relations Review,* Vol. 33 (1980), 451-469.

9. Duncan, G., and D. Leigh. "Wage Determination in the Union and Nonunion Sectors: A Sample Selectivity Approach," *Industrial and Labor Relations Review,* Vol. 34 (1980), 24-34.

10. Duncan, G., and F. Stafford. "Do Union Members Receive Compensating Wage Differentials?" *American Economic Review,* Vol. 70 (1980), 335-371.

11. Evans, J., and G. MacDonald. "On Estimating the Union-Nonunion Wage Differential in Canada." Economics Working Paper, York University, 1976.

12. Freeman, R. "Individual Mobility and Union Voice in the Labor Market," *American Economic Review Proceedings,* Vol. 66 (1976), 361-368.

13. Freeman, R. "The Effect of Trade Unionism on Fringe Benefits." Working Paper 292, National Bureau of Economic Research, 1978.

14. Freeman R. "Unionism and the Dispersion of Wages," *Industrial and Labor Relations Review,* Vol. 34 (1980), 3-23.

15. Freeman, R. "The Effect of Unionism on Worker Attachment to Firms," *Journal of Labor Research,* Vol. 1 (1980), 29-62.

16. Freeman, R., and J. Medoff. "The Two Faces of Unionism," *The Public Interest,* No. 57 (1979), 69-93.

17. Gerhart, P. "Determinants of Bargaining Outcomes in Local Government Labor Negotiations," *Industrial and Labor Relations Review,* Vol. 29 (1976), 331-351.

18. Gunderson, M. *Labour Market Economics: Theory, Evidence and Policy in Canada* (Toronto: McGraw-Hill, 1980).

19. Hendricks, W. "Labor Market Structure and Union Wage Levels," *Economic Inquiry,* Vol. 13 (1975), 401-416.

20. Hirschman, A. *Exit, Voice and Loyalty* (Cambridge, Mass.: Harvard University Press, 1970).

21. Hyclack, T. "The Effect of Unions on Earnings Inequality in Local Labor Markets," *Industrial and Labor Relations Review,* Vol. 33 (1979), 77-84.

22. Hyclack, T. "Unions and Income Inequality," *Industrial Relations,* Vol. 19 (1980), 212-215.

23. Ichniowski, C. "Economic Effects of the Firefighters' Union," *Industrial and Labor Relations Review,* Vol. 33 (1980), 198-211.

24. Kahn, L. "Union Impact: A Reduced Form Approach," *Review of Economics and Statistics,* Vol. 59 (1977), 503-507.

25. Kahn, L. "The Effect of Unions on the Earnings of Non-Union Workers," *Industrial and Labor Relations Review,* Vol. 31 (1978), 205-216.

26. Kahn, L. "Unionism and Relative Wages: Direct and Indirect Effects," *Industrial and Labor Relations Review,* Vol. 32 (1979), 520-532.

27. Kahn, L. "Union Spillover Effects on Unorganized Labor Markets," *Journal of Human Resources,* Vol. 15 (1980), 87-98.

28. Kalachek, E., and F. Raines. "Trade Unions and Hiring Standards," *Journal of Labor Research,* Vol. 1 (1980), 63-76.

29. Kochan, T., and H. Wheeler. "Municipal Collective Bargaining: A Model and Analysis of Outcomes," *Industrial and Labor Relations Review* (1975), 46-66.

30. Kochan, T. *Collective Bargaining and Industrial Relations* (Homewood, Ill: Irwin, 1980).

31. Kumar, P. "Differentials in Wage Rates of Unskilled Labor in Canadian Manufacturing Industries," *Industrial and Labor Relations Review,* Vol. 26 (1972), 631-645.

32. Lazear, E. "Why is There Mandatory Retirement?" *Journal of Political Economy,* Vol. 87 (1979), 1261-1284.

33. Lee, L. "Unionism and Wage Rates: A Simultaneous Equations Model with Qualitative and Limited Dependent Variables," *International Economic Review,* Vol. 19 (1978), 415-433.

34. Leigh, D. "Unions and Nonwage Racial Discrimination," *Industrial and Labor Relations Review,* Vol. 32 (1979), 439-450.

35. Leigh, D. "Racial Differentials in Union Relative Wage Effects: A Simultaneous Equations Approach," *Journal of Labor Research,* Vol. 1 (1980), 95-114.

36. Lewin, D., R. Horton, and J. Kuhn. *Collective Bargaining and Manpower Utilization in Big City Governments* (New York: Universe Books, 1979).

37. Lewis, H. G. *Unionism and Relative Wages in the United States* (Chicago: University of Chicago Press, 1963).

38. MacDonald, G., and J. Evans. "The Size and Structure of Union-Nonunion Wage Differentials in Canadian Industry," *Canadian Journal of Economics*, Vol. 14 (1981), 216-231.

39. Maki, D., and S. Christensen. "The Union Wage Effect Re-Examined," *Relations Industrielles/Industrial Relations,* Vol. 35 (1980), 210-229.

40. Mitchell, D. *Unions, Wages, and Inflation* (Washington: Brookings Institution, 1980).

41. Moore, W., and J. Raisian. "Cyclical Sensitivity of Union/Nonunion Relative Wage Effects," *Journal of Labor Research,* Vol. 1 (1980), 115-132.

42. Parsley, C. "Labour Union Effects on Wage Gains," *Journal of Economic Literature,* Vol. 18 (1980), 1-31.

43. Pfeffer, J., and J. Ross. "Union-Nonunion Effects on Wage and Status Attainment," *Industrial Relations,* Vol. 19 (1980), 140-152.

44. Rees, A. "The Effect of Unions on Resource Allocation," *Journal of Law and Economics,* Vol. 6 (1963), 69-78.

45. Rosen, S. "Trade Union Power, Threat Effects and the Extent of Organization," *Review of Economic Studies*, Vol. 36 (1969), 185-196.

46. Schmidt, P. "Estimation of Simultaneous Equations Model with Jointly Dependent Continuous and Qualitative Variables: The Union-Earnings Question Revisited," *International Economic Review,* Vol. 19 (1978), 453-465.

47. Schmidt, P., and R. Strauss. "The Effect of Unions on Earnings and Earnings on Unions: A Mixed Logit Approach," *International Economic Review,* Vol. 17 (1976), 204-212.

48. Slichter, S., J. Healy, and R. Livernash. *The Impact of Collective Bargaining on Management* (Washington: Brookings Institution, 1960).

49. Starr, G. *Union-Nonunion Wage Differentials* (Toronto: Ontario Ministry of Labour, 1973).

50. Swidinsky, R. "The Effect of Bargaining Structure on Negotiated Wage Settlements in Canada." Economic Council of Canada Discussion Paper 139, Ottawa, 1979.

51. Thompson, A., C. Mulvey, and M. Farbman. "Bargaining Structure and Relative Earnings in Great Britain," *British Journal of Industrial Relations,* Vol. 15 (1977), 176-191.

QUESTIONS

1. Discuss the various goals of unions and indicate the implications of these goals for their impact on wages, fringe benefits, and wage structures.

2. "The power of unions depends on the economic environment in which unions operate." Discuss.

3. Discuss the determinants of the elasticity of demand for union labour in both the construction industry and the public sector, indicating what this should imply about the ability of unions to achieve wage gains in those sectors.

4. "Unions can have no long-run impact on wages because if they did then unionized firms would go out of business." Discuss.

5. Discuss the impact of unions on the wages of *non*union workers.

6. Discuss how unionized firms may adjust their hiring standards and working conditions when faced with unions. What does this imply about the measured union-nonunion wage differential?

7. Discuss the mechanisms whereby unions may be a *response* to high wages as well as a *cause* of high wages. What does this imply about the measured union-nonunion wage differential?

8. Why might fringe benefits be a preferred form of compensation for union members even more than for nonunion members?

9. Discuss the mechanisms whereby unions may affect productivity. What does this imply about the cost to the firm that results from unionization?

10. "The study of unionization represents a fertile ground for the judicious blending of a knowledge of institutional industrial relations, economic analysis, and statistical techniques." Discuss, specifically highlighting the strengths and weaknesses of each of these areas.

KENNETH P. SWAN

12. Union Impact on Management of the Organization: A Legal Perspective

The legislation establishing collective-bargaining rights created a legal structure within which those rights must be vindicated. Aspects of that structure, especially the duty to bargain and the grievance-arbitration system, have had a direct effect on the balance between union influence and management authority in the work place.

INTRODUCTION TO THE "MANAGEMENT-RIGHTS" CONTROVERSY

The Historical Background

The advent of statutorily sanctioned collective bargaining in Canada produced a dramatic shift in power balances within unionized enterprises. Until the spread of labour relations legislation on the Wagner Act model, borrowed from the United States after World War II, the legal status of collective agreements was in considerable doubt, and unions which went for assistance to the courts were met with the argument that their hard-won agreements were legally unenforceable documents whose terms could only be implemented against a recalcitrant employer by economic self-help — that is, by resort to strikes, slow downs or picketing. Although unions were often judicially upbraided for breaching those very agreements when they took to the picket lines to compel an employer to accept their interpretation of a disputed provision (4, pp. 326-330), no other effective enforcement mechanism was available. Thus economic sanctions were necessary both at the negotiation stage, in order to induce an employer's consent to include a desired term in a collective agreement, and at the enforcement stage, to require the employer to acquiesce in the reasonable interpretation of a provision and to comply with it. Such crude methods rarely encouraged the negotiation of comprehensive agreements or the development of sophisticated interpretive approaches.

Modern Canadian labour-relations statutes, however, contain certain common features that have led to the evolution of the collective agreement as a code for relationships in the work place; a code which not only deals with pay, hours, and benefits, but which commonly limits, at least in relation to the use of human resources, the scope of managerial authority. First, there is a legal duty on employers to recognize a certified trade union as exclusive bargaining agent for a unit of employees, to negotiate in good faith, and to make every effort to conclude a collective agreement to cover those employees. Second, collective agreements are now binding in law on employers and trade unions (and on associations of either where broader-based bargaining takes place) as well as on individual employees. Third, the mechanism for interpretation and enforcement of the collective agreement is now the grievance-arbitration process, a system of informal specialist tribunals with a distinctive and burgeoning jurisprudence. Each of these ingredients has contributed significantly to the limitation of managerial freedom of action.

The duty to bargain in good faith is a duty imposed by the law and enforceable by either party against the other through a range of sanctions which has been broadened over the history of our collective-bargaining system (2). The duty includes a requirement to make every reasonable effort to conclude a collective agreement, and thus its ambit will depend upon the reach of collective bargaining. In this respect, Canadian experience has considerably outstripped that in the United States, where the concept of a requirement to bargain originated. The American jurisprudence, by the identification of subjects for bargaining as either "mandatory" (a duty to bargain can be enforced and economic weapons may be deployed) or "permissive" (bargaining need only take place by mutual consent), has effectively narrowed the range of matters that the law requires to be bargained.[1] In particular, managerial initiatives "at the core of entrepreneurial power" are not mandatory subjects of collective bargaining and remain subject to unilateral employer action, without even consultation with or notice to the union (5). Thus a wide range of management prerogative has been preserved from any legal obligation to bring it to the bargaining table.

The legal structures in Canada contain no such limitation. The Ontario legislation, for example, defines a collective agreement as including "terms and conditions of employment or the rights, privileges or duties of the employer, the employers' organization, the trade union or the employees." The breadth of this provision makes considerable encroachment on managerial control of an enterprise legally possible. Provisions in other provincial legislation are more narrowly drawn than in Ontario, but the American doctrine has simply never taken hold in Canada.[2] As a consequence, virtually any provision not intrinsically illegal may be advanced by a union for inclusion in a collective agreement and may, if rejected by the employer, be supported by strike action. The extent to which this theoretical legal potential has been converted into practical results is the subject of this chapter.

The "Management-Rights" Issue

The potential shift in the balance of control of the enterprise which the new legislation presented soon led to a debate about its practical effect, a debate no less riveting because of the prolonged and formal way in which it unfolded. Collective agreements were, under the new regimes, legally binding. They were also enforceable through the specialized labour tribunals comprising the grievance-arbitration sys-

---

1. The principal source of the U.S. doctrine is *National Labour Relations Board* v. *Wooster Division of Borg-Warner Ltd.*, 356 U.S. 342 (1958).

2. The reason is probably the decision of the Supreme Court of Canada in *Syndicat Catholique des Employés de Magasins de Québec, Inc.* v. *Compagnie Paquet Ltée.* (1959), 18 D.L.R. 2d 346 and see *Pulp and Paper Industrial Relations Bureau and Canadian Paperworkers Union* (1978), 1 Can. L.R.B.R. 60.

tem, whose decision makers (sometimes judges, more frequently academics) were pioneers in private adjudication. From the beginning, those decision makers perceived that their role was to include the articulation and application of labour-relations policy, and thus they took directions which courts would never, at least at that point in history, have pursued. Arbitrators have been encouraged to act as "labour-relations physicians," charged with interpreting collective agreements in the light of transcendent labour-relations objectives (15, pp. 16-17). Although that view has not received universal acceptance, it has had a considerable influence on patterns of arbitral decision making and has received tacit recognition by most arbitrators as an aspect of the arbitral process.

Given the legal enforceability of collective agreements and the nature of the mechanism of arbitration chosen for their enforcement, it was inevitable that philosophical issues would soon arise in the course of apparently routine interpretation disputes. For one thing, collective agreements were codes of rights and obligations negotiated in the context of an eternity of employment relationships in which employers directed and workers obeyed. What was to happen in the new system when an employer took an initiative about which the collective agreement offered no guidance and the workers balked? Was the statutory collective-bargaining structure to act only as an exception in a system where, presumptively, the job of management is to manage and the job of workers is to work; or was it a new beginning, a reallocation of human resource control from exclusive management initiative to joint administration by employer and union? The debate began in both Canada and the United States (8, 12) at about the same time in the 1950s and lasted in its original form in this country for more than a decade, only to be revived recently in a new guise.

The leading proponent of the more radical characterization of the labour-relations legislation as a new beginning was Professor Bora Laskin, now Chief Justice of Canada. In a 1953 arbitration award, he advanced this analysis:

> In this Board's view, it is a very superficial generalization to contend that a Collective Agreement must be read as limiting an employer's pre-collective bargaining prerogatives only to the extent expressly stipulated. Such a generalization ignores completely the climate of employer-employee relations under a Collective Agreement. The change from individual to Collective Bargaining is a change in kind and not merely a difference in degree. The introduction of a Collective Bargaining regime involves the acceptance by the parties of assumptions which are entirely alien to an era of individual bargaining. Hence, any attempt to measure rights and duties in employer-employee relations by reference to pre-collective bargaining standards is an attempt to re-enter a world which has ceased to exist. Just as the period of individual bargaining had its own "common law" worked out empirically over many years, so does a Collective Bargaining regime have a common law to be invoked to give consistency and meaning to the Collective Agreement on which it is based.[3]

This was, however, the high-water mark of the "shared-rights" theory of managerial authority over the employment relationship. By 1966, another prominent arbitrator was obliged to conclude that a consensus had developed in favour of a "residual-rights" theory.[4] This approach regards collective bargaining as a mere super-

---

3. *Re Peterboro Lock Mfg. Co. Ltd.* (1953), 4 L.A.C. 1499, at p. 1502 (Laskin).

4. *Re Russelsteel Ltd.* (1966), 17 L.A.C. 253 (Arthurs).

imposition of a collective agreement on the employment relationship so that virtually unlimited managerial authority is restricted only to the extent that a collective agreement expressly limits its operation. Although recent jurisprudence has softened this approach somewhat, it remains the basis on which collective agreements are now negotiated in Canada.

Its practical impact is that whatever limitation unions wish to impose on a presumptive managerial discretion to control the use of labour in an enterprise must be expressly bargained for during the negotiation of a collective agreement. That requirement, with its associated costs, has circumscribed the intrusion of union influence into the historical areas of management discretion. Since the duty to bargain in good faith only requires negotiation and not agreement, every concession coming from management in bargaining must either be bought by backing down on other demands or forced by resort to economic sanctions. In either way, collective-agreement provisions encroaching on managerial prerogatives will, if resisted by the employer, be won only at a significant cost to the union and to its members. Moreover, although it is difficult to generalize, there has been a natural employer disposition to resist vigorously any encroachment on its traditional prerogatives (9). As a result, there has been little indulgence in symbolism in this area; union power has been concentrated for the most part on limiting managerial discretion over matters directly and practically affecting critical job interests and only tentatively has it been used to assert broader influence over the actual direction of the enterprise.

UNION IMPACT ON PERSONNEL DECISIONS

The Limits of Union Influence

Because of the necessity to bargain for every encroachment on the traditional managerial prerogatives at the same time as bargaining for improvements in wages and benefits, there has been a tendency for unions to direct their primary efforts in negotiations to matters directly affecting employment. The core of union negotiating objectives has moreover been directed to improving the lot of employees actually at work, so that once wages, benefits, and related issues such as overtime schemes, sick leave, and other income-protection systems have been inserted into the collective agreement, unions have turned next to negotiating provisions to enhance the notion of "property" in a job. Under this rubric may be included protections against dismissal, termination, demotion, layoff, and involuntary transfer; all these constitute a code of prohibitions against arbitrary treatment. Also included are rights with respect to promotion and transfer. The extent and nature of negotiated protections and opportunities for employees actively at work are discussed below. First, however, the degree to which unions have succeeded in controlling employer discretion at the initiation and the conclusion of the employment relationship is reviewed.

The Hiring Process and Union Security

At the initiation stage, the involvement of unions in the hiring process has been, with a few minor and one major exception, negligible. The minor exceptions have occurred in professional or public employment, where, for example, the adequacy of hiring procedures has been a matter of concern. Although other examples exist, the prevalence of procedural requirements for hiring for teaching posts in university-faculty agreements are a paradigm for this sort of restriction on management prerogative.

The major exception is the preentry "closed shop," a form of union-security provision which requires that only union members in good standing be hired to meet the employer's labour requirements. Although, again, exceptions exist, the closed shop is often coupled with union operation of a "hiring hall," a sort of employment agency which selects union members to fill an employer's request and has the exclusive right to refer workers to the employer. Such provisions are the rarest form of union-security clauses (16, p. 393), and most unions are content either to negotiate a "union-shop" provision under which employees must become union members after hiring, or an "agency-shop" clause, where employees must pay to the union an amount equivalent to union dues whether they become members or not. In any case, to this limited extent, and in the specific industries (construction, longshoring, seafaring, and so on) in which they exist, such clauses constitute virtually the only effective intervention by unions in the process of attracting, selecting, and hiring prospective employees.

Probation and Acquisition of Seniority Status

Probationary periods of varying lengths are common practice in collective agreements. Their purpose was originally to provide management with an opportunity to assess a new employee without regard to the extensive arbitral jurisprudence on dismissal and without any union input into this process. Thus agreements often include an employer's right to "reject" or "release" an employee during the probationary period and a prohibition against such a decision becoming the subject of a grievance or of going to arbitration.

These clauses have been negotiated against a reluctance on the part of arbitrators to hold employers to strict tests of "just cause" for release of probationers. It has been widely accepted that employers have a legitimate claim to secure the most competent and effective work force available (3, pp. 385–386). The probationary period has classically been regarded as an extension of the hiring process, and without express direction from the collective agreement arbitrators have been unwilling to impose outside review on managerial decisions in this area. Thus, even in the absence of clauses excluding arbitration of grievances relating to release of probationers, arbitral deference has considerably diminished the scope for union involvement in the assessment of probationary employees.

Nevertheless, this is a volatile area of arbitral jurisprudence, and two recent trends are evident. The first is a series of cases[5] in which arbitrators have asserted authority to review the decision to release an employee against criteria which judge not only the factual basis of the employer action but also the reasonableness of the standards against which the employee was measured. Taken as a whole, this approach would recognize a special employer interest in selecting employees but would assert arbitral supervision over the standards of selection and the application of those standards in individual cases. In the most comprehensive awards, there is a clear intention to ensure that a probationary period constitutes a fair opportunity for a new employee to demonstrate ability and suitability, and thus matters such as the extent of employer direction and counselling of the new employee during

---

5. The paradigm case, but not the earliest example of this approach, is *Re Porcupine Area Ambulance Service* (1974), 7 L.A.C. 2d 182 (Beatty).

probation have been considered relevant to the propriety of the decision. Although these cases still comprise a minority of the awards on release of probationers, they appear to be the new wave. Thus, where the parties to an agreement are unwilling or unable to negotiate a specific ban on arbitral interference in selection decisions during probation, there will be at least a limited scope for arbitral review of management action in this regard.

The second recent trend directly affecting probationary employees concerns the legality of any attempt to restrict access to grievance and arbitration for such employees. Arguments have been best developed in Ontario, but may well be applicable elsewhere, that any restriction on the arbitrability of grievances is statutorily prohibited. The basis of this argument is section 37(1) of the Ontario Labour Relations Act (R.S.O. 1970, c. 232, as amended) which provides:

> 37. — (1) Every collective agreement shall provide for the final and binding settlement by arbitration, without stoppage of work, of all differences between the parties arising from the interpretation, application, administration or alleged violation of the agreement, including any question as to whether a matter is arbitrable.

If "all differences" must be submitted to arbitration, the argument continues, how can parties to a collective agreement legally provide for the exemption of an entire class of differences — disputed releases of probationers — from the operation of the arbitration procedure? This argument was first accepted by arbitrators but rejected by the courts; however, the Ontario courts have recently concluded that any disputed issue which constitutes "a difference" must be settled at arbitration if the parties are unable to resolve it earlier. Specifically, the court found that arbitral review of the release of workers on probation could be carefully circumscribed by the parties but could not be wholly excluded.[6]

The combination of these two trends in the jurisprudence probably has the result of bolstering union negotiating power on the conditions of probation. If the parties cannot simply make the problem go away by excluding all release grievances from arbitration, they will be faced with either accepting the growing tendency toward arbitral review or negotiating their own standards in the collective agreement. Since the preservation of freedom of action in posthiring selection is clearly in management's interests (a related union interest in avoiding entirely the expense of grievance administration and arbitration appears to have been foreclosed by the latest court decisions), management must propose, negotiate, and pay for — by trade-offs during negotiations on other bargaining priorities — any improvement over the developing norm of arbitral review.

This aspect of labour-management relations is an example of the interaction of the arbitration process and the negotiation process. While earlier, the way in which unions used bargaining to make inroads on management prerogatives was examined, here progress is made on another front. By pursuing grievances to arbitration and arguing for broad interpretive approaches to legislation and collective agreements, unions have exerted control over the way in which management makes its decisions. The extent of that control is limited to a voice in the process — a fair hearing and application of reasonable standards — but it may be that even such a degree of control satisfies all legitimate union objectives. Where proper manage-

---

6. *Toronto Hydro-Electric System* v. *Canadian Union of Public Employees* (1980), 80 C.L.L.C. para. 14, 035 (Ont. Div. Ct.). This decision was upheld by the Ontario Court of Appeal. Leave to appeal to the Supreme Court of Canada has been refused.

ment functions are being exercised, it may be sufficient for unions to have the power to intervene to protest abuse.

Discipline and Discharge

The classical example of the use of arbitration to curtail management power is found in the areas of discipline and discharge. For obvious reasons, protections against discharge and other disciplinary penalties have always been a high priority for unions, and it is usual to include a provision in the collective agreement permitting discharge or discipline only for "just cause," or some similar phrase. Rarely is such a provision omitted, and even when it is, some arbitrators have asserted a right to review disciplinary decisions on the basis of the common law of employment prevailing before collective bargaining, which required that cause be shown for a discharge if sufficient notice was not given. Although there are cases to the contrary, the recent court decisions on the arbitrability of grievances relating to release on probation would appear to be applicable a fortiori to discipline of employees with seniority status. Moreover, there is a growing tendency for legislatures to give a statutory right to arbitration of discipline and discharge grievances.

Whether there is a universal right to grieve against discipline or whether the almost universal collective-agreement provisions are controlling, the jurisprudence developed by arbitrators on when employers may discipline employees, what procedures must be followed, and what penalties may be exacted constitutes a comprehensive code for the exercise of management disciplinary power. The starting point was the common law of employment developed by the courts before statutory collective bargaining, but the momentum of thousands of cases pressed by unions before hundreds of arbitrators has built up a body of precedent in the last thirty years far more substantial and sophisticated than the courts were able to produce in centuries.

From the beginning, the arbitrators asserted authority not only to determine whether "just cause" as asserted by the employer existed or not, as an exercise of a fact-finding function, but also to decide what the content of the "just-cause" notion is, an exercise of a normative function in setting standards for industrial discipline. These functions were never contentious, since they grew directly from the common law of employment. Finally, however, arbitrators asserted a remedial authority to reinstate dismissed employees and to substitute a lesser penalty, thus assuming a sort of sentencing function. There was a brief period when the courts balked at this extension of arbitral authority, but legislatures soon overturned judicial objections, and arbitrators in every province except Quebec (where the problem does not seem to have arisen) have now been given an express statutory authority to substitute for a penalty imposed by an employer such a penalty as seems to the arbitrator to be just and reasonable. There is no doubt that such remedial authority is essential to the operation of the arbitration system; there is equally little doubt that the result has been a transfer of the ultimate authority in determining disciplinary penalties from the sole prerogative of management to either the arbitrator or a joint union-management decision to settle the grievance before it goes to arbitration. It is now possible to discern definite trends in arbitral approaches towards certain kinds of disciplinary issues. This is not the place to discuss the relative merits of managerial discretion and arbitral review as disciplinary mechanisms, and indeed only a few scholars have attempted any such discussion (1). It is enough to observe that all of the theoretical and doctrinal issues involved in employment discipline are now subject to arbitral control and, indeed, initiative (3, pp. 361-392). Three aspects of this development, however, merit further study here: arbitral treatment of employer-promulgated rules, the content of the doctrine of insubordination, and the evolution of "progressive-discipline" concepts. Each of these aspects has had a considerable influence on managerial control over the work force.

Company rules — Before the advent of collective bargaining, the only limits on employer authority to discharge were found in the definition of "just cause" articulated by the courts. Since, in this definition, an employee owed a duty of faithful service to an employer, a failure to obey instructions issued by an employer could constitute cause. Instructions may be give generally, as in widely promulgated rules, or specifically, in direct orders. A disobedience of direct orders raises the issue of insubordination, a flouting of symbolic authority. Merely acting contrary to general rules, without the aspect of confrontation, is less serious; nevertheless, such delinquency would have afforded just cause for discharge at common law.

Because of the outcome of the "management-rights" debate described earlier in this chapter, arbitrators have accepted that the promulgation of rules on a virtually unlimited range of subjects relating to the operation of the work place is entirely within the prerogative of management. They have, at the same time, placed limitations on the kinds of rules which may be promulgated, the obvious requirement being that the rule not be inconsistent with or contrary to the express terms of the collective agreement, since provisions negotiated into the agreement serve as checks on management action. In addition, however, arbitrators have also required that rules be clear and unequivocal; that they be expressly communicated to an employee before the company can enforce the rule against that employee; that the rules have been consistently and universally enforced; and that the express disciplinary aspect of a rule must also be communicated if a breach of the rule is relied upon to justify discharge. Finally, and most important, in addition to all of these essentially procedural requirements, arbitrators have insisted that such rules not be unreasonable (3, pp. 149-153).

By asserting authority to determine what rules are reasonable, arbitrators have placed an implied limitation on the scope of managerial action. In making that determination, they have attempted to balance the employer's interest in a safe, efficient, and orderly operation of the enterprise against the rights of individuals to be treated fairly. Although there are other examples, perhaps the most striking instance of arbitral control on employer initiation of rules is found in the "personal-appearances" cases (3, p. 150, n. 62), by which a previously generally accepted right of management to require employees to meet certain standards of neatness, dress, and comportment has been circumscribed by an assertion of an individual's right to personal freedom in matters of appearance, subject only to such legitimate employer concerns as health and safety or, in a rapidly diminishing minority of cases, a vital "public-image" problem.[7]

The reasonableness requirement has, therefore, established another way in which unions may, by appeal to arbitral powers, place limitations on the way in which managerial control over the work force is exercised. This requirement applies, of course, only to nonconfrontational disobedience of general rules. Where the symbolic authority of the employer is challenged by a direct refusal to obey a present order, different considerations apply.

---

7. See, for example, *Re Dominion Stores Limited* (1972), 23 L.A.C. 257 (Brandt); *Re Air Canada* (1975), 9 L.A.C. 2d 254 (Deverell).

Insubordination — Arbitrators have consistently held, on the basis of the proposition that "an industrial plant is not a debating society,"[8] that employees must promptly obey instructions given to them by management and test the propriety of those orders subsequently through the grievance procedure; this has been called the "obey now, grieve later" rule. In general, the rule is designed to protect the productivity of the enterprise and to ensure disciplined, orderly operation (3, p. 343). Thus the rule will, in general, apply even where the order given is clearly unreasonable or is potentially contrary to the collective agreement; redress can always be obtained, the rule assumes, by submitting and processing a grievance.

Even here, where short-term symbolic authority and operating efficiency are given priority over rights which can be vindicated elsewhere in the future, exceptions have grown up to protect individual employees from the rigours of the rules. In general, the exceptions have been based upon a corollary to the theory that employee interests can adequately be protected by the grievance procedure: where no such protection can be secured, or where it would come too late to be effective, the rule will not apply.

The entire range of particular exceptions forms a complex code of work place relationships and is expanded from time to time as new cases may require (3, pp. 347-354). Included in the code are a right to refuse to perform an illegal act, to refuse an order the obedience of which involves a reasonable fear for health and safety, and for a union official to refuse an order to neglect duties which would cause irreparable harm to other employees. In addition, some hint of a reasonableness test may be found in cases which permit employees to refuse to obey orders to alter personal appearance (such as instructions to shave off a beard) or directly related to personal privacy (such as an order to permit a physical search). Particularly where the order is to work a compulsory overtime assignment, a rather wider exception to accommodate reasonable personal excuses has grown up (3, pp. 356-358).

Finally, although the rule recognizes a general managerial authority to maintain production by requiring orderly and disciplined response to supervisory instructions, its impact will be lessened as the instructions deal with matters not directly related to production; this may be the real reason for the personal appearance exception, for example. Nevertheless, even where the maintenance of production is directly involved, the arbitral jurisprudence offers some leeway for employee, and union, challenges to the moment-by-moment supervision and direction of the work place.

Disciplinary penalties — By statutory intervention, control over the appropriate penalty to be involved in a particular case has been lodged with arbitrators. As a result, virtually every disciplinary arbitration hearing includes a plea for a reconsideration of the penalty even if it is found that some culpable conduct has occurred. Arbitrators regularly deal with the propriety of the penalty applied, and whether it is just and reasonable in all the circumstances.

The scope of arbitral review appropriate to this exercise is the subject of some debate, and a variety of statements of the correct approach may be extracted from the cases. At one extreme, arbitrators have practised deference to the managerial computation of penalty, provided that it was not made in an arbitrary, unreasonable, or manifestly unjust fashion. At the other, they have asserted a right and a

---

8. *Re Ford Motor Co.*, 3 L.A. 779 (Schulman).

responsibility to conduct a review of the penalty from first principles. In between the extremes, a compromise approach has been to ask if the penalty imposed falls within the range of reasonable disciplinary responses (3, pp. 363-364).

While no solid consensus has yet emerged, some arbitrators have begun to construct theories of industrial discipline by reference to which a specific penalty may be judged. Perhaps the most widely debated are the notions of corrective discipline and progressive discipline, which are different facets of the same theory: that industrial discipline ought to be designed to rehabilitate rather than to punish or to deter. Thus, for any given incident the appropriate penalty is one which is corrective and which will provide an employee with an opportunity to improve and adapt to the requirements of employment.[9] Similarly, where a series of minor infractions is alleged to justify a conclusion that an employee should be dismissed, arbitrators will ensure that the disciplinary response to each infraction has been appropriately chosen to produce a course of progressive disciplinary penalties leading to discharge (3, pp. 381-382).

These theoretical approaches have certainly not been universally accepted, yet they demonstrate that initiative in constructing industrial-discipline systems no longer rests solely with management. Rather, to the extent that they are able to persuade arbitrators to accept their arguments, unions have gained considerable influence not only in respect of the actual discipline imposed in specific cases but also in the formulation of disciplinary policy. Ironically, the only exception provided by the legislative enactment of arbitral review of disciplinary penalties occurs where the collective agreement itself provides a specific penalty. Thus, the only way employers can insulate a disciplinary policy from arbitral review is to bargain with the union.

In conclusion, the institution of arbitration as the mechanism for reviewing disciplinary decisions has produced a shift from an essentially management-controlled discipline function to one in which union influence may be exerted, albeit through argument in an adversarial process rather than by direct bargaining. In particular, certain aspects of the day-to-day direction of the work force have been altered by arbitral decisions in such a way as to limit supervisory direction both procedurally and substantively. Although much scope is left for managerial initiative, and there remains an element of arbitral deference to management decisions in some areas, the overall effect has been to limit the way in which management runs the enterprise.

Seniority and Its Applications

Understandably, given the factors reviewed above, the major focus for the union negotiating power unleashed by modern labour-relations legislation was the preservation of the employment relationship itself. Job security in various forms, and protected by various mechanisms, was and remains a vital concern of union negotiators. Although there are exceptions to the rule, unions have almost invariably chosen seniority as the yardstick of job security.

The origins of the seniority system are entangled with the history of the trade-union movement, and to some extent job security based on seniority has traditionally

---

9. The theory is developed and expounded in *Re Galco Food Ltd.* (1974), 7 L.A.C. 2d 350 (Beatty) and *Re Toronto East General Hospital* (1975), 9 L.A.C. 2d 311 (Beatty). An exhaustive discussion of the issues involved in arbitral review of disciplinary penalties may be found in *Re Phillips Cables Ltd.* (1974), 6 L.A.C. 2d 35 (Adams).

been a hallmark of union employment. Nevertheless, it is an idea with so much to offer that it has been generally adopted in our society as at least one factor to be considered in allocating employment benefits. Thus, priority for some employment benefits, such as first choice in scheduling vacations, may be conditioned on seniority. In addition, service-based differentials in fringe benefits may also be negotiated, so that more senior employees have longer vacations, higher pay, more sick leave protection, or greater severance pay on termination.

More importantly, seniority may also be used as a direct curb on managerial discretion, by providing an ostensibly objective basis on which to decide which of two or more employees is to be favoured in the exercise of that discretion. It appears that the original purpose of seniority systems was to prevent managerial decisions from reflecting favouritism, antiunion bias, or similar discriminatory factors. The usual applications of seniority which act as a direct check on managerial authority are controls on promotion, transfer, layoff, and recall. In these applications, seniority operates to secure a type of property right in a job (11, pp. 201-202). In a seniority system, managerial arbitrariness is prevented, so the theory goes, by the provision of a rigid, objective test to determine which employee is to get a desired promotion or transfer, or to retain work in a layoff.

Seniority is attractive because of its simplicity, its ease of application and its objectivity (13, pp. 1005-1006). It may even be encouraged by management to the extent that it encourages the retention of workers with experience and training with the company. Seniority, however, has its drawbacks, and unions have had to compromise between their own interests in demonstrable objectivity and the competing interests of management (and doubtless many junior employees) in rewarding "merit": skill, ability, qualifications, and the like. The negotiation of collective-agreement provisions which balance these interests in a mutually acceptable way has produced a number of formulations. The classical models either make the exercise of seniority rights conditional only on proof that an applicant meets a threshold of ability to perform the job, or alternatively establish a competition between applicants with seniority relevant only to break a tie and merit, and thus hybrid tests have emerged under which neither factor is clearly dominant and each must be considered and weighed in making a decision on promotion, transfer, layoff, or recall. However the test is formulated, management's rights to decide which employee is more meritorious are restricted by the extent to which seniority is inserted into the balance.

But this is not the only restriction on managerial prerogative: in addition, arbitrators have gradually developed a theory of arbitral review of the merit component of such decisions as a check on the way in which managers determine the outcome of merit tests or competitions. The development of this theory is still continuing, and the courts have recently become involved in the debate, so any conclusions drawn now about the ambit of arbitral review must be tentative. This much is clear, however: arbitrators are bound to interpret and apply the collective agreement under which they act and must hold the employer, when requested by the union, to strict compliance with the tests set out in the agreement.

At first, arbitrators were content to assure themselves that managerial decisions had been made without evidence of discrimination, bad faith, or unreasonableness. In due course, the test by which the absence of unreasonableness was determined came to be an affirmative examination of the evidence to derive a standard for reasonable decision making. This standard was still applied, however, with considerable deference to the employer's decision, since arbitrators expressed a reluctance to "second guess" the exercise of a managerial function (3, pp. 253-260). As required by an Ontario court decision[10] accepted by arbitrators in most, but not all,[11] other jurisdictions, arbitrators may no longer use findings of managerial honesty and reasonableness as a cloak for deference but must decide, on the basis of the language negotiated in a collective agreement, whether the decision made by management complies with the requirements of the test provided.

Under current arbitral review, management is restricted in its freedom to select employees to benefit by promotion, desired transfer, or recall or to be adversely affected by demotion, undesired transfer, or layoff. Management discretion is restricted by both the mathematical certainty of the seniority component and by the collective-agreement language chosen to express the merit component. Obviously, management may attempt to win more freedom of action by negotiating clauses including a broader scope for employer discretion. What evidence there is about negotiating patterns does not indicate any trend towards softer clauses relating to the application of seniority; indeed, collective agreements including a "straight-seniority" promotion or layoff clause, the form most limiting of managerial discretion, have actually increased slightly in numbers over the past few years (16, p. 391).

Thus the creation of a type of property right in a job, including both a measure of security of tenure and some right to consideration for opportunities for advancement, has resulted in the development of constraints on managerial discretion. Those constraints have been expanded by a combination of union negotiating power to require stringent collective agreements and the growth of a concept of arbitral review of the administration of the area of decision making still left for managerial initiative.

UNION IMPACT ON PRODUCTION DECISIONS

At a level beyond that relating directly to the employment of an individual worker are decisions that, while they may also have a considerable impact on working life, are directed to the management of the work place as a whole and to control of the productive processes. At this level, union bargaining power becomes diluted, and only very specific and vital concerns are usually brought to the bargaining table by unions.

Indeed, it is not unusual for unions to withdraw entirely from management decisions at this level. About three-quarters of collective agreements include a "management-rights clause" (16, p. 390), and although these may take innumerable forms, they will commonly reserve to management the right to manage and operate the enterprise, assign work, determine work methods, procedures and equipment, schedule production, and direct the work place. Even without an explicit management-rights provision, however, it is generally accepted by arbitrators that these functions, as the essence of management, properly belong to the employer and its managerial personnel (3, p. 172).

---

10. *Canadian Food and Allied Workers, Local 175* v. *Great Atlantic and Pacific Co. of Canada Ltd.* (1976), 76 C.L.L.C. para. 14,076 (Ont. Div. Ct.).

11. See, for example, *Re British Columbia Housing Management Commission* (1977), 15 L.A.C. 2d 121 (J.M. Weiler).

Because of this general assignment of functions, coupled with the "residual-rights" theory which permits management to act unilaterally on matters not covered by the collective agreement, it is generally conceded that an employer has the right not only to assign work as it sees fit among members of the bargaining unit but also to assign the work somewhere else entirely. The usual example of such a decision is "contracting out."

Contracting Out

In certain circumstances, employers may find it advantageous to have some work done by an independent contractor. Often this will involve production of a part or a subassembly and will be done in some other location. Sometimes, however, work to be done on the work site itself is contracted; the usual examples are cleaning and janitorial services, security guards, or cafeteria and food services. This is the classical case of a management decision, taken for productive reasons, potentially causing disruption to individual employees, usually in the form of redundancy or layoff. Indeed, the cases discussed earlier in which the "reserved-rights" theory was developed were all cases of contracting out.

The result of the development of the residual-rights theory was to permit management to contract out unless the collective agreement expressly forbids it. There are a very few limitations on this general right, and they are designed for the most part to deal with "sham" contracts designed only to avoid the legitimate collective-bargaining rights of the union. Once an employer can demonstrate a valid business purpose and an assignment in good faith, however, contracting out will be permitted in the absence of collective-agreement prohibitions even if the result is to wipe out the entire bargaining unit by having all of its work done on contract by others (3, pp. 180-183).

Negotiation of a prohibition on contracting out would seem to be an urgent priority for unions. The need for such clauses, however, varies from sector to sector, and their incidence depends on union bargaining power. In primary industries and manufacturing, powerful unions and abundant opportunities to contract out have resulted in specific prohibitions being negotiated into about two-thirds of all agreements (16, p. 413). Elsewhere, the incidence is lower; overall, only about half of all collective agreements include such prohibitions, although they are slowly becoming more common.

Perhaps it is obvious that a prohibition on contracting out removes a degree of freedom from the employer in its quest to make production as efficient and as inexpensive as possible. No doubt vigorous bargaining by management to avoid such clauses has contributed to their slow acceptance.

Work Assignment

Controls on the generally accepted right of management to assign work freely among its own employees arise chiefly from two kinds of collective-agreement provisions, those defining which employees are in the bargaining unit and those relating to classification, job description, and wage structures. The first controls are implicit and operate simply by applying the definition of the bargaining unit to anyone to whom work previously done in the bargaining unit is assigned. Thus, if production work is assigned to a supervisor, or office employee, the result may be merely to move that person into the production bargaining unit, thus reasserting union control over the job and its incumbent (3, pp. 183-187).

Controls of the second kind, involving classification, job description, and wage structures, are explicit and, indeed, are strictly construed by arbitrators. Nevertheless, if the parties construct a substantial and fixed classification and job-description system in the collective agreement, it may limit the right of management to assign work within the unit (3, pp. 187-202). Such provisions, however, are rare.

It should be observed, in passing, that the question of to whom a job is to be given may well be affected by the seniority-based provisions relating to promotion, transfer, and recall. Thus the placement of individuals into a reorganized production structure is likely to be subject to much more union influence than is the actual reorganization itself.

Occupational Safety and Health

Some protection for health and safety of employees has been created by permitting workers in appropriate circumstances to refuse to perform hazardous work without attracting discipline for insubordination. Given the vital importance of this issue, it is amazing how little impact unions in general have made in negotiating positive protections for health and safety. It is true that the incidence of collective-agreement provisions has now increased to the point that about 70 percent of workers are covered by some kind of clause. It is also true that some large and powerful unions have developed internal expertise and have begun concerted campaigns both in negotiations and in the public arena. Nevertheless, the usual clause is a mere recital of pious hopes or the establishment of a meaningless committee; provisions with real teeth are so rare as to be nearly nonexistent.

The reasons for this failure to negotiate meaningful solutions to such a central problem are uncertain. Some observers identify the unwillingness of unions to regard health and safety as a bargainable issue as founded on purely philosophical grounds; that is, that a safe working environment should be a basic right and not have to be bargained for. Other reasons for the lack of bargaining over safety issues include the informational and organizational difficulties in dealing with such matters in a collective agreement, or the lack of leverage over the relatively short term of a collective agreement over such long-term problems as industrial disease or toxicity (6, pp. 59-62; 7, pp. 19-22).

Whatever the reasons, legislatures have now taken the initiative, admittedly at the urging of unions among others, to set health and safety standards for industry on a universal basis. This entire area, therefore, is in the process of being removed from union influence except to the extent that unions participate in the administration, monitoring, or enforcement of the legislation.

UNION IMPACT ON STRATEGIC DECISIONS

At this final level of managerial initiative, far removed from the shop floor, any discussion of union intrusion on decision making must necessarily be discussed in terms of exceptions. Two areas deserve consideration: the limited controls unions have been able to exert over plant location and the rather more extensive union influence in matters of technological change.

Plant Location and Closing

As discussed elsewhere in this book, collective bargaining in Canada has traditionally been based on a single-employer, single-location bargaining-unit structure. The result has been that collective agreements are of local application only and do not have sufficient reach to deal with plant-location decisions. There are, of course, other bargaining-unit patterns, but even where national bargaining takes place, plant location and closing has never been a negotiating priority.

The one exception has arisen where employers have attempted to use plant location as a bargaining tool, by threatening to move production elsewhere unless negotiations produce a tolerable settlement; this tactic is often called the "runaway shop." While preserving an employer's right to relocate for valid business purposes, the Ontario Labour Relations Board has dealt with plant closures designed to defeat collective-bargaining rights with a broad application of its remedial authority. In one case, an employer had moved warehouse operations in a city to several smaller locations outside the city designed to serve exactly the same market as the closed warehouse; this was found to be an attempt to avoid a certificate for all employees in the city. The board ordered the employer either to reopen its original operation or to recognise the union as bargaining agent at all of the new locations. [12] In a similar case, where mixed motives of business efficacy and antiunion feeling were found, an employer was ordered to give affected employees first chance at jobs in the new locations and pay their relocation costs.[13]

Although these are marginal cases, they are examples of a way in which union influence can be exerted on relocation decisions, this time through the intervention of labour-relations boards. Another way is through political action, an avenue that is currently being pursued by unions concerned with plant shut-downs, particularly where foreign firms transfer production abroad in the process. By prevailing upon legislatures to enact stiff termination and redundancy pay legislation, organized labour might be able to increase the cost of shut-downs sufficiently to prevent some moving of production out of a jurisdiction. This is, of course, an exercise fraught with other costs. It is also a very indirect exercise of union power.

Technological Change

An area where rather more activity has taken place relates to decisions to alter productive processes or equipment, with resultant effects on job security. The sudden changes in employment levels produced by technological change have long been of concern to unions, and there have been attempts to bargain protections for individual employees for decades. Indeed, contracting-out clauses deal with a very similar problem.

The difficulty with technological-change disruptions is that they very seldom occur, and bargaining for them in advance requires a very long-sighted negotiation policy. Nevertheless, clauses are bargained and, perhaps as a sign of the times in the era of microtechnology and the silicon chip, they are increasing in incidence (16, pp. 390-391). The usual provisions range from a simple requirement for advance notice through requirement for consultation to a provision that reopens the collective agreement and provides for arbitration. For employees actually laid off because of the change, some agreements provide for retraining, relocation, wage guarantees, or work-sharing schemes (10).

12. *Humpty Dumpty Foods Limited* (1977), OLRB Rep. July 401.

13. *United Electrical, Radio and Machine Workers, Local 504 and Westinghouse Canada Limited* (1980), 2 Can. L.R.B.R. 469.

Collective agreements do not generally prohibit technological change but merely try to cushion its impact on employees. Once again, therefore, the emphasis is on job security rather than on entrepreneurial decisions, a pattern observed earlier. Even so, such provisions are most difficult to bargain for where they would be of most value, in unprofitable plants badly in need of updating, or in a declining labour market (14). Thus, some legislatures and Parliament have passed statutory technological-change provisions which require notice and permit a collective agreement to be reopened in mid-term to permit negotiation and, if necessary, strike or lockout action to be brought to bear on the issues arising from the proposed change. In these jurisdictions, obviously, the opportunity for the exercise of union power to intervene in technological-change decisions is considerably enhanced. Elsewhere, the existence of a binding collective agreement may prevent the use of economic sanctions, and even a negotiated reopener clause may fall afoul of the legal requirements for minimum collective-agreement terms of operation set out in the legislation. Even the most minimal protection of job security will, of course, limit managerial initiative to implement technological change. Real intervention will require hard bargaining as well as the assistance of a statutory scheme.

NEW DEVELOPMENT — THE DOCTRINE OF FAIR ADMINISTRATION

Although it is yet too early to assess the full implications of any trend, recent arbitration and court decisions suggest that some alteration may be made in the balance established when the "residual-rights" theory replaced the "shared-rights" theory with respect to managerial prerogatives. A few arbitration cases have developed a theory of "fair administration" of the collective agreement, in which arbitrators have concluded that, where management has a discretion to take action unfettered by external controls, it must nevertheless do so fairly and reasonably.

The use of this standard of arbitral review in the treatment of promotion and similar "merit" decisions has already been seen. One arbitrator has suggested that the new doctrine (which has been applied to such matters as transfers, applications for discretionary leave, and the like, where the collective agreement either vests management with discretion or is silent) is simply a general statement of the specific applications discussed.[14] Another arbitrator has announced the doctrine as the end of the "residual-rights" theory,[15] and at least one court has approved the use of the theory to establish a jurisdiction for arbitral review where the collective agreement was silent.[16]

For the moment, however, there is no consensus that employers have a generalized duty to act fairly and reasonably, in personnel decisions at least, even where the collective agreement is silent. If the theory is more widely accepted, there will be an expansion of the kind of approach already seen in arbitral review of promotion decisions, and a wider scope will be possible for union influence on management

---

14. *Re Photo Engravers and Electrotypers Ltd.* (1980), 25 L.A.C. 2d 88 (Adams).

15. *Re International Nickel Co.* (1977), 14 L.A.C. 2d 13 (Shime).

16. *Re Municipality of Metropolitan Toronto and Toronto Civic Employees' Union, Local 43* (1978), 79 D.L.R. 3d 249 (Ont. Div. Ct.). See also *Re Falconbridge Nickel Mines Ltd. and Brunner et al.* (No. 2) (1980), 28 O.R. 2d 787 (Ont. Div. Ct.).

action. As already noted, a right to challenge arbitrary personnel decisions is within the reasonable goals of unions; the doctrine of fair administration will simply provide another tool to be used to vindicate that right.

REFERENCES AND WORKS CITED

1. Adams, G.W. *Grievance Arbitration of Discharge Cases* (Kingston: Queen's University Industrial Relations Centre, 1978).

2. Adell, B.L. *The Duty to Bargain in Good Faith: Its Recent Development in Canada* (Kingston: Queen's University Industrial Relations Centre, 1980).

3. Brown, D.J.M., and D.M. Beatty. *Canadian Labour Arbitration* (Toronto: Butterworth, 1977).

4. Carrothers, A.W.R. *Collective Bargaining Law in Canada* (Toronto: Butterworth, 1965).

5. Cox, A. "The Duty to Bargain in Good Faith," *Harvard Law Review*, Vol. 71 (1958), 1401-1442.

6. Doern, G.B. *Regulatory Processes and Jurisdictional Issues in the Regulation of Hazardous Products in Canada* (Ottawa: Science Council of Canada, 1977).

7. Doern, G.B. "The Political Economy of Regulating Occupational Health," *Canadian Public Administration,* Vol. 20 (1977), 1-35.

8. Goldberg, A. "A Labour View," in *Management Rights and the Arbitration Process* (Washington: Bureau of National Affairs, 1956), pp. 118-148.

9. Joseph, P. "Management's Labour Relations Prerogatives," *University of British Columbia Law Review*, Vol. 14 (1979), 75-135.

10. Manson, A.S. "Technological Change and the Collective Bargaining Process," *Western Ontario Law Review,* Vol. 12 (1973), 173-221.

11. Meyers, F. "The Analytical Meaning of Seniority," *Proceedings of the Industrial Relations Research Association*, Vol. 18 (1965), 194-202.

12. Phelps, J.C. "Managements' Reserved Rights: An Industry View," in *Management Rights and the Arbitration Process* (Washington: Bureau of National Affairs, 1956), 102-117.

13. Schulman, H. "Reason, Contract and Law in Labour Relations," *Harvard Law Review*, Vol. 68 (1965), 999-1024.

14. Weiler, P. *Labour Arbitration and Industrial Change* (Ottawa: Task Force on Industrial Relations, 1969).

15. Weiler, P. "The Role of the Labour Arbitrator, Alternative Versions," *University of Toronto Law Journal,* Vol. 19 (1969), 16-45.

16. Wood, W. D., and P. Kumar (Eds.). *The Current Industrial Relation Scene in Canada, 1980* (Kingston: Queen's University Industrial Relations Centre, 1980).

QUESTIONS

1. What are the major legal factors which shape the content of a collective agreement?

2. In what ways have arbitration decisions altered the balance of bargaining power between union and management?

3. Explain the "residual-rights" theory. To what extent does it still affect collective-agreement interpretation?

4. How does a general requirement for "fairness" in administering a collective agreement affect negotiations to conclude an agreement?

5. What factors would influence the balance of bargaining power in respect of:
   (a) a union proposal that all asbestos insulation be removed from the employer's premises;
   (b) an employer proposal that the collective agreement include no provision relating to grievances concerning discharge;
   (c) a union proposal requiring union approval of all new manufacturing machinery to be installed by the employer;
   (d) an employer proposal that compulsory transfer from one work site to another within a province be entirely at management's discretion;
   (e) an employer requirement that all office employees wear black shoes to work?

THE UNION-MANAGEMENT RELATIONSHIP

JEFFREY GANDZ

13. Grievances and Their Resolution

Grievances may be expressions of feelings of inequity; challenges to managerial authority; communications of problems being experienced by employees, their union, or management personnel; reflections of political forces within union or management groups; or strategic and tactical manoeuvres in the ongoing process of collective bargaining.

This chapter describes the legal and administrative framework within which grievances are resolved or regulated, the factors which might influence their initiation, resolution, or regulation, and the implications of these factors for industrial-relations management.

Narrowly defined, a grievance is an allegation that one or more provisions of a collective agreement have been violated and a claim for the redress of any damages incurred as a result of that violation.

> I, John Doe, claim that I was disciplined contrary to Section 2(b) (i) of the collective agreement in that I was disciplined without just cause and suspended for three (3) days. I claim three (3) days back pay at my normal rate and the removal of the disciplinary notice from my file.

But grievances may not even allege violations of the collective agreement. Consider the following grievances which, like the one above, come from the grievance files of a large food-distribution company.

> We (the delivery drivers) claim that the loading dock of the XYZ company (a customer) is usually dirty and covered with trash. This is dangerous when we make deliveries and it should be cleaned up.

> My foreman is harrassing me. He always calls me dirty names.

> Olga_____ sorts the eggs too fast. She is costing me bonus by breaking so many. She should be told to take more care.

These grievances are communicating problems with customers, between employees and their supervisors, and between employees within the bargaining unit. In other studies, grievances have been shown to be used politically by both union and management personnel, and strategically and tactically in both contract negotiations and the ongoing, day-to-day bargaining between union and management.

The purpose of this chapter is to deal with the subject of grievances and their resolution in this broader context. First the legal and administrative framework within which grievance resolution takes place is described; then the factors influencing the initiation and processing of grievances are identified; and finally, the implications for industrial-relations management are discussed.

THE LEGAL AND ADMINISTRATIVE FRAMEWORK

Aside from federally chartered organizations, which account for only approximately 10 percent of certified bargaining units in Canada, union-management relationships fall within provincial jurisdiction. This means that the student of industrial relations in the Canadian context must cope with eleven sets of labour and labour-related statutes. While they share many common provisions, and all have their origins in the original Wagner and Taft-Hartley acts in the United States, there are significant differences. Moreover, recent developments indicate that the differences are likely to increase in the future. This section focuses on the common elements and highlights those major divergences only insofar as they affect the initiation and resolution of grievances.

No Strike or Lockout During Agreement

From the earliest Canadian labour legislation, a distinctive feature of both federal and provincial statutes has been the illegality of strikes and lockouts during the term of a collective agreement. In the Canadian federal jurisdiction and in every provincial jurisdiction except Saskatchewan, the statutes either specify that there shall be no strikes or lockouts during the term of a collective agreement or they specify that collective agreements must contain a clause providing for the final resolution of disputes by arbitration or some other means. This use of arbitration to interpret an existing collective agreement is referred to as "grievance arbitration" or "rights arbitration" as opposed to the use of arbitration to settle such things as salary increases or working conditions in a new collective agreement, which is called "interest arbitration."

The principle of resolving disputes arising during the life of a collective agreement by arbitration appears to have gained wide acceptance and legitimacy by both management and labour. Although there have been many criticisms of the arbitration process (9, 11), and although some academics have advocated an extension of the right to strike or lock out under certain conditions such as major technological change (22), there has been no ground swell of opinion in favour of abolishing this restriction on the use of the strike and lockout. Even in those North American jurisdictions in which arbitration is not mandatory, such as the important United States federal jurisdiction, there is a voluntarily negotiated mechanism in 95 percent of all collective agreements. In Saskatchewan, which alone among the provinces does not have mandatory arbitration, it is assumed to be included in collective agreements unless the agreement specifically excludes it.

Arbitration itself is only the tip of the iceberg in the grievance procedure; it is estimated that less than 2 percent of all written grievances actually reach arbitration. The majority are settled by the parties or are withdrawn before arbitration (6). However, because of the large body of general industrial jurisprudence flowing from arbitration activities, and because this jurisprudence influences the parties in their approach to grievance initiation and resolution, an understanding of the principles and practices of arbitration is an essential prerequisite for industrial-relations management.

Grievance Arbitration

When the parties to a dispute cannot resolve a dispute arising from a collective agreement, either party can request that it be arbitrated. The most common approach is for the parties to agree on a neutral third party to act either as a sole arbitrator (approximately one-third of cases in Ontario) or as the chairman of a three-person arbitration board consisting of the chairman and two nominees (or "sidesmen" as they are sometimes called), one of whom represents management and the other the union. When the parties cannot agree on an arbitrator, one is appointed by the minister of labour.

The arbitrator (a chairman of a three-person board is also usually referred to as simply the arbitrator) is usually a lawyer who is sometimes a full-time arbitrator or is, more often, a university professor who does arbitration on a part-time basis. Where disputes involve highly technical issues such as work standards or methods changes, the parties will often use consulting engineers as arbitrators, and this is usually outlined in the collective agreement. Although judges have been barred from sitting as arbitrators in Ontario since 1968, they still arbitrate in some provinces. Arbitrators currently charge $700 to $1,000 for a one-day arbitration case, and this fee is almost always shared by the parties on an equal basis. In addition, each party will bear its own costs for counsel (if used), the travel expenses and lost wages of witnesses, and other out-of-pocket costs.

A study of arbitration in Ontario showed that in a forty-two-month period, 76 percent of all arbitration awards in the private sector were made by thirteen arbitrators (8), three of whom were full-time arbitrators and the remainder of whom were law professors. This concentration of arbitration and the predominance of legally trained arbitrators is also found in the United States (18).

Most arbitrators are selected on an ad hoc basis, as and when the need for one arises. A number of organizations which have frequent recourse to arbitration have established permanent arbitrators, sometimes referred to as umpires, or panels of arbitrators from which an arbitrator for a particular case is chosen on the basis of "next in line" or "earliest availability." Such arrangements may be made either to speed up the arbitration process or to ensure the parties of an arbitrator who, by experience, understands the situation, the technology, the relationship between the parties, or an extremely complex collective agreement. While these advantages exist, there are dangers in using such permanent umpires or panels or arbitrators. Commonly cited are the problems of such arbitrators splitting their awards (one for the union, one for the management) in an effort to remain acceptable to both parties, or the fact that the arbitrator is on some form of retainer fee inducing the parties to use his "already-paid-for" services too frequently and therefore not attempt to resolve disputed issues themselves (15).

In most jurisdictions the Ministry of Labour or the Labour Relations Board keeps lists of people qualified to arbitrate and may undertake the training and education of arbitrators. Breaking into arbitration as a career is, however, difficult since parties are loath to try an untested arbitrator.

The selection of an arbitrator may take several weeks or even months since the parties may "negotiate" as to who the arbitrator should be. Experienced union and management personnel often believe that they can assess which arbitrator is likely to give a favourable ruling in a certain situation, and the practice of keeping "box scores" or detailed analyses of arbitrators' past rulings is widespread. While Professor X may be known to be lenient in assessing discipline for a person who is chronically absent, Professor Y may be known to be tough on such cases. Management may want Professor Y, the union may want Professor X — and the bargaining goes on! There is some empirical evidence that arbitrators do tend to follow certain stable patterns of judgment (8), and that their judgments are influenced by their values and beliefs (12, 3) which leads to the conclusion that selecting the right arbitrator for the right situation might improve one's chances of a successful outcome.

Once an arbitrator has been selected or appointed, a hearing date and location, usually a hotel meeting room, are arranged. The parties may be represented by counsel or may represent themselves. One study (9) indicated that management was represented by counsel in 58 percent of cases, and in the remainder the case was presented by personnel or industrial-relations managers; unions were represented by counsel in 36 percent of cases and, most often, the union case was presented by a business agent or international representative. The process usually involves the following steps:

(a) An opening statement is made by each party in which they outline the nature of the grievance and the issue(s) in dispute.
(b) The party on whom the onus of proof rests will call any witnesses who will give evidence, usually under oath, and who will then be cross-examined by the other party and may also be questioned by the arbitrator and the nominees in the case of a three-person board.
(c) The other party will then call witnesses who will also give evidence and can be cross-examined.
(d) Both parties will then present their closing arguments to the arbitrator.
(e) The arbitrator will then adjourn the hearing and, if sitting as the chairman of a three-person board, will then confer with the nominees. The arbitrator will then prepare an award if acting as a sole arbitrator or a draft award to which he will seek input from the nominees if sitting as a chairman. This written award will be sent to the parties and may be filed with the courts for enforcement if either party so requests.
(f) In the case of a three-person board the arbitrator's ruling is final although one or both of the nominees may dissent with all or part of the award.

Variations on the Arbitration Process

While the above describes a typical arbitration process, there are many variants and departures from this generalized description. Some have been provided for in legislation, others have been developed by particular union-management groups. In British Columbia, for example, the B.C. Labour Relations Board can act as an arbitration board to hear grievances if it desires. In Ontario, recent legislative amendments to the Ontario Labour Relations Act provide each party to an agreement with the opportunity to apply for expedited arbitration to the Ontario Labour Relations Board. The board will appoint a sole arbitrator to schedule and conduct a hearing and issue an award within weeks rather than the average seven months that it usually takes for the conventional arbitration process to run its course (OLRA, s.37(a)).

Under many of the federal and provincial acts governing public-sector collective bargaining or teacher-school-board bargaining, specific procedures for rights arbitration involving panels, tribunals, arbitration boards, and other arrangements have been promulgated. Both in Ontario and B.C., the labour-relations boards can intervene and appoint a grievance mediator to investigate the case and assist the parties in reaching a settlement before going to arbitration. While there has been much commentary about the impact of these legislative developments, there has been little or no research into their effects on union-management relations or the collective-bargaining system.

Some union-management teams have developed their own variants. INCO and the United Steelworkers of America, for example, have developed their own expedited arbitration system, in which cases with low monetary implications and cases which will not be used to establish precedents are referred to regularly scheduled, less formal, summary arbitration sessions in which decisions are given by a sole arbitrator usually within ten days. One of two permanent arbitrators visits the INCO Copper Cliff site once a month to hear such cases. This procedure has helped reduce the time taken to get disciplinary cases heard and has been a factor in reducing the number of cases going to conventional arbitration.

ISSUES IN ARBITRATION

There are a number of issues in arbitral practice and jurisprudence with which all students of industrial relations should be familiar.

Ownership of a Grievance

Grievances may be filed by individuals, groups of individuals, or by a union or employer. However, only the union and the employer can be the actual parties to an arbitration although the award is binding on all employees. As is sometimes said: "the union (or management) owns the grievance." This means that a union could decide to withdraw a grievance from arbitration, or indeed to take a grievance to arbitration, even if the grievor disagreed with the action, provided that the union was not denying the grievor fair representation under the labour-relations act as specified in the particular jurisdiction. Unions may decide not to prosecute certain grievances to arbitration because they consider that to do so would not be in the interests of the bargaining unit as a whole. While they may have to defend such action against allegations of unfair representation, the arbitrator can only proceed if union or management wishes to proceed.

The Role of the Arbitrator

Weiler (23) suggests that arbitrators can act as adjudicators or judges of issues in dispute or as "labour-relations physicians" bringing their knowledge, skills, and experience to bear on the problems. As judges or adjudicators they may either confine themselves to decisions which are based only on explicit or specific provisions within the collective agreement or they may delve below the words and attempt to divine the meaning of the parties when they chose a certain text. As labour-relations physicians, arbitrators may try to mediate between the parties so that they can resolve their own disputes, or arbitrators may even impose on the parties a solution which they believe will serve the good of the general public as well as that of the parties.

The overwhelming and preferred practice in Canada is for arbitrators to confine themselves to the judicial role. Once a case has passed through the grievance procedure and has been submitted to arbitration, the parties want a clear-cut, unambiguous decision. Arbitrators do not view their authority as completely open-ended, and they will generally try to address the specific issue referred to them by the parties and dispose of the problem based on their application of the legal requirements laid out in the collective agreement, the facts presented in evidence, and arguments by the parties to the dispute. However, the courts have clearly established the rights of arbitrators to decide what is "reasonable" action for managements or unions to take under the circumstances of a particular case and arbitrators are not reluctant to exercise their mandate (*Canadian Food and Allied Workers Union, Local 175 v. Great Atlantic,* 76, CLLC 14,056).

Ambiguity

Where there is a specific language in a collective agreement to cover a situation, the arbitrator will abide by that specific language. Where, for example, the language states that the senior employee must be offered first refusal for a job, the arbitrator must decide that the senior employee should have the job, for to do otherwise he would be acting outside the jurisdiction derived from the collective agreement. However, the contract language may be ambiguous, and it is this very ambiguity that often leads to grievances. For example, the agreement may say that the senior employee must have the job if suitably qualified. The phrase "suitably qualified" is ambiguous. Most agreements will refer to the rights of management to discipline employees "for just cause" — what is just is clearly a matter for interpretation. Sometimes this ambiguity is accidental in that the parties were not able to clearly establish unambiguous language when writing the collective agreement. On the other hand, it is sometimes deliberate, so that the parties have some flexibility in handling the myriad situations which might arise during the life of a collective agreement but which could not have been visualized before the agreement was signed. Sometimes, the parties are unable to agree on the actual language to be used in the collective agreement during negotiations but do not want to make the disagreement a strike issue. They may, therefore, simply decide to leave the ambiguity for an arbitrator to sort out at some future time when the need arises.

When there is ambiguity, the arbitrator will look first to the intent of the agreement. Arbitrators may look at precontract negotiations to determine the intent of the parties when they negotiated the language. They may also look at the contract as a whole to see if interpreting the ambiguity in one way would be inconsistent with other provisions in the contract.

Where the contract is ambiguous, the arbitrator will also look to the past practice in the relationship. One example is the case of an agreement in which a company agreed to "make reasonable provisions for the safety and health of its employees." If the company suddenly asked its employees to purchase their own safety gloves whereas it had previously supplied such items, an arbitrator would probably interpret "reasonable provisions" as meaning that the company should buy the gloves because of the past practice of doing so which gives meaning to the words "make reasonable provisions" (15). However, resort to looking at either intent or past practice must not overrule specific language in the collective agreement which is unambiguous. The specific language always prevails.

Contract Is Silent

There are situations in which the language of the collective agreement is silent on a particular practice. Suppose, for example, it had always been the practice for a company to offer employees "make-work" projects such as floor sweeping and tidying when there was insufficient work to do for a few hours before a shift was due to end. Suppose also that there was no language in the agreement that addressed the issue of a procedure for sending employees home in the middle of a shift if there was not enough work to do. Employers have traditionally argued that in such cases, management has a "reserved right" to do anything with respect to wages, hours of work, or conditions of employment unless these rights were specifically limited by language in the collective agreement. Therefore, according to management, they could decide to send people home in the above case.

Unions, on the other hand, have argued that in the absence of specific provisions, the status quo, that is past practice, should prevail. In Canada, arbitrators have generally held to the first of these approaches. In a large number of cases involving issues such as contracting out, the institution of time studies, experimental work, and the use of bulletin boards, management may, in the absence of any express terms in the agreement to the contrary, and if they are acting in good faith in a manner which does not jeopardize the integrity of the bargaining unit, exercise traditional management rights (2). However, there are cases in which management's right to act unilaterally has not been upheld. Where, for example, management had planned to contract out work and such plans had existed at the time a collective agreement was being negotiated but had not been revealed to the union, management was judged to have acted in bad faith and of having sought the protection of the no-strike/lockout provision of the agreement. Management was not allowed to contract out in that case (15). In another case, an arbitrator has ruled against the introduction of an incentive scheme in mid-contract on the basis that it would severely distort the negotiated wage structure. In short, arbitrators have generally followed the "reserved-rights" theory when the contract is silent but have not done so when bad faith is evident, or if the change would severely distort the negotiated agreement.

Arbitrability

One of the first questions that arises in many arbitration hearings is whether or not an issue is "arbitrable," that is, whether an arbitrator has the jurisdiction to hear the case and make a ruling. The arbitrator only has jurisdiction insofar as the issue is covered by the collective agreement. While many grievances are filled with complaints and requests such as those cited at the start of this chapter, these are not considered arbitrable since they do not allege a breach of the agreement. Furthermore, an arbitrator will usually only consider a grievance to be arbitrable if all the procedures outlined in the collective agreement, including the time limitations for filing grievances, holding hearings, and so on have been followed. However, arbitrators have generally been loath to have minor technicalities prevent them from holding that a grievance is arbitrable, preferring to seek out the merits of a grievance (2).

The Burden of Proof

Where discipline or discharge is involved, management must initiate the case and, therefore, carry the burden of establishing a prima facie case that the action or events causing the discipline took place, and that the disciplinary action was warranted. There are other cases in which management must carry the burden of proof, such as when a junior employee is given a job because a more senior employee was deemed not qualified or when there is an allegation of an illegal strike, but in most other cases the burden of proof is on the union to satisfy the arbitrator that the contract has been violated, and that the claimed redress should be given.

In rights arbitration the burden of proof is the civil rather than criminal burden of proof. In criminal cases, it is necessary to prove "beyond a reasonable doubt" that something took place. In rights arbitration, as in civil cases, there is a lesser standard of proof, and one has only to prove "on the balance of probability." If, in the arbitrator's opinion, the balance of probability is so equal that one party's case is no weaker or stronger than the other's, the arbitrator will rule against the party moving the case. So, in a discipline case in which management moves the case, the nod would go to the union, and in a case involving a work assignment, for example, in which the union moves the case, an equally balanced case would tend to be resolved in favour of management.

Precedents

Since arbitration is a quasi-judicial process and arbitration awards are in the public domain and are frequently reported and analysed in publications such as *Canadian Labour Law Cases*, it should not be surprising that a large and significant body of arbitral jurisprudence has developed. The rulings of arbitrators, labour boards, and the courts who have reviewed arbitration cases comprise a "common law of arbitration." As Brown and Beatty state it: "These awards have come to shape and direct not only the drafting of clauses in new collective agreements by providing a point of reference as to how certain problems have been determined by arbitrators in the past, but also they bear upon the resolution of future grievances" (2, p. 13).

Arbitrators will almost invariably follow a precedent established by a previous arbitrator ruling in a similar issue between the parties, unless he is prepared to show why that previous decision was wrong. Therefore, an interpretation given to a clause in a collective agreement by one arbitrator will almost always hold until that agreement is changed. If the circumstances were different, and the issues were not precisely the same, precedent might not be followed although previous decisions in similar situations will usually be considered by the arbitrator and may be influential. Some arbitrators have so succinctly or eloquently established general lines of reasoning or have established such clear decision frameworks that their awards have influenced not only other arbitrators but also the development of industrial-relations policies. For example, Weiler's (22) elaboration of the steps that must precede the discharge of an employee for persistent nonculpable absence has guided the absenteeism policies of a number of private- and public-sector organizations.

Arbitration and Other Legislation

With the proliferation of other types of legislation affecting people at work, there is a real possibility of problems arising from the concurrent jurisdiction of arbitrators, the courts, and other administrative agencies. For example, in Ontario there is a possibility that working conditions may be covered both by a collective agreement and by the Employment Standards Act. Or an employee may claim discrimination and seek redress by filing a grievance alleging a breach of the collective agreement and by lodging a complaint under the Human Rights Act. Or an employer may initiate criminal prosecution of an employee for theft while discharging him for just cause as provided for in the collective agreement.

This whole area is made even more involved by the major differences that exist in the various Canadian jurisdictions. In Ontario, for example, the Rights of Labour Act provides that no action can be brought into court where it is based on a collective agreement, and the courts have ruled that where an action rests on the interpretation of a collective agreement they do not have jurisdiction. In New Brunswick, however, where there is no legislation such as the Rights of Labour Act the courts have held that individual contracts of employment may continue to exist as long as they conform to the collective agreement and, in certain circumstances, a claim for wrongful dismissal may be heard by the courts as an alternative to arbitration. As a further variation, in Nova Scotia the courts will hear such actions only after the grievance procedure has been exhausted (2).

The issue of the interaction between arbitration and other legislation is currently confusing. Some arbitrators have rejected any reference to criminal proceedings while others will entertain them; some will delay proceedings pending the outcome of other hearings while others will proceed.

Arbitral Remedies

Arbitrators are limited to trying to right any wrong that has been done. Their powers are remedial, not punitive. An arbitrator may generally substitute a lesser penalty than one imposed by an employer although he may not do so if the language of the collective agreement specifically forbids it. For example, a suspension could be substituted for a discharge if it was found that an employee had committed an offence but did not warrant discharge because of the gravity of the offence, the employee's past record, or some other mitigating factors. If the arbitrator found that an illegal strike had taken place, damages could be assessed, or back pay and reinstatement could be ordered for an employee who had been improperly laid off. In some cases, arbitrators have issued compliance orders. For example, this has happened when an arbitrator ordered an employer to deduct union dues in accordance with the arbitrator's interpretation of the collective agreement.

Arbitrators do not hold that they have the right to assess punitive damages, and they generally restrict themselves to awarding damages for monetary losses rather than for hurt feelings, mental anguish, or the like. Furthermore, the general common-law principle that the parties should attempt to mitigate their damages has been applied by arbitrators. Even if someone is eventually found to have been discharged without just cause, the amount of back pay awarded by the arbitrator will be reduced by some amount if the person cannot show that they attempted to find alternative employment between the times they were discharged and reinstated. Here, the guiding rule is that the person sustaining damages must have made reasonable efforts to mitigate them. The discharged person, for example, need not have actually found a job and does not have to accept an inferior job, but has only to show through evidence of answering advertisements, going for interviews, or other actions that a reasonable effort was made.

The awards made by an arbitrator are binding on the parties and in most jurisdictions can be filed with a superior court for enforcement if necessary. There are, however, different procedures that must be used in the different provincial jurisdictions. In Nova Scotia, for example, the order by the Labour Relations Board is binding and can be enforced through the courts and this, in effect, amounts to the same thing as enforcing the substance of the award.

Judicial Review of Arbitration Awards

Appeal to the courts of an arbitrator's award will only be entertained by the courts on three bases: the arbitrator acted outside his jurisdiction or failed to exercise his jurisdiction; the arbitrator denied natural justice; or there was "an error on the face of the record."

Jurisdictional errors may be of several types. Arbitrators may act without the grievance-procedure steps having been followed; they may not answer the question that the parties placed before them; they may try to amend, alter, or vary the collective agreement; or they may say that they do not have jurisdiction although they do. Furthermore, they may err with respect to a finding of fact or law on any matter that is collateral to or preliminary to the exercise of their jurisdiction.

Denial of natural justice occurs when the arbitrator is biased, venal, or conducts a hearing in a blatantly partial manner. Although it is recognized that union and management nominees to a tripartite board of arbitration are there to represent their principals' interests, they are expected to act judicially, and they would not be allowed to be, say, members of the union which is a party to the arbitration or the auditors of the employer (2). Refusal to allow cross-examination, consideration of facts other than those presented in evidence, a refusal to compel the attendance of a witness, or other procedural irregularities will, if gross enough, be considered to be a denial of natural justice.

The third basis of judicial appeal of arbitration awards is rather more difficult to understand. Awards can be appealed if there is "an error on the face of the record." This would occur if, for example, the arbitrator made a gross error in interpreting an agreement such that the interpretation could not reasonably be made. In Ontario, appeals of this nature are limited to collateral issues, that is to issues other than the one submitted for arbitration. In one award, for example, the Supreme Court allowed an appeal of a discharge, not because the arbitrator had interpreted the discharge clause incorrectly, but because he had disregarded another relevant provision of the collective agreement. In those jurisdictions in which arbitration is required by statute, courts have been more willing than in other jurisdictions to entertain appeals and review awards, as well as to examine whether or not the arbitrator's interpretation of an agreement is one that it can reasonably bear.

Arguments for further limiting judicial review have been advanced by several parties, mainly those representing labour's interests. They argue that to appeal an arbitrator's award is usually a stalling tactic by management and, in that it delays the execution of justice, it is detrimental to good labour relations. Management, on the other hand, has often expressed preference for the stricter, "constructionist" approaches of the judiciary and has been unwilling to forsake judicial review.

GRIEVANCE PROCEDURES

Less than 2 percent of written grievances actually go to arbitration and, since most grievance procedures contain provisions for the verbal presentation of grievances as the first step, it is probable that somewhat less than 1 percent of all grievances ever reach arbitration (5). The vast majority of grievances are either resolved during the internal grievance procedure or are withdrawn by the parties.

A wide variety of grievance procedures has been developed by the parties to collective agreements and a typical private-sector grievance procedure has been appended to this chapter. While they have many features in common there are differences. A study (5) of 118 grievance procedures in bargaining units in Ontario found that:

(a) Most procedures (67 percent) had three steps with a range from two to seven formal stages.

(b) In 42 percent of procedures the first stage was verbal, with the grievor, usually accompanied by a steward, confronting the supervisor with the grievance. In a further 25 percent, this verbal stage preceded the first official stage of the grievance procedure, and the agreement specified that a grievance would not be considered to be a grievance until the verbal stage had been exhausted. In 17 percent of the procedures, the verbal stage was to precede the formulation of a written grievance although both were considered to be a part of the first stage. In 11 percent of the cases, the written or verbal alternative was available at the discretion of the grievor.

(c) In almost all grievance procedures, limits were imposed on the time in which the parties could file a grievance and the time in which to respond at various stages of the procedure and to initiate subsequent stages. However, there were invariably waiver clauses on such time limits, and the parties could agree to depart from the specified times. Extensive use was made of such time waivers since the response time provided for in the agreement seldom allowed for adequate time for investigating complex issues.

(d) There was extensive departure from the formal steps and restrictions in the collective agreement. Only 42 percent of the 118 industrial-relations managers in the study stated that managements always insisted on following the procedures; 48 percent stated that exceptions were sometimes made while 10 percent said that the procedure was not taken very literally.

(e) Many organizations opened up the grievance procedure to both formally phrased grievances and complaints at the early stages, and only one-third of the industrial-relations managers in the study said that the grievance procedure was used only for items specified in the collective agreement.

(f) Most of the organizations studied indicated that there was an unofficial extra step in the grievance procedure that varied in its formality. This step usually occurred after the union had said it would take a case to arbitration but before the arbitration hearing. In some cases this step became almost official as, for example, in one organization in which the management and union personnel met on the second Thursday of every month to review the cases "pending arbitration." Some of these were withdrawn, some were conceded to, others were simply left in abeyance, and others were slated for arbitration. To give some idea of the scope of such "unofficial" grievance resolution, one consumer-durables company had forty grievances officially referred to arbitration by its union in a nineteen-month period. Of these, the union withdrew eleven prior to an arbitration hearing, the company conceded to seventeen, five were compromised, and seven were actually arbitrated.

(g) In a few cases, there was extensive bargaining over cases pending arbitration, sometimes in official contract negotiations. While most of the ninety-nine industrial-relations managers questioned on this issue were opposed to such negotiations on the basis that such horse trading was both unfair to grievors and supervisors involved in the grievances and would inhibit efforts to resolve differences through the grievance procedure, many acknowledged that it went on particularly when there were backlogs of "petty" grievances prior to contract negotiations.

(h) In most procedures, provisions were made to escalate disciplinary grievances involving discharge or policy grievances involving groups of employees or the whole bargaining unit to advanced or final stages of the grievance procedure so that they could be expeditiously dealt with by more senior management and union officials.

Grievance Issues

Studies of the types of issues that are the subject of grievances tend to be restricted to looking at specific bargaining units since there is no consensus on typologies of grievance issues which would allow for interunit comparisons. Furthermore, the types of issues are likely to vary with the nature of the work, management practices, the provisions within collective agreements, and many other variables. Some sense of the issues can be derived from looking at the grievances arising in a fifteen-month period in one large basic steel-making complex with approximately 12,000 bargaining-unit members. The breakdown of disciplinary grievances, and those arising from allegations by the union of violations of provisions of the collective agreement concerning such issues as seniority and job postings, are shown in Table 1.

During this same fifteen-month period the company filed one grievance against the union for encouraging and condoning an illegal strike.

Grievance Rates

Studies of grievance rates (1, 5, 16, 19) have shown very large variations between organizations, between departments within organizations, and even between different time periods for the same organization. The reported rates have varied from 0 to 1,359 grievances per thousand employees per year (5).

Variations in grievance rates cannot be easily explained in terms of types of industry, location, or technology. For example, of three tire manufacturers in one study (5), two were producers of a similar range of tires, were located within ten miles of each other, and were organized by the same international union yet they had grievance rates of 9.5 and 87.5 per thousand employees per year respectively. In ten mines, all owned by the same company, total grievance rates varied from 108 to 840 per thousand employees per year.

Patterns of Grievance Resolution

Most grievances are withdrawn by the union as various stages of the grievance procedure are exhausted, although there is a greater tendency to pursue disciplinary grievances to the later stages of the grievance procedure than nondisciplinary grievances (5). Typical was one mining company with 1,726 first-stage disciplinary grievances filed during a collective agreement. Of these, 3.1 percent actually went to arbitration while management conceded to 20.5 percent. The remaining 76.4 percent were dropped by the union during the grievance procedure. For the same company, of 8,081 nondisciplinary grievances filed during the contract, management conceded to 20.9 percent, 1.0 percent went to arbitration, and the remaining

Table 1

Grievances in a Basic Steelworks

Issues	%	Step 2 of Total	(n = 311)	%	Step 3 of Total	(n = 155)
1. Discharges		3.8			4.5	
Absenteeism			1.9			3.2
Time card violation			0.6			
Others			1.3			1.3
2. Discipline other than discharge		45.6			56.1	
Absenteeism and lateness			14.1			20.0
Off the job			10.3			14.2
Poor work performance			10.0			4.5
Personal misconduct			8.0			15.5
All others			3.2			1.9
3. Seniority		19.6			15.5	
Layoffs and recalls			2.6			3.2
Job vacancies and promotions			15.7			11.0
Others			1.3			1.3
4. Overtime		1.0			1.9	
5. Pay		2.9			0.6	
6. Miscellaneous		27.0			21.3	
Job postings			5.8			2.5
Safety and health			3.2			1.9
Work scheduling			2.6			2.6
Foreman harassment			1.6			1.9
Work beyond job description			1.0			1.9
Work by supervisors			2.3			1.3
Others			10.5			9.2

NOTE: These data cover all written grievances (Step 1 of this unit's grievance procedure is oral) in a fifteen-month period. The data were generated, by the investigator, from records of individual grievances made available by the company.

78.1 percent were withdrawn by the union. In the case of the disciplinary grievances, 41.5 percent of those originally filed were considered at the third and final stage of the grievance procedure while 33.8 percent of the nondisciplinary grievances reached this final stage.

There is a greater propensity for disciplinary grievances to be referred to arbitration if they cannot be resolved to the union's satisfaction during the grievance procedure, particularly if discharge is involved (5). Of the 364 arbitrations recorded in the study cited immediately above, 2 of the 118 bargaining units accounted for over 50 percent. Sixty-seven of 94 bargaining units which had disciplinary grievances did not have an arbitration and 73 of 112 bargaining units with nondisciplinary grievances used arbitration.

FACTORS INFLUENCING GRIEVANCE INITIATION AND RESOLUTION

The high variance in grievance and arbitration rates have prompted many investigators to look for the factors which influence grievance initiation and resolution. From these studies have come a recognition of the multidimensional nature of grievances. They may be:
(a) A conventional form of communication between managements and employees around issues of concern to one or both of the parties;
(b) A challenge by one party to the authority, rights, or actions of the other party;
(c) A strategic or tactical manoeuvre in the ongoing collective-bargaining relationship whereby one party seeks gains at the expense of the other;
(d) A politically motivated action stimulated by the self-serving objectives of some person or faction within either union or management organizations.

Grievances as Communications

The grievance procedure is a useful channel for union and management personnel to exchange information and opinions. Indeed, in the absence of other channels such as union-management committees, or informal or formal communications sessions, the regularly scheduled grievance meetings may become the only form of communication between the union and management outside of contract negotiations. Its value as a communications channel is such that most managements allow and even encourage its use for both formally stated grievances and less formally stated complaints.

Sometimes managers may actively encourage employees to use the grievance procedure as a communications vehicle. In one case known to the author, a public-sector manager was having great difficulty in getting the back pay that was overdue to a secretary in his department. Failing in his own efforts to unblock the communications channel, which in this case involved another government department, the manager encouraged the secretary to make her feelings known through the grievance procedure knowing full well that a formal grievance would soon find its way "to the top" and action would result.

Grievances as Challenges

One way in which conflict can be expressed is through the grievance procedure. This procedure allows one party to challenge the actions of the other, to try to modify those actions, and to obtain compensation if the party has been unfairly damaged by those actions. Specifically, the grievance procedure represents the accepted, legitimate procedure to be used for ensuring compliance both with the collective agreement as written and with the traditions and widely accepted practices in the employer-employee relationship. It is not, however, the only means of trying to force such compliance. Aggrieved employees have recourse to other means to seek compliance and redress, including illegal strikes, concerted work-to-rule or other slowdown campaigns, obstruction of management actions, or noncooperation. In trying to understand the factors which influence one party's decision to challenge the authority, actions, or intent of the other, it is necessary to consider the many factors which influence actual conflict conditions, the perception by people of that conflict, the feelings that they develop about the issues, and the ways in which they decide to manifest this conflict.

Environmental factors — Many factors in the task environment of organizations might lead to one party challenging the actions or intentions of the other. In adverse economic times, when organizations are laying off employees or restructuring operations in some way, grievances alleging violations of seniority provisions, bumping rights, or work scheduling are likely to increase both because there are more of these types of activities going on and because people are likely to feel more insecure and perhaps more militant. In buoyant economic times, when the work force is being strained to capacity, there may be more grievances relating to overtime allocation, shift scheduling, standards, piece rates, or other managerial actions designed to increase production volume.

Local labour-market conditions may have significant impact on grievance initiation and resolution. A plant existing in a very tight labour market may have to draw on a poorly skilled, inexperienced work force and might anticipate a large number of performance-related problems which could be reflected in a large volume of grievances over discipline, incentive rates, or work standards.

Social or community factors may also play a role in the initiation and resolution of grievances. A high-grievance-rate department in one basic steel-making facility (16) was shown to be made up almost entirely of blacks in low-status jobs. Spurred on by a union leader who was active in the civil-rights movement in the community, this department came to reflect the general racial tensions in the community, and the grievance procedure became the outlet for the blacks' general frustrations. In communities characterized by union-management strife, the prevailing attitudes of both employees and managers may be such that they lack the degree of interpersonal respect, trust, liking or at least tolerance to allow for informal problem solving.

Technological change — Technological changes may affect both job security and job content and may result in increased grievances related to layoffs, classifications, pay, and manning. In the replacement of open-hearth furnaces by basic-oxygen furnaces in a basic steel-making facility, there were major changes in the number of bricklayers and labourers, and the nature of the jobs they did. Among other effects, the changes resulted in the lowering of the required skill of the bricklayers and, hence, a narrowing in the perceived skill differential between the bricklayers and the labourers (16). This was a source of considerable dissatisfaction to the bricklayers and resulted in a flood of grievances. In his classic study of grievances and arbitration in the bituminous-coal-mining industry, Somers (20) attributed the sharp increase in grievance rates and the use of arbitration in the 1941-1954 period to the impact of new mining technology and the accompanying shrinkage of the work force with its attendant impact on perceived job insecurity. In addition to creating specific problems with layoffs and seniority, this manpower shrinkage had induced a greater degree of militancy in the work force.

Job characteristics — A variety of job characteristics may influence the initiation of grievances and their resolution. Peach and Livernash (16) describe a "high grievance rate syndrome" which they see as being associated with: high individual-worker responsibility for quality and quantity of product; a requirement for close attention to work; difficulty in achieving quality standards; close supervision; frequent product and process changes; a work environment which is rushed or noisy and that makes informal problem solving difficult; an incentive system with many nonstandardized tasks and with many earnings and effort inequities; and a difficult-to-manage task environment with possible additional unfavourable characteristics such as physical working conditions, work pressure, and so on. Of course, since many of these conditions could easily coexist and may reinforce or counteract each other, it is difficult to develop empirical support for cause-and-effect relationships between these factors and actual grievance rates. Furthermore, when bargaining units with similar job characteristics are compared, a vast range of grievance rates are found which would suggest that if job characteristics do have an impact on grievance rates they are not overwhelming (5).

Characteristics of grievors — Several attempts have been made to examine personal characteristics which might be associated with grievors (1, 17, 21). Grievors have been shown to be generally younger, more likely to be without family responsibilities, more likely to be better educated, to have been absent more often, and to have had more suspensions, reprimands, and arrests than nongrievors. Since grievances often result from disciplinary action as a consequence of rule infraction, it is interesting to note that in one study (14) it was found that violators tended to be less well educated, less domestically stable, and to score lower on such traits as cautiousness and emotional stability. Furthermore, in this same study, it was found that rule violators tended to belong to work groups that were less cohesive than those that nonviolators belonged to. Attempts to explain involvement in grievance activity on the basis of personal characteristics are fraught with many problems. While it is sometimes tempting to think of the grievor as a young "tearaway" who has not yet settled down to responsible work, or as an activist in the union simply trying to stir up trouble, the evidence is largely contradictory, and the simple statistical relationships can often be explained in several ways. While the young employee is, perhaps, more likely to engage in horseplay in the plant or to take unscheduled absences, both of which may lead to subsequently grievable disciplinary actions by management, he is also more likely to be a victim of layoffs or classification changes which would expose him to situations in which he might have reason to grieve.

Union influences — Whereas the factors described above might influence the actual amount of conflict that can arise between union and management, it is the activity of union and management officials which often serve to draw attention to problems in the relationship and to cause them to be first perceived and then felt as conflicts by employees. Union leadership, organization, and policies influence both the actual challenge rate and resolution processes.

Peach and Livernash have suggested that union leadership constitutes "the single most conspicuous and outstanding variable in the generation and resolution of problems" (16, p. 62). They describe five types of union leadership. *Inactive* leadership provided few challenges to management and was found in low-grievance-rate departments. *Problem-solving* leadership was also found in low-grievance-rate departments, and such leaders were active but showed a preference for informal challenge and resolution, a selective approach to worker complaints, and a willingness to follow precedent. The *advocacy* form of leadership was found in high-grievance-rate departments and in departments with a high incidence of pressing grievances to late and final stages of the grievance procedure and arbitration. The advocate was extremely loyal to the union and was unwilling to compromise an issue or to drop a case. *Political* leaders differed from others in that they used the grievance procedure to advance their own position. Formal challenges, natural delays, and self-created delays in the grievance procedure were used "to dim the memory of the issue and to give the impression of great effort expended on behalf of the employee" (16, p. 69).

Finally, *radical* leadership was found to differ from political leadership in that the grievance procedure was used to advance a cause, such as civil rights, rather than personal ambition. All of the high-grievance-rate departments in this study had leaders at the department or local level who were radicals, politicians, or advocates while the low-incidence departments had either inactive or problem-solving leaders.

While the style of union leadership is an issue in grievance initiation and resolution, certain structural and policy factors also play a part. Sometimes lower-level union officials simply do not have the authority to deal with grievances, particularly if the issue involves a substantial compromise unacceptable to the grievor or the complete abandonment of the grievance. With a duty of fair representation, a decision to abandon a grievance may have to be taken at a senior union-officer level, with many unions providing for a direct appeal to the membership at large if the grievor wants the grievance taken to arbitration. Also, some unions have explicit policies that certain types of grievances, discharges for example, will always be taken to the final stage of the grievance procedure.

Management influences— Management often violates the collective agreement by intent, ignorance, or carelessness. Changes in collective agreements are often not well communicated to lower-level managers or supervisors who were not involved in their negotiation. The absence of policies and lack of training of supervisors may lead to inconsistencies in the treatment of employees in different departments. Moreover, changes in management personnel may lead to inconsistencies over time.

The leadership style, structure, and policies of management can also affect both the initiation and resolution of grievances (16). Inactive, problem-solving, and authoritarian or autocratic managers will influence the ways in which complaints are dealt with and whether they are resolved before formal grievance procedures are initiated. However, just as union leaders have limited authority to settle grievances, so do managers. Frequently grievances have to be processed through several stages in the grievance procedure before an adequately senior manager is reached.

Industrial-relations management — The involvement of specialized industrial-relations or personnel staff groups is one aspect of structure that varies widely in organizations. One study showed that the early involvement of staff groups resulted in lower grievance rates, a higher proportion of settlements at the early stage of the grievance procedure, and a higher level of oral and informal resolution. On the other hand, the readiness of staff groups to become involved directly at the very early stages of grievances may encourage line managers to "pass the buck" to such a specialized group and to avoid personal involvement in the situation creating the complaint or grievance. This is of considerable concern since the first-line supervisor, whose primary responsibilities relate to achieving short-term production objectives, tends to view grievance management as interfering with his main function.

The role taken by industrial-relations staffs also shows considerable variety (7). Some see their roles in terms of "management's policeman," trying to do their best to enforce the letter of the collective agreement, representing line management in the grievance procedure, developing support for management's actions, and protecting management's rights against erosion by the union. Others see a completely different role, acting as the employees' advocate representing employees who perceive themselves to have been treated unjustly and trying to get them a fair deal from their line managers. The most common role taken by professional industrial-relations staff is that of the mediator who tries to objectively determine the facts in a situation, to ensure that employees, the union, and the managers involved have the opportunity to present and explain their positions to each other and to propose solutions that are either acceptable to both parties or which represent some compromise. Occasionally a situation is found where the industrial-relations manager is formally or informally vested with the authority, by both management and union, to adjudicate disputes, making a fair and equitable settlement on the merits of the case. Finally, some industrial-relations staffs are not directly involved in grievance procedures unless they end up at arbitration.

The actual role to be taken by industrial-relations or personnel professionals in an organization will be a function of many factors. The basic industrial-relations philosophies in the organization, the beliefs and attitudes toward employees and the union, prior experience in grievance management, the personalities of union and management people involved in the grievance resolution process, and many other variables will influence the emergent roles and relationships.

Grievances and the grievance procedure — The structure and operation of the grievance procedure itself has also been shown to influence both the initiation and resolution of grievances. In one multiplant operation (13), in order to reduce a large volume of grievances, the process was centralized at the head office and a master agreement negotiated to cover all plants. While this improved consistency and diminished local feelings of inequity somewhat, the line managers avoided ruling on grievances, deferring to the industrial-relations department. However, the huge volume of grievances overwhelmed the central industrial-relations staff, delays ensued, and as the rank and file became exasperated with these delays even more grievances were filed. One contributor to this increased volume was the increased complexity of the new master agreement and the unfamiliarity of the line managers in the various plants with its terms and conditions. Centralization had become a mixed blessing.

Major reductions in grievance volumes, particularly at later stages of the grievance procedure, only came when the number of stages in the grievance procedure was reduced and a policy and training program initiated whereby disputes could be rapidly escalated at the local-plant level and presented in oral form to a senior manager with the authority to make decisions. The investigators concluded that this major change was responsible for reducing written grievances from 8,000 to just over 100 in two years without widespread appeasement, for major improvements in morale, and for a net reduction in the amount of time spent in grievance or complaint resolution.

The new system did create some problems. Some managers were reluctant to take on grievance-management responsibilities and the union stewards had to take more responsibility for compromising or withdrawing grievances. The whole system could not have been changed without the full commitment of senior management and union officials. On balance, however, these major structural and process changes were seen as highly beneficial by management, the union, and employees.

Grievances and Bargaining

Bargaining goes on throughout the duration of the union-management relationship, not just during the formal negotiations for a new collective agreement. The grievance procedure is used both tactically and strategically in this ongoing process.

Strategically, grievances may be used to try to get a concession that could not be achieved through formal contract negotiations. In one case study (10), workers in a tire plant filed grievances alleging violations in the safety-and-health provisions in the collective agreement. Further investigation indicated that what the employees really wanted was a downward adjustment in the production rate, and they were prepared to drop the grievances in return for such a concession. In another unreported case known to the author, a company filed a grievance against a union for an illegal strike and was awarded several million dollars in damages by an arbitrator. Management had no intention of ever trying to collect the money but they were able to trade off the claim for damages in return for important union concessions on working hours in the next set of formal negotiations.

It is not necessary to take a case to arbitration in order to achieve some concession that may significantly alter the collective agreement. Where a contract is silent or ambiguous, the actual past practice in an organization is taken into account by an arbitrator. Therefore, if a union can get management to concede to a grievance by taking a certain action, that action becomes the prevailing practice unless it is very clearly an action that is taken "without prejudice" to future behaviour. If, for example, management were to concede to a union grievance claiming that an employee should not be discharged for the theft of material of, say, less than twenty dollars in value, any subsequent decision by management to discharge an employee of similar seniority and work record in similar circumstances would probably be overturned by an arbitrator. Through the grievance procedure, the union would have succeeded in establishing de facto ground rules covering theft.

Another strategic use of the grievance procedure is related to the establishment of the bargaining agenda. Sometimes, long before formal contract negotiations actually take place, the union may file a number of grievances about issues in which they intend to seek concessions in upcoming negotiations. Although the grievances may clearly lack merit based on the wording of the current agreement, the filing of the grievance and subsequent discussions with management serve to put management "on notice" that the issue will be coming up in negotiations and might also allow the parties to explore each other's positions with respect to the issue prior to formally scheduling it on the bargaining agenda.

Sometimes the parties are unable to resolve an issue during contract negotiations, but the issue is not important enough to strike over or to delay signing an agreement. In such a case, the parties may decide to leave the issue phrased ambiguously, file a grievance when the issue arises, and either continue negotiations on it in the grievance procedure or let an arbitrator resolve the matter for them.

Tactically, grievances may be used in a number of ways. Since grievances require responses and often quite lengthy meetings, a union may decide to harass management or particular supervisors by filing very large numbers of grievances of dubious merit. Responding to such grievances ties up both line managers and staff specialists, sometimes at quite senior levels. If, as occasionally is the case, the collective agreement provides that the time spent by union officials on grievance meetings is totally paid for by the employer, the union has a costless way of tying up large amounts of management time and, in some cases, of even forcing management to take on extra staff merely to deal with such grievances. In such situations, management may be tempted to concede to a large number of grievances merely to reduce the grievance case load. In making such concessions, there is always the danger of establishing extremely costly precedents, of alienating supervisors who believe that management should stand firm against such tactics, or, indeed, of encouraging even more grievances if the union comes to believe that concessions are related to the number of grievances actually filed.

The Political Dimensions of Grievances

While a union official, such as a steward or committee member, is important in assuring that managements comply with the terms of the collective agreement, he is also the elected or appointed representative of a constituency. He is under pressure to act as the agent for members of that constituency who may feel aggrieved. It is sometimes suggested that volumes of grievances increase in periods immediately prior to union elections or are higher in unions in which there are many factions such as skilled and unskilled employees, or senior and junior employees although there is little empirical support for such assertions. The union leader may actively provoke grievances as evidence of assertiveness, or may be tenacious in the prosecution of grievances emanating from his constituents in order to demonstrate commitment to them. Even if union stewards or committee members feel that the grievance lacks merit, they may continue to press it, if there is some political gain in so doing or some political cost to dropping it (8).

It is not only on the union side that grievances may have political dimensions. Cases can be found where a manager wants a policy or procedure changed but cannot persuade more senior management to make the change; in such cases a grievance may be just the stimulus to change that is needed, and such an action may be encouraged by the change-seeking manager.

Decision Making in the Grievance-Resolution Process

Unions have to decide whether to file a grievance and how far to pursue it. Many factors enter into such decisions, including the merits of the case itself, its significance for the bargaining unit as a whole, the value of the gains if the issue is eventually decided in the union's favour or not, the political impact of the decision on the leadership of the union, and the kind of political, strategic, and tactical considerations described above. Given the range of possible influences, it is not surprising that even the most experienced industrial-relations managers sometimes express surprise at the union taking a particular case to arbitration or dropping another. The union may take a case which has only an outside chance of being successful all the way to arbitration if the stakes, financial, political, or psychological, are high enough (8).

Management faces similar decisions. Whether or not to concede to a grievance may be influenced by financial, political, strategic, or tactical considerations. Sometimes management goes to arbitration with a poor case because they need to support some lower-level decision taken by a line manager, even if the actions were clearly breaches of the collective agreement. Sometimes it is necessary to show line managers what is permissible and what is not, and an arbitrator's authoritative award may be the best way of communicating the realities of a situation to line managers. Frequently, management may refuse to concede to an insignificant demand because they fear that the precedent involved may be very costly in the future.

In their response to grievances, management must tread a narrow line. While many concessions in grievance negotiations may tend to encourage further grievances, particularly if the union appears to be making substantive gains in modifying the working relationship to the employees' benefit, steadfast refusal to make any concession could lead to discrediting the grievance procedure. If employees perceive that it is useless to grieve, but nevertheless feel aggrieved, their dissatisfaction could well be manifested in nonprocedural forms of conflict such as slow downs, work-to-rule actions, or individual aggressive or withdrawal behaviours such as absenteeism or quitting.

IMPLICATIONS FOR INDUSTRIAL-RELATIONS MANAGEMENT

Conflict is inevitable in any sociotechnical system, particularly one in which people may not share similar ideologies or philosophies. No matter how comprehensive or unambiguous the language of collective agreements, there will always be allegations of noncompliance with either the formal written agreement or the traditional policies and practices that govern day-to-day working relationships.

The objective of management should be to avoid taking actions which unintentionally contravene such provisions and practices in the first place. This involves training managers and supervisors in the letter and intent of the collective agreement, as well as familiarizing them with the established practices and culture of the work environment. Beyond that, however, it is also in management's interest to ensure that the grievance system functions as an effective communications channel and as a forum for addressing those problems which can be resolved to mutual benefit, as well as those which involve fundamental conflicts of interest. Not all conflicts are zero-sum in nature. Many so-called conflicts are misunderstandings of the actions or intentions of one of the parties. Others are problems which concern both parties and which, if information is exchanged and active search for alternative solutions engaged in, could be resolved with benefits to all involved.

Given the multidimensional nature of grievances, it is often difficult for management to understand what underlies a grievance and, therefore, to formulate the appropriate management response. In a highly politicized union, it might be tempting for management to view a grievance as political grandstanding, when it may represent some significant problem that needs attention. On the other hand, assuming that all grievances represent real problems in the work place rather than tactical or strategic manoeuvres in bargaining would be equally as naïve and lead to an overreaction by management.

The aggrieved employee is a problem for management in terms of: the reduced effort and attention to quantity and quality of work output; the contagious effect that such an employee's attitude might have on a whole work force; and the impact of that effect on such variables as absenteeism, turnover, and productivity. There would be broad consensus among managers that it is desirable for employee complaints and grievances to be resolved as quickly as possible. Managers would not want resolution to reflect concession on matters of principle or substance, appeasement for the sake of conflict avoidance, or supervisors turning a blind eye to infringements of the collective agreement because they wanted to avoid a grievance, or feared that their decisions would be subsequently overruled by more senior line or industrial-relations managers.

Grievances can be thought of as both consequences of poor union-management relationships and as contributors to the development of those relationships. Given that management wants improved relationships, there are a number of steps that can be followed to improve the grievance-management process.

Training and motivation — It is important that line managers and supervisors know both the letter and the spirit of the collective agreement. This may involve extensive training of management and supervisory personnel following the conclusion of contract negotiations. Training alone is insufficient if managers and supervisors are not motivated to resolve grievances without merely "passing the buck" to someone else. Therefore, grievance management should be incorporated as a performance criterion in performance-evaluation programs, management by objectives and other goal-setting and measurement systems. Through education of supervisors and managers, a sensitivity to both the political and bargaining dimensions of grievance activity can be developed while ensuring that all grievance activity is not attributed to such motivations.

Advance consultation — Advance consultation with the union and affected employees can be provided prior to major changes in processes, staffing, scheduling, or other activities which might be within management's prerogative in the collective agreement but which have the potential for misunderstandings or misconstructions. Such consultation may not result in satisfaction for the union or the affected employees and a grievance might ensue. However, it should prevent grievances based on misunderstandings or misconceptions.

Authority level — It is important to develop grievance procedures which both involve the parties to the grievance and bring the grievance as quickly as possible to a level of manager and union official who have the authority to do something about the issue which is the cause of the grievance. Multiple-stage grievance procedures, in which the early stages are mere formalities, are likely to contribute to even greater levels of employee dissatisfaction and alienation.

Consistency and flexibility — There is a delicate balance between the development of policies and procedures that are consistent throughout a bargaining unit but are flexible enough to allow for some autonomy for first- and second-line supervisors and managers. This requires the development of close, consultative relationships between industrial-relations professionals and line managers. The line manager must feel comfortable consulting with the industrial-relations manager while still retaining the authority to act. Failure to establish this relationship will likely result in the repetitive undercutting or overruling of the line manager by the industrial-relations staff or the loss of numerous grievances in arbitration. If this is the outcome, line managers will eventually lose all interest in grievance management. Consistency and flexibility may be established through team-building efforts focused on industrial-relations issues, the rotation of line managers through industrial-relations jobs, seminars, and training sessions. Line managers should be involved in grievance-resolution meetings and should be advised of the outcome of grievance cases and arbitrations throughout the organization, as well as in their own areas of responsibility.

Industrial-relations climate — Improving the overall industrial-relations climate should also improve grievance management. By using such approaches as preventative mediation, or single-team bargaining, managements and unions have sought to improve the levels of trust, understanding and acceptance of each other's legitimacy in the relationship.

Steps such as those described above will not eliminate grievances completely. Nor should the elimination of all grievances be viewed as desirable. Insofar as grievances may reflect genuine concerns of employees being communicated to management, they serve a useful purpose if management is alert and responsive to the messages contained in the grievances. The objective should be to clear up misunderstandings, focus on creative problem solving in those cases in which both parties can gain from such problem solving, and to identify clearly the issues which are the subject of disagreement and, therefore, to create a position from which to negotiate their resolution.

APPENDIX

The Grievance Procedure in a Consumer-Durables Company

Article 10

GRIEVANCE AND ARBITRATION PROCEDURE

10.01 The parties hereto shall meet through their authorized representatives respectively to discuss and adjust any dispute and/or grievance which may arise between the parties; every effort shall be exerted mutually to adjust any and all grievances which may arise.

10.02 The Bargaining Committee, consisting of five members, all of whom shall be regular employees of the employer, being twenty-one years of age or over, and all of whom shall have had at least one year of continuous service with the employer, shall be elected by the employees of the employer who are members of the union in a manner determined by the union; the employer shall be informed by the union of the personnel of that committee; a representative from any department may be called in when deemed necessary by either party, and may take part in negotiations until the completion of the particular grievance in question.

10.03 Any dispute or grievance between the employee and the employer shall be dealt with as follows:

(a) An employee who has a complaint may discuss it either personally or through the intervention of his steward, with his immediate supervisor.

(b) If no satisfactory solution is reached at the discussion above mentioned, such employee may put his complaint in writing and present it to his steward, and each such complaint shall be a "grievance" subject to the procedure hereinafter in this Article set forth.

(c) Stage One
A grievance may be discussed by the steward and/or the chief steward and/or the union representative with the foreman of the department in which the grievance occurred.

(d) Stage Two
If no satisfactory solution is reached at the discussion in the next preceding paragraph mentioned, such grievance may be discussed by the steward and/or the chief steward and/or the union representative with the Department Foreman and/or the Division Superintendent and the Personnel Manager of the employer within a period of not more than five working days after the discussion in the next preceding paragraph mentioned.

(e) Stage Three
If no satisfactory solution is reached at the discussion in the next preceding paragraph mentioned, such grievance may be discussed by the Bargaining Committee with the Personnel Manager, the Plant Manager and not more than three other representatives of the employer within a period of not more than five working days after the discussion in the next preceding paragraph mentioned.

(f) Stage Four

If no satisfactory solution is reached at the discussion in the next preceding paragraph mentioned, such grievance may be discussed by the Bargaining Committee and a representative of the International Union within a period of not more than five working days after the discussion in the next preceding paragraph mentioned with such representatives of the employer, not more than five in number, as the employer, may nominate for such purpose.

(g) The aggrieved employee shall be at liberty and may be required by either party to appear in person at any stage of the negotiations above set forth.

10.04 (1) Any dispute between the employer and the union as to the interpretation of this Collective Agreement and any allegation by either party that the other has violated any term of this Collective Agreement shall be deemed to be a grievance when notice in writing thereof has been delivered by the party considering itself aggrieved, to the other party, and shall be subject to arbitration as hereinafter in this Article set forth.

(2) Such grievance shall be discussed by the Bargaining Committee and at the option of the union, a representative of the International Union with such representatives of the employer not more than five in number, as the employer may nominate for such purpose.

10.05 If no satisfactory solution of any grievance in the next preceding paragraph mentioned is reached at the discussion in the said preceding paragraph mentioned, and, in the case of any grievance in Section 10.03, which arises out of a difference as to the interpretation of this Collective Agreement or an alleged violation of any term of this Collective Agreement, if no satisfactory solution of such grievance is reached at the discussion mentioned in subsection 10.03 (f), either party may refer such grievance to a Board of Arbitration by delivering to the other party, in writing, within five working days after the cessation of such discussion or within such further period as may be mutually agreed upon by the parties involved in the grievance:

(a) A statement of intention to refer the grievance to a Board of Arbitration.

(b) A fair and just statement of the subject matter of the grievance.

10.06 Both parties shall thereupon meet together, through their representatives as provided in subsection 10.04 (2), and agree upon the statement of the subject matter of the grievance in the next preceding paragraph mentioned; and such statement shall be submitted to the Board of Arbitration hereinafter provided, provided that if the parties are unable to agree upon the said statement, the party to whom such statement was delivered shall deliver, in writing, to the other party, within five working days of the delivery of such last mentioned statement or within such further period as may be mutually agreed upon by the parties involved in the grievance, a counter-statement of the subject matter of the grievance, and in such event both the statement and the counter-statement shall be submitted to the Board of Arbitration hereinafter provided.

10.07 Each party shall, not later than three days after they have agreed upon a statement of the subject matter of the grievance, or not later than three days after the delivery of a counter-statement, deliver to the other party, in writing, a statement of the name of the person nominated to represent such party on the Board of Arbitration. These time limits may be extended at any time by mutual agreement between the employer and the union.

10.08 No person may be nominated to the Board of Arbitration who has either directly or indirectly, attempted to negotiate or settle the grievance in dispute.

10.09 The two nominees on the Board of Arbitration shall, within five days of their appointment, select a third member to act as Chairman. If they are unable to agree upon a Chairman, they shall forthwith request the Minister of Labour of the Province of Ontario to appoint a Chairman.

10.10 Such Chairman, together with the two nominees above mentioned, shall then constitute the Board of Arbitration, and shall meet promptly to hear and consider the grievance with all reasonable dispatch, and the decision of the majority of the Board shall be final and binding on both parties.

10.11 Each of the parties will bear the expense of the arbitrator nominated by it; the parties will jointly bear the expense of the Chairman of the Board.

10.12 The Board of Arbitration shall wherever possible endeavour to render its decision within thirty days of the conclusion of the hearing on the dispute; provided that the failure of the Board to render its decision within the time limit specified shall not deprive it of jurisdiction or vitiate any award that may be made.

10.13 The Board of Arbitration shall not have any power to alter or change any of the provisions of this Collective Agreement, or to substitute any new provision for any existing provision or to give any decision inconsistent with the terms and provisions of this Collective Agreement.

10.14 To facilitate the above procedure, it is agreed that all the employer's representatives, up to the Personnel Manager, shall make every effort to effect a settlement of the grievance by the close of the working day following the day the grievance is presented and when they are unable to do so, shall notify the steward in writing and keep him informed as to progress being made, and final answer to be in writing.

10.15 Any member of the Local Executive Board shall be permitted to enter the factory for the purpose of negotiating or making investigation of a grievance, provided that he first requests and receives permission from the Department Foreman or Night Superintendent for each visit; when necessary, he may be accompanied by the steward from the department concerned, provided the steward can be temporarily relieved from his duties without impairing the efficiency and production of the factory; the international Representative may have the privilege of entering the factory for investigating grievances if each visit is approved and a pass is signed by the Plant Manager.

10.16 If an employee is discharged or suspended as a penalty by the employer and feels that he has been unjustly dealt with, he shall have the privilege of discussing the discharge or suspension with the union steward and/or the chief steward prior to leaving the Plant. It is understood that the foreman will inform the steward of the discharge or suspension as a penalty as soon as possible.

If the employee considers the penalty unjust, he shall, within five working days from the date of the imposition of the penalty, notify both the employer and the union in writing of his intention to process the penalty as a grievance and it shall then be considered a grievance and must be brought before the parties for discussion at the stage set forth in subsection 10.03 (f) within a period of not more than five working days from the date of receipt by the employer of notice from the employee. If no satisfactory solution is reached as a result of the application of the grievance procedure set forth in subsections 10.03 (f) and (g), the dispute shall be subject to arbitration in accordance with the provisions of Article 10.

If it is decided that the employee was unjustly discharged or suspended he shall be reinstated and shall be compensated at his regular rate of pay for time lost subject to the provisions hereinafter provided.

The Board of Arbitration will have the right to increase or decrease the penalty if they feel the circumstances justify this action and will have authority to determine the amount of pay the employee is to receive for the period of his discharge or suspension, if he is subsequently reinstated.

In calculating the amount of pay the employee is to receive if reinstated, the Board of Arbitration shall deduct therefrom any moneys earned by the employee from other employment and any Unemployment Insurance benefits received by the employee during the period of his suspension or discharge and retained by him.

10.17 Upon mutual agreement of the parties a single arbitrator may be substituted for the Board of Arbitration provided for in Article 10 and in case of such substitution all other applicable provisions of Article 10 will continue to apply so far as they are relevant.

10.18 (1) An employee will be given a copy of any notation concerning his misconduct or inefficiency at the time it is placed in his personal record. A copy of every notation will be forwarded to the Secretary of the Union by the Personnel Manager of the employer.

(2) Notations reporting offenses, exclusive of the violation of the no-strike provisions in this Agreement, not repeated within a one year period will be disregarded in the administration of discipline.

(3) Notations reporting offenses involving violation of the no-strike provisions in the Agreement not repeated within a three year period will disregarded in the administration of discipline.

REFERENCES AND WORKS CITED

1. Ash, P. "The Parties to the Grievance," *Personnel Psychology,* Vol. 23 (1970), 13-38.

2. Brown, D.J.M., and David M. Beatty. *Canadian Labour Arbitration* (Agincourt, Ont.: Canada Law Book, 1977).

3. Fleming, R.W. *The Labour Arbitration Process* (Urbana, Ill.: University of Illinois Press, 1965).

4. Gandz, J. "Grievance Arbitration: A Model for the Study of Policy Change," *Relations Industrielles/Industrial Relations,* Vol. 31 (1976), 631-654.

5. Gandz, J. "Employee Grievances: Incidence and Patterns of Resolution." Ph.D. thesis, York University, 1978.

6. Gandz, J. "Grievance Initiation and Resolution: a Test of the Behavioural Theory," *Relations Industrielles/Industrial Relations,* Vol. 34 (1979), 778-792.

7. Gandz, J. "Resolving Conflict: A Guide for the Industrial Relations Manager," *Personnel,* Vol. 56 (1979), 22-32.

8. Gandz, J., and P.J. Warrian. "Does It Matter Who Arbitrates? A Statistical Analysis of Arbitral Awards," *Labour Gazette,* February 1977, pp. 65-66.

9. Goldblatt, H. *Justice Delayed* (Toronto: Labour Council of Metropolitan Toronto, 1974).

10. Kuhn, J.W. *Bargaining in Grievance Settlement: the Power of Industrial Work Groups* (New York: Columbia University Press, 1961).

11. Laberge, R. "A Look at Arbitration of Rights Disputes," *Labour Gazette,* July 1975, pp. 443-448.

12. McGuicken, J.H., Jr. "Grist for the Arbitrator's Mill: What GM and the UAW Argue About," *Labor Law Journal,* Vol. 22 (1971), 647-664.

13. McKersie, R.B., and W.W. Shropshire, Jr. "Avoiding Written Grievances: A Successful Program," *Journal of Business of the University of Chicago,* Vol. 35 (1962), 135-152.

14. Mulder, F. "Characteristics of Violators of Formal Company Rules," *Journal of Applied Psychology,* Vol. 55 (1971), 500-502.

15. Peach, D.A., and D. Keuchle. *The Practice of Industrial Relations* (Toronto: McGraw Hill-Ryerson, 1975).

16. Peach, D.A., and E.R. Livernash. *Grievance Initiation and Resolution: A Study in Basic Steel* (Boston: Graduate School of Business Administration, Harvard University, 1974).

17. Price, J., J. Dewire, J. Nowack, K. Schenkel, and W. Ronan. "Three Studies of Grievances," *Personnel Journal,* Vol. 55 (1976), 33-37.

18. Primeaux, W.J., and D.E. Brannen. "Why Few Arbitrators are Deemed Acceptable," *Monthly Labor Review,* Vol. 98 (1975), 27-29.

19. Slichter, S.H., J.H. Healy, and E.R. Livernash. *The Impact of Collective Bargaining on Management* (Washington: Brookings Institute, 1962).

20. Somers, G.G. *Grievance Settlement in Coal Mining* (West Virginia: Virginia University Business and Economic Studies, 1956).

21. Sulkin, H.A., and R.W. Pranis. "Comparisons of Grievants and Nongrievants in a Heavy Machinery Company," *Personnel Psychology,* Vol. 20 (1967), 111-120.

22. Weiler, P.C. *Labour Arbitration and Industrial Change,* Study No. 6, Task Force on Labour Relations (Ottawa: Queen's Printer, 1969).

23. Weiler, P.C. "The Role of the Arbitrator: Alternative Versions," *University of Toronto Law Journal,* Vol. 19 (1969), 16-45.

QUESTIONS

1. What are the possible outcomes for union-management relations if the government makes arbitration less expensive by appointing more arbitrators, controlling fees, and specifying shorter hearing-completion times than the current average seven-month period?

2. As the industrial-relations manager of a company, what questions would you ask yourself about a grievance before starting to investigate it?

3. How are grievances related to contract negotiations?

4. At the start of contract negotiations, the union president approaches the industrial-relations manager and suggests that they schedule one day to go through several dozen outstanding grievances that are "pending arbitration" with a view to settling most of them before contract negotiations start. What risks are both the industrial-relations manager and the union president running in this situation?

BRYAN DOWNIE

14. Union-Management Cooperation

The purpose of this chapter is to provide an understanding of the ways in which unions and management can move to a more cooperative relationship. Mechanisms for cooperation include early negotiations, integrative bargaining, joint committees, workers' participation, and quality of work life. The types of cooperation are grouped into three categories: (a) programs to change the bargaining process; (b) programs to change the attitudes and perceptions of the parties; and (c) programs to increase productivity, worker control, and worker security. The reasons for cooperation are set forth and discussed as are initiatives by government and the problems of establishing and maintaining union-management cooperation.

The purpose of this chapter is to provide an understanding of the reasons for labour-management cooperation, the various forms it takes, and the ways government can assist the parties in attaining improved relationships. The first section of the chapter explores the need for, and growth of, union-management cooperation. This is followed by sections on the types of cooperative programs that currently exist, on their limitations, and on the role of government. Cooperation is a concept that is intellectually appealing but it is very difficult to establish in fact. The last section of the chapter, therefore, deals with the barriers to, and problems in, establishing cooperative programs.

REASONS FOR UNION-MANAGEMENT COOPERATION

Mechanisms to integrate the interests of labour and management take many forms — joint labour-management committees, Scanlon Plans, prebargaining sessions, voluntary arbitration, plant-production committees, various types of consultative bodies at the plant level, productivity bargaining, and quality-of-work-life programs. This list is by no means exhaustive. While there is no hard data on the matter, it seems clear that there are more instances of labour-management cooperation than ever before. *Business Week* (27) recently suggested that union-management collaboration is increasing. Moreover, the support for cooperation from the main actors in our industrial-relations system has increased significantly. For the first time since unions became a major force in North America, a number of U.S. union officials, such as I. W. Abel of the Steelworkers and Irving Bluestone of the Auto Workers' union, have voiced strong support for such programs. In Canada, labour leaders now are less reticent to offer support for cooperative and quality-of-work-life programs. Among officials in business and government there is also a feeling that our system of industrial relations leaves much to be desired. The view has been expressed repeatedly over the past decade that collective bargaining is archaic and that the adversary system is not working. These sentiments are expressed in the phrase, "there must be a better way."

In addition, industrial-relations experts (1, 3, 38) who seemed to be solidly in support of traditional collective bargaining have recently indicated partial reservations with respect to the adversary system. This is a significant shift in opinion. Most industrial-relations experts and practitioners in the past have stressed the sanctity of collective bargaining and have termed the adversary system an indigenous and valued part of our pluralist society. Most have held that strikes and the threat of strikes are a necessary part of our industrial-relations system. Indeed, the argument often goes further to stress that conflict is a valuable characteristic of a pluralist society.

The feeling that our industrial-relations system is not working as effectively as it should is probably due to three developments: (a) the high incidence and duration of strike activity in Canada since the mid-70s; (b) the increased public awareness of strikes, especially as a result of increased public-sector strikes; and (c) recent reductions in the growth rate of productivity and other economy-wide problems including worker alienation. In response to these phenomena, many new initiatives, which involve cooperation between the parties, have taken place.

In recent years, Canada has experienced one of the worst records of strike activity in its history (see Chapter 10), and there is a feeling that this situation could be improved through cooperative efforts. The argument that strikes account for only a small portion of total man-days lost and hence are not damaging, no longer seems to be acceptable to the public. A federal minister of labour, in particular, recently pointed out that when employees are absent because of sickness they are not absent en masse and at the same time. The latter is the case in a strike situation, and the impact is far more serious.

Some have argued that strikes and other forms of labour-management conflict are merely a reflection of society's economic malaise so that if the state of the economy were improved then industrial strife would soon dissipate. There is a strike cycle with peaks and troughs corresponding to the business cycle so that, for example, strikes increase during periods of inflation. Curbing inflation, therefore, should reduce strikes. This view, however, has been challenged. A feeling began to emerge at the time of wage-and-price controls in Canada (1975-78) that the cause-and-effect relationship may be working the other way. Rather than inflation causing additional strikes, it may be that industrial-relations unrest amplifies, if not causes, much of the economic malaise. There is a feeling that strikes and other forms of industrial unrest may add uncertainty and adversely affect expectations with respect to the economy. This, of course, continues to be a debatable issue.

There has been a related reason giving impetus to the search for more cooperative solutions. The incidence of strikes has shifted in the past decade. Growth of collective bargaining in the public sector in the 1970s meant a growing number of strikes in politically sensitive areas. Strikes by fire fighters, police, postal workers, garbage collectors, and teachers contain more potential for harm, in the public mind at least, than strikes by private-sector workers. There is a higher probability of adverse secondary effects from strikes in the public sector and of innocent third parties being directly and adversely affected. Labour problems in the public sector probably account for much of the public dismay with our industrial-relations system. One response of government has been to emphasize the importance of improved union-management relationships.

The most important reason for the emphasis on cooperation, however, may rest elsewhere. It is argued that the very nature of collective bargaining today (clearly win-lose in most cases) results in opportunities foregone for labour and management. Until recently, there were very few examples in North America of long term labour-management cooperation on a broad range of issues. As a consequence, there is a feeling that productivity and efficiency suffer in addition to worker well-being and satisfaction. Some evidence regarding this has been provided by the industrial-relations experience in Europe.

In short, union-management cooperation often is seen as at least a partial solution to our economic and social problems. To counter such contemporary problems as high energy costs, balance-of-payments difficulties, rampant inflation, government regulation, and high levels of worker alienation, both government and business have stressed the importance of experimentation in labour relations. However, some trade unionists as well as some academics (14, 15) see cooperative programs as sinister attempts by management to manipulate the work force in order to attain higher productivity. They also believe that some employers use such devices to destroy or weaken unions. It would be naïve to suggest that this is not the case in at least some isolated instances.

It is safe to conclude that both union and management agree to new approaches for reasons of self-interest. In a recent article, Wilfred List (24) has reported: "There is no sign that the CLC wants to turn its back on some form of cooperation with business in order to bring about economic improvements that would benefit its members." For unions, cooperation promises to bring increased employment security and satisfaction for its membership. Management, on the other hand, may well benefit through higher productivity, lower absenteeism, fewer grievances, and so on. For cooperation to survive or grow, there clearly must be benefits to both labour and management.

Joint cooperation may exist without government pressure, despite the underlying economic and social forces just discussed. The scope of collective bargaining has tended to expand over the years and as the parties have matured they have established joint committees to explore solutions to problems of mutual concern. These include areas such as occupational safety and health, education and training, alcoholism and drug addiction, and other similar matters.

For whatever reason — the incidence and duration of strikes, their deleterious impact on the economy and innocent third parties, low productivity growth, worker discontent, the need for employee security, and so on — there seems to be a growing recognition from government, business, and labour that there is a need for well-thought-out programs of cooperation. But while there is a disaffection with the current industrial-relations situations, it is equally true that the adversary process will remain the cornerstone of our industrial-relations system. It is an important part of our democratic society. Within the context of the adversary system, however, cooperative programs seem to be playing a larger role.

Union-management cooperation is not a new development. There are dramatic examples of cooperation that go back several decades. Healy (17) offers an in-depth case history of many of these in the United States. The purpose of the next section is to describe the various forms of union-management cooperation that have been utilized over the years. Particular emphasis is placed, nevertheless, on developments that have occurred over the past decade and on Canadian examples of union-management cooperation.

TYPES OF JOINT COOPERATION

There are three broad types of union-management cooperation elaborated in detail below: (a) programs to change the bargaining process; (b) programs to change management and labour attitudes and perceptions; and (c) programs to increase productivity, worker control, or worker security. Joint union-management initiatives often fall into more than one category, and the parties may introduce programs sequentially with certain components falling into more than one category.

Changes to Effect More Cooperation in the Bargaining Process

The behavioural dimension of the *negotiation process* obviously is important in setting the tone for a union-management relationship. By and large, collective bargaining is "crisis bargaining" with all of the trappings of win-lose conflict (low trust, biased perceptions, dysfunctional attitudes, and so on). As discussed by Fox (11), there is often institutionalized distrust. The two sides generally try to "power" one another through threats and counterthreats until a crisis is reached, usually at the strike deadline; then the parties, more often than not, rapidly shift positions and come to an accommodation. A well-known third-party neutral has described the process as follows:

> ... we are tending more and more to crisis bargaining. This is a question of strategy; how to get more out of the bargaining process, how one party can get a settlement close to its end of the range of possible settlement.
>
> The tactics on the part of both union and management seem to be that in direct negotiations meaningful concessions are withheld. Each party forms its own ideas about where it wants to go, but it doesn't tell the other party. Neither side uses conciliators or mediators properly, that is confiding in them or allowing them to use information they have been given. What happens is that both sides reveal nothing, make no offers, make no concessions — stonewall right down to the last minute, hoping that everything will fall into place, with concession begetting concession so that there is a deal. The trouble is that both parties play the same game. (39, p. 362)

As the above statement indicates, crisis bargaining is a behavioural dimension of the process and this accounts, in part, for the inflexible, legalistic and adversarial orientation of the parties. Union-management cooperation, therefore, sometimes takes the form of attempts to dampen conflict in the bargaining process. Three systems have been used to achieve this: (a) voluntary arbitration; (b) early negotiations or prebargaining; and (c) single-team or integrative bargaining.

Voluntary arbitration— There may be a relationship between the dispute-settlement mechanism used by the parties and the character of their joint dealings within, and outside of, the bargaining process. The following statement is from a union negotiator (4) who is a proponent of voluntary final-offer arbitration (italics added by author):

Each union and each company must individually choose the process and atmosphere they want. If they want a good fight — so be it. If they want a bargaining ritual — fine. But, if they want to confront issues, to come to terms, and to do it with minimum cost, then they have to give careful thought to the *kind of process* they choose. The *final weapon* to resolve disputes between them is only a part of the process, but it can, even if never used, affect the attitude of both parties in all earlier steps.

This suggests that the imposition of a sanction substitute by the mutual agreement of the parties may facilitate cooperation. This notion is somewhat contrary to the general perception that arbitration has a number of dysfunctional effects in labour relations (8). However, there is an emerging consensus in industrial relations that, while interest arbitration imposed by government as a strike substitute may be harmful to collective bargaining, voluntary arbitration is a workable option. Voluntary arbitration actually may not destroy the give-and-take of collective bargaining but, rather, it may enhance the labour-relations climate where it is used. For example, David Cole (3, p. 156), an eminent industrial-relations expert, has stated the case for voluntary interest arbitration most forcefully: "As I have said on other occasions, to insist that we cannot have collective bargaining without depending on the strike is like saying that if we renounce war we cannot have diplomacy. To me, precisely the contrary is true."

The best-known cooperative initiative along these lines has occurred between the United Steelworkers of America and the major U.S. steel companies which bargain together as an industry-wide group. In 1971, the parties signed the Experimental Negotiation Agreement (ENA). In return for a no-strike pledge by the union, a generous benefit package was offered, and there was a provision for voluntary binding arbitration of all unresolved disputes by a three-man arbitration board. The union does retain its right to strike on local-plant issues; therefore, local issues cannot be ignored in negotiations.

The arbitration procedure obviously was carefully designed. The ENA provides for an arbitration panel which contains a union advisory representative, a management advisory representative, and three impartial arbitrators jointly selected by the parties. Two of the three arbitrators must be familiar with the steel industry. There is a provision that the arbitration award must be made before the contract expiry date.

While the interest in voluntary arbitration is new, application of the concept is not, particularly in Canada. Jacob Finkleman, when he was chairman of the Public Service Staff Relations Board, noted in an address to the Electrical Contractors Association of Ontario in 1972 that in the Ontario clothing industry voluntary arbitration has been used for thirty years. It has been used in a number of teacher-school-board disputes in Ontario and by faculty and a number of universities in Canada as well.

The voluntary imposition of arbitration is potentially an extremely important step to a better labour-management relationship. It may help remove the military-type tactics, the use of bilateral threat, and the high level of mistrust often prevalent in negotiations. It saves on stockpiling and other costs associated with the actuality, or threat, of a strike or lockout. More importantly, it allows the parties the opportunity to experiment without the threat of economic sanctions over their heads.

There are those who favour innovation in industrial relations but not voluntary arbitration because they favour resolution of disputes through the efforts of the two sides alone. The idea of voluntary arbitration, however, is that it would be used rarely. This seems to work in actual practice. For example, the parties have not had to use arbitration in the U.S. steel industry and as Finkleman indicated, the number of contract disputes referred to arbitration in the Ontario clothing industry were "very, very few." But, if negotiations break down, after the parties manage to improve their relationship, they can resolve their dispute with a minimum amount of disruption and without destroying any other positive innovations that may have been introduced.

Early negotiations and prebargaining — A characteristic of adversary bargaining is the setting of "deadlines" and "conditions" for further talks. Additionally, it is not unusual for one of the parties, or both of them, to set a prescribed period of time for negotiations after which, according to the threat, negotiations will break down if settlement is not reached. Moreover, actual negotiating is often limited to a very short flurry of activity.

Research findings (23) have indicated that a sufficient period of time, and one free of deadlines, is necessary for problem solving and for "win-win" rather than "win-lose" behaviour to take place. In light of this, it is not surprising that in some relationships the parties have deliberately set aside extra time as a strategy for more cooperative and peaceful negotiations. "Early-bird negotiations," as they are referred to, have been used on numerous occasions and with success. This mechanism is also known as prebargaining, prenegotiations, or a study committee.

One of the best-known examples of providing ample negotiating time also occurred in the U.S. steel industry. In the early 1960s the Human Relations Research Committee was set up to consider problems in the industry on a more or less continuing basis. On several occasions during the 1960s, negotiations in the industry were started well in advance of contract expiry, and settlement was obtained prior to that date. The Experimental Negotiating Agreement continues that tradition by requiring that negotiations start in January even though the contract does not expire until July 31.

In Canada, at Ontario Hydro, the parties hold prebargaining meetings in late October even though the contract does not expire until March 31 of the following year. Negotiations are now started a full six weeks earlier than had previously been the case. Agreement generally has been achieved prior to the expiry of the collective agreement. Prebargaining is used at Ontario Hydro to bring together the main union and management committees and to provide an opportunity for all members to better understand technical areas such as pensions, insurance, sick leave, and costing. The meetings are used to prepare the parties by supplying them with a common understanding of the above areas as well as a common statistical and financial information base.

There are many other variations on this basic theme. For example, early bargaining took place in the 1974 Canadian Railway negotiations. Talks started, by design, in early July even though the various contracts (there were seventeen unions bargaining together) did not expire until December 31. Both sides felt that, by starting earlier, negotiations would be smoother. These talks not only ended in a negotiated settlement but it was also the first time in the history of railway bargaining that this had occurred without third-party assistance.

There is a difference between early negotiations by mutual design and negotiations that drag on, as frequently occurs in the public sector, for months or even for years. In early negotiations or prebargaining, the parties generally have a negotiation plan and timetable. It seems important to have a target date for settlement and a well-thought-out time frame for negotiations. A target date for settlement is quite different, of course, from a deadline. The latter denotes a threat and implies adverse consequences for the other side. A target is a goal to strive for, with little threat attached to it. To illustrate, a preconceived and specific time sequence for negotiations was agreed upon by both sides at Ontario Hydro. This plan contained a target date for settlement and the parties reached agreement prior to this date. The ENA in U.S. steel is definite on this point as well. National negotiations must begin in mid-January with a target date of mid-April for settlement. The parties have always reached agreement on schedule. While there was no formal plan in Canadian rail negotiations mentioned above, both sides came to the table exceedingly well prepared and had individually developed a time frame for negotiations. Their time frames were similar, and an informal target date of November 1 (two months prior to contract expiry) was agreed to by both sides. This target was missed by only a few days.

Early-bird negotiations and the setting of a target date for settlement apparently help mute the dysfunctional aspects of deadline setting. By removing deadline pressure, these two aspects in conjunction also allow the parties to consider more thoroughly items on the agenda, and they may facilitate a more thorough search for alternative solutions. In addition, the extra time available may lead the parties to interact more as a working committee than as protagonists. An example of this approach occurred many years ago in the U.S. auto industry. Chrysler and the UAW set up prenegotiation *study* committees which contributed in a major way to successful 1964 contract negotiations between the parties.

Prebargaining does not always prevent strikes, nor is it always successful. Canada Post and the Letter Carriers Union in the late 1970s undertook initiatives to improve their relationship including the utilization of prebargaining. Despite considerable improvement in their relationship, a strike did take place in 1979, although the strike lasted only a few days, and the improved relationship allowed the parties to resolve their dispute amicably and quickly.

Single-team or integrative bargaining — Walton and McKersie (37), in their seminal work on collective bargaining, break the negotiation process into four subprocesses — distributive bargaining, integrative bargaining, attitudinal structuring, and intraorganizational bargaining. Integrative bargaining is frequently referred to as problem solving. Early negotiations (or prebargaining) is an attempt to induce problem-solving behaviour by removing the deadline aspects and time pressure from collective bargaining. Cooperation may also be induced by minimizing the perceived differences between union and management groups at the bargaining table. A manifestation of adversary, or distributive, bargaining is that the parties physically group themselves in a "we-they" arrangement. Indeed, it has been found (32) that conflict is promoted by such seating arrangements. Some have noted that physical separation is a precursor to conflict. Filey (10, p. 79) for example, has stated: "Spatial arrangements will themselves provoke or elicit various forms of behaviour. Not only that but it has been found that the greater the distance between the two parties the less friendly they are perceived to be."

Single-team bargaining is a concept to induce problem solving through, among other things, a change in seating arrangements at the bargaining table. It is simply the practice of integrative bargaining and has been described as a process under which the parties to negotiations combine resources to resolve items on the agenda as if all individuals were on one team instead of on two opposing teams. By agreeing on new, more informal, less adversarial seating arrangements, it is felt that the parties will be able to introduce an improved climate at the bargaining table.

As noted, single-team bargaining is not a new idea. The notion of problem-solving behaviour in negotiations and the environmental and attitudinal components necessary for its practice were well documented by Walton and McKersie in the mid-1960s. In the early 1970s in Canada, many of the key ideas behind integrative bargaining were brought together by Mr. Tom Crossman, the personnel director for Labatt's Breweries, and put into practice in an actual set of negotiations with a bona fide trade union. A member of the union who went through the negotiation coined the term "single-team collective bargaining." Under single team there is a real attempt to make negotiations nonadversarial. No bargaining table is used in certain circumstances or, if one is necessary, a round table is introduced. The elimination of the single spokesman ploy, generally considered functional and necessary for traditional collective bargaining, is another strategy of a similar nature that was introduced by Crossman. The basic idea is to maximize informality and to minimize the "we-they" atmosphere.

Single-team or integrative bargaining was first applied to the resolution of nonmonetary items. However, its carry-over into the monetary items has been recognized. As Crossman (31) stated:

> If the single team talks have been successful, there is a strong tendency towards much greater openness on the part of all concerned. You get concerned with your trustworthiness and are careful not to be deceptive. If these attitudes carry over into the monetary talks, the negotiations are smoother and quicker.

Integrative bargaining is not limited to instances where the single-team concept is used. There are other cases where the parties have attempted to treat nonmonetary items in a cooperative fashion. Canada Post and the Letter Carriers Union, for example, utilize a process for nonmonetary items which they call problem-solving bargaining. It has been described by an official at Canada Post as "an approach to bargaining whereby union and management representatives tackle issues in a problem-solving way, that is, they negotiate without adopting the traditional policy of union demands/management counterproposal."

Integrative bargaining needs to be constantly nurtured if it is to last, and its success depends to a very great extent on the personalities at the bargaining table. There is a tendency for such efforts to fail or break down. There are a variety of reasons for this including membership apathy, relationships that become "too cozy," political pressures within the union, and economic pressures. In the early 1960s, a number of spectacular examples of institutionalized problem solving took place in the United States — the Human Relations Research Committee in the steel industry, the West Coast Modernization and Mechanization Plan, the Armour Automation Fund, the Kaiser Steel Progress Sharing Plan — to name the foremost examples. These attempts and some others were very successful. Nevertheless, as others have noted (29), many of the schemes were either discontinued or badly crippled after a few years. At the same time, many of these served their purpose and a leading practitioner in the field put the record in perspective:

No informed critic can write-off non-crisis dialogue ... The successes outweigh the failures ... As collective bargaining becomes increasingly complex, the old notion that it can be confined to a few days or weeks every two or three years with routine handling of a few grievances in the meantime, becomes progressively less realistic. (33, p. 318)

Programs to Change Attitudes and Perceptions

There is, of course, no way that conflict can be totally eliminated nor, as Coser (6) has noted, is that necessarily desirable. Healy (17, p. 284), however, based on past cooperative programs, reports that "mutual trust and respect are a cornerstone of any new approach." The two broad approaches discussed below are directed primarily at attitudinal improvement in union-management relationships through mechanisms designed to increase intergroup contact.

Organization development techniques — Attitudinal change entails a fundamental transformation in the orientation that the two sides undertake in their joint dealings — a shift from conflict to collaboration. Bringing about such change is particularly difficult under the adversary system. Experiments have been conducted which illustrate gross distortion in the perceptions of labour and management of one another and, therefore, of their *attitudes* toward one another. Research has demonstrated that labour and management stereotype each other, and as Haire states:

> ... this distortion is sufficient to give rise to considerable misunderstanding between them because of the subject matter of their conversations. It does not suggest that this is the sole source of difference of opinion between labour and management in negotiation. The kind of distortion demonstrated here should probably be viewed primarily as a barrier to communications which makes doubly difficult the problem of resolving differences of opinion or purpose. Where there is in fact substantive disagreement between labour and management, it would seem to be of particular importance to have a clear statement of the view and aim of each side. The kind of misperception illustrated here must certainly inhibit an unambiguous understanding of whatever differences exist. (16, pp. 204-206)

Some successful experiments in attitudinal change, nevertheless, have taken place. Techniques from the field of organization development (OD) have been used to change union-management perceptions. The most popular device, the "intergroup lab," has been used extensively to treat win-lose conflict between departments in organizations. This type of behavioural-science intervention in situations of intergroup conflict outside labour-management relations had been successful and impressive. The lab approach involves trying to induce problem-solving relations by cutting through the tensions and conflict existing between two antagonistic groups. The concept was first applied in union-management relations in the U.S. by Blake and Mouton and, according to reports (2), perceptions and attitudes were changed and because of this a problem-solving orientation was adopted by labour and management representatives.

In Canada, intergroup labs now have been used in a number of union-management situations. The most intensive application of the lab approach has occurred at Canada Post. Intergroup sessions were first held in September of 1976 with the Letter Carriers Union. Since that time, in addition to the Letter Carriers Union, the Association of Postal Officials of Canada, the Canadian Postmaster and Assistants Association, and the Public Service Alliance of Canada have all been involved in intergroup lab sessions. Since 1976, more than 200 intergroup labs had been held across Canada at Canada Post. These involved some 3,000 union and management personnel. Indeed, "intergroup," as it is referred to, has been used as the primary means of improving the labour-relations climate at Canada Post. It has never been utilized, however, with the Canadian Union of Postal Workers (CUPW).

"Intergroup" at Canada Post brings union and management representatives together outside the atmosphere of collective bargaining. At intergroup sessions, management and union representatives meet to uncover mutual problems regarding their relationship, confront these problems in an open manner, and collectively develop action plans to resolve them. This is similar to most consultative committees but, in the case of intergroup, ground rules are established for each session, and a facilitator is available to lend assistance and direction to each of the two parties. Also, a structure is provided to force the two groups to air their perceptions, misperceptions, and differences.

The original design by Blake and Mouton called for the two conflicting groups to work in separate rooms on the following questions: (1) What are our perceptions of the other group? (2) What are our perceptions of our group? (3) What do we think the other group's perceptions of us are? The two groups would then be asked to hold a joint meeting to confront, with the assistance of a facilitator, the similarities and differences of the two groups' lists. At Canada Post, the basic intergroup-lab concept has been modified to suit their own situation. Briefly, the first step is for both groups to reach an understanding of the attitudes, problems, and barriers that tend to separate them. Through questionnaires followed by group discussion, each party — management and union — presents to the other its consensus of the *present* and the *ideal* union-management working relationship. The discussion and elaboration that follows creates mutual understanding of the two sides and clears up many misperceptions. Each group then presents a list of problems that represent significant bottlenecks in closing the gap between the existing and ideal relationship. Finally, joint union-management teams work on bottleneck issues and develop specific action plans to resolve them.

The intergroup approach apparently has helped eliminate distrust and reduce communication barriers between union and management representatives. It has shifted attitudes on both sides and has helped the parties solve mutual problems effectively on a cooperative basis. Despite poor relationships between Canada Post and the Canadian Union of Postal Workers, the labour-relations climate between Canada Post and their other unions has improved dramatically since intergroup was introduced. There apparently has been a growing sense of mutual trust and respect and a common commitment to the overall goals of the organization among management and the leaders of the unions which have been involved in the intergroup experiments.

Intergroup labs have been used extensively in various union-management settings in the U.S. through a program introduced by the Federal Mediation and Conciliation Service. FMCS has entitled its program "Relationships by Objectives" (RBO). An identical program has been introduced by the Ontario Ministry of Labour and, more recently, the Ontario Education Relations Commission has embarked on a similar effort. The ministry's program will be discussed at greater length under the section on the role of government.

The role of OD concepts in labour relations is controversial. In at least some cases, it has been reported (35) that OD specialists have failed to understand the dynamics of the collective-bargaining process. Strauss, in a recent article (36), highlights some of the difficulties by describing two cases involving an OD intervention in labour relations.

> Blake, et al. (1946) described an inter-group laboratory as a means of handling union-management problems. As they described it, their "orientation is based on recognizing union and management disputes as symptoms of pathology in the problem solving area, diagnosing the causes that produce the symptoms, and treating the causes directly" (p. 144). In context it is clear that the authors view the "causes" of conflict as interpersonal rather than economic. In other words, economic differences are caused by poor interpersonal relations, rather than the reverse. Though the authors report four cases where laboratory programs led to improved relations, they tell us little about substantive questions at stake.
>
> In the second case, OD specialists Lewicki and Alderfer (1973) came to grief in their attempts to intervene in a difficult bargaining relationship shortly before a union election. Unwittingly they showed insufficient sensitivity to the intricacies of union politics, thus allowing themselves to become identified as management representatives.

Strauss goes on to note that despite these problems, OD insights and techniques do have applications to collective bargaining.

Industry-wide and economy-wide consultative committees — James Healy, in discussing steps the parties can take to improve relationships, has noted:

> The most critical element in the success of a creative approach to collective bargaining is an attitude on the part of both parties which is characterized by mutual determination or commitment to find a more effective way to settle their own union-management differences.... No matter the impetus the first step is for the parties to step back and look at their situation and to appraise it realistically... such an analysis demands an objective search for factual information on which the parties can agree and on an honest and perhaps *joint examination* of the "truths" and "matters of principle" with respect to particular issues upon which past positions of the respective parties were based. (17, pp. 283-284)

In the 1960s and 1970s, many joint committees were formed which brought together union and management representatives from an entire industry or, in some cases, from the domain of an entire province. The idea was to improve the attitudes of the parties by inducing interaction on matters of common concern. Joint consultation, as this usually is referred to, has been fairly actively pursued by the federal government as well as some provincial governments. Manitoba's Labour-Management Committee (Woods Committee) is one of the most successful attempts of this type. To this point, the impact of broad-based joint consultation has been minute because it has not been effectively directed at the establishment level. Kovaks points out one of the weaknesses of practising joint consultation on such a large scale:

> The employers' group does not have an organizational structure for committing them to provincial policy, and industrial relations is only one area among many to occupy the attention of management. Therefore, only by example will any experience gained through joint Provincial councils filter through to any individual employer. (21, p. 49)

Over and above that, the subject matter of such consultation is somewhat restricted. To illustrate, the focus of joint councils might be limited to an examination of labour legislation within the jurisdiction. This has positive potential but, at best, constitutes a limited form of cooperation. This is true of any experiments in tripartism which attempt to introduce change from the top. Discussions among top union, management, and government officials run the danger of being superficial due to the fact that those involved, particularly for management, generally are not the actual decision makers. Instead, they are simply representatives for the decision makers.

Broad-based consultation of the right variety, nevertheless, has proven useful. If the emphasis is on the establishment level, or, in some cases, on the industry or sector level, important changes may result. For example, through third-party or other government initiatives the parties, say, in construction, may be persuaded to sit down and work out new procedures for the prompt and informal resolution of jurisdictional disputes. This may lead to other labour-management innovations in the industry. There are many examples of industry-wide cooperation. Earlier reference was made to the Human Relations Research Committee in the U.S. basic-steel industry in the 1960s. A more recent illustration is the Joint Labour Management Committee for the Retail Food Industry which was formed in the United States. The committee seeks to aid collective bargaining through the maintenance and exchange of information on wages, collective-bargaining settlements and other matters that will assist collective bargaining. The committee also was formed for the discussion of longer-range problems including fragmented bargaining, and the need for adequate information on such sensitive areas of technological change as the automated checkout, automated warehousing, and centralized meat cutting.

Recently in Manitoba, under the guidance and assistance of the Woods Committee, labour and management in the hospital sector attempted to reform their system of collective bargaining. The parties managed to introduce a number of changes to assist the process. A more dramatic example of cooperation through consultation took place over a decade ago also under the auspices of the Woods Committee. Manitoba Hydro approached the committee concerning the labour problems that they felt might arise in connection with the Nelson River project. Through the consultative machinery of the committee, the major players in the project (Manitoba Hydro, the Manitoba Federation of Labour, the several international unions involved in construction, and several employers' associations) were able to reach a *ten-year* agreement. This assured labour-relations peace and stability for that period of time.

Programs to Induce Plant Floor Cooperation, Productivity Improvement, and Employee Security

The most dramatic increase in union-management cooperation has taken the form of joint action at the establishment level. Here, there are three broad approaches to cooperation: (1) joint labour-management committees; (2) participative schemes; and (3) quality-of-work-life innovations. In some cases, for example at establishments where the Scanlon Plan is in effect, all three of the above mechanisms may be introduced.

Joint labour-management committees— Union-management interaction within a unit on an ongoing basis *outside of collective bargaining* has been mounted to induce problem-solving behaviour, a greater degree of openness, improved productivity, and benefits for the labour force. Joint committees which operate on a year-round basis can be run with a problem-solving style and thus reduce confrontation and perhaps result in new attitudes between the parties. With such an orientation, it is hoped that innovative solutions to pressing production and cost problems will be discovered.

An illustration of this type of approach is found in a declining industry, the U.S. railroad industry. In 1974, with financial aid from the Association of American Railroads, the Federal Railroad Administration, the Missouri Pacific Railroad and various railroad labour organizations, the "St. Louis Project" began. This is a program of cooperative action outside of normal collective bargaining. It entails a program of joint labour-management experiments involving changes in operations at Missouri Pacific's (MOPAC) St. Louis terminal. The following approach has been adopted:

1. The parties jointly identify barriers to terminal efficiency and service reliability.
2. They propose changes in management and labour practices (including changes in the contract) and in government regulations that affect the operation of the terminal.
3. They conduct on-line experiments designed to test the effectiveness of the proposed solutions. The changes or experiments are considered as temporary only.
4. The cost savings become known, and the unions involved then have the option of negotiating permanent change.

The program has obvious advantages. First, it has demonstrated some clear-cut improvements in efficiency with both sides sharing in the improvement. Second, it has opened communication between local labour and management by a series of regular meetings between the employees and operating officials. It, therefore, involves many members of both groups in intergroup contact. As a consequence it may facilitate attitudinal improvement. Third, the emphasis throughout the process is on problem solving rather than confrontation.

The St. Louis project is an illustration of productivity bargaining. This involves the negotiation and implementation of formal agreements that stipulate certain changes in work rules in order to achieve greater productivity while at the same time ensuring that labour receives its share of the resulting savings. A distinction has been made (26) between productivity bargaining using a "gain-sharing" approach as against a "buy-out" approach. Under the buy-out strategy, management analyses its operations and, on its own initiative, develops a plan for productivity improvement. Management then goes to the bargaining table to negotiate change with the union. The gain-sharing approach uses an open-ended problem-solving process, and labour-management cooperation, to search out ways to improve productivity or joint benefits. Once the productivity or benefits are increased, or procedures are discovered to ensure this, the rewards are shared by the parties.

The St. Louis Project is an example of the gain-sharing approach. The gain-sharing approach has also been used in a set of teacher-board negotiations in Ontario. At Thunder Bay, through open-ended joint-committee problem solving, the parties arrived at an agreement known as the "four-over-five plan." Teachers may bank one-quarter of their salary in each of four consecutive years and take a year off from teaching in the fifth year at four-fifths of their regular salary. The leave is financed through the banking provision plus interest accumulated on the scheme. Many board and teacher groups have included this innovation into their collective agreements. The teachers gain a leave plan. A board faced with declining enrolment gains a system of dealing with teacher redundancy. Rather than having to dismiss teachers, they are able to maintain their teacher contingent and at the same time see their labour force develop professionally (through the leave provision).

The buy-out approach entails union-management cooperation at a single point in time. An example recently occurred in Canada (12) when the Goodyear Company in Toronto wanted to convert its sixty-three-year-old tire plant to radial-tire production. The parties jointly negotiated change. In return for economic and job-security concessions, the union, the United Rubber Workers, agreed to a special arrangement on productivity with the company and expressed its commitment to maintain plant costs and quality during the changeover.

The benefit to the workers from joint committees is often employment security. Joint committees were provided for in the Experimental Negotiating Agreement in the basic-steel industry in the United States. The benefits to both sides can be seen from the following description (13) of that experiment:

> Another development of the 1971 negotiations was agreement on the formation of joint advisory committees on productivity at each plant in the industry .... These committees, continued under the 1974 agreement as "employment security and plant productivity committees," have additional purposes to the improvement of productivity. They are to promote orderly and peaceful relations in the plant; promote the use of domestic steel; achieve desired prosperity and progress for its employees; and, consistent with the terms of the agreement, review matters of special concern. As the union has stressed, these joint productivity efforts are based "not on the concept of speed-up but of eliminating waste and unnecessary costs." Pointing to the substantial increase in the annual rate of output per man-hour from 1971 to 1973 and the maintenance of a relatively stable employment level, the union view was that "after three years of experience under the joint productivity program, a great many tangible results became apparent. No speed-up measures have been instituted by management. None of the feared job rearrangements materialized. Slowly the process of building mutual trust set in after the plant committees began functioning." The increase in productivity was attributed to the evening of production schedules, high level of demand and output, imports down and exports up, and the joint labour management productivity program.

Joint union-management committees differ from "participative and incentive schemes" in that, unlike the latter, the joint-action concept does not necessarily include a prearranged formula for efficiency improvement. Instead, the savings and benefits are achieved on an *ad hoc* basis.

Participative and incentive schemes — Joint cooperation through the use of some sort of participative and inventive scheme goes back many years. This was highlighted in a recent article on the subject of union-management cooperation.

> In 1940, when labour relations in the steel industry were still in a primitive state, steel union leader Philip Murray proposed an idea that was daring for the times. Instead of perpetuating conflict, labour and management should collaborate on the shop floor, Murray said. By "tapping labour's brains" — that is, seeking workers' advice on how to improve production processes — management could make labour an "active participant" in managing the work place and thus increase productivity. (34, p. 98)

It is not surprising, therefore, that one of the earliest and most successful schemes, the Scanlon Plan, was pioneered by the Steelworkers. The Scanlon Plan has an established track record that dates back four decades. The plan is named after Joseph N. Scanlon who was a steelworker and a local union president of the Steelworkers. The best-known application of the Scanlon Plan occurred at Lapoint Machine Tool Company, where the plan had a long and successful history. The best-known Canadian application is at the Hayes Dana plant in St. Thomas, Ontario, where the International Association of Machinists holds bargaining rights. Because of its success, the Scanlon Plan warrants some detailed discussion. The following description draws on the authoritative work concerning the plan by Lesieur (22).

The Scanlon Plan entails a set of principles or ideals to stimulate teamwork on the plant floor. The details of the plan are extremely difficult to describe, and there are necessary differences in the application of the scheme to various situations. Nevertheless, there are two major facets to the plan — participation and a cost-sharing formula. With respect to participation, production committees and a screening committee are generally set up. The production committees which may be formed in each department of a plant will have representation from both labour and management. The union members are usually elected by the membership while management usually appoints its members to the committee. The latter is generally a supervisor or an individual with some decision-making power within the firm. Most typically, there is not equal representation of union and management personnel on the committee. Often five or six union members will be meeting with one management representative.

The function of the *production committees* is to meet regularly, usually at least once a month, to discuss production problems in the department in an open way. There is often a formal suggestion system, and it is the job of the committee to process suggestions submitted to it by the employees in a department. The discussion will typically centre on such problems as material waste, production bottlenecks, scheduling, and work processing problems. A key aspect is that each suggestion is treated seriously, and in some cases the actual suggestor will be invited to discuss the idea with the committee.

While practices vary from committee to committee, it is often a rule that final decisions on suggestions are not taken at this level and a formal vote is not taken. It is important to point out that management reserves the right to accept or reject any suggestion filed with a production committee. Also, it should be noted that a production committee does not deal in any way with issues related to the grievance procedure or that would infringe on the collective agreement. Finally, unlike traditional suggestion systems, an *individual* reward is not paid for suggestions that are ultimately introduced. Rather, the Scanlon Plan involves a *group* incentive scheme.

All of the minutes of the production committees are forwarded to a *screening committee*. The screening committee varies in size but typically ranges from eight to twelve people, and unlike the production committees there are typically an equal number of union and management representatives on the committee. The representation from each side will often vary, but typically one of the members will be the local union president and there will be employee representatives from the areas covered by the production committee. It is important that management representatives on this committee include top decision makers within the company. Therefore the management representatives might be the president or vice-president of the company, the treasurer, a plant superintendent, and an engineer. Meetings of the screening committee are held on a regular basis (in most instances at least once a month). At these meetings, the committee determines the monthly group bonus (or deficit) which has been incurred in the most recent accounting period. They also will discuss possible difficulties faced by the plan such as changes in the economic environment or competitive factors. The various suggestions that have been accepted by the production committees are discussed and put into the record and those suggestions which have been rejected are also thoroughly discussed and decisions with respect to these are made. The screening committee, like the production committee, does not have final decision-making approval. Again, management reserves the right to accept or reject any suggestion that has been presented.

As mentioned earlier, the Scanlon Plan involves the development of a cost-sharing plan. Initially, a measurement is taken over some historical period of the relationship between total payroll in the unit and the sales value of what has been produced by that payroll. This represents the *norm* against which future comparisons will be made in calculating the bonus. When labour costs are *below* the norm, the difference between the normal payroll and the actual payroll constitutes the bonus pool. The *total* bonus is not paid out, however. Instead, a certain amount is generally set aside in a reserve to protect the company and the employees against possible deficit months in which the actual payroll exceeds the norm.

Of course, not all of the bonus goes to the employees. The bonus pool that remains after provision for a reserve is split between the employees and the company on a basis that represents the rough division between capital and labour. (Most often 25 percent goes to the company and 75 percent is paid out in immediate cash bonus to participants in the Scanlon Plan.) There are generally numerous adjustments which must be made before the bonus is paid. For example, the bonus paid to individuals as a percent of their participating payroll may exclude payments for such things as vacations and holidays. The feeling may be that the bonus should not be paid on vacation pay because only actual effort in the production process should be remunerated through the bonus system. Similarly, pay to probationary employees generally is excluded from the payroll base. Many extraneous factors, such as shifts in product mix, can dramatically affect the amount of bonus received by each employee if they are not included in the cost-sharing formula.

The purpose of the Scanlon Plan formula is not only to focus employee attention on key variables which are of critical importance to company success but also to act as a vehicle to stimulate worker participation and union-management cooperation. Other schemes such as *profit sharing* and *employee stock ownership* are designed to perform similar fuctions. The Scanlon Plan in particular, however, seems most amenable to a unionized setting. For example, Nightingale (28), in discussing the Scanlon Plan, notes:

> Under the Scanlon Plan, union officials approach the bargaining table with much more information on the company's position than under conventional arrangements. Similarly, under an effectively running Scanlon Plan, management has better insight into the union's problems. The Plan consequently can foster more collaborative labour-management relations.

The Scanlon and similar plans, nevertheless, do not invariably meet with success. Often failure is linked with the inability to pay a monthly bonus. In addition, success is difficult to maintain if the company does not continue to make technological improvements. Finally, the applications of participation schemes are limited at this point to a fairly small set of organizations. For example, there seem to be few applications for either the Scanlon Plan or other similar types of schemes in very large organizations. Moreover, to succeed, participative plans require a management style which includes Theory Y values —a belief that employees are intrinsically motivated and self-directed individuals.

Other quality-of-work-life innovations— Most of the mechanisms discussed in this chapter to stimulate cooperative relationships fall under the broad rubric of Quality of Work-Life (QWL). QWL refers to those initiatives taken in the work place which are designed to produce more cooperation and efficiency and to improve the psychological and social conditions of work. There are other options sometimes utilized to stimulate employee cooperation which fall under QWL, but they are introduced only rarely in unionized settings.

Works councils, for example, are joint bodies of employees (though not generally union officials) and management. They are more common in Europe than in North America. The elected employee representatives have codecision-making power with management on various corporate matters. This is a concept which strengthens trade unionism in the European setting but in the North American setting is more likely to be an alternative to unionism. Nightingale (28, p. 345), in making this point, has noted that: "The Works Council — Canadian Style — is based on a collaborative, rather than an adversarial relationship between labour and management, and the works council assumes many of the responsibilities of a trade union." Nevertheless, a recent report, known as the "Connaghan Report," suggests that the concept might be a way to improve labour-management relationships in Canada. At the same time, Connaghan (5) has noted that the works-council idea, if adopted in Canada, would have to be altered to suit the Canadian industrial-relations system.

Several other concepts, generally introduced as QWL initiatives, also are related to union-management cooperation in a tangential manner only. Employee stock ownership, particularly in the United States, is enjoying a miniboom (40). Employee stock ownership, however, does not necessarily imply that there will be employee or union *participation* in decision making. Indeed, there are many cases where employee-owned firms continue unilateral decision making on the part of management. There are firms, however, such as Supreme Aluminum in Toronto, that combine worker participation with profit sharing and employee stock ownership.

Self-directing (or autonomous) work groups, and shop-floor democracy through job redesign are examples of programs designed to relieve the boredom, monotony, and alienation generated by most industrial jobs. Under these systems, employees are involved in the decisions and work design specifically related to their own activities. These concepts sometimes introduce significant changes in the organization with respect to supervision and work practices. The rationale behind such concepts is that workers understand the production process they are closest to and that, in particular, they possess the most knowledge regarding their own job. Sociotechnical systems, job design, job enrichment, and job rotation are all innovations which are based on this belief. Under semi-autonomous work groups, for example, workers form their own norms about appropriate behaviour and performance. While a spirit of cooperation within such groups is the general result, and productivity often increases, these QWL concepts are more appropriately viewed as the outcome of union-management cooperation rather than as a case, or an example, of cooperation. In fact, many QWL experiments are not congruent with or may be at cross purposes with union goals and the collective agreement. Another author on this subject has written as follows with respect to trade unions and job enrichment:

> The creation of self-directing workgroups can disturb collectively bargained policies. Within self-directing groups, jobs are shared, distinctions between tasks and craft boundaries are blurred, and supervisory and non-supervisory tasks are combined. Consequently, it is important when considering job redesign to involve trade unions in the process. (28, p. 384)

This is not to say that QWL is an antithetical concept to the concept of trade unionism. However, unions have legitimate concerns with respect to such initiatives because QWL projects can be used by management for antiunion purposes.

THE ROLE OF GOVERNMENT

A large measure of responsibility for industrial relations lies in the hands of government (in Canada, provincial or federal depending upon the industry). It has been noted by Downie (9), however, that government can only encourage labour-management cooperation through very indirect means. The most direct form of government action in this area would be legislation dictating some form of worker participation. One of the purposes of such legislation would be to facilitate more collaborative relationships. However, a legislative solution has often (7) been rejected as not logical or desirable in Canada because of the nature of the country's labour and management institutions and its system of collective bargaining and government. Nevertheless, there are two forms of government assistance in this area which, while indirect, have had some impact— QWL assistance and preventive mediation.

Government can encourage labour-management cooperation through support of QWL initiatives by labour and management. Labour Canada has been engaged in such a project for several years. The program was designed to facilitate voluntary QWL experiments rather than force new initiatives on the parties. The Province of Ontario has mounted a somewhat similar program in its Ministry of Labour and recently has released an inventory of QWL innovations in Ontario (25). Through information gathering and dissemination, plus the delivery of QWL expertise when requested by the parties, these two programs have played a role in the formation of cooperative ventures at the work site. The formation of semiautonomous work groups, job redesign and job enrichment experiments, joint labour-management committees, and other related activities, as noted earlier, may help to integrate the interests of labour and management. This approach is quite different from industrial democracy or worker participation required and enforced through legislation. The provision of expertise and information with respect to QWL is a light-handed approach to facilitate change in the industrial-relations system.

Preventive mediation is another type of assistance rendered by government. Preventive mediation differs from conventional mediation in that intervention takes place before crises develop and, also, often outside of collective bargaining. In fact, preventive mediation has been called "non-crisis mediation" in that it encompasses the activities of third parties that are not related to contract deadlines. For example, a preventive mediator might be concerned with a faulty grievance procedure, consultation, or prenegotiation joint committees set up to resolve troublesome issues confronting the parties' future negotiations. Or, a preventive third party might be involved with a postnegotiation committee formed to resolve an issue that could not be resolved through regular negotiations because of the complexity of the issue.

Preventive mediation, too, is a light-handed approach to government assistance. The parties rarely will use preventive mediation prior to a very serious crisis. And, like marriage counselling, preventive mediation will not work if forced on the parties. The impact of preventive mediation, then, may depend on the persuasiveness of the conventional mediator in convincing the parties to innovate, and then on the ensuing utility to the parties of the preventive mediation process. Indeed, the conventional mediator is an important player in preventive mediation in that such a person is generally in contact with the parties when the negotiations are at a critical crisis point and can therefore encourage the future use of preventive mediation when the parties are most likely to feel the need for such assistance. William Simkin, commenting on the growth of preventive mediation in the United States, has noted the critical role of the conventional mediator:

> One important reason is that the crises disputes mediator is in an especially favourable position. He works with and lives with the parties at a time of stress when the weak points in the bargaining relationship become all too apparent to all three participants (labour, management, and the mediator). Most negotiators desire to correct such weaknesses. If the mediator has earned the respect of the parties, a hint by him may inspire a desire to experiment. Not infrequently the hints come the other way. The parties ask the mediator to assist in formulating a program designed to improve the weak spots particular to their relationship. (33, p. 329)

If preventive mediation begins, the necessary third-party skills are by no means identical to those required in crisis bargaining. The analogy is closer to a marriage counselor than a power broker. One of the cornerstones of preventive mediation, for example, is to improve communications so that each side can see its opponent's point of view more clearly. This change, in turn, may substantially reduce tension and hostility between the parties.

Such an approach may be formalized through direct government assistance. The Federal Mediation and Conciliation Service in the United States a few years ago introduced a program entitled Relationships by Objectives (RBO). As noted earlier, a very similar program which is called Relationships Improvement Program (RIP) has been introduced by the Ontario Ministry of Labour. In 1980, the Education Relations Commission, an independent government agency which oversees collective bargaining in Ontario education, initiated a formal program of preventive mediation which includes workshops on building relationships, joint committees, communications, and effective bargaining.

The purpose of each of these programs is to improve communications and to eliminate, or reduce, misperceptions between the parties. Each of the programs mentioned above utilizes some of the techniques from the field of organization development. Earlier reference was made to intergroup labs, a concept pioneered by

Blake and Mouton. Each of the government programs referred to utilizes this technique, or a variant of it, as a potential building block for improved relationships. The basic flavour of such efforts is captured in a description of an intervention conducted by the Ontario Ministry of Labour:

> The same type of program resulted in an improvement in the industrial relations climate at Livingston Industries in Tillsonburg, a firm which makes wooden crates and packs auto parts for assembly abroad. Despite a relationship going back twenty-five years, management and the union, the International Woodworkers of America, with a membership of 650, have run into almost every kind of industrial relationship problem over recent years, including lack of trust. And the poor labour relations were now seriously affecting the quality of production.
>
> The program at Livingston Industries involved bringing together top managers, first-line supervisors, International Union representatives, and shop stewards, for a three-day seminar supervised by a team of four mediators from the Ministry of Labour at a location away from the work place. Part of the theory of the program is that open discussion helps to uproot mistrust and suspicion which is often the cause of labour management problems. Each side is encouraged to express themselves very straight-forwardly about what the other is doing wrong. To help improve the relationship, each side is encouraged to offer suggestions to the other and to establish specific goals in order to accomplish the objective of the suggestion.
>
> Following the program, there has been a tremendous improvement in the attitude of both union and management at Livingston Industries and both parties are carrying out all of their commitments. These include:
>
> 1. A more responsive and open-minded attitude by the company in listening to and acting on employee suggestions and complaints;
> 2. An undertaking by the union and its members to treat all levels of management with courtesy, honesty and respect;
> 3. Union investigation of complaints before taking action;
> 4. A company commitment to give safety priorities over production;
> 5. A promise that supervisors will treat all employees with courtesy, honesty, and respect;
> 6. An undertaking by the union and its members to give more support to the company and its programs;
> 7. An agreement by the union and company to co-operate in reducing absenteeism;
> 8. A company undertaking to improve its internal communications;
> 9. An agreement by both parties to emphasize the importance of an effective safety program;
> 10. A company agreement to be more attentive to working conditions to help reduce accidents. (18, pp. 19.6, 19.7)

Government agencies are more actively involved now than ever before in attempting to engender union-management cooperation. The concepts behind preventive mediation and relationship building hold some promise. The parties, too, seem more amenable today than in the past to such experimentation. Nevertheless, there are difficulties with respect to union-management cooperation. These are discussed below.

BARRIERS AND PROBLEMS IN ESTABLISHING COOPERATIVE PROGRAMS

Whether union-management cooperation will increase or decrease in the future is uncertain. From past experience it seems clear that the amount of cooperation will fluctuate and will depend upon national, industry, firm, or establishment economic conditions. Joint cooperation typically takes place when there are internal or external pressures on the two parties for change — most typically in situations where the establishment and, therefore, the union membership, face an economic crisis.

If the above is true, a definitive trend towards greater frequency of cooperative arrangements is unlikely. Moreover, union-management cooperation, while an attractive concept, is exceedingly difficult to start and, once initiated, difficult to maintain. There are many organizational and political difficulties which serve as very real constraints to such efforts. For example, Peterson and Tracy (29) have investigated the roadblocks to problem solving by surveying negotiators with respect to this issue. They found that management negotiators felt that the nature of the union constituency was a serious limitation on the depth of cooperation that was possible. That is, the political nature of the union results in union representatives being primarily interested in cooperation on short-run, immediate-pay-off issues. They noted, too, that management negotiators felt that the fact they had to face new employee representatives every two or three years made cooperation difficult. Another group of researchers (19) investigating joint union-management safety committees also found turnover to be a problem. Specifically, they found that one of the issues facing union and management officials was to ensure the continuity of their committees.

Even a successful and time-proven cooperative plan such as the Scanlon Plan will not continue without constant nurturing and attention. A leading expert on the Scanlon Plan has stated:

> Neither the Scanlon Plan or any other scheme to increase productivity will work unless there is the will and the determination on the part of both management and labour to make it work. This is not possible unless there is good faith, mutual respect, and confidence in the hearts of all participants. (22, p. 161)

Kochan has suggested the obstacles that must be overcome in listing the necessary political and organizational conditions for successful cooperative ventures. Although writing from a U.S. perspective, his observations are directly applicable to the Canadian scene.

1. Both parties must be able to see the change programs as being instrumental to the attainment of goals valued by their respective organizations and/or constituents.
2. The internal political risks to union leaders and management officials must be overcome.
3. The programs must produce tangible, positive results in the short run and must demonstrate a high probability of being able to continue to achieve valued goals in the future.
4. The initial stimulus or pressure to embark on the program must continue to be important and the initial goals of the programs must continue to be of high priority to the parties.
5. The gains or benefits from the initial program must be equitably distributed among the workers and the employer.
6. The union must be perceived as being an instrumental force in achieving the goals or benefits of the program and the union leaders must be protected from getting over-identified as part of management.
7. The change process must be successfully integrated with the formal structure and procedures of contract negotiations and administration. (20, p. 43)

While the barriers and problems are formidable, the current interest in joint cooperation is likely to continue in the foreseeable future. There is very little empirical evidence on the fact, but there are numerous reports that both labour and management benefit from cooperation. The main benefit or value to management from cooperation often is more flexibility in managing the operation. Cooperation has sometimes resulted in the examination of inefficient operations, new flexibility in job assignments, a change in the number and duration of shifts, fewer grievances, and so on. The union membership often benefits through improved supervision, more equitable and just plant-floor practices, improved job-posting procedures, more equitable allocation of overtime, and more prompt attention to employee problems in general.

It is the promise of the above benefits that has resulted in many union and management leaders attempting to bring about basic change to their joint relationship and in government agencies actively assisting the parties in this endeavour. Through their attempts — both their successes and failures — practitioners and researchers have gained a greater awareness of appropriate strategies or approaches to facilitate change. In a study on cooperation, two researchers (30, p. 383) note that it is important in such experiments to start small, to attempt to obtain initial success, and to separate problem solving from the distributive or conventional bargaining process. It goes without saying that constant vigilance is necessary to maintain a cooperative system once it is attained. The harsh realities of the bargaining table and the economic environment, and the political realities of trade-union organization, pose formidable challenges to union and management decision makers interested in cooperative ventures.

REFERENCES AND WORKS CITED

1. *Arbitration in Essential Industries: Seven Essays in Search of a Solution* (Ottawa: Labour Canada, 1975).

2. Blake, R., H. Shepard, and J. Mouton. *Managing Inter-Group Conflict in Industry* (Houston: Gulf Publishing, 1964).

3. Cole, D.L. "Role of the National Commission for Industrial Peace," *Proceedings of the Industrial Relations Research Association,* Vol. 26 (1973), 155-158.

4. "Conference on Dispute Settlement Alternatives," *Labour Gazette,* January 1975, p. 44.

5. Connaghan, C.J. *Partnership or Marriage of Convenience? A Critical Examination of Contemporary Labour Relations in West Germany with Suggestions for Improving the Canadian Labour-Management Relationships Based on the West German Experience* (Ottawa: Department of Labour, 1976).

6. Coser, Lewis. *The Functions of Social Conflict* (New York: Free Press, 1956).

7. Crispo, J. *Industrial Democracy in Western Europe: A North American Perspective* (Toronto: McGraw-Hill Ryerson, 1978).

8. Downie, Bryan M. "The Behavioural, Economic and Institutional Effects of Compulsory Interest Arbitration." Discussion Paper #147, Economic Council of Canada, Ottawa, 1979.

9. Downie, Bryan M. "Some Thoughts on Public Policy and Industrial Peace," *Relations Industrielles/Industrial Relations,* Vol. 36 (1981), 63-86.

10. Filey, A. *Interpersonal Conflict Resolution* (Glenview, Ill.: Scott, Foresman, 1976).

11. Fox, Alan. *Beyond Contract: Work, Power and Trust Relations* (London: Faber and Faber, 1974).

12. *Globe and Mail,* August 27, 1980, p.1.

13. Goldberg, J.E. "Bargaining and Productivity in the Private Sector," in G. Somers, M. Anderson, D. and L. Soyles (Eds.), *Collective Bargaining and Productivity* (Madison, Wisc.: Industrial Relations Research Association, 1975), pp. 1-13.

14. Goldman, P.G., and D.R. Van Houten. "Uncertainty, Conflict and Labour Relations in the Modern Firm I: Productivity and Capitalism's 'Human Face,' *Economic and Industrial Democracy: An International Journal,* Vol. 1 (1980), 63-98.

15. Goldman, P.G., and D.R. Van Houten. "Uncertainty, Conflict and Labour Relations in the Modern Firm II: The War on Labour," *Economic and Industrial Democracy: An International Journal,* Vol. 1 (1980), 263-287.

16. Haire, M. "Role-Perceptions in Labour Management Relations: An Experimental Approach," *Industrial and Labour Relations Review,* Vol. 8 (1955), 204-216.

17. Healy, J. (Ed.). *Creative Collective Bargaining: Meeting Today's Challenges to Labour-Management Relations* (Englewood Cliffs, N.J.: Prentice Hall, 1965).

18. Kehoe, F., and M. Archer. *Canadian Industrial Relations* (Oakville, Ont.: Twentieth Century Labour Publications, 1980).

19. Kochan, T., L. Dyer, and D. Lipsky. *The Effectiveness of Union-Management Safety and Health Committees* (Kalamazoo, Mich.: W.E. Upjohn Institute for Employment Research, 1977).

20. Kochan, T.A. "Collective Bargaining and Organizational Behavior," in B.M. Staw and L.L. Cummings (Eds.), *Research in Organizational Behavior, Vol. II* (Greenwich, Conn.: JAI Press, 1979).

21. Kovaks, A. "Joint Labour Management Councils," in S.M.A. Hameed (Ed.), *Canadian Industrial Relations: A Book of Readings* (Toronto: Butterworth, 1975).

22. Lesieur, F.G. (Ed.). *The Scanlon Plan: A Frontier in Labour-Management Cooperation* (Cambridge, Mass.: M.I.T. Press, 1958).

23. Likert, R., and J. Likert. *New Ways of Managing Conflict* (New York: McGraw-Hill, 1976).

24. List, W. "Co-operation Benefits Labor and Management," *Globe and Mail*, June 30, 1980, p. B5.

25. Mansell, J., and R. Wilkinson. *An Inventory of Innovative Work Arrangements in Ontario* (Toronto: Ontario Ministry of Labour, 1978).

26. McKersie, R.B. "An Evaluation of Productivity Bargaining in the Public Sector," in G. Somers, M. Anderson, D. and L. Soyles (Eds.), *Collective Bargaining and Productivity* (Madison, Wisc.: Industrial Relations Research Association, 1975), pp. 1-13.

27. "A New Social Contract: A Partnership to Build the New Workplace," *Business Week,* June 30, 1980, pp. 96-101.

28. Nightingale, D.V. "Workplace Democracy: An Inquiry into Employee Participation in Canadian Work Organization." Unpublished manuscript, Queen's University, 1980.

29. Peterson, R.B., and L. Tracy. "What Factors Encourage Problem-Solving in Labour Relations," in J. Power (Ed.), *New Dimensions in Dispute Settlement,* Proceedings of the Fourth Annual Meeting of the Society of Professionals in Dispute Resolution, Toronto, 1978.

30. Peterson, R.B., L. Tracy, and A. Cabelly. *Readings in Systematic Management of Human Resources* (Reading, Mass.: Addison-Wesley, 1979).

31. Rumball, D. "One Way to Avoid Strikes: Diffuse the Confrontation Mood," *Financial Post,* November 8, 1975, p. 11.

32. Russo, N.F. "Connotation of Seating Arrangements," *Cornell Journal of Social Relations,* Vol. 2 (1967), 37-44.

33. Simkin, W.E. *Mediation and the Dynamics of Collective Bargaining* (Washington, D.C.: Bureau of National Affairs, 1971).

34. "Steel Seeks Higher Output Via Workplace Reform," *Business Week,* August 18, 1980, pp. 98-103.

35. Strauss, G., R. Miles, C. Snow, and A. Tannenbaum (Eds.). *Organizational Behavior: Research and Issues* (Belmont, Ca.: Wadsworth, 1976).

36. Strauss, G. "Can Social Psychology Contribute to Industrial Relations?" in G.M. Stephenson and C.J. Brotherton (Eds.), *Industrial Relations: A Social Psychological Approach* (New York: Wiley, 1979), pp. 365-397.

37. Walton, R., and R. McKersie. *A Behavioral Theory of Labor Negotiations: An Analysis of a Social Interaction System* (New York: McGraw-Hill, 1965).

38. Weinstein, T. "Collective Bargaining Under Scrutiny," *Labour Gazette,* January 1975, pp. 53-56.

39. Weinstein, T. "An Interview with Stanley Hartt," *Labour Gazette,* June 1975, pp. 362-364.

40. Whittingham, A. "Kicked Out and Kicking Back," *Maclean's,* August 25, 1980, pp. 32-34.

QUESTIONS

1. Union-management cooperation would seem to be a concept that most of the actors in the Canadian industrial-relations system could support. What accounts for its limited use and growth?

2. Distinguish between the various types of joint union-management committees and briefly describe their similarities and differences.

3. Do you believe that government should play a role in union-management

cooperation? If so, what action should government take in inducing union-management cooperation?

4. Concepts and techniques from organization development would seem to be very promising with respect to union-management cooperation. Comment.

5. Discuss the relationship between union-management cooperation and the quality of work life.

SPECIAL ISSUES IN CANADIAN INDUSTRIAL RELATIONS

ALLEN PONAK

15. Public-Sector Collective Bargaining

This chapter reviews the evolution, distinguishing features, and special problems of collective bargaining in the Canadian public sector. One-quarter of all Canadian workers and close to half of the country's union members are public employees. Widespread collective bargaining did not emerge until the mid-1960s, but since then bargaining coverage has become almost universal.

Experience has demonstrated that collective bargaining functions differently in the public sector than in the private sector due, in particular, to some pronounced differences in the decision-making context in which public- and private-sector employers operate. These differences, as well as other factors, have given rise to persistent problems in the areas of dispute resolution and wage determination which have yet to be resolved. Focusing on concepts and trends, the discussion places these aspects of the public-sector labour-management experience into perspective and raises questions with respect to future developments.

The spread of collective bargaining in Canada's public sector has been accompanied by controversy and challenge. The controversy has come from the highly visible nature of public-sector collective bargaining and its impact, real or imagined, on the public. Unlike most private-sector disputes, public-sector work stoppages frequently affect large segments of the general public — disrupting mail delivery, closing schools, grounding airplanes, or shutting down transit service. Even where such inconvenience is less apparent, public-sector negotiations seem to capture a disproportionate amount of media attention. Perhaps this reflects an awareness that the results of bargaining affect the citizenry too — taxes and mill rates may be increased, stamps made more expensive, or bus fares raised.

The challenge comes in fashioning a workable industrial-relations system within such a charged environment. Private-sector systems have benefited from decades of evolution and testing. Much of the private-sector framework developed slowly, in relatively obscurity, and in an era when only a small proportion of the work force was unionized and engaged in bargaining. Public-sector collective bargaining, on the other hand, seems to have emerged full-blown in a very compressed time span. Virtually all eligible public employees are covered by collective agreements. Experimentation and testing accordingly are much more difficult. The stakes are higher and the consequences of unsuccessful experiments are dramatic and far-reaching.

This chapter attempts to place the public-sector experience in an analytical perspective. Examined in turn are the size and scope of the public sector, the emergence of bargaining, the distinguishing features (compared to the private sector) of public-sector labour-management relations, and the special problems of public-sector dispute resolution and wage determination.

SIZE AND SCOPE OF THE PUBLIC SECTOR

For purposes of this discussion, the public sector is defined to include the following: (a) the federal civil service; (b) provincial civil services; (c) municipal employment; (d) health care; (e) education; and (f) government enterprises (for example, Air Canada, Hydro-Quebec). Reliable data on the extent and growth of employment within these sectors have been notoriously difficult to compile. Statistical series often are contradictory, sometimes are incomplete, and may change the definitional basis of their calculations from year to year (9). Fortunately, recent studies conducted under the auspices of the Institute for Research on Public Policy have gone a long way toward overcoming many of these data limitations (10, 13, 26). As indicated in Table 1, total public employment was estimated at slightly over two million, with education the largest component. Total public-sector employment represented 23.7 percent of total employment in Canada, a figure which was slightly higher than that in the United States (20.6 percent) and slightly lower than that of the United Kingdom (27.4 percent) (10).

Current public-sector employment levels reflect a period of growth that began after World War II. Between 1946 and 1975, public employment rose at an annual rate of almost 7 percent, growing from slightly over 400,000 employees to more than two million. The most rapid growth occurred between 1956 and 1965, and, contrary

Table 1

Public-Sector Employment (1975)

Category	Number (000's)	Percent of Total
Federal government[a]	326	15.2
Provincial government	352	16.4
Municipal government	247	11.5
Education	529	24.6
Health care	382	17.8
Government enterprises	311	14.5
Total	2,147	100.0

SOURCE: *R.M. Bird, "The Growth of the Public Service in Canada," in D.K. Foot (Ed.),* Public Employment and Compensation in Canada: Myths and Realities *(Scarborough, Ont.: Butterworth, 1978), p. 25.*

NOTE: *a. Excludes members of the armed forces.*

to popular beliefs, the slowest growth has been since 1971 (27). Furthermore, the *proportion* of public employment to total Canadian employment has increased very little since 1960, moving from 22.2 percent of total Canadian employment in 1961 to 23.7 percent in 1975 (10). This stability in the relative share of public employment in total employment indicates that since 1960 public employment has grown at approximately the same pace as private-sector employment. In other words, while the number of public employees has increased substantially, so has employment elsewhere in the economy.

Some segments of the public sector have experienced more rapid expansion than others. Since World War II, employment generally has increased most quickly in health care and education, and has grown the least in the federal civil service (27). The result of these disparate growth rates is visible in Table 1 which shows that health care and education now account for the largest share of public-sector employees. The federal public service, on the other hand, constitutes a relatively small share of total government employment, again perhaps contrary to popular conception.

Reviewing the overall data, it is clear that public employees constitute a large and significant part of the Canadian labour force. The overall number of public employees is increasing and will continue to do so. Public employment growth rates clearly have slowed, however, with the result that public employment's share of the total jobs in the economy has stabilized at around one-quarter of the labour force.

DEVELOPMENT OF PUBLIC-SECTOR COLLECTIVE BARGAINING

Public-sector collective bargaining did not emerge on a widespread basis until the mid-1960s. Prior to then, public-employee groups engaging in formal collective bargaining were the exception rather than the rule. Today the situation is totally reversed. It is very difficult to find public employees not covered by a collective agreement. Three of Canada's largest five unions operate almost exclusively in the public sector, and the level of collective bargaining in the public sector far exceeds that found in the private sector. It is estimated that almost half of all union members in Canada work in the public sector (31).

Association-Consultation

It is remarkable in certain respects that public-sector bargaining did not emerge on a broad scale much sooner. Associations of public employees have existed since World War I and public employees shared at least some of the many concerns of their private-sector counterparts in terms of salaries and employment conditions (55). But instead of placing their faith in unionism and collective bargaining, public employees turned instead to another approach. The associations that public employees formed opposed strike action and eschewed compulsory membership requirements. Most remained apart from and unaffiliated to major labour federations. Management personnel, up to the most senior positions, often played active association roles and frequently occupied positions of leadership. Most importantly, stress was laid on a variety of consultation mechanisms, as opposed to collective bargaining, as the best means for influencing salaries and working conditions of the association's members.

This approach to employer-employee relations will be referred to as association-consultation. It was the prevalent form of public-sector labour relations until the mid-1960s at which time it gave way to the more familiar union-collective bargaining approach. The transition from association-consultation to union-collective bargaining began gradually in the 1950s, accelerated in the mid-1960s, and is virtually complete today.

Before examining the association-consultation model and the transition in more detail, several points can be made at this juncture. First, it should be emphasized that not all early organizational activity among public employees followed the association-consultation model. A number of groups, such as teachers in British Columbia and outside municipal workers generally, have a long history of unionism and bargaining with their public employer (30). Until the 1960s, such groups were in the minority, however. Second, the association-consultation model should not be viewed as an either-or proposition; some employee organizations fit the model more closely than others. In fact, one might envision a continuum with association-consultation at one end and union-collective bargaining at the other. While the majority of public-employee organizations were closer to the association-consultation side of the continuum, they certainly occupied different points on the scale. The Professional Institute of the Public Service (PIPS) displayed a much "purer" form of association-consultation, for example, than did most teacher groups. Third, it is interesting to find that not all public-sector organizations today take the union-collective bargaining approach. A number of faculty associations (McGill Association of University Teachers, for example) and professional groups (for example, Management and Professional Employees Society at B.C. Hydro) adhere to the association-consultation model. Employee relations within the Royal Canadian Mounted Police also conform to a version of association-consultation (42).

The reasons contemporary public employees adhere to association-consultation are not different from the reasons early employee organizations were attracted to this approach. First, association-consultation is popular with employees (for example, faculty members) who want some participation in the setting of their employment conditions but are uncomfortable with what they consider trade union methods and tactics. Historically, many public employees fell into this category.

White-collar workers and professionals, a major component of the public sector, have traditionally viewed unionism with a great deal of suspicion (11). Other public employees believed that the nature of their public service obligations, particularly the need for uninterrupted service, precluded collective bargaining. Still other employees, appointed pursuant to patronage practices, were reluctant to "rock the boat" in any manner. Not surprisingly these employees directed their energies toward fashioning consultative arrangements which could meet their needs. As long as consultation was either promised or granted, they displayed little enthusiasm for collective bargaining. Most provincial civil servants, federal employees, teachers, nurses, and university faculty had access to some type of consultation scheme (29, 43, 57, 63, 71).

Second, association-consultation is found in situations where there is fierce employer opposition to collective bargaining. It is arguable that even if public employees had wanted to bargain with their employers, they would not have been able to do so. Until recently, most public employers strongly opposed collective bargaining for their employees. The foremost basis of their opposition lay in the concept of government sovereignty. Simply stated, sovereignty implies that government bodies are properly vested with certain powers and responsibilities that cannot be shared or taken away. Collective bargaining, it was argued, must result in a diminution of these powers by forcing, for example, revisions in government budget allocations.

On the basis of the sovereignty concept, governments contended that even if they wished to do so, they could not permit public employees to engage in bargaining. Perhaps the clearest articulation of this position was the statement of Quebec Premier Jean Lesage in 1964 that "the Queen does not negotiate" (35, p. 11). In a similar vein, Prime Minister Louis St. Laurent declared in 1951 that "there can be no bargaining agent for the nation comparable with the employer in industry. The funds from which salaries are paid in the public service have to be voted by Parliament and Parliament alone can discharge that responsibility" (29, p. 11).

Public-employer opposition also was based on concern over the effect of work stoppages. It was argued that bargaining would inevitably lead to strikes and that strikes would result in an interruption of services which the government has an obligation to provide, which were irreplaceable in many cases, and which might be essential to the safety of the population. The government of British Columbia advanced this position in a brief to a 1959 commission on employer-employee relations in the B.C. civil service, stating that "private industry is conducted for profit and may be discontinued and wound up. Government must be conducted in the best interests of the people and it cannot stop." The sovereignty and work stoppage arguments provided a strong intellectual and moral basis for opposition to public-employee bargaining. Employees may have been left with little choice but to turn to association-consultation as the most feasible way of dealing with their employers.

Third, association-consultation is an alternative for employees who face legal obstacles to their acquisition of collective-bargaining rights (for example, the Royal Canadian Mounted Police). Consistent with their opposition to public-employee collective bargaining, governments excluded many public employees from labour legislation. In contrast, following the enactment of P.C. 1003 in 1944, most private-sector employees received the benefit of protection during union activity and the ability to compel their employers to bargain with them. The majority of public-sector employees, particularly provincial and federal civil servants and teachers, had to wait until the mid-1960s to win similar legal rights.

The absence of coverage under labour legislation curtailed public-employee collective bargaining activity in two ways. First, provincial and federal statutes which followed P.C. 1003 (such as the federal Industrial Relations and Disputes Investigation Act) contained a variety of administrative procedures which facilitated the acquisition of collective-bargaining rights. The government interceded (through labour-relations boards) to define the appropriate unit for bargaining purposes, distinguish employees from managers, conduct representation votes if necessary, and generally lay out the steps a group of employees needed to follow in order to bargain with their employer. The establishment of such procedures, moreover, lent a certain imprimatur of legitimacy to the whole process.

More importantly, however, the lack of legal protection made it much easier for public employers opposed to unionism to discourage bargaining activity. Public employees had few of the protections accorded their private-sector counterparts. The implications are summarized for municipal employees excluded from labour legislation: "They (municipal employers) cannot legally forbid their employees to exercise the right to organize themselves into trade unions, to bargain collectively, to enter into contractual agreements, and to strike. However, the city can refuse to have any dealings with unions of its employees. It may discriminate against union organizers, refuse to negotiate with representatives of organized employees, threaten those who join a union with loss of employment and so on" (30, p. 25). Again, association-consultation may have been adopted as the most feasible alternative given a legal environment unsupportive of collective bargaining.

From Association-Consultation to Union-Collective Bargaining

If employee sentiments, employer opposition, and the legislative environment all seemed to favour association-consultation, what accounts for its swift demise starting in the 1960s? The answer lies mainly in problems with the "consultation" component of association-consultation. Association-consultation was predicated on the belief that consultation could provide an adequate means for employees to address their employment concerns. When this premise proved suspect, the underpinnings upon which association-consultation rested collapsed.

In the long run, consultation proved a disappointment. It contained a number of weaknesses which had not been foreseen at the outset and which ultimately created great dissatisfaction. As these problems became apparent, public-sector groups which had acquiesced to association-consultation out of necessity reconsidered. Even employees with a long-standing distaste for union-collective bargaining approaches reluctantly reevaluated their opposition as difficulties with association-consultation mounted (7).

The experience of federal government employees with the National Joint Council (NJC) is instructive in this regard (28, 29). The NJC was introduced in 1944, culminating twenty-five years of struggle on the part of federal civil service associations to establish such a consultation body. Representatives of about a dozen staff associations (Staff Side) and senior government officials (Official Side) comprised the council. Meeting as frequently as necessary, they considered matters related to "the general principles governing conditions of employment in the public service of Canada including among other conditions recruitment, training, hours of work, promotion, discipline, tenure, regular and overtime remuneration, health, welfare, and seniority" (28, p. 376). When agreement could be reached on an issue recommendations would go forth from the NJC to the cabinet. Because senior government officials (for example, Secretary of the Treasury Board) took part in council deliberations, it was anticipated that council recommendations would be accepted by the government without undue delay.

In practice, the NJC delivered something less than originally envisioned. The scope of issues which were open to consultation proved narrower than the Staff Side initially believed. In particular, wages were deemed to be outside the jurisdiction of the council, forcing associations to submit periodic salary briefs directly to the government. No mechanisms were provided in the event the Staff Side and the Official Side could not reach agreement on a particular issue. Essentially, if the Official Side said "no," there the matter rested, and the status quo prevailed. Staff associations also complained of excessive secrecy surrounding the council's deliberation. In certain cases, the Official Side would refuse to engage in meaningful discussion of an issue unless Staff Side representatives agreed not to divulge the contents and progress of the discussions. Such promises prevented staff associations' representatives from consulting even with their own constituents. Further, in the absence of the principle of exclusive representation, more than a dozen staff associations were represented on the council. The many associations often claimed similar jurisdictions and competed with one another. Thus, Staff Side representatives sometimes operated at cross-purposes, weakening their ability to achieve objectives.

Finally, in the last analysis, council decisions were only advisory. The government retained the right to reject recommendations if it was so inclined. While council recommendations were usually implemented, their implementation sometimes followed lengthy delays, preliminary rejections, and content changes in the recommendations. This absence of guarantees and the uncertainty it fostered added to the dissatisfaction of Staff Side representatives.

Less than ten years after the NJC was inaugurated some staff associations were questioning the utility of the whole process. By 1960, this questioning had turned into a chorus of support for abandoning the NJC scheme and replacing it with collective bargaining (6, 29). The National Joint Council experience was not atypical; consultation frameworks elsewhere were subject to similar tensions (63, 66, 71). As the problems with consultation gradually became apparent, the notion that consultation could serve as an adequate vehicle for addressing public-employee concerns lost credibility.

Once disenchantment with consultation set in, events followed swiftly. Staff associations began switching from a position of opposition to collective bargaining to one of advocacy. At the same time, they began to model themselves along traditional union lines, excluding management personnel from their membership, hiring full-time staff experts, eliminating no-strike clauses from their constitutions, merging with competing or complementary organizations, and in many cases affiliating with the Canadian Labour Congress.

This transformation did not occur overnight, of course, and not without some soul-searching, particularly on the part of professional groups (7, 34). Major changes in leadership often were necessary (56). Two factors considerably facilitated the transition, however. Once some momentum towards the union-collective bargaining model had been achieved, a demonstration effect emerged which accelerated developing trends. The gains made by New York City teachers following a highly publicized strike in 1961 is a frequently cited example which spurred public employees elsewhere (14). Similarly, a huge arbitration award won by Ottawa nurses in 1968 greatly heightened nurse interest in collective bargaining throughout Ontario. Also helping the transition was the general climate of social change characteristic of the 1960s. This was the era of the civil rights movement, anti-Vietnam War protests, the "Quiet Revolution" in Quebec and campus militancy. The social environment was conducive to challenges of authority and the status quo in general, making it a particularly propitious time for public employees to undertake major changes in existing norms.

The final push to full collective bargaining was accomplished with the removal of legal obstacles. Saskatchewan had set a precedent in 1944 by including civil servants under the coverage of the provincial Trade Union Act, undermining the proposition that government sovereignty was an insurmountable obstacle to public-sector bargaining (15). Other governments slowly began to accept that certain limitations in their own discretion might be necessary if rights to which public employees now felt strongly entitled were to be ensured. Misgivings about work stoppages were also partially overcome by substituting arbitration for the right to strike in many jurisdictions. Gradually, the legislative environment began to change from one hostile to the union-collective-bargaining model to one which was supportive.

The most important breakthrough occurred in 1963. Astute political lobbying by employee organizations persuaded the newly elected Liberal government of Lester Pearson to introduce collective-bargaining rights in the federal civil service; the Public Service Staff Relations Act resulted (20). Within five years over 100,000 federal employees were under collective agreements. In 1965, the Quebec Labour Code extended similar rights to all public employees in the province and 40,000 workers began bargaining for the first time shortly thereafter. One by one, similar legislative changes were made in other jurisdictions.

By 1975 the rights of virtually all public employees to engage in collective bargaining were fully established and protected by law. The access of public employees to certification procedures, conciliation machinery and labour boards, and employer acceptance of the union-collective-bargaining model implied by the enactment of the various statutes, launched one of the most sustained periods of union growth in Canadian history. Once committed to collective bargaining, public-sector organizations wasted little time exercising their newly acquired rights. The degree of existing organization eliminated the need for extensive membership campaigns which are the characteristically difficult first step when a new group seeks certification. The (former) staff associations provided a well-established base from which collective-bargaining rights could be pursued, explaining the speed with which collective bargaining spread. By the late 1970s, virtually all eligible public employees in the country were covered by collective agreements.

Conclusions on the Development of Bargaining

There are several lessons that can be drawn from both the pattern of public-sector collective-bargaining development and the fact that the public sector is now so highly unionized. First, although unionism and collective bargaining are now irrevocably entrenched, the rapidity with which collective bargaining supplanted consultation means that certain growing pains are inevitable. Important questions concerning dispute procedures, structural arrangements and wage patterns have yet to be resolved, and more experience with collective bargaining will be necessary before satisfactory answers can be found.

Second, the rise of public-sector unions has changed the shape of the Canadian labour movement. Prior to the 1960s, organized labour in this country was predominantly blue-collar, male, private sector, and U.S.-linked. This is true to a far lesser extent today. It remains to be seen how easily public- and private-sector unions can coexist within organizations such as the Canadian Labour Congress.

Third, the experience in the public sector suggests that the high degree of union penetration ultimately achieved would have been unlikely had public employees not gone through the association-consultation phase first. While adherence to association-consultation delayed collective bargaining for a considerable period, it also set the stage for almost complete bargaining coverage in a time period unprecedented in its brevity. Important insights into union growth in other sectors of the economy, particularly where white-collar workers are concerned (for example, banking), may be gained by comparing developments there to the association-consultation/union-collective bargaining transition in the public sector.

DISTINGUISHING FEATURES OF PUBLIC-SECTOR COLLECTIVE BARGAINING

As public-employee unionism spread rapidly, it became obvious that bargaining in the public sector did not work in quite the same way as in the private sector. Certain important differences between public- and private-sector employees, employers, and legislation combined to produce distinctive bargaining dynamics. While some of the public-private differences had been recognized in advance, they could not fully be appreciated until substantial bargaining experience developed. Finding acceptable ways of dealing with these differences continues to bedevil public-sector labour relations.

Employee Differences

The public sector contains a relatively higher proportion of white-collar workers and professionals than the private sector. White-collar workers filled approximately half of all jobs in the economy as a whole (that is, private and public sectors combined) in 1978 (82). Although specific comparative data are not available, information from a variety of sources (2, 26, 43, 57) suggests that white-collar employment in municipalities and government enterprises approximates the economy-wide level and substantially exceeds the economy norm in health care, provincial and federal civil services, and education. With respect to professional employees, Gunderson (39) estimates that the public sector employs two-thirds of all Canadian professionals.

Differences are more pronounced in terms of union composition. Private-sector unionism is concentrated among blue-collar employees; very few white-collar workers in the private sector are organized or covered by collective agreements. By contrast, virtually all white-collar employees in the public sector engage in collective bargaining (82). This means that private-sector unions essentially are blue-collar in nature while public-sector unionism is mainly white-collar.

These differences have several implications. The extensive literature on white-collar unionism suggests, among other things, that white-collar workers may be less strike-prone than blue-collar workers, may be less likely to file grievances, may display more interest in cooperative mechanisms, and, especially in the case of professionals, may pursue a bargaining agenda concerned with "higher-order" needs (11, 46).

Some of these propositions are supported by available data, while others are not. Strike statistics generally show that proportionately less time is lost due to strikes in the public sector than in the private sector (51). A study of the federal civil service showed that bargaining units composed of white-collar workers were much more likely to prefer arbitration (as opposed to strikes) as a means of resolving their interest disputes compared to blue-collar units (64). Another study of registered nurses revealed strong support for collective bargaining, but much weaker support for the right to strike (63).

With respect to grievances and arbitration, a recent analysis of more than 100 bargaining units revealed that white-collar employees are much less grievance prone. Among blue-collar units sampled, 98 percent had reported one or more nondisciplinary grievances, disciplinary grievances had been filed in 89 percent of the units, and in half of the units at least one grievance had been processed to arbitration during the previous contract period. Among the white-collar units surveyed, by comparison, nondisciplinary grievances had been filed in three-quarters of the units, in only 30 percent of the units had disciplinary grievances been filed, and in less than ten percent of the units had a single grievance gone to arbitration (33). Analyses of unionized faculty have also shown the incidence of grievances and arbitration to be low (8).

The collective-bargaining objectives of blue- and white-collar workers may vary as well. A British study found that white-collar workers were much more interested in worker participation programs than were blue-collar workers (76). A study of registered nurses in Ontario showed that issues relating to professional concerns (for example, in-service education) were considered more important than traditional union "bread and butter" concerns such as hours of work or shift premiums (61). On the other hand, a comparative survey of activists in an industrial union and a union of provincial civil servants showed remarkably few differences in the bargaining issues considered important and in the degree of support indicated for joint labour-management programs (62).

Another reason private- and public-sector collective bargaining patterns might differ is if the participants in two sectors were faced with inherently different costs of agreement/disagreement (16). Indeed, it will be argued below that on the *employer* side these costs are substantially different between the sectors, and that this fact produces distinctive public-sector bargaining dynamics. On the employee side, however, differences are slight.

Looking first at the costs of agreement, there is no evidence to suggest that pressure is any less on public-sector union leaders who reach what union members feel is a suboptimal agreement, compared to pressure that might be exerted on private-sector union leaders in a similar situation. The costs for negotiating a *bad* agreement are high in both sectors. On the other hand, it has been suggested that there may be differences between the two sectors with respect to the costs associated with reaching too *good* an agreement. Most studies show that public employees have little to fear from an exceptionally rich settlement since the demand for their services is price-inelastic (40). Thus, very substantial public-sector settlements should not lead to loss of jobs, unlike the situation in the private sector where an overly expensive settlement can produce job loss.

Turning to the costs of disagreement, except in extreme situations where a work stoppage forces a private employer permanently out of business, the costs of disagreement, that is, failing to reach a settlement, are similar in the two sectors. The major cost of disagreement to employees in both sectors is a temporary loss of income. There is little reason to expect that such costs have inherently different consequences for employees in the two sectors (59). It is true that many public employees operate under binding arbitration systems, but differential public-private costs of disagreement in such cases reflect dispute resolution differences rather than any special differences in the nature of the employees or their organizations.

Overall, the most important difference on the employee side of the collective bargaining equation results from the predominance of white-collar workers. Although the evidence is by no means conclusive, it suggests a less militant brand of unionism in the public sector and one more attuned to intrinsic aspects of working conditions.

Employer Differences

Most of the distinctive features of public-sector labour relations stem from differences between public employers and private employers. Decision-making structure and authority differ between the two sectors, typically being much more diffuse in the public sector. Public-sector employers are more subject to political considerations and private-sector employers to economic factors, resulting in somewhat different cost of agreement/disagreement calculations. Some public employers also enjoy an advantage unmatched by their private sector counterparts — the ability to legislate. Each of these features can have substantial implications for public-sector bargaining dynamics.

Management structure — Management responsibility for collective bargaining is much more clearly defined and established in private-sector organizations than in public-sector organizations. In the private sector, "the line of management responsibility is usually clear and direct" (18, p. 81), "authority for personnel issues is . . . concentrated at a particular point within the management structure" (14, p. 103), "representatives have broad discretion to negotiate and commit the organization on almost all matters, and the negotiators and top management constitute a closely knit team" (69, p. 78). The public sector is characterized, on the other hand, by "bewildering fragmentation of authority among numerous management officials" (14, p. 103). "Public sector responsibility is generally divided or shared, and the formal responsibility often differs from the actual" (18, p. 81).

There are several explanations for this phenomenon. First, the diffusion of public-sector management authority is to some extent deliberate, reflecting assumptions about the value of checks and balances, political versus nonpolitical decision making, and local versus central control. For example, responsibility for education decisions typically is apportioned between locally elected school boards, provincially appointed superintendents, and a ministry of education; civil-service recruitment, transfer and promotion is vested in an ostensibly apolitical civil-service commission but resource allocation remains a cabinet function; and many provinces divide responsibility for managing municipal police forces among a police chief, municipal officials, and a police board. Thus, overlapping and divided authority structures are consciously built into the system.

Public-sector funding arrangements also contribute to shared authority. Many public employers are funded from a multiplicity of sources, each of which may seek to influence the way in which the money is spent (18). Urban-transit commissions offer a good illustration of this point. Urban transit is financed through a combination of user charges, municipal subsidies, and provincial grants. Sometimes, as in Montreal, several municipalities fund a unified transit system. Accordingly, provincial governments, a variety of municipal administrations and citizen groups, as well as transit authorities themselves, all may claim some role in the collective-bargaining process and some control over bargaining outcomes. With so many claimants, actual decision-making authority invariably is dispersed.

Third, structural disunity is exacerbated by political competition. Public management officials may belong to different political parties or may view colleagues as actual or future political rivals. They may represent different constituencies or speak on behalf of different levels of government. Competition on the basis of any of these differences (that is, party, government level, and so on) is an accepted part of our political system. Thus, with little certainty that various participants on the management side will act in harmony or be seeking the same objectives, employer cohesion is further undermined.

Public management's structural complexity has important implications for collective bargaining. First, overlapping and unclear authority lines contribute to *unnecessary delay* as a variety of internal bargains have to be struck before union proposals can be dealt with. The 1975 Toronto teacher negotiations are a case in point (45). The management negotiating team contained up to forty individuals. They represented different constituencies, some were elected trustees, others were appointed officials, a number of the participants had broader political ambitions, and labour-relations experience varied considerably among bargaining team members. As a result, "the range of opinions was often very broad, and at times the committee seems to have had a great deal of difficulty in making proposal and strategy decisions and agreeing on the general approach to be taken toward the teachers" (45, p. 44). Negotiations proceeded for more than a full year, a bitter two-month strike took place, and compulsory arbitration ultimately was imposed by the provincial government.

A second consequence of public-sector management structure is what former Canadian Union of Public Employees (CUPE) president Stan Little labeled *"phantom bargaining"* (81). Referring to negotiations in Ontario health care, Little was concerned that the level of government capable of dealing with key monetary issues, the provincial government, was not a direct participant at the bargaining table.

> You are bargaining with a local administration that can hide behind the fact that the provincial government has only increased the year's budget by perhaps 7 percent. That's what we mean by the phantom at the bargaining table. We might just as well start dealing where the money is. Without that we are just going through the motions. (81, pp. 726-727)

A third implication of the diffusion of managerial authority is the opportunity it provides for the union to engage in *multilateral* bargaining. Collective bargaining normally is conceived as a bilateral process in which representatives of the union meet representatives of the employer at the bargaining table. Multilateral bargaining refers to a situation, not uncommon in the public sector, where individuals purportedly speaking for management, but not part of the management bargaining team, intervene in the bargaining process. These individuals, usually political officials but sometimes representatives of citizen groups, either intervene at their own initiative or are drawn into negotiations by the union.

To the extent a union is able to manipulate such intervention, it will frequently be able to achieve objectives not otherwise obtainable through the normal bilateral exchange at the bargaining table. The more management structure is diffused, the greater the number of potentially sympathetic individuals with authority on whom the union can call. The greater the degree of management political rivalry, or internal conflict, the more likely it becomes that the union can find someone who is unhappy with the way bargaining is progressing and is willing to intercede (47).

Most evidence of multilateral bargaining has been gathered in the United States. A recent description of Wisconsin state employee negotiations showed, for example, how in two successive rounds of bargaining the union successfully engineered "end runs" around the management bargaining team in order to deal directly with the state governor. This tactic produced further intervention by members of the state legislature and the attorney general (48).

The incidence of multilateral bargaining in the Canadian public sector has only begun to be systematically investigated. Preliminary evidence suggests that at the municipal level multilateral bargaining may be less widespread in Canada as compared to the United States (2). Multilateral bargaining is thought to be most common in health care and education (53). That some multilateral bargaining does occur in the Canadian public sector is evident from the following illustration:

> The city and the union representatives were just finishing negotiations and the city had made its final offer of thirteen percent. The union although not totally satisfied was going to take it back to their membership. Leaving the sessions the union representatives bumped into the mayor. The mayor who was characterized as an old time hand-shaking politician asked "How's it going boys?" They responded not too well as it looked like they were going to have to settle for thirteen percent. The mayor replied "Those bastards, I gave them the OK for fifteen percent!" The union promptly contacted the city negotiators and demanded the increase. Management had been holding back in case of ratification problems. The union got its fifteen percent increase. (2, p. 407)

It is probable that as public employers acquire more experience they will take steps to deal with the problems created by their own structural deficiencies. Private-sector employers, with considerably more experience with unionized work forces, have learned to devise appropriate managerial control systems to meet their labour-relations needs. A great deal of centralization at top corporate levels has resulted (49). Public-sector employers are still groping for the right formula (37). The Quebec provincial government has altered its negotiating format repeatedly in the fifteen years in which it has bargained with Quebec public employees (12, 36). The City of Vancouver and a dozen surrounding suburban communities have been trying for more than a decade to centralize full bargaining authority in an accredited employers' association. In Saskatchewan, the provincial government has managed to largely insulate itself from the bargaining process with respect to civil servants, but has been unable to achieve as effective structural arrangements in health care and education (78). It may well be, however, that the inherent nature of the public sector precludes the degree of management cohesion characteristic of the private sector.

Costs of agreement and disagreement— The point was made earlier that the costs of agreement/disagreement were quite similar between the public and private sectors on the employee side. On the employer side, however, some major intersectoral differences do exist. For the private-sector employer the costs of agreement and disagreement are reckoned mainly in economic terms. The costs of agreeing to union demands must be calculated in terms of how changes in production efficiency and overall labour costs will affect product prices, the firm's ability to remain competitive, and ultimately its profit-loss situation. The major employer costs of disagreeing to union demands stem from consequences generated by loss of production if employees withdraw their services. These consequences may include short-run revenue loss and long-term market-share decline. Bargaining behaviour must be evaluated in terms of these consequences and their ultimate profit-loss impact.

Public employers also must be cognizant of the economic costs associated with either agreeing or disagreeing with union proposals, but these costs have different implications in the case of the public employer. Profit-loss considerations usually are inapplicable, market share and competitive pressures rarely are relevant, and revenue is not generally linked in the short run to quantity of product or service provided. Furthermore, there is a political dimension to the costs of agreeing or disagreeing to union demands which is absent in the private sector. Private employers do not normally have to concern themselves with the effect their actions might have on their public popularity, while public employers ignore citizen reactions at their peril.

The differing perspectives are obvious with respect to costs of agreement. The major concern of public employers is with the political consequences of funding an increased labour bill, rather than with the profit-loss implications of higher labour costs. Alternative funding strategies might include raising additional revenue through increased taxes, user charges, or borrowing, reallocating resources internally, and restricting services (18, 44). Choosing one of these alternatives is essentially a political decision. If the wage settlement also happens to exceed guidelines which the public employer, as legislator, has itself established, further political consequences undoubtedly will have to reckoned with.

Costs of disagreement are viewed differently as well. A work stoppage normally places financial hardships on private-sector employers, but public employers may actually reap financial benefit from a strike if, as in many cases, revenue inflows are unaffected. For example, the revenue of a municipality does not cease because its road repair staff have withdrawn their services temporarily. Financially beleaguered school districts in the United States have found it advantageous to take a strike, ceasing operations for several weeks, in order to meet their operating budgets. While private-sector employers sometimes find themselves in a similar situation (for example, the 1978 Sudbury Inco strike in which Inco had significant inventories and worldwide nickel prices were depressed), the likelihood is much smaller.

Private employers, on the other hand, only rarely need to contend with citizen reaction to an interruption of services. Substitutes exist for most consumer goods and services and most private-sector strikes inconvenience only a limited number of individuals not directly involved in the dispute. The same is not true for many public-sector work stoppages, and as a result, the major cost of disagreement for government employers lies in adverse public reaction to service disruption. Where interruption of the public service involved has widespread and immediate impact, as in an urban-transit dispute, reaction is intense and cost of disagreement is high. Where the service is less visible (federal government translators are a case in point) citizen response may be nonexistent or at least muted, producing much lower costs of disagreement. In either event, public employers must assess the potential political consequences of a service disruption if they do not agree to union proposals, an assessment that private-sector employers normally do not have to make.

It is evident therefore that public- and private-sector employers make bargaining decisions under different sets of constraints, since agreeing or not agreeing to union demands produces different consequences in the two sectors. In particular, private-sector employers are likely to evaluate their bargaining strategy and resistance points in terms of an economic "bottom line" whereas public employers are more likely to be attuned to a political one.

This has several consequences for bargaining. Perhaps the most obvious is the potential created for a politicized bargaining process. Since the costs of agreement/

disagreement for the public employer are to a large extent political, strong incentive exists for each side to engage in overtly political activity in an attempt to manipulate the costs of agreement/disagreement in its favour. Teachers and hospital workers, for example, have frequently claimed that they are striking not over their wages and working conditions, but for improvement in the quality of education or health care. These are political goals over which it is difficult to disagree. Public employers, for their part, take great pains to justify such actions as back-to-work legislation in the name of the "public interest," not on grounds that such tactics enable them to achieve a particular bargaining objective.

At a different level, public-sector unions have supported particular political parties or candidates in the expectation that such support will make it difficult for these officials to oppose union bargaining demands later. Similarly, some public-sector unions have led especially bitter strikes against public employers viewed as antiunion, or at least very unsympathetic to labour, in the hope that such disputes might jeopardize the employers' reelection chances. Some of the confrontations between Quebec public employees and the Liberal government of Premier Robert Bourassa were of this type.

Second, and somewhat related to the politicization of negotiations, both sides in the public sector are more likely to attempt to use the media to present their cases directly to the public. The 1980 province-wide nurses' negotiations in British Columbia provide a good illustration. In these negotiations, the Registered Nurses' Association achieved a 50 percent wage settlement over twenty-seven months. A major factor in their success was a convincing media campaign to the effect that nurses were greatly underpaid. The effect of the campaign was to substantially reduce the employers' cost of agreement. Normally, a wage increase of this magnitude would produce substantial negative political reaction. The ability of the nurses' association to elicit public sympathy for their position meant that the political consequences of granting and funding the settlement were not nearly as unpalatable as they otherwise would have been.

Third, because the costs of agreement/disagreement cannot be calculated in terms of profit-loss considerations, market share, and competitive pressure, much greater emphasis is placed on the concept of wage (and conditions) "comparability" in public-sector negotiations. While industry and community comparisons play an important role in the private sector, the question of a firm's ability to remain competitive in light of a given contract settlement also is a critical variable. In public-sector negotiations, however, the issue of whether the organization had a good or bad year financially usually is not as germane, with the result that much greater attention must be paid to patterns and standards established elsewhere.

Legislative powers — In terms of labour relations, the federal government and the ten provincial governments play a unique dual role. On the one hand, they are the employers of significant numbers of employees, virtually all of whom are unionized and are covered by collective agreements. On the other hand, in their role of sovereign authority over all the people, they are vested with the power to formulate and implement the labour legislation under which they and their employees must interact. This dual role creates some obvious problems. One does not have to be excessively cynical to suggest that from time to time governments will find the temptation irresistible to adjust labour-relations rules in their own self-interest as employers.

Table 2

Public-Sector Labour Legislation

Jurisdiction	Private Sector	General Municipal	Police	Fire Fighters	Hospitals	Teachers	Civil Service	Government Enterprises	Additional Comments
Federal	Canada Labour Code	–	–	Public Service Staff Relations Act	PSSRA	PSSRA	PSSRA	Labour Code	Royal Canadian Mounted Police excluded from PSSRA and Canada Labour Code
British Columbia	B.C. Labour Code	Labour Code	Labour Code	Labour Code	Labour Code	Public Schools Act	Public Service Labour Relations Act	Labour Code	Dispute procedures for all public employees governed by Essential Services Disputes Act
Alberta	Alberta Labour Act	Labour Act	Firefighters and Policemen's Labour Relations Act	Firefighters and Policemen's Labour Relations Act	Labour Act	Labour Act	Public Service Employees Relations Act	Public Service Employees Relations Act	Some strike restriction for certain municipal employees (e.g. sewage)
Saskatchewan	Trade Union Act	Trade Union Act	Police Act	Fire Department Platoon Act	Trade Union Act	Teachers Collective Bargaining Act	Trade Union Act	Trade Union Act	Earliest comprehensive public-sector legislation in Canada (1944)
Manitoba	Labour Relations Act	Labour Relations Act	Labour Relations Act	Fire Department's Arbitration Act	Labour Relations Act	Public Schools Act	Civil Service Act	Labour Relations Act	1974 Special Review Committee Report (H. D. Woods, Chairman) not acted upon

Ontario	Labour Relations Act	Labour Relations Act	Police Act	Fire Department Act	Labour Relations Act; Hospital Labour Disputes Arbitration Act	School Boards and Teachers Collective Negotiations	Crown Employees Collective Bargaining Act	Crown Employees Collective Bargaining Act	
Quebec	Labour Code	Labour Code	Labour Code; Police Force Syndical Plan Act (provincial police)	Labour Code	Labour Code	Labour Code	Labour Code	Labour Code	Labour Code contains special provisions for public employees. Structure of public sector bargaining governed by Special Legislation
New Brunswick	Industrial Relations Act	Industrial Relations Act	Industrial Relations Act	Industrial Relations Act	Public Service Labour Relations Act (PSLRA)	PSLRA	PSLRA	PSLRA	Modeled closely after federal Public Service Staff Relations Act
Nova Scotia	Trade Union Act	Trade Union Act	Trade Union Act	Trade Union Act	Trade Union Act	Teachers Collective Bargaining Act	Act Respecting Collective Bargaining in the Civil Service	Trade Union Act	
Prince Edward Island	Labour Act	Labour Act	Labour Act	Labour Act	Labour Act	School Act	Civil Service Act	Civil Service Act	
Newfoundland	Labour Relations Act	Labour Relations Act	Labour Relations Act; Constabulary Act (provincial police)	Labour Relations Act; St. John's Fire Department Act	Public Service (Collective Bargaining) Act	Teacher (Collective Bargaining) Act	Public Service (Collective Bargaining) Act	Public Service (Collective Bargaining) Act	Registered nurses excluded from coverage of Labour Act

SOURCE: W.E. Wood, and Pradeep Kumar, The Current Industrial Relations Scene in Canada, 1980 *(Kingston: Queen's University Industrial Relations Centre, 1980).*

The brouhaha surrounding Bill C-22, the federal government's proposed amendments to the Public Service Staff Relations Act in 1978, illustrates well the dual-role conundrum. The amendments extended managerial exclusions significantly, provided tighter arbitration and conciliation criteria with respect to compensation, added restrictions to the right of employees to strike, and gave the employer, for the first time, the right to lock out. These proposals were bitterly attacked by the Public Service Alliance of Canada. Calling the amendments "a tragic and stupid mistake," the alliance charged that they were designed only to "strengthen the employer's negotiating power," provide the government with "a tool to control wages in the Public Service," and "to protect political interests in the event of a strike" (65). The government staunchly defended the proposals, arguing that its objectives were: "To improve compensation determination within the collective-bargaining process, to alter the mix of employees subject to the collective-bargaining process, and to protect the public interest in the event of strikes" (74).

The question of who was being more "honest" in this matter is immaterial. Undoubtedly the government was acting partially in its own self-interest as employer, but just as certainly it was responding to real public concern about the regime of collective bargaining in the federal civil service. The important issue for our purposes is the unique opportunities and special responsibilities imposed on governments which assume the dual role of employer and rule maker. The ability to exercise legislative authority to further their own ends as employers is a potent source of industrial-relations power unmatched in the private sector.

Policy and Legislative Distinctions

Public-sector legislation is characterized by incredible diversity. Consistent with practices in the private sector, each province plus the federal government retains authority for public-employee labour-relations legislation within its own jurisdiction. However, whereas private-sector legislation is guided by a generally accepted underlying set of policy considerations derived from the U.S. Wagner Act of 1935, no such consensus exists in the public sector. This leads to considerable differences in legislation both within and across jurisdictions and between the public and private sectors.

The degree of intrajurisdictional statutory differentiation in the public sector is demonstrated by Table 2. At one extreme we find Ontario in which virtually every public-sector group is covered by a different piece of legislation. General municipal employees are governed by the general private sector statute (Labour Relations Act), police and fire fighters by the Police Act and the Fire Department Act, respectively, and hospital workers fall under both the Labour Relations Act and the Hospital Labour Disputes Arbitration Act. Ontario civil servants and employees of government enterprises are covered by the Crown Employees Collective Bargaining Act and teachers negotiate under provisions of the School Boards and Teachers Collective Negotiations Act. At the opposite end of the continuum is Quebec, in which only one basic statute, the Quebec Labour Code, applies to all public employees. Even in Quebec, however, the Labour Code contains special provisions applicable to the public sector. The remaining jurisdictions fall somewhere between the Quebec-Ontario extremes.

The multiplicity of statutes reflects different policy approaches toward various public-sector groups within a given jurisdiction. In Manitoba, for example, municipal employees, police, and hospital workers can strike; teachers, fire fighters, and civil servants must submit disputes to arbitration. In Quebec, both police and fire fighters are subject to arbitration while all other public employees may legally withdraw their services. Overall, the public-sector pattern of intrajurisdictional distinctions offers a clear contrast to the private sector where there tends to be one statute and one policy approach (construction excepted) towards all private-sector employees within a particular jurisdiction.

In light of the degree of differences within each province, it is not surprising that sharp public-sector policy cleavages exist between jurisdictions as well. Employees of government enterprises, for example, are covered by general (private-sector) labour codes in six jurisdictions, but by special public-sector statutes in the remaining five. Teachers in Ontario and Quebec can bargain over virtually whatever issues they choose, but in British Columbia negotiations are restricted to "salaries and bonuses." Police in Alberta, Ontario, Quebec, and Newfoundland are prohibited from joining associations affiliated with the general labour movement; no such restrictions are placed on police elsewhere. Half of the provinces permit their civil servants to strike, the other half do not. If there is a particular pattern in all this, it is well-disguised. This kind of interjurisdictional variation again stands in sharp contrast to the situation which prevails in the private sector, where legislation across jurisdictions is more similar than it is different.

Because public-sector legislative practices are so diverse, specific comparisons between a public-sector "approach" and private-sector norms must be made cautiously. However, there are several substantive differences.

Bargaining unit determination — In the private sector, the determination of the appropriate bargaining unit usually is left to the parties involved or to the appropriate labour-relations board. Statutory guidelines are very discretionary and decisions on bargaining units are made on a case-by-case basis according to criteria (for example, past precedent in the industry, community of interests) which have evolved over time.

Under public-sector statutes, however, bargaining units frequently are determined legislatively. The preeminent example of this is found in the Public Service Staff Relations Act (PSSRA). Federal civil servants are statutorily divided into more than 100 different occupational groups, and each one of these groups is designated in the PSSRA as an appropriate bargaining unit. Very little discretion in this regard is left to the Public Service Staff Relations Board. There are accordingly 100 bargaining units certified in the federal civil service (25). A modified version of the federal approach is found in New Brunswick. At the opposite end of the spectrum, the Alberta Public Service Employees Relations Act mandates a single all-inclusive bargaining unit for civil servants in the province, and the Saskatchewan Teachers Bargaining Act, while permitting local units, requires a province-wide set of negotiations for all provincial teachers. Other provinces, for example Quebec, also have centralized bargaining structures that are established by statute for various groups of public employees.

In British Columbia, the labour-relations board has adopted a special approach toward employees of government enterprises, even though these employees are covered by the general labour code. In decisions involving the Insurance Corporation of British Columbia and the B.C. Ferry Corporation, the board departed from the criteria usually applied in bargaining unit determination, placing all employees in single comprehensive units. These decisions were justified on the ground that the public interest demanded fashioning bargaining units for public-sector employees which specifically minimized the likelihood of work stoppages. In the board's view, that goal was best accomplished by inclusive bargaining units (77).

Bargaining scope — The scope of bargaining is a second substantive area where noteworthy differences in public-private-sector policies are evident. Private-sector negotiators almost universally are free to negotiate over whatever issues they choose. Statutory requirements that bargaining proceed over "wages, hours, and working conditions" have been interpreted very liberally. Less negotiating latitude is permitted under a variety of public-sector statutes. The PSSRA renders classifications, criteria for promotion, transfer and layoff, technological change, and pensions nonnegotiable, restrictions which, some observers claim, have had a dysfunctional impact on the collective-bargaining process (5). Similar constraints on bargaining scope are found in a majority of provincial civil-service statutes. The situation in education, as noted previously, is somewhat more variable, with negotiable issues ranging from "salaries and bonuses only" in British Columbia to basically an unlimited scope in Ontario and Quebec. The negotiating scope for police and fire fighters also may be limited, particularly with respect to disciplinary arrangements and superior-subordinate relations, owing to the paramilitary nature of these services.

Dispute resolution — Dispute-resolution procedures provide the major area of substantive differences, and the one which is most controversial. Almost all private-sector employees enjoy a right to strike over the renegotiation of a collective agreement once certain preconditions have been satisfied. These preconditions are not very limiting, and typically include contract expiration, a strike vote, strike notice, and, in about half the jurisdictions, a conciliation step. Public-sector employees by comparison are much more fettered. Frequently their right to strike is removed and replaced by arbitration, even in situations, as for New Brunswick fire fighters, where basic statutory coverage is provided by the general labour code. Where strikes are permitted, preconditions are normally more severe than in the private sector. Quebec public employees cannot withdraw their services until agreement is reached on maintenance of certain functions deemed essential, federal civil servants must participate in a two-stage conciliation process before their right to strike becomes operative, and fact finding is a precondition to work stoppages for Ontario teachers.

Conclusions on Distinguishing Features

The most important distinguishing feature of public-sector collective bargaining is the special nature of the public employer. Operating in a decidedly political environment, the public employer is faced with constraints not encountered in the private sector. Some of these constraints, notably those associated with collective-bargaining structure and decision making, ultimately lie within the public employer's control and may eventually be overcome. Other constraints, such as the high cost of disagreement imposed by work stoppages which inconvenience the public, are less easily dealt with and will continue to pose difficult problems.

Distinctive legislative patterns in the public sector are not unrelated to these special employer characteristics. It would be surprising if the differences between public- and private-sector employers were not in some way reflected in policy differences between the two sectors. Mandated bargaining structures and restrictions on work stoppages are just two examples of public-sector distinctions which can be related back to special public-employer concerns. These types of policy differences are even more understandable if one recalls that the public employer, much more than the private employer, has the ability to directly influence (and even control) the direction that labour legislation will take.

There is much that public employees may find frustrating in all this. Essentially they want most of the same things sought by employees who work in the private sector. The costs of agreement and disagreement for employees differ very little between the two sectors. Yet public employees, because they happen to work for a special kind of employer, the government, find themselves operating under a very different system than employees elsewhere and are subject to a variety of special constraints. Public employees are more likely to be denied the right to strike, ordered back to work if they do strike, placed in bargaining units not of their own choosing, and subjected to special incomes-policy initiatives. And rather than being able to turn to government as the ultimate arbiter of their difficulties, public employees face the prospect of dealing with government as their employer — and thus perhaps the originator of their difficulty.

Devising an effective system of industrial relations in the public sector can only be accomplished if the very real public-sector differences are recognized and the divergent concerns of public employees, public employers, and the citizenry are accommodated. But as will be obvious from our discussions of dispute procedures in the next section, this is easier said than done.

STRIKES AND DISPUTE PROCEDURES

Of all the issues that remain contentious in the public sector, the question of public-employee strikes has been proven to be the most intractable. Opponents of strike rights for public employees make their case mainly on the grounds that public-sector work stoppages impose an unacceptable degree of inconvenience on the public at large. While private-sector disputes often do not affect third parties because they can go elsewhere for the service, this frequently is not true in the public sector. Strikes by teachers, postal workers, and transit workers, among others, inevitably spill beyond the employees and employers directly involved at the bargaining table, thus disrupting irreplaceable and heavily used services. Furthermore, as in the case of stoppages involving hospital workers, police, or lighthouse keepers, service interruptions may pose immediate danger to the health and safety of those who by necessity must rely on the struck services. For these reasons alone, it is argued, public employees should be prohibited from striking. Additionally, strike opponents variously have contended that the right to strike gives too much power to public-sector unions (ability to "hold the public up to ransom"); that public-sector strikes invariably take on political overtones, political strikes per se being undesirable and not really part of our industrial-relations system; and that the right to strike was designed for the private sector and the distinctive characteristics of the public sector therefore render it inapplicable (17, 48, 75).

These arguments have not gone unchallenged. Those who advocate strike rights for public employees suggest that damage to the public is far less extensive than commonly believed. Many public-sector employees, they point out, perform services that most people in the short run, at least, can do without (for example, research, administrative functions, weather forecasting). It is merely that the few truly disruptive disputes that do take place receive tremendous publicity, creating an impression that all public employees perform similarly vital services. In addition, techniques have been developed, such as special-notice requirements and requirements that critical employees in striking bargaining units remain at work, which can protect the public in the event that irreplaceable, or essential services are withdrawn.

The notion that the right to strike places too much power in the hands of public-sector unions is also contested. On the contrary, the financial constraints under which many public employers now operate, the decreasing likelihood of public panic in the face of service disruptions, taxpayer restlessness (if not revolt), the substantial financial savings a public employer may realize during a strike, and the degree of public concern over possible inflationary wage increases place substantial constraints on public-employee bargaining power (17, 22). Thus, the possibility of a strike plays exactly the role in bargaining that it should; namely, it tempers the demands of both parties and induces compromises necessary for a settlement.

But the foremost basis for arguments in favour of retaining the right to strike in the public sector lies in the perceived inadequacy of strike substitutes. Removing the right to strike necessarily implies replacing it with some other mechanism capable of resolving disputes. Advocates of a right to strike contend that they are not so much enamoured with the strike weapon, as they are disillusioned with the alternatives, such as arbitration and final-offer selection. Strike substitutes are criticized on the grounds that they weaken the collective-bargaining process, lead to excessive third-party intervention, and generally produce inferior collective agreements.

In light of this debate, it is not surprising that policy makers are divided in their opinion, as the diversity of disputes-resolution approaches currently in effect testifies. Union leaders tend to support the right to strike as a fundamental democratic right. However, when the legislative bill which led to the Public Service Staff Relations Act first was being discussed, most of the white-collar unions favoured arbitration over a right to strike. Professional groups such as registered nurses and unions in the protective services (police and fire fighters) have often expressed reservations about the right to strike. Employers are also divided on the issue. While less than enthusiastic about the prospects of strikes by their employees, many public employers seem even less enthralled with arbitration, which, they believe, usurps their decision-making authority (60). The Quebec government, for example, has repeatedly refused to submit public-sector disputes to arbitration, arguing that too large a portion of the provincial budget is at stake to permit a third-party decision (36). Probably the most support for the right to strike is found among third-party neutrals such as mediators, arbitrators, and industrial-relations and law professors. This is, perhaps, a bit ironic considering this is the group most likely to benefit, in terms of more demand for their services, if strikes were replaced with arbitration or a similar device.

Public-Sector Strike Record

In the five-year period from 1975 to 1979, the public sector accounted for approximately 18 percent of all time lost due to work stoppages in Canada (51). This proportion is slightly less than the overall proportion of public employees in the work force. If one considers that there are almost as many unionized public employees as private employees (though perhaps half of all public employees legally cannot

Table 3

Public-Sector Work Stoppages by Jurisdiction, 1978-1979

Jurisdiction	Percentage of Total Public Employment[a]	Percentage of Total Public-Sector Work Stoppage Time Lost[b]
British Columbia	10	6
Alberta	7	8
Saskatchewan	3	9
Manitoba	5	_[c]
Ontario	29	13
Quebec	21	51
New Brunswick	2	_[c]
Nova Scotia	3	1
Prince Edward Island	1	_[c]
Newfoundland	2	2
Federal	17	10

NOTES: a. Estimates based on data provided in D.K. Foot, and P. Thadaney, "The Growth of Public Employment in Canada," in D.K. Foot (Ed.), Public Employment and Compensation in Canada: Myths and Realities *(Scarborough, Ont.: Butterworth, 1978), Table A3.3.*
b. Estimates based on data provided in Labour Canada, Strikes and Lockouts in Canada, *1978-1979.*
c. Less than 1 percent.

strike) and that the Labour Canada data overstates public-sector strike activity by including telephone disputes, it is clear that, proportionately, public employees engage in less strike activity than do their private-sector counterparts.

A comparison of strike statistics (51) with employment data presented earlier in Table 1 indicates that in 1978 and 1979, provincial, and to a lesser extent, municipal government employees were the most strike-prone, in the sense that they accounted for a greater share of public-sector strike activity than public-sector employment. Based on this same criterion employees in education and in the federal government were the least strike-prone. Province-wide strikes by civil servants in Newfoundland in 1978 and Saskatchewan and Quebec in 1979 account for the high provincial strike totals.

On a jurisdictional basis, Table 3 reveals that the Quebec and Saskatchewan public sectors were the most strike-prone. Of the larger jurisdictions, Ontario and to a lesser extent British Columbia and the federal sector were less strike-prone.

Taken together these data suggest that for the country as a whole it is difficult to justify statements that public-sector strike activity is "excessive." Unionized public employees are less strike-prone than unionized private-sector employees. This is not to say that particular public-sector strikes do not create public hardship. The point is simply that such strikes must be placed in the context of an otherwise good record. Understandably Quebecers may fail to see things in quite the same light. Public-sector work stoppages have posed major problems in Quebec not only in 1978 and 1979, but throughout the 1960s and 1970s (12, 36). As indicated in Chapter 18 of this volume, however, Quebec's problems are to some extent unique and are imbedded in broader social and political forces. Elsewhere in Canada public-sector disputes have been kept to a much more manageable level.

Strike Substitutes

Public-sector strikes, whether excessive or not, do from time to time impose unacceptable levels of hardship on noncombatants and may, even in situations where public inconvenience is not an issue, contain a degree of political risk that elected officials are not prepared to countenance. For these reasons, policy makers have experimented with a variety of dispute mechanisms designed to remove strikes and their threat from public-sector collective-bargaining relationships.

Conventional interest arbitration — The most common and well-known strike substitute is conventional interest arbitration. Under this system, the negotiating parties, in the event they cannot reach a settlement, submit their differences to an arbitrator (or arbitration panel) who listens to arguments as to the merits of the respective positions then issues a binding award. This award becomes in effect the new collective agreement. Arbitrators are free, under the conventional-arbitration procedure, to either accept positions that the parties have submitted, or to fashion their own solution on any particular issue. They can, for example, "split the difference." The great majority of strike-substitute systems in effect in the Canadian public sector are of the conventional-arbitration variety.

There is little question that conventional-arbitration systems in Canada have been very successful at eliminating work stoppages. While occasional strikes against arbitration awards occur, sometimes with spectacular results as in the 1969 Montreal police strike, such occurrences are infrequent. Misgivings about arbitration are not based on its effectiveness at preventing strikes, but rather on the effect conventional arbitration has on the likelihood of the parties reaching agreements during negotiations (19, 68). North American industrial relations places a high premium on the ability of labour and management to resolve differences themselves through the give-and-take of the bargaining process. Almost all available evidence indicates that conventional-arbitration systems lead to a lower rate of negotiated settlements compared to systems in which strikes are permitted (64). For example, British Columbia teachers operating under a conventional-arbitration system have been able to achieve negotiated settlements 70 percent of the time (72); Ontario teachers, with a right to strike, have a settlement rate of 93 percent (23). Canadian federal civil servants who must submit their disputes to conventional arbitration manage to settle 75 percent of their negotiations; federal civil servants who can strike achieve settlements 88 percent of the time (64). Canadian municipal employees under arbitration have settlement rates of 71 percent; municipal employees who can strike settle in 93 percent of their negotiations (4).

The reduced ability of parties to settle their differences under conventional arbitration is attributable to two major factors. First, the possibility of an arbitration award being imposed often is not a sufficient threat to the negotiators to induce the tough compromises necessary to reach a settlement. The possibility of a strike, by comparison, usually is a sufficient threat. Second, conventional-arbitration systems may introduce an actual disincentive to compromise because concessions offered by a party during negotiations may be used against it if introduced as evidence before an arbitrator (79). Anything which discourages compromise during negotiations reduces the likelihood of settlements. For these reasons, and as the previous evidence indicated, the parties stand a good chance of actually using arbitration, thus not settling their differences themselves. When this happens, especially in consecutive rounds of negotiations, the parties may be left with collective agreements which are difficult to administer, not very reflective of their ongoing needs, and towards which they feel very little sense of commitment.

Closed-offer arbitration— The drawbacks of conventional arbitration have resulted in a search for other techniques which can maintain conventional arbitration's success at eliminating strikes but at the same time can lead to a higher rate of negotiated (as opposed to arbitrated) settlements. One such proposal was made by Wheeler in 1977 (79) and called closed-offer arbitration (COA). Under a COA system, parties unable to reach agreement in negotiations would, in the same manner as under conventional arbitration, submit their impasse to an arbitrator. The key operating difference under COA, however, would be that negotiating positions of the parties during bargaining could not be introduced as evidence during the arbitration hearing (for example, the union could not argue that management had offered to settle for 10 percent during negotiations). This would produce two positive effects. First, the parties would no longer be reluctant to make concessions during negotiations, since such concessions could no longer be used against them if arbitration became necessary. Thus, compromising activity, an essential ingredient in effective bargaining, would be restored. Second, because the arbitrator would be unaware of offers and proposals made during negotiations, the arbitration award conceivably could give one of the parties *less* than they were offered in negotiations (for example, an arbitrator could award an 8 percent wage increase, whereas management had offered 10 percent during bargaining). This is a possibility that is very unlikely under conventional arbitration and would impose a threat likely to help foster settlements. Although closed-offer arbitration has yet to be formally introduced as policy in any jurisdiction, it does offer some distinct advantages over conventional arbitration.

Final-offer selection — If closed-offer arbitration has not yet cleared the drawing board, another variation of conventional arbitration, final-offer selection (FOS), has successfully made the transition from theory to practice. First proposed in 1966 (68), FOS requires an arbitrator to choose either the position submitted by management or the position submitted by the union *without alteration.* Arbitrators cannot, as under conventional arbitration, split the difference between the positions submitted by the two parties: they are obliged to accept one party's position or the other's. Depending on the form of FOS used, the selection of the two positions may be made either on an issue-by-issue basis or on an entire contract basis. The idea behind FOS is that the two parties would rather make the concessions needed to achieve settlement during negotiations than face the risk of an arbitration award in which the other side's position, in its entirety, would be incorporated into the new collective agreement.

Final-offer selection has been adopted in a number of American jurisdictions but has been used to a very limited extent thus far in Canada. The American experience generally suggests that FOS is more capable of producing negotiated settlements than conventional arbitration. While the rate of negotiated settlements under an FOS system in Eugene, Oregon was only 75 percent, settlement rates were substantially higher for police and fire fighters in Michigan (84 percent), Wisconsin (86 percent), and Massachusetts (93 percent), and much higher, 96 percent, for Iowa government employees (24, 32, 54, 67). In Canada, University of Alberta academic staff use FOS to resolve salary impasses (70). Since 1971, the parties have managed to settle without arbitration only on five occasions and have had to resort to FOS four times (50).

Despite the apparent success of FOS in facilitating negotiated settlements (at least in the United States), certain concerns about the procedure have limited its more widespread adoption (21, 77). The most important concern, especially where FOS is used on an entire-contract basis, is the possibility that both parties will submit unreasonable final positions. Since the arbitrator is unable to modify the positions in any way, but must choose one or the other, the resultant award could lead to an unworkable collective agreement. This danger exists to a far lesser extent under a conventional-arbitration approach because the arbitrator can use discretion to fashion awards that ensure some degree of acceptability. Final-offer selection also can foster a win-lose mentality in bargaining which potentially can be very damaging to the labour-management relationship. Again, under conventional arbitration, where the award is likely to reflect some compromises between the final positions submitted by the two sides, a win-lose atmosphere is much less likely to emerge. Thus, though recognizing the benefits of FOS in terms of fostering negotiations, one observer states that "while it is necessary to preserve the integrity of the collective bargaining *process,* it should never be forgotten that the purpose of the process is to reach acceptable *results*" (79, p. 300).

Compromise Approaches

Choice of procedures — The drawbacks associated with various kinds of arbitration systems combined with persistent misgivings about an unfettered right to strike have given rise to some intriguing compromise approaches. The best known of these is choice of procedures (COP), an approach pioneered in 1967 under the Public Service Staff Relations Act and now in place in several American and Canadian jurisdictions (64). Under COP one or both of the parties are given the option of choosing either arbitration or a work stoppage in the event negotiations fail to produce a settlement. Depending on the jurisdiction, the choice between the two procedures is vested either unilaterally in the union (PSSRA and British Columbia), the employer (Minnesota), or is subject to joint determination (Wisconsin). The choice may be made either at the point a negotiating impasse is reached (B.C., Minnesota, Wisconsin) or prior to the start of negotiations (PSSRA).

Unlike final-offer selection, whose potential benefits had been debated in the industrial-relations literature before its practical application, COP lacked any a priori theoretical rationale when first introduced. It arose as a result of political compromises. For example, when the PSSRA was being debated by Parliament, some employee groups favoured arbitration while other employee groups adamantly argued for the right to strike. The government, in adopting COP, sought to accommodate both employee factions. The Minnesota COP framework, which vests the choice in the public employer, simply reflected the state legislature's belief that extending strike rights to public employees should be done cautiously. The hope of policy makers in all four jurisdictions, however, was that COP would produce few strikes and help foster negotiated settlements.

Experience suggests that COP has accomplished these twin policy objectives. Out of more than 3000 negotiations falling under COP in B.C., the federal service, Minnesota, and Wisconsin, strikes occurred only forty times—that is, in less than 2 percent of the negotiations. Labour and management achieved negotiated settlements, that is, neither a strike nor an arbitration award, in almost 90 percent of their negotiations. Arbitration was most likely under the PSSRA framework, possibly because the strike-arbitration choice under the PSSRA must be made prior to the start of negotiations as opposed to at the point of impasse in the three other jurisdictions. The experience with COP also showed that unions are more inclined to choose arbitration than are public employers, but that *both* parties choose arbitration over a strike procedure in the majority of cases (64).

Choice of procedures is not without its drawbacks. First, although strikes have been minimized, they have not been eliminated entirely. Legal work stoppages under the PSSRA involving postal workers and air-traffic controllers have caused significant public inconvenience. Second, giving one party the unilateral right to choose either strike or arbitration at its discretion, forcing that procedure on the other party, may create a serious power imbalance in negotiations. A consequence could be one-sided collective agreements in favour of the "choosing party." Thus, as was suggested with respect to final-offer selection, the results of bargaining under COP need to be more thoroughly analysed if the approach is to become more widespread.

Controlled strike — A second intriguing addition to the public-sector dispute framework is the concept of a controlled strike. Also first introduced under the PSSRA, it has since been adopted in British Columbia, Quebec, and New Brunswick. The controlled-strike approach permits work stoppages but requires that certain designated employees in the striking bargaining unit remain on the job to provide essential services. Under the PSSRA, the proportion of designated employees within a given bargaining unit has varied from under 1 percent of employees in the case of postal workers to over 85 percent of fire fighters. Most jurisdictions have assigned the role of designating employees to their labour-relations boards, but Quebec currently is experimenting with permitting the union to determine who is or is not essential. The Quebec approach is consistent with that taken in several European countries (1), and employee groups in other jurisdictions, notably registered nurses, also have sought the right to self-determine the question of essentiality.

In theory, the controlled-strike system should satisfy the divergent needs of policy makers, unions, and employers. The union is able to exercise its right to strike. It is under pressure to settle because the majority of its members are foregoing their pay cheques, and the employer is in partial operation. The employer is under pressure because it is unable to provide the level of service normally counted upon and further may be forced to mount a herculean effort to maintain even its limited operations. The public interest is protected because the designated employees ensure that essential services are maintained.

In practice, it becomes obvious that designating the "correct" proportion of bargaining-unit personnel is crucial to the success of the controlled-strike approach. If too many employees are designated, the pressure on the employer may be inconsequential; if too few employees are designated, public safety may be jeopardized. Unions in the federal civil service have accused the Public Service Staff Relations Board with being too conservative. In Quebec, there are fears that unions will manipulate their power over designation to great advantage.

This dilemma has been clearly illustrated by Weiler's (77) description of a controlled strike at the Vancouver General Hospital in 1976. The hospital, the largest in Canada, contains over 1800 beds and employs more than 5000 people. The dispute involved the hospital's largest bargaining unit composed of 2000 nonprofessional employees. With the strike imminent, the Labour Board was summoned to designate which employees would be required to remain on the job. Hospital management insisted that all 2000 employees were essential while the union claimed that "none of its members should be directed to scab on their own union's strike." Eventually the board designated 100 employees as essential. The hospital managed to operate 1000 of its 1800 beds through the use of administrators, supervisors, professional employees, and volunteers. The designated employees only performed specialized tasks or operated equipment indispensable to patient safety (for example, respiratory equipment). The strike lasted three weeks and ended with both the union and the employer agreeing to voluntary arbitration. During the dispute the Labour Board was accused of "playing God" and an editorial questioned whether the board chairman could differentiate a "tracheotomy from a tree farm licence." For his part, Weiler termed the experience as "unquestionably the most traumatic, the most tension-filled" of his five-year chairmanship of the B.C. Labour Relations Board (77, p. 209). Yet he still saw the controlled-strike approach as preferable to a blanket prohibition of all public-sector disputes.

Conclusion on Strikes and Dispute Procedures

"The design of a dispute resolution system requires balancing the multiple objectives of avoiding strikes, minimizing third-party dependence, and maximizing good faith bargaining, protecting the public interest and accountability of elected officials, and in the long run, building the commitment of the parties and the public to a bargaining system that forces the parties to confront their problems effectively" (48, p. 187). It is not yet clear whether these objectives can be compatibly accommodated within a single dispute-resolution system. In reviewing the array of alternatives currently available — right to strike, conventional arbitration, final-offer selection, closed-offer arbitration, choice of procedures, and controlled strike — it is apparent that some techniques come closer to meeting the ideal than others, but that there are no easy answers. Continued experimentation and research, combined with a maturation of public-sector labour-management relations, may eventually produce a consensus. The first step towards such a consensus, however, must surely be the realization that all procedures are at best imperfect and that explicit trade-offs between desirable but incompatible objectives (for example, strike avoidance and no third-party dependence) might have to be made and lived with.

WAGE ISSUES

Though less spectacular than dispute resolution, questions surrounding public-employee compensation have proven almost as troublesome. It is not an exaggeration to suggest that much of the public believes that government employees are overpaid and have been remarkably successful at winning high and unwarranted wage increases. Private employers complain that government wage settlements establish patterns which the private sector, contending as it does with profit-loss considerations, is hard-pressed to match.

Union officials counter by claiming that such allegations are untrue and that seemingly high wage increases reflect nothing more than a normal "catching-up" process (31). Furthermore, some union officials argue, even if government employees were paid more than their private-sector counterparts, there would be nothing inherently wrong about such a state of affairs. Rates of pay should reflect the social value of the work performed. "Public employees who perform work that in many cases is so essential that they are forbidden by law to strike should not have to follow rates of pay for nonessential workers" (52, p. 62). In addition, it is argued, there is no universal law which requires government to be a wage follower. On the contrary, "public employers should be free to be model employers, to be followed by the rest of the community" (52, pp. 62-63).

Public-Private Wage Differentials

Philosophies and perceptions aside, there are some fundamental institutional reasons to assume that public- and private-sector wage determination processes may differ. The most extensive work in Canada on the subject has been carried out by Gunderson (38, 40, 41) who concluded that a potential for upward wage bias exists in the public sector. This conclusion is based on reasoning that: (a) political pressure may be less stringent than the profit constraint; (b) the demand for labour is relatively inelastic compared to the private sector; (c) union wage pressures are greatest for recently unionized groups; and (d) competitive forces ensure a public-sector wage floor, but do not provide an effective wage ceiling.

Empirical evidence is consistent with theoretical expectation; public employees do earn more than their private-sector counterparts. Evidence based on the 1970 census data, the most current data set available, indicates that after other factors have been controlled (for example, education, experience, job level), male public employees earn on the average 6 percent more than male private-sector employees and that female workers in the public sector earn 9 percent more than their counterparts in the private sector (38). The public-sector wage advantage tends to be greatest at lowest skill levels. At higher occupational levels, private-sector employees enjoy a wage advantage. Fringe benefits are roughly comparable between the two sectors. Data comparing public-private wages in the United States indicate that patterns in that country are very similar to those in Canada (41).

In terms of wage trends, analyses of negotiated wage increases since 1967 show that public-sector unions have achieved slightly higher average wage increases (9.6 percent) than unions in the private sector (9.3 percent). Private-sector wage increases were higher between 1967 and 1972 and again in 1978 and 1979. Public-sector wage increases topped those in the private sector between 1973 and 1977 (41). Other data series on wage trends, however, indicate a slight narrowing of the public-private-sector wage gap since 1970 (41).

The data reviewed here are noteworthy in several respects. First, they confirm that, consistent with public expectations, government employees are better paid than private-sector employees. But the differential is slight (and may in fact be shrinking) and in all probability is a good deal less than popularly believed. Second, the evidence suggests that the public employer may be a more egalitarian employer. Women earn comparatively more in the public sector than in the private sector. Public-sector wage scales as well may be more compressed, providing employees at the low end with a comparative earning advantage in the public sector. Thus, intentionally or otherwise, government is in certain respects a "model" employer if one assumes that equal pay and "bringing the bottom up" are laudable objectives. Third, there is little support for the contention that public-sector wage settlements have outstripped private-sector wage settlements during the last decade. Differentials in this regard are very slight and subject to year-to-year fluctuations.

Wage Comparability

Whether or not, given the evidence, a problem in fact exists with respect to public-sector wage determination, many analysts and policy makers remain convinced that public-sector wages for unionized employees should not be set in the same way as in the private sector. A case in point is a recent article by Michael Walker, director of the Fraser Institute (75). Citing the potential for upward wage bias that exists in the public sector and the inconvenience caused by public-sector strikes over wages, Walker calls for the establishment of a public-sector wage board and a strike prohibition over compensation issues. He argues that "wage determination by a wage board would not only serve to protect the taxpayer from excessive gains by public employees, it would also protect public employees from inappropriate measures taken against them by government during public sector belt-tightening" (75, p. 16). Proposals similar to this have been made in the past (80), but all have foundered in the face of vigorous union opposition.

Policy makers have turned instead to the concept of comparability (58). This approach attempts to tie the compensation of public employees explicitly to the compensation of comparable private-sector employees. Accordingly, wage arguments during negotiations, conciliation, and arbitration (if required) centre on the relationship between the compensation of particular private- and public-sector employees. Conciliators and arbitrators are mandated under applicable legislation (for example, the Public Service Staff Relations Act) to give primary weight to this private-public comparison in their recommendations. Unions generally oppose legislated implementation of the comparability principle. They do not dislike the notion of comparison, per se; comparison to relevant employee groups has always been a key feature of all negotiations, private or public sector. Rather, unions see the statutory imposition of comparability as a formal admission that government must be a follower, and never a leader. Second, unions claim that excessive attention to comparability introduces rigidities into the bargaining process as "wage and fringe benefits could be placed in a computer which would then spit out 'the facts' on what changes might be allowed in a collective agreement" (52, p. 457). The third, and perhaps most important union fear, is that governments, acting in their own self-interest as employers, will manipulate statutory comparability formulas in a way that will severely damage the ability of unions to achieve satisfactory wage settlements.

Union misgivings about comparability may be overcome once several thorny technical issues in comparability are resolved. First, consensus has yet to be reached on which private-sector employees are most appropriate for comparison purposes. Should comparisons be made, for instance, against all employees in a relevant comparison group, employees who work only for "good" employers, or some combination in between; should regional comparisons be made or should comparisons be made on a national basis; and should unionized and nonunionized employees be considered or unionized employees only? How should public-sector employees for whom no private-sector comparable group exists (for example, air-traffic controllers) be treated? Should special adjustments be made in situations where the comparable private-sector group arguably has been subject to discrimination? For example, tying the salary of public-sector secretaries to private-sector secretaries may only perpetuate the low-wage status to which this virtually all-female occupation has been perhaps unfairly subjected.

Second, agreement must be reached on the range of factors to be considered in making the comparisons. Should only wage and fringe benefits be counted or should other less easily quantifiable elements be included as well? Relevant additional elements might include seniority provisions (which could have economic impact), sick leave benefits, special scheduling arrangements, call-in pay, uniform allowances, leave provisions, and overtime entitlements. Research has shown that a given level of wages may reflect trade-offs between salaries and many of the aforementioned items (3). Can these items be measured and should they?

Third, questions about data-gathering techniques must be answered. Collecting the substantial amount of information needed to make proper comparisons is time-consuming. Thus, private-sector data used for comparison purposes may not reflect current conditions, but conditions of six months or a year before. A built-in lag in public-sector wage levels would result unless some adjustment formula was incorporated. Also to be resolved is the issue of who actually performs the data collection and reporting. Should each side have responsibility for collecting its own data, should a government body be involved, or should some tripartite agency be established? Unions have expressed concern that governments may be too easily tempted to subvert agencies within the government's purview.

Conclusions on Wage Comparisons

Few quarrel with the proposition that public employees deserve to receive fair compensation for the work they perform. The question is how this "fairness" is to be achieved. Because of persistent concerns about the ability of the pure collective-bargaining model to establish appropriate public-sector wage levels, other procedures are urged. More formal reliance on wage-comparability principles seems likely. It must be asked, however, in view of data suggesting that the wage-determination problem may be more myth than reality, union opposition to any schemes which might constrain the collective-bargaining process, and the difficult technical problems involved in applying comparison formulas, whether the effort to find a "better" way to determine public-employee compensation is in fact necessary and worth the problems it might generate.

CONCLUSION

The arrival of public-sector collective bargaining has been arguably the most important development in Canadian industrial relations of the last twenty years. It has significantly increased the size and strength of the Canadian labour movement and introduced large numbers of white-collar workers and professionals to collective bargaining for the first time. It has given birth to whole new legislative schemes and launched an era of policy experimentation which continues unabated. It has placed unprecedented pressure on public-sector management to accommodate itself to the new reality of dealing with their employees through the give-and-take of the bargaining table. Perhaps most significantly, collective bargaining in the public sector has brought labour-relations problems home to the general public in a way in which private-sector developments never did.

This chapter explored the many complex issues that underlie these and other developments. It is clear from the discussion that no easy solutions exist to the various problems that confront labour, management, and policy makers in the public sector. It is hoped that this chapter has at least provided a basis which will enable the reader to critically evaluate events that continue to unfold in the public sector and to identify what the real problems are and where the possible solutions lie.

REFERENCES AND WORKS CITED

1. Aaron, B. "Procedures for Settling Public Interest Disputes in the Essential and Public Sectors: A Comparative View," in M. Gunderson (Ed.), *Collective Bargaining in the Essential and Public Service Sectors* (Toronto: University of Toronto Press, 1975).

2. Anderson, J.C. *Union Effectiveness: An Industrial Relations Systems Approach.* Ph.D. dissertation, Cornell University, 1977.

3. Anderson, J.C. "Bargaining Outcomes: An IR System Approach," *Industrial Relations,* Vol. 18 (1979), 127-143.

4. Anderson, J.C. "Determinants of Collective Bargaining Impasses: The Role of Dispute Resolution Procedures." Paper presented at a conference, Industrial Relations and Conflict Management, at the Netherlands School of Business, June 29-July 3, 1980.

5. Anderson, J.C., and T. Kochan. "Collective Bargaining in the Public Service of Canada," *Relations Industrielles/Industrial Relations,* Vol. 32 (No. 2, 1977), 234-249.

6. Armstrong, R. "Some Aspects of Policy Determination in the Development of the Collective Bargaining Legislation in the Public Service of Canada," *Canadian Public Administration,* Vol. II (1968), 485-493.

7. Bairstow, F., H. Lebel, B. Downie, and A. Kleingartner. "The Professional Employee in the Public Service of Canada," *Journal of the Professional Institute,* Vol. 52 (1973), 4-55.

8. Begin, J.P. "Grievance Mechanisms and Faculty Collegiality: The Rutgers Case," *Industrial and Labour Relations Review,* Vol. 31 (1978), 295-309.

9. Bird, R.M. "The Growth of the Public Service in Canada," in D.K. Foot (Ed.), *Public Employment and Compensation in Canada: Myths and Realities* (Scarborough, Ont.: Butterworth, 1978), pp. 19-44.

10. Bird, R.M., M. Bucovetsky, and D.K. Foot. *The Growth of Public Employment in Canada* (Scarborough, Ont.: Butterworth, 1979).

11. Blum, A.A., M. Estey, J. Kuhn, W. Wildman, and L. Troy. *White Collar Workers* (New York: Random House, 1971).

12. Boivin, J. "Collective Bargaining in the Province of Quebec Public Sector," *Relations Industrielles/Industrial Relations,* Vol. 27 (1972), 708-717.

13. Bucovetsky, M. (Ed.). *Studies in Public Employment and Compensation in Canada* (Scarborough, Ont.: Butterworth, 1979).

14. Burton, J.F. "The Extent of Collective Bargaining in the Public Sector," in B. Aaron, J. Grodin, and J. Stern (Eds.), *Public Sector Bargaining* (Madison: Industrial Relations Research Association, 1979), pp. 1-43.

15. Carrothers, A.W.R., Chairman, *Report of the Board of Reference* pursuant to the provisions of the Civil Service Act (Victoria, B.C., 1959).

16. Chamberlain, N.W., and J. Kuhn. *Collective Bargaining,* 2nd ed. (New York: McGraw-Hill, 1965).

17. Cohen, S. "Does Public Employee Unionism Diminish Democracy?" *Industrial and Labor Relations Review,* Vol. 32 (1979), 189-195.

18. Derber, M. "Management Organization for Collective Bargaining in the Public Sector," in B. Aaron, J. Grodin, and J. Stern (Eds.), *Public Sector Bargaining* (Madison: Industrial Relations Research Association, 1979), pp. 80-117.

19. Downie, B. *The Behavioral, Economic, and Institutional Effects of Substituting Compulsory Arbitration for the Right to Strike* (Ottawa: Economic Council of Canada, 1979).

20. Edwards, C. "The Public Service Alliance of Canada," *Relations Industrielles/ Industrial Relations,* Vol. 23 (1968), 634-641.

21. Feigenbaum, C. "Final Offer Arbitration: Better Theory Than Practice," *Industrial Relations,* Vol. 14 (1975), 311-317.

22. Feuille, P. "Selected Benefits and Costs of Compulsory Arbitration," *Industrial and Labor Relations Review,* Vol. 33 (1979), 64-76.

23. Feuille, P., and J.C. Anderson. "Public Sector Bargaining: Policy and Practice," *Industrial Relations,* Vol. 19 (1980), 309-324.

24. Feuille, P., and J. Dworkin. "Final Offer Arbitration and Intertemporal Compromise, or It's My Turn to Win," *Proceedings of the Industrial Relations Research Association,* Vol. 31 (1978), 87-95.

25. Finkelman, J. *The Rationale in Establishing Bargaining Units in the Federal Public Service in Canada* (Kingston: Queen's University Industrial Relations Centre, 1974).

26. Foot, D.K. (Ed.). *Public Employment and Compensation in Canada: Myths and Realities* (Scarborough, Ont.: Butterworth, 1978).

27. Foot, D.K., and P. Thadaney. "The Growth of Public Employment in Canada," in D.K. Foot (Ed.), *Public Employment and Compensation in Canada: Myths and Realities* (Scarborough, Ont.: Butterworth, 1978), pp. 45-62.

28. Frankel, S. "Staff Relations in the Canadian Federal Public Service: Experience with Joint Consultation," in J.E. Hodgetts and D.C. Corbett (Eds.), *Canadan Public Administration* (Toronto: Macmillan, 1960), pp. 370-385.

29. Frankel, S. *Staff Relations in the Civil Service* (Montreal: McGill University Press, 1962).

30. Frankel, S., and R.C. Pratt. *Municipal Labour Relations in Canada* (Montreal: The Canadian Federation of Mayors and Municipalities and McGill University Industrial Relations Centre, 1954).

31. Fryer, J. "Public vs. Private Wage Comparison," *Business Review* (1979), 17-23.

32. Gallagher, D., and R. Pegnetter. "Impasse Resolution Under the Iowa Multistep Procedure," *Industrial and Labour Relations Review,* Vol. 32 (1979), 327-338.

33. Gandz, J. "Grievance Initiation and Resolution: A Test of the Behavioral Theory," *Relations Industrielles/Industrial Relations,* Vol. 34 (1979), 778-792.

34. Garbarino, J. *Faculty Bargaining* (New York: McGraw-Hill, 1975).

35. Goldenberg, S. "Collective Bargaining in the Provincial Public Services," in J.F. O'Sullivan (Ed.), *Collective Bargaining in the Public Service* (Toronto: The Institute of Public Administration of Canada, 1973), pp. 11-44.

36. Goldenberg, S. *Industrial Relations in Quebec Past and Present* (Kingston: Queen's University Industrial Relations Centre, 1975).

37. Goldenberg, S. "Public Sector Labor Relations in Canada," in B. Aaron, J. Grodin, and J. Stern (Eds.). *Public Sector Bargaining* (Madison: Industrial Relations Research Association, 1979), pp. 259-291.

38. Gunderson, M. "Decomposition of Public-Private Sector Earnings," in M. Bucovetsky (Ed.), *Studies in Public Employment and Compensation in Canada* (Scarborough, Ont.: Butterworth, 1979), pp. 1-28.

39. Gunderson, M. "Professionalization of the Canadian Public Sector," in M. Bucovetsky (Ed.), *Studies in Public Employment and Compensation in Canada* (Scarborough, Ont.: Butterworth, 1979), pp. 81-124.

40. Gunderson, M. *Labour Market Economics* (Toronto: McGraw-Hill Ryerson, 1980).

41. Gunderson, M. "Public Sector Compensation in Canada and the U.S.," *Industrial Relations,* Vol. 19 (1980), 257-271.

42. Hardy, J., and A. Ponak. "Employee Relations in the Royal Canadian Mounted Police." Unpublished manuscript, 1980.

43. Hodgetts, J.E., and O.P. Dwivedi. *Provincial Governments as Employers* (Montreal and London: McGill-Queen's University Press, 1974).

44. Katz, H.C. "The Municipal Budgetary Response to Changing Labor Costs: The Case of San Francisco," *Industrial and Labor Relations Review,* Vol. 32 (1979), 506-519.

45. Kervin, J.B. *The 1975 Metro Toronto Teacher-Board Negotiations and Strike* (Toronto: University of Toronto Centre for Industrial Relations, 1977).

46. Kleingartner, A. "Collective Bargaining Between Salaried Professionals and Public Sector Management," *Public Administration Review,* Vol. 33 (1973), 165-172.

47. Kochan, T. "A Theory of Multilateral Collective Bargaining in City Governments," *Industrial and Labor Relations Review,* Vol. 27 (1974), 525-542.

48. Kochan, T. "Dynamics of Dispute Resolution in the Public Sector," in B. Aaron, J. Grodin, and J. Stern (Eds.), *Public Sector Bargaining* (Madison: Industrial Relations Research Association, 1979), pp. 150-190.

49. Kochan, T. *Collective Bargaining and Industrial Relations* (Homewood, Ill.: Richard D. Irwin, 1980).

50. Labour Canada. *Collective Bargaining Review,* various issues, 1972-1980.

51. Labour Canada. *Strikes and Lockouts in Canada,* 1978-1979.

52. Levine, G. "Public vs. Private-Sector Compensation: A Trade Unionist's View," *Labour Gazette,* October 1977, 453-458.

53. Lewin, D., and S. Goldenberg. "Public Sector Unionism in the U.S. and Canada," *Industrial Relations,* Vol. 19 (1980), 239-256.

54. Lipsky, D., and T. Barocci. "Final Offer Arbitration and Public Safety Employees: The Massachusetts Experience," *Proceedings of the Industrial Relations Research Association,* Vol. 30 (1977), 67-75.

55. Logan, H.A. *Trade Unions in Canada* (Toronto: Macmillan, 1948).

56. McLean, B. *"A Union amongst Government Employees": A History of the B.C. Government Employees' Union* (Vancouver: B.C. Government Employees' Union, 1979).

57. Muir, J.D. *Collective Bargaining by Canadian Public School Teachers* (Ottawa: Task Force on Labour Relations, 1971).

58. O'Connel, M. "Fair Comparison with Selected Good Employers." Unpublished discussion paper, Ottawa, 1976.

59. Phillips, P. "Theoretical Problems of Public Interest Sector Industrial Relations," *Relations Industrielles/Industrial Relations,* Vol. 31 (1976), 566-587.

60. Ponak, A. "Public Sector Dispute Resolution: An American Twist to a Canadian Approach," *Relations Industrielles/Industrial Relations,* Vol. 31 (1976), 537-553.

61. Ponak, A. "Unionized Professionals and the Scope of Bargaining," *Industrial and Labor Relations Review,* Vol. 34 (1981), 396-407.

62. Ponak, A., and C.R.P. Fraser. "Union Activists' Support for Joint Programs," *Industrial Relations,* Vol. 18 (1979), 197-209.

63. Ponak, A., and T.P. Haridas. "Collective Bargaining Attitudes of Registered Nurses in the United States and Canada," *Relations Industrielles/Industrial Relations,* Vol. 34 (1979), 576-590.

64. Ponak, A., and H. Wheeler. "Choice of Procedures in Canada and the United States," *Industrial Relations,* Vol. 19 (1980), 292-308.

65. Public Service Alliance of Canada. *The Truth About Bill C-22* (Public Service Alliance of Canada, 1978).

66. Scarrow, H. "Employer-Employee Relationships in the Civil Services of the Canadian Provinces," in J.E. Hodgetts and D.C. Corbett (Eds.), *Canadian Public Administration* (Toronto: Macmillan, 1960), pp. 385-398.

67. Stern, J., C. Rehmus, J. Loewenberg, H. Kasper, and B. Dennis. *Final-Offer Arbitration* (Lexington, Mass.: Lexington Books, 1975).

68. Stevens, C. "Is Compulsory Arbitration Compatible with Bargaining," *Industrial Relations,* Vol. 5 (1966), 38-52.

69. Stieber, J. "Collective Bargaining in the Public Sector," in L. Ulman (Ed.), *Challenges to Collective Bargaining* (Englewood Cliffs, N.J.: Prentice-Hall, 1967).

70. Swimmer, G. "Final Position Arbitration and Intertemporal Compromise: The University of Alberta Compromise," *Relations Industrielles/Industrial Relations* Vol. 30 (1975), 533-536.

71. Thompson, M. "The Development of Collective Bargaining in Canadian Universities," *Proceedings of the Industrial Relations Research Association,* Vol. 28 (1975), 257-265.

72. Thompson, M., and J. Cairnie. "Compulsory Arbitration: The Case of British Columbia Teachers," *Industrial and Labor Relations Review,* Vol. 27 (1973), 3-17.

73. Thompson, M., and L. Moore. "Managerial Attitudes Toward Industrial Relations: Public and Private Sectors," *Relations Industrielles/Industrial Relations,* Vol. 31 (1976), 359-367.

74. Treasury Board of Canada. *Proposed Changes to the Public Service Staff Relations Act* (Treasury Board of Canada, 1978).

75. Walker, M. "Independent Board Should Set Public Sector Pay," *Financial Post,* October 11, 1980, p. 16.

76. Wall, T.D., and J.A. Lischeron. *Worker Participation* (London: McGraw-Hill, 1977).

77. Weiler, P. *Reconcilable Differences* (Toronto: Carswell, 1980).

78. Wetzel, K., and D. Gallagher. "The Saskatchewan Government's Internal Arrangements to Accommodate Collective Bargaining," *Relations Industrielles/Industrial Relations,* Vol. 34 (1979), 452-470.

79. Wheeler, H. "Closed-Offer: Alternative to Final-Offer Selection," *Industrial Relations,* Vol. 16 (1977), 298-305.

80. Williams, C. "Collective Bargaining in the Public Sector: A Reexamination," *Relations Industrielles/Industrial Relations,* Vol. 28 (1973), 17-31.

81. Williams, J. "Shifting Jurisdictions, Phantom Bargaining, and Essential Services," *Labour Gazette,* November 1973, 724-729.

82. Wood, W.D., and P. Kumar. *The Current Industrial Scene in Canada, 1980* (Kingston: Queen's University Industrial Relations Centre, 1980).

QUESTIONS

1. Explain the role consultation played in the development of public-sector collective bargaining.

2. Describe the key differences between private- and public-sector management and discuss the implications of these differences for the process of collective bargaining in the public sector.

3. Some public employees fall under general private-sector labour legislation (for example, most municipal employees) while other public employees are governed by special public-sector statutes (for example, federal civil servants). Discuss the merits of the respective approaches.

4. Why is the question of dispute-resolution procedures such an important issue in the public sector?

5. "Public employees should have the right to strike." Discuss.

6. Identify the techniques suggested for either eliminating entirely or at least reducing the impact of public sector strikes and discuss their respective advantages and disadvantages.

7. Why is reliance placed on the concept of "wage comparability" in public-sector collective bargaining and what are some of the problems associated with its usage?

MARK THOMPSON

16. Collective Bargaining by Professionals

Collective bargaining by professional employees is a new phenomenon with, as yet, uncertain features. If one counts as "professionals" persons with specialized knowledge and organizational identification, there are about 1.1 million in Canada. The majority are employed in the public or parapublic sectors.

Within these sectors, most professionals bargain, but this process is still relatively rare in the private sector. Professionals have adopted bargaining to preserve elements of their status in the large organizations where they work. In a few jurisdictions, professionals are still not covered by labour codes, and these employees frequently work in managerial categories, excluding them from the protections of the law. But public-sector legislation is more permissive.

A variety of organizations represent professionals — ranging from professional associations to trade unions. However, most professionals who bargain belong to independent associations, which are usually, but not always, certified. Some organizations have become more unionlike, but the transformation is not inevitable. Initially, professionals are reluctant to engage in union tactics, and legal barriers to certification have prevented them from unionizing in a number of cases.

Collective agreements covering professionals contain features not found elsewhere, such as leave to attend professional meetings, and, in some instances, the amount or quality of service to be provided. Clauses of the latter type have been contentious in bargaining. The apparent economic impact of bargaining by professionals has not been large. Strikes have been infrequent and concentrated among nurses and teachers.

The future of bargaining by professionals is still unclear, but the relevant question is to what extent they will adopt the modes of bargaining used by other groups.

Until recently, the subject of collective bargaining by professionals would not have accounted for more than a brief mention in any book on Canadian industrial relations. Professionals generally avoided unionization and associated practices in the belief that collective action was unprofessional and that their qualifications and abilities protected their self-interest without resorting to tactics used by blue-collar workers. Events of the 1960s and 1970s have made such attitudes obsolete for many professionals, many of whom have overcome their initial reluctance to engage in collective action. Teachers, nurses, translators, and physicians, to cite only a few examples, have gained public attention by their willingness to use traditional bargaining tactics to achieve their objectives.

Since these developments are still relatively recent, many questions about bargaining by professionals remain unanswered. The forces that cause them to adopt collective bargaining are not well understood. Many different organizations represent professionals, and patterns of representation are still not firmly established. A number of legal issues have arisen in this context, and the nature of collective bargaining by professionals, including their willingness to strike, is not yet clear. But experience of the last decade does provide some tentative answers, which this chapter will present.

PROFESSIONALS IN CANADA

The definition of a "professional" has caused many observers considerable difficulty, as various groups have incorporated the word into their titles or proclaimed themselves to be "professional." However, only the traditional professions of law, medicine, and the clergy are regarded as such without question. Although discussions over the inclusion of other groups inevitably arouse controversy, debates over the meaning of the term "professional" are neither enlightening nor convincing. For the purposes of this chapter, a "professional" is someone who possesses specialized or technical knowledge, usually acquired through a formal and lengthy education program, and who has a degree of organizational identification as a member of a profession. The older (and stronger) professions have, by a combination of technical skill and organizational strength, achieved considerable control over their work environment in such areas as definition of appropriate work, regulation of entry into the profession, and administration of ethical and technical codes. New (and weaker) professions have sought similar status by political or legal means with limited success.

Unfortunately, this designation does not correspond to any source of labour force data, so it is difficult to estimate just how many professionals there are in Canada. But one scholar, using data from the 1971 census and other federal government surveys, estimated that there were approximately 1.1 million professionals in the labour force in 1971. Of these, about 70 percent were in the public or parapublic sectors, with one-third each in education and health or medicine. Other professionals are widely distributed over the private sector (18).

The employment status of specific professions varies greatly, and these differences affect their position vis-à-vis collective bargaining. If one counts employees of government-funded institutions in the public sector, virtually all teachers, nurses, and most other health professionals are employed in that sector, whereas only about 20 percent of architects, engineers, or accountants are in the public sector. The proportions of accountants and scientists in the two sectors resemble that for engineers (29).

Law and medicine, the two professions on which many others are modeled, have a long tradition of self-employment, but engineering or accountancy are mixed, with some members employed in firms providing professional services and some self-employed. Finally, a number of professions, such as nurses, teachers, or scientists, have no tradition of self-employment.

For most professions, the proportion of members in salaried status tends to increase over time. As a result of this trend, by 1971 93 percent of accountants, 99 percent of engineers, and 94 percent of all professionals were employed (6). The advent of medicare has made physicians financially dependent on government grants, even though they are formally self-employed. About 2 percent of all engineering and accounting graduates still working in engineering or accounting are self-employed. In those professions where self-employment always has been rare, principally in health care and education, the importance of government funding increased in the 1960s and 1970s. This in turn caused the installation of control and reporting systems to guarantee accountability for the expenditure of public monies.

Collective bargaining in Canadian society is a mechanism for regulating conditions of employment. While physicians and a few other self-employed professions bargain with governments over fee schedules or other terms which determine their income, such practices are outside the normal scope of labour relations. Therefore, this chapter will cover only employed professionals.

EXTENT OF COLLECTIVE BARGAINING AMONG PROFESSIONALS

Precise data on the extent of collective bargaining among professionals are not available, but a number of general statements indicate where bargaining exists. Professionals employed in the public sector normally bargain where legislation permits. Thus, the practice is virtually universal among health-care professionals and public-school and college teachers, while about half of all university teachers bargain.

Members of most professions employed in government service in nonmanagerial capacities also engage in bargaining. In Crown corporations, the incidence of bargaining by professionals is extensive, but not universal. Engineers employed by provincial hydro authorities and Atomic Energy of Canada have formed bargaining associations in several jurisdictions, for instance.

The incidence of collective bargaining in the private sector is limited. Engineers in most large private electronics, aerospace, and telecommunications companies have organized for that purpose, but they probably number less than 5,000 nationally. Even if groups like airline pilots or journalists (who have long been unionized) are counted as professionals, examples of collective bargaining in the private sector are relatively rare. Nor are there many signs that large numbers of professionals in the private sector are ready to adopt collective bargaining. At British Columbia Telephone Company, for instance, an organization of engineers and lower managers overcame strong employer resistance and obtained a representation vote but then lost the vote by a narrow margin.

THE SHIFT TO COLLECTIVE BARGAINING

During the past two decades, the incidence of collective bargaining among professionals increased dramatically. To name a few, physicians, engineers, foreign service officers, university professors, and research scientists all began collective bargaining in that period.

The reasons for this change are an important issue in the study of industrial relations. For some professionals, the transition to bargaining was gradual, as previous arrangements for discussions with management evolved into bargaining. Unlike blue-collar or industrial workers, professionals have traditionally worked in a system of consultation or "collegiality" which incorporated employee views into managerial decisions. Professionals once regarded these mechanisms as part of their professional status or a substitute for collective bargaining. Employers and supervisors have relied on the opinions of salaried professionals on many subjects, such as the methods for accomplishing assigned tasks, hiring of fellow professionals, standards of service, and so on. Inevitably such advice was also offered and sometimes accepted on such topics as merit pay increase, salary scales, or promotion standards — conventional subject matter of collective bargaining. But even those systems offering considerable scope for employee participation in decisions began to break down in the 1960s.

The motivation of professionals for adopting collective bargaining may be classified as defensive or offensive. Although few hard data on the subject exist it is logical to assume that motives are mixed for many persons and groups. However, this classification is meant to highlight the predominant forces causing professionals to undertake bargaining. The change to collective bargaining is *defensive* when professionals organize themselves to avoid inclusion in a bargaining unit or union dominated by nonprofessionals. Professionals also have taken defensive positions to avoid being placed in a relatively weak bargaining position in comparison with other employee groups in the same enterprise when fellow employees started bargaining. Although professionals often began with limited enthusiasm for bargaining, they saw little choice but to adopt this mode of relations with management.

Professionals' motives are *offensive* when they organize to achieve their own economic or social objectives through bargaining. Professionals who make such a choice look to the bargaining process as the primary mechanism for the maintenance or improvement of their conditions of work. They are willing to consider strikes or other traditional trade-union tactics and may consider alliances with other public-sector unions.

The prevalence of collective bargaining among public-sector professionals and its relative absence in the private sector is an indicator that many professionals in public agencies organized for defensive reasons. As they observed other employee groups becoming unionized in the 1960s and 1970s they saw little choice but to follow suit. But where large elements of a labour force, especially white-collar workers, remained nonunion as in the private sector, professionals have shown less interest in bargaining as well. When the shift to bargaining was under way in the federal public service after 1965, for instance, pressure for change came from blue-collar workers, especially in the post office (3). Many professionals supported bargaining because they believed (accurately) that a political decision favouring bargaining had been made, and groups choosing to remain a part of the old system of consultation would be at a disadvantage in the distribution of resources and other decisions. In an earlier era, the Registered Nurses' Association of British Columbia secured its first Labour Relations Board certificates in the late 1940s to avoid the inclusion of nurses in a comprehensive bargaining unit of unskilled or semiskilled hospital employees. Engineers employed by the City of Calgary formed an association in 1955 to stop the collection of dues for a general union of civic employees (13). Professionals in several provincial hydro corporations, who worked with unionized blue-collar and white-collar employees, saw little choice but to deal with management on a collective basis.

Professionals who undertake bargaining for offensive reasons usually respond to a real or perceived deterioration in their working conditions which often challenges basic values of professionalism — autonomy, pride in work, and economic security. Increasingly, they are employed in large bureaucratic organizations, with inevitable rules that limit highly valued autonomy in their work. Decisions on matters as trivial as starting times for work, or as significant as technical decisions are made by managers who, even when they are members of the profession, are judged more by efficiency or profit than by the quality of a product or service. One of the complaints that caused some university professors to unionize was pressure from government or administrators for "accountability," that is, greater centralized managerial control over such factors as expenditures and academic programs (30). The growth of public education in the 1950s and 1960s inevitably put school teachers into large organizations and teachers and other professionals turned to collective bargaining to reinforce their rights to participate in a variety of decisions despite pressures from administrators. (In Ontario, the number of school boards was reduced from almost 1,400 to about 124 in the late 1960s.)

During the 1950s and early 1960s, the rising demand for professionals benefited them in many ways. For professionals such as teachers, real incomes rose both in absolute terms and relative to other occupations. But this tendency stopped and was reversed in the 1970s for several professions. Earlier growth in education produced large numbers of new graduates at a time when demand for their services was decreasing. Compared to other employee groups, their economic positions declined, especially for the less well-organized professions. Overall, the relative economic position of professionals fell between the 1930s and the early 1970s despite the large salary increases many obtained in the 1960s (17). Salaries of employed professionals consistently lag behind the earnings of their self-employed colleagues by 25 to 60 percent (6).

One factor underlying the rising demand for professionals was the shift to government support for many of their activities. The advent of government-funded medical care in the 1960s effectively moved the health-care professions into the public sector. Similar developments occurred in post-secondary education and other social services. This influx of government funding for the employers of professionals has had two general consequences for collective bargaining.

First, the issue of ability to pay has been removed from employees' thinking, so that offensive motives for the switch to bargaining became more prominent. When institutions such as universities or hospitals relied on users' fees and donations, limits on the employer's resources were real, as was the risk that employees' demands would result in decreased levels of service. Perhaps more than other employees, professionals were susceptible to fears that their gains would be at the expense of persons dependent upon social services. But when the government became the ultimate source of funding, collective bargaining gained improved chances of success. Indeed employers were in a position to use pressures from their staff to support claims for budgetary increases. Gains to professionals were no longer at the financial expense of their clients (who typically are unrepresented in bargaining), but resulted from competition with other claimants on public funds.

This was the positive aspect of an expanded role for government, but a second result was negative. Budgets of publicly supported enterprises became subject to the vagaries of political processes. Large numbers of professionals are employed in "soft" service areas (that is, functions not absolutely necessary for consumers), so their salaries and working conditions suffered and employment opportunities were reduced when governments found themselves short of resources. Professionals were accustomed to a high degree of employment security and expected to be rewarded according to their abilities and efforts. But the increased role of government meant that their real income or job tenure was not dependent on performance, or even the business cycle, but rather on changes in official policies in a political environment increasingly hostile to greater government spending, thus encouraging defensive responses.

Because of the long training period for professionals, imbalances in their labour markets tend to be extreme. When demand for a certain profession is high, enrolments in professional programs rise. But by the time the increased enrolments produce a greater supply of professionals, demand often has diminished, resulting in an oversupply. This cycle of "boom and bust" has caused professionals to seek the protection of a collective agreement when their job security is threatened (17).

The motives for turning to collective bargaining just discussed, both offensive and defensive, have not influenced all professions equally and are obviously offset by other factors that induce many professionals to avoid collective bargaining. Some professionals are restricted by law from engaging in certain kinds of collective activity, a subject discussed in the next section. But there are other considerations that warrant a brief discussion.

A few professions, notably accounting and engineering, are traditional paths to management in the private sector. For example, approximately half of all professional engineers recently surveyed in Ontario are no longer working in engineering. About two-thirds of this group are probably in executive positions (29). Since persons in this and similar professions see their futures as managers, virtually a second profession, they are unlikely to favour collective representation by professionals. Vigorous advocacy of collective bargaining might damage their chances for advancement by resentful superiors, and certain social or economic grievances may be resolved by promotion. Moreover, existing organizations in such professions discourage their members from engaging in collective bargaining.

As a group, professionals tend to be conservative and do not seek confrontation or adversarial relationships. These perspectives, together with a close physical and organizational proximity to management, discourage them from turning to collective bargaining to resolve their problems.

Management normally opposes the extension of collective bargaining to new groups in the enterprise. While the extremes of past efforts to discourage blue-collar employees from unionizing are absent, this influence on the development of bargaining by professionals is undoubtedly a strong one.

LEGAL CLIMATE FOR BARGAINING

The bargaining activities of professionals present special legal problems which have affected both the incidence and conduct of collective action. For years, professionals were excluded from coverage by virtually all labour codes in Canada. The effect of this exclusion was to deny professionals legal protection of the right to organize, leaving management free to prohibit collective representation if it so desired. Four reasons for this exclusion have been identified. First, since early labour-relations statutes did not mention professionals at all, they were included in large bargaining units of unionized production or white-collar workers, a situation many professionals resented, largely on the grounds that they were unlikely to secure any recognition of their special needs or desires. When provincial powers over labour relations were restored after World War II, professionals successfully petitioned for exclusion from new statutes.

During this period, most professionals believed collective bargaining to be undignified at best, and unethical at worst. They were imbued with traditions of service and individualism which made them uncomfortable with the use of collective pressure against an employer. Customary trade union emphasis on monetary gain appeared "unprofessional" to them, so they were anxious to be excluded from labour-relations statutes.

Professionals' associations generally opposed collective bargaining for their members when speaking for them. Salaried professionals were not yet influential in these bodies and the images of the traditional (independent) professions were important role models to members of other groups.

Finally, early labour-relations statutes were written against the background of the 1930s when the rapid unionization of semiskilled industrial workers occurred. The goal of legislation was to secure and maintain the benefits of collective bargaining for blue-collar workers. There was little interest in or sympathy for the problems of more affluent professionals (1).

Gradually, the once common professional exclusions have disappeared. The conditions summarized above causing professionals to adopt collective bargaining have been noted by legislators, often after representations by salaried professionals, so that when labour-relations acts were revised, professional exclusions are dropped. In 1964, for example, the new Quebec Labour Code covered professionals for the first time. The review of Canadian labour-relations policy conducted by a federal task force in the late 1960s recommended that professionals receive full bargaining rights. The Saskatchewan Trade Union Act was amended in 1966 to provide for professional bargaining units (previously professionals were not a separate category of employee) (15). British Columbia ended professional exclusions in 1975 after a comprehensive revision of its labour-relations legislation, and Ontario gave bargaining rights to engineers, but not other professionals, in 1971. Currently, legislation in Newfoundland, Nova Scotia, Alberta, and Prince Edward Island excludes members of the medical, dental, architectural, engineering, and legal professions (26), and occasionally other professions are also identified. But such provisions are clearly exceptional and those provinces are likely to join the national pattern in time.

Legislation covering collective bargaining in the public sector was enacted in the 1960s and 1970s when a tendency to include professionals in the private sector was already evident. Moreover, professionals had long been represented collectively in informal joint councils or consultative mechanisms in many public agencies. For these reasons, only Ontario has a broad exclusion for bargaining by professionals in the public sector (12), and a review for the provincial attorney general recommended the exclusion be eliminated.

When professionals are included in the coverage of a labour code, there still exists the problem of whether or not to accord them a separate identity. Even if professionals support collective bargaining, they usually prefer separate bargaining units, either for each profession, or for all professionals. Where all professionals are to be placed in a single unit, the statute generally defines a "professional" in general terms relative to educational qualifications, type of work, and eligibility for membership in a professional society.

Legislative support for all three approaches exists in Canada. Isolating each profession in a single unit often is the least supportive policy for collective bargaining, since in many work settings members of a single profession are too few to constitute a viable bargaining unit and as a result may have very little bargaining power. Moreover, if individual professions are identified in the law, new or evolving professions may be denied protection for their efforts to secure bargaining rights. But, if one assumes that the legal climate will favour the extension of bargaining rights for professionals, labour-relations boards will probably be given the authority to determine if professionals should be included with other employees, in units confined to a single profession.

A second legal restriction facing professionals seeking to engage in bargaining is the exclusion of managers or supervisors from bargaining. Since an underlying condition of North American labour relations is an arm's-length relationship between a bargaining agent and the employer, labour codes normally exclude managers from their coverage and prohibit such persons from participating in the activities of labour organizations. Because professionals commonly have some managerial responsibilities, they may fall within this exclusion. In these circumstances, not only are certain individuals denied access to the law's protection, but the number of professionals left with employee (that is, nonmanagerial) status may be so low that a viable professional bargaining unit is impossible.

The scope of managerial exclusions in Canadian labour-relations statutes varies considerably, but again there is a general trend to extend the protections of the law. This extension is a recognition of the complexity of modern organizations, in which many persons have some supervisory function. Although professionals in the private sector who perform supervisory functions may be unable to obtain certification under labour codes, more permissive public-sector bargaining laws have enabled such professionals to engage in bargaining.

The discussion in this section applies generally to professionals except for public-school teachers. Most provinces have special legislation to regulate bargaining by teachers. Teachers organized for a variety of objectives early in the twentieth century, and many local associations obtained voluntary recognition from school boards in the 1920s and early 1930s. But employers often removed gains achieved under this system unilaterally during the depression of the 1930s. The response of provincial associations was to seek membership by compulsory law as a prelude to more formal bargaining procedures. When teachers did achieve bargaining rights, legislatures recognized their unique status, and generally enacted separate laws defining the composition of bargaining units, the scope of bargaining, and methods of dispute settlement. Only Alberta and Quebec have included teachers in their labour codes (23).

EMPLOYEE ORGANIZATIONS

The range of organizations representing nonprofessionals in collective bargaining is rather limited. Most employees who engage in bargaining belong to unions in one of three broad categories —craft unions, industrial unions, or public-sector unions. In fact, even these distinctions are less meaningful than they once were, as the differences among the types of unions are blurring.

The situation is quite different for professionals. They are represented by several different types of organizations, including the biggest public-sector unions, a large number of unaffiliated provincial associations, and many independent local bodies. Many are not certified under conventional labour-relations legislation and maintain that they are not trade unions.

For analytical purposes, organizations representing professionals can be placed on a spectrum, from nonbargaining associations at one end to "conventional" trade unions at the other. An individual organization is located on this spectrum according to the following criteria: whether it declares itself to be a trade union, by title or objectives; affilation to a provincial or national labour federation; independence from the employer for negotiating purposes; collective bargaining and protection of employees as major funtions; and a willingness to use industrial action to advance bargaining objectives (7).

Almost by definition, professionals usually belong to an association. Traditionally, these associations perform a variety of functions unrelated to collective bargaining, such as the promulgation of ethical codes, setting of educational qualifications for the profession, administering entry to the profession, and the promotion of research and in-service training for members. Some associations (rather hesitantly) have addressed "the economic status of the profession," in response to members' concern about their absolute or relative economic position. In this role, associations often begin their activities with the publication of salary surveys, then move to the publication of salary standards and model employment contracts, and occasionally engage in "black"- or "grey-listing" of employers who do not meet minimum standards (20). A final prebargaining mode of action is the presentation of salary briefs or other recommendations on salary policy to the employer on behalf of members, with the understanding that the employer retains final authority for changes in salaries.

Theoretically, licensing bodies could restrict entry to a profession in order to create an artificial shortage of labour and thereby enhance the bargaining power of their members (17). In practice, however, such policies seem unlikely, and the lack of enthusiasm of most professional associations for collective bargaining creates a presumption that they have not used their statutory powers to influence bargaining. Where salaried professionals have turned to collective bargaining as a means of protecting their interests, many turned first to their professional association as their natural bargaining agent. The response of these associations has varied considerably.

In those professions whose members are overwhelmingly in the public sector, such as teachers, nurses, or university professors, the associations accepted collective bargaining as an additional function. However, their licensing powers are seldom strong. The transition from a traditional association to association-cum-union was not always an easy one. It usually occurred when membership interest was high and numbers were sufficient to constitute a viable bargaining unit. After making the transition, a few associations, nurses in particular, faced problems in accommodating bargaining within their existing structure.

Executive positions in professional associations often attract persons who are also supervisors in the employment context. But this participation by supervisors may cause the associations to be classified as "management dominated" and thereby ineligible for certification under labour-relations legislation. This issue did not arise for the first associations that engaged in bargaining, principally teachers and some nurses, but it was raised in the 1960s and 1970s during certification campaigns of other groups.

In 1973, the Supreme Court of Canada upheld a decision of the Saskatchewan Labour Relations Board in refusing certification to a local affiliate of the Saskatchewan Registered Nurses' Association (SRNA) on the grounds that a majority of the SRNA officers traditionally were management. The court also noted that the SRNA had actively organized staff nurses to keep nurses out of general hospital unions (that is, for defensive motives) [*Service Employees International Union, Local No. 333 v. Nipawin District Staff Nurses' Association, et al.* (1973) 41 D.L.R. (3rd) 6 (Can. Sup. Ct.)].

The Supreme Court decision crystalized the contradictions some associations have experienced in combining traditional professional activities and bargaining. The emerging response of nurses has been the formation of separate organizations or semiautonomous affiliates to conduct bargaining, while the association retains its traditional functions. In 1980, for instance, the "Labour Relations Division" of the Registered Nurses' Association of B.C. separated from the parent association (11).

Teachers, both in public schools and universities, have been more successful in combining both sets of functions. Provincial teacher associations either include principals in their bargaining units or permit them to bargain separately. Therefore, the issue of employer or management domination has not been a serious one under legislation covering teachers. University-faculty associations, which traditionally welcomed membership by all persons holding faculty appointments, including deans and presidents, secured inclusion of administrators through the level of department heads or assistant deans in bargaining units, thus establishing a rational employee-management distinction. At the national level, virtually all associations belong to the Canadian Association of University Teachers (CAUT). However, slightly less than half of university faculty are unionized, a quarter bargain in nonunion status, and the rest have no bargaining activities at all. The three groups maintain an uneasy peace within CAUT, which acts as an advocate for faculty interests in many areas of higher education.

Where professional associations have had members in both the private and public sectors, their response to the interest of their members in collective bargaining has been quite different. Engineering societies, in particular, tend to oppose any move by their employee-members toward collective bargaining. The heavy proportion of managers in their membership, and traditional reliance on employers for support, gave these organizations a strong proemployer bias (4,20). Employed professionals who turned to such associations for support in their efforts to win bargaining rights encountered opposition instead. Thus, they virtually had to form independent bodies or turn to trade unions. Generally, they did the former, and when engineering societies abandoned their formal opposition to collective bargaining, the independent associations maintained separate identities. There was a perceived conflict of interest between the regulatory functions of the associations and the representative functions of the bargaining agents. Perhaps more significant was the suspicion that even if these associations were to offer themselves as bargaining agents, their natural inclination to favour employer interests would render them ineffective.

The movement to independent associations was given further impetus by the problem of supervisory exclusions. For some employee groups, managerial exclusions have been an insuperable barrier to certification, should the members desire this status. Professionals employed in provincial hydro corporations are a typical example. While most professionals employed in hydro corporations are engineers, a significant proportion exercise managerial authority. When associations formed in the 1960s and 1970s, they found that they would be forced to exclude these potential members if they sought certification. The exclusions would have weakened the association numerically and split a perceived community of interest among employed professionals. The most common response has been to enter into bargaining arrangements with employers outside labour codes whenever possible (14).

Similar arrangements have been negotiated by several university administrations and faculty associations, including those of British Columbia, Alberta and Toronto, as well as supervisors in local government in a number of municipalities. These associations faced legal barriers to certification, or simply lacked the desire to enter full-scale bargaining.

The organizations involved in such relationships have only a few characteristics associated with trade unions. They do not refer to themselves as unions, nor do they affiliate with any central labour body and their members do not think of themselves as union members. The engineering groups have formed two federations, one predominantly in Ontario and the other in Quebec, to exchange information, provide some central services, and lobby on matters of mutual interest. Lacking the legal protection of certification, the associations tend to rely on employer good will, but they are independent for bargaining purposes.

The third category of organization to represent professionals are trade unions, although again there are several different varieties. The most common type is the independent multiprofessional union. Examples include the Professional Institute of the Public Service (PIPS), which represents 18,000 professionals in the Public Service of Canada; health professionals employed in hospitals; and associations of professionals in some provincial public services. Such independent multiprofessional unions obtain certification from labour-relations boards and negotiate comprehensive agreements. They seldom affiliate with central labour bodies, but they do cooperate with professional associations to represent matters of mutual concern.

Another variety of professional union is the single-profession body. A few unions representing one profession, or perhaps a small number of allied professions, have appeared. Some have broken away from larger bodies like PIPS, but others, such as unions of residents and interns in university teaching hospitals, historically have been confined to a single profession.

Conventional unions, usually in the public sector, also represent professionals. In general, public-sector unions which have attempted to organize professionals have had limited success. However, some professions that lack bargaining power or influence before labour-relations boards have been submerged in comprehensive units. For example, many professional librarians belong to the Canadian Union of Public Employees (CUPE) in units including all library staff; nurses in small medical facilities have been put into units of hospital employees; and college teachers and other professionals belong to several provincial public service unions. Overall, the role of professionals in these unions is slight, and, conversely, the ability of the unions to attract professionals is not great, so the influence of these bodies on professionals is not substantial.

When they have their own organizations, professional unions or associations impart a style of labour relations not often found elsewhere in the Canadian industrial-relations system. They usually begin by disavowing any resort to strikes and by placing greater reliance on consultation or "rational" discussions with management. Should a dispute occur over the terms of a new collective agreement, professional unions tend to rely upon various forms of interest arbitration, but avoid use of formal grievance procedures for "rights" disputes over the terms of the existing collective agreement. They often do not honour picket lines and seldom affiliate with the Canadian Labour Congress (CLC) or any other central labour body.

Some organizations, teachers' and nurses' associations in particular, have become more militant in recent years. They now routinely threaten strikes and engage in occasional stoppages. Ties with nonprofessional unions have been established, and bargaining units including nonprofessionals have been organized. Reliance is placed less on consultation and more on formal grievance procedures dealing with management. Even terminology has changed, as organizations incorporate "union" into their titles.

Various reasons have been advanced to explain this transformation that has occurred in some — but not all — professional organizations. It is possible that all organizations which enjoy the protections of a labour code eventually will find that the pressures of bargaining force them to adopt the full range of trade-union tactics. In other words, the process of unionization creates a dynamic in which all employee organizations grow more similar, that is, "unionlike." Alternatively, the evolution may be caused by management, which often expects all unionized employees to act similarly and thus forces professionals into courses of action they would prefer to avoid. Where the employer responds more sensitively or generously to unionized professionals, transformation may be forestalled or perhaps even prevented.

CONTENT OF BARGAINING

One of the most interesting and important issues arising from bargaining by professionals is the content of these negotiations. As noted above, professionals often organize for bargaining purposes in order to gain or protect conditions of employment, such as control over their work that they associate with professionalism. Moreover, the responsibilities that professionals have in many organizations involve them in many policy decisions, such as school curricula, staffing levels, or techniques for engineering or scientific projects. Many of these decisions simultaneously affect working conditions. The possibility thus exists that professionals will seek to include "professional" subjects in bargaining, either through direct negotiations or via the grievance procedure, thereby broadening the scope of bargaining into areas usually regarded as within the authority of management (5).

Conversely, professionals are also involved in various consultative mechanisms, many of which predate bargaining. Given the generally conservative posture in bargaining of most professionals, they might well prefer to leave professional issues to such consultative mechanisms and confine negotiations to traditional "trade-union" issues such as wages, economic benefits, and grievance procedures.

In negotiations conducted under public-service labour-relations legislation, the scope of bargaining is often limited by law. However, few of the statutory restrictions apply to professional areas, but instead cover pensions, technological change, the merit principle, or staffing matters. Where legislation is not a barrier, collective agreements covering professionals normally contain the full array of economic benefits. This is to be expected, since white-collar and professional employees were often the first categories of workers to receive fringe benefits prior to widespread unionization of either blue-collar or white-collar workers.

But professionals have also won benefits not found elsewhere. More highly educated professionals, such as university professors, research scientists or teachers have negotiated sabbaticals or "career development plans" which entitle the recipient to release from normal duties at partial pay to pursue programs of study or research aimed at enhancing skills. These provisions grew out of common practice in universities and other educational institutions prior to the arrival of bargaining, but formal negotiations have often improved the financial terms of such sabbaticals and have established them as a right rather than a privilege.

Newer provisions negotiated by nonteaching professionals cover attendance at scientific or technical congresses or seminars. For example, the agreement covering research scientists in the federal government contains the following provision of this type:

> In order that each employee shall have the opportunity for an exchange of knowledge and experience with his professional colleagues, the employee shall have the right to apply to attend a reasonable number of conferences or conventions related to his field of specialization. The Employer may grant leave with pay and reasonable expenses, evaluating registration fees to attend such gatherings, subject to budgetary and operational constraints as determined by the Employer. (8, pp. 31-32)

In the same vein, agreements have covered paid leave to write examinations and grants to cover the purchase of professional books and journals.

But such provisions are in keeping with the content of bargaining among certain blue-collar employees. Leaves for professional development have an educational purpose and may revitalize the recipient's mental outlook, but they are also another form of paid time away from work. Support for attendance at conferences is not radically different from normal practice when employees are sent to training sessions, and grants to cover books resemble tool allowances. None of these provisions affects the authority of management or is inconsistent with administrative practice in most organizations employing professionals.

Other clauses bargained by professionals are also consistent with trade-union behaviour but pose a greater challenge to management. Most unions attempt to control the workload assigned to their members by job descriptions, negotiations over the speed of assembly lines, or by grieving what they consider excess demands. While professionals often work in environments in which they largely determine their own pace, others, such as teachers or nurses work in circumstances where an administrative decision regarding workload is necessary. In the latter circumstances, workload is expressed in such terms as pupil-teacher or patient-nurse ratios. Professionals are accustomed to setting qualitative standards for their own performance and so naturally resist being placed in a situation where they are unable to perform well. When they are asked to look after more patients or pupils than they can adequately care for or teach, they object on professional grounds that the quality of the service they are being asked to render will deteriorate. But managers regard work assignment as their right and may accuse organized professionals of malingering (or "feather-bedding" in traditional union terms). Moreover, management typically regards decisions concerning the overall capacity of an enterprise or facility as central to its "mission" or a matter of public policy. Employers, therefore, typically resist any attempts by organized professionals to regulate the distribution of work (19). While rhetoric on both sides of this question is heated, there is a fundamental clash between professional and managerial values behind the debate.

Not all professionals raise these issues at the bargaining table, however. In British Columbia, for instance, where teachers are legally precluded from negotiating working conditions in connection with salaries, they rely on consultative procedures or political pressure to achieve their objectives in an informal fashion. In Alberta, where teachers have the right to bargain over such matters, they seldom do so, apparently preferring to rely on procedures outside of formal bargaining. However, in Ontario, teachers in about one-quarter of all agreements have negotiated detailed provisions covering class size, and nurses are seeking "professional-responsibility clauses," which guarantee access to expedited arbitration when nurses are assigned more patients than they can care for properly (28).

A potentially more contentious area in bargaining by professionals is the issue of professional judgment and autonomy on questions unrelated to workload. Again, professionals assert that their competence and expertise entitle them to certain prerogatives and protections, while employers are concerned about the erosion of their authority. Disputes in this area become especially heated when ethical questions arise. A few examples may illustrate the dimensions of this issue.

University professors have incorporated into collective agreements CAUT standards on academic freedom, which protect faculty who espouse unpopular views from disciplinary action. Since academic freedom is a well-established feature of Canadian university life, the negotiation of these clauses provoked little controversy, although their application in specific cases is troublesome. Professional librarians have put the Canadian Library Association "Statement of Intellectual Freedom" into their collective agreements, partly as a protection against community censorship or restriction on the acquisition and circulation of materials (28). The tradition of professional autonomy is much less accepted in public libraries than in universities, so there is clear potential for conflict between administrators responding to community pressures and professionals with a sense of responsibility to their peers. Similarly, an agreement negotiated by professionals at Atomic Energy of Canada incorporated the Association of Professional Engineers of Ontario code of ethics (29).

An excellent example of a clause incorporating this principle of professional responsibility is in an agreement negotiated by the British Columbia Government Professional Employees' Association:

> The Employer recognizes that a professional employee must conduct his work in a
> manner consistent with the standards of conduct, codes of ethics and by-laws estab-

lished by his appropriate professional licensing body. The Association recognizes that the Employer may, from time to time, differ with professional employees and/or their licensing bodies as to what actions, policies, etc., are most consistent with the public interest. However, no professional employee will be disciplined for refusal to append his name, signature and/or seal to an instructed course of action which conflicts with his professional responsibilities, provided that in such a case the professional employee will, upon request, be required to prove the violation of the relevant professional standard or code and the Employer shall have the right to seek alternative advice. (2, p. 5)

The same principle arises over the supervision of professionals. In many large organizations, this issue does not arise, since a manager-professional supervises a technical department. But where a number of professions are found in the same organization, such as a hospital, members of one profession may be supervised to a degree by nonprofessionals or members of another profession [cf. *Re Lions Gate Hospital and Health Sciences Association of B.C.*, 1979, unreported (Thompson)]. In these cases, the possibility for conflicting judgments on professional issues is real, with managers being forced to choose between two professions, who may be represented by different unions but are almost surely supported by separate associations.

This discussion has concentrated on extensions of the scope of collective bargaining, but the degree to which professionals will seek to expand bargaining is uncertain. For example, many agreements negotiated by professional groups treat a number of subjects in a cursory manner, leaving wide authority with management or relying on joint consultation to resolve differences. Merit- or incentive-pay decisions are often left to management. An agreement covering research officers employed at the National Research Council (including Canada's only living Nobel Prize winner) permitted the Council to pay employees at rates beyond schedules contained in the agreement (10). The agreement negotiated by an uncertified association covering engineers and professionals at B.C. Hydro and Power Authority permits management to award merit-pay increases without challenge through the "redress" (that is, grievance) procedure (9). A number of agreements bargained by nonunion university faculty have similar provisions. Other personnel actions commonly left to managerial discretion include promotions, transfers, and performance appraisals.

Survey research of two quite different groups of professionals only adds to the uncertainty about the bargaining strategy of professionals. According to one study (25), a group of nurses in Ontario ranked "professional" goals in bargaining (for example, better procedures for clerical evaluation of nurses, joint nurse-physician liaison committees, reduction of nonprofessional tasks) above economic goals (for example, shift differentials, higher salaries, more time off on weekends). This study implies that nurses will attempt to bargain over professional issues related to workload and policy. But a survey of university faculty in British Columbia revealed much less interest in bargaining over noneconomic items (for example, teaching evaluation, committee assignments, procedures for selecting department chairmen) than salaries, pensions, sabbaticals, and so on (24).

Several factors may explain these differences. The Ontario nurses had negotiated substantial salary increases prior to the survey, so their responses may have been affected by the circumstances of that period. Had they been anticipating salary increases in forthcoming negotiations, their replies might have been quite different. Faculty have a variety of opportunities for influencing university policy, so they see little need to bargain over these matters. If one applies that principle to other groups, it would be expected that professionals do wish to be heard on many policy issues, but their desire to bargain depends on their perception of their influence through other channels. Finally, it may be that professionals tend to begin bargaining over basic economic matters, but expand the scope after acceptable standards in these areas are met.

RESULTS OF BARGAINING

There is little information on the specific outcomes of bargaining by professionals in Canada. American studies suggest that the impact of unionization on wages in the public sector has been mixed, but that it is probably less than the 10 to 15 percent advantage typically found in the private sector (22). Canadian research has found that the public sector rewards the educational backgrounds of its employees less than the private sector, but that the overall wage advantage is about 7 percent in favour of the public sector, weighted in favour of lower-paid employees (16). Because professionals are disproportionately employed in the public sector where they occupy higher-pay jobs, these findings suggest that the impact of bargaining on professionals' salaries has not been great, and that professionals who turned to bargaining to counteract their declining relative economic position will continue to concentrate on monetary issues at the bargaining table.

Strikes by professionals are infrequent and have been concentrated among teachers and nurses. In 1979, for example, there were four strikes by college or university teachers (all in Quebec), four by public-school teachers (three in Ontario and one in Alberta), and two by health professionals (one each in Newfoundland and Quebec) (21). Because of their novelty and impact on segments of the public (parents of school children or hospital patients), strikes by professionals attract unusual attention. An especially interesting aspect of strikes by professionals are the issues in contention. A group of Toronto residents and interns not certified under the Labour Relations Act struck briefly in 1980 to win the right, not to strike, but rather to have arbitration to resolve salary disputes. Calgary school teachers struck in 1980 to support demands for class preparation time. Nurses employed in British Columbia by the provincial government won salary parity with hospital nurses after a brief stoppage.

Overall, it appears that professionals are reluctant to strike, but strikes are more likely to occur over noneconomic issues than salary or related items. It also seems that professionals file fewer grievances than other employees, though there is only scattered evidence on this point. In British Columbia, professionals account for about 5 percent of all arbitrations, roughly equivalent to the proportion of organized professionals covered by the provincial Labour Code. The majority of these cases is from the hospital sector. Approximately 1,700 managers and professionals employed in the B.C. Hydro and Power Authority did not even demand a formal grievance procedure for several years. After one was included in their agreement, fewer than five grievances were filed annually. A survey of 55,000 American cases submitted to arbitration revealed only 23 involving the discipline of professionals, only one of which was actually arbitrated (31). Presumably, these findings reflect the relatively peaceful nature of labour relations among professionals and the availability of consultative procedures to resolve potential grievances.

To date, the most important issue in arbitral jurisprudence involving professionals is the question of professional standards. Based on a limited number of cases, one arbitrator observed that professionals are expected to meet higher standards of responsibility than other employees, but they may not refuse assignments on professional grounds in the absence of specific contract language (28). However, when the terminology covering work assignments for professionals is quite similar to that used for other employees, the presumption that different criteria apply to professionals may be challenged [*Re Surrey Memorial Hospital and Registered Nurses' Association* of B.C. (1979) 24 L.A.C. (2d) 342 (Thompson)].

CONCLUSIONS

Many of the issues raised by a survey of collective bargaining by professionals in Canada can be summarized in a single question: To what extent will professionals bargain in the same fashion as other groups? More specifically, will the organizations representing professionals eventually adopt the tactics and structures of labour unions, either by joining existing unions or evolving independently? Will private sector professionals choose collective representation in proportions comparable to the public sector or other private-sector employees, or at a lower rate than either? Will professionals adopt policies toward the scope of bargaining and the use of economic coercion similar to those of other organized groups?

It is still too early to answer these questions with any confidence. Comparative data suggest that in virtually all Western nations white-collar workers are more difficult to unionize than blue-collar workers, though there is a strong correlation of the success of unions in organizing the two groups. Experience also indicates that public-sector employees are unionized more readily than those in the private sector. But when organized, white-collar workers often avoid close ties with the mainstream of the labour movement, and they are generally less militant (27). This separation from other organized workers may derive from the basic motive of white-collar employees in organizing — to preserve the distinctions between themselves and other employees as long and as well as possible. But in Canada and elsewhere professionals have been willing to adopt the tactics of trade unions.

The past fifteen years demonstrated that professionals will embrace collective bargaining, reluctantly at first, but permanently. The next fifteen years may show what the results of bargaining will mean to professionals, their employers, and their clients.

REFERENCES AND WORKS CITED

1. Adams, G.W. "Collective Bargaining by Salaried Professionals," in P. Slayton and M.J. Trebilcock (Eds.), *Professions and Public Policy* (Toronto: University of Toronto Press, 1978), pp. 264-278.

2. *Agreement between the Public Service Commission and the British Columbia Professional Employees' Association,* June 20, 1975.

3. Arthurs, H.W. *Collective Bargaining by Public Employees in Canada: The Five Models* (Ann Arbor: Institute of Labor and Industrial Relations, University of Michigan-Wayne State University, 1971).

4.   Bailey, C.M. "The Experience of the Engineering Profession with Collective Bargaining." Paper prepared for the National Conference on the Professions and Public Policy, Faculty of Law, University of Toronto, October 15-16, 1976.

5.   Bairstow, F. "New Dimensions in Public Sector Grievance Arbitration." Paper presented to the National Academy of Arbitrators meeting, April 7, 1978.

6.   Beatty, D., and M. Gunderson. "The Employed Professional," *Working Paper No. 14* (The Professional Organizations Committee, Ministry of the Attorney General, Province of Ontario, Toronto, 1979).

7.   Blackburn, R.M., and K. Prandy. "White Collar Unionization: A Conceptual Framework," *The British Journal of Sociology,* Vol. 16 (June 1965), 111-122.

8.   *Collective Agreement and Salary Administration Plan, Scientific Research Group, Treasury Board and Professional Institute of the Public Service,* January 9, 1975-June 17, 1976.

9.   *Collective Agreement between British Columbia Hydro and Power Authority and Management and Professional Employees Society of B.C. Hydro,* December 1, 1979-November 30, 1981.

10. *Collective Agreement between the National Research Council of Canada and The Professional Institute of the Public Service of Canada, Covering Employees in the Research Office and Research Council Officer Grades,* expiring June 30, 1975.

11. "Complete Separation Approved," *RNABC News,* Vol. 12 (November 1980), p. 3.

12. Federation of Engineering and Scientific Associations. "Rights Denied: Collective Bargaining for Professional Employees in the Ontario Public Service: A Brief to the Government of Ontario" (FESA, Toronto, 1980.)

13. *Federation of Engineering and Scientific Associations File,* Vol. 7 (October-November 1980) p. 2.

14. Fraser, D., and S. Goldenberg. "Collective Bargaining for Professional Workers: The Case of the Engineers," *McGill Law Journal*, Vol. 20 (1974), 456-479.

15. Goldenberg, S.B. *Professional Workers and Collective Bargaining* (Ottawa: Task Force on Labour Relations, 1968).

16. Gunderson, M. "Decomposition of Public-Private Sector Earnings Differentials," in M.W. Bucovetsky (Ed.), *Studies in Public Employment and Compensation in Canada* (Toronto: Butterworth, 1979), pp. 1-28.

17. Gunderson, M. "Economic Aspects of the Unionization of Salaried Professionals," in P. Slayton and M.J. Trebilcock (Eds.), *Professions and Public Policy* (Toronto: University of Toronto Press, 1978), pp. 247-263.

18. Gunderson, M. "Professionalization of the Canadian Public Sector," in M.W. Bucovetsky (Ed.), *Studies in Public Employment and Compensation in Canada* (Toronto: Butterworth, 1979), pp. 81-124.

19. Helsby, R.D. "Scope of Bargaining Issues with Professional Issues," in R. Adelman (Ed.), *Proceedings of New York University Thirty-First Annual National Conference on Labor* (New York: Bender, 1978), pp. 275-294.

20. Hoffman, E.B. *Unionization of Professional Societies* (New York: The Conference Board, 1976).

21. Labour Canada. *Strikes and Lockouts in Canada 1979* (Ottawa: Labour Canada, 1980).

22. Mitchell, D.J.B. "The Impact of Collective Bargaining on Compensation in the Public Sector," in B. Aaron, J.R. Grodin, and J.L. Stern (Eds.), *Public Sector Bargaining* (Washington: Bureau of National Affairs, 1979), pp. 118-149.

23. Muir, J. *Collective Bargaining by Canadian Public School Teachers* (Ottawa: Task Force on Labour Relations, 1968).

24. Ponak, A.M., and M. Thompson. "Faculty Attitudes and the Scope of Bargaining," *Industrial Relations,* Vol. 18 (1979), 97-102.

25. Ponak, A.M. "Unionized Professionals and the Scope of Bargaining: Testing Some Assumptions," *Industrial and Labor Relations Review,* Vol. 34 (1981), 396-407.

26. Rose, A. "Professional Income and Government Restraint Programs: The Case of the Employee Professionals," in P. Slayton and M.J. Trebilcock (Eds.), *Professions and Public Policy* (Toronto: University of Toronto Press, 1978), pp. 290-300.

27. Sturmthal, A. "White Collar Unions — A Comparative Essay," in A. Sturmthal (Ed.), *White Collar Trade Unions* (Urbana: University of Illinois Press, 1967), pp. 365-398.

28. Swan, K.P. "Professional Obligations, Employment Responsibilities, and Collective Bargaining," *Interchange*, Vol. 9 (1978-79), 98-110.

29. Swinton, K. "The Employed Professional," *Working Paper No. 13* (The Professional Organizations Committee, Ministry of the Attorney General, Province of Ontario, Toronto, 1979).

30. Thompson, M. "The Development of Collective Bargaining in Canadian Universities," *Proceedings of the Twenty-Eighth Annual Winter Meeting, Industrial Relations Research Association* (Madison: IRRA, 1976), pp. 257-265.

31. Unterberger, I., and S.H. Unterberger. "Disciplining Professional Employees," *Industrial Relations,* Vol. 17 (October 1978), 353-359.

QUESTIONS

1. Distinguish between defensive and offensive motives for the organization of professionals for bargaining.

2. Why have so many professionals chosen to be represented by independent associations instead of trade unions?

3. What is the significance of managerial exclusions to the organizations of professionals for bargaining?

4. Why did public policy discourage the unionization of professionals? What caused the changes in this policy?

5. What do you believe to be the future of bargaining by professionals? Will these employees act more like union members, or will they develop a distinctive mode of bargaining?

JOSEPH B. ROSE

17. Construction Labour Relations*

The purpose of this chapter is to discuss the various aspects of industrial relations in the construction industry. It begins by examining the characteristics of the industrial-relations system, particularly those factors which distinguish it from other industries. This is followed by an analysis of the external and internal sources of instability in construction and the various attempts by provincial governments to remedy the situation. The willingness of the parties to come to grips with these issues, and predictions about the future direction of industrial relations in construction, are also explored.

The past two decades have been accompanied by a number of significant developments in construction labour relations. During the sixties, the industry experienced a sharp increase in strike activity and wage settlements which outpaced those in other industries. As this pattern continued into the seventies, policy makers across Canada began to grapple with possible imperfections in the collective-bargaining system, notably its fragmented bargaining structure. This led to the passage of legislation designed to rationalize and centralize the bargaining system. The eighties will undoubtedly produce additional challenges for negotiators in the construction industry. Chief among them will be continued high rates of inflation, forecasts of modest growth in construction activity, an increase in nonunion competition, and the maturation of centralized bargaining structures and bargaining agencies.

This chapter examines the evolution of collective bargaining in construction over the past twenty years and assesses the prospects for labour-management stability in the coming decade. Five broad areas are discussed: (a) the industrial-relations system in construction; (b) the external and internal sources of instability in industrial relations; (c) public policy and labour-management relations; (d) work stoppages and wage rates; and (e) the industry's capacity to tackle pressing problems in the coming decade.

*I would like to thank Anna Bakerspigel for research assistance in the preparation of this manuscript.

THE INDUSTRIAL-RELATIONS SYSTEM

Dunlop's (3) model of the industrial-relations system in construction in the U.S., which stresses the importance of economic, technical, institutional, and historical factors, is generally applicable to the Canadian situation. The industry is characterized by local product markets and substantial specialization. The construction product is unusual in that it is immobile, dispersed geographically, and variable in size and composition. The diversity of the construction product is exhibited by the number of branches or sectors found in the industry, for example, road building, pipelines, residential, and industrial construction. Market and technological factors have had a profound impact on contractor and trade-union organization and the collective-bargaining process. Accordingly, wages and other conditions of employment have been established on an individual-craft and area-wide basis. The technological requirements of construction activity necessitate the recruitment of a highly skilled pool of labour.

Under these circumstances, contractors and unions have negotiated contract provisions to allocate employment opportunities, through such devices as the union hiring hall and travel arrangements, and they have utilized jointly sponsored training and apprenticeship programs to meet their manpower requirements. In addition to these special requirements, public policy governing various facets of labour-management relations has developed in a manner distinguishable from most other industries.

Contractor Organization

The construction industry is comprised of a large number of small, usually labour-intensive firms. Although there are differences among sectors in the degree of competition, the industry is generally regarded as highly competitive and business failures are quite common. Both general and specialty trade contractors are organized into a multiplicity of local, regional, provincial, and national associations. These organizations perform a number of functions, including the operation of bid depositories, lobbying with various levels of government, and handling labour relations for member firms. Employer associations display considerable variation in size and structure. For example, there are associations with broad constituencies (for example, they include union and nonunion firms, as well as suppliers and architects), and organizations which are limited to a specific sector (road building) or trade division (mechanical trade associations). There are also contractors who steer an independent course and are not affiliated with an association (23).

What is of particular interest is the logic of employers delegating their collective-bargaining rights to an association. Understanding this arrangement is important because it represents a departure from the standard pattern of single-company bargaining found in this country (1). Coordinated bargaining was embraced by contractors in order to establish uniformity of wage rates in the local product market. Employer alliances were seen as necessary to stabilize labour-management relations in the industry because of the highly competitive nature of the industry, the preponderance of small employers, and the tremendous strength of the building trades unions (18). Consequently, the responsibility for collective bargaining was vested in local employers' associations. Given the diversity of employer organization and the craft structure of construction unionism, numerous collective agreements were negotiated within a given product market.

The last decade has witnessed a significant change in employer organization. Specifically, the responsibility for collective bargaining has shifted from local contractor organizations to provincial multitrade associations whose sole function is to handle industrial relations. The formation in 1969 of the Construction Labour Relations Association of British Columbia (CLRA) became the model for employer organization in most other jurisdictions of Canada (21). These new bargaining agencies were created because there was a need to develop greater professional expertise in industrial relations and because many multipurpose employer organizations failed to place sufficient priority on collective bargaining. As a consequence, divisions occurred within local employer associations. This factor and the lack of coordination among employer bargaining agents enabled unions to exploit weaknesses in employer organization.

Construction Trade Unionism

Construction is a highly unionized industry. In 1977, union membership in Canada stood at 303,000 workers or approximately two-thirds of the construction work force (25). Construction unions play a key role in the labour market through wage negotiations and contract provisions dealing with subcontracting and work rules. In addition, through the closed shop (where individuals are required to join the union prior to employment) and the hiring hall (where the union controls referral of workers to employers), the union strongly influences the entry of workers into the industry. Construction unionism is deeply rooted in the principle of exclusive work jurisdiction, and the unions have strengthened their claim to specific work "by obtaining recognition as the source of manpower for employers doing the work" (15, p. 45).

Most construction trades are organized into seventeen craft unions jointly affiliated with the Canadian Labour Congress (CLC) and the American Federation of Labour-Congress of Industrial Organizations (AFL-CIO). Construction unions are grouped into an intermediary body at the national level known as the Advisory Board for the Building and Construction Trades in Canada (similar to the Building and Construction Trades Department of the AFL-CIO). With the exception of a few independent unions, such as the Christian Labour Association of Canada, the only serious challenge to the supremacy of the international building trades has come in Quebec. The internationals (which are affiliated with the Quebec Federation of Labour) are in direct competition with affiliates of three French-Canadian federations, which are organized along regional and industrial lines as opposed to a craft basis. These latter organizations are estimated to represent between 30 and 40 percent of the construction labour force in the province (8).

During 1981, a further split within the Quebec construction labour movement occurred which has reverberated throughout the CLC. The conflict erupted when the QFL granted a haven to a 12,000-member unit of electrical workers which had broken away from the International Brotherhood of Electrical Workers (IBEW). The failure of the CLC to take action against the QFL so angered the building trades that two of its representatives resigned from the CLC Executive Board. In addition, the 400,000 members of the building-trades unions in Canada began withholding their dues (an amount equal to 18 percent of the CLC's income).

This is not the only issue in dispute. At CLC conventions the building-trades unions have supported a system of proportional representation similar to that of the AFL-CIO. They believe that the present system, which gives each local union equal representation regardless of size, is unfair and gives too much power to public-sector unions.

The dispute has now reached a critical juncture in which the building trades are weighing a decision to withdraw from the CLC, and the labour federation is considering expelling them. Not only do the parties appear to be far apart, but CLC President Dennis McDermott feels the showdown may be long overdue. If the two groups go their separate ways, it could have profound implications for construction labour relations and the Canadian labour movement. For example, if the CLC sets up a rival building-trades organization, will this encourage a breakaway movement from the international unions? There is already some indication that this might occur in British Columbia and Quebec (13). Organizational rivalry between the two groups would undoubtedly have a spill-over effect on collective-bargaining outcomes and strike activity. Furthermore, if the breakaway movement spread beyond construction, and the position of international unions was significantly weakened, it would alter the face of unionism in this country. Indeed, the mere departure of the international building trades from the CLC, probably the most conservative element within the labour federation, would signal a new direction for Canadian labour in the eighties. Whether organized labour can resolve its internal conflicts will bear watching in the coming months and years.

Another important change in union organization has been the centralization of decision-making responsibility for collective bargaining. Historically, local unions have enjoyed considerable autonomy to negotiate collective agreements. However, as employers delegated this function to centralized employer associations and to provincial, single-trade associations, the locus of union decision making became more centralized. For example, in British Columbia and Quebec, provincial councils are responsible for negotiations. In Ontario, province-wide union councils have been established on a single-trade basis. Even in the absence of formal council bargaining, there is some evidence that individual locals and individual trades are more actively coordinating their bargaining activities.

Notwithstanding these developments in collective bargaining, local unions still enjoy a considerable amount of autonomy from their international organizations. While many policy decisions, such as guidelines on apprenticeship and admissions, are made at central headquarters, the local is responsible for deciding how these policies will be implemented and enforced. Consequently, the business agent is the central figure in the local union.

> He is responsible for the day-to-day operations of the union, enforcing contractual and informal agreements on working conditions, handling individual grievances, protecting craft jurisdiction, and matching available workers with employers' requests. On major policy questions such as admissions standards and wage objectives, his role is critical. (5, p. 307)

Because members and contractors alike are dependent on the business agent, and internationals are reluctant to interfere in local affairs, these union officials wield more power than "any single officer in an industrial union" (24, p. 240).

The Role of Government
The uniqueness of the construction industry and the peculiarities of its industrial-relations system have created a set of relationships which are distinguishable from other industries. These differences have been reviewed extensively elsewhere (3, 23)

and are only summarized here, with particular emphasis on the role of the government.

Prevailing wage (or "fair wages") legislation — In most jurisdictions, these laws require employers working on government-financed projects to pay the prevailing wage rate in a particular geographic area. The primary purpose of these laws is to ensure that government-financed projects do not undermine local wage rates. Since prevailing wage rates are usually based on negotiated settlements, they have a tendency to protect the unionized sector from nonunion competition. A broader approach has been adopted in Quebec, where the government may extend, by decree through extension legislation, the working conditions (including wages) contained in the provincial agreement to all employers and employees in the industry (8).

Apprenticeship and training — The provincial labour departments play an active role in establishing the qualifications and standards applicable to apprenticeship and journeyman training. In addition to government financing of training, many collective agreements in the industry establish training funds which are jointly administered by the parties. There are also programs to promote labour mobility. For example, there is the interprovincial "Red Seal" certificate which signifies a worker has passed the appropriate examinations and is a fully qualified journeyman. The Canada Employment and Immigration Commission administers a Mobility Program, which provides financial assistance to unemployed workers to travel to or relocate in areas where work is available.

Bargaining rights — Labour-relations boards play a broader role in determining bargaining rights in this country than in the United States. This is because public policy in Canada provides greater support for certification (as opposed to voluntary recognition). In addition, most labour-relations boards have the authority to confer exclusive bargaining rights on employer associations under accreditation legislation.

Dispute resolution — A major source of conflict in the construction industry is jurisdictional disputes, involving interunion conflicts over the assignment of work. The prevalence of these disputes is influenced by the insecurity of employment generated by technological change and the competition among individual craft unions for job opportunities. While some of these disputes are referred to the Impartial Disputes Board in Washington, D.C., the parties have frequently relied on public tribunals (for example, labour-relations boards) to resolve these disputes. A new jurisdictional disputes procedure has been adopted in British Columbia (the "Assignment Plan") which is financed by the industry and empowers an impartial umpire to settle disputes and establish work assignment guidelines.

Specialized treatment — Several provincial labour statutes have separate sections to deal with labour-management relations in the construction industry. In addition, a number of labour-relations boards have established separate panels for the construction industry to build up expertise in specialized areas such as employer accreditation, hiring-hall procedures, secondary picketing, and jurisdictional disputes.

Joint consultation — In an effort to promote labour-management consultation, several provincial labour laws provide for the establishment of advisory panels in the construction industry. These tripartite committees have been involved in studying ways of improving construction labour relations and assisting provincial governments in the formulation of public policy. For example, in Ontario, the Construction Industry Review Panel was instrumental in bringing single-trade, province-wide bargaining to fruition. In British Columbia, a similar body success-fully developed the Assignment Plan for handling jurisdictional disputes.

Common Ideas and Values

While labour and management in construction have fought many pitched battles, there is no denying their common outlook toward the industry and the industrial-relations system.

> They [construction workers] tend to be tied more to the craft and the union than to a single work place or enterprise. They exalt skill and technical knowledge of the craft and industry. They think in terms of craft jurisdiction. Compared with other workers they tend to accept layoffs and discharges as inherent in the operation of the construction labor market. They tend to be relatively conservative on economic and social issues; their differences with contractors or superintendents, many of whom have come from the ranks, are confined largely to compensation. They tend to believe that all employees in the same craft or classification should receive the same compensation regardless of the branch of the industry; this often complicates the task of organizing and makes difficult the relations between the labor organizations and contractor associations. Contractors and workers and their organizations oppose seniority; they seldom resort to third party arbitration; they oppose industrial unionism, and they continue to believe in traditional jurisdictional concepts. (3, p. 264)

The shared beliefs of labour and management are further reinforced by the fact that many contractors came up through the ranks of construction labour and still others float between the two worlds of contractor and employee.

SOURCES OF CONSTRUCTION INSTABILITY

Construction has a reputation for being a strike-prone industry in which skilled tradesmen are paid higher wages than their counterparts in other industries. During the sixties, time lost due to work stoppages was three times higher than the previous decade and hourly wage rates more than doubled in the same period. While some observers have commented that there are "no accepted standards by which to measure how high wages should be, or how many strikes are too many" (15, p. 26), policy makers generally believed that the collective-bargaining record of the construction industry was the worst in Canada.

Most explanations of labour-management instability in construction have stressed the importance of economic and bargaining structure variables. For example, Mills described the problem in terms of favourable economic conditions and the fragmen-tation of collective-bargaining.

> In times of economic expansion, the decentralized bargaining structure of the indus-try is conducive to high settlements. Leapfrogging of wage rates by craft and area creates a continued upward pressure on wages. The militancy of union membership, together with the existing bargaining mechanisms, fueled the search for higher wage settlements, and inflationary economic conditions generally sustained them. (15, p. 61)

This section deals with the external and internal sources of instability and how they influence wage bargaining and strike activity.

External Sources of Instability: The Market for Construction

A number of years ago the Economic Council of Canada undertook an exhaustive study of instability in the construction industry (4). Notwithstanding the positive long-run relationship between changes in gross national product and construction expenditures, construction is a volatile sector which is extremely vulnerable to cyclical and seasonal fluctuations. While the industry is subject to many destabilizing influences not all branches of construction are equally affected by the same stimuli. For example, residential construction is particularly sensitive to the availability of mortgage money and credit conditions, whereas nonresidential construction is dependent on business expectations and government spending on such items as schools, hospitals, and electric-power projects. In addition, weather conditions in Canada can determine the length of the construction season and impose limits on certain types of construction work.

Cyclical and seasonal fluctuations have a profound impact on the construction work force. Employment insecurity is easily demonstrated by examining unemployment data and the frequency of layoffs among the trades. The unemployment rate in construction is generally two to three times higher than the national average and can fluctuate from 6 percent in the peak summer months to over 20 percent in winter. Moreover, since most tradesmen do not work for a single employer but move from project to project, they also experience a considerable amount of frictional unemployment. The combined effect of these factors prompted the Economic Council of Canada to conclude that construction workers experience four times the employment insecurity of manufacturing employees (10).

The employment dislocation experienced by construction tradesmen helps to explain why unions place such a high priority on wage bargaining and do not hesitate to strike in support of their wage goals. While many have decried the high wage rates paid in construction — the average hourly wage rate in 1979 was $11.05 — unions have justified them in terms of "the skill composition of the construction workforce, intermittence of employment, the relatively low level of nonwage benefits and the arduousness and danger of construction work" (6, p. 336). They also note that high hourly wage rates are necessary to provide income security and are not necessarily synonymous with high annual incomes. When one takes into account such factors as skill composition, hours worked, and supplementary benefits, the annual income of construction workers is not disproportionate to those employed in other industries (5, 10). Construction trades have accepted layoffs and unemployment as a way of life in the industry, in exchange for high hourly rates of compensation.

Internal Sources of Instability: Fragmented Bargaining Structure

As construction activity expanded in the sixties, the building-trades unions began to exert their power and exploit weaknesses in the decentralized bargaining structures in the industry. The superiority of union bargaining power was recognized in both the U.S. and Canada. For example, Foster and Strauss noted:

> The balance of power in building trades bargaining is generally recognized to be heavily weighted in favor of the union. Even the earliest studies of construction labor relations pointed up the relative lack of cohesion on the employers' side. The unions' advantage stems primarily from the structural characteristics discussed above. In the first place, most contractors' associations are composed of large numbers of small, undercapitalized employers. Prolonged work stoppages may threaten

these firms' solvency. Thus pressure builds from within the association to meet the union's demands, particularly since each employer knows that his competition will have to operate under the same conditions. A second important factor is the localized nature of most bargaining relationships. In this situation many union members are frequently able to find work in nearby jurisdictions, thus mitigating the economic pressure on the union to scale down its demands. (5, p. 310)

Thus, construction unions were in a position to use their strength and leapfrog wage settlements within and among labour markets.

The fragmentation of bargaining structure prior to the introduction of employer accreditation legislation was related to a variety of factors. Voluntary multi-employer alliances could easily be exploited by the unions. The selective use of the strike and picketing weapons frequently stripped contractor associations of their ability or willingness to resist union demands. Intraorganizational conflicts were common and loyalty to an association's bargaining goals frequently left much to be desired. In the absence of leadership and cohesion within the contractor community, employer associations were no match for their seasoned union counterparts.

Even in those situations where contractor groups were unified, they frequently did not hold all bargaining rights for unionized employers in an area. Nonassociation contractors were able to work out arrangements with unions whereby they would pick up the terms and conditions of employment negotiated by the association in exchange for a union promise not to disrupt their operations. This phenomenon placed added pressures on local employer groups to settle on the unions' terms.

There was also a general lack of cooperation among employer bargaining agencies. Specifically, bargaining goals and policies were rarely coordinated on a multi-trade basis, among local and regional associations or across sectors of the industry. Consequently, most collective agreements were negotiated between a local employer association and a local craft union and covered the work jurisdiction of the craft and the geographic area of the local. The cumulative effect was to create a "vast network of agreements of varying geographic scope, applicable to differing sectors or branches of the industry" (3, p. 263).

There have also been special bargaining structures created for large construction jobs or "megaprojects." In some cases these arrangements have been legislatively imposed, for example, the Athabasca Tar Sands, while in other instances they have been voluntary, for example, petrochemical and dam projects. Another approach has been to legislatively create a separate branch of the industry, such as the electrical-power-system sector in Ontario. In most instances, megaproject agreements are negotiated between the owner-client or the general contractor and the international unions. The contracts (known as national "free-ride" agreements) frequently contain a no-strike/no-lockout provision for the duration of the project and stipulate that wages, hours, and working conditions will be referenced to external collective agreements.

The proliferation of autonomous bargaining agencies and the narrow scope of most bargaining led to intensified wage competition among negotiation units and more frequent industrial conflict. Policy makers were alarmed for two reasons. First, they recognized the strategic importance of construction to the economy and were concerned that labour unrest would have a detrimental impact on growth and development policies. Second, they believed construction wage settlements were inflationary and would set a pattern for other industries.

Table 1

Employer Coordination and Bargaining Structure

Type of Accreditation	Employer Coordination			Bargaining Structure				
	Total Number of Collective Agreements 1977	CLRA[a] Agreements 1977	Other[b] Employer Association Bargaining Agents 1977	Province-Wide Agreements 1967-68		Province-Wide Agreements 1977		Proportion of Employees Covered by Province-Wide Agreements (%) 1977
				No.	%	No.	%	
By sector								
British Columbia	50	47	1	8	40	32	64	90
Nova Scotia	31	30	1	1	10	6	20	17
Newfoundland	11	8	3	9	100	10	90	95
Quebec	1	1	0	0	00	1	100	100
By trade								
Ontario	232	6	158	6	09	23	10	25
Alberta	36	18	15	4	10	6	17	20
New Brunswick	18	0	10	0	00	5	28	22
No accreditation								
Saskatchewan	17	14	2	4	16	13	76	82
Manitoba	9	7	2	11	100	8	89	84

SOURCE: 1967-68 figures are based on a study of selected trades and are reported in Gordon W. Bertram, "The Structure and Performance of Collective Bargaining Systems," in Construction Labour Relations, H. Carl Goldenberg and John H.G. Crispo (Eds.), (Ottawa: Canadian Construction Association, 1968), pp. 416-519. The 1977 data covers all building trades and is contained in Construction Collective Agreements — Summaries published by the Canadian Construction Association.

NOTES: a. Refers to a province-wide Construction Labour Relations Association.
b. Refers to the number of employer associations that were signatory to the non-CLRA agreements.

THE GOVERNMENT RESPONSE

In contrast with the U.S., in Canada the government response to labour-management instability in construction has been to restructure employer and union bargaining agencies and to broaden the scope of bargaining.

The Reform of Bargaining Structure: Broader-Based Bargaining

The adoption of employer accreditation in most provinces has had a positive impact on employer unity. Although accreditation schemes vary in scope and impact, they have provided legal cohesion for employer associations by: (a) bringing nonassociation firms within the bargaining unit; (b) prohibiting firms in the unit from bargaining individually and reaching an agreement or understanding with a union; (c) outlawing national "free-ride" agreements in several provinces; and (d) in some cases banning selective strikes. By strengthening an association's control over members, accreditation sought to remove an internal source of instability. The evidence suggests it has done just that. Not only have employer associations displayed unity in taking strikes, but in several provinces accredited associations have even imposed industry-wide lockouts in response to selective strikes (23).

The impact of accreditation on the scope of bargaining varies from province to province, reflecting two distinct approaches to the determination of the appropriate employer bargaining unit for accreditation.

> The first is known as trade accreditation and is based on existing bargaining rights. Under this scheme the bargaining unit normally corresponds to the sector and geographic area specified in an existing collective agreement between an employer association and a trade union. Alternatively, the sector approach permits an association to seek accreditation in any sector and area for which it claims support. (23, p. 69)

Under the latter scheme, the potential for broader-based bargaining would appear to be better.

A comparison of the changes in bargaining structure between 1967 and 1977 is presented in Table 1. Although interprovincial variations exist, employers have increasingly coordinated their bargaining through a single bargaining agency (CLRA), and the geographic scope of bargaining shows signs of moving from the local and regional level to a provincial level. This is indicated by one study of bargaining structure in construction:

> In the 4 provinces where sector accreditation exists, CLRA organizations now negotiate about 95 percent of all collective agreements and, with one exception, province-wide bargaining covers 90 percent of the construction workforce. In Nova Scotia, bargaining takes place over two broad geographic areas and these regional agreements embrace the vast majority of construction workers. Under trade accreditation, CLRA organizations were signatory to less than 50 percent of all collective agreements and there was a proliferation of other contractor associations engaged in collective bargaining. Fragmentation was most pronounced in Ontario where 159 associations were signatory to 232 collective agreements (only six were negotiated by CLRAO). In addition, the extent of province-wide bargaining is substantially less in these provinces, as most negotiations are conducted on a metropolitan or a regional basis. (23, p. 91)

Table 2

Public Policy and Bargaining Structure by Province, 1980

Province	Geographic Scope of Bargaining	Employer and Union Coordination	Bargaining Patterns
Quebec	Compulsory province-wide bargaining	Compulsory coordination by employers and unions	A single industry-wide agreement is negotiated between a single employer association and a trade-union federation.
British Columbia	Supports wider-area bargaining but does not require it.	Voluntary employer coordination through accreditation; council bargaining can be imposed on unions.	Separate provincial agreements are negotiated for most trades, with CLRA and the Bargaining Council coordinating talks.
Newfoundland	Same as above	Accredited employer association may coordinate bargaining wherever it claims majority support. No provisions for union coordination.	CLRA bargains on behalf of employers in the building sector. Provincial agreements are negotiated with individual unions and no formal coordination exists on the union side.

Nova Scotia	Same as above	Same as above	Same as above, except CLRA negotiates regional agreements.
Manitoba	No provision	No provision	Bargaining is largely province-wide and coordinated by CLRA. Unions bargain separately.
Ontario	As of 1978 province-wide bargaining is required in the industrial, commercial, and institutional sector.	Union and employer coordination by trade is required.	Bargaining occurs on a single-trade, province-wide basis; no multitrade coordination.
Saskatchewan	Encourages province-wide bargaining	Same as above	Bargaining is province-wide and coordinated by CLRA.
Alberta	Permits province-wide bargaining	Employer coordination is permitted on multitrade basis; no provision for union coordination.	Bargaining is fragmented by trade and area, although CLRA coordinates bargaining for other employer associations.
New Brunswick	Preserves existing scope of bargaining	No provision	Bargaining is uncoordinated and fragmented by trade and area.

Since 1977 accreditation laws have been modified even further and public policy has directed its attention at union bargaining agents. For example, Ontario and Saskatchewan now require single-trade, province-wide bargaining by designated employer and union bargaining agencies in the industrial, commercial, and institutional sector. In British Columbia, the building-trades unions formed a multitrade provincial bargaining council after the B.C. Labour Relations Board exhorted them to do so.

The brisk pace of legislative reform in construction often makes it difficult to present an up-to-date account of the impact of public policy. Table 2 outlines the legal framework for broader-based bargaining in terms of: (a) the geographic scope of bargaining; (b) the degree of employer and union coordination; and (c) the extent of compulsion used to designate bargaining units and bargaining agents. Several patterns are evident. Quebec is the only province where compulsion is widely used to achieve broader-based bargaining: legislation has established a highly centralized and integrated collective-bargaining system requiring one multitrade industry-wide collective agreement between a single employer and union bargaining agent. In British Columbia, provincial multitrade bargaining has also been achieved, but without sacrificing the parties' freedom of choice; the broadening of bargaining structure has been achieved largely on a voluntary basis and, although individual trade agreements are negotiated, formal coordination exists on both sides of the table. Elsewhere the pattern is mixed. Ontario and Saskatchewan actually *require* province-wide bargaining by single trade (although this pattern exists voluntarily in several other jurisdictions) but stop short of requiring employers and unions to coordinate their bargaining on an industry-wide basis. Moreover, in those provinces which initially adopted trade accreditation and have not instituted changes to that system (Alberta and New Brunswick), bargaining has remained decentralized and coordination is not as well developed.

In summary, there are few statutes which actively encourage centralized and coordinated bargaining on an industry-wide basis in construction. Nevertheless, the realignment of public policy over the last decade or so has nudged the parties in this direction. Thus, as we enter the eighties, the scope of bargaining is significantly broader than it was a decade ago and the decision-making authority of employers and unions has been centralized.

The Quebec System: Centralized Bargaining by Decree

Because the Quebec system of construction labour relations differs from the North American model in several respects, it is worth highlighting some of its distinctive features. Its main distinguishing characteristic is the decree system, which enables the government to legislatively extend privately negotiated terms and conditions of employment to other parts of the industry. Originally, these terms were extended to the entire industry in a region; presently there is a single provincial decree. Thus, working conditions in construction are determined by a mix of collective-bargaining and a form of labour standards established by government.

From its inception, the decree system encouraged industry-wide bargaining at the regional level. Both the impracticality of trying to apply working conditions on a trade-by-trade basis and the inherent difficulties of enforcing numerous separate decrees prompted the unions to bargain on a multitrade basis.

Originally the administration and the enforcement of the decree was assumed by a joint labour-management committee (parity committee). The logic of this arrangement was based on the parties' familiarity with the industry and their ability to enforce their own working conditions. However, this system began to experience difficulties, and in 1975 an independent agency was formed to assume these duties (known as the Office de la construction du Québec — OCQ).

Unlike other provinces, labour and management were responsible for establishing vocational qualifications (through the parity committees). In 1969, however, this responsibility was taken over by the government. Another unique feature of manpower control in the province is the reduced status of hiring halls. In 1975, the OCQ was given "full responsibility for the placement of workmen in the construction industry" (8, p. 8). The complexity of the Quebec system and the frequency of government intervention in this sector makes it difficult to provide a concise up-to-date review of its salient features. Accordingly, primary emphasis is placed on the development of its centralized bargaining system.

In 1968, the Construction Industry Labour Relations Act (Bill 290) was passed. It sought to unify and rationalize the system by stabilizing union and employer organizations and encouraging more centralized bargaining. This was achieved in two ways. First, the law designated which labour organizations and employer associations could act as bargaining agents in the industry. Bill 290 eliminated union certification and established compulsory union membership in the building trades to overcome recognitional problems when there was union rivalry. (Presently, construction workers may designate the labour federation they wish to represent them six months prior to the termination of the provincial agreement.) Second, it established *compulsory* industry-wide bargaining on either a regional or a provincial basis. Although some of the rules governing the decree were modified, the principle of this system remained essentially the same.

Since 1968, Bill 290 has been amended more than fifteen times to refine various deficiencies in construction labour relations. Many of these changes were instituted following the Cliche Commission inquiry into union practices in the construction industry. These included regulations governing the internal affairs of unions, the imposition of trusteeships on several unions, the licensing of contractors, and other changes. The bargaining system was modified further to require: (a) a single province-wide agreement for the entire industry; (b) all contractors in the province joining the Association of Building Contractors of Quebec (ABCQ), the exclusive employer bargaining agent designated by law; (c) the employee association (or associations) which claims majority support concluding the provincial agreement; and (d) once the provincial agreement is concluded, its forming the basis of a provincial decree.

There can be little doubt that in Quebec the government has been an active participant in shaping the labour-relations system. It is also evident that labour-relations policy has embarked on a new course. Specifically, the abandonment of trade-union certification and the statutory imposition of bargaining agents and multitrade, province-wide bargaining constitute significant departures from the North American model. To what extent have these modifications perfected the bargaining system? One knowledgeable observer argues that collective-bargaining has been destroyed rather than advanced: "In a way, one can say there has been no collective agreement negotiated and actually signed by the parties since the passage of Bill 290" (8, pp. 124-125).

Table 3

Work Stoppages in Construction, 1950-1979

Period	Number of Strikes	Number of Workers Involved	Man-Days lost	Man-Days Lost in Construction as a Percentage of All Industries
1950-1959	363	108,454	1,870,132	10.5
1960-1969	1,054	316,234	5,108,000	16.8
1970-1979	832	668,395	12,473,640	17.1
1950-1979	2,249	1,093,083	19,451,772	16.1

SOURCE: Canada Department of Labour, Strikes and Lockouts in Canada, *1950-1979.*

BARGAINING OUTCOMES: STRIKES AND WAGE RATES

Previous studies of construction work stoppages have produced several important findings. First, in Canada and the U.S., construction accounted for about 15-20 percent of total strike activity in the postwar period (9, 12, 20), although it only accounted for about 7 percent of the nonagricultural labour force. There is evidence that strike proneness is related to decentralized bargaining patterns and union structure.

> Still, craftsmen's unions in construction, also a localized industry, are more strike prone than other unions in the sample or other unions in localized markets. This, we argue, reflects in part the high degree of subordinate autonomy made possible by characteristics of the industrial relations system in the construction industry. (19, p. 214)

Construction disputes tend to occur more frequently and involve fewer workers than work stoppages in other industries. This is primarily due to the high incidence and small size of noneconomic work stoppages (for example, disputes over grievances and work assignment) that dominate construction (12).

A detailed breakdown of construction strike data is presented in Table 3. Between 1950 and 1979, man-days lost in construction represented about one-sixth of the total for all industries. It is noteworthy that both the number of workers involved and the time lost attributable to construction disputes have increased over the past three decades. There is other evidence of a worsening strike picture. During the seventies, the average size and duration of construction disputes exceeded the all-industry average. Although the relative frequency of construction strikes declined in this period, the relative severity of these disputes more than doubled and rose to three times the national average (23).

The worsening strike picture in Canadian construction can be contrasted with the American situation. During the seventies, the number of construction man-days lost in Canada more than doubled over the sixties, whereas in the U.S. the increase was a modest 10 percent. This difference is largely due to the fact that construction work

Table 4

The Number, Average Size, and Duration of Work Stoppages in Construction by Type of Strike, 1960-1969 and 1970-1979

Stoppages	Number of Stoppages				Average Size (Workers Involved)		Average Duration (Days)	
	1960-1969		1970-1979		1960-1969	1970-1979	1960-1969	1970-1979
	No.	%	No.	%				
All stoppages	656	100	483	100	300	895	16.2	19.0
Stoppages over:								
Economic issues	343	52.3	233	48.2	604	2,114	22.5	24.6
Working conditions	150	22.9	87	18.0	339	556	5.8	5.2
Union organizing and security	71	10.8	13	2.7	257	210	12.6	6.5
Jurisdiction	71	10.8	31	6.4	388	605	8.0	5.7

SOURCE: Canada Department of Labour, Strikes and Lockouts in Canada, 1960-1979. Not all work stoppages are recorded in this publication, since only disputes involving 100 or more workers are listed individually (with reasons). In construction, about 60 percent of work stoppages are recorded individually.

stoppages are significantly larger and slightly longer in this country (23). Also, construction strikes represent part of a national trend of increased labour-management conflict during the seventies in Canada, whereas most measures of American strike activity have remained stable. In addition, in the U.S. the adoption of a special wage-controls program for construction workers in the early seventies (16) and the significant inroads made by nonunion contractors (17) have undoubtedly had a stabilizing influence on collective bargaining in that industry.

The most important aspect of construction disputes is revealed by examining the composition of strike activity over the past two decades. In Table 4, work stoppages are divided into the following categories: (a) total — including a residual category; (b) economic — wages and supplementary benefits; (c) working conditions — job security, grievances, and other noneconomic factors; (d) union organizing and security — recognitional disputes and union security issues; and (e) jurisdictional — interunion and intraunion conflict (12). The data indicate that a substantial proportion of all work stoppages involve noneconomic disputes. These strikes are significantly smaller in size and shorter in duration than the average for the industry as a whole. What is particularly noteworthy is that while the composition of strike activity remained about the same in these two decades, the increased conflict of the seventies is primarily due to an expansion of negotiating units. The average size of disputes over wages was three-and-one-half times greater in the latter period (604 workers involved in the sixties and 2,114 in the seventies). When the data is disaggregated and interprovincial comparisons are made, it is found that economic disputes are significantly larger and longer in provinces where centralized bargaining is practised. In essence, aggregate measures of construction strike activity are increasingly reflecting the structure of bargaining on wage issues.

While inflation has undoubtedly increased union wage demands and rank-and-file militancy, this factor alone cannot account for the differences in strike activity between Canada and the U.S. The centralization of bargaining structures in Canada, while motivated by a desire to achieve labour peace, has been accompanied by severe short-run conflict. Nowhere is this better illustrated than in British Columbia, where four consecutive centralized rounds of bargaining produced industry-wide shutdowns. As indicated by Kochan:

> Efforts to change a bargaining structure increase the probability of a strike because change may affect the long-run balance of power in the bargaining relationship. Therefore, it is something worth fighting for. Because of the longer-run strategic importance, these strikes tend to last well beyond what any model would estimate, solely on the basis of the short-run gains and savings achieved by either party. (11, p. 261)

The rising tide of industrial conflict was also accompanied by hefty wage settlements throughout most of the seventies. A comparison of average hourly wage rates in construction and manufacturing between 1950 and 1979 is presented in Table 5. Several trends are discernible. First, wage increases in construction have been larger than those in manufacturing, and the differential between these two industries rose from 2 percent in 1950 to a high of 53 percent in 1977. Second, the wage explosion which occurred between 1965 and 1970 subsided briefly in the early seventies only to record double-digit gains between 1974 and 1977. The average annual increase in construction wages in the seventies was 11.3 percent or about 0.5 percent higher than in the sixties. Third, following the introduction of mandatory

Table 5

**Average Hourly Earnings in Construction and Manufacturing,
1950-1979**

| Year | Construction | | Manufacturing | | Construction as Percentage of Manufacturing |
	Wage	% Increase	Wage	% Increase	
1950	$ 1.06	—	$ 1.04	—	101.9
1951	1.19	12.3	1.18	13.5	100.8
1952	1.32	10.9	1.30	10.2	101.5
1953	1.44	9.1	1.36	4.6	105.9
1954	1.48	7.8	1.41	3.7	105.0
1955	1.52	7.7	1.45	2.8	104.8
1956	1.65	8.6	1.52	4.8	108.6
1957	1.84	11.5	1.61	5.9	114.3
1958	1.86	1.1	1.66	3.1	112.0
1959	1.93	3.8	1.73	4.2	111.6
1960	2.03	5.2	1.79	3.5	113.4
1961	2.06	1.5	1.83	3.3	112.6
1962	2.14	3.9	1.88	2.7	113.8
1963	2.23	4.2	1.95	3.7	114.4
1964	2.34	4.9	2.02	3.6	115.8
1965	2.53	8.1	2.12	4.9	119.3
1966	2.80	10.7	2.25	6.1	124.4
1967	3.12	11.4	2.40	6.7	130.0
1968	3.33	6.7	2.58	7.5	129.1
1969	3.71	11.4	2.79	8.1	133.0
1970	4.21	13.5	3.01	7.3	139.9
1971	4.75	12.8	3.28	9.0	144.8
1972	5.15	8.4	3.54	7.9	145.5
1973	5.66	9.9	3.85	8.8	147.0
1974	6.43	13.6	4.37	13.5	147.1
1975	7.53	17.1	5.06	15.8	148.8
1976	8.68	15.3	5.76	13.8	150.7
1977	9.77	12.6	6.38	10.8	153.1
1978	10.28	5.2	6.84	7.2	150.3
1979	11.05	7.5	7.43	8.6	148.7

Average Annual Increase in Wages (%)

1950-1960	6.7	5.6
1960-1970	10.8	5.4
1970-1979	11.3	10.6

SOURCE: Statistics Canada, Review of Man-Hours and Hourly Earnings, *1950-1970 and* Employment, Earnings and Hours, *1971-1979.*

wage-and-price controls in late 1975, the rate of growth in construction wages subsided. Indeed, over the last several years, the construction wage advantage declined, indicating that these settlements were more in line with those negotiated in other sectors. The moderation in wages and strike activity following the lifting of controls in 1978 appears to have been temporary, however, as both measures increased in the 1980 round of negotiations. Finally, wage settlements in the seventies were substantially higher in Canada than in the U.S. While both countries experienced high rates of inflation and economic slowdowns, it appears that the recession of the mid-seventies was deeper and longer in the U.S., and the presence of construction wage controls and nonunion competition restrained wage settlements (22).

One might ask why there has not been a moderating trend in wages as bargaining became increasingly centralized. To begin with, Mills and others have commented that bargaining structure is an intervening variable in the relationship between the external environment and bargaining outcomes (11, 15). Consequently, factors such as construction demand, employment growth, and inflation have had an important bearing on wage outcomes. There is, nevertheless, some fragmentary evidence indicating that centralized bargaining has constrained wage settlements during upswings in construction activity. Unfortunately, this influence has frequently been achieved at a considerable cost, namely widespread industrial conflict (23).

While the level of wage settlements has remained relatively high, centralized bargaining has had an impact on internal wage structures. A comparison of wage settlements in centralized and decentralized bargaining structures reveals two notable differences (23). First, while the wage differential between the highest- and lowest-paid trades is declining throughout the country, this compression is occurring most rapidly in those provinces where the *change* in bargaining structure is the greatest, for example, British Columbia, Quebec, and Nova Scotia. The second impact is found in the stability of intertrade rankings in the wage hierarchy. Under centralized bargaining there is greater stability and fewer shifts in the relative wage structure by individual trades. These results can be explained by the fact that broader-based bargaining has led to common expiry dates within provinces and across-the-board settlements have impeded union efforts to leapfrog wages. In those provinces where the geographic scope of bargaining is not province-wide or negotiations are not coordinated on an industry-wide basis, intertrade wage competition is more intense.

A LOOK AT THE FUTURE

If the past decade can be characterized as a period of structural change, the eighties should provide a testing ground for assessing the efficacy of centralized collective bargaining. The next decade is likely to witness continued economic instability and stagflation, and an increase in nonunion and own-account construction, that is, construction work undertaken by an owner using his own employees rather than contracting work out to a construction firm. These developments will pose a significant challenge to the industry and more particularly to the ability of labour and management to conclude reasonable settlements and maintain industrial peace. In this section, several areas are explored which will receive increased attention in the coming years.

Bargaining Structure

The development of centralized and coordinated bargaining is likely to continue across Canada in the next decade. For all practical purposes, province-wide bargaining is now practised in all but a few provinces. Although the degree of employer and union coordination varies considerably, there is a strong likelihood that employer alliances will be solidified and that multitrade bargaining through trade-union councils will evolve on either an informal or a formal basis. The traditional opposition of the building-trades unions to an "industrial structure" for bargaining may dissipate if they can be persuaded that reorganization need not interfere with their legitimate craft interests and autonomy.

> The creation of a multi-trade council would be for bargaining purposes only and need not interfere in other craft union functions. Moreover, a system of two-tier bargaining could be developed to ensure that trade issues are negotiated prior to the commencement of talks on industry-wide issues. With contractors having organized themselves into provincial, multi-trade organizations, and with concerns mounting about own-account and nonunion competition, the pressures to accept some form of coordinated bargaining will grow stronger. (23, p. 176)

If the experiment with council bargaining in British Columbia proves successful, it may well set the pattern for unions elsewhere in Canada just as CLRA became the model for employer associations. If the parties cling to the status quo and strike activity escalates, the government may feel compelled to impose these changes.

A major unresolved bargaining-structure issue is how to handle megaprojects, many of which operate outside the existing collective-bargaining system in major building construction. Many of these projects are under agreements that prohibit strikes or lockouts, and wages and employment conditions are based on those negotiated in the surrounding areas. The vast size of these projects, both in terms of cost and manpower requirements, has tempted several governments to draft special legislation removing these work sites from the existing collective-bargaining system, for example, the Athabasca Tar Sands. The impact of these megaprojects on industrial relations elsewhere in the industry is now being examined in a major study consisting of five case histories including the Lorneville Area Project (New Brunswick), James Bay (Quebec), Bruce Nuclear Power Development (Ontario), the Athabasca Tar Sands (Alberta), and the British Columbia dam projects. One question being investigated is whether megaprojects are a haven for strikers involved in local work stoppages. If they are, then unions can mitigate the cost of a work stoppage by transferring strikers and pressuring local associations to reach an agreement on their terms. An assessment of this and other issues will help to determine whether these large projects should be treated differently for industrial-relations purposes.

Nonunion Competition

The growth of nonunion (open-shop) and own-account construction is widely discussed in Canada, but there is unfortunately little empirical evidence of its magnitude. In the U.S., the open-shop movement has been documented and is making deep inroads into the industry. Indeed, the evidence now suggests that the preponderance of new construction is nonunion. This phenomenal growth has been attributed to high rates of compensation, costly work rules and strikes in the unionized sector, the emergence of strong nonunion associations, and major construction users considering the open-shop alternative to be less costly and more reliable (7). As labour costs and strike activity increased in the U.S. during the sixties, the disparity between the union and nonunion sector increased. This intensified management opposition to new union organizing, and it prompted many large, traditionally union firms to go "double-breasted," that is, to set up separate nonunion divisions (11).

Considering the strike and wage record of Canadian construction in the seventies, how do we explain the absence of an open-shop movement paralleling that of the U.S.? One possible explanation is that there is frequently a time lag between the occurrence of events in the two countries. Several Canadian employer associations have conducted surveys which they claim indicate an emerging nonunion presence. While these studies are subject to methodological limitations, there appears to be an emerging consensus that open-shop work is making inroads and will continue to grow. What is less clear is the potential of such a movement. The absence of a national open-shop association, such as the Associated Builders and Contractors in the U.S., and the larger role of government in the Canadian economy suggest that nonunion competition will not grow as large or as fast as in the U.S. What may pose an even greater challenge is own-account construction (where employers use their own employees to perform construction-related duties). For example, in British Columbia the building-trades unions recently protested the construction of a saw-mill by members of the International Woodworkers of America. Elsewhere there is evidence that municipal and provincial work forces are performing work which was previously contracted out.

There can be little doubt that labour and management will have to weigh the potential impact of increased competition. While many unions are sceptical about management statistics on the growth of nonunion competition, both sides would be adversely affected if the American pattern is repeated here. If the parties fail to explore avenues for stabilizing labour costs and strike activity in the future, owner-clients will actively consider the nonunion and own-account alternatives.

Bargaining Outcomes

The evolution of broader-based bargaining may facilitate increased labour-management cooperation and a reduction in labour strife. This hypothesis is based on two considerations. First, the parties will begin to assume the responsibility that goes with centralized power. While the implementation of broader-based bargaining has been far from peaceful, the realignment of bargaining structures appears to be in its final stages of development. What is critically important is how the parties respond to the consolidated structures which are now in place. The fact that negotiations are now in the limelight, and external pressures on the industry are mounting could help to alleviate economic conflict in the long run. While it is still recognized that the industrial-relations system is vulnerable to external sources of instability and that the strike will not become obsolete, there is a good chance that the severity of industrial conflict over the last twenty years will not be repeated in the eighties.

The second possibility for improved labour-management relations rests on the parties' ability to reduce the sources of noneconomic conflict. This could be achieved by promoting greater uniformity in contract language and moving to standardize employment conditions across areas and trades. The intent would not be to destroy real distinctions based on craft identity but to rationalize those disparities based on fragmentation and bargaining power. For example, such conditions as overtime, room and board allowances, travel pay, and grievance and arbitration procedures lend themselves to standardization. The variation in contract terms found on many projects often leads to claims of inequitable treatment and illegal work stoppages. Moreover, the problem is frequently compounded by the lack of uniformity in contract administration. Centralized bargaining should help to standardize terms and conditions of employment and improve grievance handling.

There will also be an increased reliance on joint labour-management committees. Centralized bargaining will undoubtedly provide a forum in which the industry's top leaders can exchange ideas on major industrial-relations problems. For example, the jurisdictional-disputes plan hammered out in British Columbia represents a major achievement in construction labour relations. Not only has the industry designed an expeditious procedure which is well-suited to local needs, but it is believed to have had a salutary effect on work stoppages over job assignments (2). It would not be difficult to envision other issues being removed from the distributive bargaining table and approached on an integrative or problem-solving basis. A few examples include: (a) a comprehensive job-evaluation study to rationalize the construction wage structure; (b) determining means of improving productivity, for example, a relaxation of restrictive union work rules in exchange for a guaranteed annual number of hours of work, (c) developing more sophisticated safety and training programs; and (d) exploring how alternative dispute-settlement procedures might reduce labour-management conflict, for example, expedited grievance arbitration.

Clearly, tackling these issues and resolving them will require a long-run strategy and commitment. External threats to unionized construction will not by themselves stimulate the parties to take action on all of these issues. For example, notwithstanding the nonunion threat in the U.S., efforts to institute productivity bargaining have not been uniformly successful (14). But as the centralization process matures, and the structural apparatus is put in place to deal with pressing problems, we can expect the parties to respond on an industry-wide basis. Even if their response is motivated by a pure survival instinct, we can be cautiously optimistic that the winds of change are blowing across the industry. This is not meant to suggest that labour-management relations will be instantly stabilized. What we can expect to see is a more sophisticated and rational approach to collective bargaining and industrial relations in the construction sector.

REFERENCES AND WORKS CITED

1. Christy, R.J. "The Structure of Collective Bargaining," in S.M.A. Hameed (Ed.), *Canadian Industrial Relations* (Toronto: Butterworth, 1975), pp. 187-204.

2. Collingwood, L. "Developments in Construction Industrial Relations," *British Columbia Department of Labour Research Bulletin,* July 1979, pp. 12-15.

3. Dunlop, J.T. "The Industrial Relations System in Construction," in Arnold R. Weber (Ed.), *The Structure of Collective Bargaining* (New York: Free Press, 1961), pp. 255-277.

4. Economic Council of Canada. *Toward More Stable Growth in Construction* (Ottawa: Economic Council of Canada, 1973).

5. Foster, H.G., and G. Strauss. "Labor Problems in Construction: A Review," *Industrial Relations,* Vol. 11 (1972), 289-313.

6. Foster, H.G. "Wages in Construction: Examining the Arguments," *Industrial Relations,* Vol. 11 (1972), 336-349.

7. Foster H.G. "Industrial Relations in Construction: 1970-1977," *Industrial Relations,* Vol. 17 (1978), 1-18.

8. Hebert, G. *Labour Relations in the Quebec Construction Industry, Part 1: The System of Labour Relations* (Ottawa: Economic Council of Canada, 1977).

9. Jamieson, S. "The Third Wave Reconsidered— Labour Unrest and Industrial Conflict in Canada, 1960-1975." Paper presented at the meetings of the Canadian Industrial Relations Research Institute, Fredericton, New Brunswick, June, 1977.

10. Jenness, R.A. *Manpower in Construction* (Ottawa: Economic Council of Canada, 1975).

11. Kochan, T.A. *Collective Bargaining and Industrial Relations* (Homewood, Ill.: Richard D. Irwin, 1980).

12. Lipsky, D.B., and H.S. Farber. "The Composition of Strike Activity in the Construction Industry," *Industrial and Labor Relations Review,* Vol. 29 (1976), 388-404.

13. List. W. "CLC Faces Internal Battle With Building Trades," *Globe and Mail,* September 29, 1980, p. B2.

14. Maloney, W.F. "Productivity Bargaining in Contract Construction," *Labor Law Journal,* Vol. 28 (1977), 532-538.

15. Mills, D.Q. *Industrial Relations and Manpower in Construction* (Cambridge: Harvard University Press, 1972).

16. Mills, D.Q. "Construction Wage Stabilization: A Historic View," *Industrial Relations,* Vol. 11 (1972), 350-365.

17. Northrup, H.R., and H.G. Foster. *Open-Shop Construction* (Philadelphia: Industrial Research Unit, University of Pennsylvania, 1975).

18. Pierson, F.C. "Recent Employer Alliances in Perspective," *Industrial Relations,* Vol. 1 (1960), 39-55.

19. Roomkin, M. "Union Structure, Internal Control and Strike Activity," *Industrial and Labor Relations Review,* Vol. 29 (1976), 198-247.

20. Rose, J.B. "A Note on Industrial Conflict in British Columbia's Construction Industry," *Relations Industrielles/Industrial Relations*, Vol. 31 (1976), 309-315.

21. Rose, J.B. "Construction Labour Relations Associations in Canada," *Relations Industrielles/Industrial Relations,* Vol. 22 (1977), 35-49.

22. Rose, J.B. "A Canadian View of Labor Relations in Construction," *Industrial Relations,* Vol. 18 (1979), 156-172.

23. Rose, J.B. *Public Policy, Bargaining Structure and the Construction Industry* (Toronto: Butterworth, 1980).

24. Strauss, G. "Business Agents in the Building Trades: A Case Study in a Community," *Industrial and Labor Relations Review,* Vol. 10 (1957), 237-251.

25. Wood, W.D., and P. Kumar (Eds.), *The Current Industrial Relations Scene in Canada, 1979* (Kingston: Industrial Relations Centre, Queen's University, 1979).

QUESTIONS

1. What distinguishes industrial relations in the construction industry from other industries?

2. What factors help to explain the strike proneness of the construction industry?

3. Assess the efficacy of government legislation to stabilize labour-management relations.

4. Why might we expect wage determination in the construction sector to be different from other sectors?

5. Discuss the pros and cons of centralized versus decentralized bargaining in construction.

6. Discuss the future outlook for labour-management relations in the construction industry.

JEAN BOIVIN

18. Labour Relations in Quebec

This chapter examines the relationships between employers and employee organizations in Quebec, identifying the particular features of the Quebec industrial-relations system and emphasizing those characteristics which differ from the rest of Canada. A brief presentation of the specific sociopolitical and ideological contexts precedes the formal description of labour-relations practices.

Given the unique situation of trade-union diversity prevailing in Quebec, the origin, development, structure, and ideology of the labour movement are analysed in detail. Quebec's labour legislation is compared with that of the rest of North America, centring on both the general role of the state in labour relations and specific aspects of labour legislation such as antistrikebreaking provisions or the unique administrative machinery of the Labour Court.

The last section of the chapter is devoted to collective bargaining. Emphasis is placed on the structure of employer-employee organizations and on strikes and lockouts. Special attention is given to construction and to public sectors where labour-relations practices are quite different from those prevailing in the rest of Canada.

Is the Quebec industrial-relations system different than the Canadian industrial-relations system or do all the considerations which have been put forth about the latter apply to Quebec? Although strong arguments can certainly be raised by advocates of both interpretations, this chapter takes for granted that many of the fundamental characteristics of the Canadian industrial-relations system prevail in Quebec, but that there are nonetheless specific conditions and practices which are unique to the Quebec situation.

This chapter addresses the following aspects of industrial relations in Quebec: the environment in which labour relations exist; the development of labour organizations; the structure and membership of major labour federations; the legislative framework; the collective-bargaining process with special emphasis on construction and the public sector; and some perspectives on the future of labour relations.

THE ENVIRONMENT OF LABOUR RELATIONS

Although the general nature of the Canadian environment also applies to Quebec, a number of specific characteristics merit special consideration.

The economic environment in Quebec tends to have the similar problems of high inflation and unemployment that have plagued the rest of Canada. In fact, Quebec's unemployment rate tends to be slightly higher than the average rate in Canada, although income per capita in Quebec is about average. Quebec's economy relies heavily upon the development of natural resources and upon labour-intensive industries, such as textiles. However, the most obvious difference between Quebec and the rest of Canada is that the population is over 80 percent French-speaking and possesses a specific cultural background and tradition. This situation accounts for the perennial political turmoil over the type of relationships that should exist between the Quebec and Federal governments.

On more practical grounds, this cultural specificity has led to a somewhat different political setting than elsewhere in Canada. For example, at the provincial level, the Conservative Party ceased to exist in the 1930s as it was replaced by a new nationalist party — the Union Nationale — which was to rule Quebec's destiny for many years. In fact, this party formed the government between 1936 and 1940 and between 1944 and 1960 under the strong (some historians even say "authoritarian") leadership of Prime Minister Maurice Duplessis. The Union Nationale was also the party in power from 1966 to 1970, but much of its nationalist program was taken over by a new party — the Parti Québécois (PQ) — which was formed in 1967 by dissident members of the Liberal Party and other nationalist elements in Quebec society. The PQ gained strength rapidly and in 1976 defeated the Liberals who had been in power since 1970.

Federally, the Liberals have tended to dominate Quebec, with the Social Credit party being second in importance. The left-wing New Democratic Party has seldom had much support in Quebec, in part because the Parti Québécois has embraced some left-wing programs. The PQ tends to have strong support of union members, a fact which is reinforced by the official endorsement of this party by the Quebec Federation of Labour. However, despite some measures such as the increase of the minimum wage to the highest level in North America, it remains to be seen how far this party is willing to go in the direction of endorsing a strong socialist program. The Parti Québécois' electoral platform is above all a nationalist one and its socialist outlook (to the extent that such a term can be used) is a by-product of nationalism. Although it draws support from left-wing elements in society, the population supports the party either because it is also strongly nationalist, or because there is little chance for a truly socialist party to emerge in Quebec in the short run.

The Quebec labour movement gives the impression of extreme radicalism, without a shared ideology between labour, management, and government. Despite the bitterness of certain spectacular strikes and the words ordinarily used by some union leaders to depict management and government officials, there is no reason to believe that a minimal set of common values shared by the parties is less likely to be found within Quebec's industrial-relations system than elsewhere in Canada. Three factors support this assessment.

First, the perception of a radical union leadership occurs because of the variety of central labour organizations in Quebec, in contrast to the predominance of a single central organization, the CLC, outside Quebec. In this latter situation, radicalism has more difficulty finding official or institutionalized expression since a single organization comprising many different elements will most likely put a check on radical leaders, or at least on radical platforms. On the other hand, where a plurality of central labour organizations exists it is very likely that one or more organizations will be officially dominated by radical elements, accounting for a more publicized form of radicalism in Quebec.

Second, despite the expressed radicalism of many union leaders, grass-roots members do not usually share the same aggressiveness towards the "system" or even towards their employers. Even if they are ready at times to engage in militant action, it is seldom that workers deliberately try to jeopardize the source of their jobs and incomes.

Third, in Quebec, as in the rest of Canada, parties of the extreme left have seldom received much of the popular vote, at least not over the last twenty years.

Thus, while there are some substantial differences in the social and political environments between Quebec and the rest of Canada, the economic and general labour-relations environments in these two contexts are similar. The political and cultural differences tend to have their strongest influence on the development and radicalism of Quebec labour.

DEVELOPMENT OF LABOUR ORGANIZATIONS: THE FORMATIVE YEARS

Early Beginnings: A Nucleus of Local Organizations

Most historians use 1816 as a starting point to trace the presence of labour organizations in Canada. That was the year the government of the Province of Nova Scotia enacted legislation the specific purpose of which was to outlaw coalitions of workers. However, the first union of which there is a definite record was a boot-and-shoe workers' organization in Montreal in 1827. On a more permanent basis, the printers were the first occupational group in Canada, as in the United States, to establish permanent organizations. As early as 1827, a group of printers in Quebec City had established a combined trade-union-mutual-aid society that regulated wages in their trade, cared for their sick, and provided social and recreational aid for their members (16, p. 12).

The period between 1827 and 1836 saw many craftsmen form their own trade associations; the carpenters were probably the most active group. In 1833, they created the Montreal Mechanics Mutual Protective Society, whose major objective was to reduce daily working hours from twelve to ten. Other trades which joined in this movement for the reduction of the work-day were stonecutters, masons, shoemakers, journeymen bakers, and cordwainers.

This first wave of organization in Quebec, which paralleled similar developments in Ontario and in the Maritimes among the same trades, led to the short-lived existence of municipal labour councils such as the Montreal Trades Union (1834), which is probably the first attempt at a multitrade organization in Canada.

Although all the trade unions referred to above operated strictly on a local basis, their most salient feature was that they possessed the fundamental characteristics of permanent organizations. Their members had to pay dues which were used mainly to provide for social benefits but also, at times, for strike pay. They elected delegates or representatives to take care of the organization. Moreover, proceedings of local meetings were kept in official records.

Despite these early successes, the period 1840 to 1860 was not favourable to the development of labour organizations in Quebec. Few new locals were created and many of the old ones collapsed, usually in times of economic recession, with some reappearing during the recovery of the economy. Until the 1860s, the leadership of most of these trade unions was assumed by skilled craftsmen from Europe, especially Britain. In fact, the British Amalgamated Society of Engineers even established a local in Montreal in 1851.

However, the impetus for the second wave of unionization which occurred in the 1860s was provided by the action of American trade unions which "chartered" locals in major Canadian cities. Increased mobility and competition between Canadian and American workers, as a result of the gradual integration of product markets on both sides of the border, provided a strong incentive for local unions to join together into "international" organizations. The Iron Moulders Union was the pioneer when it established a local branch in Montreal in 1861, and it was soon followed by the printers', the cigarmakers', and the shoemakers' unions. The construction of railway lines across the border also facilitated the early growth of international unions in rail transportation.

Despite the growing importance of international organizations, a number of purely Canadian trade unions were also created at the same time. This was the case of the most important labour organization in Quebec City in the nineteenth century — The Ship Labourers' Benevolent Society — formed in 1857. The presence of such organizations, which have preferred to remain outside the "international" labour movement, is certainly not confined to the boundaries of Quebec. However, either the leadership or the bulk of the membership of these autonomous Canadian bodies usually have originated in Quebec.

Consolidation of Trade Union Structures

The next step in the evolution of the labour movement, after the creation of local organizations, has always been the establishment of local councils, usually in major urban centres. The function of these bodies is to further labour objectives, such as reduction in hours of work, which are common to different trade unions. A council was formed in Toronto in the early 1870s, in support of the nine-hour work-day. This episode is a landmark in Canadian labour history, since the widespread agitation which accompanied the activities of the Toronto Trades Assembly induced the Canadian government to pass new legislation that freed unions from liability under common law for conspiracy in restraint of trade. It was also the Toronto Trades Assembly, which later became the Toronto Trades and Labor Council, that took the initiative of establishing a Canadian labour federation. This organization, whose formation constitutes the third and final step in the organic development of national labour movements, came into existence in 1886 as the Trades and Labour Congress of Canada (TLC).

There is nothing specifically relevant to Quebec in these particular developments, except that local councils on the model of the Toronto Trades and Labor Council were also established in most major cities and that Quebec union members widely participated in the formation of the TLC.

The Rise of a National Labour Movement

One of the major characteristics of the newly formed TLC was that it accepted among its ranks not only the locals of various international unions but also members of purely Canadian unions and members of the Noble Order of the Knights of

Labor. This latter organization had come into existence in Philadelphia in 1869. It attempted to organize all types of workers, skilled and unskilled, into local general labour unions or "trade assemblies" and, in major urban centres, "district assemblies." The Knights grew very rapidly in the United States; however, by the end of the century they had died out, due mainly to the fierce competition of the international unions. The Knights had better success in Canada where they survived more than a decade after their collapse in the United States.

Although the Knights of Labor established local and district assemblies throughout Canada, the bulk of their membership came from Ontario and Quebec. In fact, from 1881, when the first local assembly was formed in Hamilton, to 1887 there were more assemblies in Ontario than in Quebec. However, even if no precise statistics exist on the membership of the Knights of Labor after this year, it is quite probable that the figures would show a decline for Ontario and an increase for Quebec in the next decade (13, p. 86).

The Knights of Labor had been very active in the creation of the Montreal Trades and Labor Council in 1886, which they dominated until a rival organization — the Montreal Federated Trades Council — was created in 1897 with the support of the AFL. This conflict between the Knights and international unions in Montreal would extend itself to the national organization and would lead to the expulsion of the Knights of Labor and other purely Canadian unions from the TLC in 1902. Immediately after the 1902 TLC Convention, the Knights of Labor assemblies that had been expelled, together with a number of purely Canadian dual unions (that is, those whose jurisdiction conflicted with that of an international union), joined to form a new nationalist labour federation — the National Trades and Labour Congress whose name would be changed to the Canadian Federation of Labour in 1908. This organization defined itself as a truly authentic Canadian body and its ambition was to take over the TLC's place as the major labour federation in Canada. However, it did not achieve this goal since the most members it ever had was 20,000 in 1906 (17, p. 226) and by the start of World War I it was almost extinguished.

The Birth of a Confessional Labour Movement in Quebec

Of the twenty-three organizations which were expelled from the TLC, sixteen came from Quebec and were mostly composed of French Canadians. One of the major reasons for the growth problems of the new CFL was that its Quebec membership would gradually turn down their affiliation to join a new type of organization — the confessional trade union.

These trade unions were established as a result of the involvement of the Catholic church in labour relations. Although the first formal confessional trade union was established in 1912, the origin of the Catholic labour movement can be traced as far back as the 1900-1901 strike in Quebec City shoe industry which involved 5,000 workers and twenty-one employers. The strike was only settled after an arbitration award issued by the archbishop of Quebec. The basis of this award was to set the pattern for the kind of workers' organizations that would later be called "confessional unions," namely that each local organization should have a chaplain as advisor for the conduct of its affairs; that the organization should recognize the common interests of workers and employers; that it should resort to conciliation and arbitration procedures rather than rely on the strike weapon to resolve its conflicts with management; and that it should be vowed to the defence of nationalist (French Canadian) values.

The church's interest in workers' organization arose because of its antipathy towards the values and practices of international trade unionism. This position is clearly expressed in a pastoral letter written by Archbishop Bruchési in 1903:

> With the greatest anxiety do we see the labor organizations of our city seeking for affiliation with foreign associations. The majority of the leaders and members of those international unions have nothing in common with our temperament, our customs and our faith. (1, p. 53)

Among the first concrete actions taken by the church to turn workers away from international unions was the formation of "social movements" such as the Action sociale catholique de Québec in 1907 and l'école sociale populaire de Montréal in 1911. These movements, which brought together laymen and priests, sought an amelioration of working conditions by developing a strong sentiment of Christian solidarity among the population. The leaders of these movements soon began to be directly involved in the organization of formal trade unions. Hence, the first confessional trade union, La fédération ouvrière mutuelle du Nord, was established in Chicoutimi in 1912 at the instigation of Archbishop Eugène Lapointe, who feared the presence of international-union organizers in the region.

The same pattern was followed in major industrial centres where the strong involvement of Catholic priests and bishops promoted the formation of confessional trade unions to challenge the locals of international unions. An informal convention was held in 1918 in Quebec City in which the delegates expressed the necessity to unify all the confessional trade unions into one provincial organization. This objective was reached three years later when the Confédération des travailleurs catholiques du Canada (CTCC) was established at a convention held in Hull. The founding convention was attended by 220 delegates who came from eighty trade unions, eight study circles, and four central councils (Quebec, Montreal, Granby, and Hull). The new organization claimed to represent some 26,000 members.

THE EVOLUTION OF LABOUR ORGANIZATIONS: 1921-1980

The Transformation of the CTCC

Spokesmen of other unions repeatedly charged that confessional unions were undercutting union standards, selling out to employers, and using their members as strikebreakers. These charges are supported by statistics showing that between 1915 and 1936 only 9 of the 507 officially reported strikes in Quebec involved confessional unions. Starting with World War II, however, the CTCC underwent significant changes in policy and practices. The rapid industrial expansion drew large numbers of French Canadians into major urban centres where they came into contact with other workers. This led the CTCC to remove the "Catholic-only" clause from its constitution in 1943. Vigorous organizing campaigns by the TLC and the CCL unions in Quebec also forced the Catholic organizations to be more militant. New and more aggressive lay leaders like Gérard Picard and Jean Marchard took over top executive positions in the CTCC and members of the clergy played a correspondingly less active part in the organization.

This new militancy brought the CTCC into conflict with the Duplessis regime on more than one occasion. The most dramatic confrontation occurred in the violent strike of Asbestos workers in 1949, an event which many historians consider to be the major turning point in the evolution of the Catholic confederation. While the seven-month strike ended without tangible gains for the workers, the CTCC emerged with new strength and prestige. It became the main rallying force during the 1950s in pressing for long-overdue social and political reforms in Quebec.

Union Mergers . . . without the CTCC

At the time of the union mergers which brought an end to the rivalry between the AFL and the CIO in the United States and their junior bodies in Canada — the TLC and the CCL — the CTCC was urged to join the movement of unification. The new Canadian Labour Congress was established at the joint convention of the TLC and CCL in April 1956. At the convention and at the convention of the CTCC in September of the same year, resolutions were passed in favour of affiliating. Joint committees were set up with representatives of the two major labour bodies, and numerous meetings were held in an effort to reach agreement. However, negotiations broke down and organized labour in Quebec remained divided.

The major impediment to affiliation was that the CTCC wanted to affiliate as a unit, in order to preserve its distinct character and identity, while the CLC was structurally designed to accommodate individual unions organized on the basis of particular trades or industries. Accepting the CTCC's viewpoint would have meant tolerating "dual unions" within the CLC which was contrary to its constitution. An affiliation along craft or industry lines would have meant that the CTCC's membership would be gradually overtaken by the CLC's strong affiliates, among which were the locals of international unions against whom the CTCC had always fought. Thus, instead of reaching unity, the Quebec labour movement continued to be prone to rivalry and conflict between the two main union bodies, the CTCC and the CLC's new Quebec Federation of Labour.

This rivalry did not completely rule out cooperation between the two central organizations in Quebec, as was apparent in the highly publicized copper mining strike in Murdochville in 1957. The strike, which involved the United Steelworkers of America, once again involved the openly hostile stance of the Duplessis regime against militant unionism, as was the case with the Asbestos strike in 1949. This time the CTCC gave strong moral and material support to the strikers who were fighting a subsidiary of a large multinational corporation. In fact, the relationships between the CTCC and the old industrial unions of the CLC had always been very close. Reliable union sources confirmed that the top QFL leadership, being dominated by former TLC affiliates, did not agree with the public demonstrations that were organized against the company and the Duplessis government during the Murdochville strike. These people were nonetheless "convinced" by more militant elements within the QFL to give their support.

Another major landmark in the evolution of the Quebec labour movement was the strike of the CBC producers in Montreal in 1959. Some observers consider this event as the beginning of the Quiet Revolution, a period which is associated with the end of the Duplessis regime in 1959 and with the emergence of the Liberal government of Jean Lesage from 1960 to 1966. The strikers, including the noted journalist René Lévesque, achieved an important precedent concerning union recognition of professional and supervisory employees in the public service, despite lack of support from most of the English network's producers. The apparent indifference of the federal government and of English-speaking Canadians to the prolonged shutdown of the French-language radio and television network, coupled with the hostility of CLC

Table 1

**Membership of Labour Organizations in Quebec,
Selected Years 1956-1978 (thousands)**

	Provincial Federations				
Year	CLC[a]	QLF[b]	CTCC-CSN[c]	CIC-CEQ[d]	CSD[e]
1957	250	92	100		
1960	250	99	94	30	
1964	250	111	141	42	
1966	325	141	204	54	
1972	342	233	219	70	21
1978	420	300	178	85	42

SOURCE: Fernand Harvey, (Ed.), Le mouvement ouvrier au Québec *(Montreal: Boréal Express, 1980), p. 287.*

NOTES: a. *Canadian Labour Congress. Most members of the CLC are also members of one of the four largest provincial federations.*

b. *Quebec Federation of Labour.*

c. *Confédération des travailleurs catholiques du Canada prior to 1960, thereafter the Confédération des syndicats nationaux.*

d. *Corporation des instituteurs et institutrices catholiques du Canada prior to 1967, thereafter the Corporation des enseignants du Québec, until 1974, thereafter Centrale de l'enseignement du Québec.*

e. *Centrale des syndicats démocratiques.*

parent-union executives toward their French-language locals during the strike, encouraged the latter to secede and join the CTCC. It also killed prospects for a future merger of the two central federations.

At its 1960 convention, the CTCC dropped the last vestiges of its identification with the Catholic church and renamed itself the Confédération des syndicats nationaux (CSN). It subsequently took important steps to reorganize and centralize its structure (such as establishing a single strike fund financed by all its affiliates) in order to be in a better position to compete with the QFL's affiliates.

The Quiet Revolution and Its Aftermath

The CSN grew rapidly in size and influence during the 1960s under the Quiet Revolution. It benefited most from the organization of professional and other salaried employees in the public service, but it also won jurisdiction over CLC-QFL affiliates on many occasions. As indicated in Table 1, total membership in the confederation more than doubled between 1960 and 1966. Moreover, the political influence of the CSN was tremendous during the Liberal government of Jean Lesage. The alliance of political, intellectual, and union leaders who had fought against the Duplessis regime was suddenly in power after the 1960 election. One of the major achievements of this alliance was the enactment of the Labour Code in 1964, considered by many to be the most liberal piece of labour legislation in Canada at that time. One of its features was that it granted the right to strike to all public-service employees except police and fire fighters. The Labour Code also explicitly gave civil servants the right of association and granted them the right to bargain with, and to strike against, the government, provided that essential services were maintained. However, one specific article forbade civil servants to join a labour organization officially committed to a political party. Since this would apply specifically to the QFL which supported the NDP, many observers considered that the Liberal government had directed the civil servants — a substantial group of some 30,000 members — to join the CSN.

After the departure of CSN president Jean Marchand for Ottawa in 1965, where he eventually became a very influential minister in Pierre Trudeau's Liberal cabinet, the new leaders who came to power showed a much greater propensity for radical, even revolutionary viewpoints. In contrast to Marchand's charismatic and authoritarian leadership, the new president, Marcel Pépin, let the major professional federations and affiliated trade unions decide their own courses of action, even at the risk of placing the CSN in tight situations, as was the case, for example, in the 1966 general strike by hospital workers or the strike by Montreal transit workers during Expo 67. These two strikes, as well as others, were very unpopular and contributed to discrediting the image of the CSN among the population.

On the other hand, the political or ideological orientation of the CSN increasingly became defined by a group of influential radical elements within the organizations. This became particularly apparent in 1971 when the Confederal Bureau of the CSN unanimously adopted a manifesto entitled "Il n'y a plus d'avenir pour le Québec dans le système économique actuel" ("There is no longer a future for Quebec in the present economic system"). This was followed a few months later by the publication of another document entitled "Ne comptons que sur nos propres moyens" ("Let us rely only on our own means"), which presented a quasi-Marxist interpretation of capitalist imperialism in Quebec. Although this document was widely distributed (over 100,000 copies were printed), and despite the fact that a group of a dozen militants had organized consultations throughout various levels of the organization in order to have it adopted as the official political program of the CSN, the leadership did not present the document for ratification at the 1972 convention. It chose not to do so because the level of participation at consultative meetings had been very low and because it would have created considerable disagreement among some delegates.

Nonetheless, given the wide publicity which accompanied these documents, and taking into consideration the kinds of statements made by union leaders during such spectacular conflicts as the 1972 public-sector general strike, many people did believe that the CSN's official ideology was that expressed by these documents.

The Opposition of Organized Labour to the Liberal Government: 1970-1976

The early 1970s were a period conducive to radicalism and the QFL adopted a much more radical political stance in its official documents. In 1971, it ceased to officially support the NDP as the "political arm of labour" and became a strong critic of the Liberal government. Such radicalism, within both the CSN and the QFL, served to reduce rivalry between the two bodies and redirect their efforts towards policies of mutual accommodation and cooperation. This new trend was strengthened by a series of strikes where, at mass meetings sponsored by the two federations, resolutions were passed calling for concerted action in organized labour's struggles with the provincial government and private employers. The two best examples were provided by the 1971 strike at the newspaper *La Presse* where a mass rally in the streets of Montreal brought 12,000 people to the Forum, and by the 1972 "Common Front" negotiations which resulted in the most massive strike in Canadian history and jail sentences for the leaders of the three federations. The "Common Front" had been formed by the CSN, the QFL, and the teachers' organization— the Corporation des enseignants du Québec — to bargain jointly with the provincial government on behalf of more than 200,000 teachers, hospital workers, and civil servants.

One important aftermath of the growing radicalism was a serious split within the CSN. In May 1972, while President Marcel Pépin was still in jail, three members of the five-man executive council called a meeting of dissident union leaders who strongly disagreed with the ideologies expressed and tactics followed by the prevailing leadership of the CSN. One month later, the Centrale des syndicats démocratiques (CSD) was born. It drew approximately 30,000 of the 235,000 members affiliated with the CSN with most people coming from the textile, metalworking, and construction industries. On the other hand, in September of the same year, 30,000 civil servants also pulled out of the CSN but decided to remain an independent labour organization rather than to join either the QFL or the CSD. One year later another 5,000 workers in the aluminum industry also left the CSN and formed another independent organization, the Fédération des syndicats du secteur aluminium.

From late 1972 until 1976, the labour scene was very complex in Quebec since, at the same time the QFL and CSN leaders were making concerted efforts in public-sector negotiations and in official condemnation of the Liberal government, a very fierce rivalry continued to exist between affiliates of the two labour bodies in the construction industry. This competition was particularly strong at the James Bay hydroelectric project. The QFL's strong construction affiliates had been granted exclusive rights to represent James Bay workers, although this arrangement between government officials and QFL construction unions was never made public. CSN organizers, who had access to the site nonetheless, tried to sign up construction workers. In retaliation, some QFL affiliates' business agents damaged machinery, equipment, and buildings resulting in costs of over five million dollars.

A few months later, the same construction locals launched an "indexation campaign" by calling a general strike in the construction industry in order to force employers to reopen their collective agreements. The strike was obviously illegal but it received full approval from the QFL's top executives who did not want to lag behind the CSN, whose affiliates had already successfully engaged in similar actions in some public utilities such as the Montreal Urban Community Transit Commission. In addition, the construction general strike could be used to divert attention from the James Bay situation. The magnitude of the strike demonstrated the strength of QFL construction unions and deterred the government's will to proceed with an inquiry commission. However, even though some monetary gains were made by construction strikers, the government nevertheless established a commission which was presided over by Judge Robert Cliche.

Despite this harsh competition between unions in the construction industry, the QFL and CSN strongly opposed the Liberal government without, however, endorsing the PQ formally in the 1973 election. This election occurred in the aftermath of the 1972 public-sector general strike and the PQ, whose commitment in favour of the "labour cause" was clear, certainly suffered from the strong lack of popularity of the labour movement.

The landslide victory of the Liberal Party and the passage of labour legislation which was considered antiunion brought a movement of unity between the three major labour federations. In an act of solidarity with the CSN, QFL and CEQ leaders decided to boycott all consultative committees where the government tried to appoint a delegate from the CSD. The boycott also applied to any kind of formal public appearance such as conventions and television programs. Moreover, at the request of the CEQ, the three organizations agreed to engage in unity discussions. A joint committee was set up to further union solidarity and to coordinate labour struggles at the local level.

The PQ's Electoral Victory and Its Consequences for Organized Labour's Unity

Although the general conventions of the three federations agreed on the principle of labour unity and condemned certain forms of interunion rivalry, nothing concrete ensued from these unity talks. This failure reflected the interunion rivalry which prevailed in the construction industry and the fact that in the 1976 election, the QFL officially gave its support to the PQ while the CSN and the CEQ refused to do so. The electoral victory of the PQ contributed to the widening gap since the CSN and the CEQ continued to criticize the PQ, while the QFL publicly emphasized the benefits for the labour movement of dealing with a government which had a "favourable prejudice" towards the working class.

The relationship between the QFL and the PQ has nothing to do with that which prevails in most other provinces between the NDP and provincial labour federations. The QFL support of the PQ is a kind of "moral endorsement," and it was made only for the 1976 election. It is not at all sure whether it will still be given in forthcoming elections, although it was reiterated in 1981.

The similarity of ideological orientation between the CSN and CEQ led the political and technical staffs of these two organizations to undertake a project of unity between the two labour bodies. However, the respective memberships were far from sharing the same views, as can be shown from the resolutions which were adopted by both 1978 conventions, and which, although reaffirming the virtues of union solidarity, considered any formal merger as premature.

TRADE-UNION STRUCTURES AND MEMBERSHIP

The evolution of an independent and distinct labour movement in Quebec has led to a complex structure of trade-union organization in Quebec today. This structure will be examined with respect to the major central bodies.

The Quebec Federation of Labour

Numerical importance— As its other counterparts throughout Canada, the QFL is composed of members of international and national unions who are affiliated with the Canadian Labour Congress (CLC). Since the decision to affiliate with a provincial labour federation is voluntary according to the CLC's constitution, the QFL does not comprise the whole CLC membership in Quebec. The exact number of QFL members is very difficult to establish, not only because affiliation is voluntary, but also because, as is often the case with labour organizations, many locals do not declare the exact number of members when they have to pay their per capita dues.

Although the QFL's top officials claim that their organization has succeeded in affiliating approximately 80 percent of the CLC membership in Quebec, a study has revealed that, as of 1977, only about 50 percent of the 417,228 CLC union members were in locals that had paid their dues to the QFL (6, p. 14). It must be said, however, that this figure excludes some 51,800 construction workers whose locals had refused to pay their dues to the QFL for reasons that will be explained below. Since most of these locals had always been affiliated with the QFL, a more realistic view of the numerical importance of this organization should include these construction workers.

As indicated in Table 1, the CLC has always been the most important labour federation representing unionized workers in Quebec throughout the period 1956-1980. Even today, the QFL has more affiliated members than either the CSN, the CSD, or the CEQ. In fact, one of the major achievements of the QFL since the 1956 merger has been to substantially increase the number of its "voluntary" affiliates: from a mere 30 percent of the CLC membership in the 1950s, the QFL has raised its share to approximately 70 percent in the 1970s. Hence, even if the QFL is "only" a subsidiary body in its role as a provincial federation of the CLC, it is nevertheless the most important Quebec-based labour organization in numerical terms.

Special status within the CLC — The particular context of trade-union pluralism and cultural specificity in Quebec inevitably leads an organization like the QFL to behave like an independent labour body. Unlike other provincial federations which have achieved a monopoly status in their respective jurisdictions after the formation of the CLC in 1956, the QFL must also compete with three major labour organizations to obtain the allegiance of union members. This unique situation has gradually led QFL leaders to ask for additional powers and more autonomy from their parent body, the CLC. It has also led the QFL to take actions which are not allowed by the CLC constitution but which have been more or less tolerated until now.

As early as 1967, the QFL leadership developed the argument that CLC success in Quebec depended on a strong provincial federation. In practice, this meant that the CLC should recognize that the QFL was in a better position than the CLC to understand the specific needs and problems of Quebec workers. But to be successful in attracting workers to CLC unions, this organization would grant the QFL more power, autonomy, and money.

The CLC leadership was rather slow to understand this message but the QFL finally achieved its goal at the 1974 CLC convention in Vancouver where the delegates accepted the three major requests made by the Quebec delegation, namely: (a) that the QFL would henceforth assume full jurisdiction over labour-education services in Quebec, a prerogative which is exercised by the CLC in all other provinces; (b) that the CLC agrees to bargain with the QFL to permit the latter to recoup funds for services for which Quebec union members pay but from which they receive no return whatsoever because of linguistic, cultural, or political differences, such as unilingual newspapers; (c) that the CLC yields to the QFL full jurisdiction over local labour councils, which implies jurisdiction over the staff providing the appropriate services and the corresponding sums of money.

Although it took considerable time to realize these resolutions, the QFL has been able to increase its presence in most regions where it was either weak or nonexistant. This was accomplished through the hiring of additional union staff appointed to local councils and through the expansion of education services to its members.

According to the CLC constitution, a provincial federation can only affiliate local organizations that are already affiliated with national or international trade unions which in turn are affiliated with the CLC. However, in recent years, the QFL maintains among its affiliates organizations which are not members of an international trade union. Such is the case of at least four local unions in the textile industry and of a substantial group of electricians in the Fraternité interprovinciale des ouvriers en électricité (FIPOE).

When asked to justify this irregularity, QFL leaders have always publicly affirmed that the situation was only "temporary." The rationale for the QFL action was that "members of these locals were dissatisfied with the services provided by their international union; given the possibility that these workers could join the CSN or any other rival organization, the QFL keeps them within its ranks, pending their final decision either to return to their former organization or to affiliate with any other CLC member organization" [19, Chap. 3, Art. 5 (f)].

There are situations, however, which seem to be more permanent than temporary. For example, the Fédération interprovinciale des ouvriers en électricité is nothing but a rival of the International Brotherhood of Electrical Workers whose local in Quebec was, until very recently, also affiliated with the QFL. The Building Trades Department of the AFL-CIO is now pressing both the CLC and the QFL to rectify the situation of dual unions within the latter organization. It is actually withholding construction unions' dues payments to the CLC in retaliation to the QFL's tolerance of FIPOE among its affiliates. The crisis has had serious repercussions within the QFL since the leadership has decided to defy the Building Trades Department by refusing to expel FIPOE and by encouraging other construction locals to seek direct affiliation. However, a strong proportion of construction locals has decided to support the position of the Building Trades Department. Clearly it is very difficult to predict a solution that can settle this complex issue.

The Confédération des Syndicats Nationaux

The organizational structure of the CSN is like that of any other labour federation. Local trade unions are affiliated with local labour councils and "professional federations" which are the equivalent of national or international unions. These two bodies together with local trade unions send delegates to the biannual convention which elects the top senior officials. Two intermediate bodies also take care of the CSN's administration between biannual conventions: the Confederal Bureau which is made up of the top senior officials and an equal number of representatives (22) from the professional federations and local labour councils, and the Confederal Council which includes all members of the Confederal Bureau plus sixty-five representatives designated by local labour councils and fifty-three representatives from the professional federations. This latter body meets four times a year while the former meets every month.

Even though the 1976 convention has increased the representation of professional federations in the proportions described above, the structure of the CSN remains "highly political" due to the strong weight which has been given to local labour councils. It is well-known that while professional federations are more oriented toward bread-and-butter issues, local labour councils are functionally oriented toward broader political issues. Hence, the decision to adopt such a structure reflects the kind of role which the militant union members want the CSN to play in Quebec society.

Table 2

CSN Membership by Professional Federation, 1976

Professional Federation	Membership	Percent of Total
Social affairs[a]	49,193	30.5
Public service[b]	28,301	17.5
Construction	19,394	12.0
Mines, metalworking, chemical	18,814	11.7
Commerce	13,263	8.2
Pulp and paper, forest industries	12,111	7.5
Teachers	9,500	5.9
Salaried professional	6,879	4.3
Communications	1,818	1.1
Directly chartered locals	2,186	1.3
Total	161,459	100.0

SOURCE: François Delorme et Gaspar Lassoude, Aspects de la réalité syndicale québécoise *(Gouvernement du Québec: Ministère du travail et de la main-d'oeuvre, 1978), p. 34.*

NOTES: a. *Includes mainly hospital employees.*
b. *Includes mainly municipal and school-board employees.*

Since the CSN was the great beneficiary of the unionization of public-sector workers during the 1960s, it is not surprising to find that more than half of its membership is composed of such workers. According to Table 2, union members from the federations of "social affairs" workers, public servants, teachers, and salaried professionals accounted for 58 percent of the total CSN membership in 1976. Adding the commerce and communications federations yields 67.5 percent of the CSN membership working in the tertiary sector of the economy, thus indicating that this labour organization is predominantly one of white-collar workers. This is in contrast to the QFL which is predominantly blue-collar.

Contrary to the typical North American model of craft unions, the CSN does not affiliate construction workers on a trade-by-trade basis. Rather all its members in this sector, whether they are carpenters, electricians, labourers, and so on, are grouped within a single industrial-like professional federation. As discussed in Chapter 17, this type of union structure is in conformity with the legislation which regulates labour relations in the construction industry.

While the QFL has its share of problems with the Building Trades Department of the AFL-CIO, the CSN's major challenge today consists of preventing some extreme-left elements from gaining too much influence inside the organization. The new CSN president, Norbert Rodrigue, saw fit, at the 1978 convention, to publicly criticize people "who are not genuine trade union members and who are trying to divert the labour organization from its fundamental purpose" (sic). It seems that these "outside elements" are taking control of a growing number of local trade unions, and there is very little that the CSN can do about it since this organization has always respected the autonomy and "sovereignty" of local trade unions.

Despite the formal denunciation of these "active minority groups" by the CSN leadership, the ideological language used by CSN leaders has a lot in common with that of the people whom they are officially criticizing. For this reason, it is very difficult to predict if the autonomy of the CSN with respect to outside political groups will be preserved as it has always been in the past, or if on the contrary, the CSN will gradually lose its political and ideological independence. One factor, in the end, may be decisive: because of its internal problems the CSN has lost membership since the early 1970s. In the period 1970-1977, almost all union members who left one of the three major labour federations to become independent were formerly from the CSN and most of these workers came from the public sector (8, p. 30).

The Centrale des Syndicats Démocratiques

The Centrale des syndicats démocratiques was created in 1972 on the same model as the CSN. The bulk of its membership originates from three major industrial sectors: metalworking and chemical products (9,991 members), textile (8,918), and clothing (7,217). In 1976, there were also 13,862 workers who were members of directly chartered locals in commerce, construction, and medical and social services (6, p. 33).

The CSD wants to remain absolutely neutral vis-à-vis political parties. It does not profess any particular social doctrine, and its has even adopted an article in its constitution whereby it would require a referendum of the whole membership to engage the organization in a particular ideological orientation.

The Centrale de l'Enseignement du Québec

Teachers' unionization dates as far back as 1936, and the first provincial federation was formed ten years later. The Corporation des instituteurs et institutrices catholiques du Canada had a very rough time — as did most other union organizations — during the Duplessis regime. It dropped its confessional designation in 1967 and became the Corporation des enseignants du Québec (CEQ). The year 1967 also saw the first teachers' confrontation with the provincial government, which led to the first special legislation to end a wave of teachers' strikes throughout the province.

At the beginning of the 1970s, the CEQ went through a substantial ideological reorientation similar to that which occurred within the CSN. In fact, the ideology of the two unions is very similar, thus explaining the merger talks which have recently occurred. Associated with this reorientation was the transformation of the organization from a "corporation," in which membership was mandatory according to a governmental charter, and which was restricted to elementary and secondary-school teachers, into a genuine "labour" organization. This meant that after the CEQ asked the government to revoke its charter it had to seek certification from all its existing local units according to the rules provided in the Quebec Labour Code. However, by doing so, the CEQ opened its ranks to all categories of workers in the field of education, from the janitor to the classroom teacher and from the elementary to the university level. As a consequence, the CEQ became involved in representation elections for certain categories of employees alongside the CSN, the CSD, and the QFL's affiliates. Nonetheless, in 1976, elementary and secondary-school teachers still constituted 94 percent of the CEQ membership (6, p. 32).

Independent Labour Organizations

In 1978, there were 194,827 workers who were members of independent organizations (8, p. 17). This number represented 21 percent of the total union membership. Although this percentage was still lower than the Canadian figure, 25 percent for the same year (8, p. 3), it must nevertheless be considered as quite substantial given the numerous alternatives for affiliation which are offered to unionized workers. Moreover, what is more alarming from the standpoint of major labour federations is the fact that this number is increasing rapidly over time, since the percentage was 17 percent in 1976 and 15 percent in 1975 (6, p. 13).

STATE INTERVENTION AND THE EVOLUTION OF LABOUR LEGISLATION

Labour legislation in Quebec is a complex network of regulations dealing with: (a) general working conditions; (b) relationships between employers and employee organizations; (c) health and safety at the work place; and (d) vocational training and manpower policies. In these broad general terms, the legal framework of labour relations is similar to that prevailing elsewhere in Canada and in North America. However, a specific examination of each piece of legislation illustrates some unique features indicating that Quebec is a sociopolitical entity different from the rest of North America.

Historical Antecedents and State Intervention in Quebec

Quebec has borrowed from both the Canadian and American experiences but it has also drawn from European countries and, as regards public-sector bargaining, it has created its own model. Quebec initially followed the general Canadian pattern by adopting the Conciliation Act in 1901 on the model of a 1900 federal law providing for voluntary conciliation at the request of both parties. It also adopted, in 1932, a law which made conciliation mandatory in certain industries affecting the public and which postponed the right to strike during the conciliation period. This legislation was almost a carbon copy of the 1907 federal law (Loi Lemieux) which had been declared unconstitutional in 1925. Finally, when the basic statute providing for collective-bargaining rights in Quebec was enacted in 1944, it was also a replica of federal legislation, and that of other provinces.

Despite these similarities in the basic general framework, the pattern in Quebec differs from that in the rest of Canada because of two particular laws. The 1934 Collective Agreement Decrees Act gives the minister of labour the power to extend the terms of a collective agreement to all employees and employers in a given sector of the economy. A joint committee of employer and employee representatives has the responsibility of supervising the administration of the decree. This extension legislation, which finds its inspiration in France and Belgium, is mostly used in industries characterized by a large number of small employers, such as groceries, shoe manufacturers, garment production, and barber shops. Its major objective is to prevent unfair competition from nonunion employers by equalizing labour costs throughout the whole industry. There are actually some fifty decrees covering 108,000 employees in Quebec (21, p. 34). This figure does not include construction which is also covered by a decree but under separate legislation — the Construction Industry Labour Relations Act of 1968.

Another unique aspect of labour legislation is the 1924 Professional Syndicates Act which permits a group of individuals to incorporate and protect the assets of their organization. Even if this legislation has very little use today, it permitted labour organizations to be granted some form of legal protection at a time when collective bargaining had not received official sanction by public authorities. This legislation, modeled on similar legislation adopted in France in 1920, came at the request of the CTCC's leadership, despite the opposition of international unions which preferred to rely on their own strength to deal with employers.

The new Labour Code adopted in 1964 during the Quiet Revolution was considered by many observers as the most liberal piece of labour legislation in North America. However, a close examination of the provisions of the act would confirm that this statement is a gross exaggeration. In fact, what the legislation did was to consolidate many old laws into one basic statute. Practically the same principles which guided the Labour Relations Law of 1944 reappeared in the Labour Code. The procedure dealing with the settlement of industrial disputes was simplified in such a way as to suppress the mandatory arbitration process which followed the conciliation period, but the latter remained as a necessary prerequisite to the exercise of the right to strike. The really outstanding feature of the Labour Code, and what made it look extremely liberal, was the granting of the right to strike to all public employees with the exception of police and fire fighters. In this regard, Quebec was the first government in North America to allow the right to strike in the public sector. Most other jurisdictions had restrictive legislation (or court interpretations) applying to public-sector employees. A notable exception was the government of Saskatchewan which had always considered public-sector employees as identical to private-sector employees from the standpoint of labour legislation. In the next few years, Quebec was to be followed by the Canadian federal government, five provincial governments and two American states. However, this "liberal legislation" soon became outmoded, so much so that the PQ government saw fit to present major amendments in 1977 in order to catch up with the labour legislation of other provinces.

CHARACTERISTICS OF QUEBEC'S CURRENT LABOUR LEGISLATION

The Public Sector

Aside from granting public-sector employees the right to strike, the Labour Code of 1964 also included all public-sector employees, with the exception of the provincial police, under its coverage. This same administrative machinery, therefore, applies to both private- and public-sector employees, contrary to the situation prevailing at the federal level where a separate law regulates government labour relations — the Public Service Staff Relations Act — and a separate administrative agency — the Public Service Staff Relations Board — supervises the legislation.

In the Quebec Labour Code, the major restrictions pertaining to the public sector are those of Article III, and those added in the 1977 modifications of the legislation and which are limited to services where the government is a direct party in negotiations, namely the civil service, education (with the exclusion of universities), and social affairs.

The original Article III, which still applies to all public services where the provincial government is not a party in negotiations, stipulates that: (a) strikes are prohibited unless the association of employees concerned has acquired the right to strike and has given at least eight days' prior written notice to the minister of labour of the time when it intends to have recourse to a strike; (b) whenever the lieutenant-governor-in-council (the provincial cabinet) thinks a threatened or actual strike in a public service endangers the public health or safety, he may appoint a board of inquiry to inquire into the dispute (although this board must confine itself to ascertaining the facts and cannot make any recommendation whatsoever); (c) upon the petition of the attorney general after the appointment of the board of inquiry, a judge of the Superior Court, if he finds that the strike imperils the public health or safety, may grant an injunction to prevent or terminate the strike; (d) this injunction must cease not later than twenty days after the end of the period of sixty days within which the board of inquiry must file its report; and (e) educational services, as well as any other services the loss of which may imperil health or safety, are covered by this section.

The new amendments of 1977 were introduced after the PQ had set up an Inquiry Commission (5) to examine the whole system of collective bargaining in public services where the provincial government is a party of interest. The government drew heavily, but not exclusively, on the recommendations of the commission to enact two pieces of legislation, one dealing with collective-bargaining structure (Bill 55), and the other with the process of bargaining (Bill 59). This latter legislation was thereafter included in the Labour Code as a separate chapter. It deals with issues such as representation elections, public information (where a special panel of five to seven members is created with the mandate to report to the public the respective bargaining positions of the parties), the distribution of bargaining matters between local and provincial levels, the calendar of negotiations, and essential services (where another panel is established to inform the public of the situation prevailing in cases of work stoppages in health institutions).

This last issue of essential services in health-care facilities was obviously the most delicate and the most controversial, since the government was often accused of having handed the unions the power to unilaterally determine the number of employees that should be considered "essential" on a particular work site. In fact, Article 111.10 stipulates that the parties at the local level must bargain over the number of employees to be designated as essential, and this agreement must be sent to the panel referred to above. Should the parties disagree, the same article allows the local union to transmit to the employer and to the panel its own list of designated employees 180 days prior to the expiration of the collective agreement. In the event of a strike, which may occur at the termination of the contract as long as a two-day written notice has been sent to the minister and to the other party, the local union's list should prevail. However, a safety valve is provided in Article 111.12 since the lieutenant-governor-in-council can suspend the right to strike for a period not exceeding thirty days if such actual or threatened strike imperils the public health or safety.

The Civil Service Act regulates the civil service but clearly affirms the jurisdiction of the Labour Code over collective bargaining in the civil service. However, as is often the case in other jurisdictions, the scope of bargaining is more restricted than in other areas of employment since such items as classification schedules, pension plans, and the "merit principle" are explicitly excluded from collective negotiations.

The Labour Court

Another original aspect of Quebec's labour legislation has to do with its administrative machinery. A 1969 amendment to the Labour Code replaced the traditional Labour Relations Board by a three-tier system of "investigator," "investigation commissioner," and "chief investigation commissioner" to deal with certification matters and unfair labour practices. The 1977 amendments of the Labour Code changed these titles to "certification agent," "labour commissioner," and "general labour commissioner."

On top of this three-tier system rests a Labour Court which, in addition to the other matters that are declared by law to be within its competence, shall have jurisdiction, to the exclusion of any other court, to hear and decide: (a) appeals regarding any decision of a labour commissioner who closes a case, and any decision of the general labour commissioner; and (b) cases of first instance in any penal prosecution brought under the Labour Code.

The eleven members of the Labour Court are appointed by the lieutenant-governor-in council from among the judges of the provincial court, after consultation with the General Council of the Bar of the Province of Quebec and the Advisory Council on Labour and Manpower. The court sitting in appeal may confirm, amend, or quash any decision referred to it and render the decision which, in its opinion, should have been rendered in the first place. Every decision rendered by the court other than in penal matters shall be without appeal. The court and each of its members sitting in penal matters shall have the same powers as one or more justices of the peace.

The Labour Court was created, in part, to act as a specialized tribunal to handle the appeals of decisions of labour commissioners. Since this judicial body would be composed of persons with expertise in human and labour relations, the hope was for a substantial reduction of civil suits. However, experience has shown that such cases are still very frequent, even more so than in other provinces which use a less sophisticated system of labour-relations boards to administer their labour legislation.

The Suppression of "Bona Fide" Recognized Associations

The 1969 amendments of the Labour Code which introduced the Labour Court also contained a rather unique provision, at least in Canada, in that it no longer permitted "bona fide" associations recognized by employers to conclude valid collective agreements. Only "certified" associations can now legally bargain on behalf of a group of employees in Quebec. That is, voluntary recognition by the employer of the union is no longer permitted.

The original intent in imposing such a restriction was to prevent the formation of company unions. However, an important side effect of this decision was to create legal difficulties for associations of professionals or supervisors which had been entering into genuine collective agreements with their employers for many years. Recognizing this problem, the government immediately enacted special legislation to validate collective agreements which were covering engineers for the City of Montreal and Hydro-Quebec (Bill 36). Nonetheless, the consequence of this decision was to halt the development of trade unionism among professionals and supervisors which had started with some success during the 1960s.

Voluntary Conciliation

The 1977 amendments of the Labour Code, introduced by the new PQ government in the form of Bill 45, resulted in voluntary conciliation. This was designed to enhance the collective-bargaining process, since it was admitted by all interested parties that the previous mandatory scheme was just a technical formality, prior to the exercising of the right to strike, that deprived the conciliation intervention of its usefulness. Voluntary conciliation permits a trade union to obtain the right to strike or the employer the right to use a lockout immediately at the expiration of the collective agreement. At any time during negotiations, one party can ask for conciliation and the minister of labour must, upon such request, designate a conciliation officer. On the other hand, the minister can also appoint a conciliator, without one being requested.

By adopting the 1977 amendment, the Quebec government completely erased any form of restriction on the right to strike in the private sector. It went back to the original philosophy of the American Wagner Act, rather than relying on compulsory conciliation and arbitration procedures that had been introduced on the model of British and Australian legislation.

Representation Elections and First Collective Agreements

The liberality of Quebec's legislation is exhibited by the fact that the 1977 amendments contained in Bill 45 permit certification agents to hold representation elections if the employee association can demonstrate that it represents between 35 to 50 percent of the proposed bargaining unit. Moreover, the certification agent can grant certification even if there is still disagreement as to the inclusion or exclusion of some employees within the bargaining unit. In such a case, the general labour commissioner appoints a labour commissioner to settle the issue but such litigation cannot prevent the parties from starting to negotiate.

In addition to this last provision, which was introduced to prevent employers from using delaying tactics that thwarted unionization, the legislation, in the case of a first collective-bargaining relationship, stipulates that one party can ask the minister of labour to appoint an arbitration panel if conciliation has failed to produce positive results. This arbitration panel, if it finds that at least one of the parties has not bargained in good faith, can issue a binding award that determines the content

Table 3

**Requests to Appoint Arbitration Panels
in Cases of First Collective Agreements
(February 1978 to December 1979 inclusive)**

Outcome of Request	1978	1979
Conflicts settled before the award	11	14
Awards rendered	11	7
Certifications canceled	11	1
Cases under study by the minister	5	10
Cases suspended	4	1
Requests rejected by the minister	3	0
Requests withdrawn	2	2
Cases pending before an arbitration panel	7	10
Total	54	45

SOURCE: Michelle Girard, "L'arbitrage des premières conventions collectives," Le Marché du travail *(juillet 1980), p. 43.*

of the collective agreement. Such an agreement should be for a period of not less than one year and not more than two years.

Table 3 gives a breakdown of the various outcomes of the requests for arbitration of a first collective agreement.

The following conclusions can be drawn from these figures. First, arbitration panels, which must try to reach an agreement between the parties before rendering their awards, have been successful in achieving this goal in one case out of four (twenty-five out of ninety-nine). Second, although twelve certifications have been canceled, these were probably situations where an employee association was just about to die out and tried to use the new provisions of the law as a last resort, since eleven of these cases occurred in 1978 and only one in 1979. Third, very few requests have been formally rejected by the minister of labour, in fact only three, but this figure must be interpreted keeping in mind the fifteen cases which were still under study as of December 31, 1979. In these instances, the minister of labour has decided not to appoint arbitration panels even if he did not formally reject the requests. We can make the hypothesis that conciliation was still under way or that the requesting party was not in a position to seek further remedial procedures under the legislation. Finally, only eighteen awards were rendered, including two cases where the arbitration panels decided not to impose a collective agreement because the requesting party had not proved that it had bargained in sufficient good faith. This small number of arbitration awards, which represents less than 1 percent of the first collective agreements signed during the period covered by the study, seems to indicate that the parties prefer to reach an agreement on their own rather than have a third party impose one upon them.

Agency Shop and Antistrikebreaking Provisions

The 1977 amendments (Bill 45) of the Labour Code also resulted in a legislated agency shop and in antistrikebreaking provisions, two features that are unique in Canada. Article 47 of the Labour Code legislated the agency shop by requiring that all employees within a bargaining unit pay a sum equivalent to the union dues whether they are members of the union or not. This type of provision is often found in collective agreements, but it was the first time in North America that a government has made it compulsory for all employers whose workers are unionized.

The most controversial issue of the 1977 amendments introduced by Bill 45 was certainly its antistrikebreaking provisions. According to Article 109.1, employers cannot use the services of other persons to do the work usually done by their own employees if the latter are in a situation of legal strike or lockout, in the following circumstances: (a) if the "new" employees have been hired in the period between the date when the negotiations started and when the strike or lockout ended; (b) if these employees are already part of the bargaining unit affected by the interruption of work, unless an agreement between the parties or a special court order or legislative action has decided otherwise; or (c) if these employees are already in the employ of the same employer in another plant. Moreover, the employer cannot use members of the struck bargaining unit in any other of its establishments not affected by the work stoppage. However, a paragraph tending to soften these rather harsh restrictions says that nothing should prevent employers from taking the necessary measures to avoid the destruction or serious deterioration of their movable and immovable property.

Upon application, the minister may dispatch an investigator to ascertain whether or not Section 109.1 is being complied with and, according to Article 142.1 of the Labour Code, any person who contravenes Section 109.1 is guilty of an offence and is liable to a fine of not more than 1,000 dollars for every day or part of a day during which the offence continues. There is nothing in the law which specifies that the report of the investigator should be used as prima facie evidence for further procedures. In practice, one of the following tends to happen: the union may file a complaint to the Labour Court for the execution of article 142.1; it may also seek injunctive relief from the Superior Court to prevent the employer from using strikebreakers; or it may use both recourses simultaneously. On most of these occasions, however, the requests filed by the unions refer to the report of the investigator appointed by the minister of labour.

A summary compilation made by the Department of Labour and Manpower of seventy-eight investigatory reports as of April 1980 produced the following results: in fourteen cases, the conflict was settled prior to the time when the report was submitted in writing to the minister of labour; in twenty-nine cases, the investigators concluded that no strikebreakers were used by employers; and in thirty-five cases they came to the opposite conclusion. It is interesting to note the major arguments developed by investigators. For instance, they usually consider that the employer is not using strikebreakers if the persons doing the work of regular employees are supervisory personnel even if these persons come from another establishment owned by the same employer. They have also accepted some form of subcontracting but only if the company doing the work is legally related to the struck plant. On the other hand, they have considered subcontracting as a violation of the law when there is no legal partnership between the two companies.

This last issue is very controversial because the courts have started to develop an interpretation which is contrary to the one mentioned above. In the few cases where the Superior Court was asked by the union to grant an injunction to stop an employer from subcontracting, most judges have developed the rationale that the employer was entitled to do so since article 109.1 contemplated only "physical persons" and not "legal persons" like corporations.[1] This line of thought was also accepted by a judge from the Labour Court who refused to fine an employer according to the provisions of article 142.1 for the same reason.[2]

Such a restrictive interpretation of the antistrikebreaking provisions of the law — if it is accepted as jurisprudence — will certainly reduce the impact which the legislators originally contemplated. It is, however, too soon to make a final judgment on the matter since there are some instances where the Labor Court has fined an employer[3] and the Superior Court has granted injunctive relief.[4]

1. *Syndicat des imprimeurs de Thetford-Mines (CSN) et al.* c. Jos T. Beaudoin ltée et al. (District de Megantic, dossier no. 235-05-000278-78); *Travailleurs unis du pétrole, local 2* c. *Shell Canada ltée* (District de Montréal, dossier no. 500-05-002335-808); *Union internationale des employés professionels et de bureau, local 57* c. *Drummond Business Forms* (District de Drummond, dossier no. 405-05-000370-79).

2. *Gilees Ouellet* c. *Zeller's ltée,* Tribunal du travail, 29 septembre 1980, dossier no. 700-28-000001-806.

3. *Raymond Charbonneau (Travailleurs unis du pétrole, local 1)* c. *Shell Canada ltée,* Tribunal du travail, 30 mai 1980, dossier no. 500-28-000064-808.

4. *Métallurgistes unis d'Amérique, syndicat local 6833 (FTQ)* c. *Société d'énergie de la Baie James* (district de Montréal, dossier no. 05-012-371-793), 2 août 1979.

Conclusion on Labour Legislation

Generally speaking, the philosophy of the Quebec Labour Code, except for its agency shop and antistrikebreaking provisions, follows the major principles of all collective-bargaining statutes in Canada. What does distinguish Quebec's labour legislation, however, is the frequent intervention of the state through the imposition of "special legislative frameworks" for certain groups of employees. This is illustrated by the decree system, the separate labour-relations legislation for construction, the special bargaining structure for the public sector and the separate regime of labour relations for provincial police.

Some observers question this habit of governing "by exception," a situation which creates confusion as a result of the conflicting interpretations of various statutes. Many have even asked for the establishment of a special inquiry commission on labour relations, but every government has refused to undertake such an overall revision of industrial-relations practices in Quebec.

COLLECTIVE-BARGAINING STRUCTURES

In construction and in the public sector, the structure of collective bargaining is much more centralized in Quebec than elsewhere in Canada or the United States. However, except for these two particular sectors, the overall picture of collective-bargaining structures in Quebec seems to be in conformity with that existing in the rest of North America. This conclusion is illustrated in Table 4. The most frequent bargaining situation involves one employer in one plant dealing with one local trade union. This is the case in 91.1 percent of the collective agreements, although these agreements cover only 43.9 percent of the total number of employees. This substantial difference can be explained largely by the impact of provincial negotiations in the public sectors of education and social affairs (categories 8 and 9) where less than one percent of the collective agreements cover 35.9 percent of employees. For the private sector, however, decentralized bargaining prevails.

The most important exceptions to this decentralized pattern of bargaining are: textiles, where one union holding many certifications is dealing with different employers (category 6 in Table 4); retail food, where one union also holding many certifications is bargaining with a single multiplant employer (category 4 in Table 4); and automobile sales, where collective bargaining takes place between an association of employers and different local unions (category 7 in Table 4).

A labour lobby (mostly from the QFL) currently is attempting to convince the government to amend the Labour Code in such a way as to facilitate multiplant or multiemployer certification. However, strong opposition has originated from the most representative employers' associations such as the Conseil du patronat du Québec and the Centre des dirigeants d'entreprises. The government has refused to commit itself to centralized bargaining even though this was part of its electoral platform in 1976.

STRIKES AND LOCKOUTS

As Table 5 indicates, strike activity is unusually high in years such as 1972, 1976, and 1979; these were years when there were considerable public-sector negotiations

Table 4

**Distribution of Collective Agreements and Employees Covered
According to the Type of Bargaining Structures[a], October 1980**

Certification Identification	Collective Agreements		Employees Covered	
	Number	Percent	Number	Percent
1. One employer, one plant, one union, one certification	3,681	91.1	301,441	43.9
2. One employer, one plant, more than one union, more than one certification	3	[b]	563	—
3. One employer, more than one plant, one union, one certification	124	3.0	75,545	11.0
4. One employer, more than one plant, one union, more than one certification	61	1.5	13,606	1.9
5. More than one employer, one plant, one union, more than one certification	5	—	1,369	—
6. More than one employer, more than one plant, one union, more than one certification	78	1.9	35,581	5.2
7. More than one employer, more than one plant, more than one union, more than one certification	7	—	2,014	—
8. Provincial collective agreements in education	19	—	111,751	16.3
9. Provincial collective agreements in social affairs	16	—	134,192	19.6
10. Others	46	1.1	9,978	1.5
Total	4,040	100.0	686,040	100.0

SOURCE: Data provided by the Department of Labour and Manpower, Quebec, October 23, 1980.

NOTES: a. *The Construction Industry Decree is* excluded *from these data.*
b. *Indicates less than 1 percent.*

involving the provincial government. The sudden increase in the number of strikes in 1974 and 1975 reflects the battles for indexation fought by many unions as a result of the substantial increase in the rate of inflation which accompanied the abrupt rise in the price of oil. This phenomenon was not peculiar to Quebec but was felt throughout Canada.

Statistics provided by the Department of Labour and Manpower for the year 1979 also indicate other interesting patterns of strike activity. Strikes and lockouts are heavily influenced by a few major industrial disputes; of the 384 strikes and lockouts which started in 1979, the 13 most important ones account for two-thirds of man-days lost. The average duration of work stoppages was 60.2 days in the private sector, and 27.3 days in the public sector. There seems to be a negative relationship between the size of the bargaining unit and the duration of strikes. Most work stoppages are relatively brief, with a little less than 50 percent of the strikes and

Table 5

Strikes and Lockouts in Quebec, 1966-1979

Year	Number	Workers Involved	Average Size[a]	Man-Days Lost	Percent of Working Time Lost
1966	137	90,984	664	2,175,417	0.50
1967	143	145,452	1,017	1,653,370	0.37
1968	128	26,552	207	1,113,906	0.25
1969	141	103,235	732	1,296,639	0.28
1970	126	73,189	581	1,490,690	0.32
1971	134	48,747	364	615,671	0.13
1972	147	352,130	2,395	3,480,144	0.71
1973	199	74,372	374	1,810,343	0.34
1974	390	190,277	488	2,690,483	0.29
1975	362	185,765	513	3,555,558	0.62
1976	315	607,818	1,930	6,583,488	1.15
1977	299	61,466	206	1,433,421	0.24
1978	354	126,026	356	1,869,461	0.33
1979	384	199,714	520	3,658,886	0.60

SOURCES: For 1966 to 1976: François Delorme, Gaspar Lassonde, et Lucie Tremblay, Grèves et lock-out au Québec: un aperçu de leur situation *(Gouvernement du Québec: Ministère du travail et de la main-d'oeuvre), pp. 24-25; for 1977 to 1979: Gouvernement du Québec, Ministère du travail et la main-d'oeuvre,* Grèves et lock-out au Québec: 1979 *(Gouvernement du Québec: Ministère du travail et la main-d'oeuvre), Table II.*

NOTES: a. *Calculated by dividing the total number of workers involved by the number of strikes.*

lockouts covering 70 percent of the employees involved lasting 14 days or less (11, pp. 3-4). Finally, most industrial conflicts (77 percent) are categorized as strikes, compared to lockouts (16 percent) or "strikes and lockouts" (7 percent). Although there are relatively few strikes with lockouts, those that occur tend to involve large numbers of workers — an average of 1,082 compared to 547 under strikes and 111 under lockouts (11, pp. 3-4).

THE CONSTRUCTION INDUSTRY

Bargaining Structure

The structure of collective bargaining in the Quebec construction industry is unique in North America. Its legal framework dates as far back as 1934 since construction was one of the industrial sectors where the Collective Agreement Decrees Act applied. Collective bargaining occurred on a multitrade basis at the regional level and the minister of labour would extend, by decree, the terms of the collective agreement to all employers in a given geographical area. Until 1970, there were fifteen decrees throughout the province. Some trade unions would bargain individually in a number of regions and obtain additional advantages which were not provided in the decree, but these situations were rather exceptional.

This system was in force until 1968 when the government imposed a new legal framework, the Construction Industry Labour Relations Act (Bill 290). The legislation retained the multitrade bargaining and the extension principles of the old decree system, but it established a compulsory industry-wide structure of bargaining through bargaining agents designated by law. One purpose of the act was to reduce the fierce rivalry between locals of international unions affiliated with the QFL and the regional associations affiliated with the CSN; therefore, traditional trade-union certification under the Labour Code was eliminated and a system of representative associations was introduced. Although the original legislation was designed to permit collective bargaining either on a regional or a provincial basis, the first negotiations after the expiration of the old decrees were conducted on a provincial basis and numerous subsequent legislative amendments reinforced centralized bargaining in the industry.

Union and Employer Associations

There are some forty local unions representing twenty-three different trades affiliated with international organizations whose jurisdictions may cover a city, a region, or the whole province. These trade unions have always been (until recently) affiliated with the QFL. The Conseil provincial des métiers de la construction (Provincial Council of Construction Trades), more frequently called QFL-construction, is the official representative for all construction trades outside as well as inside the QFL. It sponsors organizational campaigns against rival unions in the industry and acts as a lobbyist to the provincial government. As with similar bodies in other jurisdictions, it holds a charter from the AFL-CIO's Building Trades Department. Contrary to this typical organizational pattern, CSN and CSD construction workers are grouped into a single multitrade federation. The CSN and CSD organizations represent, respectively, 24 and 7 percent of organized construction workers in Quebec, compared to 68 percent for the QFL.

On the employer side, legislation adopted in 1975 (Bill 47) provided for a single contractors' association — l'Association des entrepreneurs en construction du Québec (The Association of Building Contractors of Quebec, or ABCQ). The legislation, which first stipulated that all contractors had to affiliate directly to ABCQ, was amended in 1978 to allow affiliation on the basis of employer groups which already represented the three main sectors of the industry (industrial and commercial, residential, road building and engineering), and two trade associations (electricians and pipe mechanics).

On the employers' side the ABCQ is designated as the sole bargaining agent for all contractors. However, on the union side, the legislation has tried to reconcile the basic majority-rule principle (which requires exclusive jurisdiction under the Labour Code) with the reality of pluralism which has always prevailed in the construction industry. To do so, the legislation stipulates that the most representative associations can come to an agreement which will be extended by decree to the whole industry. However, any association which represents more than 15 percent of the workers in the industry can participate in the discussions at the bargaining table.

The severe internal conflict which has just emerged within QFL-construction as a result of the refusal of the QFL leadership to expel "dual" unions and which has led the Building Trades Department to withhold the construction trade unions' per capita payments to the CLC, will probably alter the representativeness of the bargaining agent on the union side. The QFL-construction leadership has lined up on the side of the Building Trades and against the top leadership of the QFL who now recommends that the local trade unions disaffiliate from QFL-construction and join a new organization, the Conseil Québécois des métiers de la construction (Quebec Council of Construction Trades). However, this new union body has no legal existence from the standpoint of the Construction Labour Relations Act since this legislation explicitly recognizes the Provincial Council of Construction Trades as the official bargaining representative. That is why the QFL leadership has asked the government to amend the Construction Labour Relations Act in order to permit the recognition of the new Quebec Council of Construction Trades.[5]

The Quebec Construction Board

Under the decree system, the parties which have negotiated the collective agreement also have the responsibility for supervising its administration through a joint committee. When the new Construction Labour Relations Act was passed in 1968, the fifteen or so joint committees were replaced by a single provincial body — the Quebec Construction Commission (QCC). The principle of parity between employers and employees was maintained and representatives of all interested parties composed the new administrative machinery.

The justification for this administrative structure rests on the idea that the parties which have negotiated the agreement are in a better position than anybody else to supervise its application. This may be true in principle but, in practice, some very important problems can arise. For example, the members of a joint committee are in a conflict of interest when they have to take action against competitors who have violated the decree. The Cliche Commission was able to demonstrate several cases of favouritism in the administration of the QCC. In addition, the CSN began boycotting the QCC. For these reasons, in the aftermath of the Cliche Report, the government enacted legislation (Bill 47) which, among other things, replaced the QCC by a new body independent of employers and employees — the Quebec Construction Board.

The QCB possesses the same powers and exercises the same functions as the QCC including: inspecting the records and construction sites of employers to make sure that the decree has not been violated; providing salaries which were not paid at the decreed rate; making regulations for the administration of the Construction Labour Relations Act and prosecuting parties that default; and financing itself through a deduction of one-half of 1 percent of both construction workers' salaries and employers' payrolls. The major difference between the new QCB and the previous QCC is that QCB administrators are five independent members appointed by the lieutenant-governor-in-council for a period of five years.

Job Security and Hiring Practices

One of the most important characteristics of the construction industry is the occasional nature of employment. Many employees do not work with the same employer on a regular basis, their work is often seasonal, and they have to move from one construction site to another. That is why construction workers are less closely

---

5. The government answered this request by special legislation which ordered that a vote be taken among QFL construction affiliates. The results were the following: 70 percent were in favour of the new organization and 30 percent showed their preference for international affiliation.

related to their employers than they are to the industry in general and to their trade union, which is generally the major source of employment through its hiring hall. In addition, a substantial portion of construction workers is composed of "marginal" employees who are sporadically driven into the industry to get supplemental income and who provide employers with additional labour in certain periods. As a result of this competition from marginal workers, regular workers are often deprived of jobs which they could have otherwise obtained. If we add the fierce competition which exists between rival unions, it is not surprising that a permanent feeling of job insecurity has always existed among this work force.

The James Bay incident was the obvious pretext for the establishment of a Commission of Inquiry (the Cliche Commission) on certain illegal practices in the industry, but most observers considered the creation of this Commission as a good opportunity to examine all aspects of labour relations in construction. After all, the record of collective bargaining had not been enviable, since both the 1970 and 1973 negotiations ended in a deadlock, with the government unilaterally imposing the terms of the decree on the parties in 1970, and enacting special legislation in 1973 (Bill 9) to overrule the veto exercised by CSN-construction on the proposed agreement reached by the majority QFL-construction unions and employers' associations.

The commission held public hearings, received briefs from all interested parties, and sponsored specific studies from specialists in the field. Out of these testimonies came the conclusion that the chronic situation of job insecurity was probably the most important cause of labour-relations problems in the industry. In order to improve this situation, the commission made some recommendations which can certainly be considered as unorthodox (not to say revolutionary) from the standpoint of North American industrial-relations practices. These recommendations can be summarized in the following principles. First, trade-union hiring halls would be replaced by a single centralized placement service under the direct control of a new independent administrative machinery — the Quebec Construction Board. The board would be entitled to issue work permits to "professional" construction workers rather than to "marginal" workers. Second, a system of regional priority would be enforced to give construction workers in a specific area priority over outsiders. Finally, a system of income security, modeled on that of the longshoring industry, would be established.

The Liberal government of the time received the Cliche Report circumspectly since the latter had unveiled dubious relationships between the Liberal Party organization and some union organizers who seemed to have closer links with organized crime than with the labour movement. The government nevertheless put into legislation many of the commission's recommendations, including the creation of the QCB and a single employers' association — the ABCQ. However, on the delicate question of job security and hiring practices, the government did not commit itself but preferred to "pass the buck" to the QCB by giving it the task of making appropriate regulations on hiring.

The proposed regulations were submitted to the minister of labour and manpower in June 1976, and they were received rather coldly. It is impossible to predict what the Liberal government would have done with them because it was replaced by the Parti Québécois after the election of November 1976. The change of government, and the later replacement of the first PQ minister of labour and manpower after eight months in office, brought considerable delay. However, the regulations were finally adopted in September 1977, becoming effective on July 1, 1978.

These regulations retained most of the basic principles established in the Cliche Commission's recommendations except that they did not abolish trade-union hiring halls and did not mention anything specific about income security. Their application after two years, nevertheless, has enabled the achievement of two of the commission's major objectives. Violence which accompanied union rivalry for potential members has been eliminated, and construction jobs have been restricted to "professional" construction workers. This last outcome is attested to by the fact that while 250,000 individuals had worked at least one hour in the construction industry in 1974, this number was reduced to 120,000 in 1979. In addition, in 1979, the average income of construction workers was raised by 12 percent over the previous year despite the substantial decrease of activities in this industry.

The regulations on hiring are as follows. Every construction worker must be a member of a trade union. A worker who wants to change union allegiance can do so every three years, six months before negotiations for the renewal of the decree. A worker must hold a work permit — the key to the system — issued by the QCB. There are two basic types of permits. The "A" permit is issued to every person who has worked at least 1,000 hours in the construction industry in the last two years, or 5,000 hours in the last five years. An "A" permit is also issued to a person who has reached the age of fifty and who has worked at least 2,500 hours in the last five years. In order to maintain an "A" permit, a person must have worked at least 100 hours in the construction industry in each of the five years preceding the date of renewal of the permit. This provision allows an individual who has been ill or injured for a period of time to remain in good standing. A "temporary" permit is issued to a worker who cannot qualify for an "A" permit, but who is working in the industry at the date of the renewal of the permit. The QCB can issue, on request, a temporary permit to any person who has been offered a job by an employer registered with the QCB, provided that there is no worker holding an "A" permit available in the same trade or for the same job. In addition, a "special" permit is issued in certain situations where there is no employee already holding a work permit, and there is also an "apprentice" permit.

Employers must always respect regional priority, whether they hire at the gate, through a trade-union hiring hall, through the QCB, or through a private agency. Every worker has a right to appeal a decision concerning the work permit to a neutral "hiring commissioner" from outside the QCB. The QCB regulations did not abolish trade-union hiring halls but did submit them, as any other private hiring agency, to a code of ethics which proscribes a series of discriminatory or otherwise illegal practices.

Even if industrial conflict has not dissipated and additional problems have been created as a result of the internal conflict within the QFL, the new regulations on hiring have had a positive effect on the crucial issue of job insecurity, and competition over potential union members has been conducted in a more democratic and less violent fashion. In its totality, the record of labour relations in construction is definitely better than it was five or ten years ago.

THE PUBLIC SECTOR

Another unique feature of labour relations in Quebec involves its particular collective-bargaining practices in sectors where the provincial government is directly or indirectly involved. Contrary to the situation in construction where a separate legislative framework regulates labour relations, the public sector is regulated by both the general labour legislation and by Bill 55 which determines the structure and scope of bargaining in three important sectors — education, social affairs, and quasi-governmental corporations such as Hydro-Quebec and the Quebec Liquor Board.

Bargaining Structures

There are approximately 340,000 public employees whose compensation and conditions of work are determined almost simultaneously every three or four years. These workers represent 13 percent of the Quebec labour force and, as of June 30, 1978, their total wage and fringe benefits accounted for approximately half of the province's budget.

In the civil service where the government is the direct employer, there are eight bargaining units. The most important ones are those of white-collar civil servants (28,875 members), blue-collar workers (11,000 members), and professionals (6,500 members), the first two being represented by the same union — the Syndicat des fonctionnaires provinciaux du Québec.

In social affairs, even though there exists some 680 different certifications for general (white- and blue-collar) employees, 240 certifications for nurses, and 417 certifications for other professionals and technicians, there are only nine formal bargaining units according to Bill 55. The CSN represents 65,000 out of 95,000 general employees and the QFL, 24,000. Nurses are mostly represented by an independent organization — the Fédération des syndicats professionnels d'infirmières et d'infirmiers du Québec — which claims 14,000 members. However, two other independent organizations also exist — the Fédération québécoise des infirmières et infirmiers and the United Nurses of Montreal — with approximately 5,000 members each.

In education (outside the university system), certifications are also issued on a local basis and the CEQ represents 198 groups of primary- and secondary-school teachers (65,000 members) while the Provincial Association of Protestant Teachers represents 27 (7,600 members), and the Provincial Association of Catholic Teachers represents 20 (3,900 members). At the collegiate level, the CSN represents 5,800 teachers and the CEQ 600. Certifications are also issued for nonteaching professionals and for clerical employees in both the school-board and collegiate systems, with the CSN being the most important organization in these sectors. As in social affairs, the number of bargaining units in education is considerably less than the number of certifications. Specifically, there are only 20 units, usually one for each occupational category and each labor organization mentioned above.

As regards quasi-governmental corporations, the QFL, through the Canadian Union of Public Employees, represents the 12,000 employees of Hydro-Quebec while the 2,600 workers of the Quebec Liquor Board are represented by an independent organization. The 4,000 members of the Provincial Police Department have a special legislative framework which will not be discussed here.

Bill 55 explicitly established the role of the government at the various bargaining tables, and it also determines the commanding position of the Treasury Board which must approve the wage policy of every public employer contemplated in the legislation. For all intents and purposes, the respective ministers of education and social affairs are coemployers with the appropriate employers' associations such as the Quebec Catholic Federation of School Boards and the Quebec Hospitals Association. Although the government is not directly involved in negotiations of quasi-public bodies such as Hydro-Quebec or the Quebec Liquor Board, the Treasury Board must, nevertheless, approve the latter's wage policy. Major provisions of collective agreements are bargained at the provincial level but local or regional negotiations on other issues such as individual teacher workload come after the provincial negotiations.

Despite the absence of legal prescriptions to this effect, a very important informal bargaining structure has existed since 1972 when the various labour organizations decided to present a "Common Front" to the government. A great deal of the unions' strategy during these negotiations relied on their concerted efforts to force the government to bargain key issues, such as wage policy, job security, and pension plans, at a single centralized bargaining table. Although the Liberal government of Prime Minister Bourassa originally refused the idea, it finally yielded to the Common Front demand. Since then, every bargaining round has been characterized by these centralized discussions which are always concomitant to the formal sectoral bargaining (centralized bargaining that goes on in each separate element of the public sector).

The Dynamics of Bargaining

Even if generalizations tend to be hazardous, we can say that each of the three bargaining rounds which occurred since 1972 comprised the following elements. First, the Common Front was always able to get a strike mandate from its members. In 1972, there was an eleven-day general strike which ended after special legislation was enacted and which was followed by the jailing of the leaders of the Common Front for contempt of court. In 1975-76, civil servants who had left the Common Front and disaffiliated from the CSN settled their collective agreement with the government before the Common Front, to prove to their members that they could get a good deal without resorting to strike action. But it turned out that the Common Front got an even better deal, although once again after special legislative interventions were taken in both the fields of education and social affairs. In 1978-79, civil servants and nurses, whose contracts expired one year before those of the Common Front, resorted to partial strikes and the government retaliated with partial lockouts against some civil servants. However, these negotiations were not terminated before the Common Front got its strike mandate, and a general strike was enjoined through special legislation (Bill 62).

Secondly, there has always been some type of civil disobedience by union members who have either not respected injunctions, as in 1972, or simply challenged special back-to-work legislation, as was the case in 1979 when CSN union members in social affairs refused to go back to work after the enactment of Bill 62. It was during this period of civil disobedience, however, that a settlement was finally reached, and the government did not sue the union leaders who had broken the law.

Thirdly, sectoral bargaining has always been a lengthy process and the composition of the employer team at the bargaining table is largely responsible for this situation. The employer side consists of two equal partners — the government and the appropriate employers' association — each having formal veto powers. In practice, however, bargaining deadlocks can only be resolved when the Treasury Board gives its consent. But even then, after the government representatives have the mandate to accept a specific compromise, they have to convince their partners at the bargaining table, a task which is not always easy since their partners are often elected officials such as school-board commissioners.

Finally, after an agreement has been reached at the sectoral level, local or regional negotiations must start, and the possibility of further disruption of public services always persists. For example, strikes over local bargaining which prevented schools in the Three Rivers region from opening in September 1980 resulted in back-to-work legislation (Bill 113).

Some Prospects

Despite considerable improvements in the wages and working conditions in the public sector, the Common Front has been plagued with internal divisions. Civil servants, professional employees of the government, Hydro-Quebec workers, Quebec Liquor Board employees, and Catholic School Teachers, who were part of the 1972 Common Front, are now bargaining on their own. The 1975 Common Front took a long time getting under way because of the rivalry between the CSN and the QFL in the construction industry. The 1979 experience saw the QFL publicly criticize the CSN's decision not to respect Bill 62. Nonetheless, from the standpoint of union strategy, the Common Front formula has been sufficiently successful to be unlikely to be abandoned.

On the other hand, the constant use of the strike weapon, in such vital sectors as hospitals, is generating a backlash of public opinion against public-sector unions. The government is under pressure to act because the opposition is becoming more and more inclined to recommend the abolition of the right to strike in this sector.

CONCLUDING OBSERVATIONS

In the near future, the main issues in collective bargaining in Quebec will probably revolve around three themes: access to trade unionism; the possibility of an autonomous labour movement in Quebec; and the public consequences of collective bargaining.

Access to Trade Unionism

In Quebec, approximately 35 percent of the paid work force is unionized. In the private sector, however, only slightly more than 20 percent of paid workers are unionized, a figure that is comparable to the Canadian average.

Since the unions can hardly increase their membership by making gains in the public sector, which is already extensively unionized, they must rely on further inroads into the private sector to enhance their strength. That is why major labour organizations in Quebec have proposed an amendment to the Labour Code to permit multiemployer certification in order to facilitate the unionization of employees in industries characterized by numerous small firms engaged in tight competition such as retail food, textiles, and local transportation.

In these sectors, where employees are working at close to minimum-wage levels, the structure of the industry and the requirements of the Labour Code make unionization very difficult. Union leaders affirm that the poor working conditions of these employees could be substantially ameliorated as a result of unionization.

The government has in fact been sensitive about the wages and working conditions in some "soft" sectors, but it has preferred to provide remedies through minimum-standards legislation. For example, Quebec's hourly minimum wage of $3.65 in 1980 is the highest in North America, and new legislation on minimum standards will permit a nonunionized employee who might have been unfairly dismissed to appeal the employer's decision before a Minimum Standards Board.

The Autonomy of the Quebec Labour Movement

The situation which has already been depicted within the QFL is a good indication of the degree of "self-government" which is aimed at by some influential union leaders in Quebec. In cases where the international organization does not intervene in local unions' affairs, the relationships with the parent body are good. Such is the case with the Steelworkers or the Automobile Workers. Yet the idea of an organization which could be totally independent from its American counterpart is not new, since a formal separation has already been achieved in the cases of paper workers, communication workers, and brewery workers. However, in these instances, the severance was accomplished by mutual agreement between the parties, and it applied to the whole country.

The latest events in the construction industry may be the first step towards the creation of a new autonomous union organization which could eventually bring together all other Quebec labour federations. However, such unity will be hampered by the fierce historical rivalry between QFL and CSN affiliates and the major ideological differences which have led to the creation of the CSD and a substantial number of independent organizations.

Impact of Collective Bargaining on the Public

Private-sector bargaining does not have many negative effects on the public because of the decentralized nature of the process, and because alternate goods and services usually are available. Even if some particular work stoppages may receive spectacular coverage from the media, the overall record is satisfactory. The situation could be more severe under centralized sectoral bargaining as in construction, since the whole sector could be shut down.

The adverse effect on the public could be even more severe in the public sector because of the essential nature of many services, the lack of alternative services elsewhere, and the fact that a warfare syndrome exists in Quebec since the centralization of the bargaining structure has brought the ritual confrontation between the Common Front and the government every three or four years. The unions have tried to adapt their strategy to the public reaction by sometimes using rotating or partial strikes instead of resorting to general walkouts, but the cumulative effect over the years has created a great deal of resentment in the population against public unions whose members are certainly not the most exploited in society. For these reasons, the issue of the right to strike in the public sector will be of constant concern in the years to come.

REFERENCES AND WORKS CITED

1. Babcock, Robert. "Samuel Gompers and the French-Canadian Worker, 1900-1914," *The American Review of Canadian Studies*, Vol. 3 (1973), 47-66.

2. Barbash, Jack. "The American Ideology of Industrial Relations," *Proceedings of the Industrial Relations Research Association 1979 Annual Spring Meeting*, 453-457.

3. Boivin, Jean. "The Evolution of Bargaining Power in the Province of Quebec Public Sector, 1964-1972." Ph.D. dissertation, Cornell University, 1975.

4. Boivin, Jean. "Règles du jeu et rapport de force dans les secteurs public et para-public québécois," *Relations Industrielles/Industrial Relations*, Vol. 34 (1979), 3-19.

5. Commission d'étude et de consultation sur la révision du régime des négociations collectives dans les secteurs public et para-public, Yves Martin et Lucien Bouchard, Commissaries. *Rapport Martin-Bouchard* (Gouvernement du Québec: Editeur official du Québec, 1978).

6. Delorme, François, and Gaspar Lassoude. *Aspects de la réalité syndicale québécoise* (Gouvernement du Québec: Ministère du travail et de la main-d'oeuvre, 1978).

7. Delorme, François, Gaspar Lassonde, and Lucie Tremblay. *Grèves et lock-out au Québec: 1966-1976. Quelques précisions sur les modes de compilation* (Gouvernement du Québec: Ministère du Travail et de la main-d'oeuvre, 1977).

8. Delorme, François, et Diane Veilleux. *Les syndicats indépendants au Québec: un aperçu de leur situation* (Gouvernement du Québec: Ministère du travail et de la main-d'oeuvre, 1980).

9. Gaulin, Robert. "L'expérience de la négociation du front commun des secteurs public et para-public: une évaluation syndicale," in Noel Mallette (Ed.), *La gestion des relations du travail au Québec* (Montreal: McGraw-Hill, 1980), pp. 571-594.

10. Girard, Michelle. "L'arbitrage des premières conventions collectives," *Le Marché du travail* (juillet 1980), 40-53.

11. Gouvernement du Québec, Ministère du travail et de la main-d'oeuvre. *Grèves et lock-out au Québec:* 1979 (Gouvernement du Québec: Ministère du travail et de la main-d'oeuvre, 1980).

12. Harvey, Fernand (Ed.). *Le mouvement ouvrier au Québec* (Montréal: Boréal Express, 1980).

13. Harvey, Fernand. "Les chevaliers du travail, les Etats-Unis et la société Québécoise, 1882-1902," in Fernand Harvey (Ed.), *Le mouvement ouvrier au Québec* (Montreal: Boréal Express, 1980), pp. 69-130.

14. Hébert, Gérard. *Labor Relations in the Quebec Construction Industry, Part 1: The System of Labor Relations* (Ottawa: Economic Council of Canada, 1977).

15. Hébert, Gérard. "La négociation du secteur public provincial: histoire et cadre institutionnel," in Noel Mallette (Ed.), *La gestion des relations du travail au Québec* (Montreal: McGraw-Hill, 1980), pp. 547-569.

16. Jamieson, Stuart. *Industrial Relations in Canada* (Toronto: Macmillan, 1973).

17. Lipton, Charles. *Histoire du syndicalisme au Canada et au Québec 1827-1957* (Montreal: Editions Partie-Pris, 1976).

18. Martin, Yves. "Le cadre juridique de la ronde de négociations collectives de 1979 des secteurs public et parapublic: le rapport Martin-Bouchard," in Noel Mallette (Ed.), *La gestion des relations du travail au Québec* (Montreal, McGraw-Hill, 1980), pp. 596-608.

19. Quebec Federation of Labour, *Constitution and By-Laws as Amended by the XVth Convention* (Montreal: QFL, 1977).

20. *Rapport de la Commission d'enquête sur l'exercice de la liberté syndicale dans l'industrie de la construction* et *Recueil des annexes*, Juge Robert Cliche, président (Gouvernement du Canada: Editeur official du Québec, 1975).

21. *Le travail: point de vue sur notre réalité* (Gouvernement du Québec: le sommet économique du Québec, 1977).

QUESTIONS

1. Discuss the importance of ideology in Quebec's industrial-relations system.

2. Describe the philosophy of early confessional unions.

3. Compare the relationships between the CTCC-CSN and the Quebec government before, during, and after the "Quiet Revolution."

4. Compare the respective attitudes of the CSN and the QFL vis-à-vis the Quebec government before and after the Parti Québécois' electoral victory of 1976.

5. Explain the special situation of the QFL within the CLC.

6. Explain the similarities and differences in the general legal framework for labour relations between Quebec and the rest of Canada.

7. What are the most outstanding features of the Quebec Labour Code, as recently amended?

8. Can we say that collective-bargaining structures are more centralized in Quebec than elsewhere in Canada?

9. What major factors have accounted for the high level of strike activity in the years 1972, 1975, 1976, and 1979?

10. Describe the collective-bargaining system in Quebec's construction industry.

11. Explain the major characteristics of the hiring system in the construction industry.

12. Identify the formal and informal structures of bargaining in the public sector and explain the dynamics of the last three rounds of negotiations.

ROY J. ADAMS

19. Industrial-Relations Systems in Europe and North America

The chapter considers the major industrial-relations systems differences between the United States and Western Europe and examines Canadian practice in light of the comparison. Particular topics include the development of the labour movement and the reasons for the different strategies chosen by trade unions; employer and government reactions to the emergence of organized labour; current structures and practices of job regulation and the results of the systems in terms of industrial conflict and terms and conditions of employment.

Perhaps the most significant fact of this age is the productive capacity of modern economies. Twentieth-century society produces goods and services at a rate which could only be imagined during other periods of history. This situation is the result of the Industrial Revolution which "took off" in the latter part of the eighteenth century. In its wake, the process of industrialization produced enormous changes in society. Modern industrial-relations systems are one result of the process (45).

In this chapter, focus is limited to Western Europe and North America which have proceeded through a similar industrial evolution and have arrived at comparable levels of industrialization. Each adheres to liberal democratic principles and depends heavily upon the market for the production and distribution of goods and services. The labour movement in both North America and Western Europe is free from government and employer control, and it relies heavily on collective bargaining to establish terms and conditions of employment (36).

Despite these similarities each country has developed a unique industrial-relations system. From a global perspective, however, two major patterns—the American and the European—stand out from the diversity of detail. Although Canadian practice is similar to the American, on many dimensions Canada stands between Europe and the United States. Thus, an examination of these two general modes of industrial relations may provide considerable insight into the system of industrial relations in Canada.

THE DEVELOPMENT OF THE LABOUR MOVEMENT

Modern-day labour movements trace their roots to local organizations which began to appear in the eighteenth century. These organizations typically were founded by craftsmen such as printers, shoemakers, shipwrights, seamen, tailors, cigar makers and bakers (68, 41, 44, 30). Many began as friendly societies whose original purpose was mutual insurance against death, unemployment, sickness, and retirement. When employment problems were experienced as a result of inflation, recession, or the introduction of new technology, these societies chose spokesmen to present petitions to the employer regarding the situation. Work stoppages tended to be spontaneous protests directed towards the employer and sometimes towards government authorities. Trade unions were fragile, blossoming in good times and wilting during depressions. In the early years, they were faced with substantial opposition from employers and from governments.

As industrialization proceeded, the economic concepts of free trade, free enterprise and competition began to win favour. In several countries, unions were outlawed as conspiracies in restraint of trade (44). Employers frequently refused to deal with unions arguing that they were an infringement on the legitimate rights of the owner. Labour was regarded as a commodity to be purchased and sold on the free market. The Protestant Ethic, derived from Calvinism, suggested that one's economic destiny depended solely upon one's ability to work and save. Poverty, once considered to be an inevitable phenomenon, now was regarded as the reward for sloth (26). The unemployed were often arrested as indigents and made to labour in workhouses.

Despite these negative forces, union membership and influence slowly grew. Periodic outbreaks of labour protest resulted in the overturning of the various laws against union activity during the latter part of the nineteenth century. The right of association and the right to strike were eventually won. In 1868, the first national trade-union federation to endure was established in Great Britain. During the next thirty years, union federations came into being in most of the countries of Europe and North America.

To counter the political and legal obstacles of the era, these emerging labour movements required a philosophy or ideology to justify their existence and provide direction. At this critical juncture, Karl Marx put forth his grand sociopolitical theory of economic evolution (35, 20). He argued that capitalist society was composed essentially of two classes: workers (who depend on wages for their living) and capitalists (owners of the means of production). The income of the capitalist results from their expropriation of a part of the value added to raw products by labour — value which should, according to Marx, rightfully go to the worker. Over time, the capitalist class would be reduced in size as a result of competition and economic cycles, and workers would become conscious of the exploitative nature of capitalist society with its tendency to create class divisions. Eventually, workers would overthrow the remaining capitalists and set up a socialist government which would, in time, fade away into classless communism. Unionism, in Marxist thought, was a necessary step towards communism, but a labour strategy designed only to win better terms and conditions of employment could not succeed because of the competitive dynamics of the economic system. A political strategy was required. Moreover, because capitalist philosophy and class power pervaded every aspect of society including education, religion, government, and the press, capitalism could be replaced only by a complete and violent overthrow of the system.

Fundamental Marxism was challenged, embellished, or limited by other socialist intellectuals. Democratic Socialists, like the British Fabians, accepted the Marxist dictum that a political strategy was appropriate for labour but they believed that political change could be brought about by democratic means. They urged workers to seek change within the context of democracy (74). Syndicalists, on the other hand, were opposed to party politics. They accepted the Marxist proposition that capitalism could only be defeated by drastic means but felt that the general strike should be used as the principal tool (47).

Between 1870 and 1920, the mainstream of the labour movements in Europe adopted some combination of these ideas. In some countries, labour or socialist parties acted as the central body for the unions for several years. In others, unions were instrumental in founding political parties (68).

The growing acceptance of socialist ideals gave rise to counter movements. The Catholic Church was particularly concerned with the antireligious and violent nature of the Marxist philosophy. In 1891, Pope Leo XIII issued the encyclical *Rerum Novarum* which stimulated the establishment of trade unions based on Christian principles. The result was the development of a Christian trade union movement which acquired importance in several European countries including France, Italy, Belgium, Holland, and Germany (28).

Marxist thought, however, also inspired several North American union movements including the Industrial Workers of the World, The One Big Union, and the Workers' Unity League. In the United States, the American Federation of Labor (AFL) in 1886 established principles which would be adopted by the majority of American unionists. Rejecting all variants of socialism, the AFL strategy was to organize skilled craftsmen into strong unions, one for each trade, capable of winning job and income security from employers by the application of bargaining power. The AFL did not seek major social change. Rather, it accepted the capitalist system, rejected the idea of any alliance with a political party, and distrusted any government action. On the political front, it would seek to "reward friends and punish enemies."

Socialists condemned this "exceptional" approach for being misguided, elitist, and hard-hearted. In the 1920s, American "exceptionalism" found a champion in Selig Perlman, a reformed socialist and professor at the University of Wisconsin. Perlman argued that socialist intellectuals were not really concerned with the well-being of "flesh-and-blood" workers (60). Instead, they saw the world in terms of abstract forces and abstract masses of labour. European unionists, according to Perlman, were beguiled by the elegant and grandiose schemes of the socialists and had failed to recognize the real needs of workers. American unions were mature and realized, contrary to socialist thought, that workers have no desire to capture the government or to manage industry. Workers were interested only in their job and income security and consequently had fashioned unions capable of meeting these modest ends. Perlman also suggested that because of conditions special to the U.S., the AFL approach was appropriate. He implied that any other approach would not have been successful.

Over time, the pillars of U.S. labour ideology would weaken and a few would fall. Thus, when the unskilled began to organize en masse during the 1930s, the AFL decided to give up its elitist craft-union approach and to organize unskilled and semiskilled workers. The alternative was to become overshadowed by the rapidly expanding Congress of Industrial Organizations (CIO). The tenet of "one-union-for-one-jurisdiction" weakened substantially in 1955 when the AFL and CIO merged. In several industries, both an AFL and a CIO union were taken into the new AFL-CIO.

From its formation in the 1930s, the CIO provided considerable support to the Democratic Party, and since the 1955 merger the alliance between the Democratic Party and organized labour has continued for the most part. On its own, the AFL-CIO has been much more active politically than was the old AFL. However, the idea that the primary aim of unions is to win better terms and conditions of employment for its own members, an approach known as "pure-and-simple" or "business" unionism, still pervades the thought of the American labour movement (31).

In Canada, the labour movement had developed no firm philosophy by 1900. There were political-reformist unions affiliated to the U.S.-based Knights of Labor, "pure-and-simple" unions (some affiliated to the AFL and some purely Canadian), and unionists who adhered to various shades of socialism.

In 1902, the AFL pressured the Canadian Trades and Labour Congress (TLC) to expel dual unions and adopt a craft-union strategy. The TLC reluctantly did so but did not accept the antipolitical attitude of the AFL. Many active Canadian unionists were British immigrants who brought their labour ideology with them. In 1906 when the British Labour Party officially came into being, largely as the result of the initiative of the British Trades Union Congress, the TLC gave its support to the formation of provincial labour parties in Canada. However, they were not success-ful. In 1918, when the British Labour Party was reorganized and "accepted for the first time a socialist objective" (27, p. 148), the TLC gave its support to the develop-ment of a national labour party in Canada. A federal party was formed, but in 1923 it was taken over by Communists and union support was withdrawn. An enduring alliance between the Canadian Confederation of Labour (CCL) and the Co-operative Commonwealth Federation (CCF), which had been formed in 1933 without signifi-cant union support, was forged in 1943. (The CCL came into existence in 1940 and merged with the TLC in 1956 to become the CLC.) Today, the Canadian Labour Congress (CLC) supports the New Democratic Party, the successor to the CCF, which has a philosophy similar to the British Labour Party or the Social Democratic Parties of Scandinavia and Germany. Within the CLC, however, there are both business unionists and many who subscribe to socialist objectives (34, 55).

The "exceptional" strategy chosen by the U.S. labour movement has long been a focus of thought in America. Sturmthal (67, 69) suggests three factors as critical determinants of labour strategy: the nature of the problems faced by workers, the membership base of the labour movement, and the state of the labour market. American workers considered their major problem to be job and income security. European workers had similar security problems, but they also had political prob-lems which American workers did not have. During the nineteenth century, the great majority of workers in most European countries did not have the right to vote, did not have ready access to education, and were treated by those in power as an inferior class of human beings. Differences of dress, speech, social behaviour, and other vestiges of feudal society emphasized adherence to classes. In contrast, the American equalitarian ethic "stressed the ideas of classlessness, individual initia-tive, and opportunity" (12, p. 1403). Even though real upward mobility was probably no better in America than it was in Europe, equalitarian ideology persisted (49).

The AFL considered its problem to be primarily economic rather than political.

Therefore, it decided to limit membership primarily to workers who had a critical position in the production process. Since the American economy was developing rapidly, these workers were often in short supply and thus had significant economic bargaining power. On the other hand, because it was representative of only a small fraction of society, the political power of the AFL was modest at best. In Europe, where the dominant problems were considered to be political, the labour movements organized broadly. By doing so they weakened their potential economic bargaining power but became more influential politically.

Over time, the labour movements on both sides of the Atlantic have changed their strategies somewhat. Today, the AFL-CIO is much more politically active than was the old AFL. In Europe, trade unions are heavily engaged in economic bargaining with employers although they continue to pursue political objectives. One would expect these changes from Sturmthal's theory. Since the 1930s, the U.S. government has intervened more deeply in the economy. Thus, more issues important to workers are being determined politically. Moreover, in the 1930s the membership base of the American labour movement expanded significantly and now is representative of a wider constituency. In Europe, as the economies grew, collective bargaining expanded since the forces of supply and demand for labour more often favoured unions (51).

Although they provide considerable insight, the theoretical perspectives of Sturmthal and Perlman are not entirely satisfactory. For example, one is left with the impression that the U.S. and European labour movements were both appropriate and successful within their respective milieus. In many respects, however, the AFL approach was not successful. Because of its exclusionist nature, the majority of American workers did not receive the benefits of its efforts. Moreover, social legislation in the U.S. developed at a much slower pace than in Europe, in part because of the lack of political pressure from a strong, broad-based union movement. Nevertheless, the AFL did survive. In the individualistic, equalitarian environment of the U.S., perhaps that is the best that could be expected.

The state of the labour market was certainly an important factor in the development of collective bargaining, but other factors were also important. For example, the achievement by labour of political power put pressure on European employers to come to terms with the labour movement and establish regular patterns of interaction. Moreover, as Sellier (66) has demonstrated, it was not the lack of economic bargaining power that thwarted the development of collective bargaining in France. Rather, the continual intervention of the state into labour relations fostered a dependence on government action. Labour leaders, imbued with the syndicalist ideology of direct worker action, spurned the idea of developing administratively sound organizations for the purpose of negotiating with capitalist employers.

An additional factor noted by Sturmthal — the migration of ideas — has been important in Canada. Since its emergence, the labour movement has been pulled between the moderate, democratic socialism of Great Britain and the nonpolitical approach of U.S. labour. Perhaps because of the British link, moderate socialism is more acceptable in Canada than in the U.S. Nevertheless, many Canadian unionists subscribe fully to the U.S. approach. The current situation is a compromise. The Canadian Labour Congress endorses the New Democratic Party as the party with policy objectives most consistent with aims of trade unionists. However, there are no functional links at the central level. Local unions may affiliate to the party, but the majority have chosen not to do so. Only a minority of Canadian unionists vote for the NDP in federal elections. The link between unions and political parties in Canada remains controversial (9, 56).

In Quebec, the Canadian and Catholic Confederation of Labour was part of a wider movement set in motion by *Rerum Novarum*. Over time, the confederation has evolved from Church-dominated, to "pure-and-simple," to quite radical during the 1970s. Interestingly, the Catholic Union movement underwent a similar evolution in France. Whether the similarity of development was coincidental or causal has yet to be determined (42, 11, 2).

EMPLOYERS IN INDUSTRIAL RELATIONS

In Continental Europe, worker political action was successful and labour-socialist parties grew rapidly in the early decades of the twentieth century (44). The very different strategic decisions taken by labour movements in North America and Europe produced divergent employer reactions.

Socialist ideology threatened the fundamental existence of the capitalist system. Realizing that they could not destroy the labour movement, European employers established associations with the objective of stabilizing relations with the unions. These associations eventually drew together under national federations which represented the industrial-relations interests of employers to government, to the public, and to union federations. In many countries, employers' associations decided (often under government pressure) to recognize unions as legitimate bargaining agents for workers on a broad scale. "Basic agreements," providing such recognition, were recorded in Denmark during the 1890s, in Sweden in 1906, in Germany and parts of British industry in the post-World War I era, and in Switzerland and France during the 1930s (53, 71, 50, 21). In return for recognition, unions were expected by employer associations to negotiate agreements on an industry-wide basis.

A major objective of this strategy was to reduce or check the potential influence of unions at the work place. European employers were prepared to negotiate industry-wide agreements with unions but they were not prepared to allow unions to interfere with the day-to-day management of the firm.

Employer reactions to unions were entirely different in the U.S. Because unions organized narrowly along craft lines and accepted the maxims of capitalism, they did not acquire political power and thus did not pose a threat to fundamental employer interests. As a result, employers generally concluded that they might, indeed, be able to check or destroy the unions. Where associations were formed, their main priority often was to stay union-free, negotiating with the unions only if forced to do so (52). Under such circumstances, unions were generally forced to seek recognition on a plant-by-plant basis, and the process of recognition took on the characteristic of a battle for the hearts and minds of the workers involved. Where the union won such a struggle, it was typically powerful enough to require management to sign a collective agreement which, over time, became increasingly elaborate. This development gave nonunion companies more reason to oppose unions because, unlike Europe, union recognition did come to imply significant union incursion into day-to-day management authority (12). In Canada, the employer reaction and the resultant plant-by-plant struggle for recognition was very similar to the U.S. situation.

When worker protest grew during the 1930s, the U.S. government set out to develop a procedure for orderly union recognition, consistent with the pattern of collective bargaining which had developed to that point. The Wagner Act (the National Labor Relations Act of 1935) was the result. It created a procedure whereby union organizations could acquire government certification as bargaining agent for groups of employees on a plant-by-plant basis. Canadian governments were slow to follow the U.S. lead, but during the war years the Canadian federal government issued an Order in Council (P.C. 1003) which contained principles similar to those in the U.S. This document became the basis of federal and provincial labour laws enacted after the war (77).

The American Wagner Act of the 1930s initially encouraged employer recognition of trade unions. It was formally supportive of collective bargaining; it made illegal many employer unfair labour practices designed to penalize employees for union sympathies, and it compelled intransigent employers to negotiate once unionized. However, the Taft-Hartley Act of 1947 gave approval to employer attempts to convince employees to reject trade unions and collective bargaining. Subsequently, few employers recognized unions voluntarily, and union organizing campaigns continued to be an open struggle for the loyalty of the workers involved. Unionization came to be thought of as a punishment for management failure. Consequently, the possibility of the U.S. system evolving in the direction of European models became very remote. Since they had good prospects of remaining "union-free," nonunionized employers were provided with no incentive to associate with unionized employers for the purpose of dealing with unions. Indeed, many formed groups openly hostile to the fundamental existence of trade unions, a development which would not be tolerated in Europe (1).

Thus, in the U.S. the extent of employer organization for industrial-relations purposes is much less than in Europe. Although associations do exist in some industries, particularly those characterized by small unionized firms whose bargaining power relative to unions is low, most U.S. employers conduct labour-relations policy individually. It has been estimated that about 80 percent of U.S. collective agreements are limited to employees of a single company and about two-thirds are limited to a single plant (22). There is no U.S. employer federation having prominence and authority regarding social matters which is comparable to the federations which exist in most European countries (12).

In Canada, the situation is similar to that in the U.S. (17). However, in recent years the gap created by the disunity of business has become an issue. Several provinces have legislated accreditation procedures whereby a group of employers may form an association for bargaining purposes and receive government sanction as a bargaining agent. In the construction industry, employer fragmentation has been particularly problematic, and some provinces have passed legislation requiring multiemployer bargaining (64). Recently, the federal government appointed a commission to recommend ways in which government might encourage more multiemployer bargaining (62).

The difficulties created by the lack of a national employer organization with authority to speak for business have been recognized by the federal government, which has encouraged business to move towards a more united approach (3). In 1977, the Business Council on National Issues (BCNI), an organization composed primarily of chief executive officers of large corporations, was founded. Membership included representatives from the Canadian Manufacturers Association and the

Canadian Chamber of Commerce. The objective of the BCNI is to pursue business interests in government policy at the national level. The organization has also pursued a consultative approach with organized labour and has reached consensus with the Canadian Labour Congress on some public issues (16).

In contrast to Europe, employer organization in Canada is still in its infancy. The great majority of Canadian firms do not belong to the BCNI, nor does the organization have the will or desire to attract a significantly expanded membership. In the view of some business leaders, the formation of a broad-based national employers' organization, competent to express the views of business on employee-relations matters, would suggest a recognition of fundamental class divisions in society.

JOB REGULATION

Canada and the United States

In Canada and the U.S., as noted above, the dominant bipartite job-regulation process is collective bargaining between a single union and a single employer. In some industries (for example, shipping, construction, railways, hospitals) multi-party, centralized negotiations have developed but decentralized collective bargaining is more characteristic of the North American industrial-relations systems. Other typical attributes include written, formal collective agreements covering the entire range of negotiated issues; strong union organizations at the work place with important duties; and well-developed grievance procedures ending in binding arbitration.

West German Illustration

These arrangements are unusual in comparative international perspective. The following example from West Germany (4, 32, 57, 10) illustrates common themes found in much of European bargaining. The principal union federation in West Germany is the German Federation of Trade Unions (DGB). Unlike most of its European counterparts, it is apolitical. However, its pre-Nazi predecessor had close links with the Social Democratic Party, and many German union leaders continue to be active socialists. When the DGB was reconstituted after World War II, in order to discourage factionalism and to encourage the widest base of membership, it decided not to officially endorse a political party. That goal was only partially met. West Germany also has a small Christian Federation (CGD), an Association of German Civil Service Officials (DBB), and a German Salaried Employees Union (DAG). However, about 80 percent of all union members belong to DGB-affiliated unions. The DGB is composed entirely of industrial unions with the largest affiliate being IG Metall, the Metalworkers' Union.

On the other side of the labour market, the industrial-relations interests of employers are pursued by the German Employers Confederation (DBA). It is composed largely of associations of employers organized by industry. Approximately 90 percent of all German private enterprises (employing about 95 percent of the work force) belong to an employers' association and most are affiliated to the DBA.

Union-management collective bargaining is typically conducted between an industrial union and an employers' association. The resulting collective agreements are binding on employers in given provinces or regions of the country. In the metalworking industry, bargaining for wages typically takes place annually between the employers' association and IG Metall. For steel companies, jobs in the industry are broken into eight categories and, for each category, minimum wages, average increases, overtime rates, and other generally applicable wage issues are negotiated. In addition to the wage contract, IG Metall has ten or more other contracts with the association on specific issues. There are, for example, agreements regarding the procedures which an employer must follow with respect to layoffs, vacations, technological change, apprenticeships, union shop stewards, and the humanization of work. These agreements do not expire at the same time, and some last for up to five years.

The employers' association also negotiates with a DAG white-collar union. However, most white-collar workers are, in fact, in IG Metall and the negotiations with the white-collar union tend to follow the dominant pattern. Legally, collective agreements apply only to union members. As a matter of practice, however, the terms are applied to all relevant employees regardless of union status. As in Canada, unions are not permitted to strike for higher wages while a wage agreement is in effect.

Within the metalworking industry, white-collar workers have a choice of joining IG Metall, which is affiliated to the DGB, or the white-collar union affiliated to the DAG. The workers might also become members of the Christian trade union. Thus, in the same office, different clerks might belong to different unions such as Metall, DAG or the Christian union; others may not belong to any union. There are no mandatory union membership provisions in German collective agreements. German unions do not believe in compelling people to join, and such agreements would probably infringe the right of free association (32).

Most relevant employers in the metalworking industry belong to the employers' association. However, through extension legislation the terms of the agreement may be extended to nonmembers, based on joint approval by the union and the employer association.

Within each individual enterprise, there is the need to deal with numerous additional employment issues including actual hours of work, wage-payment procedures, holiday scheduling, piece-rate systems, recruitment and selection standards, job classification, transfers, and individual dismissals. In West Germany such issues are not negotiated by a local union but rather are established unilaterally by the employer or negotiated by a works council elected by all relevant employees, whether union members or not. German law requires the establishment of such councils. However, since enforcement procedures are lax there are many companies (especially small firms) in which there is no functioning council. These bodies have no formal connection with the union, but IG Metall is entitled to nominate candidates to the council, and in practice most councillors are active trade unionists. The councils are not permitted to call a strike but impasses concerning most issues may be taken to binding arbitration. In addition to negotiating substantive terms and conditions of employment, the councils also monitor the collective agreements and the application of employment law such as human rights and labour standards.

German workers with a grievance may turn to their supervisor, works councilor or shop steward, or they may go directly to the local union office. In recent years, IG Metall has made strenuous efforts to establish a network of union shop stewards in plants but even where they do exist their functions and stature are restricted. Workers may also take their grievance to the Labour Court if no satisfaction is received from their initial efforts. A worker who does so most likely will ask the union to present the case. The courts are manned by professional judges, familiar with labour law and practice, appointed only after consultation with employers and unions. The labour courts will entertain grievances, not only over the application of the collective agreement, but also on alleged infringements of law or agreements between works councils and employers. Before handing down a judgment, the courts attempt to conciliate disputes (53).

Other European Illustrations

In West Germany, the major union federation (DGB) does not negotiate collective agreements with the Employers' Federation (DBA) but in several European countries bargaining at this centralized national level does take place. In Sweden, for example, the LO (the Social-Democratic Labour Federation) negotiates a "frame" or national centralized agreement with the Swedish Employers Confederation (SAF) (29). This agreement calls for an average increase in the wage bill of employers and may have more detailed provisions for certain categories of workers such as women, youths, and supervisors. Within the frame, more detailed agreements are negotiated at the industry level and within the confines of the industry agreements still more detailed agreements are reached between local union "clubs" and enterprise or plant management. Works councils, set up not by law but by union-management agreement, also exist in the enterprise. Their function is to discuss nonconflictive issues of joint concern to workers and companies rather than to negotiate distributive issues of substance. In addition to periodic wage bargaining the LO and the SAF have also concluded several long-term agreements on such issues as industrial conflict, safety, training, layoffs, and work study (15).

Tripartism, Political Bargaining, and the Social Wage

Over and above their direct negotiations, trade unions and management organizations are able to exert a considerable amount of influence on social policy. Formal, tripartite consultation regarding government policy takes place in several countries. In Holland, for example, the Social-Economic Council, consisting of union, management, and Crown-appointed public members, advises the government on policy initiatives. The government is required by law to consult the council on all important social and economic issues, and consensus recommendations from the council generally become government policy (76). In Sweden, important employment issues are investigated by ad hoc commissions on which union and management organizations always have representation. As in Holland, government rarely rejects consensus recommendations (75). Through such agencies, labour and management in many European countries engage in what amounts to the negotiation of socioeconomic policy (19, 40, 72, 59).

In recent years, a more explicit form of what has been called "political bargaining" has come into existence (63). This type of bargaining always includes trade unions and the government as parties and may include employers and other interest groups such as farmers and professionals. Political bargaining leads to a "social contract" which may or may not be included in one or more specific documents. A social contract typically consists of two parts. The unions agree to restrain wage demands and strikes, and government agrees to some package of social legislation which may consist of "action on agricultural and other prices, corporate dividends, food prices, housing, rents, industrial-relations arrangements, industrial government, aids to industry, private and public investment policy, profits and other incomes, social benefits and services, and taxes" (7, p. 6). For example, the social contract which was in effect in Great Britain during the mid-1970s called for union wage restraint in return for food subsidies, a rent freeze, pension and tax reform, the establishment of a Conciliation and Arbitration Service, an Employment Protection Act, an investigation of income distribution and of workers' participation on boards of directors (18), and the abolition of the Industrial Relations Act which had been introduced over union objections by a previous Conservative government.

Works Councils and Workers' Participation in Management

Works councils are found in most European countries. In some cases, they have their basis in law, in others through collective agreements (23, 14). In several countries, they came about because of the vacuum created by the generally successful employer strategy of seeking multiemployer bargaining. In Germany, Holland, and France the unions were not able to establish a viable shop-floor presence. When councils were first proposed the unions were suspicious because they feared that the councils would usurp their collective-bargaining functions and therefore reduce union influence. Employers feared that councils would make inroads into managerial prerogatives. On the other hand, the council idea was consistent with the socialist philosophy of class representation. From the employers' perspective, it was better to deal with a council of representatives elected by all employees rather than with outsiders.

For many decades the arrangement worked in favour of the employer who, by and large, was able to dominate the councils and conduct business as usual (6, 25). However, political pressure for reform built up during the 1950s and 1960s, and during the 1970s the councils were strengthened significantly in several countries. Moreover, European labour movements began to demand significant worker input into more general management policy dealing with production lines and schedules, plant closures, financial administration, investments, mergers, and organizational changes. To socialist labour movements, workers' participation in management (if not worker's control of industry) had long been an objective. During this period, unions began to mobilize their energies to advance towards this goal. The result has been laws both strengthening works councils and also requiring the appointment of workers' representatives to the boards of large corporations, much to the chagrin of management (37). The process has gone furthest in West Germany where workers have parity with stockholders in choosing directors in the coal and steel industry and near parity in other large companies. Despite the fears of business, labour-management parity on German boards has not resulted in economic disadvantage to the firms. The workers' representatives have acted responsibly. In fact, explosive situations have been avoided because the employment implications of issues such as the introduction of new technology and plant closures have been seriously taken into account at an early stage (4).

Other Features of European Industrial Relations

Multiple unionism, another common feature of European industrial-relations systems, resulted from the controversial choice of socialism as the doctrine of much of the labour movement. This, in turn, led to a proliferation of counter-socialist and apolitical union organizations as well as the fragmentation of the Left. Because of this political factionalism, union security clauses and exclusive representation of the North American variety are not workable.

Another notable characteristic of European practice is the existence of collective-bargaining-extension legislation whereby certain provisions of a collective agreement, negotiated by a group of employers and employees, is extended by law throughout the industry. Such procedures free employers from low-wage competition and allow the unions to be of benefit to more than their own membership. Moreover, the existence of these clauses helps to explain why employer associations in Europe have generally been successful in attracting most large corporations into membership. In order to influence decisions which affect their work force, companies must be association members. Moreover, if they stay out of the association the unions may be able to concentrate pressure on them to grant concessions over and above the industry standards. Characteristically, small employers are less likely to be associated. Even if they were to join, they would still wield only a small amount of influence on association bargaining policy (38). In contrast, employer associations in North America are most prevalent in industries characterized by small employers who individually have little power against strong unions. Extension-of-agreement provisions and the propensity of employers to apply union rates to everyone also reduce the attractiveness of union membership. Thus, in Holland, Germany, and France, where unions do not have a strong position in the work place and non-union members receive all of the benefits of collective bargaining without having to pay union dues, union membership is relatively low despite widespread union recognition.

Labour courts are also found in most European countries. They perform functions similar to private arbitrators or arbitration boards but their jurisdiction is much broader. In most countries, the labour courts hear cases regarding disputes over the application of work rules whether such rules were established by custom and practice, statute, collective agreement, or by an agreement between the works council and the employer. Since union recognition is not a significant issue throughout most of Europe, agencies similar to North American labour-relations boards are rarely found.

As in Sweden, national collective bargaining takes place in several European countries including Austria, Norway, Denmark, Belgium, Holland, France, and Ireland. It was a logical step in a long-term process of the rationalization of collective bargaining. In these countries, it is clearly understood that collective bargaining may have a serious impact on the operation of the economy. Thus, negotiations which apply to the entire economy, and take the likely impact of collective bargaining on the economy into account, make sense. National negotiations are also a logical concomitant of socialist ideology. If one purports to represent an entire class, it is sensible to negotiate agreements applicable equally to that class.

Policy consultation and political bargaining are also characteristic of general European practice, and influencing public policy has long been a labour priority. Union-management bargaining and influencing public policy are alternative methods for achieving the same result. Thus, to the individual, a tax decrease as a national public policy may have the same effect as a wage increase attained through collective bargaining. However, since provisions introduced by legislation are usually more universal, they are often preferred by European unions.

North American Parallels

In North America there are no tripartite consultative mechanisms with the stature and influence of those in Europe. Many consultative bodies, such as the Economic Council of Canada, do exist. However, no tradition has been established which obliges government to seek consensus and to follow through on the decisions arrived at as a result of the consensus decisions.

Recent North American developments have been moving to some extent in a European direction. During the 1970s, the Canadian Labour Congress argued forcefully for a greater say in policy making, and the federal government in Canada has consulted with the unions to a much greater extent. To date, however, little of concrete substance has emerged (24).

In 1979, a form of social contract labeled the National Accord was worked out in the U.S. between the AFL-CIO and the federal government (5). Although the AFL-CIO did not give firm assurances of wage restraint by all of its affiliates, it did agree to participate on a tripartite Pay Advisory Committee which established wage guidelines. In return, the Carter administration committed itself to several policy objectives including a full-employment strategy, action to protect American jobs from foreign competition, and improvement of the quality of the human environment. Although not explicitly stated in the accord, organized labour expected prompt action on full employment. However, in an election year, the winds of politics convinced the administration that a balanced-budget strategy was more important than a full-employment strategy, and it reneged on the understanding. With the election of Ronald Reagan in 1980 the accord became moot.

European-style vehicles of industrial democracy, such as works councils and worker representation on boards of directors, generally have not been considered necessary or attractive to North American unions. Most believe that strong local unions and hard bargaining provide workers with a substantial say in establishing those work rules in which they are most interested. Nevertheless, recent developments have tended towards European models. Some Canadian provinces have recently passed laws requiring the establishment of health and safety committees in all relevant work places whether a union is involved or not (78). These committees are similar to works councils in Germany, although they have a very limited mandate. The idea of union representation on boards of directors also gained a foothold as a result of the recent Chrysler negotiations in which the president of the United Auto Workers was provided with a board seat.

The convergence has not been all in one direction. Thus, the push by European unions to establish a firmer presence at the work place is a move in the direction of the North American norm. Moreover, several European unions have, in recent years, become concerned about free-riders— workers who receive all of the benefits of union efforts without contributing to the union financial base which makes those efforts possible. As a result, the unions have been experimenting with various forms of security (43). In Belgium, for example, employers provide unions with a financial subsidy in return for the maintenance of industrial peace. The unions utilize this money to underwrite dues payments. Throughout Europe, the checkoff of union dues has become fairly common.

INDUSTRIAL CONFLICT

As Table 1 indicates, the number of days lost due to industrial conflict in Canada and the U.S. exceeds that of most industrialized countries. This widely publicized observation has given rise to much popular discussion. On the basis of such figures it is often stated that "Canada's industrial relations record is the worst among

Table 1

**Volume, Frequency, and Duration of Industrial Conflict,
Annual Averages, 1969-1978**

Country[a]	Days Lost Per 1000 Paid Workers (Volume)	Number of Strikes Per Million Workers (Frequency)	Days Lost Per Worker on Strike (Duration)	Workers Involved Per Strike (Size)
Italy	1,603	294	3	2,086
Canada	924	105	14	618
Australia	604	1,029	2	556
U.S.	539	72[b]	17	448
U.K.	471	120	8	489
Denmark	253	75	6	582
Belgium	247	63[b]	10	375
France	205	210	2	539
West Germany	53	n/a	6	n/a
Sweden	47	20	9	255
Norway	47	11	10	426
Holland	35	6	6	979
Austria	11	n/a	2	n/a

SOURCE: *Derived from International Labour Office,* Yearbook of Labour Statistics *(Geneva: ILO, 1979) and Organisation for Economic Cooperation and Development,* Labour Force Statistics 1967-1978 *(Paris: OECD, 1980).*

NOTES: a. *Ranked from high to low in terms of strike volume.*
b. *1969-1977 only.*

industrialized nations except Italy" (54, p. 1). However, when one disaggregates the available strike data a clearer picture of Canada's situation emerges.

With respect to the frequency and length of strikes, three patterns of strike activity stand out in Table 1. In France, Italy, and Australia strikes are frequent but are usually very short. In Sweden, Holland, and Norway strikes are very infrequent and of moderate length. The popular belief that strikes occur more frequently in Canada and the U.S. than abroad is not borne out by the data. In fact, strikes occur with only moderate frequency. Of the eleven countries for which data is reported, Canada ranks fifth and the U.S. seventh in the incidence of strikes per million workers. However, North American strikes tend to be of longer duration than elsewhere. Strike volume (that is, man-days lost due to strikes) is high because of the combination of moderate strike frequency and long duration (54, 46).

The position of Canada and the U.S. near the top of the strike-volume charts is of relatively recent origin. Before World War II, many countries including Sweden, Norway, Britain, Denmark, and Holland experienced higher overall levels of industrial conflict (33). By the late 1950s, it appeared that strikes were "withering away" (65). Hibbs, however, has recently demonstrated that since World War II strike volume has decreased to very low levels in some countries and has increased in

Table 2

Mean Strike Volume[a]
Before and after World War II

Country[b]	1918-1938	1944-1972	Change
Norway	2,079	100	−1,979
Sweden	1,713	40	−1,673
U.K.	1,210	210	−1,000
Netherlands	700	50	− 650
Denmark	810	170	− 640
Belgium	500	370	− 130
Italy	690	710	+ 20
France	500	630	+ 130
Canada	400	550	+ 150
U.S.	500	700	+ 200
Finland	510	730	+ 220
Japan	50	300	+ 250

SOURCE: Derived from D.A. Hibbs Jr., "On the Political Economy of Long Run Trends in Strike Activity," British Journal of Political Science, *Vol. 8 (1978), 153-175.*

NOTES: *a. Average number of days lost per year due to strikes.*

        b. Ranked from high to low in terms of the change in strike volume.

others. (See Table 2.) It was also shown that the level of industrial conflict is closely related to the change in socialist-labour and Communist Party cabinet representation and to the size of the public budget. In countries with a high "social wage" (as represented, for example, by the level of social services), Hibbs (33, p. 165) argues that "political competition and conflict between left-wing and right-wing parties in the electoral arena (and political market place) has, to a great extent, replaced industrial bargaining and conflict between labour and capital in the private sector (the economic market place) as the process shaping the final distribution of national income." On the other hand, in "countries governed more or less continuously by bourgeois parties of the centre and right, the state budget or public economy remains comparatively small," and "the economic marketplace is therefore the primary locus of distributional conflict in these nations" (33).

From an industrial-relations perspective, Hibbs' findings may be interpreted somewhat differently. In European countries with a low level of industrial conflict, a large part of the total labour package is legislatively determined (8). In part, this is the result of the competition of political parties. However, much social legislation is the result of consensual agreements on the part of labour, management, and government, given effect through law. In very broad terms, industrial-relations decision making in Europe begins at the national level where general consensus is sought over the distribution of the national product. Consensus agreements at the national level are elaborated at the industry level and later at the local level. For several reasons, strikes are an unlikely result of high-level negotiations. National bargaining requires a high degree of professionalism. The parties are constrained to take into account the consequences of their decisions on the economy. If they did not do so they would lose credibility and, therefore, political and social support. Moreover, an irresponsible use of power could result in higher rates of inflation, or the precipitation of recession, outcomes which would have negative consequences for their constituents. Failure to agree at the national level might result in the shutdown of the economy.

The available data suggest that few breakdowns occur at centralized levels of bargaining in Europe. If they did so one would expect many thousands of workers to be involved in each strike. However, the data indicate that the size of strikes in Europe is about the same as in North America (last column of Table 1). One may conclude that when strikes do take place in Europe they generally occur at lower levels in the bargaining structure. Since many issues have been taken out of contention at higher levels, the range of issues in dispute is likely to be narrow.

In Canada and the U.S., where bargaining is concentrated at the establishment level, the scope of the issues to be negotiated is much wider. Thus, the stakes are higher and the bargaining process is probably more complicated, resulting in larger and more detailed agreements. Considering such circumstances, North American bargaining works remarkably well. However, when strikes do occur they tend to be long and drawn out. On the other hand, strikes which occur at lower levels of multilevel bargaining systems are relatively short. In the most successful multilevel systems, both the duration and incidence of strikes are lower than in predominantly single-level systems.

Industrial-relations experts in North America have long presumed that conflict is primarily a problem of the bargaining process. They have, therefore, spent an enormous amount of time and effort seeking to develop techniques such as conciliation, arbitration, "med-arb," fact finding, and final-offer selection. In international perspective, however, the problem appears to be largely one of the structure of bargaining. As long as decentralized bargaining continues in North America, it is unlikely that the overall level of conflict will be reduced to levels common in Northern Europe.

TERMS AND CONDITIONS OF WORK

Compensation and Purchasing Power

Workers in the U.S. and Canada who belong to strong trade unions receive total compensation which is equivalent to or better than that of workers in most other nations. Average wages in the U.S. and Canada have historically exceeded those in other nations. During the 1970s, however, the North American wage advantage over Europe eroded substantially. As indicated in Table 3, in some European countries manufacturing wages now exceed those in the U.S. and Canada, and most countries have closed the gap substantially.

Calculations based on wages alone do not necessarily reflect living standards because of differences in the cost of living. In general, while the wage gap between Europeans and North Americans has been reduced substantially, the purchasing power of wages is still greater for Americans than Europeans. For example, one survey indicated that the index of purchasing power for major cities was 102 in the

Table 3

**Indices[a] of Hourly Wages
in Manufacturing, 1967-1977**

Country[b]	1967	1972	1977
Denmark	57	73	116
Norway	49	65	108
Canada	79	94	106[d]
Sweden	64	82	103
U.S.	100	100	100
Switzerland	43	57	87
West Germany	41	60	85
Belgium	36	50	85
Netherlands	34	50	84
Finland	39	42	64
France	30	38	55
Austria	24	33	55
Britain	41	49	48
Italy	25	36	43[c]

SOURCE: Wages and Total Labour Costs for Workers, International Survey 1967-1977 *(Stockholm: Swedish Employers' Confederation, 1979). Hourly wages include time rates, piece rates, shift supplements, overtime payments, regularly paid bonuses and premiums and payments for leave, public holidays, and other paid individual absences.*

NOTES: *a. Calculated as the hourly wages in the particular country, expressed as a percentage of the hourly wages in the U.S. The original data from which the indices were calculated were presented in Swedish currency (ore) per working hour.*

        b. Ranked from high to low based on wages in 1977.

        c. Figure for 1976.

        d. Canadian rates temporarily exceeded those in the U.S. in the mid 1970s largely because of a short-term Canadian exchange-rate advantage.

U.S., 96 in Canada, and 71 in Europe, with only a few European cities like Zurich, Geneva, and Amsterdam approaching the U.S. average (73).

North American unions have also been successful in negotiating extensive fringe benefits such as vacations, holidays, sickness insurance, pensions, supplementary unemployment insurance, and severance benefits. Through collective bargaining and grievance procedures, unionized North American workers have been able to participate in the establishment and administration of procedures for job classification, discipline, transfers, layoffs, promotions, subcontracting, manning schedules, plant location, and the effects on employees of technological change (48). Most North American experts consider the grievance procedure and the body of private work-place law flowing from published arbitrators' reports to be a major accomplishment (31). Decentralized bargaining provides individual workers with the opportunity to participate closely in decision making regarding these issues (13). Thus, the strategy of North American unions to focus most efforts on winning concessions from individual employers has provided significant benefits to the workers involved. These benefits have been most substantial in those cases where union bargaining power is strongest. North American legislation (unlike works-council law in West Germany, for example) does not require management to reach agreement with worker representatives on issues in dispute. Where management power exceeds that of the union involved, many of the issues listed above have remained within the discretion of the employer. Contrary to Europe where works-council legislation and board representation provide most employees with a legal right to participate in managerial decisions via elected officials, a large percent of North American workers have no collective representation rights whatsoever. They may opt for unionization if they so choose but to do so is often thought to be disloyal, insulting, and openly critical of the employer.

Extent of Unionization

The majority of employees in North America do not belong to trade unions as noted above, largely because of employer opposition and the structure of the law. As a result, most workers depend on individual bargaining and the action of legislators as their methods for participating in employment decisions. Table 4 presents estimates of comparative union density in several countries. The Europe-North America differential in terms of worker coverage under collective agreements is, however, much larger than the table would suggest. For example, in Germany and the Netherlands most workers are covered by collective agreements even though the level of unionization is low.

Managerial Discretion

Until recently, North American unionists have had a clear advantage over their European counterparts in terms of their ability to hold management accountable for

Table 4

Trade Union Density, 1976
(Union Membership as Percent of Nonagricultural Workers)

Country[a]	Density	Country	Density
Sweden	82-83	Netherlands	39-40
Finland	78	West Germany	40
Belgium	70	Canada	37
Denmark	65	Switzerland	37
Norway	63	United States	28-29
Great Britain	51-52	France	25

SOURCE: Everett M. Kassalow, "Industrial Conflict and Consensus in the U.S. and Western Europe," in B. Martin and E.M. Kassalow (Eds.), Labour Relations in Advanced Industrial Societies, Issues and Problems *(New York: Carnegie Endowment for International Peace, 1980). The estimate for France is from Hugh Clegg,* Trade Unionism Under Collective Bargaining *(Oxford: Blackwell, 1976).*

NOTES: a. Ranked from high to low in terms of density.

its decisions related to the terms and conditions of employment and to participate in those decisions. Although European coverage of the work force was greater, the participatory procedures were weaker. However, with the introduction of new legislation granting works councils more rights and providing workers' representatives on boards of directors as well as union efforts to strengthen their work-place organizations, the situation may be significantly changing. Clearly the opportunity of European workers to participate in management decisions has been improved considerably while there have been few such gains in North America.

Social Benefits

The early, intensive, and continuous political efforts of European labour have produced substantially better social benefits than have the relatively recent and more modest efforts of the U.S. and Canadian labour movements. As indicated in Table 5, relative to other industrialized countries, the U.S. has the lowest social wage, as represented by expenditure on social security as a percent of gross domestic product. In Canada, where a unified labour movement has pursued a consistent policy of lobbying and party support for the past twenty years, the social wage is somewhat higher. Unlike the U.S., for example, Canada has universal medical coverage and legally mandated holidays and vacations with pay.

In European countries, the political strategy of labour was put into effect earlier and was more thorough. It was also more successful. Labour and social-democratic parties have contested the primacy of moderate and conservative parties at the national level for several decades. As a result, the social wage in most European countries is considerably higher than in either Canada or the U.S.

North American workers also have less job security than their European counterparts. Unemployment rates in Canada and the United States have exceeded those in Europe for many years, although recently unemployment in a few European coun-

Table 5

**Expenditures on Social Security Benefits[a]
as a Percent of Gross Domestic Product, 1973-1974**

Country[b]	Percent	Country	Percent
Sweden	23.9	France	19.1
Holland	23.9	Austria	17.4
Denmark	20.5	Norway	17.2
Italy	19.7	U.K.	13.6
Belgium	19.4	Canada	13.5
West Germany	19.4	U.S.	11.7

SOURCE: The Cost of Social Security, Ninth International Inquiry, 1972-1974 *(Geneva: ILO, 1979).*

NOTES: *a. Social security is defined to include medical care, sickness benefit, unemployment benefit, old-age benefit, employment-injury benefit, family benefit, maternity benefit, invalidity benefit, and survivor's benefit.*

      b. Ranked from high to low in terms of percent of gross domestic product spent on social security.

tries has climbed. To some extent, the differences are due to factors originating outside of the industrial-relations system. For example, labour forces have been growing faster in North America than in Europe. But industrial-relations customs and laws are also, in part, responsible. For example, employers in Canada and the U.S. regularly lay off workers during brief downturns in the economy whereas such practices are considered unacceptable in many European countries (61).

Political Strategy and the Public Interest

The political strategy of European labour has also paid off in other ways. For example, labour movements in Europe are more integrated into society, and they are considered to be essential institutions of democracy. Labour and management in Europe are often referred to as social partners. Although both sides vigorously pursue their own interests in the industrial-relations arena, they also respect the public interest and attempt to cooperate in pursuing compromises in the general interest.

In contrast, North American industrial-relations systems are adversarial in nature. Organized labour's position in society is less well assured. Self-interest is pursued more narrowly and the public interest in union-management relations is less often and less explicitly taken into account. As noted above, recent research suggests that the level of industrial conflict is largely a function of these differences in industrial-relations systems. In European countries, which have a low level of industrial conflict, trade unions are more legitimate, labour and management pursue a cooperative strategy taking account of the public interest, collective bargaining is more centralized, and a larger part of the total compensation package is decided in the political arena.

In summary, with respect to the terms and conditions of work, the vigorous political strategy pursued by European labour has produced a social wage and general benefits considerably higher than those of the U.S. and Canada where the dominant emphasis of organized labour has been on decentralized bargaining with employers. On the other hand, North American business unionism has produced more worker influence on managerial decisions at the work place but only for a minority of workers. This situation has been changing during the past few decades as North American labour has become more politically active and European labour has more forcefully pushed for more workers' participation in management.

REFERENCES AND WORKS CITED

1. Adams, R.J. "Solidarity, Self-interest and the Unionization Differential between Europe and North America," *Relations Industrielles/Industrial Relations,* Vol. 29 (1974), 497-511.

2. Adams, R.J. "Discussion of Politicization of Canadian Labor Unions," *Industrial Relations Research Association Proceedings,* Vol. 29 (1976), 116-118.

3. Adams, R.J. "A Case for an Employers' Organization in Canada," *Labour Gazette,* Vol. 77 (1977), 153-156.

4. Adams, R.J., and C.H. Rummel. "Workers' Participation in West Germany: Impact on the Worker, the Enterprise and the Trade Union," *Industrial Relations Journal,* Vol. 8 (1977), 4-22.

5. *AFL-CIO News,* October 6, 1979, p. 6.

6. Asplund, C. *Some Aspects of Workers' Participation* (Brussels: International Confederation of Free Trade Unions, 1972).

7. Barkin, S. "Social Contracts in Europe," *Free Labour World,* May-June 1977, p. 6.

8. Barkin, S. "The Total Labor Package: From Wage Bargain to Social Contract," *Journal of Economic Issues,* Vol. 11 (1977), 339-351.

9. Bercuson, D.J. "Canadian Labour and Political Action: Past and Present," *Quarterly Review of Canadian Studies,* Vol. 4 (1976), 86-96.

10. Bergmann, J., and W. Muller-Jentsch. "The Federal Republic of Germany: Cooperative Unionism and Dual Bargaining System Challenged," in S. Barkin (Ed.), *Worker Militancy and its Consequences, 1965-1975* (New York: Praeger, 1975), pp. 235-276.

11. Boivin, J. "The Politicization of Canadian Labor Unions: An Inevitable Phenomenon," *Industrial Relations Research Association Proceedings,* Vol. 29 (1976), 107-115.

12. Bok, D.C. "Reflections on the Distinctive Character of American Labor Laws," *Harvard Law Review,* Vol. 84 (1971), 1394-1463.

13. Brooks, G.W. "Unions and the Structure of Collective Bargaining," in A. Weber (Ed.), *The Structure of Collective Bargaining* (Glencoe, Ill.: Free Press, 1960), pp. 123-140.

14. Carby-Hall, J.R. *Worker Participation in Europe* (London: Croom Helm, 1977).

15. Carlson, B. *Trade Unions in Sweden* (Stockholm: Tidens Forlag, 1969).

16. "Chief Executives Form Organization to Discuss General Economic Issues and Sponsor Research," *Globe and Mail,* April 6, 1977, p. B1.

17. Christy, R.J. "The Structure of Collective Bargaining," in S.M.A. Hameed (Ed.), *Canadian Industrial Relations: A Book of Readings* (Toronto: Butterworth, 1975), pp. 187-204.

18. "Chronicle," *British Journal of Industrial Relations,* various issues.

19. Clark, J. "Concerted Action in the Federal Republic of Germany," *British Journal of Industrial Relations,* Vol. 17 (1979), 242-258.

20. Clark, T., and L. Clements (Eds.). *Trade Unions under Capitalism* (Glasgow: Fontana/ Collins, 1977).

21. Clegg, H.A. *The System of Industrial Relations in Britain* (Oxford: Blackwell, 1972).

22. Cohen, S. *Labor in the United States* (Columbus: Merrill, 1975).

23. Commission on Industrial Relations. *Workers' Participation and Collective Bargaining in Europe* (London: IIMSO, 1974).

24. Dodge, W. (Ed.) *Consultation and Consensus: A New Era in Policy Formulation* (Ottawa: Conference Board in Canada, 1978).

25. Dufty, N.F. *Changes in Labour-management and Relations in the Enterprise* (Paris: OECD, 1975).

26. Dunlop, J.T. "The Development of Labor Organization: A Theoretical Framework," in R. Marshall and R. Perlman (Eds.), *An Anthology of Labor Economics* (Toronto: Wiley, 1972), pp. 5-16.

27. Flanders, A. *Trade Unions* (London: Hutchinson, 1968).

28. Fogarty, M. *Christian Democracy in Western Europe, 1820-1953* (London: Routledge and Kegan Paul, 1957).

29. Forseback, L. *Industrial Relations and Employment in Sweden* (Stockholm: The Swedish Institute, 1976).

30. Galenson, W. *Comparative Labor Movements* (New York: Russell, 1962).

31. Galenson, W., and R.S. Smith "The United States," in J.T. Dunlop and W. Galenson (Eds.), *Labor in the Twentieth Century* (New York: Academic Press, 1978), pp. 11-84.

32. Gunter, H., and G. Leminsky. "The Federal Republic of Germany," in J.T. Dunlop and W. Galenson (Eds.), *Labor in the Twentieth Century* (New York: Academic Press, 1978), pp. 149-196.

33. Hibbs, D.A., Jr. "On the Political Economy of Long Run Trends in Strike Activity," *British Journal of Political Science,* Vol. 8 (1978), 153-175.

34. Horowitz, G. *Canadian Labour in Politics* (Toronto: University of Toronto Press, 1968).

35. Hyman, R. *Industrial Relations: A Marxist Introduction* (London: Macmillan, 1975).

36. International Labour Office. *Collective Bargaining in Industrialized Market Economies* (Geneva: ILO, 1974).

37. International Labour Office. *Social and Labour Bulletin,* various issues.

38. International Organization of Employers. *Structure, Scope and Activities of National Central Employer Organizations* (London: International Organization of Employers, 1970).

39. Isbester, F. "Quebec Labour in Perspective, 1949-1969," in R.U. Miller and F. Isbester (Eds.), *Canadian Labour in Transition* (Scarborough, Ont: Prentice-Hall, 1971), pp. 240-266.

40. Janne, M.H., and G. Spitaels. "Belgium: Collective Bargaining and Concertation Mold a New System," in S. Barkin (Ed.), *Worker Militancy and its Consequences, 1965-1975* (New York: Praeger, 1975), pp. 154-193.

41. Kassalow, E.M. *Trade Unions and Industrial Relations: An International Comparison* (New York: Random House, 1969).

42. Kassalow, E.M. "The Transformation of Christian Trade Unionism: The Recent Evolution of the French CFDT," *Industrial Relations Research Association Proceedings,* Vol. 24 (1971), 186-197.

43. Kassalow, E.M. "The Closed and Union Shop in Western Europe: An American Perspective," *Journal of Labour Research,* Vol. 1 (1980), 323-348.

44. Kendall, W. *The Labour Movement in Europe* (London: Penguin, 1975).

45. Kerr, C., J.T. Dunlop, F. Harbison, and C.A. Myers. *Industrialism and Industrial Man* (New York: Oxford University Press, 1964).

46. Kinsley, B.L. "Trends in Canadian Strikes 1917-1972," *Labour Gazette,* Vol. 76 (1976), 28-33.

47. Landauer, C.A. *European Socialism,* 2 vols. (Berkeley: University of California Press, 1959).

48. Lewin, D. "The Impact of Unionism on American Business: Evidence for an Assessment," *Columbia Journal of World Business,* Vol. 13 (1978), 95-96.

49. Lipset, S.M., and R. Bendix. *Social Mobility in Industrial Society* (Berkeley: University of California Press, 1959).

50. Lorwin, V. *The French Labor Movement* (Cambridge: Harvard University Press, 1954).

51. Losche, P. "Stages in the Evolution of the German Labor Movement," in A. Sturmthal, and J.G. Scoville (Eds.), *The International Labor Movement in Transition* (Urbana, Ill.: University of Illinois Press, 1973), pp. 101-122.

52. McCaffree, K.M. "A Theory of the Origin and Development of Employer Associations," *Industrial Relations Research Association Proceedings,* Vol. 19 (1966), 56-68.

53. Malles, P. *The Institutions of Industrial Relations in Continental Europe* (Ottawa: Information Canada, 1973).

54. Malles, P. *Canadian Industrial Conflict in International Perspective* (Ottawa: Informetrica Ltd. 1977).

55. Miller, R.U. "Political Affiliation of the Trade Unions," in S.M.A. Hameed (Ed.), *Canadian Industrial Relations: A Book of Readings* (Toronto: Butterworth, 1975), pp. 59-70.

56. Morton, D. "Time to Talk: The Labour-NDP Marriage," *Canadian Forum,* February 1976, pp. 12-15.

57. Muller-Jentsch, W., and H.J. Sperling. "Economic Development, Labour Conflicts and the Industrial Relations System in West Germany," in C. Crouch and A. Pizzorno (Eds.), *The Resurgence of Class Conflict in Western Europe since 1968* (London: Macmillan, 1978), pp. 257-306.

58. Organization for Economic Cooperation and Development. *Collective Bargaining and Government Policies* (Paris: OECD, 1979).

59. Panitch, L. "The Development of Corporatism in Liberal Democracies," *Comparative Political Studies,* Vol. 10 (1977), 61-90.

60. Perlman, S.A. *A Theory of the Labor Movement* (New York: Macmillan, 1928).

61. *Report of the Commission of Inquiry on Redundancies* (Ottawa: Labour Canada, 1979).

62. *Report of the Inquiry Commission on Wider-based Collective Bargaining,* Frances Bairstow, Chairman (Ottawa: Labour Canada, 1978).

63. Reynaud, J.D. "Industrial Relations and Political Systems: Some Reflections on the Crisis in Industrial Relations in Western Europe," *British Journal of Industrial Relations*, Vol. 18 (1980), 1-13.

64. Rose, J.B. *Public Policy, Bargaining Structure and the Construction Industry* (Toronto: Butterworth, 1980).

65. Ross, A.M., and P.T. Hartman. *Changing Patterns of Industrial Conflict* (New York: Wiley, 1960).

66. Sellier, F. "The French Workers' Movement and Political Unionism," in A. Sturmthal and J.G. Scoville (Eds.), *The International Labor Movement in Transition* (Urbana, Ill.: University of Illinois Press, 1973), pp. 79-100.

67. Sturmthal, A. "Economic Development and the Labour Movement," in A.M. Ross Jr. (Ed.), *Industrial Relations and Economic Development* (London: Macmillan, 1966), pp. 165-181.

68. Sturmthal, A. *Comparative Labor Movements* (Belmont, Cal.: Wadsworth, 1972).

69. Sturmthal, A. "Industrial Relations Strategies," in A. Sturmthal and J.G. Scoville (Eds.), *The International Labor Movement in Transition* (Urbana, Ill.: University of Illinois Press, 1973), pp. 1-33.

70. "Sweden Ends Work Stoppage," *Globe and Mail,* May 12, 1980, p. B2.

71. Taft, P. "Germany," in W. Galenson (Ed.), *Comparative Labor Movements* (New York: Russell, 1952), pp. 277-283.

72. Thompson, A.W.J. "Trade Unions and the Corporate State in Britain," *Industrial and Labor Relations Review,* Vol. 33 (1979), 36-54.

73. Union Bank of Switzerland. *Prices and Earnings Around the Globe.* Geneva, 1980.

74. Webb, S., and B. Webb. *Industrial Democracy* (London: Longman, 1920).

75. Wheeler, C. *White-collar Power* (Urbana, Ill.: University of Illinois Press, 1975).

76. Windmuller, J. *Labor Relations in the Netherlands* (Ithaca, N.Y.: Cornell University Press, 1969).

77. Woods, H.D. *Labour Policy in Canada,* 2nd ed. (Toronto: Macmillan, 1973).

78. Wood, W.D., and P. Kumar (Eds.). *The Current Industrial Relations Scene in Canada, 1979* (Kingston: Queen's University Industrial Relations Centre, 1979).

QUESTIONS

1. The North American labour movements have emphasized an "economic" strategy for seeking their goals while the approach of continental European labour movements has been more political. What have been the practical consequences of these different strategies on the conditions of the average worker?

2. A typical North American collective agreement might contain a management's-rights clause, a union-security clause, actual wages to be paid per job class, seniority provisions regarding promotions and layoffs, and a grievance procedure ending in binding arbitration. How would these same issues be handled in a typical European situation? Use examples from at least two countries.

3. Sturmthal's thesis in "Economic Development and the Labour Movement" may be thought of as an attempt to resolve the differences between Marxist philosophy and Perlman's "Theory of the Labour Movement." How does Sturmthal go about doing this? Is his thesis convincing?

4. In Europe today, the great majority of employers accept trade unions as necessary and legitimate institutions. Contrarily, large numbers of North American employers continue to resist unionism and do not recognize the necessity of trade unions. What factors account for these differences?

5. Works councils are common agencies of job regulation in Europe but they do not exist in North America. Why have they appeared in Europe and not North America? What functions do they serve? What advantages and disadvantages do they have over the North American approach to these same functions?

6. Collective bargaining has been described as the American approach to industrial democracy. What advantages and disadvantages does American-style collective bargaining have over other forms of industrial democracy found in Europe?

7. What is a social contract? What forces have given rise to the use of social contracts in Europe?

8. Describe the present-day pattern of industrial conflict in Canada and at least two other countries outside of North America (these two countries should exhibit patterns different from each other). Provide an explanation for these three patterns.

9. In some developed countries, industrial conflict has increased in the long run; in others it has decreased. How may these different patterns be explained?

10. Most North American IR experts explicitly or implicitly assume that industrial conflict is primarily a problem of the bargaining process. How well does this assumption hold up against the international experience?

11. What are the differences in the "social wage" between the typical European country and North America? To what extent are these differences due to variation in the IR systems? What is the relationship between the social wage and the volume of industrial conflict?

12. What advantages did European employers see in pursuing multiemployer bargaining? In light of the European experience, why have North American employers, by and large, rejected multiemployer bargaining?

FRANK REID

20. Wage-and-Price Controls in Canada*

The two main reasons for the surprise imposition of a three-year controls program in October 1975 were: (a) wage settlements and inflation had increased dramatically, and an intolerable rise in unemployment would result from combating inflation using restrictive monetary and fiscal policy alone; (b) the government may have seriously misread labour market conditions because of a change in frictional and structural unemployment.

Studies show that, due to controls, wage settlements dropped by three or four percentage points more than otherwise predicted. Although it was the dramatic AIB (Anti-Inflation Board) rollbacks that made headlines, most of the effect of the controls program was on negotiations prior to submitting settlements to the AIB. The average rollback was substantially less than 1 percent in each year of the program.

Profit margins were restrained mainly by market conditions rather than by controls. The inflation rate of nonfood items dropped steadily throughout the program, and inflation of food prices (mainly outside the scope of controls) dropped sharply the first year but then rose again. On average, wages increased by 2 percent per year faster than prices, indicating that Labour's fear that controls would be an attack on workers was not realized.

A comprehensive three-year program of wage-and-price controls on the Canadian economy was announced as a complete surprise in a national television address by Prime Minister Pierre Trudeau on October 13th, 1975. The program imposed mandatory limits on wage increases in all private-sector firms with more than 500 employees, construction industry firms with more than 20 employees, and all public-sector employees.

The impact on industrial relations was dramatic. For three years, the controls program suspended free collective bargaining for all major groups in Canada. It was unquestionably the most important single change in government policy affecting industrial relations in the postwar period.

*I am indebted to Allan Maslove for helpful comments.

The labour movement had long opposed controls. It had refused to cooperate in the government's attempt in 1969-70 to introduce voluntary restraint through the Prices and Incomes Commission, and it reacted quickly to condemn the mandatory controls. Less than a month after the beginning of the controls program, the Ontario Federation of Labour passed the following resolution at its annual convention in Kitchener in November 1975:

> The Ontario Federation of Labour is firmly opposed to the federal government's so-called anti-inflation program. We believe that it is ill-conceived, outrageously inequitable, shamelessly one-sided, patently dishonest, highly undemocratic, un-workable and even, possibly unconstitutional. (OFL *Policy Statement*)

Most professional economists rejected the use of wage-and-price controls, regarding them as ineffective in controlling inflation and as having adverse effects on resource allocation. Even Prime Minister Trudeau and the Liberal Party had strongly opposed controls in the 1974 federal election in the previous year. Controls were a major election issue and the Liberals won reelection on a platform opposing controls.

In the face of this widespread opposition, why did the government decide to impose controls? An answer to this question requires an examination of the economic situation leading up to controls, and this is the first topic discussed. The actual structure of the controls program is then discussed, followed by an analysis of the effects on wage settlements, inflation, strike activity, contract duration, and union organizing. Some concluding comments on the impact of the program and comparisons with experiences in other countries are contained in the final section.

WHY CONTROLS WERE IMPOSED IN CANADA

The government's main consideration in imposing controls was the rise in inflation and wage settlements in 1974 and 1975. As Table 1 shows, during 1974-75 there was a sharp rise in the Canadian inflation rate and an even more dramatic rise in the level of wage settlements in contracts negotiated in the 1974-75 period. During this period, wage settlements were in excess of 15 percent per year compared to increases in the range of 6 to 10 percent in the 1967-1973 period. Initially, the prevailing view was that the inflation was externally generated and temporary. By 1975, however, the high level of wage settlements suggested inflation had become more internally generated and entrenched.

Since the large settlements in 1974-75 were one of the main reasons for the implementation of controls it is important to understand their cause. Research has shown that average wage settlements in the economy are related to economic conditions, inflationary expectations, and the need for catch-up wage increases (4, 9, 18). With regard to the first point, when economic conditions are booming, unions are in a stronger bargaining position and tend to negotiate higher wage settlements, other things holding constant. On the second point, if a high rate of inflation is expected over the life of the contract then the negotiated settlement tends to increase by roughly an equivalent amount. The reason is that workers need an increase to protect the purchasing power of their wages and when firms are in an inflationary environment they are in a better position to grant larger wage increases because they will be anticipating an increase in the price of the goods or service being produced. (In economic terms, an increase in expected inflation shifts

Table 1

Average Settlements in Major Collective Agreements,[a]
Inflation, and Unemployment

Year & Quarter	Wage settlements, Manufacturing		Wage settlements, All sectors		Inflation	Unemployment
	All agreements	Agreements without COLAs[b]	All agreements	Agreements without COLAs[b]		
1967: 1	7.1	—	8.7	—	2.1	3.7
2	8.2	—	8.7	—	4.9	3.7
3	7.9	—	7.7	—	5.5	3.7
4	7.6	—	8.0	—	2.7	4.2
1968: 1	9.3	—	8.5	—	4.8	4.4
2	7.9	—	8.1	—	2.8	4.5
3	7.2	—	7.9	—	3.7	4.5
4	7.0	—	7.2	—	5.3	4.5
1969: 1	6.4	—	7.2	—	3.4	4.3
2	8.2	—	7.4	—	6.5	4.4
3	9.4	—	7.9	—	3.9	4.4
4	9.1	—	8.2	—	4.0	4.6
1970: 1	8.5	—	8.7	—	4.1	4.9
2	8.0	—	8.1	—	2.6	5.8
3	8.8	—	9.0	—	0.9	6.2
4	8.1	—	8.4	—	1.0	6.1
1971: 1	7.2	—	7.8	—	2.4	6.2
2	8.1	—	7.8	—	4.7	6.3
3	8.6	—	8.2	—	4.8	6.1
4	6.8	—	7.5	—	4.3	6.1
1972: 1	7.5	—	9.2	—	5.1	5.9
2	7.9	—	7.7	—	2.8	6.1
3	9.4	—	8.9	—	6.8	6.4
4	9.3	—	6.9	—	5.5	6.5
1973: 1	9.1	—	9.9	—	7.9	5.9
2	10.0	—	9.4	—	8.5	5.4
3	9.5	—	10.2	—	10.1	5.4
4	7.2	—	9.8	—	8.5	5.5
1974: 1	12.9	14.0	11.9	11.8	10.2	5.2
2	11.7	14.9	13.1	13.4	12.8	5.2
3	13.4	15.0	14.8	15.4	10.7	5.3
4	14.0	24.0	17.5	19.1	12.0	5.7

Table 1 (continued)

Average Settlements in Major Collective Agreements,[a]
Inflation, and Unemployment

Year & Quarter	Wage settlements, Manufacturing		Wage settlements, All sectors		Inflation	Unemployment
	All agreements	Agreements without COLAs[b]	All agreements	Agreements without COLAs[b]		
1975: 1	15.0	17.9	18.2	18.5	9.5	6.7
2	15.7	16.6	18.8	20.8	8.2	6.9
3	12.6	18.4	17.1	20.3	12.6	7.0
4	14.0	14.6	14.8	13.5	8.7	7.1
1976: 1	11.7	12.3	14.1	14.7	6.2	6.8
2	9.7	10.1	10.8	11.3	5.6	7.0
3	9.3	9.3	9.4	10.2	4.8	7.3
4	5.9	9.2	7.9	8.7	6.8	7.4
1977: 1	7.1	7.4	8.4	8.5	9.4	7.9
2	6.4	7.6	8.0	8.4	8.8	7.9
3	7.2	7.6	7.4	7.5	7.6	8.3
4	7.3	7.3	7.1	7.3	9.5	8.4
1978: 1	6.6	7.4	6.6	6.9	8.2	8.4
2	6.5	7.2	6.4	6.4	9.2	8.5
3	6.4	8.2	6.9	7.4	9.2	8.5
4	7.5	8.3	7.8	8.0	6.2	8.2
1979: 1	7.5	8.3	7.1	8.1	9.0	7.9
2	7.2	9.1	8.2	8.2	10.5	7.6
3	10.4	10.5	9.0	9.0	7.9	7.1
4	5.3	10.4	8.1	9.5	9.2	7.3
1980: 1	8.3	10.7	9.0	9.4	8.9	7.4
2	8.0	11.1	10.2	10.9	11.1	7.7

SOURCE: *Wage settlements data are from Labour Canada's* Wage Developments. *The unemployment rate is seasonally adjusted and revised to the new Labour Force Survey definitions introduced in January 1976, Statistics Canada catalogue 71-201 (1979), p. 24. The inflation rate is the quarter-to-quarter percentage change in the Consumer Price Index at an annual rate, Statistics Canada catalogue 11-003.*

NOTES: a. *Bargaining units of 500 or more employees, excluding construction.*

b. *COLA provisions were not common in the 1967-73 period, and a separate series for agreements without COLA was not published in that period.*

Figure 1

**Canadian Unemployment-Vacancy
Relationship, 1953-78**

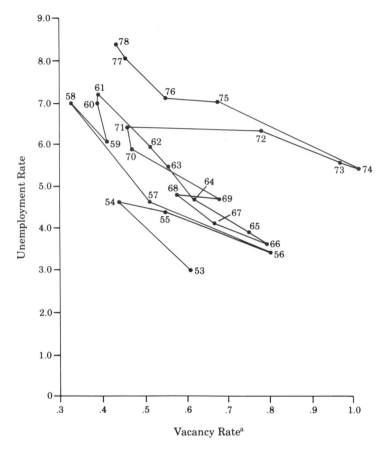

SOURCE: *Frank Reid and Noah M. Meltz, "Causes of Shifts in the Unemployment-Vacancy Relationship: An Empirical Analysis for Canada,"* Review of Economics and Statistics, *Vol. 61 (1979), 470.*

NOTES: a. *The vacancy rate is calculated as the number of vacant jobs as a percentage of the number of jobs. Vacancy
data are from Statistics Canada's Job Vacancy Survey from the beginning of the survey in 1971 until its
termination in 1978. Prior vacancy data are the Economic Council of Canada series constructed by Denton
et. al. (11) to link the National Employment Service data, the Help Wanted Index and the Job Vacancy
Survey data in a consistent series.*

up both the supply and demand curves of labour.) On the third point, wage settlements will also tend to increase if an unexpected increase in inflation over the
previous contract has reduced the purchasing power of the wage below the level
which was anticipated by the union and management during the previous negotiations. In this case, a "catch-up" increase is needed just to restore the real wage to its
"equilibrium" level.

To what extent can these factors account for the high level of wage settlements in the 1974-75 period? As indicated previously, the inflation rate did rise just prior to this period and, although this explains part of the increase in wage settlements, the rise in the inflation rate was not enough to explain all of the increase.

The usual measure of economic conditions in the labour market is the unemployment rate. Table 1 shows that in the year just prior to controls, the unemployment rate had risen to quite high levels compared to the rates that existed during the mid-1960s. A high unemployment rate normally indicates a weak labour market and, other things equal, would tend to reduce rather than increase wage settlements.

The occurrence of such high wage settlements during what appeared to be a recession created a feeling in government that long-standing economic relationships had broken down, and the economy was out of control (14, p. 11). Government felt that dramatic and highly visible action was needed and resorted to a controls program.

Although the high wage settlements in 1974-75 were somewhat of a puzzle at the time, subsequent economic research offers an explanation. What appears to have happened is that in the early 1970s a substantial change occurred in the relationship between the unemployment rate and conditions in the labour market. Figure 1 plots the Canadian annual unemployment rate against an alternative measure of labour market conditions, the job vacancy rate. The data are for the period 1953 to 1978, and the numbered points in the figure indicate years. During the period 1953 to 1971 the points lie in a downward sloping band known as the unemployment-vacancy curve. During booms, the economy moves to the lower right-hand end of the curve characterized by a low unemployment rate and a high job-vacancy rate. During recessions, the economy moves to the upper left-hand end of the curve with a high unemployment rate and a low job-vacancy rate. The height of the curve is determined by the amount of structural and frictional unemployment in the economy.

During the 1950s and 1960s, there appears to have been a slow upward drift of the unemployment-vacancy curve followed by a pronounced upward shift in 1972. Research on the causes of this shift suggests that the two main factors were an increase in structural unemployment resulting from the changing demographic composition of the labour force and an increase in frictional unemployment resulting from the substantial changes in the Unemployment Insurance Act in 1972 (21). The important point is that after the upward shift in the unemployment-vacancy curve a "boom" in the economy was characterized by a substantially higher rate of unemployment than prior to the shift.

The government was not aware of this dramatic shift in the unemployment-vacancy curve when it made the decision to implement controls because the historical job-vacancy rate series was not constructed until 1975 by Denton et al. (11). For this reason, the government's decision to implement controls may have been influenced by a serious misreading of labour-market conditions at the time. Looking only at the unemployment rate in 1974, one could easily conclude that the economy was in a recession, and the labour market was very weak. Looking at the job vacancy rate, however, suggests that the economy was in one of the strongest booms in the postwar period. The view that the precontrols period was a boom is also supported by other measures, such as capacity utilization in manufacturing and deviation of real GNP from its trend rate of growth (3, p. 19). When this information is combined with the rise in the inflation rate in the early 1970s, the high wage settlements of 1974-75 become much easier to understand.

Figure 2

**Actual and Predicted Wage
Settlements, Canadian Manufacturing,
1967:1 to 1978:3**

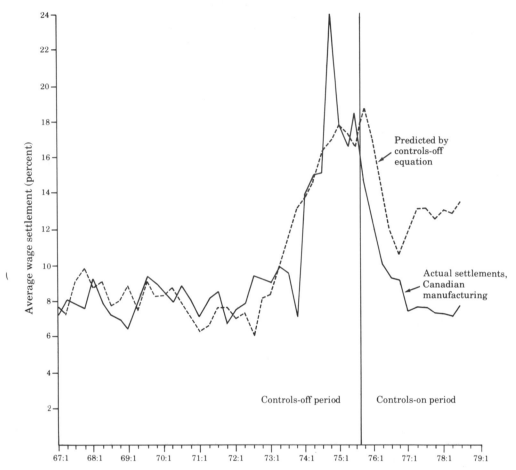

SOURCE: *Frank Reid, "The Effect of Controls on the Rate of Wage Change in Canada,"* Canadian Journal of Economics, *Vol. 12 (1979), 219.*

These qualitative arguments are also supported by quantitative research using formal statistical methods. Several studies which use the vacancy rate as the measure of labour market conditions (rather than the unemployment rate) are able to explain the rise in settlements in the 1974-75 period. For example, Figure 2 shows the actual level of wage settlements in Canadian manufacturing and the predicted level using a multiple regression analysis. The regression model is able to explain about 75 percent of the total variation in settlements over the period including the large increase in 1974-75.

It was mentioned earlier that most economists were opposed to the use of wage-and-price controls. This partly reflected a general concern over government intervention in a market economy and partly a concern that controls would have no long-term effect on inflation if the underlying causes of inflation were not addressed. Most economists (monetarists and nonmonetarists) would agree that reducing the rate of growth of the money supply is a key element in controlling inflation and that a sufficiently restrictive monetary and fiscal policy would *eventually* restrain inflation without controls.

The government was aware of these arguments but it was also very concerned about the severe and prolonged recession which could result from adopting highly restrictive policies. The way that restrictive monetary policy restrains inflation is to create a recession and increase unemployment. This restrains wage settlements and changes in labour costs and eventually restrains price changes. The "short-run" rise in unemployment resulting from such policies, however, could require a severe recession for several years to significantly reduce inflation using monetary policy alone. In a situation in which there is a high expected inflation rate and in which the government adopts a restrictive monetary policy, controls can be used as a complementary policy in an attempt to bring actual and expected inflation down directly with a less severe rise in unemployment than would occur if the restrictive monetary policy were used alone (19).

In addition to economic and political considerations concerning the desirability of controls, there is a question as to whether the federal government had the constitutional right to implement the program. Jurisdiction over wages and prices is normally a provincial matter under the property and civil rights section of the B.N.A. Act. The federal government, however, argued that it had authority under the "peace, order and good government" provision of the B.N.A. Act which could be invoked in an emergency situation or a matter of urgent national concern. The matter was referred to the Supreme Court of Canada which upheld the "national emergency" argument but disallowed the "serious national concern" argument (14, pp. 42-43).

THE CANADIAN CONTROLS PROGRAM

The program of wage-and-price controls was part of a broader policy initiative to restrain inflation. An Anti-Inflation Program consisting of four components was specified in the government's white paper, *Attack on Inflation: A Program of National Action,* which was tabled in the House of Commons on October 14, 1975. The first component was the continuation of restrictive fiscal policies, which had been announced in the budget of June 1975, and the reduction in the rate of growth of the money supply by the Bank of Canada. Although these policies were regarded by the government as essential in controlling inflation, it was not prepared to use them as the only policy: "The government has repeatedly emphasized its rejection of the use of severe monetary and fiscal restraint to stop inflation at heavy immediate cost in terms of unemployment and forgone output" (5, p. 4). The second component was a more specific commitment to limit the rate of growth of total government spending (including provincial and municipal spending) to the rate of growth of gross national product. Structural policies to make product markets more competitive and collective bargaining less fragmented comprised the third component. The final component of the program was the formation of an Anti-Inflation Board (AIB) to directly control increases in prices and incomes. The AIB was not officially established until the passage of the Anti-Inflation Act in December 1975. The act, however, was made retroactive to October 14th, 1975.

The language of the act gave the impression that the AIB would attempt to achieve voluntary restraint of changes in income. The duties of the board specified in the act were to "endeavour through consultations and negotiations with the parties involved to modify such changes so as to bring them within the limits and spirit of the guidelines" (6, section 12). The act also established an administrator, however, to deal with cases where the AIB could not obtain "voluntary" compliance. The administrator had the power to enforce the board's decision or a modification of it. It became apparent during the first year of the controls program that the administrator might impose even more severe restrictions on wage increases than the board (1, p. 60). As a consequence, less than 2 percent of the board's decisions on wage increases above the guidelines (358 of 22,340 decisions) were referred to the administrator (2, p. 7). The Anti-Inflation Act also established an appeal tribunal to which decisions of the administrator could be appealed.

As indicated earlier, the Anti-Inflation Act covered all employees in the federal government and federal agencies, private-sector firms with over 500 employees, and construction firms with over 20 employees. It did not apply directly to employees of provincial governments or employees under provincial jurisdiction such as those in municipal government, the health sector, and the education sector. The act, however, specified that provinces could enter the program either by placing employees under the jurisdiction of the federal act or by administering parallel acts. All provinces except Quebec and Saskatchewan "opted in" to the federal program by passing legislation retroactive to October 14, 1975. Quebec administered its own compulsory controls program with provisions identical to the federal program. In November 1976, the new Parti Québécois government was elected, however, and in March 1977 the Quebec program was terminated after less than one and one-half years of controls. Saskatchewan implemented a system of voluntary restraints on its employees and was the only province without a compulsory controls program.

Although the program applied only to private-sector firms with more than 500 employees, there would typically be several separate employee groups within one firm: office workers, executives, and various bargaining units within the plant. It was therefore possible for the controls to apply to a group which was very small, even consisting of only one employee.

Although firms with less than 500 employees were not covered by controls, it was felt that the smaller firms would be strongly influenced by settlements at the larger ones and the controls would thus have an indirect effect on wages in the whole economy.

The AIB was to control prices and wages in accordance with guidelines specified in the *Anti-Inflation Act Regulations* published in conjunction with the act. There were three components to the guidelines for maximum wage increases. The first was a "basic protection factor" of 8 percent in the first year of the program, 6 percent in the second year, and 4 percent in the third year. These figures equalled the government's target for maximum increases in the price level during the three years of the controls program.

To make the program more attractive, the regulations also specified that if the actual inflation rate exceeded the target rate during the first year of the program then the basic protection factor would be raised by an equal amount in the second year. Similarly, the basic protection factor for the third year would be increased if inflation exceeded its target in the second year (7, section 46). The White Paper stated that no decrease in the basic protection factor would occur if inflation was below the target rate (5, p. 21), although this provision was not specified in the official regulations.

During the first year of the program, the inflation rate was only 6.23 percent, about 1.75 percentage points below the guideline, but during the second year of the program inflation rose to 8.77 percent, about 2.75 percentage points above the guideline. Under the regulations, the basic protection factor in the third year should have been increased by 2.75 percentage points. At this point, however, the government reneged on its promise and changed the rules to specify that no increase in the basic protection factor would be allowed in the third year (1, p. 64).

A "national productivity factor" of 2 percent per year comprised the second component of the wage guidelines. The productivity factor reflected the fact that, on average over the two decades prior to the controls period, wage increases had exceeded price increases by 2 to 3 percent per year as a result of long-term productivity growth.

The third component of the guidelines was an "experience adjustment factor" which took into account the size of the wage increase the group had achieved prior to controls. If in either the contract prior to controls or the two-year period prior to controls (whichever was longer) the group's average annual settlement exceeded the annual inflation rate, plus 2 percent, then the group's guideline would be reduced by this amount over the three years of controls, subject to the restriction of a maximum 2-percentage-point decrease per year. Similarly, the experience rating factor could increase a group's guideline to allow a "catch-up" of a maximum of 2 percent per year if it had fallen behind during the period prior to controls. The experience-rating factor implied considerable flexibility since a group's guideline could vary as much as 2 percent above or below the basic-target increases of 10 percent the first year, 8 percent the second, and 6 percent the third. Because of the large wage settlements in the economy prior to controls, the average experience-rating factor was negative in all three years resulting in average guidelines over the three years of the program of 9.7, 7.4, and 5.6 percent (2, p. 8).

In an attempt to increase the equity of income distribution, the *Regulations* also specified that the average increase for any group could not exceed $2400 and no restriction would be placed on increases of up to $600 per year or increases to bring the average wage rate of the group up to $3.50 per hour.

The guidelines applied broadly to virtually all forms of compensation to prevent avoidance by negotiating increases in fringe benefits rather than wages. If COLAs were negotiated, they were to be costed by assuming inflation over the life of the contract would equal the target inflation rates.

One of the more difficult problems in designing the program was the treatment of "increments" received for years of service which are specified in some contracts, particularly in the public sector. Such increments would not increase unit labour costs for an employer in a steady-state situation in which the average age of its employees is constant. In that situation, the savings from the replacement of high-wage retiring employees by low-wage new employees would offset the cost of the increments to the rest of the employee group. Since restraint of labour costs was the objective of the Anti-Inflation Program, logic suggests that such increments should not be included in the percentage increase to which the guidelines apply. The same logic implies, however, that if a firm has a constant mean age it will not matter if the increments are included because the AIB guidelines apply to aggregate labour costs for the employee groups. In a steady-state situation, the existence of increments will not result in an increase in aggregate labour costs.

The *Anti-Inflation Regulations* (section 49), however, specified that an increment should be included unless "a condition of the payment of the increment [is that it] shall only be paid if the employee to whom it is payable has improved or added to the skills or knowledge required by the employee in the performance of the duties of the job." The AIB considered each case separately but tended to exclude increments from the calculations if there was a significant discretionary element in their payment. In a May 1976 decision involving secondary-school teachers in the Essex County Board of Education in Ontario, the AIB limited the teachers to the arithmetic guideline but excluded increments from the calculations. The Ontario Secondary School Teachers Federation appealed the ruling to the administrator who upheld the arithmetic guideline but also ruled the increments should be included in the calculations, resulting in an even harsher judgment than that handed down by the board. In further series of appeals, the decision to include the increments was rejected by the appeal tribunal but confirmed by the federal court and finally by the Supreme Court of Canada (1, p. 58).

The AIB was given discretionary power to approve wage increases above the guidelines if the contract had expired prior to October 14th, 1975, and negotiations were not concluded until after that date. The board had also had discretion to approve increases above the guidelines if an historical relationship existed. The *Regulations* define an historical relationship as existing where wage rates of another group in the same industry were related for two years prior to controls in terms of level and timing of increases. The existence of an historical relationship, however, did not necessarily imply an increase to fully restore the relationship.

The regulations also specified that wage increases to remove restrictive work practices or to eliminate sex discrimination were not subject to controls. Also exempt were increases necessary to recruit employees for positions which had been vacant for three months or longer.

For self-employed professionals, the same principles applied as for salaried employees. Fees could not be increased more than necessary to increase the net income of the professional by either $2400 or the arithmetic guideline.

Prices were not controlled directly under the Anti-Inflation Act. Instead, prices were controlled indirectly by restraining the rate of change of unit labour costs and imposing a rather complicated set of rules controlling profits. Since the effect of controls on industrial relations is the main focus of this chapter only a brief outline of the profit controls will be given. The basic idea was to restrain profits to the average share of national income which had existed over a lengthy time period prior to controls. Profit margins in the precontrols period had been somewhat above their long-run trend but calculations indicated that restraining profit margins to .95 of their precontrols rate would restore the long-run share (1, p. 110). To accomplish this goal, price increases were restricted to the absolute dollar increase in costs. This would leave absolute profits unchanged from the year prior to controls (with an unchanged output) and, because of increasing price, profit *margins* expressed as a percentage of sales would decline somewhat. For example, if initially a firm earned x dollars profit per $100 of sales and prices increased by 6 percent (the average target over controls) then x dollars of profit on $106 of output would result in a profit margin equal to 100/106 = .943 of the previous margin. Firms which were unable to allocate costs to individual products were required to price such that their profits did not exceed .95 of the precontrols level.

A check was made at the end of each fiscal year to ensure that the firm had priced at the required level. If its profit exceeded the target level, the "excess revenue" was required to be returned to the market through subsequent adjustments approved by the AIB. There were also special rules for firms with exceptionally low profits in the base period, extraordinary productivity gains, export sales, as well as for firms in the retail and financial-insurance sectors. During the third year of the program, these profit rules were modified somewhat.

THE EFFECTS OF CONTROLS

Two effects on wage settlements can be distinguished — the amount of rollback by the AIB and the effect on negotiated settlements prior to submission to the AIB. Although the amount of the AIB rollback is obvious, the amount and even the direction of the effect of controls on negotiated wage settlements is unclear. On the one hand, negotiated settlements may be reduced to more closely comply with the AIB "guidelines." Unions may feel there is little advantage in risking a strike to negotiate a large settlement which will then be rolled back by the AIB. On the other hand, negotiated settlements may increase if companies feel there is less advantage in risking a strike to obtain a low settlement because a low settlement will subsequently be imposed by the AIB. Furthermore, if both parties anticipate that the AIB will roll back part of the excess over the guideline, it would be possible for the negotiators to build this into the settlement with the result that the rolled-back settlement would be roughly equal to what the parties would have negotiated in the absence of controls. Another argument is that if the guideline is set too high it may act as a floor rather than a ceiling, tending to increase settlements that otherwise would be below the guideline.

An assessment of the net result of these various effects on wage increases requires an examination of the empirical evidence during controls. The data in Table 1 show a clear drop in wage settlements following the introduction of controls in the fourth quarter of 1974. This drop cannot be attributed entirely to controls, however, because other things were not held constant when controls were introduced. In particular, a restrictive monetary and fiscal policy was adopted, and this would also tend to reduce wage settlements.

To determine the effect of controls requires an economic model to determine how much settlements would have dropped if the same economic conditions in the labour market had existed without controls. Three studies which have attempted to answer this question, using somewhat different economic models, have all found that settlements during controls were substantially below what would have been predicted without controls (4, 10, 18). In Figure 2, the broken line shows the level of wage settlements that would have been predicted during the controls period on the basis of the relationship between settlements and economic conditions prior to controls. Clearly, the actual settlements are lower than predicted, by about four and one-half percentage points, a substantial and statistically significant amount. Such a finding does not "prove" that the effect was due to controls — it may have been due

Table 2

**Effective Rate of Compensation Increases,
By Program Year, Sector, and Union Status**

			Effective Rate of Increase		
	No. of Cases	No. of Employees	Proposed Increase	Guidelines	Effective Rate
October 14, 1975 to October 13, 1976					
Public					
Nonunion	7,229	367,250	8.5	9.1	8.3
Union	2,336	711,097	10.8	9.8	10.1
Total	9,565	1,078,347	10.0	9.5	9.5
Private					
Nonunion	16,683	1,199,738	9.0	10.0	8.9
Union	3,753	711,307	11.0	9.3	9.7
Total	20,436	1,911,045	9.8	9.8	9.2
Public and private					
Nonunion	23,912	1,566,988	8.9	9.8	8.8
Union	6,089	1,422,404	10.9	9.5	9.9
Total	30,001	2,989,392	9.9	9.7	9.3
October 14, 1976 to October 13, 1977					
Public					
Nonunion	7,252	350,750	6.7	7.4	6.6
Union	2,799	998,220	7.4	7.3	7.3
Total	10,051	1,348,970	7.2	7.3	7.1
Private					
Nonunion	17,464	1,429,011	7.0	7.7	7.0
Union	6,032	1,192,905	7.8	7.1	7.1
Total	23,496	2,621,916	7.4	7.4	7.0
Public and private					
Nonunion	24,716	1,779,761	7.0	7.6	6.9
Union	8,831	2,191,125	7.6	7.2	7.2
Total	33,547	3,970,886	7.3	7.4	7.1

Table 2 (continued)

	No. of Cases	No. of Employees	Effective Rate of Increase		
			Proposed Increase	Guidelines	Effective Rate
October 14, 1977 to April 13, 1978					
Public					
Nonunion	3,820	125,570	5.2	5.5	5.2
Union	1,285	451,110	5.5	5.5	5.4
Total	5,105	576,680	5.4	5.5	5.3
Private					
Nonunion	8,789	764,120	5.5	6.0	5.5
Union	2,778	537,374	5.6	5.3	5.2
Total	11,567	1,301,494	5.6	5.7	5.4
Public and private					
Nonunion	12,609	889,690	5.5	5.9	5.4
Union	4,063	988,484	5.5	5.4	5.3
Total	16,672	1,878,174	5.5	5.6	5.3

to some other event which occurred at the same time. In the absence of knowledge of any other major events which could supply an alternative explanation, however, the effect may be tentatively attributed to controls.

The study by Auld et al. (4) showed that most of the restraining influence of the AIB was through its impact on negotiated settlements before they were submitted to the board. Reflecting this effect, and the restrictive economic conditions which existed, is the fact that approximately 70 percent of the increases submitted to the AIB over its life were at or below the arithmetic guideline (2, p. 3).

Table 2 shows the average wage increase submitted, the average guideline, and the average approved wage increase during each of the three years of controls. The data is also broken down by public and private sector and by union and nonunion group. As previously indicated, the average guidelines for all sectors during the three years were 9.7, 7.4, and 5.6 percent. The data also indicate that in each year of the program the average guideline for public-sector groups was lower than the average for private-sector groups, reflecting the large settlements of some public-sector groups prior to controls, particularly workers in the health and education sectors.

Another striking pattern is that in each year and for both the public and private sectors, the average proposed settlement of nonunion groups was below their guideline, and the average for the union groups was above their guideline. The rollbacks of settlements above the guidelines and the existence of a substantial number of settlements below the guideline resulted in the average wage increase approved by the board being below the average guideline in each year of the program.

Several authors have discovered through statistical analysis that when the board was required to make a decision on a negotiated settlement which was over the guideline, its approved settlement tended to "split-the-difference" in a fairly predictable way (12, 14, 15, 17). Maslove and Swimmer (14) hypothesize that this behaviour is a rational response to the board's conflicting desires to exercise restraint but also to avoid adverse public opinion that might result if settlements were rolled all the way back to the guideline.

On the basis of their regression analysis of AIB decisions, Maslove and Swimmer show that public-sector groups received awards of about one-half percentage point less than private-sector groups with equal guidelines and negotiated increases (14, p. 101). The results also show that, within the public sector, approved awards to certain quasi-public groups (such as hospital service workers and school caretakers) were a full percentage point lower than awards to federal and provincial employee groups who had equal guidelines and negotiated settlements (14, p. 142).

Controls applied to total compensation, including fringe benefits, so the guidelines could not be avoided simply by negotiating increases in fringes rather than wages. It is possible, however, that controls may have been partially avoided by negotiating changes in items which are virtually impossible to cost, such as union-security provisions. There is, however, no evidence on the importance of such changes.

A similar argument at the national level is made by Lipsey (13). He argues that in future when controls are imposed the government may attempt to gain the support of the labour movement by implementing changes in labour legislation which may have long-term detrimental effects on society. He cites the implementation of universal closed-shop legislation in Britain as an example of such an occurrence.

Table 3 shows that the rate of change of average hourly earnings declined during the three years of the program. Because controls did not affect deferred increases in multiyear contracts negotiated prior to October 1975 and because they did not directly control increases in firms with less than 500 employees, the increase in average hourly earnings in the economy exceeded the wage targets of 10, 8, and 6 percent in each year of the program. Through the effect on new settlements the controls did reduce unit labour cost increase by an average of about 2 percent per year below what would have occurred without controls (4). The program's target of unit labour cost increases of 8, 6, and 4 percent was, however, somewhat unrealistic.

Table 3 also shows that the annual rate of change of the CPI declined from 11.10 percent in the two years prior to controls to 6.23 percent in the first year of controls and then rose to 8.77 and 8.67 percent in the final two years. This unusual pattern resulted mainly from the behaviour of food prices which actually dropped during the first year of controls and then increased by substantial amounts in the second and third years. The rate of change of the CPI for all items excluding food declined steadily from a 10 percent rate prior to controls to a 6.42 percent rate in the final year, consistent with the steady decline in the rate of change of average hourly earnings. Since food prices were generally not under the control of the AIB (in spite of the board's attempt to take credit for the first year drop in food prices) these figures suggest that, although the board did not achieve its target inflation rate, it was partially successful in reducing the rate of price increase for commodities within the scope of the program by about 2 percent per year.

Table 3

**Average Annual Rates of Change
of Wages and Prices in Canada**

Period	Guide-line	Approved Settlements	Hourly Earnings	CPI	Real Hourly Earnings	CPI Exfood	CPI Food
			(in percent)				
Oct. 55-Oct. 75	—	—	6.63	3.79	2.74	2.54	3.14
Oct. 73-Oct. 75	—	—	14.74	11.10	3.28	10.04	13.84
Oct. 75-Oct. 76	9.7	9.3	12.98	6.23	6.35	9.08	−0.90
Oct. 76-Oct. 77	7.4	7.1	10.64	8.77	1.72	7.30	12.73
Oct. 77-Oct. 78	5.6	5.3	7.02	8.67	−1.51	6.42	14.55
Oct. 75-Oct. 78	—	—	10.19	7.88	2.14	7.59	8.57
Oct. 78-Oct. 80	—	—	10.05	10.09	0.00	9.35	12.49

SOURCE: Guideline and average settlement are from Anti-Inflation Board Final Report (Ottawa: Supply and Services, 1979). Other series are from the Canadian Statistical Review, various issues.

NOTE: Rates of change are shown for average hourly earnings in manufacturing (Hourly earnings), The Consumer Price Index (CPI), average hourly earnings deflated by the CPI (Real hourly earnings), and the food and non-food components of the CPI.

Average annual percentage rates of change are calculated allowing for compounding.

"Guideline" is the average guideline for all cases submitted to the AIB in each year. "Approved settlement" is the average increase approved by the AIB in each year.

The AIB's profit controls required 0.32 billion dollars of excess revenue to be returned to the market place (2, p. 11). This amount equalled only about one-quarter of 1 percent of total revenues so one would not expect a noticeable effect on inflation from this factor alone. If firms were pricing as required by the board, however, excess revenue would not be generated. The effectiveness of the profit controls thus cannot be judged by the amount of excess revenue.

Figures from Statistics Canada show a slight decline in profit margins during controls, and figures for the firms under the AIB's jurisdiction show a somewhat larger decline (2, p. 71). As before, however, this may be partly or totally due to the recession rather than the controls directly. Wilson and Jump (23) use an economic model to predict what would have happened to prices and profits without controls. Their results show that the increase of prices and profits was normal, given the actual increase in unit labour costs. This suggests that the profit controls had no direct restraining effect but that prices were restrained through the effect of controls on wages and unit labour costs.

One of the government's concerns was that a "wage bubble" might occur when controls were lifted. The data in Table 1 show a gradual increase in new wage settlements following the removal of controls but this seems to be a result of the rise in inflation following controls rather than an explosion of wages. The data in Table 3 indicate that in the two years following the removal of controls the increase in

Table 4

Work Stoppages and Duration of Agreements

	Person-Days Lost[a] as Percent of Working Time	Percent of Settlements Involving a Work Stoppage[b]	One-Year Agreements as a Percent of All Agreements[c]
1960	0.06	—	—
1961	0.11	—	—
1962	0.11	—	—
1963	0.07	—	—
1964	0.11	—	—
1965	0.17	—	—
1966	0.34	—	—
1967	0.25	12.4	—
1968	0.32	13.9	14.8
1969	0.46	11.7	19.7[d]
1970	0.39	10.9	7.4[d]
1971	0.16	14.4	5.6
1972	0.43	13.0	12.1
1973	0.30	18.3	10.6
1974	0.46	15.6	27.6
1975	0.53	12.7	46.9
1976	0.55	13.5	51.4
1977	0.15	5.5	69.0
1978	0.34	6.3	52.7
1979	0.34	11.2	29.8
1980	0.39[d]	12.3[d]	22.1[d]

SOURCE: *Person-days lost are from* Strikes and Lockouts in Canada, *settlements involving a work stoppage are calculated from the* Collective Bargaining Review, *and the percent of one-year agreements is from* Wage Developments in Major Collective Agreements, *all published by Labour Canada.*

NOTES: a. *Includes all stoppages involving ten or more person-days.*
   b. *Bargaining units of 500 or more employees, excluding construction.*
   c. *One-year agreements are those of eighteen months or less duration.*
   d. *Due to data availability, figures for these years refer to first nine months of the year.*

average hourly earnings has just kept pace with inflation resulting in no growth of real wages. A firm answer to the question of a wage bubble, however, must await tests using a model to predict what would have happened without controls.

The data in Table 3 indicate that average wage increases exceeded price increases over the three years of the program, resulting in real wages increasing by an average of 2.14 percent per year. This was roughly equal to the target rate of increase of real wages. It suggests that the labour movement's fear that the controls would serve only as an attack on workers was not substantiated by actual experience during the program.

Controls might also affect the amount of strike activity in the economy. On the one hand, the labour movement's strong opposition to controls might have made unions more militant and resulted in an increase in strike activity. On the other hand, if unions felt the AIB would roll back most or all of any settlement above the guideline, it would remove much of the economic incentive to strike.

Two measures of strike activity in Canada are shown in Table 4. The percentage of work time lost due to strikes and lockouts is the most commonly used measure and although it is a comprehensive measure, it suffers from the defect that much of the variation in the series is due to variation in the number of collective agreements expiring each year. Comparison of the three "controls years," 1976, 1977, and 1978, to the noncontrols years does not lead to a definite conclusion. Person-days lost as a percent of working time dropped to 0.15 in 1977 but this may not be due to controls since low levels were also recorded in 1971, 1965, 1963, and 1960.

The series showing the percentage of settlements involving a work stoppage is not affected by the number of expiring agreements and is a more sensitive measure of strike incidence. In the noncontrols years in Table 4, work stoppages occurred in an average of 13.2 percent of settlements, and the incidence never fell below 10 percent. In 1976, the first year of controls, stoppages occurred in 13.5 percent of the agreements, about equal to the average in the period without controls. In the second and third years of controls, however, the incidence of work stoppages dropped to 5.5 and 6.3 percent. Although a formal test requires a model to predict what would have happened without controls, these figures strongly suggest that controls reduced the incidence of strikes to less than half its usual level during the second and third years of the program.

As a result of restrictions imposed by controls, one would expect unions to press for shorter contracts to prevent the effects from being carried into the postcontrols period. This expectation is confirmed by the data in Table 4 showing that the percentage of one-year contracts was higher during each of the three controls years than any of the years without controls.

The Anti-Inflation Program may have reduced the effectiveness of unions in organizing new bargaining units for two reasons. First, the controls on wage increases may have reduced the potential gain in income from joining a union. Second, the more frequent negotiations resulting from shorter contract duration and other complications in negotiating during controls may have reduced the amount of time union staff could devote to organizing. After examining the time series on certifications by the Ontario Labour Relations Board, however, Stewart Saxe (22) concludes that the AIB had no discernible effect on organizing activity.

CONCLUSIONS

The analysis in this chapter shows that the AIB was partially successful in achieving its primary goal of reducing inflation. Its target levels for inflation were not attained but, as a result of restraint on unit labour costs, price increases were reduced by about two percentage points per year below what they otherwise would have been. Unfortunately, part of this effect was offset by rises in food prices which were largely outside the scope of the controls program.

An examination of the figures for work stoppages suggests that the Anti-Inflation Program reduced work stoppages during the second and third year of the program. The controls also resulted in shorter contracts being negotiated, but controls do not seem to have had a significant impact on union organizing efforts.

There does not appear to have been significant misallocation of resources resulting from the direct government interference in setting relative wages and prices. The most significant allocative effects appear to be the administrative costs of the board itself, and the time and resources expended by those complying with the controls.

The conclusion that the Anti-Inflation Program was partially successful in restraining wage settlements and inflation contrasts with the conclusion that a somewhat similar program in the U.S. was unsuccessful in this respect (20). In August 1971, President Nixon imposed mandatory controls on wage-and-price increases, reversing previous government policy which had been adamantly opposed to controls. Phase I of the program was a ninety-day freeze during which a more elaborate controls program was designed. During the freeze period, wage increases specified in existing collective agreements and increases in new settlements were deferred, but the effect of this restraint on wage increases was completely offset by an "explosion" in wages when the deferred increases took effect at the end of the freeze period.

Phase II of the U.S. program included a pay board with discretionary power to approve wage settlements in major collective agreements which exceeded a 5.5 percent guideline. Although actual wage increases during Phase II were close to the guideline, predictions using an economic wage determination model indicate that this would have occurred even without controls. In retrospect, it appears that the guideline was set too high with the result that controls exerted little independent restraint on wage inflation.

In Phase III, the U.S. government moved to a voluntary application of controls which were generally regarded as ineffective. For this reason mandatory controls were reestablished in Phase IV of the program. Wage increases averaged 7.2 percent during Phase IV, substantially above the 5.5 percent guideline but substantially below the 9.2 percent which, it is predicted, would have occurred without controls. The partial success of the Phase IV controls was, however, offset by an explosion in wage increases following the termination of controls in April 1974. A possible explanation for this explosion is the lack of complementary restrictive monetary and fiscal policy, causing pressure for prices to increase during Phase IV and resulting in a decline in the growth of real wages. The resulting wage explosion was necessary to restore real wages to their equilibrium level.

Incomes policies of various kinds have also been tried in a number of European countries with mixed success. For example, evidence cited in (16) evaluating eleven periods of controls in Britain indicates that four periods were completely ineffective and seven periods were partially effective in restraining wage inflation. By international standards, the Canadian Anti-Inflation Program was one of the more successful attempts at controls.

Opinions on the Canadian controls program, are, however, greatly affected by personal values. The controls program was deeply resented by many people who believe strongly in the virtues of the free market, including a large proportion of the economics profession. Organized labour was also adamantly opposed to controls from the beginning and took the unprecedented step of organizing a one-day general strike in protest. Even though, in retrospect, the labour movement's fears appear to have been unfounded, implementation of controls in the face of this opposition imposed severe strains on both the social fabric and the industrial-relations system in Canada. It is not an easy task to weigh these costs against the economic benefits which resulted.

REFERENCES AND WORKS CITED

1. Anti-Inflation Board, *Chronicles of the Anti-Inflation Board* (Ottawa: Supply and Services, 1979).

2. Anti-Inflation Board, *Final Report* (Ottawa: Supply and Services, 1979).

3. Anti-Inflation Board, *Inflation and Public Policy* (Ottawa: Supply and Services, 1979).

4. Auld, Douglas et al. "The Impact of the Anti-Inflation Board on Negotiated Wage Settlements," *Canadian Journal of Economics*, Vol. 12 (1979), 195-213.

5. Canada, Minister of Finance. *Attack on Inflation: A Program of National Action* (Ottawa: Supply and Services, 1975).

6. Canada. *Anti-Inflation Act*, Bill C-73 (Ottawa: Supply and Services, 1975).

7. Canada. *Anti-Inflation Act Regulations* (Ottawa: Supply and Services, 1975).

8. Canada, Department of Labour. *Wage Developments Resulting from Major Collective Bargaining Settlements* (Ottawa: Department of Labour, various issues).

9. Cousineau, J.-M., and R. Lacroix. *Wage Determination in Major Collective Agreements in the Private and Public Sectors* (Ottawa: Economic Council of Canada, 1979).

10. Cousineau, J.-M., and R. Lacroix "L'impact de la politique canadienne de contrôle des prix et des revenus sur les ententes salariales," *Canadian Public Policy*, Vol. 4 (1978), 88-100.

11. Denton, Frank et al. "Patterns of Unemployment Behaviour in Canada," Discussion Paper 36 (Ottawa: Economic Council of Canada, 1975).

12. Foot, David K., and Dale J. Poirier. *The Compensation Decisions of the Anti-Inflation Board: An Empirical Analysis* (Ottawa: Supply and Services, 1980).

13. Lipsey, Richard G. "Wage Price Controls: How to Do a Lot of Harm by Trying to Do a Little Good," *Canadian Public Policy*, Vol. 3 (1977), 1-13.

14. Maslove, Allan M., and Gene Swimmer. *Wage Controls in Canada 1975-78* (Montreal: Institute for Research on Public Policy, 1980).

15. Osberg, Lars. "A note on the wage decisions of the Anti-Inflation Board," *Canadian Public Policy*, Vol. 3 (1977), 377-80.

16. Reid, Frank. "Canadian Wage and Price Controls," *Canadian Public Policy*, Vol. 2 (1976), 103-113.

17. Reid, Frank. "AIB Wage Rollbacks: Tests and Implications of the Linear Rotation Hypothesis," Working Paper 7704 (Centre for Industrial Relations, University of Toronto, 1977).

18. Reid, Frank. "The Effect of Controls on the Rate of Wage Change in Canada," *Canadian Journal of Economics*, Vol. 12 (1979), 214-227.

19. Reid, Frank. "Unemployment and Inflation: An Assessment of Canadian Macro-economic Policy," *Canadian Public Policy*, Vol. 6 (1980), 283-299.

20. Reid, Frank. "Control and Decontrol of Wages in the United States: An Empirical Analysis," *American Economic Review*, Vol. 71 (1981), 108-120.

21. Reid, Frank, and Noah M. Meltz. "Causes of Shifts in the Unemployment-Vacancy Relationship: An Empirical Analysis for Canada," *Review of Economics and Statistics*, Vol. 61 (1979), 470-475.

22. Saxe, Stewart D. "The Effect of the Anti-Inflation Act on Trade Union Organizing" in *Proceedings of the 16th Annual Conference of the Canadian Industrial Relations Association* (Saskatoon: Canadian Industrial Relations Association, 1979).

23. Wilson, T.A., and G.V. Jump. *The Influence of the Anti-Inflation Program on Aggregate Wages and Prices: A Simulation Analysis* (Ottawa: Supply and Services, 1979).

QUESTIONS

1. In December 1973, two years prior to his implementation of controls in Canada, Prime Minister Trudeau expressed opposition to controls on the grounds "that wage and price controls are unfair to the rank and file of labour" and that a reduction in labour's share of national income through controls is "of great and fundamental concern to me" (*Toronto Star*, December 14, 1973, p. 1). Discuss the actual effect of controls on workers under Trudeau's Anti-Inflation Program of 1975-78.

2. Empirical evidence shows that in cases where it had discretionary power, the AIB tended to roll back about two-thirds of the excess of a negotiated settlement over the arithmetic guideline. Explain how such a pattern, if it became widely known, would be expected to affect wage negotiations and strike activity.

3. Problems of high inflation and unemployment are likely to recur in the 1980s. In what circumstances would controls be likely to be reintroduced, and what lessons about the design of a controls program can be learned from the 1975-78 experience?

4. If controls were effective in reducing the rate of wage and price change while they were in force, explain the circumstances which would lead to an "explosion" of wage-and-price increases following the removal of controls.

5. Suppose that initially all product and labour markets are in equilibrium with an expected inflation rate of 15 percent and with all prices, wages, and other costs rising at 15 percent per year. That is, all demand curves and cost curves are shifting upward at this rate. Also assume productivity growth is zero for simplicity. Assume that the government then imposes controls which reduce the rate of increase of wages and other factor costs to 10 percent per year but have no direct effect on prices. Assuming that firms attempt to maximize profits and that all product markets are perfectly competitive, what will be the amount of the increase in price, output, absolute profits, real profits, and real wages? How would your analysis be affected if all product markets were monopolies?

6. Was the Anti-Inflation Program a success? Explain.

HARISH C. JAIN

21. Employment and Pay Discrimination in Canada: Theories, Evidence, and Policies

This chapter consists of three parts. The first part reviews the internal labour market, the dual labour market, and the human-capital theories, and the empirical evidence pertaining to the theories. The second part describes and analyses pay- and employment-discrimination legislation in Canada. In the third part, conclusions and policy implications are discussed.

Minority employment is perhaps the most significant and complex human-resource problem faced by management since the early 1960s. Public policy in all jurisdictions in Canada attempts to eliminate discrimination in the work place on the basis of race, colour, sex, and numerous other grounds. Employment barriers based on sexual orientation also are increasingly being called into question; at least one province has already outlawed such discrimination. Affirmative-action programs are coming increasingly into vogue to boost the employment, training, and promotion opportunities of minorities and women. Such programs have raised questions as to whether the goal of public policy should be to promote equal treatment or equal achievement in the work place (69).

Canada is the only country that has incorporated the International Labour Organization's (ILO) Equal Remuneration Convention No. 100 adopted in 1951 (2, 3) requiring equal pay for work of equal value, as opposed to the more usual requirement of equal pay for equal work. Currently, in Canada, this controversial equal-value legislation is operative only in areas of federal jurisdiction covered under the Canadian Human Rights Act (43). Quebec is the only other jurisdiction that has similar legislation (equal pay for equivalent work) in its human-rights legislation.

For the purpose of this chapter, the most important and intriguing aspect of discrimination based on race and sex is that both the existence and proposed remedies for it have been defined to a considerable extent in terms of the internal and external labour markets (45). Thus, such discrimination has been viewed, in part, as an economic phenomenon which lends itself to amelioration by legally mandated equal-employment policies and practices (16).

Since it is difficult, if not impossible, to isolate the precise extent of discrimination at the macrolevel because of variations in personal characteristics and establishment variables, detailed analysis of the operation of local labour markets and individual enterprises and establishments then becomes crucial. Here a feature of recent empirical work has been the emphasis placed on the internal labour market (ILM) and the related concept of the dual labour market (DLM). This is, in fact, highly relevant to equal-opportunity legislation not only because it is at the level of the individual organization that the laws are to be applied, but also because the legislation appears to have certain features which are consistent with a dualist interpretation of the operation of the labour market, and the emphasis on equality of training and promotion opportunities is most appropriate and significant in the context of a well-developed internal labour market (75).

This chapter is divided into five parts. In the first three parts, the internal-labour-market, the dual-labour-market, and the human-capital approaches are examined as they relate to discriminatory behaviour. The empirical evidence relating to these concepts is also summarized. In the fourth section, equal-employment and equal-pay legislation are discussed. Finally, the significance of labour-market structuring for equal-employment legislation is examined, the limitations of the legislation in dealing with these issues are discussed, and the policy implications of the analysis are considered.

THE INFLUENCE OF INTERNAL LABOUR MARKETS ON EMPLOYMENT OF MINORITIES

Doeringer and Piore (23, p. 1) defined the internal labour market as "an administrative unit. . .within which the pricing and allocation of labour is governed by a set of administrative rules and procedures." This is distinguished from the external labour market (ELM) where wages are determined by market forces. The two markets are, however, linked at various job levels which constitute ports of entry and exit to and from the ILM, while other job levels are reached by transfer and promotion of existing employees. This distinction is crucial as far as the minority worker is concerned because current employees are likely to be given preferential treatment over outside job applicants because of factors such as possession of skills and knowledge that are specific to the enterprise. Workers in the ELM may not be aware of the existence of job opportunities in the ILM, even if they possess the requisite skills. Furthermore, were they to succeed in gaining entry to the ILM, such workers may remain disadvantaged because of their lack of seniority.

The extent to which discrimination manifests itself is a consequence of the operation of the ILM. This involves two main aspects: (a) the extent to which enterprises with well-developed ILMs fail to hire workers of equal ability as a consequence of cheap screening devices or "excessive" use of credentials; and (b) the extent to which workers in certain disadvantaged groups fail to advance through the organizational hierarchy.

Barriers to Entry into the Internal Labour Market
In the extreme case of an ILM in which workers are recruited at the lowest job level, and all higher-graded jobs are filled by means of internal promotion, expected lifetime productivity becomes more of a consideration in hiring decisions than

productivity in the initial job grade. Therefore, assuming that it is not practicable to hold certain workers at the initial job grade, the costs of defective hiring procedures are exacerbated (54). Hiring practices may be expected to be more elaborate in the context of the ILM, but employers may still be forced to utilize "rule-of-thumb" techniques, particularly where assessment of productivity is difficult if not impossible prior to entry into the ILM, and these techniques may work to the disadvantage of minority groups. Aspects of hiring procedures which are relevant in this context include the following:

Screening devices — Employers are said to be using a "cheap screen" when they automatically distinguish between individuals displaying a particular, readily ascertainable characteristic (such as race or sex), without evaluating other characteristics and attributes of the individuals. Spence (70) has noted that while some characteristics observable to the employer prior to hiring are subject to manipulation by the individual, others are not. Thus, while education and training can be acquired, race and sex are unalterable. Alterable characteristics may be referred to as "signals" and unalterable ones as "indices" (70). Employers often draw inferences about productivity from indices because the latter are presumed to be correlated with productive capacity within the population. This process may be referred to as "statistical discrimination." However, as Aigner and Cain (4) point out, race and sex discrimination are a consequence of *group* discrimination rather than discrimination among individuals, which is inevitable even where there is no "discriminatory" intent. Discrimination may also be present in relation to signals since these are frequently only proxies for underlying attributes.

Credentialism — To some extent, education may also be used as a screen in the same way as race or sex. It is possible that employers may demand educational requirements which are higher and often unrelated to actual job performance (41). One explanation for credentialism is that higher educational requirements serve as an effective screening device for reducing applicant numbers to a manageable size for personnel decision making, although this in itself hardly seems adequate to explain the phenomenon. Whatever the explanation, this constitutes a barrier for persons with less than the required level of education who are excluded from employment not because they cannot perform the work but simply because they fall outside the employer's hiring requirements (41).

Employment tests and interviews — Employment tests, which lead to hiring and promoting only those who achieve a predetermined minimum score, are rarely validated in terms of job performance. Further, a test could be differentially valid, as evidenced by disproportionate rejection rates among race and sex groups. McCormick and Ilgen (51) point out, however, that differential validity is much less common than was originally assumed, and when differential validity does exist, the direction of the differences is such that the selection system is detrimental to the majority group almost as often as it is to minority groups.

Interviews are the most widely used method of selecting employees despite research indicating that they have limited reliability and validity because of their highly subjective nature (50, 74, 77). As a consequence, the interview process is vulnerable to the personal biases, prejudices, and belief in stereotypes on the part of the interviewer. Interviewers may, therefore, form unfair evaluations of minority-group members even when the candidates are substantially similar to nonminority applicants with regard to their job qualifications.

Arvey's (8) extensive review of the literature relating to unfair discrimination in the employment interview revealed that females are generally given lower evaluations than males who have identical qualifications. In some studies, for instance, the interviewer gave lower evaluations to females being considered for traditionally male-oriented jobs, and significantly more females than males were recommended for a traditionally female-oriented job (8).

Narrow channels of recruitment — Some firms tend to establish rather narrow and stable channels of recruitment including referral of friends and relatives by present employees (23, 76). Reliance upon a narrow set of recruitment channels has advantages both to the employer and potential employee, producing applicant characteristics resembling those of the incumbent work force. Relatives and friends can provide a clear picture of prospective employment for the applicant, thereby reducing the costs of trial and error and job search. These benefits encourage the continuance of any set of recruitment channels once they are established, and discriminatory recruitment practices may continue to yield employment patterns, excluding minority workers and women from certain high-level jobs long after discriminatory intent has been removed.

Misconceptions — Where behaviour is based on misconceptions, such as a mistaken belief that members of a minority group are less productive than members of the employed group, the absence of minorities from employment means that there is no disconfirming experience. A minimum quota may be a useful policy device in this context. However, if the barrier is based upon prejudice such a change may not take place. Where failure to hire is based upon misconceptions or, more specifically, a failure to revise stereotypes on the basis of labour-market changes, then legislation which overrides employer hiring standards need not distort the allocation of labour and might even improve it. Such behaviour, however, suggests that suboptimal hiring policies were being pursued.

Trade unions — As Doeringer and Piore (23) have suggested, trade unions have some responsibility for rules in the internal labour market. To understand the influence of unions upon employment discrimination, it is important to distinguish between *enterprise* internal labour markets within a particular establishment and *craft* internal markets that cover many establishments. Unions in the former are known as industrial unions and in the latter as craft unions. In enterprise markets, management, rather than the industrial union, plays the predominant role in initiating recruitment and selection decisions, and in most instances it is managerial activity which must be reviewed when discriminatory practices are being eliminated. In craft markets, the craft union usually plays an active role in the recruitment and selection decisions. Thus, for example, in the construction industry the unions control the hiring hall, and it is union activity therefore which must be monitored (23).

There are three ways in which the supply of labour may be restricted in order to maintain a wage differential in one occupation over another demanding similar skills (22). First, unions may negotiate higher-than-equilibrium wages in an occupation and prevent employers from offering lower wages despite the existence of a queue of qualified applicants. Second, unions may control hiring through "hiring halls" as noted above. Third, licensing bodies sanctioned by government may impose qualifications for entry into an occupation which are higher than performance of the job requires. Each of these methods implies some form of rationing, a form which depends on whether it is the employer, the union, or a licensing body which actually carries out the rationing function. Dodge (22) notes that possible forms of rationing include nepotism, high levels of education and training, tests of ability on entry, and entry fees.

The Woods Task Force on Labour Relations (14), The Economic Council of Canada (39), and the Royal Commission Inquiry into Civil Rights in Ontario (64) have all expressed concern over the possible use of licensing by unions and professions as a restrictive device. In craft markets, unions define trade jurisdictions for their members and have entrance requirements and competence tests to meet their obligations under closed-shop contracts. They restrict entrance to apprenticeship programs through apprentice-journeyman ratios and artificially long training periods. Hence, with respect to craft unions, the licensing of trades merely reinforces those measures which the unions themselves have developed to protect and improve the economic position of their members. In this respect, trades licensing extends a stamp of public approbation to these policies, which, as noted earlier, cannot in actuality be defended as being in the public interest (40).

The effect of these restrictions will be to limit opportunities for minority workers, since they may, on average, possess lower educational qualifications than the rest of the population. Furthermore, existing employees in such occupations will resist any attempts to remove such indirect discrimination which reduces competition for their jobs and hence enables them to maintain artificially high wages (46).

Barriers to Advancement within the Internal Labour Market

At the postentry level, the ILM is concerned with the numerous transactions that occur inside an organization affecting employees in such matters as promotion, demotion, or transfer. Discrimination may occur with respect to each of these factors including the level at which an individual is hired, the rate of wage increase once hired, and the rate at which he or she moves up through the organizational hierarchy. Discrimination may also be related to conscious and unconscious personnel policies related to personal characteristics of employees such as race, sex, marital status, education, and experience.

Several studies, using human-capital models, have examined discrimination within establishments. Malkiel and Malkiel (49) examined male-female pay differentials among the 272 (professional) employees in a single U.S. establishment. They concluded that women with the same training, experience, and other characteristics as men were assigned to lower job levels, but within levels it was difficult for discriminatory organizations to give male and female employees the same titles and pay them different amounts (49). A study of professional employees in an organization in the United Kingdom came to a similar conclusion; where women were promoted, they were assigned to less responsible jobs at lower salaries, and there was some evidence of discrimination in terms of access to higher job classifications (17).

In an effort to study discriminatory patterns in more than one organization (15), three internal labour markets were contrasted. In addition, both blue-collar and nonmanagerial white-collar employees, and both race and sex were included, and more important, the rate of progression from one job level (grade) to the next was measured. Four patterns of discrimination were found: time-of-hire grade discrimination but no posthire discrimination for minority workers; time-of-hire, posthire wage discrimination, and posthire grade discrimination for females; in incentive-pay jobs, females receiving grade promotions as rapidly as males who began at the same level, but tending to remain lower in each grade's pay range; and female workers in incentive-pay jobs beginning below comparable males, and then falling further behind in terms of grade but not in terms of wage.

Other studies of internal labour markets have found that length of service within the company was a powerful predictor of pay (while experience outside the company was not), and that allocation to grade as well as progression within a grade differed among groups according to individual characteristics, such as marital status tending to favour married males as opposed to married females (67).

Minority-group workers and women may be denied promotion by restrictive promotion criteria, by limitations upon the posting and bidding arrangements for internal recruitment, by restricting both minorities and women to the lower-paying job classifications and mobility clusters, and by discriminatory seniority systems.

Seniority in a unionized company refers to seniority in a bargaining unit. The unit describes the specific territory — occupation, craft, department, multiplant, multiemployer and so on — to which a collective agreement applies. Unit seniority refers to seniority as a principal criterion of selection, promotion, layoff, recall, and so forth. For example, various separate functions in a plant (within the same bargaining unit) may be designated as departments for seniority purposes. Generally, transfers between departments are not permitted except where they involve a promotion. Transfer between departments may also result in a loss of seniority since departmental seniority systems base employee rights not on the date of hire, but the date of assignment to that department. Thus, it becomes increasingly costly to the individual to move across departments as one accumulates seniority. Women, for example, might be placed in those departments requiring a low level of skill and men into those requiring a high level of skill. This may give rise to segregated seniority rosters in which women are restricted to the less promotable jobs.

Thus, in unionized companies, if males acquire more seniority than females they will obtain higher earnings, larger fringe benefits, easier access to overtime, preferred jobs and promotable jobs, and a lower possibility of layoff through the operation of "last-in-first-out" systems. Seniority systems, therefore, have the serious disadvantage of perpetuating existing unfavourable minority-employment patterns. If women are the last to be hired during the recovery phase of the business cycle, they will be the first to be laid off in the recession phase (46).

THE INFLUENCE OF DUAL LABOUR MARKETS ON EMPLOYMENT OF MINORITIES

The concept of the DLM broadens the analysis from the ILM to a consideration of the ELM and attempts to deal more specifically with mobility, or the lack of it, between these two sectors. The simple DLM theory states that the labour market can be divided into two quite distinct sectors. The primary labour market is characterized by high wages and fringe benefits, skilled jobs with opportunities for further training and promotion, employment stability, and high levels of unionization. By contrast, the secondary labour market has the opposite characteristics. A high concentration of white adult males is to be found in the primary market, while there is a disproportionate number of females, young workers, immigrants, minority employees, and other minorities in the secondary sector (32).

Mobility barriers prevent the movement of workers from the secondary to the primary labour market. In the case of race, such barriers will include not only overt discrimination by employers and unions but also the culture of the ghetto itself (29, 47). "Statistical discrimination" will occur where certain workers are trapped merely because their superficial characteristics resemble those of secondary workers.

Secondary markets may be expected where it is costly to create a well-developed ILM, it is difficult or unimportant to reduce turnover, job security is not valued highly, and unions are weak. The job satisfaction and performance of disadvantaged workers will be influenced by a number of factors in the social system including the characteristics of the organization providing the job, community organizations, informal peer groups, and family circumstances. Behavioural scientists generally agree that behaviour is a product of expectancies about behaviour-reward contingencies and the attractiveness of these rewards. Thus, low rates of job turnover, absenteeism, or tardiness would occur when workers believe that remaining on the job leads to desired rewards. It is not unreasonable to suggest that desired rewards will most frequently be forthcoming in the primary market and least often in the secondary market (45).

A process of self-selection by the disadvantaged may operate to create occupational segregation. Some workers may not apply for particular jobs or to particular firms (18), perhaps because of a high propensity to quit and the wage structure favouring those with low quit rates, or because of a lower level of productivity than the minimum required for entrance to a particular job or for advancement within it. Some individuals may also have misconceptions about the value of their own labour-market characteristics.

As Cain (12) has noted in relation to segmented-labour-market theories, there is no single clearly developed model of the DLM which can be subjected to rigid empirical testing. Nevertheless, some empirical studies have attempted to detect the existence of DLMs, with mixed results. Bosanquet and Doeringer (10), Edwards et al. (24), Osterman (56), and Rumberger and Carnoy (65) have found strong or partial support for the DLM theory. On the other hand, studies by Andresani (6), Flanagan (29), and Rosenberg (63) have found virtually no support for the dual-labour-market model.

THE HUMAN-CAPITAL APPROACH TO EMPLOYMENT OF MINORITIES

According to the advocates of the human-capital approach (40), many minority workers and women lack "human capital" such as education or training. Thus, it is not only the structure of the economic environment in which individuals and minority groups work (as suggested by dual-labour-market theory), but also the characteristics of individuals which keep them in low-income, low-level jobs.

In this approach, it is generally assumed that the individual is free (and sufficiently well-informed) to invest in the acquisition of skills where the rate of return is greatest. Rosen (61) has suggested that the theory of human capital is at heart a theory of "permanent" earnings. The fact that attention is focused on lifetime rather than current earnings means that it is particularly appropriate for the analysis of ILMs. Education and training are at the heart of the human-capital approach, the former normally being undertaken prior to entry into the labour force and imparting general skills upon which a return is recouped over the working lifetime, and the latter being undertaken during the years of work. Moreover, to the extent that productivity is improved simply by doing a job, earnings will be related to experience (44). Where there is a well-developed ILM, length of service with the enterprise will be more highly correlated with earnings than outside experience. In general, studies at the level of the establishment or the unit of employment (15, 17, 28, 33, 34, 49, 56, 62, 66, 68) have been able to explain between approximately 50 and 90 percent of the variance in earnings for the various sex and marital-status employment groups. Education and experience are highly significant in most but not all equations, while age is sometimes significant. This is in line with other studies where seniority was the most important determinant of individual earnings and age was, in most cases, not significant (59). The explanatory power of the human-capital model seems remarkably high in some equations given the relatively small number of independent variables in the model.

Earnings and occupational differentials should be viewed only as tentative indices of the extent of pay and employment discrimination against minorities and women (2, 3). One might argue that the studies generally excluded direct measures of male-female differences in performance, turnover, and absenteeism. If adequate data were available and were included in estimation procedures, the actual extent of pay and employment discrimination might be lower than indicated by the empirical studies (2, 3). On the other hand, adjusting for personal characteristics such as education, training, and skills neglects the feedback effects of labour-market discrimination. Minorities and women might have less incentive in acquiring such human-capital attributes if they expect postentry discrimination in labour markets. Bergmann (9) too argues that men and women have unequal access to occupations caused by sex stereotyping of occupations, unequal opportunities for education, and, they are subject to discriminatory practices of employers and unions. This results in "overcrowding" of women into certain occupations, in turn exerting a downward pressure on wages. Thus, to adjust for occupational differences in male-female earnings differentials is to mask the effects of employment discrimination (9).

Thus, there appears to be a controversy over the accuracy of the estimates of pay and employment discrimination (2, 3). It is clear that even the most conservative estimates do indicate considerable pay and employment discrimination against minorities and women. Clearly, elimination of such discrimination should be an important goal in a society like Canada's which is committed to social and economic equality for all its members. Even apart from this, employers may need to face up to the problem out of pure economic necessity. Over the past several decades, the female labour-force-participation rate has significantly increased from 21.8 percent in 1931 to 47.8 percent in 1978, while that of males declined from 87.2 to 77.9 over the same period (3, 58). These trends are expected to continue in the future, so that the female labour force will increasingly constitute a critical source of labour supply. It is imperative, therefore, that employers develop nondiscriminatory pay and staffing systems to attract, retain, and motivate female employees.

PUBLIC POLICY

Equal-Pay Legislation

In 1951, the ILO adopted the Equal Remuneration Convention (No. 100) embodying the principle of equal remuneration for men and women workers for work of equal value. Article 3 of the convention recommends the use of job-evaluation methods (objective appraisal of jobs) as a key to measuring work value. The concept of work of equal value is:

> so abstract and lacking in precision that it allows the bodies responsible for implementing it quasi-discretionary powers of appreciation, with the implied risk that arbitrary, ill-founded and consequently unpalatable decisions may be taken. Job evaluation may be the "essential tool" whereby effect may be given in practice to the principle of equality based on work of equal value. (26, p. 55)

Federal labour laws in Canada cover only about 10 percent of the labour force, with provincial governments having jurisdiction over the remaining 90 percent (27). All jurisdictions in Canada have laws which require equal pay for equal work within the same establishment, without discrimination on the basis of sex. These provisions have been incorporated either in human-rights legislation (federal jurisdiction, Alberta, British Columbia, New Brunswick, Newfoundland, Northwest Territories, Prince Edward Island, and Quebec) or in labour-standards legislation (Manitoba, Nova Scotia, Ontario, Saskatchewan, and Yukon Territory).

At the federal level, equal-pay legislation was first put into effect in 1956 and amended in 1967. It required equal wages for men and women performing the same or similar work under the same or similar working conditions on jobs requiring the same or similar skill, effort, and responsibility. This legislation remained in effect until 1977 at which time it was replaced by the Canadian Human Rights Act embodying the equal-value principle. According to the new legislation, men and women performing work of equal value (regardless of whether the work is similar or dissimilar) must be paid equal wages. The act goes on to elaborate how the value of work may be assessed. Section 11(2) of the act specifies that in assessing the value of work performed by employees employed in the same establishment, the criterion to be applied is the composite of the skill, effort, and responsibility required in the performance of the work and the conditions under which the work is performed (2). Quebec legislation calls for equal pay for equivalent work.

Compared to the federal and Quebec jurisdictions, the provincial jurisdictions in Canada follow a narrow definition of equal work. The legislation in various provincial jurisdictions defines equal work in terms of "same work," "similar work," or "substantially the same work." In six of the twelve jurisdictions (Ontario, Nova Scotia, New Brunswick, Newfoundland, Prince Edward Island, and Saskatchewan), the legislation also specifies the factors on which equality of work may be established. These factors are education, skill, experience, effort, responsibility, and working conditions.

The legislation in a majority of jurisdictions provides for a general exception permitting differentials between male and female pay based on any factor other than sex. In other jurisdictions, specific exceptions are listed which include seniority, work experience, and merit.

A number of court decisions have helped to provide a more precise interpretation of equal-pay legislation in Canada (2, 48). In the Greenacres Nursing Home case in 1970, the Ontario Court of Appeal ruled that "the same work" did not necessarily imply "identical work," and also that job comparisons should be based on work actually performed rather than on formal job descriptions or terms of employment. In the Riverdale Hospital Case in 1973, the concept of equal work was broadened even further. In this case, the Ontario Court of Appeal ruled that: (a) different job titles do not necessarily indicate different work; (b) slightly different job assignments do not make the work unequal; and (c) within an occupation, as long as some men do the same work as women, equal pay is justifiable for the whole occupation. The last point was further clarified in a case in which the Saskatchewan Court of Appeal considered whether the fact that only five out of forty-six male caretakers performed work similar to female cleaners could be considered a sufficient number within the provincial equal-pay legislation. It ruled that such a number could be viewed as sufficient and that "some" employees being paid a rate of pay higher than others doing similar work was sufficient to warrant equal pay (2, 48).

The courts have also dealt with what might properly constitute "a factor other than sex" in justifying male-female pay differentials. In two separate decisions at the federal level — the C.T.V. Television Network case in 1975 and the La Société Radio-Canada case in 1977 — the court ruled that differences in the quality of work as assessed by management are sufficient to justify unequal pay. The court acknowledged that such an assessment might be subjective and thus might involve an error of judgment; however, the court held that it was not within the competence of the judiciary to review management's judgment. The courts have also ruled on whether the existence of two separate bargaining units could be considered "a factor other than sex" to permit pay differentials between them. The Alberta Court of Appeals in the Gares case in 1976 decided against it (2, 48).

Equal Employment

In 1958, the ILO adopted the Discrimination (Employment and Occupation) Convention (No. 111) which was ratified by Canada in 1964. Each ratifying country undertakes to promote equality of opportunity and treatment in employment with the aim of eliminating discrimination.

Discrimination includes any distinction, exclusion, or preference on the basis of race, colour, sex, religion, political opinion, or national or social origin which may impair such equality. The terms "employment" and "occupation" also include access to vocational training and the terms and conditions of work.

As in the case of equal remuneration, all jurisdictions in Canada have introduced human-rights legislation to provide equal employment opportunity (13).

Prohibited Grounds and Coverage Under the Laws

As Table 1 indicates, in Canada the prohibited grounds for discrimination in employment include race, religion, colour, national or ethnic origin, age, sex, sexual orientation, marital status, and conviction for which a pardon has been granted. Several provinces and the federal jurisdiction have also included physical handicap. Generally, the relevant statutes apply to employers, employment agencies, and trade unions and, in some jurisdictions, to self-governing professions. Discrimination is prohibited with respect to advertising, terms and conditions of employment, including promotion, transfer, and training.

Interpretation of Antidiscrimination Laws

Legal definition — The Canadian Human Rights Act has borrowed the legal definition of discrimination from U.S. case law and British antidiscrimination legislation. This concept is known as indirect discrimination. In the U.S., the concept was articulated by the Supreme Court in the *Griggs v. Duke Power Co.* case in 1971. The court unanimously endorsed a results-oriented definition of what

Table 1

Predominant Prohibited Grounds of Discrimination in Employment by Jurisdiction in Canada, 1980

Jurisdiction	Race	National or Ethnic Origin	Colour	Age	Sex	Marital Status[b]	Physical Disability	Sexual Orientation	Language	Religion	Pardoned Offence
Federal	X	X	X	X	X	X	X			X	X
Alta.	X	X	X	X	X	X				X	
B. C.[a]	X	X	X	X	X	X				X	
Man.	X	X	X	X	X	X	X			X	
N. B.	X	X	X	X	X	X	X			X	
Nfld.	X	X	X	X	X	X				X	
N. S.	X	X	X	X	X	X	X			X	
Ont.	X	X	X	X	X	X				X	
P. E. I.	X	X	X	X	X	X	X			X	
Que.[c]	X	X	X		X	X	X	X	X	X	
Sask.	X	X	X	X	X	X	X			X	
N. W. T.	X	X	X		X	X				X	
Yukon	X	X	X		X	X				X	

NOTES: a. *B.C. enumerates grounds but these are not meant to be limiting.*
  b. *Marital status includes "family status" in Manitoba and "civil status" in Quebec.*
  c. *Other prohibited grounds include mental deficiency in Quebec, political belief in several jurisdictions etc.*

constitutes employment discrimination. The court indicated that intent does not matter; it is the consequences of an employer's actions that determine whether it may have discriminated under Title VII of the Civil Rights Act. In this case, the court struck down educational requirements and employment tests on two grounds.

First, these requirements could not be justified on the grounds of business necessity since they were not valid or related to job performance. Second, they had an adverse impact since they screened out a greater proportion of blacks than whites. However, if business necessity could be proved — that is, if the educational and testing requirements that had a disproportionate or adverse impact on minorities were in fact related to job performance — then the practice was not prohibited. Thus, a disproportionate or adverse impact is not sufficient to outlaw credentialism, tests, and other hiring standards. Business necessity is the prime criterion in hiring and promotion decisions (47).

U.S. case law has already had considerable impact in Canada. In 1978 in Ontario, a board of inquiry hearing the complaint of *Singh vs. Security Investigation Services Ltd.* ruled in favour of Mr. Singh. He was refused a job as a security guard because he wore the turban and beard required by his Sikh faith. The board found that the "employer bore no ill will towards Sikh people. . .had no intention to insult or act with malice. . .and did not have the intention or motive of discrimination" (20). The board, however, found that the effect of the employer's policy which required that their security guards be clean-shaven and wear caps was to deny employment to Sikhs. It ruled that intention was not necessary to establish a contravention of human-rights legislation.

Similarly in January 1979, another Ontario board of inquiry decided in the case of *Ann Colfer vs. Ottawa Police Department* that the department's minimum-height requirement of five feet, ten inches "virtually eliminates women as police constables," as only 5 percent of females in Canada are that height or taller. This height-and-weight (160 pounds) requirement, the board declared, had a disproportionate effect upon female gender relative to the male gender (20).

Class-action suits — In the U.S., class-action suits can be filed on behalf of a large number of persons in addition to the individual actually filing the charge. This ability to file a class-action suit has enlarged the scope of both investigation and remedies to cover all persons "similarly situated" who have suffered as a result of the same discriminatory practices. Thus, the class members have a common interest and a common grievance (21, 47). A notable example was the class-action suit filed on behalf of discriminatees by an employee of the Bowman Transportation Company. In this case, the Supreme Court of the United States (1976) found that the company had discriminated against black workers in hiring, transfer, and discharge. The court declared that the remedy for in-hire discrimination is the employment of the discriminatees with full seniority back to the date of their application for work. The basis for retroactive seniority is that merely to order an employer to recruit a job applicant who has been refused employment unlawfully falls short of a "make-whole" remedy. This is but one example of a number of cases brought by an individual employee and decided in favour of the affected class of employees in a particular company or industry (47).

In Canada, recent legislation in Saskatchewan (the human-rights code proclaimed in August 1979) provides for class-action suits; similarly the Canadian Human

Rights Act at the federal level is being interpreted in the same light. However, court cases or board-of-inquiry or tribunal decisions typical of the U.S. are rare.

Affirmative-action programs — One of the important features of the federal and several provincial human-rights statutes is the provision of affirmative-action programs. Although the provision is not new in the Canadian context, it is at present being increasingly patterned after the U.S. Executive Orders. Affirmative action is a deliberate, structured approach to improving work opportunities for minority groups and women. This approach involves a series of positive steps undertaken by employers to remove barriers to employment and achieve measurable improvement in recruiting, hiring, training, and promoting qualified workers who have in the past been denied access to certain jobs (42, 47).

In seven of the provinces in Canada — British Columbia, Manitoba, Nova Scotia, New Brunswick, Ontario, Saskatchewan, and Prince Edward Island — and at the federal level, there are explicit provisions for the adoption of "special" programs or measures, that is, affirmative-action programs, and explicit provision that these are not to be considered to be in contravention of the relevant antidiscrimination statutes (60).

There is some evidence of voluntary affirmative-action programs in the private and public sectors. Several large Canadian business organizations such as the Royal Bank of Canada (43, 73), Canadian National, and Bell Canada (42), have established affirmative-action programs to promote and accelerate training and promotional opportunities for women. This is also the case within the public sector at the federal as well as Ontario government level (19, 25, 44, 72). A survey of 1804 firms with 100 or more employees in Ontario (1, 44) revealed that 372 firms (20.6 percent) claimed to have a formal affirmative-action program as defined by Ontario Women's Bureau criteria, while another 338 firms (18.7 percent) reported informal affirmative-action activities. The service industry, which employs 40.5 percent of Ontario's total female labour force, reported the highest number of formal affirmative-action programs; larger firms — those employing 1,000 or more — and U.S. subsidiaries (48.8 percent relative to 36.7 percent of Canadian-owned firms) reported a greater incidence of affirmative-action programs (1, 44). Despite these voluntary programs some critics have charged that the majority of Canadian organizations have taken little or no affirmative action. For instance, Moore and Laverty have criticized the human-rights legislation in Canada for its insufficient strength in stimulating affirmative-action programs (52).

One way to increase the incidence of affirmative-action programs is through contract compliance. Several large resource developers, such as Amok as well as Eldorado Nuclear in Saskatchewan and Syncrude in Alberta, have established affirmative-action programs to recruit, employ, and train native people (44, 53). Amok, in particular, has been required by the surface-lease agreement entered into in 1978 between the company and government of Saskatchewan to undertake a comprehensive program for native people. The agreement spells out in detail the intent, goals, timetables, mechanisms, and preferences Amok must make available to northern residents in employment, contracting, and purchasing practices. The agreement also specifies the minister's powers to enforce the agreement, which ultimately includes termination of the lease. This type of agreement is also conceivable under the Pipeline Agency Act, by which the federal government has recently approved the building of the Alaska Gas Pipeline by the Foothills Company. Thus, in resource-based industries, especially in "megaprojects" such as the James Bay project in Quebec where native-employment programs have been successful, affirmative action is increasingly becoming part of contract compliance (44).

Enforcement — In the enforcement of both the equal-pay and equal-employment legislation, the method common to all jurisdictions is investigation based on employee complaints. However, in some jurisdictions human-rights commissions may file a complaint or commence an investigation on their own initiative.

All the acts provide for the settlement of complaints, if possible, by conciliation and persuasion. They provide for an initial informal investigation into a complaint by an officer who is directed to endeavour to effect a settlement. If conciliation fails, a board of inquiry may be appointed in most jurisdictions. Such a board may issue orders for compliance, compensation, and so on. This order may be appealed to the supreme court of the province on questions of law or fact or both. The federal jurisdiction allows an appeal by either the complainant or person complained against, where the original tribunal had fewer than three members to a Review Tribunal (37, 42)

In actual practice, the emphasis has been to concentrate on the issue of bringing about a satisfactory settlement rather than establishing legal guilt (36). This is true in Canada as a whole, and the Ontario legislation has been the prototype of statutes in most other jurisdictions.

Guidelines and decisions of the boards of inquiry — Most jurisdictions in Canada forbid employers from asking either in an application form or in an employment interview direct or indirect questions that could be interpreted as discriminatory. All human-rights commissions (except the Newfoundland Commission) have issued guidelines. For instance, in Ontario, the guidelines draw a distinction between preemployment and postemployment inquiries. In some cases, a question which could be construed as a violation of the code if asked of an applicant prior to being hired may be appropriately asked after being hired, so long as the information is necessary, for instance, for personnel record keeping and is not used for discrimination in employment on the restricted grounds (38, 44, 47).

According to the Ontario guide, the following inquiries are prohibited at the prehiring stage: *race or colour:* race, colour, complexion, colour of eyes or hair; *creed:* religious denomination or customs, recommendation or reference from clergymen; *nationality, ancestry, place of origin:* birthplace, birth or baptismal certificate, place of birth of parents, grandparents or spouse, national origin. In addition, employers are prohibited from asking such information as: (a) clubs and organizations which would indicate race, creed, colour, nationality, ancestry, or place of origin; (b) name and address of closest relative; (c) willingness to work on any particular religious holiday; and (d) military service (outside Canada). Request for information about race, creed, colour, age, sex, marital status, nationality, ancestry, or place of birth can be made, however, if they are bona fide occupational qualifications and requirements for the position or employment (38, 44, 47). Although these guidelines are helpful, they have generally not been subjected to test in the board-of-inquiry hearings or settlements.

Decisions of the boards of inquiry in Canada by prohibited grounds of employment discrimination — In Canada, board-of-inquiry cases have touched upon a number of aspects of discrimination. Considerations that are no longer relevant for claiming exemption under human-rights legislation include (44, 47): (a) lack of female accommodation, toilet, and washroom facilities (*Jean Tharp v. Lornex Mining Corporation Ltd.*); (b) male-dominated work; (c) marital status (*Kerry Segrave v. Zellers Ltd.*); (d) work being too physically demanding (for a female); and (e) working alone in the evenings for women (*Betty-Anne Shack v. London Drive-Ur-Self Ltd.*)

The most significant and interesting of these cases is *Kerry Segrave v. Zellers Ltd.* (September 22, 1975). The complainant alleged that he was refused employment and training because of his sex and marital status by Zellers Ltd. The applicant arranged for an interview with Zellers in response to an advertisement in the Hamilton *Spectator* for personnel-manager and credit-manager trainees. He was interviewed by a female management trainee who told him that the salary would not be attractive for a male; her district manager had told her that "we could get an executive at half price by getting rid of men." She also told him that they did not hire men because women would not go to them with their problems. The applicant then expressed interest in the credit-manager trainee position. He was given a preliminary interview for the position, but was not processed further because of his "undesirable" marital status. He had been divorced three months before and Zellers took this as "a sign of instability in his background which could cross over into his business life as well." The board of inquiry ordered that Zellers direct its personnel managers that in all hiring practices men and women should be treated equally, and that all references to marital status in the selection steps be deleted. Zellers was ordered to be prepared to submit any current directives guiding the hiring of personnel to the Ontario Human Rights Commission. They were also ordered to administer the employment tests to Mr. Segrave who, if he passed the tests, was to be offered a job and compensated for his period of unemployment as well as for general damages (44, 47).

CONCLUSIONS AND POLICY IMPLICATIONS

In this chapter, three approaches to labour-market discrimination against minority groups and women have been examined. These are the ILM, DLM, and the human-capital approaches. In the ILM approach, various studies have highlighted the extent and significance of ILMs with the possibilities of various types of discrimination relating both to entry into particular labour markets, characterized by the use of race or sex as a cheap screening device, and to advancement within such a market, characterized by poorer jobs for the same personal characteristics. In the human-capital approach, studies of particular establishments or organizations suggest that over 50 percent of the variance in earnings can be explained by differences in personal characteristics. In the DLM approach, investigators have stressed the role of dual labour markets in excluding minority workers from the advantage of primary markets even where they possess the necessary skills, but the empirical evidence seems to be more consistent with a labour-market-segmentation approach which stresses lack of mobility between a variety of different markets rather than simply from the secondary to the primary market. However, whether or not the DLM approach is descriptive of labour markets in practice, this perspective appears to have had some influence on the form in which antidiscrimination laws have been applied — notably in relation to the concepts of indirect discrimination, class-action suits, and affirmative-action programs. Indeed, these concepts seem equally applicable to the ILM approach (45). The ILM approach, as noted earlier, emphasizes the crucial role of staffing practices in perpetuating discriminatory behaviour.

The role of barriers to entry and to advancement within the organization may have strengthened as a result of the development of internal labour markets in line with the growth in firm size and rising capital intensity. As noted earlier, internal labour markets pose problems for minority groups because they imply that preferential treatment would be given to incumbents with regard to promoted posts, and acquired seniority rights may be limited to majority workers. Added to this, minority workers may be relegated to the secondary sector of dual labour markets, where they may develop poor work habits, making them less desirable employees and to some extent exclude themselves from applying for primary jobs through a process of self-selection. As far as barriers to entry are concerned, employers may use sex or race as a cheap screening device which may be discriminatory for certain members of minority groups who would turn out to be desirable employees if they were only offered a job. Similarly, excessive use of credentialism (job selection based on educational qualifications) may mean that hiring standards are set in excess of job requirements and minority workers are excluded from certain occupations to a disproportionate extent. Similar problems may arise with respect to employment tests and interviews in so far as they are not properly validated against actual job performance and with respect to channels of recruitment where they are sufficiently narrow to arbitrarily exclude minorities. Employers should also guard against the possibility that they hold misguided or stereotyped views of the relative performance or value of the various groups. For example, misconceptions may be important in relation to barriers to advancement where there is no experience of minority workers being employed in senior positions. Married women in particular will be adversely affected through discontinuous work experience in obtaining job advancement, so that it is important to assess accurately the significance of experience in determining the actual performance of workers in particular jobs. Thus, entry and training requirements should be carefully established and maintained only if they are truly necessary employment or promotion prerequisites (35, 44).

It would, therefore, seem sensible for employers to develop clear equal-opportunity policies in order to ensure that they are not discriminating by default of appropriate action. This would give them some safeguard in the event of their policies being challenged in the courts. For instance, organizations must issue clear instructions regarding the employment interview through their personnel departments. Interviews should be structured as much as possible, and only questions of direct relevance to the job should be asked (35, 44).

Organizations should keep in mind that over the years substantial validity evidence has accumulated for many of the predictors. Generally, in employment tests, ability tests, and work-sample tests — relative to personality and interest tests — produce the most favourable validity evidence. References, recommendations, and interviews generally have been found to be less valid as predictors of job success. Choices of predictors to be used in staffing systems should be governed by the nature of the job and the validity of the predictors. Staffing systems can be improved considerably by the use of standardization to obtain reliable information, and by the validation process (35, 44).

There would appear to be three broad types of human-resource policies which might be utilized to assist minority workers. First, taking labour supply and demand as given, one might attempt to make the labour market operate more efficiently by means of placement activities, worker counseling, and labour mobility or related measures, which would be appropriate regardless of the structure of labour markets. Second, one might attempt, consistent with the human-capital approach and the general findings reported in this paper, to upgrade the labour supply of minority workers by means of greater investment in education and training (5). Third, following the labour-market-segmentation approach, one might recommend solutions lying on the demand rather than the supply side, with a requirement for government employment and expenditure policy to favour those in the secondary sector. This would include equal-opportunity and affirmative-action programs.

If equal-opportunity and affirmative-action programs are to work, they have to be effective. However, the little empirical evidence that does exist points to only a limited impact of such legislation (30, 31, 34). Another indication of the limited impact is the small number of complaints filed (2, 3, 71). Ignorance of the legislation, lack of resources, and fear of employer reprisals have apparently kept the number of complaints down to artificially low levels.

Critics (11, 47) have suggested changes in both the scope and enforcement of such legislation in Canada in order to improve its effectiveness. Instead of the case-by-case approach adopted by most human-rights commissions, class-action suits, routine investigation of firms, and contract compliance have been advocated.

Given the multiplicity of factors operating in the ILM, equal-opportunity legislation may be a necessary but not sufficient condition for the elimination of inequality between majority and minority groups within the labour force (5, 42, 45). For instance, empirical studies suggest that the employment effects of affirmative-action programs in the U.S. were positive but quantitatively small, and that the effect in terms of relative occupational position was negligible (30, 31). Legal approaches are limited because they operate only on the demand side of the problem (that is, employer side) and do little to change supply (that is, education and training of minorities) (42, 69).

Education and training of minorities and women for professional and managerial jobs require lead time. Thus, the lowering of racial and sex barriers does not in itself ensure a supply of qualified people to take advantage of new opportunities. While employers, unions, and other institutions can be compelled to stop discrimination against minorities and women, they cannot be compelled to recruit them actively or train them. This suggests the need for supportive policies such as improvements in education and training, the achievement of sustained levels of employment, and a more equal division of labour in the household.

REFERENCES AND WORKS CITED

1. *Affirmative Action for Women in Ontario: Survey of the Incidence and Scope of Affirmative Action Activities for Women in Ontario: A Summary* (Toronto: Ontario Ministry of Labour, Research Branch and Women's Bureau, 1980).

2. Agarwal, N.C. "Pay Discrimination: Evidence, Policies and Issues," in H.C. Jain and P.J. Sloane, *Equal Employment Issues: Race and Sex Discrimination in the U.S.A., Canada and Britain* (New York: Praeger, forthcoming).

3. Agarwal, N.C., and H.C. Jain. "Pay Discrimination Against Women in Canada: Issues and Policies," *International Labour Review*, Vol. 117 (1978), 169-177.

4. Aigner, D.J., and G.G. Cain. "Statistical Theories of Discrimination in Labour Markets," *Industrial and Labor Relations Review*, Vol. 30 (1977), 175-187.

5. Alexander, A.J. "Income, Experience and Internal Labor Markets," *Quarterly Journal of Economics*, Vol. 88 (1974), 63-85.

6. Andresani, P.J. "Discrimination, Segmentation and Upward Mobility: A Longitudinal Approach to the Dual Labour Market Theory." Mimeographed, Temple University, Philadelphia, 1976.

7. *Annual Report of the Ontario Human Rights Commission, 1978-1979* (Toronto: Ontario Human Rights Commission, n.d.).

8. Arvey, Richard D. *Fairness in Selecting Employees* (Reading, Mass: Addison-Wesley, 1979).

9. Bergmann, B.R. "Occupational Segregation, Wages and Profits When Employers Discriminate by Race and Sex," *Eastern Economic Journal*, Vol. 1 (1974), 103-110.

10. Bosanquet, N., and P. Doeringer. "Is There a Dual Labour Market in Great Britain?," *Economic Journal*, Vol. 83 (1973), 421-435.

11. Bruner, A. "Rights Board Is Inflexible and Slow, Critics Say," *The Globe and Mail*, October 2, 1980, p. 5.

12. Cain, G.G. "The Challenge of Segmented Labour Market Theories to Orthodox Theory: A Review," *Journal of Economic Literature*, Vol. 14 (1976), 1215-1257.

13. *Canada and the International Labour Code* (Ottawa: Labour Canada, 1978).

14. *Canadian Industrial Relations* (Ottawa: Queen's Printer, 1969).

15. Cassell, F.H., S.M. Director, and S.I. Doctors. "Discrimination within Internal Labour Markets," *Industrial Relations*, Vol. 14 (1975), 337-344.

16. Chamberlain, Neil, Donald Cullen, and David Lewin. *The Labor Sector,* 3rd ed. (New York: McGraw-Hill, 1980).

17. Chiplin, B., and P.J. Sloane. "Personal Characteristics and Sex Differentials in Professional Employment," *Economic Journal*, Vol. 86 (1976), 729-745.

18. Chiplin, B., and P.J. Sloane. *Sex Discrimination in the Labour Market* (London: MacMillan, 1976).

19. D'Avignon, Guy, et al. *Report of the Special Committee on the Review of Personnel Management and the Merit Principle* (Ottawa: Minister of Supply and Services Canada, 1979).

20. Day, S. "Affirmative Action: The Distribution of Well-Being," *Canadian Human Rights Reporter*, April 4, 1980, pp. c-13 — c-16.

21. Dewees, D.N., J.R.S. Prichard, and M.J. Trebilcock. *Class Action as a Regulatory Instrument* (Toronto: Ontario Economic Council, 1980).

22. Dodge, D.A. "Occupational Wage Differentials, Occupational Licensing and Returns to Investment in Education: An Exploratory Analysis," in S. Ostry (Ed.), *Canadian Higher Education in the Seventies* (Ottawa: Economic Council of Canada, 1972).

23. Doeringer, P.B., and M.J. Piore. *Internal Labour Markets and Manpower Analysis* (Lexington, Mass.: D.C. Heath, 1971).

24. Edwards, R.C., M. Reich, and D.M. Gordon (Eds.) *Labour Market Segmentation* (Lexington, Mass.: D.C. Heath, 1975).

25. *Equal Opportunities for Women in the Public Service of Canada* (Ottawa: Public Service Commission of Canada, n.d.).

26. *Equal Remuneration, General Survey by the Committee of Experts on the Application of Convention and Recommendations* (Geneva: ILO, 1975).

27. "Equality of Opportunity and Pluralism in a Federal System: The Canadian Experiment," *International Labour Review*, Vol. 95 (1967), 381-416.

28. Ferber, M.A. "Sex and Race Differences in Non-Academic Wages in a University," *The Journal of Human Resources*, Vol. 11 (1976), 366-373.

29. Flanagan, R.J. "Segmented Market Theories and Racial Discrimination," *Industrial Relations*, Vol. 12 (1973), 253-273.

30. Flanagan, R.J. "Actual Versus Potential Impact of Government Anti-Discrimination Programs," *Industrial and Labor Relations Review*, Vol. 29 (1976), 486-507.

31. Goldstein, M., and R.S. Smith. "The Estimated Impact of the Anti-Discrimination Program Aimed at Federal Contractors," *Industrial and Labor Relations Review*, Vol. 29 (1976), 523-543.

32. Gordon, D.M. *Theories of Poverty and Underemployment: Orthodox, Radical and Dual Market Perspectives* (Lexington, Mass.: D.C. Heath, 1972).

33. Gordon, M., and T.E. Morton, "The Staff Salary Structure of a Large Urban University," *The Journal of Human Resources*, Vol. 11 (1976), 374-382.

34. Gunderson, M. "Male-female Wage Differentials and the Impact of Equal Pay Legislation," *Review of Economics & Statistics*, Vol. 57 (1975), 462-470.

35. Heneman, H.G., D.P. Schwab, J.A. Fossum, and L.D. Dyer. *Personnel/Human Resource Management* (Homewood, Ill.: Irwin, 1980).

36. Hill, D.G. "The Role of the Human Rights Commission: The Ontario Experience," *University of Toronto Law Journal*, Vol. 19 (1979), 390-401.

37. *Human Rights in Canada Legislation 1978* (Ottawa: Labour Canada, 1978)

38. *Human Rights in Employment: A Guide for Employers, Employees, and Employment Agencies* (Toronto: Human Rights Commission, n.d.)

39. *Interim Report on Competition Policy* (Ottawa: Queen's Printer, 1969).

40. Jain, H.C. *Disadvantaged Groups on the Labour Market and Measures to Assist Them* (Paris, OECD, 1979).

41. Jain, H.C. "Is Education Related to Job Performance?," in H.C. Jain (Ed.), *Contemporary Issues in Canadian Personnel Administration* (Scarborough, Ont.: Prentice-Hall, 1974), pp. 106-109.

42. Jain, H.C. "Discrimination in Employment: Legal Approaches Are Limited," *Labour Gazette*, Vol. 78 (1978), 284-288.

43. Jain, H.C., and D. Carroll (Eds.). *Race and Sex Equality in the Workplace: A Challenge and an Opportunity* (Ottawa: Minister of Supply and Services Canada, 1980).

44. Jain, H.C., and P.J. Sloane. *Equal Employment Issues: Race and Sex Discrimination in the U.S.A., Canada and Britain*, (New York: Praeger, forthcoming).

45. Jain, H.C., and P.J. Sloane. "The Structure of Labour Markets, Minority Workers, and Equal Employment Opportunity Legislation," *International Journal of Social Economics*, Vol. 7 (1980), 95-121.

46. Jain, H.C., and P.J. Sloane. "Trade Unions and Discrimination," in H.C. Jain and P.J. Sloane, *Equal Employment Issues: Race and Sex discrimination in the U.S.A., Canada and Britain* (New York: Praeger, forthcoming).

47. Jain, H.C., and P.J. Sloane, "Race, Sex and Minority Group Discrimination Legislation in North America and Britain," *Industrial Relations Journal*, Vol. 9 (1978), 38-55.

48. Knoppers, B.M., and L.L. Ward. "Equal Pay and Quebec's Charter of Human Rights and Freedom," Faculty of Law, McGill University, Montreal, May 1978.

49. Malkiel, B.G., and J.A. Malkiel. "Male and Female Pay Differentials in Professional Employment," *American Economic Review*, Vol. 63 (1973), 693-705.

50. Mayfield, E.C. "The Selection Interview: A Re-evaluation of Published Research," *Personnel Psychology*, Vol. 17 (1964), 239-260.

51. McCormick, E.J., and D. Ilgen. *Industrial Psychology*, 7th ed., (Englewood Cliffs, N.J.: Prentice-Hall, 1980).

52. Moore, J., and F. Laverty. "Affirmative Action: A Sadly Passive Event," *Business Quarterly*, Vol. 41 (1976), 22-26.

53. *Native Employment Programs of Amok Ltd., Syncrude Canada Ltd., Eldorado Nuclear Ltd.* (Ottawa: Canadian Employment and Immigration Commission, 1979).

54. Newman, J.N. "Discrimination in Recruitment: An Empirical Analysis," *Industrial and Labor Relations Review*, Vol. 32 (1978), 15-23.

55. Oaxaca, R.N. "Theory and Measurement in the Economics of Discrimination," in L.J. Hausman, O. Ashenfelter, B. Rustin, R. Schubert, and D. Slaiman (Eds.), *Equal Rights and Industrial Relations*, (Madison, Wisc.: Industrial Relations Research Association, 1977), pp. 1-30.

56. Osterman, P. "Sex Discrimination in Professional Employment: A Case Study," *Industrial and Labor Relations Review*, Vol. 32 (1979), 451-464.

57. Osterman, P. "An Empirical Study of Labour Market Segmentation," *Industrial and Labour Relations Review*, Vol. 28 (1975), 508-523.

58. Ostry, S., and M. Zaidi. *Labour Economics in Canada*, 3rd ed. (Toronto: MacMillan, 1979).

59. Rees, A., and G.P. Shultz. *Workers and Wages in an Urban Labour Market* (Chicago: University of Chicago Press, 1970).

60. Robertson, Peter C. "Some Thoughts About Affirmative Action in Canada in the 1980s." Paper prepared for the Canadian Employment and Immigration Commission, February 15, 1980.

61. Rosen, S. "Human Capital: A Survey of Empirical Research, in R. Ehrenberg (Ed.), *Research in Labour Economics* (Greenwich, Conn.: JAI Press, 1977).

62. Rosenbaum, J.E. "Hierarchical and Individual Effects on Earnings," *Industrial Relations*, Vol. 19 (1980), 1-14.

63. Rosenberg, S. "Male Occupational Standing and the Dual Labour Market," *Industrial Relations*, Vol. 19 (1980), 34-49.

64. *Royal Commission Inquiry Into Civil Rights, Vol. 3* (Toronto: Queen's Park, 1968).

65. Rumberger, R.S., and M. Carnoy. "Segmentation in the U.S. Labour Market: The Effects on the Mobility and Earnings of Whites and Blacks," *Cambridge Journal of Economics*, Vol. 4 (1980), 117-132.

66. Siebert, W.S., and P.J. Sloane. "The Measurement of Sex and Marital Status Discrimination at the Workplace," *Economica*, Vol. 48 (1981), 125-142.

67. Sloane, P.J., and W.S. Siebert. "Hiring Practices and the Employment of Women."

Paper prepared for the Manpower Services Commission, Paisley College of Technology, 1977.

68. Smith, S. "Government Wage Differentials by Sex," *The Journal of Human Resources*, Vol. 11 (1976), 185-199.

69. Smith, Arthur B., Jr. "The Law and Equal Employment Opportunity: What's Past Should Not Be Prologue," *Industrial and Labor Relations Review*, Vol. 33 (1980), 493-505.

70. Spence, A.M. *Market Signalling: Informational Transfer in Hiring and Related Screening Processes* (Cambridge, Mass.: Harvard University Press, 1974).

71. *The Status of Women in Canada* (Ottawa: Information Canada, 1970).

72. *The Status of Women Crown Employees* (Toronto: Ontario Ministry of Labour, 1979).

73. Tucker, P.H. "Equal Opportunity: Royal Bank," in H.C. Jain and D. Carroll (Eds.), *Race and Sex Equality in the Workplace: A Challenge and an Opportunity, Proceedings* (Ottawa: Minister of Supply and Services Canada, 1980), pp. 99-102.

74. Ulrich, L., and D. Trumbo. "The Selection Interview Since 1949," *Psychological Bulletin*, Vol. 63 (1965), 100-116.

75. Wachter, M. "Primary and Secondary Labor Markets: A Critique of the Dual Approach," *Brookings Papers on Economic Activity*, Vol. 3 (1974), 637-680.

76. *Women in the CBC: Report of the CBC Task Force on the Status of Women* (Toronto: CBC, 1975).

77. Wright, O.R. "Summary of Research on the Selection Interview," *Personnel Psychology*, Vol. 22 (1969), 391-413.

QUESTIONS

1. Compare and contrast the concepts of the internal labour market, the dual labour market and human capital. What can you learn from these concepts about the staffing policies and practices of employers?

2. Discuss the concept of affirmative-action programs in the Canadian context. What are its pros and cons?

3. Discuss the legal concepts of indirect discrimination and class-action suits. What is Canada's experience in applying these concepts?

4. What is the potential for discrimination by industrial and craft unions against minorities and women? Discuss the pros and cons of their current practices.

5. What should employers do to protect themselves against any pay- and employment-discrimination lawsuits? What specific recommendations can you propose to improve employers' staffing practices?

JOHN CRISPO

22. The Future of Canadian Industrial Relations

This chapter surveys current trends and prospective developments in industrial relations. After commenting on the climate within which industrial relations are conducted, the chapter focuses on the labour movement and on management activities Subsequently, the article reviews subjects ranging from wage-and-price controls to Western-European-style industrial democracy.

It is presumptuous for any one person to claim to perceive the future of anything so complex as the Canadian industrial-relations system with any degree of precision. There are too many variables involved, and they are too susceptible to change. At the most, this article represents a survey of some current developments and trends in our industrial-relations system. Only to a limited extent does this approach permit any sort of definitive assessment of what lies ahead.

Aside from denying any pretension as a so-called futurist, I should make it clear what I mean by our industrial-relations system. As the first section of this chapter will reveal, I prefer to interpret it in a broad and comprehensive manner encompassing much more than collective bargaining. Since it is not feasible to cover all of the components of our industrial-relations system, the labour movement — its numbers, structure, and philosophy — receives the most attention. Considerably less attention is devoted to developments on the management side. Some time is also devoted to the role of law and public policy, to labour demands in collective bargaining, to controls and inflation, and to the prospects for Western-European-style industrial democracy in this country.

THE INDUSTRIAL-RELATIONS SETTING

Forecasting the future of industrial relations is difficult because it is part and parcel of the general socioeconomic-political setting within which it operates. Unless one fully appreciates what is likely to happen to that environment, one cannot begin to comprehend what is going to transpire in industrial relations. For example, observers of the industrial-relations scene periodically become obsessed with the notion that it is in real trouble. Whenever this assessment has any validity, it virtually always reflects a similar state in society at large.

524

Industrial relations is seldom a sufficiently strong phenomenon by itself to upset society. By and large, the influence runs strongly the other way. This underscores the point that it is difficult to understand where industrial relations is heading unless it is first understood where society is heading.

Possible future changes in some general environmental elements in Canada could have a profound effect on the future direction of our industrial-relations system. If the current pressure for more decentralization of power within our federal-provincial system comes to fruition, it cannot help but lead to further decentralization within what is already a highly decentralized industrial-relations system.

One can also speculate on the impact a permanent slow down in our rate of economic growth would have on our industrial relations. Generally speaking, our method of sharing the spoils of economic progress may be described as a "trickle-down" system under which the privileged leave enough crumbs on the table to satisfy a solid majority of the masses. This approach appears to work well as long as there is sufficient growth being generated to satisfy both ends of the income distribution. Without such growth, there would be considerable pressure for a real redistribution of income and wealth, something that has never really been contemplated — let alone experienced.

Such pressure would doubtless give rise to much more social strife and tension — potentially even class warfare — than this country has ever known. Our industrial-relations system could hardly avoid being caught up in this process with obvious consequences for such factors as work stoppages.

Still more far-fetched — but not to be ruled out — are the implications, for our industrial-relations system, of a breakdown in the democratic and pluralistic way of life. If liberal democracy does not survive (and no one would claim it is on the ascendancy in the world at large), there is no way that our industrial-relations system will remain intact. No totalitarian regime, be it of the left or right, has ever accepted the relatively free and unfettered form of collective bargaining which is the hallmark of our industrial-relations system.

Unless one makes some assumptions about the key variables that have been mentioned, not much can be said about the future course of industrial relations. The perspective of this chapter is to adopt a rather cautious and conservative approach and to assume that there will not be any profound changes in the major environmental forces which shape our industrial-relations system.

THE LABOUR MOVEMENT IN CANADA

For any analysis of the future of industrial relations, there are three major aspects of the labour movement in this country which warrant attention. The first of these pertains to its potential for growth, the second to its intractable structural defects, and the third to its ambivalent philosophic leanings.

The White-Collar Challenge
The only significant question relating to the growth of the labour movement in Canada is its prospect for more fully organizing white-collar workers. For reasons which are not altogether clear, the Canadian labour movement has been able to organize almost twice the proportion of its potential membership than has its

American counterpart. In the last twenty years, the U.S. labour movement has witnessed its share of the labour force shrink from about one-third to just over one-fifth. In contrast, unions in Canada have more than held their own, relatively speaking, now representing between 35 and 40 percent of their prospective members.

Nonetheless, except in the public service, the Canadian labour movement has failed to make substantial inroads into the white-collar work force. The white-collar citadels of banking, commerce, and finance remain virtually union-free, and the immediate outlook does not bode well from a union point of view.

Increasingly, the larger white-collar employers appear determined to avoid unions at virtually any cost. Besides engaging in some subtle and not-too-subtle tactics designed to discourage their employees from joining unions, they are resorting to more refined and sophisticated means to instill in their employees the feeling that they will be treated as well without a union as they would be with one. In effect, some of these employers are literally buying off their employees to prevent them from unionizing. They have apparently decided that the flexibility and freedom they enjoy without a union is worth a compensation package not unlike that which would exist if they were organized. This is a difficult strategy for the labour movement to counter. Clearly, it has yet to devise an effective response.

Whether or not unions eventually are able to organize workers in banking, commerce, and finance may well depend on broader social forces. As it becomes more obvious that many so-called professionals such as doctors are really unionized and that many other groups in society, like farmers with their marketing boards, have collective devices with which to advance their common interests, the mass of white-collar workers too may decide they need to band together. If and when they do, however, they may decide to form their own unions separate and apart from the rest of the labour movement.

The Structural Problem

Historically, the labour movement in Canada has never represented a cohesive and unified force. Traditionally, it has also been characterized by a great deal of decentralization and fragmentation. One of the factors which has contributed to these problems has been the presence of international unions. Although saddled with an excess of blame on this score, this unique Canadian phenomenon has aggravated the domestic causes of structural difficulties.

The case for blaming international unions for these difficulties has been weakened by the gradual decline in their share of the organized work force in this country. They now only represent about 50 percent of organized workers in Canada as opposed to 75 percent two or three decades ago. In addition, much has been done to Canadianize this country's sections of international unions, including the establishment of separate and distinct Canadian regions or sections, the creation of meaningful Canadian policy conferences, elections of the top Canadian officers by the Canadian members, and the maintenance of staffs in Canada adequate to service the membership here. However, none of these unions have yet constitutionally conceded the right of their Canadian members to run their own financial affairs or to secede. Although these concessions may be too much to expect of any such institutions, nothing less will satisfy the ultranationalistic critics of international unions.

As significant an obstacle as these unions may have presented to structural reform of the Canadian labour movement, it probably would not have taken place easily even in their absence. To illustrate, one need only cite the historical existence of rival unionism in Quebec, especially in the form of the French-Canadian-based Confederation of National Trade Unions (CNTU).

Today, Quebec's special place within confederation is reflected by the unique position which the Quebec Federation of Labour (QFL) enjoys within the Canadian Labour Congress (CLC). Unlike the other provincial federations of labour, some years ago the QFL was granted special powers in the areas of education and organizing. Building on that precedent, the QFL has acquired more and more authority within its jurisdiction. Now it charts its own course within Quebec, almost to the point of ignoring the CLC. Recently, for example, it defied the latter's constitution by taking under its wing a breakaway group from one of the building-trades unions.

Another measure of the weakness of the structure of the Canadian labour movement is its decentralization. The CLC has almost no control over its affiliates who consider it little more than a mouthpiece for organized labour.

The determination of the affiliates to guard their autonomy became dramatically clear a few years ago when the CLC convention adopted a manifesto designed to show that there was a positive side to its condemnation of wage-and-price controls. This manifesto indicated that organized labour must be granted a meaningful voice in national policy formulation if the right of collective bargaining was going to be sacrificed under wage-and-price controls.

However, by calling for a vague form of tripartism, the manifesto gave rise to the impression that in return for more centralized power at the national level, the CLC would be quite prepared to trade off some of the autonomy of its affiliates in the collective-bargaining arena. As suspicion of this possibility spread, the CLC affiliates rallied their forces to condemn the manifesto in one provincial federation of labour convention after another. By the time of the next CLC convention, the manifesto was a dead issue. Regardless of the rationale behind their actions, the affiliates were once again making it crystal clear that they would countenance no compromising of their independence by their national labour front.

As one looks ahead, it is difficult to be optimistic about any meaningful reforms in the structure of the Canadian labour movement. Its very unity is in question, as evidenced by the fact that most of the building trades are withholding their per capita taxes from the CLC. At issue is what they take to be their jurisdictional integrity as well as a range of philosophic differences.

If, as now seems likely, the building trades withdraw from the congress, this could mark the beginning of an even more divisive realignment. Assuming the building trades pull out, that will leave a congress potentially dominated by the public-service unions. Under such circumstances it is possible that the industrial affiliates may also pull out. It is not inconceivable, therefore, that the Canadian Labour Congress could split into at least three separate groups — building trades, industrial unions, and public-service unions. If this should happen then more individual unions might decide that, like the Teamsters, they would be better off on their own.

Meanwhile, paralleling what seems to be happening in the country as a whole, power within the labour movement may gravitate more and more to provincial and regional levels. The QFL precedent could be emulated to a lesser degree in other parts of the country. Certainly, there are already signs of the British Columbia Federation of Labour playing a much more active, and perhaps independent, role in that province.

These suggestions about the future structure of the Canadian labour movement represent more of a fear than a forecast. Nonetheless, as drastic as the consequences could prove for all concerned, current trends are such as to indicate that it is going to prove exceedingly difficult to retain whatever unity the labour movement now enjoys.

Labour's Philosophical Dilemma

In addition to being in difficulty on the structural front, organized labour is also in trouble on the philosophical front. This is because labour's traditional commitment to social reform does not find much support among its more prosperous members. It is almost as if the success of organized labour in the collective-bargaining arena could prove to be its undoing in the political sphere.

Historically, the labour movement in Canada has had a strong political leaning towards the left. Indeed, in the absence of the labour movement, it is hard to imagine what force in Canada would begin to offset the entrenched power of the political right.

Basically, unions in Canada have only two realistic choices with respect to their general philosophic outlook. On the one hand, there is business or "bread-and-butter" unionism, which concentrates almost exclusively on utilizing collective bargaining to better the terms and conditions of employment of its members. To the limited extent that it involves itself in politics, this type of unionism concentrates on labour laws of immediate concern to its collective-bargaining activities and not on the general reform of society.

Another realistic form of unionism is based on business unionism but combines it with a degree of social unionism. No union in Canada can survive if it does not put the income and job security of its members first. But it is possible, as most of the industrial and public-service unions have demonstrated, to go far beyond this narrow approach. If only as a kind of "fringe benefit" for their leaders, union members in Canada will support, or at least tolerate, their unions involving themselves extensively in social causes, even to the point of backing the New Democratic Party (NDP).

More radical forms of unionism are not likely to survive in Canada in the absence of some of the drastic changes in the environment alluded to earlier. As long as workers have a growing stake in a relatively prosperous, healthy, and stable socioeconomic-political system, they are unlikely to support unions whose objectives include radical social reform or revolution. Such workers have too much to lose if things go wrong.

It is even difficult for the labour movement in this country to mount and sustain meaningful support for the NDP. Relatively few workers display much loyalty to the NDP even though it almost always champions their causes, shows by example what can be done when it is elected, and forces the Tories and especially the Liberals to remember their left wings lest they be outflanked.

There is no easy way out for the labour movement when it comes to its philosophical and political dilemma. It has to put the collective-bargaining interests of its members first but in doing so it risks losing their commitment to any real social reform.

Without a real crisis in society this dilemma may only grow more difficult to resolve in the future.

EMPLOYERS AND THEIR ORGANIZATIONS

On the employer side, few major developments can be anticipated even where they might be highly desirable. One can expect continuing professionalization of the industrial-relations and personnel functions within virtually all large organizations. Most employers of any consequence have discovered that they can no longer afford to neglect these areas.

As indicated earlier, this will mean more refined and sophisticated antiunion or union-free campaigns in many unorganized sectors. Within organized enterprises, there will remain some emphasis on ousting the unions involved, but the major stress will be placed on more effective relations with the unions now in place. In both union and nonunion situations, employers will continue to show more interest in various types of quality-of-working-life (QWL) experiments.

Employer associations can be expected to play a more active part in situations where individual firms are vulnerable to union divide-and-conquer measures which lead to various forms of leapfrogging and whipsawing. After years of runaway settlements, the major breweries are once again pulling together in most of the provinces in order to present a common front to their unions. Only in B.C. has this process been aided and abetted by accreditation of employer associations, which is only available to contractors in the construction industry in the other provinces.

At the national level, employers still lack an effective champion of their point of view. Instead, a host of management organizations profess to speak for the employers' cause. Besides the Chamber of Commerce and the Canadian Manufacturers' Association, there is the Business Council on National Issues (BCNI) and the Canadian Federation of Independent Businessmen, not to mention numerous groups like the Canadian Construction Association which represent particular industries. Except in B.C., this lack of employer unity at the national level continues to prevail at the provincial level as well.

Employers in B.C. have made the greatest progress in terms of providing a united front on issues of common concern. The Employers Council of British Columbia has no counterpart anywhere else in the country. For a variety of reasons, employers in B.C. have discovered that it pays to work together in industrial relations as well as other areas. As a result, they share information, meet regularly, and lobby and speak out in a manner quite unique to their jurisdiction. One important manifestation of their efforts is the biweekly meeting which takes place among all the major spokesmen for employers in their dealings with organized labour. Attending these meetings are representatives of the federations which bargain for groups of employers in the province as well as those from the few major employers, such as B.C. Hydro, which still negotiate on their own.

The basic thrust of these and other activities of the Employers Council of British Columbia is not antiunion. Indeed, the council came out strongly against "right-to-work" legislation when the Social Credit government was under strong pressure from its right-wing elements to move in that direction. Rather than being antiunion, the council is intended to ensure that employers in B.C. are able to deal with their organized workers on a more intelligent and united basis. However, there is no real sign of employers in the other provinces following the example of their B.C. counterparts. For the foreseeable future, therefore, employers are likely to remain as divided as ever.

LABOUR LAW AND PUBLIC POLICY

The basic legal framework for the conduct of labour relations in Canada is now too well entrenched to yield to any radical departures in the absence of some fundamental changes in the environment. From a legislative point of view, about all that one can anticipate is some relatively minor tinkering.

Two recent examples of such tinkering which may spread further are the provision by law both for the agency shop (compulsory automatic payment of dues for union and nonunion members of the bargaining unit) and for first agreement arbitration. The agency shop began in Quebec while the imposition of first collective agreements on recalcitrant employers got its start in B.C. Both provisions have already spread to other jurisdictions and seem likely to spread still further.

Related areas where changes may occur in the application and interpretation of labour law include the duty of fair representation and the duty to bargain in good faith. With respect to the duty of fair representation, unions are required to represent, in a nonarbitrary manner, all members of the bargaining unit, irrespective of their minority status or, in fact, whether or not they are members of the union. In this area, labour boards may show an increasing disposition to regulate the internal affairs of unions, even in the absence of a comprehensive bill of rights for their members. With respect to the duty to bargain in good faith, labour boards may well choose to meddle even more than they have in the collective-bargaining process, in spite of the difficulties of proving a failure on the part of unions or management to bargain in good faith.

Probably the most meaningful innovation in labour-relations legislation is to be found in British Columbia where the labour-relations board has been empowered to realign and restructure obsolete bargaining units. This long overdue provision has enabled the board to introduce effective joint bargaining by union councils on a province-wide basis both in the construction industry and in B.C. Railways. Unfortunately, this welcome initiative seems unlikely to be emulated elsewhere because of government reluctance to move against the entrenched vested interests which favour the status quo.

If there are to be any significant retrograde steps in labour law and public policy in this country, they are likely to revolve around the right to strike. No one in Canada needs to be reminded of our abysmal strike record. Although this trait is part and parcel of our adversarial industrial-relations system, and in fact causes surprisingly little real damage, it provides ample justification for those who would like to curtail the right to strike.

Especially sensitive to criticism are the advocates of the right to strike in the public service, a right which prevails in this country much more widely than in most others. If the right to strike is to be rolled back, the process undoubtedly will begin in the public sector. However, the right to strike may prevail if only because the alternative is not particularly attractive. The only real alternative is some form of compulsory arbitration and its record is hardly appealing, even in the face of an occasional disruptive public-service shutdown.

LABOUR DEMANDS AND THE ECONOMIC OUTLOOK

It is important to link labour demands with the economic outlook because the former is so strongly influenced by the latter. After a long period of prosperity, for example, it is not surprising that unions should begin to place less emphasis on their usual priorities. Normally, wages and hours of work are the primary issues. As progress is made in these areas, however, unions tend to place more emphasis on other basic issues such as occupational health and safety and on more esoteric goals such as anniversary and birthday holidays and paternity leave.

Demands such as these tend to fade into the background again when the economy worsens. The current combination of inflation and unemployment has forced unions once again to concentrate on the fundamentals. Money has to be the priority because it takes so much more just to stay even in real terms. At the same time, reduced hours become more appealing in the forlorn hope that they will reduce the level of unemployment. In fact, about all they can do is convert unemployment into underemployment, albeit spread around on a more even basis.

Perhaps some rough equivalence of sacrifice among its own ranks is about all labour can hope to accomplish when it comes to unemployment or underemployment. Labour would doubtless like to apply the same principle across the board when it comes to bearing the costs of inflation. Unfortunately, it finds it difficult, if not impossible, to do so given the strength of marketing boards, professional guilds, and other powerful interest groups in society.

CONTROLS AND INFLATION

Given the present rate of inflation, our political leaders may once again become so desperate as to resort to some form of wage-and-price controls. They may do this despite a domestic and foreign record under controls which indicates that at best they only appear to cope with the problem in the short run. In the meantime, they contribute to all manner of anomalies, distortions, and inequities, as well as undermining the collective-bargaining process.

The alleged purpose of controls is to curb excessive increases in wages, salaries, fees, and profits from working their way through the system. The problem is that the prescription does not really fit the diagnosis, except perhaps on a temporary basis. Assuming excessive increases in income and costs are a problem, the challenge is to get at their underlying causes. Otherwise, as in the case of controls, one is only dealing with their symptoms. Where it can be demonstrated that particular groups in society, including particular unions, are extracting unduly large increases from the system, then the real challenge is to reduce the powers and privileges which permit those groups to extract such increases. Despite the futility of controls as a solution to any underlying aspect of the problem of inflation, they cannot be ruled out because politicians want to *appear* to be doing something about the problem.

THE OUTLOOK FOR INDUSTRIAL DEMOCRACY

North Americans have long believed that their collective-bargaining system, with its comprehensive collective agreements and elaborate grievance procedures, represents the epitome of industrial democracy. This is now being questioned because of a variety of other means available to Western European unions and workers to influence decision making within their countries.

In particular, labour and social-democratic parties are much more potent forces within Europe than is the NDP in this country. In addition, Europe has experienced more industrial democracy in its various forms — economic, representational, and shop floor. Economic democracy represents the different efforts which are being made in various Western European countries to provide workers with a significant share in the ownership of capital. Known as workers'-asset or capital formation, the idea is to provide workers with some equity ownership in business by compelling companies to apply a portion of their profits to the development of some form of mutual trust fund for employees.

Representational democracy takes many forms. At the national level, it usually involves unions in the formulation of major socioeconomic-political decision making through multipartite economic and social consultative bodies. At the level of the firm, representational democracy has become almost synonymous with the concept of codetermination or union and worker representation on company boards. In addition, most Western European countries require works councils at the company and office or plant levels.

Shop-floor democracy incorporates the many efforts which are being undertaken to make work more edifying, meaningful, and satisfying, if not productive as well. These efforts range from relatively simple concepts such as job rotation to more advanced ones such as semiautonomous work groups.

The relevance of these forms of industrial democracy to Canada remains a question. Because of differences in attitudes and institutions, it is difficult to transplant social experiments from one jurisdiction to another. Nevertheless, a number of developments are already occurring in North America which clearly fall under the rubric of industrial democracy of the Western European style.

With respect to economic democracy, North American workers already have far more potential than their European counterparts to influence the policies and priorities of many large companies. This is because North American workers through their unions could have a major voice in the investment of massive pension funds. Although most North American unions and workers have yet to pursue this potential for any other purpose than the maximization of the return on their investment, there are increasing signs of other goals and objectives emerging. As this happens, the problem of the trust relationship will come to the fore. If the trustees of pension funds are to invest them for purposes other than traditional ones, the law will have to be changed to permit such action.

With respect to representational forms of industrial democracy, it is hard to predict what will happen. Attempts to form anything like a national economic and social council have made little headway in this country. The most recent attempt to create such a body was thwarted by the government's imposition of wage-and-price controls. Even in the absence of such aberrations, there are many obstacles in the way of progress in this area.

To a large extent, both labour and management remain, in the main, opposed to or at least sceptical of codetermination. Nonetheless, the Chrysler precedent suggests that this concept is not to be ruled out in North America when circumstances prove desperate enough. Moreover, at some point it seems likely that the reticence of North American unions towards codetermination may give way to a more favourable attitude if only to garner the information and insight board memberships would provide.

Works councils would have little role in North America since their function is for the most part played by our local unions. Western European unions are not built upon the local union structure which underpins our unions. Consequently, works councils in Europe fill a necessary void which does not exist here. The attributes of those councils could be provided by local labour-management committees or by Scanlon Plans, which involve wages being formally related to productivity increases.

Shop-floor democracy, at least in the name of quality of working life, is gradually becoming the "in thing" in Canadian industrial relations. Ontario, for example, now has a quality of working life centre fronted in large measure by some of the leading labour people in the province. There is no doubt that some very positive developments are occurring under the banner of quality of working life. Some misgivings and reservations remain, however, if only because of its use by some companies as part of their overall programs to avoid unionization.

In general, industrial democracy of the Western European style would seem to have a mixed future in Canada. Some forms of industrial democracy, such as the quality-of-working-life movement, are almost universal in their applicability. Others, such as codetermination, depend very much upon deeply entrenched attitudes and values which are not readily transferable from one country to another.

CONCLUSION

Canada's industrial-relations system is as much its own product as are the varying forms of industrial democracy of Western Europe. Our industrial-relations system is far from perfect, but neither is it worth changing simply for the sake of change.

My own forecast of the outlook for the Canadian industrial-relations system is a simple one. It may not be the best system in the world, but it's far from the worst. I would neither advocate, nor predict, any profound changes in the system unless the environment within which it operates is radically altered. If that should happen then the outlook for industrial relations, as well as the rest of our socioeconomic-political system, will become totally unpredictable. I, for one, do not like to contemplate the result.

QUESTIONS

1. What current developments in society at large do you see having the greatest impact upon our industrial-relations system?

2. Are any of these developments likely to have a dramatic or drastic effect upon our industrial-relations system?

3. What do you believe are the most significant challenges confronting the Canadian labour movement?

4. How well equipped do you believe the labour movement is to cope with these challenges?

5. How well equipped are employers to deal with unions?

6. How would you change our laws and public policies that are designed to cope with industrial relations?

7. How best can organized labour respond to the challenge posed by inflation?

8. Under what circumstances may we see more experimentation with Western-European-style industrial democracy in this country?

JOHN B. KERVIN

Appendix 1.
The Canadian Switch Company
Collective-Bargaining Simulation

This simulation, which can be played in either a short or long version, introduces players to the process of collective bargaining — from preparation to agreement. A unique scoring scheme reflects the different objectives and concerns of union and management teams and introduces uncertainty about the opposing team's resources and priorities.

INTRODUCTION TO THE SIMULATION

This section describes the requirements, procedures, and rules for playing the Canadian Switch Company collective-bargaining simulation. The details for the short version of the simulation are provided first; instructions for playing the longer version are given at the end of this section.

Game Requirements

A group of ten players, six union and four management, is needed to play the simulation (although this can be reduced to nine or eight by dropping one player each from the union and the management team in that order). If individuals are left over after a class has been divided into groups of eight, nine, or ten, these persons can be assigned as observers and allowed to monitor the negotiations and caucus meetings of a single group. By having access to both management and union teams in their private meetings, observers can follow the course of negotiations and provide useful information and insights in the class discussion following the simulation. An instructor or "referee" is also required to select or approve team data options, designate the strike-deadline time, resolve rule disputes, record the time each group reaches agreement, and receive copies of each group's agreement and point scoring.

The short version of the simulation is designed so that it can be played in one or two full days. Alternatively it can be spread out over a number of days by playing two or three hours per day. The simulation begins with a short session in which players are divided into groups, and groups into union and management teams. Each team then meets so that its members can select their roles. These preliminaries will take from a half an hour to an hour. Following this, each person will require approximately one or two hours in order to become familiar with his or her role and the data. Each team meets again for a period of two to four hours to review its data, choose priority or costing options (if this has not been done by the instructor or referee) and plan its strategy for the upcoming bargaining. The negotiations themselves (including time for team caucuses) will require from four to six hours. For approximately the last hour of this period, a strike will be in effect. (The instructor will designate the total time available for bargaining and the strike-deadline time.) Thus the total time for the simulation will range from about seven-and-a-half to thirteen hours.

The space requirements for the game will depend upon how many groups are bargaining. Ideally, each group should have a negotiation room and two caucus rooms, one for each of the teams. An alternative is to have one of the teams caucus in the negotiation room. However, this is less satisfactory as it does not allow the players to spread out their materials and leave them behind to go to negotiations. Every effort should be made to avoid putting two teams in the same caucus room no matter how large, even if both are management or union. The distractions will be too great and the temptation to compare progress irresistible.

The basic materials required to play the simulation are found in this appendix. In addition, players will find a calculator of great help in costing and other arithmetic calculations. It is suggested that each team keep a bargaining book in which to record the specific demands and counteroffers on each side and the arguments pertaining to each issue. A sample page is shown in Figure 1.

Figure 1

Sample Page of Bargaining Book

Issue: *Skill Bonus*   **Team:** *Union*

Present Situation: *none in present contract*

Union Demand: *25¢*

Data: *Acme Tool — 20¢ in last contract 11 months ago*
    Dunn Video — 2% of hourly rate — would give Tool and Die I a bonus of about 22¢

Negotiation Record:

        11:15 — 1st meet — they reject — too costly — only half of local companies
             included a bonus in latest contract.
        11:45 — willing to give 5¢
        12:05 — we lower demand to 23¢
        12:30 — we offer to go to 15¢ — if they drop job-posting change
        12:45 — they offer 12¢
         1:15 — settle at 12¢

General Situation and Remaining Issues

In the short version of the simulation, negotiations begin with the parties in the following position: in a series of six previous meetings they have negotiated and reached agreement on all but five issues. The "signed-off" issues include such points as minor revisions to the contract language, modifications of the grievance procedure, and some major issues concerning overtime-work assignments. As well, some benefit improvements were negotiated, and the two teams have agreed to a one-year contract.

The parties are now down to the final five issues on which agreement has yet to be reached. Conciliation has come and gone, the strike deadline is not far off. The union has already taken a strike vote and 86 percent of the members have voted to walk out if a satisfactory agreement is not obtained. The task of both teams is to reach a satisfactory agreement, before the strike deadline if possible. The issues which are to be bargained are:

1. *Wages.* The current average wage is $6.26 an hour.
2. *Skill bonus.* The last bonus for skilled employees was 10¢ per hour, given two years ago.
3. *Holidays.* The current contract provides for eleven paid holidays per year.
4. *Dental plan.* At present, the company pays 50 percent of the premium for a basic preventive dental plan.
5. *Job posting.* At present, the company posts (gives its employees preference for) the original job vacancy and the first two vacancies arising out of current employees transferring to fill those vacant jobs.

Procedures

Team and role selection — Begin the simulation by dividing into groups of eight, nine, or (preferably) ten persons. Extra persons left over should be designated as observers. One person (or the class instructor) can serve as referee. For example, a class of fifty-four could be divided into three groups of ten and two groups of nine for a total of forty-eight players in five groups, a referee, and one observer assigned to each group.

Within each group, players should be designated as management or union as follows: for groups of size ten, six union and four management; in groups of size nine, five union and four management; and in groups of size eight, five union and three management. Each team should then meet briefly while the members select the roles they want to play.

The management roles are:

President and general manager: chief negotiator, quiet but forceful, believes in gentlemanly manners and fair play.
Industrial-relations consultant: earnest, ambitious, likes the sense of competition and wants to win.
Personnel manager: open, friendly, easy to get along with, believes in the benefits of cooperation.
Production manager: (drop this role if only eight in group): business-like, down-to-earth, concerned mostly about productivity.

The union roles are:

National representative: chief negotiator, business-like and realistic, concerned both with the employees' situation and the union's health as an organization.

Local president: friendly, outgoing, well-liked, tries hard to get something for everybody.

Chief steward: hard-working, ambitious, has a good competitive instinct.

Machine-shop steward: quiet, reasonable, sincere, believes in a cooperative approach.

Shipping-department steward: mistrustful of management, thinks things should be much better than they are.

Production-department steward: (drop this role if nine or eight in group): open-minded, observant, quiet but could get very involved.

If playing with nine in the group drop the production-department steward from the union team. If playing with eight also drop the production manager from the management team.

Individual preparation— After participants know their team and roles, study the rest of this chapter and in particular the appropriate role description. Review the data on the issues to be negotiated and make whatever costing or statistical-data preparations are necessary. Make up a bargaining book for the issue(s) of most concern and think about which of the issues should have priority and what the minimum or maximum position should be. Also look over the role descriptions and data for the other team to get some idea of the opposition and their particular concerns. Plan to spend up to two hours or more on this initial preparation.

It should be noted that in some cases four optional sets of figures are available, designated by the letters *a, b, c,* or *d.* Each of the teams or the referee will choose for each case which option is to be used. Thus, for its own data or situation each team will know the exact figures, but for the other team's data all the team will know is the range covered by the options. This uncertainty is a realistic representation of the actual situation in collective bargaining.

Team preparation — Once the individual preparations are completed, the team can meet to plan for the upcoming negotiations. A number of topics need to be considered. For both union and management teams, the first task is to determine which priority option or costing option will be used in the negotiations. The choice that must be made for each team is listed in Table 1. If the referee is making the choices, get the priority or costing option from him. If your team is making its own choice, start by considering the possibilities and deciding which one is preferable. Then notify the referee of your choice. (No changes are allowed once negotiations have begun.) In neither case should you allow the other team to learn which option you are using. This information would give them a considerable advantage at the table.

For the union team the most important task is to develop initial demands on the issues. Each member of the team should discuss the relative importance of each issue and the minimum position on it. Also begin to consider what concessions and trade-offs might be made. Another task is to prepare the data supporting each demand and decide who will speak on each issue as it comes up for discussion. One option is to have the chief negotiator do all the speaking; another is to allow a different member to speak on each particular matter.

On the management side, the most important task is to become aware of the overall financial situation and cost implications of each issue. While specific costing will have to wait until exact union demands are known, this is a good time to get a general idea of costs and of where the company would like to spend its money. At the same time, an initial response to the union demands can be roughed out for

Table 1

Data Option Choices

Management Costing Options

(NOTE: All management costing options must be chosen from a single group: a, b, c, or d.)

Item	a	b	c	d
Cost of items previously settled (in ¢ per hr.)	8.1¢	7.6¢	7.3¢	6.9¢
Maximum increase in labour costs (in thousands)	$571	$553	$536	$518
Target increase in labour costs (in thousands)	$474	$461	$448	$435
Dental-plan surcharge	+10%	+5%	−5%	−10%

Union Priority Options

(NOTE: Each scoring scheme puts different emphasis on different issues, as shown by the maximum number of points an issue can earn the team. Select one of the four scoring options to indicate your team's priorities.)

Issue	a	b	c	d
Wages:	45	60	30	45
Bonus for skilled employees:	5	5	10	5
Holidays:	5	10	5	10
Dental plan:	5	5	10	5
Job posting:	5	5	5	10
Membership support:	15	5	20	10
Settlement time:	20	10	20	15

later refinement once the union's position is known. Also, data should be gathered on what the competition is doing so that, for each issue, the best position and the maximum the company would be willing to concede can be determined.

Both teams should also consider what general tasks to assign their members. For example, one or more persons are often designated as observers whose task it is to watch the other side carefully for signs of tension, resistance, weakening, and so on. Another person is usually assigned the job of costing. On the management side, this person will know the exact costs; on the union side this person will have to work with whatever data is learned at the table. Still another person might be assigned to consider what strategy the team might follow, what the strategy of the opposing team appears to be, and how best to counter it. Strategies typically involve the use of bluffing and threats, the rate of concessions, and how tough a position to take. It is also frequently the case that one person is designated to note the arguments made by the other side, to prepare counterarguments, and give these to the chief negotiator. This person might be given responsibility for the bargaining book, combining the pages individual team members have previously prepared.

Meetings and caucuses — The first team to finish its preparations should send a representative to the other team's caucus room to arrange a mutually suitable time for their first bargaining meeting. At this meeting, the union should present its demands and make initial arguments. The management team should make sure it understands clearly the union position and the reasons for its position.

At any time, either team can call a caucus to do further preparation or to discuss its strategy or changes in its position. Bargaining sessions and caucuses continue in this fashion until agreement is reached. At some point, negotiations may reach the strike deadline (announced previously by the instructor or referee) without having yet obtained an agreement. If this happens, the two teams should take a short five- or ten-minute breathing spell and then resume negotiations with the strike in progress. In most games, the strike deadline will come about an hour before the time for the simulation expires.

The simulation exercise ends when agreement is reached or when time runs out. If agreement is obtained, the teams should jointly write out and sign a "Memorandum of Agreement" in which details of the settlement of the five issues are spelled out. This should be taken immediately to the referee who will note the time of settlement in relation to the strike deadline for point-scoring purposes. Each team should then calculate its points and submit to the referee a sheet outlining its scoring calculations. If time runs out, the two teams are considered to have reached a deadlock at which point mediation would be required to settle the dispute. In this case, bargaining stops and both teams earn zero points. Details of the point scoring are provided below. The procedures for the game are summarized, step by step, in Table 2.

Rules

The rules for playing the simulation are fairly straightforward. If any disputes arise, take them to the referee whose word will be final.

1. Players are not allowed to "manufacture" data. However, you may use real information (if available to both teams) beyond what is given here *provided* it does not contradict simulation data.
2. You must not contact members of the other team except as authorized by your chief negotiator.
3. Do not compare notes with persons taking part in other groups during the simulation.
4. Continue to negotiate until a settlement is reached or time runs out.
5. Bargain in good faith and make every reasonable effort to reach an agreement.
6. While outright lying and deception are never good tactics in negotiations, you are not compelled to tell "the whole truth and nothing but the truth." However, keep in mind that lack of credibility can make it virtually impossible to reach agreement.
7. Amendments to these rules are permissible as long as both sides agree and the referee approves.

Point Scoring

When negotiations end, each team calculates its point score using the information given below in the management and union data sections. Each team has a possible maximum of 100 points, although you will find it almost impossible to achieve a score close to 100. These points represent dollars, personal satisfaction, "political credit," productivity, union-membership needs, and other considerations. Thus they

Table 2

Summary of Procedures

Players	Instructor/Referee
Before Negotiations:	
Meet with your team to select your role.	Divide class into groups and groups into union and management teams. Assign observers and referee.
Study your role, general information, data, and rules.	Announce strike-deadline time and end-of-simulation time.
Initial team meeting.	Assign negotiation and caucus rooms.
Arrange time of first negotiation session with other team.	Select option for each team (options can vary from group to group) and inform teams, or allow them to select and inform you of their choices. The option choices are given in Table 1.
During Negotiations:	
Negotiate and caucus as necessary.	Resolve any rule disputes that arise.
After Negotiations:	
Draw up and sign "Memorandum of Agreement." Take it to referee.	Note time of settlement on each "Memorandum of Agreement" and inform teams.
Calculate team points, using referee's time ruling. Give referee a copy of calculations.	Check team point calculations.

do not reflect only the monetary value of wages and benefits. In calculating your own points and estimating your opponents', there are three aspects to keep in mind. The first is the absolute value of your points — the higher the value, the better you are representing your constituency (union members or company stockholders). The second consideration is the difference between your points and the other teams — the greater the difference in your favour, the more you are "out-negotiating" them. The third aspect is the total sum of your points and theirs. The greater the value of this sum, the more joint benefit you are both deriving from negotiations. As you can see, these aspects represent three different motives negotiators may bring to the table. You must decide which motive has priority for you.

Postgame Discussion

The value of this simulation is greatly enhanced if afterwards the players and observers discuss the process and outcomes. To begin the discussion, use the point scores to identify similarities and differences among teams and groups. Three types of comparisons are useful: among the different union (and management) teams, between the union and management teams within each group, and the group totals.

The absolute values of the scores of all the union teams (and all the management teams) reflect how well constituency interests have been represented. As a general rule, any team scoring less than 50 points has not served its constituency very well.

Such negotiators would certainly be replaced in the next round! The players on the highest- and lowest-scoring teams should discuss their experiences, and the observers who watched them should give their interpretations of the outcomes.

In some groups, the two teams will score very close to one another; in other groups the differences in scores will be substantial. If the union and management teams score within five points of each other the resulting contract is probably fairly equitable. If the difference is greater than five, one side has done better at the expense of the other. Here again it would be interesting to have the members of "winning" and "losing" teams discuss the situation as they saw it. Their experiences should be compared with those of team members whose scores were close to their opponents'.

Finally, you will note differences in the total group scores (sum of union and management team). The greater this total, the greater the joint benefits the two teams derived from the negotiations. In general, a joint score of 110 or less is indicative of a relatively low joint benefit and suggests that negotiators were not paying much attention to opportunities for both sides to gain.

It would be worthwhile using these point comparisons to illustrate the merits of different views negotiators might take towards their bargaining. Should a negotiator be concerned only with how well he or she does and ignore the other team's outcomes? Should a negotiator try to do better than the other team and maximize the difference in their outcomes? Or should a negotiator be primarily concerned with their joint benefits? Each of these positions has its advantages and its problems. For example, differences are important since there is considerable potential loss of face in being seen to be "out-bargained" by the opposing side, but on the other hand there is little merit in outpointing the other team if both sides are on the brink of bankruptcy as a result.

It should be noted that the scoring scheme is designed so that a gain for one side does not always mean a corresponding loss for the other. In some cases, the two teams can agree on a particular compromise which gives both of them a reasonable number of points. In such cases, the sum of their points is greater for this compromise than for some other settlement which might give one team a few more points but lower the total sum of their points. The idea of trying to maximize joint outcomes in negotiations is an important one and represents the cooperative element in effective bargaining. While it should not outweigh the importance of getting a reasonable settlement from your own team's point of view, attention to cooperative aspects, when appropriate, leads to better and more stable labour relations.

Once the differences between teams and groups have been identified, the class can discuss the factors that led to these differences. Observers are important here because they can often identify turning points in negotiations or significant events which affected the eventual outcomes. Other topics which might be considered in the postgame discussion include: What kind of strategy would each team adopt if it were to play the simulation again? Does it help to take a rational approach and try to reach agreement as "reasonable" people? How much disagreement was there within each team, and how did these disagreements get settled? How effectively did each team divide up such tasks as negotiating, costing, recording, observing, and so on? How effective is it to open with a very tough position? How effective is it to make concessions slowly as opposed to quickly? What effect did the time deadlines have on negotiations? General discussion of this kind can contribute a great deal to the educational value of the simulation and can help the players understand some of the noneconomic factors underlying the process and outcomes of collective bargaining.

Long Version

The longer version of this simulation is designed to provide players with a more in-depth exposure to the collective-bargaining process. The requirements for a referee, observers, and number of players are identical to the short version. However, because it may take six weeks or longer to play this version, the simulation should be started early in the term. The instructor or referee should designate a "strike deadline" about a week before the time allotted for the simulation expires. Space requirements can be left up to the individual groups, but if possible some set of rooms should be available on a regular basis for teams to schedule bargaining sessions.

The opening situation for the long version is that negotiations to renew the contract between Canadian Switch Company and Local 123 of the Canadian Union of Factory Workers have not yet begun. Following the formation of teams and selection of roles, each group is to obtain two copies of current contracts from at least four unionized firms (preferably manufacturing) in the area. (Some overlap among groups may be necessary, but complete duplication should be avoided. The referee should check each group's selection of contracts to prevent duplication.) One copy should be given to each team. The union team then selects from *one* contract up to fifteen new or existing *additional* clauses to negotiate as long as these clauses do not duplicate or contradict the five issues in this simulation. The union team then notifies management in writing of its intention to bargain with a view to modifying the current agreement. This notice should also indicate which additional clauses are to be bargained and from which contract they are taken. (The remaining contracts are to be used for comparative purposes.) The two teams should then schedule their initial bargaining session within fifteen days of receipt of notice (or alternatively, follow provincial practice as set out in the provincial act governing labour relations).

Each team then gathers all the data on these issues it can from the company, the union, and other sources. This field research represents an important component of the learning experience of the simulation. The union should focus on what they feel the employees of Canadian Switch need, and what employees in other companies are getting. The management team should also gather comparative data and attempt as well to determine the cost implications of revising the additional clauses.

In some cases, costing these clauses will require additional assumptions. In these cases, the management team will prepare four reasonable alternatives and submit them to the referee. The referee will select one for the management team and give all four options to the union team who will then have a rough idea of the situation although not the exact data. For example, if the union notifies management that paid vacation entitlements are to be negotiated (for example, they intend to ask for four weeks' vacation after ten instead of twelve years of service), management must know the distribution of employees by years of service in order to cost this item. The company team would then prepare four options (such as given in Table 3) and submit them to the referee, who will select one for the management team and give all four to the union team.

Other procedures for the long version are similar to the short version described above. You should plan on one or two negotiating sessions a week, perhaps increasing the frequency as the strike deadline approaches. When you reach agreement, scoring is done as described above on the basis of the five issues in the short simulation. The additional issues in the long version are taken into account through their added costs to management. In the long version, ignore the "cost of items previously settled" and substitute the cost increases of the additional items as negotiated. As you can see from Table 1, this means that management has between 6.9 and 8.1 cents an hour to spend on the additional items.

GENERAL INFORMATION

The Company

Canadian Switch Company is a medium-sized manufacturing company with its only plant located on the outskirts of Anontown, a city with a population of approximately 100,000. The company produces several types of electrical switches which are purchased by appliance and machinery manufacturers for use in their products. Canadian Switch has been in business for eighteen years and currently employs in its plant 291 men and women plus office, sales, and management staff. Many of these employees have been with the firm for over a decade.

The company faces competition from another slightly larger firm in the Anontown area plus a handful of other firms located in Ontario, Quebec, and British Columbia. The general feeling among employees is that sales and profits have been relatively good for the past six or seven years. However, there is a current danger of declining markets because of the general economic situation and fewer sales of the appliances and machinery which use parts from Canadian Switch. Despite this potential decline in sales, the company installed some new machinery about ten months ago which seems to have increased productivity, but no one is quite sure by how much. The company does not divulge overall productivity or sales figures to its employees, but they are told in general terms through the company newsletter how things are going. Occasional rumours about sales and overall productivity performance come from the office staff.

The work force on the plant floor numbers 291 employees, consisting of 183 men and 108 women. Thirty-two employees are skilled, all but two of these are males. The other employees occupy nonskilled (unskilled or semi-skilled) job classifications. In times of normal operation the plant runs with two shifts, day and afternoon.

The Union

The Canadian Union of Factory Workers, CUFW (known as "Cuff-W" for short) Local 123, represents employees in three plants in the Anontown area: Canadian Switch, Switch International (a competitor), and National Appliance Company (a firm producing small electrical appliances). The second of these has 345 members in the bargaining unit, the third has approximately 250. CUFW has been representing Canadian Switch employees for fifteen years. During that time there have been three strikes. The last occurred four years ago and lasted twenty-four days. It resulted in a two-year contract. Other than that, the last five contracts have all been for a one-year term.

Local 123 has a national representative who is paid by the union and whose responsibilities include several other locals. The president of the local works half-time at his union duties (for which he is paid from local dues) and half-time at Canadian Switch. Both these persons are automatically members of the union

Table 3

**Four Optional Years-of-Service
Distributions for Canadian Switch Employees**

	Options							
	a		b		c		d	
Years of Service	Skilled	Non-skilled	Skilled	Non-skilled	Skilled	Non-skilled	Skilled	Non-skilled
1	2	42	—	33	2	29	5	56
2	3	39	1	32	3	23	6	42
3	3	24	3	33	3	24	—	37
4	2	23	7	24	2	29	—	21
5	1	18	4	25	3	28	4	15
6	—	14	1	21	2	22	3	18
7	—	12	1	22	2	29	—	12
8	2	13	—	13	3	18	—	11
9	3	18	3	9	1	13	—	9
10	4	15	—	10	—	10	—	14
11	2	14	2	14	2	11	4	6
12	—	—	—	—	3	—	—	—
13	—	11	—	1	1	4	—	8
14	—	3	3	3	2	9	5	—
15	2	3	—	8	—	7	—	4
16	4	8	—	7	2	—	—	3
17	2	2	2	3	1	3	—	3
18	2	—	5	1	—	—	5	—

bargaining committee. Other union officials in the plant include eight stewards and a chief steward. Four of these were elected to the present bargaining committee: the chief steward, a steward representing skilled employees, and two stewards representing nonskilled workers.

In ratifying last year's agreement only 58 percent of the employees, the lowest ratification margin in recent years, approved the contract at a rather noisy meeting. This had led to some thought that there may be a strike this year. Employees lost ground to inflation in the second year of the two-year contract (three years ago), and the general feeling is that they have not been able to recover this in the two sets of negotiations since. Two years ago, Canadian Switch provided its largest wage increase ever, 58 cents per hour across the board, but a number of employees, especially the younger ones, felt that it still was not enough. Last year's wage increase of 50 cents was slightly above the inflation rate. Some employees are talking about replacing CUFW with another union, one that might be more successful in winning larger wage increases. The general feeling is that if wage gains are not substantial this year another union would have a good chance of having CUFW decertified and replacing it.

Table 4

Summary of Current and Recent Contracts

Contract	Term	Wage Increase	Percentage Equivalent	Bonus for Skilled Employees	Value of Improvements	New Average Wage	Consumer Price Index for Previous 12 months
	(Years)	(¢/hr)	(Percent)	(cents)	(¢/hr)	(dollars)	
1 year ago	1	50	8.7	—	16.2	6.26	8.4
2 years ago	1	58	11.2	10	8.1	5.76	12.2
4 years ago (2nd year)	2	40	8.4	10	10.1	5.17	8.6
4 years ago (1st year)	2	25	5.6	10	4.3	4.76	5.8
5 years ago	1	26	6.1	—	3.6	4.50	5.6
6 years ago	1	22	5.5	—	3.2	4.24	4.8

Table 5

Annual Record of Grievances for Past Six Years

Period	Number of Grievances	Number of Arbitrations
Present year	32	4
2 years ago	22	2
3 years ago	24	0
4 years ago	16	2
5 years ago	25	2
6 years ago	13	0

Recent Agreements and Current Situation

Table 4 summarizes the contents of agreements from the last five sets of negotiations. The current average wage at Canadian Switch is $6.26 per hour. For skilled employees the average wage is $8.16, for nonskilled the average rate is $6.02. The bottom rate, for the position of Janitor II, is $5.12. The top rate is for Tool and Die maker I: $9.58 per hour. Table 5 gives the number of grievances and arbitrations for the past few years as an indicator of general labour-management relations.

The unemployment rate in the Anontown area is currently at the provincial average; not many firms are hiring new employees, but so far layoffs have been relatively few and far between. No one is quite certain what the inflation, economic, and unemployment situation will be in the near future, but it is generally felt that Anontown will be close to the provincial average.

Background to Bargaining

This section contains some general information about bargaining that will help make your negotiations more realistic. The topics include how the union negotiating team treats different kinds of issues, the general objectives of the management and union teams, the role of personality and personal goals, and the process and outcomes of negotiating.

Issues — Unions generally bring three types of issues to the bargaining table in their initial set of demands. The first includes essential issues on which important gains must be made in order for union members to ratify the new contract. Failure on these issues would result in considerable loss of face for the union negotiators and could quite possibly lead to a strike, membership unrest, and instability in the union leadership, something companies generally try to avoid. The second group of issues includes those the union would like to make some advance on, but they are not essential to ratification. They are issues which may be important only to small groups of members or "icing-on-the-cake" issues which would turn a good contract into a generous one. The third group of issues includes trade-off items on which the union does not expect to make substantial gains. Trade-off issues themselves are of three different kinds. First are the demands which can be dropped later on in the bargaining to provide leverage for other more important gains. These are issues for which some good arguments can be made but for which there is no strong feeling among the union leadership or membership. The second set consists of political issues which must be raised because they are seen as essential by one or more groups among the membership. Some real effort must be made in arguing these issues, but it is not expected that substantial gains will always result. Finally, trade-off issues include "signal" items which tell management that although they are not essential in this particular round they will be bringing these issues back to the table in succeeding years, and the union will expect substantial gains in the future.

Management objectives — In collective bargaining, management is concerned with maintaining control of the production process and keeping costs down. The reason for the former is that management always wants to be able to assign work to employees as it sees fit in order to minimize costs, maximize efficiency, and produce the greatest return on investment. It is also generally true that the company is not trying to get rid of the union or to cause embarrassment to the union leadership. If the latter results, the consequence is likely to be instability and a change of leadership leading to the kind of uncertainty that management tries to avoid. Management negotiators would like to settle without a strike but would not be willing to sacrifice unduly costs or control. Management negotiators normally have a fairly specific idea of what would constitute a satisfactory agreement, taking into account both what they are able to afford and what the competition is doing.

Union objectives — The union team's objectives in collective bargaining are usually more complex than management's since most unions operate in a more or less democratic fashion and have to juggle the potentially competing interests of their members. Thus, while union negotiators would generally like to avoid an unnecessary strike, it is possible that some may be willing to strike over an issue they see as important but other union negotiators may not. Union concerns fall into two major groups: the wages and benefits they can win for their members, and protection for the union itself, particularly its survival as an organization. This latter concern involves such items as union security, mandatory dues checkoff, closed-shop clauses, and similar aspects of the contract that provide the union with both money and assurance that it is not likely to be decertified. It is generally true that union negotiators do not seek confrontation for personal or ideological reasons, although it happens from time to time that members of union negotiating committees do have conflict as a personal objective, since unions are political organizations.

While company negotiators are concerned with what they can afford and what the competition is paying, union representatives present data that provide comparisons with other firms, argue the particular needs of their members (such as dental plans) and raise general issues such as inflation. Union negotiators are also aware that the reason people join unions in the first place is often not financial gain, but rather to avoid arbitrary control on the part of management, for example discipline or work assignments subject to a foreman's prejudices. Limiting management's arbitrary control is therefore always a union concern at the bargaining table.

Personal objectives — Individuals at the bargaining table often have personal goals and concerns which will affect the process and outcome of negotiations. Most negotiators want to do a good job and win approval from their own constituency, directors and other management, or the union membership. It is also true that one's sense of self-esteem is involved in the bargaining, and individuals vary in terms of the importance of approval from others. (This may also include approval from members of the opposing team.) Negotiations may also affect the future of negotiators. On the management side, this may involve promotion; on the union side, election to more important positions. All these kinds of issues are referred to as intangibles: they do not appear on the list of demands, they are not directly bargained at the table, but they play an important role in negotiations nonetheless.

Negotiation process and outcomes — Formal bargaining starts when the union negotiators give their demands to management. The first few meetings are normally spent clarifying these demands so that management can cost them. At this stage, the union presents its initial data and arguments supporting the demands. The next major phase begins when management gives its first reply (which may be partial or total) to the union demands, and negotiating begins in earnest. Union negotiators present their arguments based on employee needs and comparison data; management negotiators reply with other comparison data and cost arguments. Gradually the items are whittled down, beginning with the noncost items. As agreement is reached on each clause it is "signed-off" — the new wording is written out and initialed by the chief negotiators, although final approval may be conditional on an acceptable total agreement. The final stage of bargaining begins when a small number of issues are left, usually the major monetary items plus the nonmonetary items on which agreement could not be reached earlier.

The process of bargaining up to this point consists of two kinds of movement the parties make toward each other's positions. The first is *trade-offs*. For example, the union agrees to drop one demand in return for management's granting another. The second kind of movement is *concessions*. For example, management will increase what it is willing to offer by a small amount after the union lowers its demands somewhat, with the two parties gradually getting closer to agreement. During the final phase, *packaging* becomes particularly important. The items are no longer treated one at a time but are combined into packages which the sides try out on one another, making trade-offs and concessions until agreement is reached.

When an agreement is finally achieved, the management team will normally have already secured approval from higher management for the cost of that particular contract. The union usually takes the proposed contract back to its membership for a ratification vote. If agreement is not reached and a deadlock occurs the parties normally go to conciliation (compulsory in most provinces), and if a conciliation officer or board is unable to bring the parties together, a strike or lockout may legally be called. In an effort to end the conflict, the more intensive and lengthy intervention of a mediator may occur in the period just prior to the strike (after conciliation) or after a strike is under way. In some jurisdictions, notably the public sector, the parties may choose (or be obliged) to submit their differences to an arbitrator who will then decide the terms of the contract on the basis of briefs submitted by the parties.

MANAGEMENT DATA AND NEGOTIATOR ROLES

In this section, brief sketches of the characteristics and concerns of the four management negotiators are provided. Data needed to argue management's position in the bargaining and details on scoring your negotiation results are also included.

Become familiar with the role you are playing and the data relevant to your concerns. Also look over the roles of the other members of your team and examine the union-negotiator roles and data.

You have a choice of four options representing financial aspects of your situation. A summary of these options is given in Table 1. Note that all four choices must be made from the same group (that is, all *a* or *b,* and so on). The referee may make a selection for you to ensure that different groups are playing with different situations, or the choice of option may be left up to your team. If this is the case, you must notify the referee of your choice before negotiations begin. In no case should you allow the other team to learn which data you are actually using. This would give them an unfair advantage in determining your position and they could take advantage of you in negotiations. Of course, there is nothing to stop the other team from reading your data options; however, they will learn only the approximate range of your costs and resources.

Negotiator Roles

General manager— You have been president of Canadian Switch for twelve years. Your manner is basically quiet although forceful, and you strongly believe in gentlemanly manners and fair play at the bargaining table. Your main concerns in negotiations are wages, total cost of the package, the time it takes to settle, and whether or not there is a strike. With respect to wages, you would like Canadian Switch to be paying somewhere in the middle of the range of current rates. You know that wages that are too low will not attract the best employees nor keep those that you have, and wages that are too high will diminish profits. Basically you want your wage settlement to be fair, not generous. You have the same concern with the total cost of the settlement. You strongly believe that there is only so much money in the pot and that it is up to the union to decide how they want benefits allotted. The company went out on a limb last year and purchased some new machinery because it was offered at a bargain price, even though you cannot presently utilize its capacity. If the market turns around in the next two years, it will have been a wise investment. However, until then you have to tighten your belt. There is just no fat left for generous wages or benefits. Finally, you are concerned about the amount of time it takes to reach a settlement, and whether or not there will be a strike. You would like very much to finish negotiations early and get back to managing the company, which is your "real" job. However, to settle early might cost you more than it is worth, and you will go down to the wire to avoid too generous a settlement. On the other hand, a strike would be a real problem particularly if it were prolonged and resulted in canceled sales. Nevertheless you realize the grim possibility that a strike may be necessary in order to convince the union that you do not have a lot of money to spread around.

Industrial-relations consultant — You are a junior member of a consulting firm replacing a recently retired and much respected member of your firm who had previously worked with this company. One of your main concerns is to keep Canadian Switch as a client. Your approach to negotiations is earnest and ambitious. You like the sense of competition and want to win by getting a settlement with only a moderate wage increase. You know that a short strike may be necessary to achieve this. One of your major beliefs is that management rights must be protected. This firm made a mistake in past negotiations by giving in on job posting. The current situation is that not only the original job vacancy but also the first two vacancies created by people moving into that job from other jobs in the plant must all be posted so that present employees get the first opportunity to fill each vacant position. This is a very time-consuming procedure and means that the company cannot easily go outside the plant to recruit better employees. As a result, you want job posting to be a "take-back" item with only the original job vacancy being posted.

Personnel manager — Since arriving at the plant three years ago you have established good relationships with most of the employees and the union leaders. They seem willing to trust you, and you feel you can trust them although you realize that some conflict is inevitable. Your own major concerns in this set of negotiations are the bonus for skilled employees and job posting. You believe that a ten-cent bonus is necessary to hold and attract skilled workers who are in short supply. You also realize that the regular employees tend to be suspicious and resentful of this bonus. The skilled employees at the bargaining table know that you are in favour of the bonus, and you have to be careful that they do not take advantage of you and press for a ridiculously high amount.

Job posting is a major concern for your department. As things stand now, when a job becomes permanently vacant because an employee quits, retires, or dies, the vacancy is posted for a week so that current employees get first opportunity to apply for it. If a current employee takes the job, this creates another vacancy, which is also posted, and if a current employee takes that job, his vacancy is also posted. The fourth and subsequent vacancies are not posted which means that the company can promote a current employee immediately without having to consider a number of applicants or can seek a new employee outside if it does not feel that anyone else is qualified. Because of this very cumbersome procedure, you find that much of your department's time is spent in the routine of interviewing and filling these jobs. In addition, the second and third postings seem to create competitive feelings among the employees that you feel are not good for morale. You would like to see the second and third postings removed. This would solve the morale problem as well as making work in your department more efficient and productive.

Production manager — You were promoted to the position of production manager less than one year ago. Your approach to all aspects of your job is business-like and down-to-earth. Through negotiations you want to keep costs down and productivity up. As you see it, four issues are important: the union's holiday demand, the bonus for skilled employees, job posting, and settling without a strike. The latter is of the utmost importance if you are to maintain your production schedule and not fall behind in fulfilling some important contracts. For the same reason you are reluctant to see another holiday added to the present eleven. Each holiday means that work schedules have to be juggled so that you can maintain productivity. If necessary, you will insist on a "floater" holiday which each individual employee takes at a time of his or her choosing after notifying the supervisor. This places much less burden on work schedules and is something that you might be able to live with.

You realize that a bonus paid to skilled workers is absolutely necessary to keep them motivated and prevent them from leaving for better-paying jobs. You feel that a more effective way around the problem of maintaining wage differentials between skilled and nonskilled employees would be to give a percentage wage increase rather than the same across-the-board amount for everyone, and you have decided to press for the percentage increase in negotiations. Finally, you would like to see requirements for job posting reduced from three to only the primary job. The current situation takes too much time, is too disruptive, and hinders productivity.

Management Data

The following tables provide important data the management team needs to make its case at the bargaining table. Table 6 gives basic information about the work force at Canadian Switch, and Table 7 gives estimates of the amount of money available to pay for improvements to wages and benefits. These estimates are based on information about sales possibilities in light of the current economic situation. You

Table 6

Work Force at Canadian Switch

	Males	Females
Skilled	30	2
Nonskilled	153	106
Totals	183	108
	Total: 291	

Table 7

Anticipated Funds Available
for Labour-Cost Increases

Targeted labour-cost increases:

	Option:		
		a.	$474,000
		b.	$461,000
		c.	$448,000
		d.	$435,000

Maximum funds allotted in current budget:

	Option:		
		a.	$571,000
		b.	$553,000
		c.	$536,000
		d.	$518,000

NOTES: 1. *Calculate target and maximum values in cents per hour per employee. (You will use these values, TARGET and MAX respectively, in calculating your team score.)*

2. *Canadian Switch calculates all labour costs on the assumption that the average employee is paid the equivalent of 2200 straight-rate hours per year, including vacations and holidays.*

(E.g., 2080 hours at straight-time plus 60 hours double-time per year equals 2200 paid hours per year.)

3. *For example, to calculate TARGET for option c:*

$$\frac{448,000}{2200 \times 291} = 70.0 \mathcal{c}/hr.$$

are to work with the maximum amount of funds allotted in the current budget. It is possible to exceed this maximum at the cost of a reduction in the preferred profit level and return on investment. On the other hand, to the extent that labour costs fall below the maximum (and it is strongly expected that they will) the company can use those funds for needed capital investment.

Table 8 provides the necessary details for costing the four monetary issues under negotiation.

For details of wages the competition is paying, check the information in the union's data section. Note that your major comparison group is Switch International, a plant in the immediate Anontown area. Their contract is due to expire in another six months, and you should be wary of being "whipsawed" — a situation where a wage gain in one plant is used to get a larger gain in the second which in turn is used for an even greater increase in the first and so on.

Table 8

Management Costing Information

Items Previously Settled:

	Option:	a.	8.1¢/hr.
		b.	7.6¢/hr.
		c.	7.3¢/hr.
		d.	6.9¢/hr.

Wages:

If a percentage increase is granted, apply percentage to the current average wage to determine cents-per-hour cost.

Bonus for Skill:

Number of skilled employees: 32

Average skilled wage: $8.16

Take value of bonus, multiply by number of employees receiving it, and divide by total number of employees to determine cents-per-hour cost.

E.g., for an 8¢ bonus:

$$\frac{8 \times 32}{291} = 0.9¢/hr.$$

Holidays:

For each fixed holiday, work must be made up in overtime at 1.5 times the wage rate. Thus, the equivalent cost is to pay each employee an additional 12 straight-rate hours per year.

For each floating holiday, work can be made up by others in regular time, thus each employee is paid an additional 8 hours per year.

E.g., the cost of a fixed holiday is:

$$\frac{12 \times \text{NEW WAGE RATE}}{2200}$$

Table 8 (continued)

Dental Plan:

Assume: 189 employees on family plan
83 employees on single plan
19 employees nonsubscribers

Company now pays 50% of basic-plan premium.

Premium surcharge:

Option:	a.	10%
	b.	5%
	c.	5% less (a discount)
	d.	10% less (a discount)

Annual Total Premium (per subscriber):	Family	Single
Basic plan (preventive care only)	$142.80	$49.44
Regular plan (includes fillings, etc.)	194.40	64.08
Comprehensive plan (includes orthodontics)	298.08	72.24

E.g., present cost to company:

$$\text{Surcharge} \times 50\% \times \frac{(83 \times \$49.44) + (189 \times \$142.80)}{2200 \times 291}$$

NOTES: All costs are expressed in terms of cents per hour per employee. All costing is based on the assumption that the average employee works the equivalent of 2200 straight-rate hours per year.
Current average wage rate is $6.26 per hour.
Number of employees is 291.

Management Team Scoring

As Table 9 shows, seven different items contribute to the negotiation score for the management team. The points for these items represent a combination of dollar costs, management control, productivity, and team satisfaction with negotiation outcomes. In deciding your negotiation strategy, it is a good idea to look over the point distribution and study carefully what point outcomes your team will get for settlements of different kinds. Wages are the largest single factor in the management team's point score, and together with the total cost of the package wages make up the majority of possible points. The next largest contribution to your point total will be the settlement time. Note that here you can gain as many as twenty points or lose up to twenty-five. The remaining items (bonus, holidays, dental plan, and job posting) can each earn a maximum of five to ten points. If you fail to reach agreement by the end of the game you receive no points.

UNION DATA AND NEGOTIATOR ROLES

In this section, you will find brief sketches of the characteristics and concerns of the six union negotiators, data needed to argue the union's position in the negotiations, and information for scoring your negotiation results. You should become familiar with the role you are playing and the relevant data. You should also read the roles of

Table 9

Management-Team Scoring

Item	Maximum
1. **Wages:**	
1 point for each cent less than 70¢	30
2. **Bonus for Skill:**	
5 points minus 1/2 point for each cent above or below 10¢	
5 points for a percentage (instead of across-the-board) wage increase	5
3. **Holidays:**	
5 points if no charge	
3 points for an additional floater holiday	
2 points for an additional fixed holiday	
0 points if more than one additional holiday	5

4. **Dental Plan:**

Percentage Company Pays

	25	33	50	67	75	100	
Basic	5	5	5	4	3	1	
Regular	5	5	4	2	1	0	
Comprehensive	5	4	1	0	0	0	5

Item	Maximum
5. **Job Posting:**	
10 points if primary job vacancy only	
6 points if primary and one subsequent for some jobs, or other major improvement	
5 points if primary and one subsequent for all jobs, or other substantial improvement	
3 points if primary, one subsequent for all jobs and second subsequent for some jobs; or other minor improvement	
0 points for no change	10
6. **Settlement Time:**	
20 points if two hours or more before strike deadline	
18 points if one hour or more before strike deadline	
15 points if less than one hour before strike deadline	
10 points if less than 20 minutes after strike deadline	
−5 points if 20 minutes or more after strike deadline	
−25 points if 40 minutes or more after strike deadline	20
7. **Total Cost:**	
1 point for each cent less than MAX	
Add 5 points if within 5.0¢ of TARGET	25
Total maximum points	100
No points if no agreement by end of game	

the other members of your team and examine the management-negotiator roles and the management data. Note that your team must decide which of four issue-priority scoring options will represent your situation. A summary of these options is given in Table 1; further information is available below in the section on union-team scoring, and in Table 11. This decision should be made at your initial union-team meeting, and the referee should be notified. Alternatively, the referee will tell you which option you are to use. In no case should you allow the other team to learn which option you are actually using. This would give them an unfair advantage in determining your position and would allow them to take advantage of you in the negotiations. Of course there is nothing to stop the other team from studying your scoring schemes, however they will learn only the broad range of your priorities rather than the exact nature of the priorities themselves. In this respect, the game is much like real-life collective bargaining.

Negotiator Roles

National representative — You are the chief negotiator and an employee of the Canadian Union of Factory Workers, which has its head office in Toronto. Your job is to take care of union business in four different locals, one of which is Local 123 in Anontown. Your approach to negotiations is business-like, and you are sympathetic to the concerns and needs of the employees at Canadian Switch. On the other hand, you must also be realistic. You do not know just how much money the company has to play with, but it is not likely to be enough for a record-breaking contract. In any event, too large a settlement creates other problems; it means there is less room to move up next year and that other locals will expect the same gain even though they cannot get it, both of which situations are embarrassing to the union. As usual, wages are your major concern together with the need to maintain comparability within the three plants in the local. The 65-cent settlement six months ago at Switch International is the target you will be shooting for in these negotiations. Another problem you foresee is the possibility of a strike. Last year, National Appliance employees went on strike for three months and as a result there is not much money around, either locally or at union headquarters, for another lengthy strike in this local. However, you feel that if absolutely necessary the union can afford to support a relatively short strike with decent strike pay.

Local president — As president of CUFW Local 123, a position you have held for the past seven years, you represent employees at all three plants in the local and rely on their support for annual reelection. You are well-liked, friendly, and outgoing and have not had any opposition in the last four elections. You work half-time as a skilled electrician at Canadian Switch and half-time in the union office. Half your wages are paid from local dues. Your most important concern in these negotiations is wages, and you also want to make sure that the final contract includes something for everybody. You do not want to see any dissatisfied groups in the local. For this reason, the issue of another bonus for skilled workers is a problem. You realize that the skilled employees want that bonus and that the company seems willing to pay it; however you also realize that many of the nonskilled workers are suspicious and resent the skilled workers getting a larger increase than they themselves get. What is more problematic is that you yourself are a skilled employee.

Chief steward — You are a hard-working skilled employee from the maintenance department at Canadian Switch. You have been chief steward for three years and have your eye on the local presidency in the next union elections. You sense that there is a great deal of dissatisfaction among the employees in all three companies in the local. One firm, National Appliance, had a lengthy strike last year, and you think that this set of negotiations may end in a strike as well. If so, this will certainly help your chances in the election. The particular issues you think are most important are wages, a dental plan (you and many of the other skilled employees are at the age where your children need substantial dental work), and the job-posting issue which the teams were not able to agree on in earlier meetings. You are aware that management wants to reduce the number of postings, and your competitive instinct tells you that by "hanging tough" on this issue you can trade it off for higher wages at the eleventh hour.

Machine-shop steward — You are an older skilled employee who has been with Canadian Switch for eleven years. Your approach to negotiations is to try to get reasonable benefits and wages for your fellow employees but not to put management in a position where they may have to cut back. You know that profits are important to keep the company going. You tend to be quiet about most matters, but other employees respect your sincerity and honesty. As well as an increase in wages, you feel that skilled employees really deserve a bonus this year, as wage differentials with nonskilled workers have been steadily decreasing. You would also like to see an improvement in the dental plan for those employees with families needing more than preventive dental work. The present basic plan only pays for checkups, routine X-rays, and other preventive work. It does not even cover fillings, which the regular plan would. Best of all would be the comprehensive plan, which pays for crowns, bridges, and children's orthodontia. You think that the comprehensive plan is the one Canadian Switch should have.

Shipping-department steward — You have been working in the shipping department at Canadian Switch in a nonskilled position for the past five years. You tend to be mistrustful of management's motives. You believe that too much time is spent worrying about profits and not enough about the wages, benefits, and working conditions of people in the plant. For example, management seems to want to pay a bonus to skilled employees, while you think the money would be better spent on everybody's wages or on better safety equipment. In addition, you really think that a few holidays would be an important benefit and would give employees a chance to get out of the plant more often and enjoy themselves with their friends or families.

Production-department steward — You are a nonskilled employee who has been with Canadian Switch for three years. You have recently become interested in what goes on beyond the plant floor and are hoping to learn more about union matters. You know that some members of the committee are on the conservative side while others seem to be more radical. So far you have decided to keep an open mind and just watch what happens. The negotiation issues which are of most interest to you are wages, the bonus for skilled employees (which you do not quite see the need for), and holidays. In particular, you and many of your fellow workers would like to see two more holidays added to the eleven that you now get, and this is something you want to press for during negotiations.

Union Data

The two important tasks of the union negotiating team are to find data comparing their situation with that of comparable companies in order to support their demands and to decide what priorities these different demands will have. It is clear that more ground will have to be given on some issues than others; an important task is to

Table 10

Comparison Data by Issue

Company	Number of Employees	Current Wage: Janitor II	Current Wage: Tool and Die Maker I	Most Recent Increase	How Long Ago
		(dollars)	(dollars)	(cents)	
Canadian Switch	291	5.12	9.58	50	1 yr.
Switch International	345	5.02	9.86	65	6 mos.
National Appliance	250	5.10	9.70	62	10 mos.
Acme Tool (same region)	134	4.82	9.49	50	11 mos.
Bolt Auto Parts (same region)	240	5.80	10.12	49	8 mos.
Dunn Video Equipment (same region)	93	5.08	(not available)	63	1 mo.

Table 10 (continued)

Company	Last Strike and Duration	Last Skill Bonus	Paid Holidays	Dental Plan, Company Share	Job Posting
Canadian Switch	4 yrs.–24 days	2 yrs.–10¢	11	basic–50%	primary + 2
Switch International	7 yrs.–13 days	6 mos.–15¢	12	basic–33%	skilled: primary only nonskilled primary + 1
National Appliance	10 mos.–3 mos.	10 mos.–10¢	11 (1 floater)	basic–75%	primary only
Acme Tool (same region)	2 yrs.–12 days	11 mos.–20¢	12	regular–100%	primary only
Bolt Auto Parts (same region)	8 yrs.–5 mos.	2 yrs.–10¢	11	regular–50%	primary + 2
Dunn Video Equipment (same region)	6 yrs.–14 days	13 mos.–2% of hourly rate	11	comprehensive–50%	primary + 1 (limited to 1 application per employee)

decide the relative importance of the issues for the bargaining team, for the union, and for the members.

Table 10 provides comparison data by issue from the other two firms in Local 123 and from three other manufacturing companies in the Anontown region. This table reflects information the union team can get from existing contracts and from employees of these other companies. The section below on scoring deals with the second task: choosing issue priorities.

Union-Team Scoring

As Table 11 shows, the union team's negotiating score is made up of seven different items, with four different scoring schemes to choose from. The union team will select one of these schemes at its initial meeting (or alternatively the referee will assign one). The points for each scoring scheme represent the concern of union negotiators with getting a good wage settlement and the importance attached to other items. Each scoring scheme represents a slightly different set of priorities. For example, wages are most important in scoring scheme *b* and least important in *c*. The bonus and dental-plan issues are more important in *c* and membership support (which is the result of a high wage settlement approaching the recent 65 cents at Switch International) is least important in scheme *b*.

In deciding your negotiation strategy, you should examine carefully the scoring scheme and try several typical settlements to get a feeling for how different kinds of agreements will contribute to your overall team score. Note that in the settlement-time item you can lose points by settling too early (which might make the rank-and-file members suspicious that the team had not tried hard enough) or by going into a lengthy strike (anything twenty minutes or longer!). If you fail to reach agreement by the end of the game you receive no points.

Table 11

Union-Team Scoring

Item	Maximum
1. **Wages:**	
a. $1^{1}/_{2}$ points for each cent more than 50¢	45
b. 2 points for each cent more than 50¢	60
c. 1 point for each cent more than 50¢	30
d. $1^{1}/_{2}$ points for each cent more than 50¢	45
All options: add 5 points if more than 57¢ (but do not exceed point maximum)	
2. **Bonus for Skill:**	
a. 1 point if no bonus	
5 points minus $1/_2$ point for each cent below 15¢	5
b. 3 points if percentage wage increase	
5 points minus $1/_2$ point for each cent below 15¢	5

Table 11 (continued)

c. 5 points if percentage wage increase
    10 points minus ½ point for each cent below 20¢   10

d. 1 point if percentage wage increase
    5 points minus ½ point for each cent below 15¢   5

3. Holidays:

	No Change	One Floater	One Fixed	One Floater & One Fixed	Two Fixed	Maximum
a.	0	3	3	5	5	5
b.	0	9	9	10	10	10
c.	0	4	4	5	5	5
d.	0	5	6	8	10	10

4. Dental Plan:

Options a, b, d: Percentage Company Pays

	25	33	50	67	75	100	
Basic	0	0	0	2	3	4	
Regular	0	1	4	5	5	5	
Comprehensive	1	2	5	5	5	5	5

Option c:

	25	33	50	67	75	100	
Basic	0	0	0	4	8	9	
Regular	0	3	8	9	10	10	
Comprehensive	3	4	9	10	10	10	10

5. Job Posting:

	Option			
	a	b	c	d
No change	5	5	5	10
Minor change (e.g., third posting removed for some jobs)	4	4	4	8
Substantial change (e.g., third posting removed entirely)	3	4	3	6
Major change (e.g., third posting removed, second partially removed)	1	2	1	3
Posting for primary vacancy only	0	1	0	1
Maximum points:	5	5	5	10

6. Membership Support:

	Wage Gain						
	60¢	61¢	62¢	63¢	64¢	65¢ or more	Maximum
a.	2	5	8	11	13	15	15
b.	2	3	3	4	4	5	5
c.	2	5	8	12	16	20	20
d.	2	4	6	8	9	10	10

Table 11 (continued)

7. **Settlement Time:**

	Option			
	a	b	c	d
1 hour or more before strike deadline	−5	−5	−5	−5
Less than 1 hour before strike deadline	5	5	5	5
Less than ¹/₂ hour before strike deadline	20	10	18	15
Less than 20 mins. after strike deadline	18	5	20	8
20 mins. or more after strike deadline	−5	−5	−5	−5
40 mins. or more after strike deadline	−25	−25	−25	−25
Maximum points:	20	10	20	15

Total maximum points   100
No points if no agreement by end of game

NOTE: All *choices must be the same option: a, b, c, or d.*

THE USE OF COLLECTIVE-BARGAINING SIMULATIONS

The use of simulations as a teaching method is gaining increasing and well-deserved attention. The major reasons for this popularity are the sense of involvement that students feel and the multitude of puposes that simulations can serve. In particular, collective-bargaining simulations can provide an introductory overview of the process and phases of negotiations, elementary training for individuals who are going to be taking part in collective bargaining, or specialized training to increase selected skills for those who already have negotiation experience. An appropriate simulation can also provide each player with the opportunity for personal assessment of organizational skills, verbal abilities, interpersonal sensitivity, how well he or she operates under stress, and other traits important for skillful and effective bargaining.

The simulation presented above is intended to meet the first of these objectives — a broad educational overview of the bargaining process. Those who use it should gain an understanding of the nature of the process and the role of a multitude of factors — economic, political, social, and personal — in determining bargaining outcomes.

As one can infer from the variety of purposes which simulations serve, there is equally wide variation among the games themselves. They differ with respect to degree of realism, length of time it takes to play, the phases of the bargaining process they encompass and particularly the emphasis they give to the different phases of collective bargaining. For example, different games give different emphasis to preparation, tactics, handling conflict, political factors, reaching agreement and so on. For reasons of time, no simulation can give equal attention to all possible elements. In the brief bibliography which follows at the end of the chapter, the major emphasis of each simulation is noted in order to allow you to choose which ones might best serve your needs.

SELECTED AND ANNOTATED BIBLIOGRAPHY
OF COLLECTIVE-BARGAINING SIMULATIONS

1. Albright, W.P. *Collective Bargaining: A Canadian Simulation*, 2nd ed. (Waterloo, Ont.: Wilfrid Laurier University, 1979). This simulation is written from a management point of view and has a strong emphasis on costing preparation and the relationship of management bargaining objectives to the economic health of the firm. Approximate playing time: twenty hours.

2. Lewiski, J., and G. Swimmer. "A Collective Bargaining Simulation," in S.M. Hameed (Ed.), *Canadian Industrial Relations: A Book of Readings* (Toronto: Butterworth, 1975). This simulation emphasizes the company's financial position and includes some political pressure on the union side. Approximate playing time: three meetings over one week or about ten hours.

3. Phillips, G.E. "The Yourtown Public Library System" in *Labour Relations and Collective Bargaining* (Toronto: Butterworth, 1977). A small-bargaining-unit public-sector game with an emphasis on costing. Approximate playing time: fifteen hours.

4. Richardson, R.C. *Collective Bargaining by Objectives* (Englewood Cliffs, N.J.: Prentice Hall, 1977). Four separate games (two private-, two public-sector) emphasizing the formulation and pursuit of systematic bargaining objectives. Approximate playing time: ten-twenty hours each.

5. Swimmer, G.R., and A.M. Maslove. *The Northville Simulation: Municipal Collective Bargaining* (Toronto: Institute of Public Administration of Canada, 1980). This simulation focuses on political and economic factors affecting public-sector bargaining. Approximate playing time: three weeks of preparation and one week (three sessions) of bargaining. In short version, six hours.

QUESTIONS

1. What are the ways in which the underlying concerns of union and management negotiators differ?

2. "One of the disadvantages unions face at the bargaining table is democracy!" Comment.

3. In preparing for negotiations, what are the major tasks facing each negotiating team (or its support staff)?

4. Discuss the importance of time deadlines in helping negotiators reach an agreement.

5. Discuss the advantages and disadvantages of the three major orientations negotiators may adopt towards their bargaining: getting the best possible deal for one's own side, out-negotiating the other team, or finding the settlement that gives each team a fair deal.

Appendix 2
Grievance Arbitration Cases

These cases were developed by Professors Frank Collum and Rick Jackson, School of Business, Queen's University and are used with permission.

WEST MEMORIAL HOSPITAL
v.
ONTARIO HOSPITAL EMPLOYEES ASSOCIATION (OHEA)

Background — West Memorial Hospital was built in 1975 to serve the residents of one of Metropolitan Toronto's boroughs. It is a 200-bed hospital specializing in chronic care. When the hospital was first opened, three separate trade unions organized specific groups of employees in the hospital. The nurses were organized by a nurses' association. A national public service union organized the maintenance and other nonprofessional health personnel such as orderlies, kitchen, and laundry staff. The third group of organized employees in the hospital were the health professionals and related personnel, including therapists and laboratory technicians.

Ontario Hospital Employees Association (OHEA) is the certified bargaining agent for health professionals and technicians at the West Memorial Hospital. The OHEA was established in 1970 and by 1978 had twenty-two locals in various hospitals throughout Ontario with a total membership of just over 1,000. The OHEA bargains with hospitals on a multibargaining unit basis, that is, there is only one collective agreement for several bargaining units in various hospitals. The collective agreement that covers the employees at West Memorial Hospital that are members of the OHEA also applies to OHEA members at four nearby hospitals.

The collective agreement, which was settled through binding arbitration, came into force on February 1, 1978 and will remain in force for two years.

The incident — Ahamad Rashid was a laboratory technician hired by West Memorial Hospital in 1975 after having completed his training at a local community college. He worked at the hospital from the first day it opened until he allegedly voluntarily terminated his employment on August 18, 1978, or alternately was discharged by the hospital on that same day. This is the only issue in dispute.

The grievor claims that he did not voluntarily leave the employ of the hospital but was unjustly discharged from his employment by his immediate supervisor, the

564

head of laboratory services in the hospital. The hospital administration claims that the grievor voluntarily quit his employment at the hospital.

The grievor had worked at the same job since he was first hired. There was no documentary evidence in his employment file to indicate that his work performance was unsatisfactory until an entry was made in the fall of 1977. Hospital-wide performance appraisals were begun in the fall of 1977. They were to be undertaken every six months thereafter. On the occasion of the first performance appraisal, the grievor's supervisor had written that the grievor's work performance was below that expected by an employee with his position and experience. At that time, the grievor was told that he must improve his work performance over the next year. It seems that the grievor did not improve his work performance but continued to work as he had from the time of his hiring. The grievor's supervisor said nothing more to him until August 1, 1978, when he summoned the grievor into his office. The supervisor told the grievor that his work performance had not improved since they last discussed it in the fall of 1977. The grievor said nothing in reply except that he was always trying to do the best job he could but nobody was helping him at his job. The supervisor stated that he did not require the kind of help he was talking about because he had supposedly learned the required techniques in school before he had even come to work at the hospital.

The supervisor told the grievor that he did not think the grievor could do the work he was supposed to be qualified to do. He stated that he could do nothing for him but give him the option of resigning or be "fired." He said to the grievor that he would recommend resignation because it would give him a better chance of finding another job in the same occupation. The supervisor asked the grievor what he wanted to do. The grievor said that he would resign. The supervisor remarked that he felt sorry for him but he had been warned. He further said that the grievor should not have any trouble finding a job elsewhere and that he would take care of the resignation details for him. The supervisor said that it would take effect on the following Friday, August 18, 1978.

The grievor left his supervisor's office but returned later in the afternoon to say that he had changed his mind and said he wanted to stay at West Memorial Hospital and would improve his work performance so that the supervisor would no longer be disappointed with him. The supervisor told him that it was too late for that and showed him the termination notice form he had filled out for him to go to the administration office. The supervisor apparently convinced the grievor at that time that it was too late for the grievor to change his mind because the grievor read the form and signed it, as was required.

Before the grievor finished his work assignments for the day he spoke to some other technicians in the laboratory who suggested that he see the union committee-person in the department. The grievor explained to her what had transpired and she advised him to file a grievance immediately. The union representative processed the grievance which alleged that the grievor had been unjustly discharged. The laboratory supervisor denied the grievance, categorically stating that the grievor had not been fired but had voluntarily terminated his employment. He showed the union representative the termination notice form that the grievor had signed and pointed to the reason for termination entry on the form which was written in as "quit."

The OHEA took the grievance to the completion of the grievance procedure without any settlement. The hospital administration said that the grievor was not discharged but had voluntary terminated his employment, the evidence being the grievor's signature on the termination notice form. Arbitration proceedings were undertaken by the union pursuant to the collective agreement. The grievor ceased working on the Friday as per the document that the grievor had signed, August 18, 1978.

During the grievance meetings, the administration representatives told the union representatives present that the hospital would not be replacing the grievor with anyone because within the year they thought they would have to lay off someone in the laboratory because of budget cutbacks. The grievor was approximately in the middle of the seniority list at his job position.

E.W. WHEELER MANUFACTURING CO. LTD.
v.
AMALGAMATED METALWORKERS UNION, LOCAL 1278

Background — E.W. Wheeler Manufacturing Co. Ltd. (the company) is a wholly Canadian-owned manufacturer of steam generating equipment for industrial uses (for example, boilers). The company's only plant is located in Southwestern Ontario and employs normally about 1,000 hourly rated employees in its production facility. The production facility is divided into three main areas or "shops," as the company refers to them. These are the plate, tube, and boiler shops. There is also a foundry and two service departments, maintenance, and traffic. The plant is organized so that there are six departments in all: the three shops, the foundry, and traffic and maintenance departments. Each department is headed by a general foreman with between three and twelve foremen reporting to him.

The Amalgamated Metalworkers Union (AMU) is an international trade union based in the United States representing primarily workers in the manufacturing and mining industries. It has just over one half million members in Canada and the United States with 150,000 members located in Canada alone. The AMU was one of the first trade unions to organize workers in the industrial sector. Local 1278 is composed of the hourly rated production workers at the E.W. Wheeler Manufacturing Company in Cambridge, Ontario. It is one of five locals of the AMU in Cambridge. Local 1278 has a full-time union president whose salary is paid by the company as part of the negotiated benefits under the collective agreement.

The tube shop in the company's plant produces the tubing requirements for the manufacturing of boilers. This involves fabricating steel tubing produced by suppliers and painting it for assembly in the boiler shop. The tube shop also produces special tubing requirements for other company products.

There are approximately 150 hourly rated employees in the tube shop which operates seven days per week on a three-shift basis. The work requires both skilled and semi-skilled tradesmen. The AMU has six shop stewards and one chief steward in the tube shop. The chief steward works the day shift (08:00 to 16:30) Monday through Friday. The six shop stewards work on various shifts throughout the week. There is at least one steward on each shift throughout the week.

During the previous year, there had been a vigorous campaign by some union members in the tube shop to replace the chief steward and some of the shop stewards, but these efforts failed at election time. The chief steward and five of the previous six shop stewards were returned in the annual elections. One of the incumbent shop stewards decided not to try for another term. A significant group of about fifteen tube-shop employees tried to elect some of their group as chief steward or shop steward but only one of their candidates was elected, replacing the retiring shop steward. The mainstays of this militant group worked in the paint-room area of the tube shop. The new steward also worked in the paint room.

The new shop steward was an active member in the union but had only worked in the plant for three years after immigrating from Europe. After having been elected as a shop steward by the tube-shop workers he went to the training seminars provided by the AMU for its newly elected shop stewards. He had completed this program by the time the events in question took place.

The incident — On May 16, 1978, the new shop steward was working the afternoon shift (16:30 to 24:00) in the paint room. There were eight other workers working in the paint room on that shift. The new shop steward was the only shop steward working in the tube shop on that shift. This was the first occasion where the new shop steward was the sole steward working on a shift.

The new shop steward had been instructed at the training seminars about what to do in the event that something more serious than a first-step grievance occurred. In the event of a serious problem in the tube shop, a steward would first contact the chief steward of the tube shop if he was available. Upon failing to reach him, a steward would then call the local president and failing to locate him he would contact any other member of the local's executive committee.

On the evening of May 16, 1978, the tube shop was supervised by three foremen. One of the foremen oversaw the production work in the paint-room area of the tube shop. The work activity in that area of the tube shop during the afternoon shift involved the final painting of a particular quantity of tubing which was urgently required in the boiler shop to complete a specially constructed boiler for one of the company's best customers, a provincially owned public utility. The general foreman of the tube shop had promised to have his department's part of the job completed by the end of the week. To accomplish this the paint shop would have to complete their work on the materials by the next morning (May 17, 1978). The night shift and afternoon shift had to work steadily to complete the painting on time.

May 16, 1978, had been a very stormy day. It had rained continuously throughout the day but had stopped shortly after 17:00. The temperature had climbed to about 20°C in the afternoon with the temperature only dropping slightly by the time the afternoon shift began (down about 2°C). After the rain had stopped, it had gotten extremely humid in the paint-room area. Whenever it became humid, the working conditions in the paint shop would become barely tolerable because of the use of spray-painting equipment. When conditions got as bad as they were on this occasion, it was normal practice to discontinue painting until the humidity dropped, since even with protective masks the air in the paint room prevented those painting from working comfortably and, in particular, caused workers to cough and perspire greatly. The company provided all the safety equipment required by law to operate the painting equipment. The necessary equipment was being used at the time by those working in the paint room.

About halfway through the afternoon shift, the men operating the painting equipment began to complain about the uncomfortable conditions in the paint room. The foreman told them how important it was to complete the painting that evening. The work was at a critical stage in the painting process because the primer paint had been applied and a special sealer coat had just been applied which required the immediate application of the final coat to bond it to the sealer coat. If the final coat of paint was not applied the tubing would have to be totally redone. An accurate cost of wasted materials would be $9,780.00.

The new shop steward was one of the men painting at the time. He approached the foreman of the paint room and told him that the conditions were too unhealthy to continue work, and he should assign the men in the paint shop to other work until the conditions improved. The foreman told him that was not possible because of the urgent need to finish the painting so as to complete the work for the next day. Also, he reminded the shop steward that the work completed on the materials would be wasted if the painting was not completed. The shop steward told him if he did not assign the painters to other work he would tell them to quit painting until conditions improved. The foreman told him he had no authority to do that and that it would be a violation of the collective agreement to refuse to continue working as directed by management, that it would constitute a strike or a refusal to work.

Evidence indicated that on that evening the conditions were truly bad in the paint room, but not intolerable for short periods of time. In fact, on previous occasions when conditions were just as bad or worse, the painters would paint for half an hour then discontinue for half an hour. The foreman suggested that the painters work in that mode but the shop steward refused to allow the painters to continue at all and told them to quit painting completely. The painters were not reassigned to other work and spent the rest of the shift in the lunch-room with the shop steward. The materials were not usable because of the long delay until other workers could continue on the night shift (00:00 to 08:00). Totally new materials had to be produced to replace the unusable tubing that was not properly painted.

The company took action against the shop steward and the other painters who refused to continue painting. The shop steward was given a one-month suspension, and the others were reprimanded. The company sent a statement of the cost of the unusable materials to the AMU and filed a grievance under Article 20 of the collective agreement (Company Grievances). claiming the full cost of the damaged materials resulting from the "illegal" work stoppage. The AMU did not feel that it was obligated to compensate the company for this loss. The AMU grieved the shop steward's suspension but that is not in issue at this arbitration hearing. The union's grievance is still pending.

INTERNATIONAL BAUXITE CORPORATION OF CANADA LTD.
v.
ALL CANADIAN MINEWORKERS UNION (ACMU), LOCAL 867

Background — International Bauxite Corporation of Canada Ltd. (the company) is a subsidiary of a multinational mining corporation based in New York. It is the only Canadian subsidiary of the parent company. The company operates the only bauxite mine in all of Northern Ontario. Bauxite is the principle raw material used in the production of aluminium. The mine is located approximately fifty miles north of Sudbury, Ontario. It employs approximately 1,560 hourly rated employees, all of whom must belong to the All Canadian Mineworkers Union (ACMU) because of a union-shop arrangement in the collective agreement.

The company has in recent years been facing stiff competition from foreign producers of bauxite, mainly in South America. The mine has been operating at full capacity for the last two years however, and a large inventory of bauxite has resulted. The company's profitability has suffered because of the foreign competition and also a drop in world demands for aluminium.

The ACMU is a national union with its head office in Sudbury, Ontario. It has only been in existence for five years. Since 1973, the ACMU has organized six separate groups of mineworkers in Northern Ontario. Two of these groups had previously been organized by a large, well-known international union. The hourly rated employees of the company were one of these groups. In 1976, ACMU signed its first collective agreement with the company. This two-year agreement terminated at the end of 1978.

Local 867 represents all the hourly rated employees of the company at the mine and processing plant in Northern Ontario. The processing plant is adjacent to the mine and employs approximately one-third of the hourly rated workers. The employees in both facilities form one bargaining unit. Seniority is not based company-wide but plant-wide. In other words, there is a separate seniority list for the processing plant and one for the mine itself. In effect then, seniority within the bargaining unit is divided between the mine and the processing plant workers. In the event of a layoff, the layoffs take place individually within the processing plant and the mine.

The incident — The company had been operating the mine and processing facility at full capacity for the past two years because the demand for bauxite was extremely strong. The manpower to staff the mine and processing plant consisted primarily of semi-skilled and unskilled workers. Since the mine first came into operation, the company had a difficult time finding people to fill its manpower requirements. Recently, the supply of capable workers to fill the company's needs has exceeded the demand.

With declining sales of bauxite and a growing stockpile of raw materials, the company found it necessary to cut production by 20 percent. This decrease in production meant that 12 percent of the company's production staff had to be laid off (both mine and processing plant workers). Exactly 180 hourly rated employees were laid off on July 1, 1978.

On July 2, 1978, the ACMU filed a group grievance for the 180 workers under Article 27 of the collective agreement alleging that the layoffs were improperly carried out because each employee laid off was entitled to ninety days notice of the layoffs and only eighty-one days notice was actually given. The company contends that on April 1, 1978, it announced to its employees that 180 hourly rated employees would be laid off, thereby giving the required ninety days notice under the collective agreement and the law. Notice was sent to the ACMU president on April 1, 1978, that there was to be a substantial layoff effective July 1, 1978.

The ACMU president and executive committee interprets the collective agreement to say that separate notice must be given to each employee that is to be laid off ninety days before the effective date of the layoff. Written notice was received by the individual employees ten days after the notice was given to the union executive. The ACMU contends that the company owes each laid-off employee the amount that they would have earned for regular time worked if they had worked their usual shifts.

Under Article 12 of the collective agreement, the company shall outline in writing its plan to lay off regular employees ninety days before said plan becomes effective. It goes on to say that each employee shall be given written notice that he/she is to be laid off.

The company contends that the written notice to the union is the only notice that must be given ninety days in advance of the layoff and written notice to each employee must be given within a reasonable time before the layoff because the collective agreement is not specific about giving notice to individual employees.

The union pursued the issue through all stages of the grievance procedure within the requirements. The company denied the grievance at each stage stating that the ninety-day requirement only applied to giving notice to the union which it did within the requirements of the collective agreement.

The union executive felt that this issue should be tested by arbitration because in the new round of bargaining for a collective agreement the ACMU wanted a 120-day notice provision to replace the 90-day and wanted to know whether or not the 90-day notice requirement presently contained in the collective agreement applied to notices given to individual employees. Notice of the ACMU's intention to take the matter to arbitration was sent to the company on Aug. 7, 1978.

On July 1, 1978, 180 employees were in fact laid off. The ACMU contends that all 180 employees laid off are entitled to be paid for the time that they would have normally worked during the period from July 1 through July 9 inclusively. It would be no small task to estimate what each and every laid-off employee would have earned during this period considering such factors as: overtime, absenteeism, shift premiums, holiday pay, and vacation pay. The ACMU feels that a payment of six days' wages at each employee's regular rate of pay would be fair compensation for the company's alleged infringement of the collective agreement.

APPENDIX A

Article 27 — Grievance Procedure for Group Grievances

Grievances affecting a group of employees, an entire department, or the plant as a whole, may be taken up by the union at the first level of the grievance procedure competent to deal with the group, department, or plant. Thereafter, if satisfactory solutions are not reached, the matter may be processed through the remaining steps of the grievance procedure to arbitration.

Group grievances must be signed by at least four (4) employees.

Article 12 — Layoff (Fifty or More Bargaining-Unit Employees)

In the event that the company finds it necessary to reduce staff due to lack of work, bargaining-unit employees shall be laid off in reverse order of seniority.

The company shall outline its plan to lay off regular employees in writing ninety (90) days before said plan becomes effective. Also each employee affected by the plan shall be given written notice that he/she is to be laid off.

NATIONAL PULP AND PAPER CO. LTD.
v.
EASTERN ONTARIO PULP HAULERS ASSOCIATION (EOPHA)

Background — National Pulp and Paper Ltd. (the company) is one of the five largest manufacturers of newsprint in Canada. It operates seven mills across Canada and two mills in the United States. The company supplies newsprint to some of the major tabloids in the northeastern part of the United States and on the west coast of the United States and Canada. The company has negotiated collective agreements with various trade unions since the early 1940s. One of the newest groups that the company has had to bargain collectively with are not "employees" at all really, but are dependent contractors. Under Section 1(1) (gb) of the *Ontario Labour Relations Act* an employee *under the act* includes a dependent contractor. A dependent contractor is defined under s. 1(1) (ga) of the act. The company for many years has undertaken with owner-operators of pulpwood rigs (a type of tractor-trailer unit) contracts for transporting pulpwood from the forests to the pulp mills. The truck owner-drivers organized themselves into a bargaining unit which was certified by the Ontario Labour Relations Board in 1974.

The Eastern Ontario Pulp Haulers Association (EOPHA) is a trade union. It was formed in 1973 to represent the dependent contractors that haul pulpwood for the National Pulp and Paper Company Ltd. in Eastern Ontario. There are fifteen drivers in total. Each and every driver owns the truck that he uses to haul pulpwood.

Since 1974, National Pulp and Paper and the Haulers Association have entered into one-year collective agreements. The collective agreements followed the calendar year, commencing on January 1, and terminating December 31. The history of agreements between the parties has been that their agreements are not highly detailed and do not incorporate as many areas of mutual concern as do most collective agreements. The collective agreement for the year 1978 contained provisions almost entirely concerned with monetary items, specifically rates of pay and monetary benefits (such as OHIP premiums and a health-care plan) paid by the company. Aside from the required provisions under the *Ontario Labour Relations Act,* R.S.O. 1970, as am. the only nonmonetary provisions in the collective agreement not required by statute concerned seniority and job protection. Article 10 in the collective agreement contains the seniority provisions. Article 12 guarantees each owner-operator the specified number of loads of pulpwood per year as promised in the individual contracts.

Each driver has a separate contract with the company. A term of each individual contract guarantees a certain amount of work each year (a guaranteed number of loads of pulpwood per year). They go on to state that the company does not guarantee work in every month of the year but is only required to provide a minimum amount of work within the year. The individual contracts are for a one-year period and follow the calendar year as does the collective agreement.

Article 10 of the collective agreement states that seniority shall govern in allocating loads to each contractor. The collective agreement does not say anything about the effect this might have on the individual contracts. Also under Article 10, choice of vacation is by seniority.

The incident — On November 10, 1978, the grievor was told that he would only be required for three loads in the following week (November 13 — November 17). One load amounts to a full eight hours of work. This was not unusual for these drivers because the loads varied throughout the year and from week to week. The grievor had loads on Monday, Tuesday,. and Thursday of that week. On the other two days, he assumed that there would probably be only five or six loads in all. The grievor was seventh highest in seniority in the bargaining unit of fifteen drivers. At the time, the grievor thought that only drivers with higher seniority than his would be working on Wednesday and Friday of that week.

The grievor worked the three days during the week of November 13-17. On Friday November 24, 1978, the grievor received his payment for the work performed during the preceding week. At the same time as he was picking up his cheque, two other drivers were also picking up their cheques. In the course of conversation with these two drivers, the grievor found out that one of these two drivers had worked a full five-day week while the other had worked four days during the week. The driver who had worked five days was second highest in seniority but the one who worked four days was only eighth on the seniority list. The grievor upon finding this out immediately knew that he rightfully should have received the additional load before that driver because of his greater seniority.

The grievor on Monday November 27, 1978, before leaving the plant yard in the morning to pick up a load of pulp logs, went into the yard supervisor's office to speak to the yard supervisor and see why the junior driver received the load he should have received. The yard supervisor explained to him the part of the individual contract which states that an independent contractor is entitled to so many loads per year. He then told the grievor that there had been fewer loads than expected, subsequently the driver who was given the load would probably not be given the minimum number unless he gave this load to him. At that point in time, the grievor had already surpassed his guaranteed minimum number of loads. As the supervisor explained it, when there had been a shortage of loads through the year it seemed that the grievor had always got the last load and the one after him on the seniority list always got left without one.

The yard supervisor clearly stated that if the other driver did not get one more load, if there was a shortage of work, the company would not be able to reach its commitment to the other driver and would then have to pay the junior driver for the balance not received but entitled to under the individual contract. The grievor accepted the yard supervisor's explanation at that time but still did not see why it should matter when he still was entitled to preference over the other driver under the collective agreement.

The grievor was not satisfied with the supervisor's explanation and decided to talk to the association president who was also the most senior driver. The association president told him that under the collective agreement he had a right to the load in question and should grieve the matter claiming compensation from the company for the lost load. At that time, the grievor filled out a record of grievance form and the association president took it and went to see the yard supervisor about the matter. The supervisor told the president the same story as he told the grievor, not giving the president any satisfaction. The association president then took the grievance to the second and final step in the grievance procedure, presenting the grievance to the plant manager who was the yard supervisor's immediate superior. He was told by the plant manager that the company had to honour the contract made with the other driver by providing him with a minimum number of loads each year. This year there was a great danger that the company could not meet this commitment unless the company skipped over the grievor and gave the other driver the last load in the event of a shortage of work.

The grievance procedure was complied with by the association (including all time limits). The association met to decide whether or not it could afford to take the matter to arbitration since it would be quite costly. The arbitration clause in the collective agreement required a single arbitrator to decide any arbitrable issues. The membership decided (all fifteen members in attendance) that the association owed it to the grievor to pursue the issue all the way to arbitration. It was also decided that letting this incident go by would only encourage the company to further violate the collective agreement. Notice was duly served upon the company that the association was taking the matter to arbitration as per the collective agreement.

APPENDIX B

Article 10 — Seniority
Seniority shall govern in matters affecting availability of work. When there are not enough loads for every driver, those with the most seniority shall be given preference.

Seniority shall govern in a choice of vacation period between bargaining-unit members.

Article 12 — Job Protection
Bargaining-unit members are guaranteed the specified number of loads of pulpwood per year as promised in their individual contracts.

CANADIAN TELECOMMUNICATIONS SERVICES LTD.
v.
COMMUNICATIONS EMPLOYEES INTERNATIONAL UNION, LOCAL 1278

Background— Canadian Telecommunications Services Ltd. (the company) provides telephone-answering service throughout most of Canada. It has offices in most major Canadian centres including Toronto. The company's employees come within the provincial labour relations board's jurisdictions. Not all of the company's offices are organized but most are, particularly in the larger cities. The company deals with a variety of trade unions, both national unions and international unions.

Communications Employees International Union (CEIU) is an international trade union based in New York City. As of January 1, 1978, it had just under 86,000 members in Canada and the United States. Only 3,600 of its members are in Canada. Local 1278 is the only local of the CEIU in Toronto. There are currently 42 CEIU members in the local. All members of this local are employed by the company in its Toronto office. The CEIU is the certified bargaining agent for all employees of the company in Metropolitan Toronto below the position of office supervisor, excluding employees in the sales branch. The bargaining unit was certified by the Ontario Labour Relations Board in June of 1963.

The company and CEIU entered into a renewal collective agreement on March 30, 1977. It was to be in force for a period of two years.

The employees in the bargaining unit work on a three-shift basis. The day shift is from 08:00 to 16:00, the evening shift is from 16:00 to 00:00 and the night shift is from 00:00 to 08:00. All three shifts are staffed seven days per week. Choice of shift assignment by an employee is based on the accumulated seniority of an employee. Every four weeks all bargaining-unit employees have to choose the shifts they want to work in the next four-week period, starting with those employees with the highest seniority. Normally each employee would be scheduled to work forty hours in any given week. A list is posted two weeks in advance of the commencement of each new four-week period showing the employees and their assigned shifts for the period.

Employee turnover has been relatively high in the Toronto office, approximately 48 percent per year. Because of this there has been a large degree of change with employees' choice of shifts as they accumulate seniority. This is the reason for posting a list and following such a procedure.

A memorandum was permanently placed on the employees' bulletin board directly above the place where each new list is posted setting out employee shift assignments. It is dated January 14, 1977, and is signed by the office manager. It states that all employees in the Toronto office are required to check the list each month before the commencement of a four-week period to see that their shift assignments are correct. It further states that failure to do this by the commencement of the work period will result in the employee waiving any right to change his or her shift assignments once the four-week period has started (see Appendix C).

The list is normally posted more than two weeks before each four-week period commences, usually on the Friday afternoon immediately before the Monday that is exactly two weeks before the period's commencement.

On average, there are twelve bargaining-unit employees scheduled for any day shift, twelve scheduled for any evening shift, and six scheduled for the night shift.

The incident — The grievor had gone home ill on the morning of Friday April 28, 1978, due to a severe headache accompanied by a slight fever. The grievor was to start a three-week vacation on the following Monday May 1, 1978.

The shift assignment list was posted as usual that Friday afternoon by the assistant to the office supervisor, a bargaining-unit member. The list was compiled and completed by the assistant. It had been approved by the office supervisor. No changes were made to the list while the grievor was on vacation. The four-week period began before the grievor returned from her vacation, with the list unchanged from when it was first posted.

The grievor returned from her three-week vacation in the second week of the four-week work period. Because she had over ten years seniority, the grievor had third choice of the shift assignments. Her preference had always been Monday through Friday on the day shift (08:00 to 16:00). For the last three years she had worked primarily the day shift as well as a few extra overtime hours whenever they were available. The grievor never worked more than three hours overtime when she had already worked an eight-hour shift in the same day. She was aware that it was her responsibility, according to the memorandum, to check her scheduled hours for each four-week period before it was to begin, but she had gotten out of the habit of checking the schedule. The grievor knew that she could always have the day shift when she wanted it because there are always more than three employees required for the day shift on any given day.

Upon returning from her three-week vacation, the grievor worked the day shift, Monday through Friday, for the next two weeks. She did not check the list for the period up to that point in time. An error had been made in the shift assignments that the grievor had requested. The error had not then been brought to her attention by management nor her fellow workers.

Unknown to the grievor, she was scheduled to work the evening shift (16:00 to 00:00) during the last week of the four-week period. She happened to look at the schedule on Monday of the last week during her lunch break, after one of her coworkers mentioned to her that she was scheduled to work evenings that week. The grievor immediately crossed off her evening hours on the list and wrote in "08:00 to 16:00" in its place. She continued to work the day shift until Thursday of that week without incident.

Late Thursday afternoon between approximately 15:00 and 16:00 three fellow employees, scheduled to work the evening shift, phoned in to say that they would not be coming in to work. The assistant to the office supervisor looked at the schedule to see who else was supposed to work and noticed the change made to the schedule. The assistant approached the grievor and asked her if she had changed the schedule. The assistant told her she had no right to change the schedule and would have to work the evening shift because they were short-handed. The grievor objected and said that there was no way she possibly could. Further discussion continued until the grievor said she would work half the shift (16:00 to 20:00) for full payment of a whole eight-hour shift at her regular rate of pay. The assistant said: "I guess that's fair." The office supervisor was taking two of his vacation days the next day and the following Monday and had at the time of the discussion departed from his office for the next four days.

The grievor worked the half-shift and punched out at the time clock at 20:00 for the day. On the Friday following, the grievor worked the day shift, completing work at 16:00. On the following Tuesday, the office supervisor, in the normal course of his weekly routine, looked at the time sheets of his office staff for the previous week and noticed the eight-hour evening shift worked by the grievor on the previous Thursday. The supervisor questioned his assistant about the entry, thinking it was an error. When informed as to the correctness of the entry by his assistant, he persisted in his inquiry because it was so unusual for any employee to work such a long work-day and for the grievor in particular. The assistant admitted that there had been some trouble and a special arrangement had to be made at the time. At this point the office supervisor was quite confused about what had gone on and summoned the grievor and his assistant into his office to sort the matter out.

The office supervisor came to the conclusion that although the grievor should not have been scheduled to work afternoons, it was up to the grievor to inform him or his assistant, as per the memorandum, of the error so that adequate arrangements could have been made to have sufficient workers on hand for all three shifts. He concluded that the grievor would have to be paid time and one-half for the hours worked, thinking that the grievor worked a whole extra eight-hour shift, as per the collective agreement. The grievor was not entitled to be paid at the regular rate of pay for the whole 16:00 to 00:00 shift, but must be paid at time and one-half the regular rate of pay for the grievor. Clearly at this point the office supervisor did not have a true picture of the situation. Neither the assistant nor the grievor said anything about his interpretation of the situation.

Upon checking the time cards later that day and finding that the grievor had not worked the full shift, the grievor and assistant were called back into the supervisor's office. At this point the supervisor was very angry at both employees. The grievor and assistant were both reprimanded for the way the time sheets were handled in the circumstances. A record of the reprimands was placed in both employees' files.

The grievor went to the office's union steward on Wednesday, the following day, contending that the supervisor had been unfair with her by not paying her what he said she was entitled to and also by blaming her for the error in the time sheet, resulting in the notice being placed in her employment record. The union took the grievance through all steps of the grievance procedure.

As far as the reprimand was concerned, the union did not feel that it alone was worth taking to arbitration, however the incident gave rise to the issue of whether management could deny the grievor her rights to working her preferred shift even though the four-week period had commenced and an error had been made which affected the grievor's shift assignment. The union executive thought this incident was an opportunity to challenge management's right to cut off a bargaining-unit member's right to preference in shift assignment at a certain point in time when the collective agreement was silent on the matter (that is, the collective agreement did not say that management could do this specifically).

The union executive decided to take this opportunity to confront the issue of management denying an employee the right to exercise his or her rights under the collective agreement beyond a certain point in time.

APPENDIX C

Canadian Telecommunications Services Ltd: Memorandum

TO: All Toronto Office Employees   **DATE:** January 14, 1977
FROM: Office Manager
SUBJECT: Work Scheduling

Due to a large amount of confusion concerning shift assignments in recent weeks, it has become necessary to establish a standardized procedure for verifying the fact that each employee has been given the correct choice of shifts according to their accumulated seniority.

From this date onward, each employee in the Toronto office is required to check the list posted for each four-week period *before* the commencement of a four-week period to see that their shift assignments are correct. In the event that there has been some kind of error made, failure to bring this to the attention of management by the *commencement* of the work period will result in the employee waiving any right to change their work assignment from that posted on the list. This action is taken pursuant to Article 7 of our current collective agreement with CEIU: "Management Rights."[1]

Office Manager

[1] No change was made in this provision when a new collective agreement was entered into in March 1977.

APPENDIX D

Article 7 — Management Rights

The company has the exclusive right and power to manage its operations in all respects and in accordance with its commitments and responsibilities to its customers, to conduct its business efficiently and to direct the working forces, and without limiting the generality of the foregoing, it has the exclusive right and power to hire, promote, transfer, demote, or lay off employees, and to suspend, discharge, or otherwise discipline employees for just cause. The company agrees that any exercise of these rights and powers shall not contravene the provisions of this agreement.

Article 14 — Shift Assignments

Shift assignments shall be posted for each four-week period at least two weeks in advance of the commencement of the period.

Seniority shall apply for the purpose of choosing shifts for an employee's work week.

Each work-week commences on Monday at 08:00.

Index

References to individual authors are listed at the end of each chapter.